THE GLORY AND FALL OF THE MING DYNASTY

Emperor T'ai-tsu, the Hung-wu Emperor of the Ming Dynasty, who reigned from 1368 to 1398. Reproduced from the Collections of the Library of Congress.

The Glory and Fall of the Ming Dynasty

By Albert Chan

UNIVERSITY OF OKLAHOMA PRESS
NORMAN

Library of Congress Cataloging in Publication Data

Chan, Albert, 1915–
  The glory and fall of the Ming dynasty.

  Bibliography: p. 403
  Includes index.
  1. China—History—Ming dynasty, 1368–1644.   I. Title.
DS753.C4825   951'.026   81–43640
                                        AACR2

Longum iter est per praecepta; breve et efficax per exempla.

L. A. Seneca, Ep. VI, 5

PATRI DANIELI FINN, SJ

Praeceptori Dilectissimo

et

Ingeniosissimo

CONTENTS

MAPS AND ILLUSTRATIONS

PREFACE

This book has had many friends. In its Ph.D. dissertation form it was finished in 1953. I had had Prof. Yang Lien-sing for director and I had done my work under his guidance and with his suggestions. I also approached Prof. Francis Cleaves frequently for advice on Mongol history. Later when the late Prof. Serge Elisséeff, then director of Harvard-Yenching Institute, suggested that I should have it published I judged revision and further development necessary to make the book more factual and readable. I went therefore to Japan in the summer of 1958 where I worked in several of the great libraries in Tokyo, Kyoto and Tenri. My trip was most rewarding, for in Japan I was able to consult numerous books and manuscripts, many of them rare and not available elsewhere. The Naikaku Bunko and the Tōyō Bunko were eminently helpful.

Revision meant re-writing and re-arrangement. I used to mail the revised script chapter by chapter to Dr. L. C. Goodrich, formerly Professor of Columbia University, New York, the most careful of scrutinizers, who apparently went through every page word by word. The questions he raised tried me hard, but the book benefited.

The Harvard-Yenching Institute very generously offered financial help for the printing of the book, but I had to find a publisher. A happy chance led me to Mr. Savoie Lottinville of Oklahoma University Press. To him and to his successors I owe thanks for understanding cooperation.

In 1969 I left Hong Kong for Europe to do research in various archives and libraries. When I returned in 1976 the book was still unpublished and I was too busy to attend to the revision of the bibliography, which the lapse of seven years had rendered necessary.

Fortunately, the friend in need arrived—Prof. Joseph Sebes of Georgetown University, Wash., D.C. In his conscientious way, he went through the manuscript once more. Like Dr. Goodrich, he would let nothing pass unquestioned. His probing ranged from punctuation to the largest constructive suggestions. I owe him thanks above all for bringing the bibliography up to date. The few months he stayed with us made the book what it is now.

Dr. Glen W. Baxter, a friend since the Harvard days, has taken great interest in my work from the beginning. His help, as administrator of Harvard-Yenching Institute, has always been positive and his interest has been unfailing. He showed himself determined to see the book in the press before his retirement.

To all these, and to many others who gave practical help and encouragement—particularly to A. Birmingham and T. F. Ryan to name but two—I wish to express my warmest thanks. They have added much to the value of this book. The mistakes and errors that remain are all my own and I take full responsibility for them.

Hong Kong   ALBERT CHAN, S.J.

INTRODUCTION

This work is a development of a dissertation which I wrote in 1952 while at Harvard. Some years of research had made me intensely interested in the history of the Ming dynasty, so I continued this research and now the accumulation of material and the encouragement of friends have prompted me to produce this book.

The past almost half a century has witnessed a rebirth of the study of Ming history. In the year 1935 there appeared in the *Rikishigaku kenkyō* 歷史學研究 an article in which Matsumoto Yoshimi 松本善海 called attention to the fact that the history of the Ming dynasty had not been given due attention by scholars.[1] Now, almost half a century later the study of the Ming dynasty is being taken up with increasing eagerness by younger historians, who realize fully the importance of the Ming dynasty both in the internal history of modern China and in the history of the Chinese relations to the rest of the world. A century ago the scholar Chu I-hsin 朱一新 (1846–1894) pointed out that the closer a historical period is to us the greater the influence it exercises on us. "Hence", he said, "we must study the history of our (i.e. the Ch'ing) dynasty and we should also be familiar with the history of the Ming dynasty. All that occurred after the Chia-ching 嘉靖 (1522–1566) period should be studied from a wide variety of sources not excluding miscellaneous historical writings: the government and its policy, the people and the society of those days, foreign relations and military activities, are all historical sources for us."[2]

This revival was already sorely needed during the first half of the Manchu period, but scholars were not encouraged to delve into the history of the Ming dynasty. The Manchu rulers were uneasily conscious of their humble origin, for they remembered that they had been subjects of the Ming government and knew that they were regarded by contemporary Chinese as merely a barbarian tribe. The legitimacy, moreover, of their rule in China was always debatable. Hence they tried to suppress all the documents and books by Ming authors that contain allusions to things better forgotten. In the K'ang-hsi (1662–1722) and Ch'ien-lung (1736–1795) reigns a literary censorship was instituted to prevent unfavorable criticism of the government.[3] Prudent scholars, therefore, thought it safer to leave aside the history of the Ming dynasty and study the history of earlier dynasties or, preferably, the blameless classics. Thus for over two centuries little progress was made in the study of the history of the Ming dynasty.

Toward the end of the 19th century, however, the Manchu government relaxed the literary censorship, and books on the late Ming period began to appear. A powerful impetus was given to such studies when a collection of official documents dating from the late Ming and early Ch'ing periods was discovered in the palace archives at the beginning of the present century.[4] This discovery was of inestimable value to historians engaged in the reconstruction of Ming and Ch'ing history. The reprinting of primary sources and the discovery of Ming documents have, of course, helped greatly to clear up many hitherto disputed points.[5]

When I was writing my dissertation in 1952, not one of the general histories of China then published gave an adequate account of the Ming dynasty. Of the histories dealing specifically with the Ming dynasty, only a single volume published by Japanese scholars gave a really good outline of the whole Ming period in China and of contemporary happenings in neighboring countries.[6] Twenty-three years ago, however, (1957) the Ming-tai shih 明代史 or A History of the Ming Dynasty written by Meng Sen 孟森 was published by Prof. L. S. Yang in Taipei. This can fairly be called the first history of the Ming dynasty to be published in Chinese. The book itself is not new—it was written almost forty-five years ago—but it is still good. Mr. Meng, one of the greatest of modern specialists on the history of the Ming and the Ch'ing dynasties, was widely known for his profound and scholarly knowledge of Chinese history. The Ming-tai shih, originally written as a sort of text-book for Mr. Meng's students of Peking University, is a general history of the Ming dynasty describing all important events and all important government institutions. Since he intended his book to be a text-book, the author aimed at giving all the important facts a student should know about the

Ming dynasty, especially on the political side. He gave, however, very little about the economic and social sides of Ming history.

In recent years, articles on Ming history have begun to appear in great numbers in periodicals and journals. Wolfgang Franke has published two articles summarizing the work being done by scholars up to the 1950s on the history of China in the 15th and 16th centuries.[7] Much of this recent work deals with the economic and social conditions. Thus the *Shih-huo pan-yüeh k'an* 食貨半月刊 has published a number of articles dealing with the economic conditions of the Ming dynasty, and the voyages of the renowned eunuch Cheng Ho have been studied by Chinese, Japanese and Europeans.[8]

Several Chinese scholars have specialized in Ming history. Three of these are especially notable, Wu Han 吳晗 and Wang Ch'ung-wu 王崇武, who have written much on Ming history in general, and Liang Fang-chung 梁方仲, who has confined his studies very largely to the economic institutions of the Ming dynasty. Mr. Wu's biography of Ming T'ai-tsu is an admirable introduction to the beginnings of Ming history. Mr. Wang has published a critical study on the invasion of Nanking by which the Yung-lo emperor seized the throne from his nephew.[9]

Japanese scholars have written abundantly on various aspects of Ming history, with, of course, special attention to relations between Japan and the Ming government. Many of them have added a great deal to our understanding of such major historical events as the Japanese pirate raids along the Chinese coast in the 16th century, the invasion of China by Hideyoshi and the Ming court officials' attempt to secure Japanese help after the fall of Peking in 1644.[10] A glance at the list of recent studies of the Ming dynasty in the *Tōyō shiryō shu-sei* 東洋史料集成 shows that the scope of such studies has widened greatly since the war: contemporary Japanese scholars are now deeply interested in the Ming dynasty especially in its economic and social side.[11] Special mention is due to Shimizu Taiji 清水泰次 whose detailed studies have been perhaps the most remarkable contribution made to the revival of Ming history especially in all that concerns economic institutions.

The contribution made by European and American sinologues to Ming studies has been smaller than their contribution to the study of other dynasties. Until the 1940's their contribution was very small indeed. In 1934 Henri Maspero wrote a short article analysing the cause of the fall of the Ming dynasty and giving a clear chronological account of the events pertaining to that fall.[12] This article, written as an introduction to a book on the Manchu emperors, was based mainly on the *Ming-shih*, admirably organized, but since the writer was interested primarily in the immediate causes of the fall of the dynasty, the remote causes are not fully treated.

Since the war, however, scholars of a younger generation have increasingly become interested in the study of the Ming dynasty. Their research covers a wide field: examination and translation of original documents and study of diverse points of Ming history. Wolfgang Franke is perhaps the most prolific writer in this field. His articles on Ming problems have appeared in a number of periodicals both in Europe and in the Far East. Still more valuable are his bibliography of and his articles on modern writing on Ming history. The works by Charles O. Hucker and O. Berkelbach van der Sprenkel on the governmental organization of the Ming are important helps toward understanding how the Ming government was run. C. R. Boxer has published a number of books on the relations between the Chinese and the Portuguese of the second half of the Ming. Articles on philosophy, on literature, and on many other aspects of the Ming dynasty have also been published.[13]

The Ming dynasty, coming between that of the Mongols (1280–1368) and that of the Manchus (1644–1912), was the only native dynasty to rule between the 13th century and the Revolution of 1911. It ranks as a comparatively modern empire: many of its government institutions and much of its social organization greatly influenced the Manchus and, to understand the Manchu system of government and the social organization in the China of the Manchu days, we must look to the Ming.

The second half of the Ming period coincided with the period when Europeans were beginning to set up in East Asia trading posts, many of which eventually became colonies. Hence the study of the Ming dynasty is closely linked with the study of Europe in the East after the discovery of the new route.

The European adventurers in China were soon followed by missionaries who were among the first Europeans to reach the Chinese capital and were the first of all Europeans to communicate with the scholars of the Celestial Empire. Through them there was spread in China a knowledge of western civilization which slowly but continually influenced Chinese thought.[14] The missionaries were the first European sinologues. They made a serious study of Chinese culture and their writings on this subject attracted the attention of European savants and helped to prepare the way for the Era of Enlightenment in Europe.[15]

In a discussion of the sources of Ming history, the early Ch'ing scholar Ch'üan Tsu-wang 全祖望 (1705–1755) said that the late Ming historical sources alone numbered nearly a thousand works. Historians writing under the Ming dynasty left a good number of historical writings in their own time. Thus, the *Chi lu hui pien* 紀錄 彙編, which contains a collection of historical writings by contemporary Ming scholars, is still an important work of reference, especially for the early part of the Ming dynasty. Several scholars wrote general histories of the Ming dynasty from the time of the founder to the reign in which they were living. Others wrote histories of one or more emperors—the *Huang-ming t'ung-chi* 皇明通紀 of Ch'en Chien 陳建, the *Ming-chi pien-nien* 明紀編年 of Chung Hsing 鍾惺, the *Liang-ch'ao chuan-hsin-lu* 兩朝傳信錄, and the *Chia-ching i lai chu-lüeh* 嘉靖以來注略 of Hsü Ch'ung-hsi 許重熙, to give but a few examples. Then there are miscellaneous writings of contemporary scholars. Often these are not histories of the Ming dynasty but rather personal notes suggested by their studies, or remarks on government or social problems of their times. Writings of this kind survive in great abundance, but care is needed in using them. Since they are private writings, the authors were often guided by their own personal tastes and views, especially when the problems treated had some reference to themselves. We find clear examples of this in the writings of supporters and opponents of the Tung-lin party 東林黨.

Another difficulty in the private sources of Ming history, as in all Chinese history, is that the historians often seek to edify their readers, to draw a moral by exalting the virtuous and condemning the wicked. Often in their zeal they paint their heroes as perfect, leaving out all their shortcomings. Their narrations thus become one-sided and to form a fair judgement, one has to read the opposite side of the story if it can be found. Again, it is quite common for historians to write only about what they consider "great events", leaving aside many things that we should be interested in nowadays—the living condition of the people, their daily customs, their amusements and so on. There are books like the *Wu tsa-tsu* 五雜俎 or the *Yeh-huo-pien* 野獲編 that give information on these points, but they are rare. It is only by painstaking labor, by churning over the miscellaneous sources, that we can form a picture of the life of the time.

Of the official documents written in the Ming dynasty the most important perhaps is the *Ming shih-lu* 明實錄 or *Veritable Records* of the Ming dynasty. Since the time of the T'ang dynasty it had been a common practice for the heir to the throne to compile a chronological history known as *Shih-lu* of his predecessor. The main sources of the *Ming shih-lu* were the documents of the Six Boards and other government documents such as the memorials to the throne by different ministers and official gazettes. Learned opinion has always been divided as to the value of the *Shih-lu*. Some of the Ming scholars considered it unreliable, but the great historian Wan Ssu-t'ung 萬斯同 (1638–1702) held it in high esteem and considered it the fundamental source for the history of the Ming dynasty.[16] Today we still consider the *Shih-lu* a most important source for the history of the Ming dynasty.

Another important official historical document is the *Hui-tien* 會典, a book on government institutions. The Wan-li revised edition of the *hui-tien* (1587) in 228 chüan, giving a full account of government institutions as they were in the Wan-li period, is indispensable for the student of Ming history. The *Ming hui-yao* 明會要, compiled in the 19th century by Lung Wen-pin 龍文彬 (1830–1893) in 80 chüan, is of much the same nature as the *hui-tien* but it is classified according to subjects, and the historical development of each institution is more clearly shown.

In 1739, the *Ming shih* or History of the Ming Dynasty was published for the first time. This work, begun in 1678 by order of the K'ang-hsi emperor, had taken over sixty years to complete. No other dynastic history undertaken by a Chinese government ever took so long to finish and very few were compiled under such propitious circumstances. The historians engaged in the work were among the most eminent scholars of the time. The time was the most peaceful part of the Ch'ing period, the country prosperous, and the emperors and scholars were able to devote their leisure to study. Then too, the fall of the Ming was still a recent event: many eye-witnesses were still alive, many facts could be easily verified either by these eye-witnesses or from the abundant official documents or from the traditions of contemporary society.

Among the eminent scholars who compiled the *Ming shih* perhaps the most outstanding was Wan Ssu-t'ung, who worked on it for thirteen years. Nominally he was no more than an unofficial member of the Historiographical Board, but in reality he was the director-in-chief of the whole work and is said to have gone through the drafts of scholar compilers, correcting whatever he thought was not in accordance with the truth. He held the opinion that private historical writings are often better than official ones since official histories are produced in a hurry by the work of many and so are likely to neglect what is important or to lack coordination. To Wan Ssu-t'ung was ascribed what was regarded as a *Draft Ming History* 明史稿 in 500 chüan, based on the *Shih-lu*. Unfortunately this is no longer extant.[17]

There is, however, a popular tradition that Wan's manuscript came into the possession of Wang Hung-hsü 王鴻緒 (1645–1723), sometime director-in-chief of the Historiographical Board, who, after altering some passages, reduced it to 310 chüan and submitted it to the throne in 1723 as his own work under the original title, *Ming-shih-kao*.[18]

When the *Ming shih* was presented to the throne in 1739, the director-in-chief, Chang T'ing-yü 張廷玉 (1672–1755), said in his preface that the work was based on Wang Hung-hsü's *Ming-shih-kao*. Wang's work, he said, was the fruit of collaboration among eminent scholars over a period of thirty years and, therefore, covered the Ming dynasty quite completely and with full treatment of all the events.[19] If we admit with Chang T'ing-yü that the *Ming-shih-kao* is derived from that of Wan Ssu-t'ung, then the *Ming shih* too is ultimately based on the *Shih-lu*.

Despite its high reputation the *Ming shih* has its defects, the most serious of which is the omission of all mention of Manchu relations with the Ming empire. As we have said already, the Manchus started as a small tribe and remained a subject tribe throughout the Ming period. Their relation with the Ming government can be traced back to the Yung-lo reign (1403–1424) and the *Shih-lu* makes frequent mention of communications between the two. In the *Ming shih*, however, these facts are all passed over in such a way that one can hardly discern the truth. The first serious conflict between the Ming government and the Manchus occurred in the Wan-li reign and both the *Shih-lu* and private historical sources give accounts of it. And yet when the *Ming-shih* was compiled these sources were ignored and accounts based on the early Manchu documents were used instead. The compilers must have known that they were sinning against all the canons of scholarship but what else could they do placed as they were under the vigilant eyes of the Manchus? Wan Ssu-t'ung certainly had good reason to decline an appointment as an official on the Historiographical Board. One can also understand why scholars of an older generation—Ku Yen-wu 顧炎武 (1613–1682) for instance and Huang Tsung-hsi 黃宗羲 (1610–1695)—actually refused to collaborate with the Manchu government. Indeed, the tendency of modern scholars is to hold that the whole of the *Ming shih* should be revised, especially the portion dealing with the sequel to the fall of Peking in 1644, where the activities of the late Ming princes are mentioned very briefly and as matters of no significance.[20]

The Chinese historians were very reserved when they came to speak about foreigners, trying to omit them altogether, or if that was impossible, mentioning them as cursorily as possible. This is under-standable: the people of that time regarded foreigners as barbarians, and consequently as of no importance. Thus speaking of Ricci, the *Ming shih* tells us that he came from I-ta-li-ya (Italy), a country that had never had communication with China. Clearly the historian knew nothing of the earlier appearances of Italy (under a different name) in the history of China. To him such a country meant little or nothing. This disregard of foreigners accounts for many regrettable gaps in our knowledge of the history of China. How fascinating the voyages of Cheng Ho 鄭和 must have been! Yet we might know nothing at all about them were it not for the three little accounts of Ma Huan 馬歡, Fei Hsin 費信 and Kung Chen 鞏珍. Macao in the 16th and 17th century must have been a very interesting city and yet there was no full account of it until the Ch'ien-lung period when the *Ao-men chi-lüeh* 澳門紀略 was written. The *Tung-hsi-yang k'ao* 東西洋考 has left us only very scanty descriptions of the south sea countries.

We know little of what the Chinese thought of the outside world, but we are fairly well supplied with the complementary knowledge of what foreigners thought of China. The early European missionaries have left us some of their accounts of the China they saw. They were voyagers in an entirely new world and their curiosity was aroused by everything. The diary of Ricci and the Journal of Trigault give us much interesting information about the Ming empire which Chinese historians had passed over as needing no mention. Their letters to Europe gave foreigners' impressions of the Chinese government, its people and its society. Through their writings we see how the Christian Church developed in China among the intellectuals and the common people, how even the emperors themselves were interested in it and how empresses, court ladies and eunuchs became Christians and opened communication with Europe. Often they throw light on historical events which Chinese historians might have deemed unim-portant or dismissed as mere hearsay. Take, for example, the notorious arch-rebel, Chang Hsien-chung 張獻忠, about whom contemporary writers had written so much and of whom later generations had so much to tell, the subject of so many legends and of so few historically accurate descriptions that many readers have been inclined to wonder if we have any certain information about him. But a Jesuit missionary, Father Gabriel de Magalhães (1609–1677), who as a prisoner of Chang Hsien-chung's was an eye-witness of his cruelty, has left us a diary describing his experiences while in captivity.[21] Documents of this kind are a great help toward understanding the character of Chang Hsien-chung and the state of Szechuan province at the end of the Ming period.

These foreign historical sources should certainly be used side by side with the Chinese sources for the reconstruction of Ming history. This is especially true of the second half of the dynasty for which there is no lack of first hand references. The recent publication "Jesuitas na Asia" by J. M. Braga tells us that there must still be many such historical treasures in the libraries and archives in Europe and elsewhere.[22] If this material were collected and put at the disposal of contemporary scholars we should be in a position to write a much more satisfactory history of the Ming.

Originally my dissertation was entitled: "The Decline and Fall of the Ming Dynasty, A Study of the Internal Factors." But now that I have doubled it in size and added much material I am tempted to call it "A General History of the Ming Dynasty", yet the book is not a general history: it does not narrate Ming history chronologically as does Mr. Meng Sen's *Ming-tai shih*. My purpose has been to study the Ming dynasty in its origin, its governmental system, its economic problems, the society and people of the time, and then to analyse the causes of its fall. Even in this last I have made a detailed study only of the internal causes. I am aware of and have touched briefly on the external causes, including the most important, the Manchu invasion. This, however, is a subject which, in my opinion, may more appropriately be considered in connection with the history of the Ch'ing dynasty. It has in fact already been extensively studied by modern scholars Chinese and foreign. Such references as I make to the Manchus are intended merely to clarify the points I am discussing.

Historians differ widely in their view on the causes of the fall of the Ming empire. Some attribute it chiefly to the eunuchs, others to rebels, others still to the Manchu invaders. The author of the *K'ou-shih pien-nien* 寇事編年 went so far as to enumerate more than forty causes for the fall of the Ming empire.[23] Most of these were immediate causes which, no doubt, helped to a certain extent to explain the fall of this great empire. But a dynasty that had lasted nearly three centuries could not topple over without warning, and the causes of its fall cannot have been so simple. Why is it that the empire did not fall during the Wan-li reign, the most critical period in its history? At that time the country was invaded from all directions: the Japanese were raging along the coast of China and there was serious conflict between the Chinese and Japanese governments over Korea. The Mongols and the Manchus were in a state of ferment along the northern and northeastern borders and the Manchus inflicted terrible damage on the Chinese troops towards the end of the reign. Inside the empire the abuses and the atrocities of the eunuchs had caused many revolts everywhere, and the strife between the Tung-lin Party and the eunuchs led to the murder or the imprisonment of many eminent ministers. Yet the dynasty survived this catastrophic reign, only to fall in the reign of the Ch'ung-chen emperor, undeniably the best of the later Ming emperors and the only one who might have been expected to restore the old glory of the dynasty.

In this study I have attempted to find adequate reasons for the fall of the Ming Empire. To do this, it has been necessary to go back to the early emperors and to the government institutions of the early days of the dynasty.

As often happens on the accession of a new dynasty, new government institutions were established to meet new circumstances. These served the state well for a while, but gradually they ceased to function satisfactorily, either because of the inability of the government to maintain them or because they were no longer suited to changing times. The abuses that were allowed to creep in helped to ruin the government machinery. This approach to the study of the fall of the Ming empire has not, so far as I know, hitherto been attempted. Consequently, to undertake it should be both interesting and profitable.

As I have said above, the material for the history of the Ming dynasty is abundant. First-hand sources, though rare for some periods, are available, and secondary sources were multiplying when I was starting my dissertation. I was so fortunate as to have had access to two first-class libraries, the Harvard Yen-ching Institute Library and the Widener Library from which I was able to obtain almost all the books I needed. On occasions Mr. K. M. Ch'iu, librarian of the Harvard Yen-ching Institute Library, borrowed periodicals for me from the Library of Congress. For this I am most grateful. A trip to Japan in 1956 proved very fruitful. In the Tōyō Bunko and Naikaku Bunko I was delighted to find rich treasuries of rare books on the Ming dynasty written and published by contemporaries. In the Tōyō Bunko I saw for the first time the *Kuo Ch'üeh* 國榷 which I was eager to read. It was a manuscript copy transcribed from the *Tung-fang wen-hua hui-so* 東方文化會所 copy in Peking.[24] The Naikaku Bunko has perhaps the richest of all collections of books on the Ming dynasty by Ming authors. There I found not only books on the history and geography of the Ming dynasty but also miscellaneous works and novels, all in Ming editions. Here and there one finds short narrations which in themselves may seem insignificant but if taken together serve to illustrate some of the points in history that official writings omit.

Basically, I have used official compilations such as the *Ming shih*, the *Ming shih-lu*, etc. Then I have consulted works of late Ming contemporary historians such as the *Ming-shih chi-shih pen-mo* 明史紀事本末, the *Tsui-wei lu* 罪惟錄, the *Ming-shih ch'ao-lüeh* 明史鈔略, the *K'ou-shih pien-nien* 寇事編年. This last book deserves special mention since it was compiled from the official gazettes of the Ch'ung-chen reign, memorials of government officials, and private records of contemporaries. Private diaries and letters by their very nature are often less guarded and therefore frequently record the truth more plainly. For this reason I have tried to make use of them in so far as they are available. Finally, the *Ming-mo nung-min ch'i-i shih liao* 明末農民起義史料, compiled in 1952 by Peking University, contains many first-hand documents concerning the revolts of the Ch'ung-chen period.

Critical studies by modern scholars on the government institutions of the Ming were consulted in so far as they were available to me. The articles of Liang Fang-chung and Shimizu Taiji have helped me greatly in explaining the economic system of the dynasty. Then there is the article of Hsieh Yü-ts'ai 解毓才 on the *wei-so* system, an excellent study based on historical documents.[25] Similar to Mr. Hsieh's article are the writings of Wang Ch'ung-wu on the military and merchant settlements.[26] Other articles such as the studies on the censorate system and the Imperial Academy by Yü Teng 于登 and Wu Han also deserve mention.[27]

The only noteworthy recent work on the revolts of the late Ming period is the *Wan-Ming min-pien* 晚明民變 by Li Wen-chih 李文治. Mr. Li's book is both very readable and well documented. He tells us in his preface that it was written during the war when important documents were not always available. He had, however, the compensatory help of contemporary specialists on the history of the dynasty. Mr. Li pays great attention to the revolts of the people from 1627 to 1644 and discusses at length the economic conditions of the period. Since his book does not claim to be a study of the fall of the Ming dynasty, the author omitted many of the causes. Nevertheless this book has been of great help to me, especially in the chapter on the revolts of the people.

The Hung-wu emperor was outstanding not only as the founder of the Ming dynasty but also as one of the greatest emperors in the history of China. The solid foundation he laid kept the dynasty in being for nearly three centuries. Hence he is frequently mentioned in this book especially in the parts dealing with government institutions. His son the Yung-lo emperor, though a usurper, followed the same lines as his father. He was able to carry out his father's unfinished work to strengthen the foundations of the dynasty. For this reason he too is mentioned time and again. The Wan-li and Ch'ung-chen emperors are mentioned equally frequently, not however because they were great but because under them the dynasty raced to its end. In the Sung dynasty when Ou-yang Hsiu 歐陽修 (1007–1072) wrote the biographies of the royal music directors (伶官傳) he started with this exclamation: "O, how often did we not attribute the rise and fall of an empire to the will of Heaven, and yet is it not true that it also greatly depends on the human will?" That will be the conclusion too of all who study the history and the decline of the Ming dynasty.

NOTES

[1] Matsumoto Yoshimi 松本善海, "Poverty of the Historical study of the Ming dynasty" 明史研究の貧困, *Rekishigaku kenkyū* 歷史學研究, 4, (Sept., 1935) 5.

[2] Liu I-cheng 柳詒徵, *Kuo-shih yao-i* 國史要義, (Shanghai, 1948) 201.

[3] Yao Chin-yüan 姚覲元, *Ch'ing-tai chin hui shu-mu szu chung* 清代禁毀書目四種, (*Wan yu wen-k'u* 萬有文庫 second series); *Ch'ing-tai wen-tzu-yü tang* 清代文字獄檔, (Peiping, 1931–1933); Inaba Kunzan 稻葉君山, *Koki cho no monji-goku* 康熙朝の文字獄, *Kinsei shina ju-ko* 近世支那十講, (Tokyo) 493; L. C. Goodrich, *The Literary Inquisition of Ch'ien-lung*, (Baltimore, 1935).

[4] Lo Fu-yi 羅福頤, "Ch'ing nei-ko ta-k'u ming-ch'ing chiu tang-an chih li-shih chi ch'i cheng li" 清內閣大庫明清舊檔案之歷史及其整理, *Ling-nan hsüeh-pao* 嶺南學報, 9, (1948) 1; Hsü Chung-shu 徐中舒, "Nei-ko tang-an chih yu-lai chi ch'i cheng li" 內閣檔案之由來及其整理. This article can be found in the first volume of the *Ming Ch'ing shih-liao*, first series 明清史料甲編 "Ming ch'ing tang-an chuan hao" 明清檔案專號, *Chung-kuo chin-tai ching-chi shih yen-chiu chi-k'an* 中國近代經濟史研究集刊, vol. 1, 2; Lo Chen-yü 羅振玉, "Nei-ko ta-k'u tang-ts'e" 內閣大庫檔冊, *Yü-chien-chai ts'ung-shu* 玉簡齋叢書, (1910).

[5] The *Ming Ch'ing shih-liao* 明清史料, i.e., *Historical sources of the Ming and Ch'ing dynasties*, contain a number of important documents from the archives of the Peking palace. Six series have been published by the *Bulletin of the Institute of History and Philology* 中央研究院 歷史語言研究所, 1930–1932; 1936; 1936; 1951; 1953–1954.

[6] *Min no kobo tō sai reki no tozen* 明の興亡と西力の東漸, (*Toyo bunkashi taikei* 東洋歷史 大系, series 5) (Tokyo, 1934). There is also a good article on the Ming dynasty in the *Tōyō rekishi dai-ji-ten*, (Tokyo, 1941) vol. 8, 145–186.

[7] Wolfgang Franke, "Der gegenwärtige Stand der Forschung zur Geschichte Chinas im 15 und 16 Jahrhundert," *Saeculum*, Band 7, Jahrgan 1956, 413–441. The following issue gave the second part of the same article.

[8] Cheng Ho-sheng 鄭鶴聲, *Cheng Ho i-shih hui-pien* 鄭和遺事彙編, (Shanghai, 1948); Chu Hsieh 朱偰, *Cheng Ho* 鄭和, (Peking, 1956); Wu Han 吳晗, "Shih-liu shih-chi ch'ien chih chung-kuo yü nan-yang" 十六世紀前之中國與南洋, *Ch'ing-hua hsüeh-pao* 清華學報 11, (1936) 1; Liu Ming-shu 劉銘恕, "Cheng Ho hang-hai shih-chi chi tsai t'an" 鄭和航海 事蹟之再探, *Chung-kuo wen-hua yen-chiu hui-k'an* 中國文化研究彙刊, (Peking, 1943) 3,

131–170; Aritaka Iwo 有高巖 "Tewa no nankai kei-ryaku" 鄭和之南海經略, *Rekishi to chiri* 歷史と地理, 1, (1918) 2, 4, 5; Yamamoto Tatsurō 山本達郎, "Cheng Ho's Expeditions to the South Sea under the Ming dynasty" 鄭和西征考, *Tōyō-gakuhō* 東洋學報, 21, (1934) 3, 68–98; 4, 36–86; Paul Pelliot, "Les grands voyages maritimes chinois au debut du XVe siècle", *T'oung Pao* 通報, 30, (1930) 237–452; J. J. L. Duyvendak, "The True Dates of the Chinese Maritime Expeditions in the Early 15th Century", *T'uong Pao*, 34, (1938) 341–412.

[9] Liang Fang-chung 梁方仲, *Ming-tai liang-chang chih-tu* 明代糧長制度, (Shanghai, 1957); Wu Han 吳晗, *Yu seng-po tao wang-ch'üan* 由僧鉢到王權, (Chungking, 1944). This book was later revised and published under the title *Chu Yüan-chang chuan* 朱元璋傳, (Kirin, 1949); Wang Ch'ung-wu 王崇武, *Ming Ching-nan shih-shih k'ao-cheng* 明靖難史事考證, (Shanghai, 1948).

[10] Akiyama Kenzo 秋山謙藏, "Wo k'ou, the Japanese Pirates" 倭寇, *Rekishigaku Kenkyū* 歷史學研究, 3, (January, 1935) 3, 51–55; Nakamura Tokugōrō 中村德五郎, "Nichi min ko-wa haretsu no temmatsu" 日明媾和破裂之顛末, *Shigaku zasshi* 史學雜誌, 8, (1897) 10, 11, 12; Ishibara Michihiro 石原道博, *Mimmatsu shinso Nippon kitsu-ikusa no kenkyū* 明末清初日本乞師の研究, (Tokyo, 1945); cf. also Wang Yi-t'ung 千伊同, *Official Relations between China and Japan* (1368 1549), (Cambridge, 1953).

[11] *Tōyō shiryō shu-sei* 東洋史料集成, (Tokyo, 1956) 218–228. One book worth mentioning particularly is the *Mınshi Shokka-shi Yakuchu*, or the Economic History of the Ming Dynasty. The original text is translated from the Ming-shih and carefully annotated by Wada Kiyoshi and a number of Japanese scholars. It was published in 1957 by the *Tōyō Bunko* in two volumes.

[12] Henri Maspero, *Etudes Historiques*, (Paris, 1950); cf. also Wolfgang Franke, who has published an excellent bibliography on Ming historical writings: *Preliminary Notes on the Important Chinese Literary Sources for the History of the Ming Dynasty* (1368–1644), (Chengtu, 1948); "Addenda and corrigenda to the Preliminary Notes on the Important Chinese Literary Sources for the History of the Ming Dynasty (1368–1644)", *Studia Serica*, vol. IX, part 1, (Sept. 1950) 33–41; other articles on the Ming history by the same author can be found in the *Monumenta Serica* and *Sinologische Arbeiten*.

[13] Wolfgang Franke, "Yunglos Mongolei-Feldzüge", *Sinologische Arbeiten*, III, (Peking, 1945) 1–54; Id., "Chinesische Feldzüge durch die Mongolei in Frühen 15 Jahrhundert", *Sinologica*, III, (Basel, 1952) 81–88; Id., "Zur Lage der vier Sari-uigurischen Militardistrikte An-ting, A-tuan, Ch'u-hsien und Han-tung in der frühen Ming-Zeit", *Silver Jubilee volume of the Zinbun-Kagaku-kenkyusyo*, (Kyoto University, Kyoto, 1954); Id., "Yü-chien, Staatsman und Krieg-minister 1398–1457", *Monumenta Serica*, XI (1946) 87–122; Id., "Ein Process gegen Yü-chien in Jahre 1457", *Studia Serica*, 6, (Chengtu-Peking, 1947) 193–208; Id., "Zur Grundsteuer in China während der Ming Dynastie," *Zeitschrift für vergleichende Rechtswissenschaft*, 56, (1953) 93–103; Charles O. Hucker, "The Chinese Censorate of the Ming Dynasty including an Analysis during the Decade 1424–1434", *Far Eastern Quarterly*, (1950); Id., "The Traditional Chinese Censorate and the New Peking Regime", *American Political Science Review*, 45, (1951) 1041–1057; Id. (ed.), *Chinese Government in Ming Times, Seven Studies*, (Columbia University Press, New York and London, 1969); The seven studies contained in this work are 1: "Ming Local Administration" by Lien-sheng Yang 楊聯陞, pp. 1–21; 2: "Yuan Origins of the Wei-so System" by Romeyn Taylor, pp. 23–40; 3: "Policy Formulation and Decision-Making on Issues Respecting Peace and War" by Jung-pang Lo, pp. 41–72; 4: "Fiscal Administration During the Ming Dynasty" by Ray Huang, pp. 73–128; 5: "Ming Education Intendants" by Tilemann Grimm, pp. 129–147; 6: "Academies and Politics in the Ming Dynasty" by John Meskill, pp. 149–174, and 7: "The Ming Dynasty Bureaucracy: Aspects of Background Forces" by James B. Parsons, pp. 175–231; Id.; *The Ming Dynasty: Its Origins and Evolving Institutions* (Michigan Papers in Chinese Studies No. 34, Ann Arbor Center for Chinese Studies, The University of Michigan Press, 1978); O. Berkelbach van der Sprenkel, "High Officials of the Ming. A note on the Ch'i Cheng Nien Piao of the Ming History", *Bulletin of the School of Oriental and African Studies*, 14, (1952) 325–334; Tilemann

Grimm, "Das Neiko der Ming-Zeit von die Anfänge bis 1506", *Oriens Extremus*, 1, (1954) 139–177; Heinrich Busch, "The Tung-lin Shu-yüan and its Political and Philosophical Significance", *Monumenta Serica*, XLV (1955) 1–163; Barbara Krafft, *Wang Shih-chen (1526–1590), Ein Beitrag zur Geistegeschichte der Ming-Zeit.* (Dissertation, Hamburg, 1955). C. R. Boxer, *South China in the 16th Century; The Narratives of Galeoto Pereira, Fr. Gaspar da Cruz and Fr. Martin da Rada, 1550–1575,* (Hakluyt Society, 1953); Id., *Fidalgos in the Far East 1550–1770. Facts and Fancies in the History of Macao,* (The Hague, 1948); Cyril Birch, "Feng Meng-lung and the Ku chin hsiao shuo", *Bulletin of the School of Oriental and African Studies,* XVIII, (1956) 64–83; Id., "Some Formal Characteristics of Hua-pen story", Ibid. DVII, (1955) 346–364; L. Carrington Goodrich (ed.), *Dictionary of Ming Biography,* 2 Vols. (New York, Columbia University Press, 1976); Romeyn Taylor, *Basic Annals of Ming T'ai-tsu,* (San Francisco: Chinese Materials Center, 1975); Edward L. Farmer, *Early Ming Government: The Evolution of Dual Capitals,* (Cambridge: Harvard University Press, 1976).

[14] Henri Bernard, S.J., *Le Père Matthieu Ricci et la société chinoise de son temps 1552–1650,* (Tientsin, 1937); Id., *Matteo Ricci's Scientific Contribution to China,* (tr. by Edward T. C. Werner) (Peiping, 1935); Id., *Aux portes de la Chine; les missionaires du seizième siècle, 1514–1588,* (Tientsin, 1933); Hsiang Ta 向達, "Ming ch'ing chih chi Chung-kuo mei-shu so shou hsi-yang chih ying-hsiang" 明清之際中國美術所受西洋之影響, *The Eastern Miscellany* 東方雜誌, 27, (January, 1920) 1, 19–38; Fang Hao 方豪, *Chung hsi chiao-t'ung shih* 中西交通史, (Taipei, 1954) vol. 4–5; Yabuuchi Kiyochi 藪內清, "Seiyo temmon-gaku no tozen" 西洋天文學の東漸, *Tōhō gakuhō* 東方學報, 15 (Kyoto, 1945) 2, 1–22.

[15] A. H. Rowbotham, *"China and the Age of Enlightenment in Europe", Chinese Social and Political Science Review,* 19, 176–201; D. F. Lach, *China and the Making of Europe;* Id. "China and the Era of Enlightenment", *Journal of Modern Library,* (1942) XIV, 209–223; R. F. Flewelling, "China and the European Englightenment", *The Personalists,* (1937) Winter number; Ch'en Shou-yi 陳受頤, "Sino-European Cultural Contacts Since the Discoveries of the Sea Route: A Bibliographical Note", *Nankai Social and Economic Quarterly,* 8, (April, 1935) 1, 44–74; Virgile Pinot, *La Chine et la formation de l'esprit philosophique en France (1640–1740),* (Paris, 1932); Martino Pierre, *L'Orient dans la literature Française au XVIIe et au XVIIIe siècle,* (Paris, 1906).

[16] Wu Han 吳晗, *Tu-shih cha-chi* 讀史劄記, (Peking, 1956) 156–234 "Chi Ming-shih-lu" 記明實錄; Chao Shih-wei 趙士煒, "Shih-lu k'ao" 實錄考, *Fu-jen hsüeh-chih* 輔仁學誌, 5, 1 and 2; Ch'üan-shou 泉壽, "Chao-hsien so ts'ang ti Ming-shih-lu" 朝鮮所藏的明實錄, *Ta-kung-pao t'u-shu fu-k'an* 大公報圖書副刊, 6, (Dec., 1933); Asano Tadasuke 淺野手允, "Min jitsu-roku zakko, ei-in-hon o chu-shin to shite" 明實錄雜考—影印本を中心として, *Hoku ajia gakuhō* 北西西亞學報, 3, (1944); Wolfgang Franke, "Zur Kompilation und Überlieferung der Ming Shih-lu", *Sinologische Arbeiten,* I, (1943) 1–46; Id., "Weitere Beitrage zur Kompilation und Überlieferung der Ming Shih-lu", *Sinologische Arbeiten,* II, (1944) 1–29; "Nachtrag zur Kompilation und Überlieferung der Ming Shih-lu", *Sinologische Arbeiten,* III, (1945) 165–168; Id., "The Veritable Records of the Ming Dynasty," *Bulletin of the School of Oriental and African Studies,* (July, 1956); A. C. Moule & Chung Kei-wen, "The Ta Ming Shih-lu" 大明實錄, *T'oung Pao,* 35, 289–323; L. C. Goodrich, "A note on the Ta Ming Shih-lu," *T'oung Pao,* 36, (1940) 81–84.

[17] In the "Eminent Chinese of the Ch'ing Period" edited by A. W. Hummel (Washington, 1944) vol. II, 803, it says: "The National Library of Peiping possesses a manuscript *Ming-shih kao,* in 416 *chuan,* which the officials of the Library attribute to Wan Ssu-t'ung, and of which they caused a transcript to be made for the Library of Congress."

[18] *Ch'ing-shih kao* 清史稿, 227; Liang Ch'i-ch'ao 梁啓超, *Ch'ing-tai hsüeh-che cheng-li chiu-hsüeh chih tsung-ch'eng-chi* 清代學者整理舊學之總成績, (*Tung-fang wen-ku hsü-pien* 東方文庫續編 series) (Shanghai, 1933) C. 6; Chin Yü-fu 金毓黻, *Chung-kuo shih-hsüeh-shih* 中國史學史, (Shanghai, 1957) 114, 13 ; Hou Jen-chih 侯仁之, "Wang Hung-hsü Ming-shih lieh-chuan ts'an-kao" 王鴻緒明史列傳殘稿, *Yen-ching hsüeh-pao* 燕京學報, 28, (June, 1939) 213–238; Ch'en Shou-shih 陳守實, "Ming-shih kao k'ao-cheng" 明史稿考證, *Kuo-hsüeh lun ts'ung* 國學論叢, I, (June, 1927) 237–259; Wang Huan-piao 王煥鑣, "Wan

chi yeh hsien-sheng hsi-nien yao-lu" 萬季野先生繫年要錄, *Shih-ti tsa-chih* 史地雜誌, 1, (1937) 2, 11–22; Meng Sen 孟森, "Wan Chi-yeh hsien-sheng ming-shih-kao pien-wu" 萬季野先生明史稿辯誣, *Shih-ti tsa-chih* 史地雜誌, (1937) 2, 7–9; "Wan Chi-yeh Ming-shih-kao liu-san mu-lu" 萬季野明史稿流散目錄, *Kuo-feng pan-yüeh-k'an* 國風半月刊, 4, 6 (I forgot to locate the name of the author of this article.)

[19] *Ming shih* 明史, (ts'e 1); Wang Sung-wei 王頌蔚, *Ming-shih k'ao-cheng chun-i* 明史考證擷逸, (Chia-yeh-t'ang 嘉業堂 edition).

[20] *Ming-tai-shih*, 2–3; Li Chin-hua 李晉華, "Ming-shih tsuan-hsiu kao" 明史纂修考, *Yen-ching hsüeh-pao chuan-hao* 燕京學報專號, 3, (1933); Huang Yün-mei 黃雲眉, "Ming-shih pien-tsuan k'ao-lüeh" 明史編纂考略, *Chin-ling hsüeh-pao* 金陵學報, 1 (Nov. 1931) 2, 323–360; Ch'en Shou-shih 陳守實, "Ming-shih chüeh-wei" 明史抉微, *Kuo-hsüeh lun-ts'ung* 國學論叢, 1, (Oct., 1928) 4, 111–148; Wu Han 吳晗, "Ming-shih hsiao-p'ing" 明史小評, *T'u-shu p'ing-lun* 圖書評論, 1, 9. 21–26; Wu Yü-ts'ang 吳雨蒼, "Hsiu-cheng ming-shih shang-ch'üeh" 修正明史商榷, *Kuo-chuan yüeh-k'an* 國專月刊, 1, 1; Chu Hsi-tsu 朱希祖, "Pien-tsuan Nan-ming-shih ti chi-hua" 編纂南明史的計劃, *Chung-yang yen-chiu-yüan yüan wu yüeh-pao* 中央研究院院務月報, 2, 2.

[21] Louis Pfister, S.J., *Notices Biographiques et Bibliographiques sur les Jésuites de l'ancienne Mission de Chine 1552–1773*, (Shanghai, 1932) 1, 232–235, 252, de Magalhães wrote about his captivity under the title: *Relação das tyranias obradas por Cang-hien Chungo famoso ladrão da China, em o anno 1651*; Hsü Tsung-tse 徐宗澤, "Chang Hsien-chung ju ch'uan yü Yeh-su-hui shih" 張獻忠入川與耶穌會士, *The Eastern Miscellany*, 43, (July, 1947) 13, 45–48.

[22] J. M. Braga, *Jesuitas na Asia*, (Macao, 1959). This is a collection of some copies of the original documents which were kept in the Colegio da Madre de Deus in Macao in the 18th Century. In 1742 the Jesuit Provincial gave instructions to Brother João Alvarez to have those documents copied with the intention of sending them to the Holy See which seems to have manifested a desire to see them just at the time when the question of the "Chinese Rites" was being debated. Brother Alvarez with the assistance of seven copyists completed the work between 1744 and 1748. The collection consists of 63 codices altogether about over one thousand pages in folio. Somehow these documents never went to Rome but eventually came into the possession of the Biblioteca do Palacio da Ajuda de Lisboa. The publication of Mr. Braga is the catalogue of these documents. It was published in the *Boletim Diocesano*, and is still being continued. A glance through this catalogue reveals that these documents deal with the history of the Jesuit Mission in the East. There is a good deal on China of the late Ming and early Ch'ing period. It can well be called the *Ming Ch'ing shih liao* from western sources.

[23] Tai Li 戴笠 (floruit 1670), *K'ou-shih pien-nien* 寇事編年, (*Hsüan-lan-t'ang ts'ung-shu* 玄覽堂叢書) (Nanking, 1947) (ts'e 5).

[24] There is a new edition of the *Kuo-ch'üeh* published in six volumes, 104 *chüan* at the end of 1958 by the Ku-chi ch'u-pan-she 古籍出版社, Peking. This edition is based on the *Yen-fen ts'ao-t'ang* 衍芬草堂 and the *Pao-ching-t'ang* 抱經堂 manuscripts and was corrected and punctuated by Chang Tsung-hsiang 張宗祥.

[25] Hsieh Yü-ts'ai 解毓才, "Ming-tai wei-so chih-tu hsing-shuai-k'ao" 明代衛所制度興衰考, *Shuo-wen yüeh-k'an* 說文月刊, 2, (1924) 9, 10, 11, 12.

[26] Wang Ch'ung-wu 王崇武, "Ming-tai ti shang-t'un chih-tu" 明代的商屯制度, *Yü Kung pan-yüeh-k'an* 禹貢半月刊, 5, (1931) 12, 1–15; Id., "Ming-tai ti min-t'un tsu-chih" 明代的民屯組織, *Yü Kung pan-yüeh-k'an* 禹貢半月刊, 7, (April, 1937) 1, 2, 3 combined issue, 231–238.

[27] Yü Teng 于登, "Ming-tai chien-ch'a chih-tu kai-shu" 明代監察制度概述, *Chin-ling hsüeh-pao* 金陵學報, 6, (Nov., 1936) 2, 109–117; cf. also Sakurai Yoshiro 櫻井芳朗 "On the Formation of the Yü-shih, Censor system of China" 御史制度の形成, *Tōyō-gakuhō* 東洋學報, 23; Wu Han 吳晗, "Ming ch'u ti hsüeh-hsiao" 明初的學校, *Ch'ing-hua hsüeh-pao* 清華學報, 15, (1948) 1; Yü Teng 于登 "Ming-tai kuo-tzu-chien chih-tu k'ao-lüeh" 明代國子監制度考略, *Chin-ling hsüeh-pao* 6, (Nov., 1936) 2, 109–117.

EMPERORS OF THE MING DYNASTY
(1368-1644)

Dynastic Title	Title of Reign	Years of Reign
T'ai-tsu 太祖	Hung-wu 洪武	1368–1398
Hui-ti 惠帝	Chien-wen 建文	1399–1402
Ch'eng-tsu 成祖	Yung-lo 永樂	1403–1424
Jen-tsung 仁宗	Hung-hsi 洪熙	1425
Hsüan-tsung 宣宗	Hsüan-te 宣德	1426–1435
Ying-tsung 英宗	Cheng-t'ung 正統	1436–1449
T'ai-tsung 太宗 ⎫ Ching-ti 景帝 ⎭	Ching-t'ai 景泰	1450–1456
Ying-tsung 英宗	T'ien-shun 天順	1457–1464
Hsien-tsung 憲宗	Ch'eng-hua 成化	1465–1487
Hsiao-tsung 孝宗	Hung-chih 弘治	1488–1505
Wu-tsung 武宗	Cheng-te 正德	1506–1521
Shih-tsung 世宗	Chia-ching 嘉靖	1522–1566
Mu-tsung 穆宗	Lung-ch'ing 隆慶	1567–1572
Shen-tsung 神宗	Wan-li 萬曆	1573–1620
Kuang-tsung 光宗	T'ai-ch'ang 泰昌	1620
Hsi-tsung 熹宗	T'ien-ch'i 天啓	1621–1627
Szu-tsung 思宗	Ch'ung-chen 崇禎	1628–1644

THE GLORY AND FALL OF THE MING DYNASTY

China under the Ming Dynasty: places mentioned in the text.

THE MING EMPIRE IN ASCENDANCY

CHAPTER ONE

The Conquest of an Empire

In the year 1351, a group of laborers while working along the old course of the Huang-ho in Huang-ling-kang 黃陵岡 Shantung, dug up a stone statue. All gathered round to examine this curious discovery, and they found that the figure had only one eye and that it had on the back an inscription which read: "Despise not this stone figure, one-eyed though it be; its appearance will herald rebellion throughout the empire." Rumors spread rapidly, and soon the whole countryside was in a ferment. People now suddenly saw the meaning of a rustic song which no one had been able to interpret till then, for the words of this song were almost identical with those inscribed on the back of the statue: this surely was a sign that the end of barbarian rule was at hand.[1] Historians knew who was the author of the song and were not impressed; but the simple people, judging only from the facts before them, regarded the omen as decisive. Besides, there were plenty of signs that the Yüan dynasty was declining, and since the accession of the ruling emperor, nature had been lavish in providing bad omens: landslides, floods and drought. On several occasions the emperor had issued edicts in which he accepted responsibility for these calamities, yet things continued to grow worse. According to the ancient tradition of the country this showed that Heaven had withdrawn its mandate from the reigning house and transferred it to some more favored line. In consequence, numerous soldiers of fortune came forward, each ready to announce himself the chosen one.

The fall of the Mongol dynasty, however, was gradual and the blame for it should not be laid to the sole charge of the last emperor; rather should one seek the causes for the decline in some of the earlier emperors. When a few years later, in 1369, some of the ministers of the Yüan dynasty came to pay homage to the founder of the supplanting dynasty, the new monarch asked them to name the good and bad points of the Yüan government. One of them having replied that leniency could be said to have been both the good and the bad feature of the Yüan government, the monarch said that he agreed that leniency was the virtue on which the preceding dynasty had built its power, but he could not agree that leniency was the cause of its fall. Too much pressure on the people, he said, causes them to revolt, whereas leniency tends to pacify them. What was wrong with the Yüan government was the pursuit of pleasure by the Mongol court and it was this that had caused its ruin; not leniency but laxity was the fatal fault.[2] Not long after this the new monarch issued an edict calling for the compilation of a history of the Yüan dynasty. The promulgation of this document was the occasion of a fuller statement of his opinion on the cause of his predecessors' fall. In an audience with ministers, he said: "In the beginning of the Yüan dynasty the tradition of the court was simple and government was not allowed to become oppressive, so that people might have a chance to recover from their sufferings. This period came to be known as the age of peace.

"However, later generations of the imperial house neglected their duties, while officials usurped power, and this caused revolts throughout the empire, bringing perpetual distress to the people. There may indeed have been some individuals of good character and some loyal ministers; but they were not trusted. Thus came the ruin of the empire. . . ."[3]

This diagnosis by the founder of the Ming dynasty was perfectly correct. Of the eleven Mongol monarchs who ruled in China, only Khubilai could be called really capable; the rest were mediocre and were often inclined to be at once tyrannical and pleasure-seeking. Moreover, during the 109 years of Mongol rule in China only Khubilai and the last monarch, Togan-Temour, had long reigns—35 years each, with the combined reigns of the other nine totalling only 39 years, an average of four years each. Many of them came to the throne as mere boys: Rintchenpal (Ning-tsung 寧宗) 1332, for example, was only seven when he succeeded and he reigned for less than a month. Inevitably the control of the government fell into the hands either of the queen mother or of nobles and ministers, and constant strife among these rulers led even to the murder of emperors. In consequence the authority of the government declined very rapidly. The succession of weak emperors, none of whom was given sufficient time to consolidate his power, must be considered one of the chief causes of the short life of the Yüan dynasty.

Emil Hevelaque, writing on the general character of the history and civilization of China, noted a point of similarity in the histories of all oriental monarchies: they were always at the peak of their power immediately after an invasion. In Egypt, India, Persia, and China alike, the foundation of an empire, or its renewed expansion, followed on the infusion of new blood and the emergence of a great barbarian leader from some neighboring nomad tribe. The people, having lost all fighting spirit under rulers enfeebled by luxurious court life, found themselves helpless in the face of the invading force. The conquerors in turn, though strong at first, were absorbed by the civilization of the vanquished. Little by little they too lost their vigor and their martial spirit. Thus foreign dynasties nearly all ended in the same way. When faced with a revolt of native brigands or an invasion by a vigorous barbarian race, these effete descendants of the earlier conquerors were found to have become as feeble as their own subjects; they were then swept away as rapidly as their ancestors had arrived.[4]

As early as the Chou dynasty (1122–255 B.C.) China had suffered invasion by barbarians from the border lands. In the days of the Han dynasty such invasions became a menace. Towards the end of the Eastern Han, war-lords fighting among themselves employed many barbarians as soldiers and so gave them an opportunity to move gradually into the country and settle among the Chinese. As long as the government was strong, the newcomers were peaceful, but with the outbreak of internal strife they became uncontrollable. In consequence the beginning of the 4th century saw the ruin of the Chin empire and the partition of the country into many small states. The Toba tribes conquered the entire north and founded the Wei dynasty, which lasted from A.D. 386 to 557. The T'ang dynasty witnessed the rise of the Turks in the desert but the vigorous T'ang government succeeded in holding them in subjection and even made use of them several times to put down internal revolts.

Under the Sung dynasty the country was not so fortunate: the Khitans, a people of Mongol tongue, who in the last years of the T'ang had founded an empire later to be known as the Liao dynasty in what is now Mongolia and Manchuria, constantly menaced the northern frontier and early in the tenth century actually occupied part of China proper.

Another newcomer was the Hsi Hsia 西夏 state, founded by a Tangut people in the later years of the T'ang. Ultimately their territory covered the present Kansu and part of modern Shensi. The Sung government, whose military power had never been impressive, tried to pacify its neighbors by promising tribute and yielding territory. This was a policy that could not succeed. Accordingly the Sung formed an alliance with the Juchens, a people of Tungustic stock and ancestors of the Manchus.

For a short time this policy prospered: the Juchens overthrew the Khitans in 1123. Soon, however, they turned their arms against the Sung themselves, capturing Pien-liang 汴梁, capital of the Sung empire (the modern K'ai-feng, Honan province) in 1127. This, however, was not the end of the Sung. The reigning emperor and his father, who had abdicated two years before, were carried into exile together with their families, but one of the sons of the reigning monarch managed to escape and was raised to the Sung throne at Lin-an, the present Hang-chou. The Juchens, however, who had established their empire in 1115 under the title of Chin 金, now extended their power to the two banks of the Yellow River.

While the Sung were still confronting the Chin, there was born in Mongolia, not far from the Onon River, a great leader, Genghiz Khan, who was to found the mighty Mongol empire. The Mongols, at first subject to the Juchens, were destined to destroy the Chin empire in 1234, though not till after the death of Genghiz Khan himself (1227). The Sung thus survived the Chin and continued to hold out south of the Yangtze; but the Mongols, who had occupied the whole of the north, were relentlessly pressing southwards and in 1279 Khubilai Khan overthrew the Sung dynasty and unified the whole of China under the dynastic rule of Yüan.

Instead of consolidating the empire which he held, Khubilai imitated his grandfather's misguided ambition for territorial expansion. Scarcely had he unified the whole of China when he turned his attention to the conquest of Japan. The two expeditions which he sent to Japan ended in disaster and he was equally unsuccessful with his ventures in Cambodia, Annam, and Java. All these military expeditions were a heavy financial drain on the treasury, and the great Khan had to look to his ministers to raise revenues for him. Men like Ahmad, Lu Shih-jung 盧世榮 and Sanga may have been able ministers of finance, but they were corrupt, and risings amongst the people soon gave proof of deep dissatisfaction with the Yüan administration.

A more fundamental cause of the speedy decline of the Yüan dynasty was the corrupt behavior of Lamaist monks. Under the patronage of Khubilai, Lamaism had become the religion of the

Mongols and monasteries of considerable size were built in Mongolia and northern China. The Mongolian nobles had the greatest respect for the Lamaist monks, and successive emperors of the Yüan dynasty were so lavish in their gifts to them that one of the ministers, Chang Yang-hao 張養浩 (c. 1308) complained that two thirds of the budget of the empire was being spent on the monks.[5] Their number increased rapidly and many of them led lives that were far from monastic, committing crimes of every kind with complete disregard of public opinion. Moreover, they gave their protection to scoundrels who preyed upon the poor.

The extravagance of the emperors caused the gravest financial embarrassment and this was made worse by the unlimited inflation of the paper currency. Towards the end of the dynasty, paper notes were issued daily in profusion to meet the needs of the moment and soon they lost all value and became so much waste paper.[6] The *Hsin Yüan-shih* tells us that a note of ten ting 錠 (50 taels) would not buy one picul of grain, and people were forced to return to a barter system.

By the middle of the 14th century the corruption of the Yüan government was becoming more and more evident, and rebellions were breaking out everywhere against the exactions of officials. A special source of discontent was the introduction of quasi-racial distinctions under the Mongol regime. The people of the empire were divided into four categories: Mongols, Se-mu 色目, Han-jen 漢人, and Nan-jen 南人, ranking in that order. The Se-mus were immigrants from Turkestan and from countries to the west, including Europeans; the Han-jen were the Chinese of northern China together with the Khitans and Juchens; Nan-jen were southerners who had lived under the Sung dynasty. The Mongols were well aware of the discontent of the Nan-jen and spared no effort to keep them under control; but, as the proverb says, "A hungry man is an angry man," and there were many willing volunteers for any rebellion against the imperial authority.

In 1348 Fang Kuo-chen 方國珍, formerly a salt dealer, became a pirate and constantly robbed the imperial transports. Three years later a certain Han Shan-t'ung 韓山童, head of the White Lotus sect,[7] gathered a large number of followers who met under pretence of religious worship. They put forward prophecies that chaos was coming to the empire, that Maitreya had been born in Honan province, that the "King of Light" was about to appear and would rule over the whole empire. Han Shan-t'ung was acclaimed as a descendant of the Sung emperor, Hui-tsung, who would expel the barbarians from China and restore the ancient glory of the Sung dynasty. This secretly organized conspiracy was cut short by an unexpected government raid in which Han lost his life; but one of his followers, Liu Fu-t'ung 劉福通, escaped and eventually managed to collect an army of over ten thousand men. At the same time Hsü Shou-hui 徐壽輝, a clothes dealer, rose in Hu-kuang (now Hunan, Hupeh), and Kuo Tzu-hsing 郭子興, son of a fortune-teller, in Hao-chou (now in Anhui). Both of these joined Liu Fu-t'ung, the combined forces being known as the Red Army since the soldiers wore red turbans. In 1355, Liu Fu-t'ung met Han Lin-erh 韓林兒, son of Han Shan-t'ung, and proclaimed him emperor of the Sung dynasty under the title Hsiao Ming-wang 小明王, "Junior King of Light." The Red Army met no resistance and was welcomed enthusiastically by the people; but quarrels broke out among the leaders, discipline became relaxed among the rank and file, and the people turned against them. Taking advantage of the dissensions of the rebel leaders and the disillusionment of the people, the government succeeded in regaining some of the lost ground.

The quarrels among the leaders of the Red Army led to the founding of many petty "kingdoms" or "empires." Hsü Shou-hui occupied Hu-kuang and proclaimed himself emperor with the dynastic title of T'ien-wan 天完, establishing his capital in Han-yang in 1355. Two years later one of his generals, Ming Yü-chen 明玉珍, a farmer by origin, moved to Szechuan where he founded the kingdom of Hsia 夏. Hsü was killed by another of his generals, Ch'en Yu-liang 陳友諒, a former fisherman, who now established for himself the kingdom of Han 漢 in Wu-chang, Hupeh. In Kiangsu, Chang Shih-ch'eng 張士誠, a salt trader, gathered ten thousand men of the same trade and after taking a few cities near Yang-chou he set up the kingdom of Chou 周. Finally, Kuo Tzu-hsing, the fortune-teller's son whom we mentioned above, established himself in the territory of Feng-yang, Anhui, with the title Ch'u-yang wang 滁陽王. Thus China was carved up among war-lords.

In the spring of 1355 Kuo Tzu-hsing died and the command of his army passed to Chu Yüan-chang 朱元璋, one of his most successful generals, who had gained the confidence of Kuo and received his adopted daughter in marriage. He was thus a man of considerable importance, but at this time no one could have dreamed that he was to become the founder of one of the great dynasties of China. Like Kuo Tzu-hsing he was a native of Hao-chou, then in Honan province; unlike him he was the son of a farmer. In 1344, plague carried off both his parents and two of his brothers; he and another brother survived but they were so poor that they had to beg for land in which to bury their relatives. Famine was raging in the locality, so at the age of seventeen, in order to keep himself alive, he decided to become a Buddhist monk in a local monastery. Even in the monastery, however, life was not easy and before long the abbot announced that owing to the famine the monks would have to disperse. Chu left the monastery and kept alive by begging in the neighboring districts. After three years, however, he returned to the monastery and stayed there for several years.

At length, stirred by news of the risings that were taking place all over the empire, Chu threw off his Buddhist habit and enlisted as a soldier under Kuo Tzu-hsing, who, we are told, was so impressed by him that he made him his personal guard. Chu's sympathy with the poor and his friendliness towards his subordinates made him very popular. On the death of Kuo Tzu-hsing, Chu proceeded to gather around him men of military and administrative talent and he soon displayed a farsightedness that distinguished him from the other rebel leaders. Moreover, while these war-lords were content with the territories they had conquered, he envisaged the conquest of the whole empire. It is related of him that a scholar once told him that if he would succeed he must observe three principles: build strong city walls, gather a store of grain, and be slow to assume titles. Again, another advised him to make Chin-ling the foundation of his dynasty, and to devote himself to relieving the sufferings of the people rather than to securing personal gain, as the other war-lords were doing.[8] All this advice he followed faithfully. When he had taken Chin-ling, he fortified it and made it his headquarters; he protected the farmers and encouraged them to grow grain; finally, until his power had been consolidated, he chose to be regarded as a supporter of Han Lin-erh, who claimed descent from the Sung emperors. At this time when the feelings of the people were so bitter against the Mongols as foreign enemies, this prudent behavior must have won Chu Yüan-chang great credit.

The capture of Chin-ling was a wise move. Since all the neighboring provinces were occupied by war-lords, it was protected from direct Mongol attack. Chu Yüan-chang thus got time to strengthen his forces and to perfect the administration of his government. Meanwhile, he kept a close watch on the struggles between the war-lords and the government army, and whenever he saw a city left defenseless, he dispatched a force to capture it. Thus, within a few years, he became one of the most powerful leaders south of the Yangtze River.

Chu Yüan-chang now felt himself strong enough to turn his attention to the war-lords, the most formidable of whom were Ch'en

Yu-liang and Chang Shih-ch'eng. Ch'en held the Hu-kuang and Kiangsi provinces and had a strong army and navy; Chang held Kiangsu and Chekiang and had command of rich resources. In 1360, Ch'en sought an alliance with Chang, but Chang refused the offer. In the following year Chu Yüan-chang's navy defeated Ch'en's in Kiangsi, and to avenge this defeat Ch'en Yu-liang set off from Wu-chang in 1363 with 600,000 men. With one third of that number, Chu Yüan-chang met him at Lake P'o-yang in Kiangsi. The desperate struggle that followed was already going in Chu's favor when Ch'en himself received a mortal wound and died. This practically ended the struggle. Ch'en's son was set up by his father's troops as king but he surrendered to Chu in the following year.

Chu Yüan-chang now turned south to the present Kiangsu and Chekiang, both ruled by Chang Shih-ch'eng. Chang was an attractive character, generous and easy of approach, but lacking in foresight. After conquering present Kiangsu and Chekiang, he had settled in Su-chou and lived in luxury there, leaving the administration entirely in the hands of his younger brother and a few ministers, whose crimes and follies soon reduced the government to chaos. In 1366, Chu Yüan-chang's armies took northern Kiangsu; in the following year they moved south and took Su-chou, few of the ministers and generals of Chang having the courage to resist. Chu Yüan-chang's armies promised safety to government officials and respect for the lives and property of the people, and this hastened the collapse of Chang Shih-ch'eng. When Su-chou fell after a seven-month siege, Chang himself was captured, but committed suicide rather than face his conqueror. The same year, 1367, saw the surrender of Fang Kuo-chen, and when Fukien, Kuangtung and Kuangsi surrendered in the following year, 1368, most of south China was under the rule of Chu. In the autumn of that same year, 1368, the Mongol capital, Ta-tu, was captured, and by 1369 Chu Yüan-chang held the whole of China with the exception of Szechuan, conquered in 1371, and Yünnan, which did not fall until 1382.

It was time now to think about the establishment of a new empire. In the previous twenty years, many had essayed this, some claiming descent from the Sung emperors, others resting their pretensions on supposed divine revelation, but all had failed. No doubt Chu Yüan-chang himself had pondered over these abortive attempts. He was intelligent and was a good organizer, but above all he possessed that deep common sense and practical wisdom so often found in men of peasant stock. Early hardship had steeled him to meet the vicissitudes of life and his years in the monastery had given him the habit of calm reflection on what lay before him. He knew how superstitious the people around him were and he did not hesitate to turn this to his own advantage by weaving a web of preternatural glory round his name, as his biography of the lunatic fairy Chou shows.[9] Many legends and fairy stories about him survive in popular lore; some of these are even recorded by his biographers. Thus it is related that before he was born his mother dreamed of two Taoist monks who gave her a pill; after she had taken this she gave birth to Chu, and on the night of his birth the sky above the house became so red that the villagers rushed to see if there was a fire. Again it was said that when he was on his wanderings as a monk, whenever he became ill two men in scarlet appeared at his side and remained with him until he was well again. One night when he had lost his way, a crowd of children appeared and addressed him as "Your Majesty"; when he shouted at them, they disappeared.[10] Such tales had a great effect on the simple people, who took them as sufficient proof that Chu had been sent by heaven to deliver the poor from their miseries.

For his part, Chu Yüan-chang lost no opportunity of winning the good-will of the people. Thus, in 1356, after the capture of Chen-kiang, he summoned the elders of the city and said to them: "The misrule of the Yüan government has caused riots throughout the empire and I have come with the sole purpose of delivering the people from their miseries. Let all of you understand this and remain at peace. If among you there are men of virtue and talent, I shall be happy to employ them. I shall not hesitate to abolish any law which may be hurtful to you, and I will see to it that you do not suffer injustice at the hands of minor officials."[11]

The success of Chu Yüan-chang owed much to the strict discipline which he enforced over his officers and soldiers. We are told that in 1359, before moving his forces towards east Chekiang, he made the following address to his subjects: "One can, it is true, capture a city by armed force, but to calm a tumult one must employ kindness. Lately, my army marched on Chi-ch'ing 集慶 (Nanking) and because I maintained good discipline, I took it without difficulty. Now that we have captured Wu-chou 婺州 we should do our best to rule it wisely so as to win over the people. When other provinces hear of this, they will be the more willing to submit to our authority. It always pleases me greatly when I hear that my generals have captured a city without unnecessary shedding of innocent blood. When a general learns that bravery does not consist in killing, he not only confers a great benefit on the country, but also ensures that his descendants shall be blessed."[12]

The scholar Chao I 趙翼 (1727–1814) drew up a formal comparison between the founder of the Ming and the founder of the Han dynasty and found so close a similarity between them that he concluded that the founder of the Ming had imitated Liu Pang 劉邦, the founder of the Han. Certainly the resemblance is striking. These two were the only ordinary subjects to become emperors in the whole history of China; both came from the modern Anhui province; both were men of sound common sense with a gift for organization. When conversing with Chu Yüan-chang, his ministers often quoted to him the achievements of the founder of the Han, and Chu himself often had before his mind the example of Liu Pang. Once he pointed out to one of his ministers that Han Kao-ti (i.e. Liu Pang) had risen from among the people to oppose the tyranny of the Ch'in government, that his dominant spirit had compelled the war-lords to submit to his authority, and that eventually he became master of the whole country. In his own time, he went on, many leaders had led revolts against the misrule of the Yüan government but all had failed through lack of discipline and want of organization.[13] He himself had regarded these things as necessary conditions for success. From the beginning of his military career he had deliberately made it his aim to train his generals and soldiers to respect his authority.

We have an example of this last in the biography of Hu Ta-hai 胡大海. When the Ming forces had captured Wu-chou, Chu Yüan-chang, perhaps to save rice, at once issued an order forbidding the making of wine. Ta-hai's son violated this order and Chu in a rage ordered him to be executed. At that very moment Ta-hai was besieging some cities in Chekiang and some of the ministers tried to save the life of the son for the sake of the father, but Chu would not listen to their plea. ''I would rather see Ta-hai turn against me,'' he said, ''than lessen my own authority.''[14]

NOTES

[1] *Hsü Tzu-chih t'ung-chien* 續資治通鑑, 210, (Shanghai, 1888) (ts'e 56) 2a; cf. *Yüan Shih*, 66, Han-fen-lou 涵芬樓 ed. Shanghai, 1916) (ts'e 18) 10b.

[2] Hsia Hsieh 夏燮 (floruit 1840), *Ming t'ung-chien* 明通鑑, 1, (Tien-shih-chai 點石齋 edition, 1903) (ts'e 1) 9b.

[3] Ibid., 10a.

[4] Emile Hevelaque, *La Chine*, (Paris, 1928) 109–110.

[5] *Hsin Yüan-shih*, 243, (Kai-ming shu-tien 開明書店 ed.) 461; *Hsü Tzu-chih t'ung-chien* 190, (ts'e 54) 4a; Ibid., 197, (ts'e 54) 3b.

[6] *Hsin Yüan-shih*, 74, 174; cf. H. Yule, *The Book of Ser Marco Polo*, (edited by Henri Cordier), London, 1926, I, Bk. 2, 423–430; Lü Szu-mien 呂思勉, *Chung-kuo t'ung-shih* 中國通史, (Shanghai, 1948) 1, 229–230; Chao I 趙翼 (1727–1814), *Erh-shih-erh shih cha-chi* 二十二史劄記, 30, (Wen-yüan shan-fang 文淵山房 ed., 1902) (ts'e 5) 61 ab.

[7] The White Lotus is a Buddhist sect which was started in A.D. 384 by the monk Hui-yüan 慧遠 (A.D. 334–416). In its beginning a good number of Confucian scholars adhered to it. Under the tolerance of religions of the Mongols the White Lotus sect was free to build and propagate its belief. In 1308, however, for the first time the practice of this sect was forbidden and their temples were ordered to be destroyed. According to a modern writer and others, the teaching of the White Lotus sect of that period was already adulterated with Manichaeism and the Maitreya sect. The prohibition only drove this sect to underground activities and after that it became a secret society, and in the eyes of governments of later dynasties, illegal. They began to make trouble at the end of the Yüan dynasty. Toward the end of the Ming dynasty, again an uprising took place under the T'ien-ch'i 天啓 reign (1621–1627). During the later years of the Ch'ien-lung and Chia-ch'ing reigns (1775–1805) great insurrections were started by them. They remained a menace to the Ch'ing government till the end of the dynasty. Cf. *Tōyō rikishi dajiten* 東洋歷史大辭典, 7, 303–304; Wu Han 吳晗, *Tu-shih cha-chi* 讀史劄記, (Peking, 1956) 257–258; *Ming-chiao yü Ta-Ming ti-kuo* 明教與大明帝國.

[8] Ku Ying-t'ai 谷應泰 (died after 1689), *Ming-shih chi-shih pen-mo* 明史紀事本末, *(HKCPTS)*, A. 2.

[9] *Yü chih Chou-tien hsien-jen chuan* 御製周顛仙人傳, *(Chi-lu hui-pien* 紀錄彙編, photographic reprints from the Ming edition by the Commercial Press, Shanghai, 1938) (ts'e 2) chapter 6.

[10] Kao Tai 高岱, *Hung-yu lu* 鴻猷錄, *(CLHP)*, 1, (ts'e 22) 3a.

[11] *Ming t'ung-chien*, 1, (ts'e 1) 4b.

[12] Ibid., 1, (ts'e 1) 9a.

[13] *Erh-shih-erh shih cha-chi*, 32, (ts'e 6) 6b, 7a; *Ming t'ung-chien, chien chi* 前紀, 3, (ts'c 1) 19b, 20a.

[14] *Ming shih*, 133, (ts'e 48) 7b.

CHAPTER TWO

Government

POWER STRUCTURE

Chu Yüan-chang founded the Ming empire in 1368. As the official style of his reign he chose Hung-wu 洪武; accordingly, he himself was known as the Hung-wu emperor. Like all the founders of dynasties he tried to lay a solid foundation for the rule of his descendants. As we have already pointed out, the Hung-wu emperor realized that one of the main causes of the fall of the Mongol dynasty was the lack of authority among the emperors. Nobles and officials, civilian as well as military, were constantly fighting for power and even dared to defy the imperial authority itself. Moreover, when a young emperor came to the throne, there was always danger that the empress dowager would try to dominate the policy of the government. This violent rivalry for power had inevitably weakened the central authority, and this in turn was the source of abuses among major and minor officials.

To obviate such weaknesses the Hung-wu emperor determined to establish absolute government. He was in no way tied to imitation of the imperial traditions of more recent times, for he had ascended the throne from among the people and had taken for his model the founder of the Han dynasty. Nevertheless his scheme of government naturally followed traditional lines. In the early days of his reign when affairs were still unsettled, he was satisfied to adopt the system of the Yüan dynasty. But he gradually introduced changes and a new government system emerged, bearing all the special characteristics of the new dynasty.

First of all, he tried to reverse all the Mongol customs which he considered to have been a great hindrance to good government. In the second month of his reign he issued an edict ordering the people to return to the dress worn under the T'ang dynasty. He then tried to forbid personal use of Mongolian names which had been popular under the Yüan dynasty. Changes of this kind, however, are always difficult to enforce, and at the end of the first year of his reign a censor reported that the people of the capital were still stubborn in their adherence to Mongol practices. In an edict issued four years later the emperor declared that there was further necessity for purifying the morals and customs of the people, "since," he said, "in towns and villages people are still infected with the customs of the Mongols."[1]

The Hung-wu emperor realized clearly the importance of education. Good citizens must know how to behave properly and this implies knowledge. He was equally aware that officials of integrity could be found only from among well-trained men. He himself, it is true, had very little education in his early days, but he had never ceased to perfect himself after the Confucian ideal ever since his first rising against the Mongols. Most of his advisers were scholars of high standing, who kept on grounding him in solid Confucian principles. Under their influence the monarch himself turned into a man of culture, able to compose essays and poems as well as any learned man of his day. His calligraphy, moreover, proved him a gifted artist. Under the encouragement of the emperor and the advice of his ministers, scholarship gradually returned to the flourishing state it had enjoyed under the Sung dynasty. The examination system also was given a solid foundation which was to last till the end of the 19th century. All of this we shall mention again in later chapters.

Let us now turn to the founder of the Ming dynasty and study the means by which he managed to consolidate his authority and make himself absolute ruler of the empire. By a common paradox, he had learned to rule by obeying strict discipline himself. In his early military career when he first enlisted under Kuo Tzu-hsing he distinguished himself both by bravery and by absolute obedience to orders. This was the secret of his rapid rise to leadership among the revolutionaries. As a young leader still largely unknown to the outside world he submitted humbly to the authority of Han Lin-erh, whose pretensions to descent from the Sung emperors had won him great prestige and many followers. Though in all this the Hung-wu emperor was no doubt actuated by shrewd political motives, nevertheless his actions gave an impression of sincerity and so helped him greatly in expanding his own power. In the eyes of the people he was the model of what a soldier should be. More than once in biographies of him we are told that he won the hearts of the people by enforcing good discipline in newly conquered cities. "When I was still a Mr. Nobody in the army," he used to amuse his subjects by saying in later years, "I was disgusted to notice how among the leaders there was such lack of discipline. Later on I was promoted to the command of an army in which all the soldiers were newly enlisted. One day when I was leading them out to fight, two of the men disobeyed me. I immediately ordered them to be executed. From then on, all submitted to my commands with trembling and no one dared violate my orders. Nothing is impossible to a man of strong will."[2]

The Hung-wu emperor's low origin made him sensitive to what others might say about him. Although he was a good friend to scholars and showed great respect for them, he always remained suspicious of them. They were, in general, men who lived by ideals and could easily be disappointed by real life. They were adept in sarcasm and frequently indulged in subtle plays upon words for which it was almost impossible to bring them to book. The name Chang Shih-ch'eng, for instance, was said to have been given by a certain scholar to a war-lord. It was taken from a passage in *Mencius* (Book II, "Kung-sun Chow" 公孫丑, Part II, Chapter 12, section 7) in which Yin Shih 尹士 is quoted as saying "士誠小人哉," meaning "I (i.e. Yin Shih) am indeed 小人 hsiao-jen a narrow-minded man," or a "mean person." It was obvious that in giving the name Shih-ch'eng to the war-lord, the scholar intended to indicate that he was 小人 in one or other of its opprobrious senses, probably the second. Under the title "Literary Inquisition in the Early Ming Dynasty" Chao I gives a number of instances of ministers losing their lives simply because the Hung-wu emperor suspected them of *lèse-majesté*. Some of these were accused of having alluded in their writings to the fact that the monarch was an usurper, others to the fact that he had been a Buddhist monk.[3]

To demonstrate that the emperor had absolute power over his ministers, the Hung-wu emperor adopted a Mongolian punishment, beating at court (t'ing-chang 廷杖). This punishment had originated in the Sui dynasty (518–618 A.D.) and was practised throughout the Yüan dynasty, when the nomad Mongols had no respect whatsoever for their ministers.[4] A writer who lived in the early years of the Ch'ing dynasty has left us an account of this torture:

"On the day fixed for the administration of a public beating at court, a eunuch was always called upon to supervise the proceedings.

All the court officials lined up in their red uniforms. On the left stood the eunuchs and on the right the emperor's body-guard, thirty men on each side. Below stood a hundred soldiers wearing P'i-i 襞衣, with wooden clubs in their hands. After the mandate of the emperor had been read, a man came with a sack of hemp which he put over the shoulders of the victim, so fastening it that the victim could move neither to the left nor to the right. Another fastened the victim by his feet, pulling them apart and leaving the buttocks of the victim ready to receive the beating. The victim's head and face were made to touch the ground and his mouth was covered with dust.

"The majority of those who received the beating died as a result. If they happened to survive, as much as a picul of dead flesh had to be removed. Recovery took several months."[5]

The emperor's control extended even to the checking of dangerous thoughts. One day when reading the book of Mencius he came across the passage in which Mencius says to King Hsüan of Ch'i, "When the prince regards his ministers as his hands and feet, his ministers regard their prince as their belly and heart; when he regards them as dogs and horses, they regard him as any other man; when he regards them as the ground or as grass, they regard him as a robber and an enemy." (*Mencius*, Book IV, "Li Lou" 離婁, Part II, Chapter 3, verse 1). Such independent ideas did not please the monarch, who required perfect submission from his subjects. Accordingly an order was given that Mencius' tablet should be removed from the temple of the sages. The reason given for this act was that such things as had been said by Mencius were not proper when said by a minister to his king. The monarch, we are told, was so angry that he declared the crime of lèse-majesté would be committed by any minister who dared to take up the defense of Mencius. But Mencius and his teaching had been popular among the Confucian scholars since the Sung dynasty and it was not possible to get rid of him so easily. The Hung-wu emperor therefore set up a committee to discuss the writings of the sage. Ultimately the book was purged and eighty-five sections were cut out and were never again to be included in the examination papers.[6]

Towards the end of his reign the emperor suffered a tragic loss which caused him deep sorrow. The heir apparent, a gentle and good-natured man on whom the emperor had placed all his hopes, died (1392) before his father. The emperor was then close to seventy and his grandson, who would succeed him, was still a mere boy. Like the founder of the Han dynasty, the Hung-wu emperor had ascended the throne through good fortune. Many of his followers who had fought bravely for him were now in high positions and were men of long experience in military affairs or experts in administration. What special right had the emperor to leave the throne to his descendants? Was it not possible that, if he were to die suddenly, a *coup d'etat* would oust the little boy emperor and undo all his grandfather's work? By day and by night this problem anguished his soul. Finally, he made up his mind to destroy his most influential ministers. This liquidation had begun, it is true, in 1380, twelve years before the death of the heir apparent. But the loss of his son seems to have strengthened greatly the Hung-wu emperor's determination to get rid of influential members of his government.

During the Hung-wu reign the emperor himself instituted two great trials, in which two ministers were condemned for treason and executed. One of the victims, Hu Wei-yung 胡惟庸, prime minister up to the time of his death, was condemned in 1380. The other, Lan Yü 藍玉, general of the army, was condemned in 1393. Both trials involved thousands of people; in the first over thirty thousand were said to have been executed, and in the second not less than fifteen thousand. Chao I judges it unlikely that so many were found guilty in either trial. He is especially skeptical about the figures given for the first case, the trial of Hu Wei-yung, which was not begun till more than ten years after the execution of the culprit. Having studied the character of the Hung-wu emperor, Chao I does not hesitate to say that these trials must have been pretexts used by the emperor to get rid of all whom he considered undesirable.[7]

Both the condemnation of Hu Wei-yung and that of Lan Yü seem to have originated in a struggle for power between the emperor and his subjects. Hu Wei-yung's biographer tells us that Hu had been preparing his way to the throne by repeated attempts to get rid of loyal subjects of the Hung-wu emperor and to make friends of those who he thought might be of great help to him. Like his master, he too made use of stories of strange happenings to win popularity for himself. It was put about that stones in the shape of bamboo shoots had sprung up mysteriously from the well in his native home at Ting-yüan 定遠, present Hopei. It was also reported that on many nights people had seen shining from the tombs of Hu's ancestors a bright light that reached the sky. The populace regarded these as good omens. The Hung-wu emperor must have recalled the ruses which he had himself employed and felt them dangerous when they were employed by others. Had Hu not committed the crime of treason, this alone would have cost him his life.

Lan Yü's ambitions were still more unmistakable. The author of the *Huang-Ming t'ung-chi* 皇明通紀 narrates that before a certain expedition Lan went with ten or twelve of his officers to bid farewell to the Hung-wu emperor. The monarch, while discussing military strategy with Lan, ordered the officers to retire. He gave the order three times, but no one paid the least attention. When Lan Yü saw this he merely twitched his sleeve and all vanished at once. The monarch was alarmed and saw in this incident a powerful motive for getting rid of his too powerful general.[8]

The Hung-wu emperor was also anxious to solve several problems concerning empresses, concubines, and eunuchs. Throughout the history of China, these three classes had caused a great deal of trouble to successive governments. The monarch himself was well aware of this, especially from his study of the history of the Han dynasty, the founder of which he admired so much and imitated so closely. Shortly after the death of Han Kao-tsu the dynasty he founded was nearly brought to destruction by the ambitions of the Empress Lü, who tried to introduce her relatives as a new dynasty. Fortunately for the Han a few of their loyal ministers put up strong opposition and through their efforts the Han dynasty was restored.

Later emperors were not so lucky. Towards the end of the Western Han period, and throughout a great part of the Eastern Han, many emperors came to the throne as mere boys. The empress dowagers, shrinking from the burden of rule, often sought help from their relatives, who naturally saw in this a glorious chance for getting control of the government. When the emperors reached maturity they found themselves powerless and naturally turned for help to the eunuchs, who were so close to them. The struggles between these two parties usually resulted in great disasters for the empire. The court officials too were often involved in the struggle. Thus in A.D. 8 Wang Mang 王莽, nephew of the empress dowager, deposed the boy emperor and declared himself founder of a new dynasty.

The second half of the second century saw an increase in the power of the court women and in the baleful influence of the eunuchs. To check the influence of the eunuchs, the relatives of the empress sought help from the court ministers and the scholars. Before long thousands of scholars were involved in the struggle. At first the eunuchs seemed to have the upper hand, but eventually they were defeated and slaughtered. The decay of the government had gone too far, however, and the Han dynasty fell soon afterwards.

Knowing all this, the Hung-wu emperor was very strict with the eunuchs. In the year 1369 he issued an edict to the Board of Civil

Office in which he discussed at length the office of the eunuchs: "We read in the *Chou Li* that the number of eunuchs employed (in the court) was less than one hundred. Thereafter their number increased to several thousand and in consequence they caused a great deal of trouble. Although we are not now able to restore the ancient tradition, we should take precautions to prevent abuses. Eunuchs should be employed only to perform household tasks. If you look for men of integrity among them you will scarcely find one or two among a hundred. If you try to use them to find out something for you, you yourself will be blinded. If you give them responsible work to do, they will cause you a great deal of trouble. It would be best to make them fear the law. Never give them a chance to excel in anything, otherwise they will grow proud and will get out of control. If they are kept in fear of the law, they will learn to become discreet (in their conduct) and this will keep them away from disorders."[9]

The Hung-wu emperor was so fortunate as to have had a good wife, the Empress Ma, the adopted daughter of Kuo Tzu-hsing, as we saw above. During their early days, the future empress shared all the hardships of her husband and on many occasions lent him invaluable help. We are told that she was intelligent and was fond of reading, and her kindness well known to all her subjects. One day, in conversation with the emperor, she asked whether the people were satisfied with the new government. The impatient monarch thought it improper for a woman to be so inquisitive about affairs that did not concern her sex. But she retorted: "Your Majesty is now the father of the people and I am the mother. Would it be considered improper for parents to inquire how their children are faring?" By making remarks of this kind she did a great deal of good for her subjects. Shortly after the accession of the Hung-wu emperor he wanted to honor her by giving official rank to her relatives, but she declined firmly, saying that for good government one must employ good ministers whereas her relatives might know nothing about governing, and elevation to the official ranks might be for them only a temptation to do evil.[10]

The Hung-wu emperor, however, knew perfectly well that the goodness of his wife was exceptional. Women can also be ambitious, as history has abundantly proved. For the sake of the newly founded dynasty and for the good of his descendants, he determined to lay down strict rules for empresses, concubines, and court ladies. In the first year of his reign he ordered the compilation of historical lives of exemplary women and instructions on the good behavior of women. Four years later (1372) a red tablet bearing good advice for empresses and concubines was hung in the palace.

A palace administrator (Shang-kung 尚宮) was appointed to look after the needs of the court ladies. When anything was needed by them the palace administrator had first to go to the emperor for his approval. A eunuch was then appointed to make a report. Only when all this had been done might provisions be obtained from the ministers who had charge of supplies. The death penalty was incurred by all who dared to violate this rule. Furthermore, court ladies who sent messages outside the court without permission of the emperor might also incur the death penalty. Strangest of all was the rule that court ladies who fell ill were not allowed to call in physicians; they were allowed, however, to communicate their symptoms to the physicians and so obtain the appropriate medicines.[11]

Through the efforts of the Hung-wu emperor the policy of the government began to take form, and gradually he was able to concentrate all authority in his own person. He gave such vitality to the new empire that the government machine which he had built ran smoothly and was not to stop for nearly three centuries. In later periods, it is true, his successors made changes, introducing new practices or doing away with systems that were no longer serviceable. Yet substantially the structure of the government remained unchanged throughout the whole Ming period.

The *Ming shih* tells us that the Ming system of government was modeled on the Han and T'ang pattern, and that in its early days the dynasty borrowed a great deal from the Mongol regime. As years went on, however, it developed a system of its own. In the central government, the most outstanding change was the abolition of the office of chief or prime minister and the consequent elevation of the emperor to the position of sole dictator. The emperor could now treat his ministers as his servants and there was no one to check him. Since its establishment under the Ch'in dynasty, the office of chief or prime minister had played a vital role, helping greatly to make the government independent of the control of the aristocracy. Imperial house succeeded imperial house, but the direction of government remained largely in the hands of the chief ministers, who often acted in the interests of the people. The influence of the emperors and that of the chief ministers were complementary and extremes were thus avoided.

Ever since the Ch'in dynasty, the day to day direction of affairs had been entirely in the hands of the chief minister. He supervised all the other departments, and all military and legal matters, and made decisions about the promotion and demotion of officials. Up to the Sui dynasty the office of the prime minister was entrusted to one man. The Sui effected a notable change. The exercise of the prime minister's power was divided among three departments: the Shang-shu sheng 尚書省, Men-hsia sheng 門下省, and Nei-shih sheng 內史省. When the T'ang dynasty succeeded the Sui, this system was retained, but the Nei-shih sheng was transformed into the Chung-shu sheng 中書省. Whenever an important order was given, an edict of the emperor was required. Usually, however, the emperor did not write it himself but left it to the Chung-shu sheng to prepare for issue. As soon as the draft of the edict was completed it was sent to the Men-hsia sheng whose duty was to censor it. If the officials of the Men-hsia sheng thought it unsatisfactory, the edict might be sent back to the Chung-shu sheng for redrafting. If the Men-hsia sheng approved of the draft, it was sent to the Shang-shu sheng whose function was to execute the order. The Shang-shu sheng was the largest organization in the central government under the T'ang dynasty. Under it were the Six Boards of: Civil Office, Rites or Ceremonies, Revenue, War, Punishments, and Works. The Board of Civil Office, or Li pu 吏部, dealt with the employment of officials (candidates had of course to pass the examinations before they could be appointed to government work): the board could appoint officials only up to the fifth rank; appointments to higher rank were made by the prime minister (ch'eng-hsiang 丞相). The Board of Revenue or Hu pu 戶部 dealt with the civil administration of the country. All questions of education and religion came under the Board of Rites or Ceremonies or Li pu 禮部. The Board of War or Ping pu 兵部 dealt with military affairs, the Board of Punishments or Hsing pu 刑部 with legal problems, and the Board of Works or Kung pu 工部 with public works.

Under the Sung dynasty the office of the prime minister was nominally what it had been under the T'ang, but in reality all power was centralized in the Chung-shu sheng. The reason for this change was that of the three departments only the Chung-shu sheng had its office in the palace. The Shang-shu and the Men-hsia sheng remained outside the palace and so lost close contact with the emperor. However, the power of the prime minister declined greatly under the Sung dynasty. Military affairs, for instance, were transferred from the control of the prime minister to that of the Shu-mi yüan 樞密院. Even matters of finance had their own department independent of the prime minister and independent departments were set up for the examination of candidates and the employment of officials. It is clear that the emperors of the early Sung dynasty tried to weaken the power of the prime minister. This could even be seen in court etiquette. Under the T'ang dynasty when the emperor gave an audience to his ministers, the prime minister was always given a seat, but from the Sung dynasty onward he too had to stand like the rest of the ministers. This undoubtedly helped to make the emperors look more dignified and more unmistakably absolute.

Of these three departments, the Yüan dynasty retained only the Chung-shu sheng. All the Boards of Civil Office that had exercised the prime minister's powers under the Sung were absorbed into the Chung-shu sheng, the Shang-shu sheng being thus reduced to merely administrative status. For military affairs there was the Shu-mi yüan, and for the inspection of the government there was the Censorate. Nominally the Chung-shu sheng was subordinate to the Chung-shu ling 中書令 ; in reality all authority in the department was exercised by the two ministers (left and right).

At the beginning of the Ming dynasty the Chung-shu sheng was retained as the sole department of the prime minister. In 1380, however, when Hu Wei-yung was executed, the Hung-wu emperor came to the conclusion that the office of the prime minister was too powerful; to his mind it was tantamount to a usurpation. Accordingly he abolished this "troublesome" office and announced his determination that it should never be restored by his descendants. "In the future," said the monarch, "if any of my subjects dares to suggest the restoration of a prime minister, let him be punished and cut into pieces, and let his whole family also be put to death."[12]

As we have seen, so long as the office of the prime minister existed, the prime minister was the head of the political organization, and even the emperor had to respect his position. In the Han or T'ang period the central government was so organized that the powers of the emperor and those of the prime minister were clearly separate. Great though the difference between the two might be, one could still say that the emperor was not absolute. But now, with the office of the prime minister abolished, the emperor became the sole head of the government. The Six Boards, formerly subordinated to the prime minister, were made directly responsible to the emperor. The emperor could now look down upon his ministers as his servants and there was no one to check him. He considered a minister good if he was ready to carry out imperial commands; otherwise, no minister could find favor with his monarch.

Theoretically, the emperor had gathered all power into his own hands; in practice, however, he could not attend to everything and had to look for some way of sharing the toil. Accordingly, the Hung-wu emperor created the Nei-ko 內閣, or Grand Secretariat. The function of this office was merely to supply to the emperor personal secretaries who would take down orders exactly as dictated by him. Sometimes the emperor might seek their views, but he was free to accept or to reject them. The position of the Nei-ko was far from being an exalted one; it ranked only as the fifth grade, three grades lower than the heads of the Six Boards.

Emperors were kept exceedingly busy so long as they continued to direct everything concerning the government, to receive all reports and to make all decisions. The early Ming emperors found it necessary to hold court three times every day. For the Hung-wu emperor, a farmer's son who had spent a great part of his life in military activities, court life may have seemed easy. Even the Yung-lo emperor (the third Ming), who had fought to gain the throne for himself, may have found court life bearable. But for later emperors who had grown up accustomed to an easy life, the burden of government proved too heavy. The simplest way of evading onerous duties was to leave everything in the hands of the Grand Secretaries. Unfortunately the Nei-ko had never been an office of high rank and it did not look well to see an official of low rank exercising high authority. In order to avoid this inconvenience the Grand Secretary was usually given an additional office as head of one of the Six Boards, and thus he was able to act as leader of the rest of the ministers without impropriety. From the time of the Yung-lo emperor onwards the power of the Grand Secretaries was constantly on the increase, but the rank of the Nei-ko remained always in the fifth grade till the end of the Ming. It could never be compared with the rank of the prime minister, which had always been far more dignified. The creation of the Nei-ko system was one of the distinguishing marks of the Ming dynasty but the system was retained by the Manchus when they came to rule China.[13]

Another important office in the central government of the Ming dynasty was the Tu-cha yüan 都察院, or Censorate. The title Yü shih 御史 is found in the *Chou li* and in the annals of the Ch'in dynasty, but it is a matter of dispute whether the office corresponded to the office of the same name of later date. However, the Yü shih or Censor of the kind we are now dealing with certainly existed under the Han dynasty. Among their various functions as censors was to supervise the morals of officials. Sometimes, also, they acted as judges or as police. On special occasions they were sent out as inspectors of official accounts.[14]

A special characteristic of the censors was that, although they were subordinated to a higher authority, they were independent of that authority when exercising their powers. Perhaps because they were the "eyes and ears" of the emperor, they were directly responsible to him alone. Under the T'ang dynasty it sometimes happened that censors even refused to obey legitimate imperial orders. This was, without doubt, audacious, for they, like the rest of the ministers, were not protected by the law, and were always at the mercy of the monarch. Still they often escaped the penalties of audacity; in some way it was sensed that they were backed by public opinion; it was, moreover, their duty to admonish and to criticize. For this reason emperors of different dynasties were chary of ill-treating their censors and thereby winning a reputation for small-mindedness.[15]

Under the Ming dynasty the Yü-shih t'ai 御史臺 or Censorate had its name changed to Tu-cha yüan 都察院. The chief censor of Yü-shih ta-fu 御史大夫 was thereafter known as Tu-yü-shih 都御史 and the vice-censor or Chung ch'eng 中丞 came to be known as Fu tu-yü-shih 副都御史. The *Ming shih* tells us that it was the function of the Tu-yü-shih to maintain order and good customs among all the officials; to direct the affairs of all the provinces; to impeach corrupt ministers and to recommend the promotion of good officials, to report on harmful doctrines or theories that might upset society. Finally, at the trials of serious criminals they were to act as judges along with officials of the Board of Punishment and the Grand Court of Revision.[16]

Among the different grades of censors under the Ming dynasty was the Chien-ch'a yü-shih 監察御史, an innovation of the Hung-wu emperor which played an important part throughout the dynasty. The main duty of censors of this grade was to report on corrupt officials. They presided at examinations for government candidates and inspected accounts and various departments. Often they were sent to the provinces where they examined everything thoroughly, from the local administration to the manner of living among the people. They then made their reports to the emperor and were allowed to make whatever remarks they wished. When meetings were called in court to discuss important affairs, the Chien-ch'a yü-shih always had the privilege of participating.[17]

Thus, the censor system developed greatly under the Ming dynasty. During the Hung-wu period the number of Chien-ch'a yü-shih alone rose to one hundred and ten. Though they were not high in rank (only seventh grade) they had an influential position and were quite independent of the rest of the Censorate. Because of the importance of their office, the Chien-ch'a yü-shih were always carefully selected and candidates had to be men of talent and great experience. Hence metropolitan graduates who had just passed the examinations were never selected.

The Chi-shih-chung 給事中 was another highly important court office under the Ming dynasty. This office is said to have originated under the Ch'in dynasty. In the early days great scholars or nobles were selected for it and it was their duty to be at the side of the emperor to advise him. By the time of the Sui dynasty their duties had multiplied and can be summarized as follows: (1) to serve as advisers to the emperor, (2) to make suggestions on divers questions of government, (3) to inspect memorials sent by officials to the throne, (4) to correct mistakes in these memorials, (5) to serve as librarians and curators of the archives. Under the T'ang dynasty the duties of the Chi-shih-chung became still more extensive. They included even the decision of important law suits, the revision of unjust sentences, examination of the talents and moral qualities of officials, and the censorship of books in the imperial library. Under the Mongols, however, this office lost its extensive functions and was largely confined to the writing of memorials on the daily life of the emperor.

When the Hung-wu emperor came to the throne, he restored the office of the Chi-shih-chung to its old status, after the T'ang and Sung pattern. There were, however, two important differences; first, under the T'ang and Sung dynasties, the Chi-shih-chung had been subject to the Men-hsia sheng, but in the Ming dynasty it was an independent department; second, it became the duty of the department to admonish the emperor for his misdeeds and to criticize the affairs of the government and the conduct of officials.

The power of the Chi-shih-chung under the Ming dynasty was extended to the Six Boards, with six new officials known as Liu-k'o chi-shih-chung 六科給事中. Each individual member was appointed according to his knowledge of the affairs of any one of the Six Boards. Before any order of the emperor was made public it had first to go before the Shang-shu of the board with which the matter might be concerned. But before the Shang-shu could put the imperial order into execution he had to seek the approval of the Chi-shih-chung, and if the latter thought it unsuitable he could signify his disapproval. When this happened, the document was returned and was either totally rejected or put aside for amendment. Usually each Chi-shih-chung dealt with the affairs of his own Board, but if the case happened to be of concern to all the Six Boards, then the

Chi-shih-chung might deal with the matter as a body. They participated in important court meetings and their opinions were always respected. When, as sometimes happened, they disapproved of a proposal, even the Shang-shu of the Six Boards could do nothing. Thus, though the rank of the Chi-shih-chung was low (only seventh grade), the power it exercised was momentous. In its own way, it even tried to check the authority of the emperor, which seemed boundless in those days.[18]

The Six Boards and the Tu-ch'a yüan were known collectively as the Ch'i ch'ing 七卿 or Seven Ministries. Sometimes to them were added the T'ung ch'eng ssu 通政司 and the Ta li ssu 大理司, bringing the number to nine. They were then called the Chiu ch'ing 九卿, or Nine Ministries. The T'ung ch'eng ssu, or Office of Transmission, was a department which received documents addressed to the throne and transmitted imperial documents. The Ta li ssu, or Grand Court of Revision, was the supreme court. The Shang-shu of the Board of Punishment, the Tu-ch'a yüan and the Ta li ssu were known collectively as the San fa-ssu 三法司, the three juridical departments. Neither the T'ung ch'eng ssu nor the Ta li ssu could compare in importance with the Seven Ministries. Nevertheless, all of the Nine Ministries were independent of each other and each had the emperor as its sole head.

In the early days of the Ming dynasty the system of local government still followed the pattern of the Yüan dynasty, which was known as the Chung shu hsing sheng system 中書行省制. It should be noted that the geographical division of the provinces under the Yüan government was a derivative of the lu 路 system of the Sung dynasty. Towards the end of the reign of the Emperor Shen-tsung 神宗 (1068–1077) (Northern Sung) the country was divided into twenty-three lu. Throughout most of the Southern Sung period there were sixteen lu. Each lu had four officials, one each for civil and military administration, financial problems, legal questions and public works, and they long remained the highest authority within the province. But in the Yüan dynasty a Hsing chung shu sheng 行中書省 was placed over the lu and controlled it. As we have seen, the highest organ of government under the Yüan dynasty was the Chung-shu sheng, at the head of which was the prime minister. The prime minister's office in the capital was called Tu sheng (都省), i.e. the sheng that was in the capital. The Hsing chung-shu sheng (called Hsing sheng for short), or movable sheng, governed the province in which it was found as the representative of the prime minister. The reason for the establishment of the Hsing sheng was, we are told, the anxiety of the Mongols to have all the provinces in the country under the direct control of the government. Hence, strictly speaking there was no local government under the Yüan dynasty; the provinces were governed by the Hsing chung-shu sheng which was no more than an agent of the Chung-shu sheng. In 1376 the Hung-wu emperor abolished the Hsing chung shu sheng system and set up in its place the Ch'eng hsüan pu cheng shih ssu 承宣布政使司. Throughout the dynasty there were thirteen Ch'eng hsüan pu cheng shih ssu. They were subordinated to the Chung-shu sheng until 1382, when, the latter having been abolished, they were put under the Six Boards.

A Pu cheng ssu had charge of the civil administration of a whole province. Under it were the Fu 府, or prefectures, Chou 州, or second-class prefectures, and Hsien 縣, or districts. In each province there were two other offices on the same footing as the Pu ch'eng ssu: the An ch'a ssu 按察司 in charge of legal affairs and the T'i hsing an ch'a ssu 提刑按察司 in charge of military affairs. These three offices were independent of each other; together they were known as san ssu 三司.[19]

In extraordinary circumstances the Tu-yü-shih were sent to inspect the provinces, with the title of Hsün-fu 巡撫, and with power over the provincial governments. The office was not a permanent one and though ministers were often appointed to it, as soon as the need was over the appointment was canceled. A Hsün-fu was properly concerned with civil administration, but at times it might also take charge of military affairs.[20]

Besides the official class, kuan 官, there were also sub-officials, known as li 吏, who formed a class quite distinct from the officials. They were employed by the officials to take charge of the archives and copy documents, to collect taxes, to examine and make reports on lawsuits, to direct ceremonies, and to supervise public works. In the early days of Chinese history, however, there was very little distinction between the kuan and the li. Under the Han dynasty, for instance, the head of a government department was called kuan, and the other officials were called li, and it was not uncommon for a li to be chosen as prime minister. Under the T'ang dynasty, the distinction between the kuan and the li became sharper, and at the beginning of the Sung dynasty (989) the Emperor Ta-tsung went so far as to issue an edict forbidding li to enter public examinations for higher government offices.

This prohibition seems to indicate that at least some of the li then had pretensions to learning. By the end of another century this learned tradition had died out. Ma Tuan-lin 馬端臨 (c. 1200) says that in his time scholarship and the office of sub-official were unrelated and that the sub-officials knew only how to write documents and were employed as ordinary messengers: their intellectual standard was low and their integrity was questionable. In 1273 Khubilai Khan, in consequence of a report made by one of his ministers on the district sub-officials, ordered all sub-officials to save their free time for the study of the ancient classics and of history. According to the report they used to give up their studies shortly after the age of ten to become sub-officials. Lacking all moral education they frequently violated the laws and had to be punished. It was hoped that study would help to reform their characters.

From the T'ang dynasty onwards, sub-officials were confined to the lower ranks, and eventually they were excluded from the official class. Scholars who had received a good education seldom aspired to such an office. Hence the government found itself employing un-qualified men who were usually despised by the scholars. Yet the sub-officials, despised though they were, had great influence in government administration. Governors were often strangers to the customs and traditions and at times to the dialects of the people whom they were to rule; they had, therefore, to rely to a large extent on the sub-officials for information. If the sub-officials were men of low character (as they usually were), they could easily deceive their superiors, and, as experts in administration, they were often able to do what they pleased in matters of government.

Chang Yang-hao 張養浩, an official who lived in the early part of the Yüan dynasty, wrote a book entitled *Mu min chung-kao* 牧民忠告, or *Some Advice for Rulers*, which deals with the problem of the sub-officials. "Since the sub-officials assist the officials in their adminis-trative work," he wrote, "it is clear that they are indispensable. The nature of their office brings them into close contact with their superiors and it is to be feared that after a while they will lose their respect for them. And since they are indispensable they are prone to do what may be illegal. Such are the defects of our days. It is necessary, therefore, for us to maintain our dignity in order to make them respect our authority. And to prevent them from doing what may be illegal it is necessary for us to examine all cases personally. Dignity does not mean a stern appearance; it means preventing sub-officials from making gifts to us. Again, examining all the cases ourselves does not imply hair-splitting; it implies rather a logical approach to what we do. . . ." He then advised superiors not to allow their sub-officials to make unnecessary acquaintances among the people or to have contact with well-to-do families, lest they should reveal information about the government or cause law suits or perhaps seek favors.[21]

At the beginning of the Hung-wu reign, because of the urgent need for officials, the system of recommending capable citizens was adopted: all officials had the privilege of recommending citizens whom they considered fit for office. The candidates thus recommended were employed as government officials, without distinction among metropolitan graduates, students of the imperial academy, and government clerks (sub-officials). During the Yung-lo reign, however, government clerks were forbidden to hold the office of censor. Seemingly this monarch had realized that if government clerks, already expert in transacting official business, were appointed to the office of censor, they could easily become corrupt, since no one would find it easy to check them. The same monarch, moreover, forbade the sub-officials to take examinations for the metropolitan graduate degrees. These prohibitions must have put an end to the ambitions of the sub-officials for higher positions. From then onwards they had to be content with their lowly rank, which had no attraction for learned scholars or members of higher society. The scholars, who regarded their own class as socially distinguished, had nothing but disdain for the plebeian sub-officials and treated all things connected with their office as necessarily low and unworthy of study. The sub-officials, for their part, despised the scholars' ignorance of the affairs of real life. This mutual contempt helped to widen the cleavage between the two classes.

When the Hung-wu emperor ascended the throne, he was fully aware of the state of the country: the poverty of the people as a result of the maladministration of the Mongol government, and the corruption of the officials and sub-officials. In particular, he knew that the sub-officials were the enemies of the poor, and because of this he established strict control over them, punishing their misdeeds with severity. He did not, however, rely on punishment alone: if they behaved well he did not hesitate to reward them generously. He tried also to establish close contact with the people. Tax collectors were chosen from among honest farmers. They were granted frequent audiences with the emperor and reported directly to him the conditions of their localities. During the Hung-wu reign it was the duty of the head officials of provinces and prefectures to report to the emperor personally at fixed periods. We are told that after their audiences the emperor used to exhort them, saying: "We have but now restored order in the country, and you can see that the people are exhausted both physically and economically. They are like young birds learning to fly, or like seedlings newly planted. Do not pull the feathers off the one or hurt the roots of the other. Only an honest man knows how to discipline himself and to be charitable to his neighbors. The selfish man would rather benefit himself at the expense of others. I warn you against this."[22] Of course, perfect compliance with this imperial advice was too much to hope for; but the emperor's severity toward corrupt officials and the effective censorial system served as a check on the conduct of the government officials.

IMPERIAL RELATIVES

The emperor's relatives formed an imperial clan consisting of the descendants of the acknowledged founder of the Ming dynasty himself and the families of his empress and his concubines. The Hung-wu emperor realized that those who had helped him to conquer the Mongols were men of very varied social origins. Although most of them remained loyal to him, he trusted none of them absolutely. He tried to place one of his sons in every province as a prince or a royal general. Princes so employed were furnished with large armies and were allowed to build fortresses, especially along the borders, where it was their duty to protect the empire from foreign invasion. Thus, to prevent attacks from the Mongols, nine princes were placed along the Mongolian border. Each of these princes held a strategic point and had anything from three thousand to eighty thousand soldiers. In their assigned territories these princes had the privilege of building their own palaces and appointing their own palace officials; in rank they came next to the emperor himself: even nobles and imperial officials had to prostrate themselves before them. Yet, in spite of the great honor they enjoyed, they possessed, strictly speaking, no territory. Outside their palaces, civil government officials were appointed directly by the emperor to rule over the people. The princes, therefore, had no jurisdiction over the people. Every year they received ten thousand piculs of rice and other presents.

Far-sighted though the Hung-wu emperor was, he never saw that this system contained the seeds of disaster. Yet disaster came less than five years after his death. In 1398, shortly after Hung-wu's death, some of the ministers felt that the power of the uncle princes might endanger the authority of the boy emperor who had succeeded the great founder of the dynasty. They suggested the disarmament of these imperial relatives. This provoked a revolt on the part of the uncles led by the fourth uncle, Yen Wang 燕王, the future Yung-lo emperor. Yen Wang, the most powerful of all the sons of the founder of the dynasty, was then ruling in what is now Peking, then known as Peiping. Under pretext of getting rid of ministers of bad influence at court he marched with a great force on the capital. After fierce resistence the capital fell and the young emperor disappeared, probably killed during the burning of the palace.

Yen Wang then succeeded his nephew as the third emperor of the Ming dynasty, the style of his reign being known as Yung-lo (1403–1424). The circumstances of his own accession had taught him the danger of relying too much on the princes. Hence he made a rule that they were to receive only salaries and titles of honor, without real authority or any share in any government offices. Strict measures were taken to prevent conspiracies of princes against the emperor. Thus, princes were not permitted to visit one another, and, without the express permission of the emperor, could not even visit the tombs of their ancestors. These precautions proved effective: during the rest of the Ming dynasty there were comparatively few princely revolts.[23]

All through the Ming dynasty the imperial relatives formed a special class. Apart from the heir, all the sons of the emperor had to leave the capital as soon as they were grown up, and to settle down in the provinces assigned to them. An annual salary was given to each and to his descendants down to the eighth generation. But both the salary and the accompanying rank fell with each generation. After the eighth generation the imperial descendants no longer ranked as nobles. In the early days of the dynasty the salary of the princes was large, each receiving fifty thousand piculs of rice yearly. But this was later cut to ten thousand piculs, and was often paid half in rice and half in paper money. Towards the middle of the 16th century the number of imperial descendants became so great that it was practically impossible for the government to keep to the fixed salary, which therefore often had to be reduced.

The families of the empresses and the imperial concubines were regarded as less important than the emperors' descendants. We have seen how strict was the attitude of the Hung-wu emperor towards court ladies, and how his admirable empress would never consent to her relatives becoming court officials. This policy was fairly well maintained by the later emperors, and no serious trouble was ever caused by the empresses or their relatives. They were excluded from the management of the government and were quite content with their incomes, which they received in the form of government farms. Later, they were given rice instead. The ranks and salaries accorded to relatives of the empresses and concubines were purely personal and were not inherited by their descendants.

EUNUCHS

Etymologically, the word "eunuch" (*eunē* bed + *ekhō* hold) denotes one who has charge of women's apartments. The term, however, is applied particularly to one who has been castrated for service as an attendant in a harem. In the West, this barbarous custom of castration seems to have had its origin in Africa, but it became customary in the oriental monarchies and among the Greeks and Romans. In China the employment of eunuchs for court service was more common. If the book *Chou Li* 周禮 can be trusted, it was practiced as early as the Chou dynasty (1100 B.C.)[24]

Emasculation weakened the characters of the eunuchs, and their constant association with court ladies made them still less virile. In general, they were men of little or no education, but by flattering service often won favor with the emperors, which was a dangerous development when an ignorant man was in power. Towards the end of the Ch'in dynasty (210 B.C.) control of the government fell into the hands of the eunuch Chao Kao 趙高. The same thing happened at the end of the Eastern Han and again at the end of the T'ang, when civil war nearly broke out. As for the eunuchs in the Ming dynasty, many historians have not hesitated to list them among the causes of the downfall of the dynasty. We shall deal with this more fully in a later chapter.

In the history of China there were four sources from which eunuchs could be obtained for court services. Firstly, many were taken from the border tribes, especially during the Ming dynasty. In 1460, during a battle against the Miaos in South China one thousand five hundred and sixty-five boys were captured and castrated for service as eunuchs. The notorious eunuch Wang Chih 汪直 himself came from the Yao tribe in Kuangsi. Secondly, there were those who were sent as tribute to the imperial court: during the Yüan and Ming period they were sent not infrequently from Korea and Annam (Indo-China). Thirdly, there were those who, because of some serious offense, had suffered the punishment of castration, and were then put to serve in the palace as eunuchs. Finally, a good number of the eunuchs came from the poorer classes; some, being unable to find any other service or livelihood, castrated themselves that they might be received into the imperial service as eunuchs; others, being unable to support a large family, had some of their children castrated with

the intention of sending them to the court as eunuchs. Not infrequently it happened that these eunuchs became so powerful that
their families eventually shared their influence and benefits.

At the beginning of this chapter we had a glimpse of the damage
done by the eunuchs to the Han dynasty. This was by no means a
unique case. Towards the end of the T'ang dynasty the eunuchs were
said to have ruined this great empire. Towards the end of Sung this
wretched class of men caused no less trouble to the government. Yet
the eunuchs of the Ming dynasty surpassed all others in infamy. This,
however, belongs to a period subsequent to the reign of the Yung-lo
emperor, and we shall deal with it in a later chapter.

As we have said above the Hung-wu emperor, knowing the
character of eunuchs, was severe with them. In 1384 he had the
following inscription engraved on an iron tablet in front of the
palace: "Eunuchs are forbidden to interfere with government
affairs. Those who attempt to do so will be subjected to capital
punishment." Shortly before his death he ordained that eunuchs
were no longer to wear the uniform of government officials and that
their rank should not exceed the fourth degree. Officials of all
departments were forbidden to communicate with eunuchs by
written documents.

Unfortunately these wise commands of the founder of the dynasty
were disobeyed almost immediately after his death. We are told that
when the Yung-lo emperor usurped the throne of his nephew he had
to rely on the help of the eunuchs, chiefly because most of the court
ministers had remained loyal to his nephew. After his success he
rewarded the eunuchs by giving them high rank and by showing
them special favor, even putting some of them in charge of military
affairs. In 1426, there occurred the unsuccessful rebellion of Prince
Kao Hsü 高煦, second son of the Yung-lo emperor. The rebel prince
seemed to be popular among the court ministers and for this reason
the Hsüan-te 宣德 emperor preferred to trust the eunuchs who used
to spy for him. In the days of the Hung-wu emperor a strict order had
been given that no eunuch was to receive any education; but now,
through the favor of the Hsüan-te emperor, a classroom known as
the Nei shu-fang 內書房 was opened and four of the Han-lin College
were appointed to teach the two to three hundred eunuchs who were
then about the age of ten. As a result some of these eunuchs later
became secretaries of the emperor and often had communication with
court officials.[25] The consequences were to be serious, though this
was not foreseen at that time.

PALACE GUARDS

Apart from the eunuchs the Chin-i-wei 錦衣衛 or palace guards also need mentioning. In the early days of the dynasty their regiment was known as Yi-luan-ssu 儀鑾司 but in 1382, the name was changed to Chin-i-wei. The primary function of the guards was to safeguard the person of the emperor, but they also acted as his spies. The guards were instituted by the founder of the dynasty and originally numbered only five hundred.[26] Later on, their numbers increased so greatly that the Chia-ching emperor thought it well to order the disbanding of over thirty thousand eight hundred of them.[17] In fact, however, their number never decreased very much. The commanders were chosen from among persons of merit, and according to Wang Shih-chen 王世貞 (1526–1590) most of the palace guards were chosen from the influential families of the capital. They in turn employed in their service warriors, vagabonds, and people of all classes of society, to the number of between one hundred and fifty and one hundred and sixty thousand men. We are not surprised to read in the *Ming shih* that by themselves they formed an independent army.[28]

Not only did the palace guards act as spies for the emperor; they also had had the right to arrest criminals and suspects and throw them into the prisons they had built. The compiler of the treatise on the Chin-i-wei in the *Ming shih* writing after the destruction of the system, still seemed to feel the horror of the prisons built by the palace guards, and did not hesitate to call them the most cruel of all inventions. Indeed, even the founder of the dynasty, though himself the originator of this organization, felt in his later years remorse for having let such prisons continue to function. In 1393, he ordered the abolition of the Chin-i-wei prisons. Before his death, he ordered that all the instruments of torture left in these prisons should be destroyed and that thenceforth the only prisons were to be those controlled by the Board of Punishments.[29] But when the Yung-lo emperor came to power, he relied greatly on the Chin-i-wei and reopened their old prisons. From then on, the prisons of the palace guards and the eunuchs' prisons existed side by side and rivaled each other in infamy.

THE MING CODE

The legal code drawn up in the time of the Hung-wu emperor was considered one of the great achievements of the era. The *Ming shih* mentions that as early as 1364, the monarch had started to draft a code of laws. Revisions were made in 1373 and 1389, and the final promulgation throughout the empire was made in 1397. This code was known as Ta-Ming lü 大明律. Elsewhere we are told that more than twenty scholars were assigned to the drafting of the code. The emperor took great care over the whole project and in his instruction to the ministers told them that the code of laws should be comprehensive and intelligible, so as not to leave any loophole for sub-officials to misinterpret the law by playing on the words. The 1364 draft consisted of 285 articles and 145 ordinances. That same year one of the ministers was commissioned to write a commentary on both laws and ordinances in order to make sure that the people understood them. This first draft was promulgated. Unfortunately it was not very successful. In 1369, a censor reported that many of the people were still ignorant of its interpretation. Accordingly he suggested that they be instructed twice monthly on the code, arguing that if the law was made clear to the people they would fear it and would guard against violating it. The Hung-wu emperor, however, did not share his minister's opinion, believing that the people should be instructed in the practice of moral virtues rather than in the fear of the law. This aspect of the Ta-Ming lü was based on Confucian ideas and remained one of the factors dominating the law of China until the end of the nineteenth century.

The Ming code laid great emphasis on family relations, and interpreters of the law were chosen preferably from among Confucian scholars who were well versed in the classics. When the Ta-Ming lü was revised in 1389, the monarch's grandson, who participated in this task, petitioned his grandfather that wherever there was a clash the claims of the "five relationships" should prevail over those of strict justice. The monarch thought this reasonable and accordingly thirty-seven articles were changed. Later on, when the young man succeeded to the throne, he recalled this fact and went further, instructing the ministers of the Board of Punishments that to govern the people by means of the law was less perfect than to govern by moral principles.[30]

The first code was drafted on the base of the code of the T'ang dynasty. We are told that the Hung-wu emperor realized that the Mongols did not follow the traditional Chinese code but used instead a species of common law and that corrupt officials could easily take advantage of such law to wrong the people. He decided, therefore, to have a fixed code and he judged that the code of the T'ang dynasty was the best model to follow. The *Ming shih* mentions that the emperor himself took part in the revision of the first draft in 1373. Whenever his ministers presented a chapter of the newly compiled code, he would have it posted on the wall of the palace, read it carefully, and make amendments himself.

Soon, however, the code based on that of the T'ang dynasty ceased to please him. He was not primarily a lover of ancient tradition but sought rather to make his institutions practical and well suited to the needs of the time. In this spirit he kept on revising his code up to the year before his death, and by 1397, when the Ta-Ming lü was finally promulgated, it excelled the T'ang code in content and the body of the law was well organized.

The Ta-Ming lü, which comprised criminal and administrative as well as civil law, was divided under seven main heads: general, civil, fiscal, ritual, military, criminal, and laws concerning public works. The general section dealt with principles applying to the whole code; the civil section dealt with the system of government and the conduct of magistrates; the fiscal section with such problems as census, land taxes, and marriage; the ritual section with social ceremonies and religious functions; the military section with military administration, the stable, couriers, and the protection of the palace; the criminal section with the punishment of wrongdoers; and the laws concerning public works dealt with the digging of dikes and examination and repair of buildings.

In general, the Ming code followed the ancient tradition. In their hearts the people of that time still believed in the theory of the "Five Elements" and held that the punishing of criminals had great influence on nature. Thus in 1368, the Hung-wu emperor published an edict to the effect that the sentences on condemned criminals should be carried out after autumn, lest an untimely execution should be offensive to nature. In the same way in the second year of Hung-chih (1489) an edict ran as follows: "We realize the serious effect that penalties have on the people. If the sentences are just the people willingly submit to them and even nature is in accordance with them. But if a wrong sentence were passed on an innocent person, forthwith nature would be offended and disasters would undoubtedly follow. Of late the capital has suffered from rain and flood and in Nanking there have been strange phenomena and thunder storms. These have given us great anxiety and we began to ask ourselves whether they are results of wrong sentences. . . ." In 1585, the minister of the Board of Punishments pointed out to the throne that "the Ta-Ming lü was revised by Kao huang-ti himself when he had the laws posted up along the two corridors (of the Palace). But of late orders have been given for the revision of cases in which sentence has not yet been passed, and for the changing of sentences in cases giving death sentences. This is equivalent to saying that the lü is not applicable. We think that these (unjust sentences) must have been the cause of the untimely rain and snow of last winter and the frequent occurrence of disasters."[31]

In addition to the Ta-Ming lü, the Ta-kao 大誥 also had the force of law. We are told that in the early days of the dynasty many of the people, unaccustomed as yet to the ways of the new administration, failed to act according to the new law. The emperor himself therefore conceived the idea of compiling a collection of concrete cases to instruct the people, and to help them to understand this collection. The new laws, known as the Ta-kao, were first published in 1385. Two supplementary series were published in the following year and were known as erh-pien 二編 and san-pien 三編.

The augmented Ta-kao was taught in schools and the people were encouraged to study it. Prisoners who possessed a copy or who had knowledge of the contents received a remission of part of their sentences. Two years before his death (1395) the Hung-wu emperor expressed his wish that in legal matters his descendants should follow the Ta-Ming lü and the Ta-kao exclusively, illegal procedures being strictly forbidden.[32] It should be noted that besides the lü the Hung-wu emperor also instituted the li 例. The lü were the cardinal and unalterable principles of law (jus stratum). The li were supplementary statutes which modified and extended the original law, adapting it to the time and circumstances. These were continually added to, and continually revised.

The earlier successors of the Hung-wu emperor seem to have enforced the Ta-Ming lü conscientiously. The Yung-lo emperor was especially noteworthy for his exact observance. Shortly after his accession to the throne an edict was issued to the effect that in criminal procedures the Ta-Ming lü was to be followed. In 1412, one of the ministers reported that in criminal cases some of the penalties for certain moral offenses seemed too light and he petitioned to have these penalties made heavier. The emperor refused to consider this proposal saying that a law must be just and permanent: if it could be altered at will, the people would lose confidence, even if the newly imposed penalty was just.[33] Unfortunately, that admirable consistency did not last. The emperors after the Hsüan-te period often neglected their duty and cunning sub-officials were frequently able to apply the li instead of the lü and by this means to make profits for themselves. The li began to grow and to ramify.[34] In the Hung-chih reign an order was given to the President of the Board of Punishments to revise the li with the help of other ministers. We are told that the ministers in charge of the revision were men of good character and that their sense of justice helped to restore the code.[35]

The Ming code, in many ways an admirable code, often suffered in execution owing to the frequent intervention of the emperors, the eunuchs and the Chin-i-wei. Emperors who possessed the supreme power often acted according to their personal likes and dislikes. The founder himself did not succeed in avoiding arbitrary innovations. Beating at court, for instance, a cruel institution, was introduced by him after the example of the two emperors of the Sui dynasty (A.D. 581–617) and was widely practiced throughout the whole Ming period. In their heyday ch'ang and wei (see above) rendered the Board of Punishments powerless. They freely arrested innocent people and subjected them to the most cruel tortures in order to force them to make false confessions, and the judges dared not utter a word for fear of the eunuchs and the Chin-i-wei. These, in turn, would seek to please the emperor if he was interested in the case; otherwise they would act according to their own pleasure. It is not surprising, then, to find ministers warning their masters not to interfere with the action of the judges. Thus, in his memorial, Liu Ch'iu 劉球 (1392–1443) reminded the Cheng-t'ung emperor that in ancient days those who held supreme power did not intervene in criminal cases lest their known predilections should hamper the causes to justice. "But of late," he went on, "I have noticed that the sentences of the judges have been altered by order of Your Majesty; heavy sentences have been made light and vice versa. The judges, on their part, dare not to say anything and during the trials they try to find out the views of Your Majesty and act accordingly. Under these circumstances it is impossible not to pass unjust sentences. . . ."[36]

In the T'ien-ch'i reign, when the power of the eunuchs was at its zenith, the Chin-i-wei put themselves at the disposal of the eunuchs and worked with them for the destruction both of the landlord class and of the common people. The *Ming shu* says that sometimes an innocent person would be arrested, tried immediately in a vacant temple, and, under cruel torture, stripped of all he possessed. Those who worked for the ch'ang and wei monopolized all the privileges of the yamen and took bribes openly. Even low officials came into possession of great wealth, sometimes to be reckoned in tens of thousands of silver taels.[37] The Ch'ung-chen emperor's deep distrust of his ministers had provided an occasion for the ch'ang and wei to entrench themselves in power. The *Ming shih* gives a very dark picture of this period: " . . . At the doors of the gentry there were always several spies. The gentry, in consequence, used to retire early and get up late. They dared not open their mouths in public. When the guards happened to pass by their door they instantly felt as if robbers were approaching. Government officials tried to share their loot. In the capital, spies, sent by the rebels, went about disguised as laborers and salesmen, and not a soul dared to reveal the secret. While the nobles and well-to-do were thus living in great anxiety, the unscrupulous followers of the ch'ang and wei went about seeking favors. If they were even slightly offended the innocent offender was subjected to false accusations. Often a single word in a letter became the cause of more than ten persons being involved in a trial. . . ."[38] According to a memorial prepared by the Grand Secretary Fan Fu-ts'ui 范復粹 in 1641, over a hundred and forty government officials were then in prison.[39] In these circumstances, it was clearly beyond the power of the Board of Punishments to enforce justice.

NOTES

[1] *Ming t'ung-chien*, 1, (ts'e 1) 8b; *Huang-ch'ao pen-chi* 皇朝本紀, (Chi-lu hui-pien 紀錄 彙編 ed., reprinted by Han-fen-lou, Shanghai, 1938), (ts'e 3) 39b.

[2] *Ming t'ung-chien*, (Ch'ien-pien 前編 ed.) 4, (ts'e 1) 31a.

[3] *Erh-shih-erh shih cha-chi*, 32, (ts'e 6) 6b–8a.

[4] Wu Han 吳晗, *Yu seng-po tao huang-chuan* 由僧鉢到皇權, (Chungking, 1944), 151–152.

[5] Ch'ien Mu 錢穆, *Kuo-shih ta-kang* 國史大綱, (Chungking, 1944) 467, where the author quotes from *Wei Shu-tzu wen-chi* 魏叔子文集.

[6] *Ming t'ung-chien*, (Shanghai, 1958) 4, (ts'e 1) 298; Wu Han 吳晗, *Tu shih cha-chi* 讀史劄記, (Peiping, 1956) 326–321 and note 1.

[7] Chao I, op. cit., 32, (ts'e 6) 8b–9b.

[8] *Huang-Ming t'ung-chi* 皇明通紀, 3, (Japanese edition, 19th cent.?) (ts'e 2) 32ab.

[9] *Ming hui-tien* 明會典, (Wan-yu-wen-fu ed.) 39, (ts'e 14) 17.

[10] *Ming shih*, 113, (HFL), (ts'e 43) 3a–6b; *Ming-shih chi-shih pen-mo*, 14, (WYWK), (ts'e 2) 66–67.

[11] *Ming shih*, 113, (ts'e 43) 1a–2a.

[12] Cha Chi-tso 查繼佐, *Tsui-wei lu* 罪惟錄, (photographic reprint by the Commercial Press) (Shanghai, 1928) 27, (ts'e 18) 2a.

[13] Concerning the office of the prime minister and the Nei-ko system, cf. *Wen-hsien t'ung-k'ao* and the *Hsü Wen-hsien t'ung-k'ao*, under *chi-kuan k'ao* 職官考; *Li-tai chih-kuan piao* 歷代職官表, (*Kuo-hsüeh chi-pen ts'ung-shu* 國學基本叢書, Shanghai, 1930), 1–4, (ts'e 1) 1–96; *Ming shih*, 72, ts'e 25) 4a–6a; Chien Mu, *Chung-kuo li-tai cheng-chih te-shih* 中國歷代 政治得失, (Hong Kong, 1952); Kao I-han 高一涵, *Chung-kuo nei-ko chih-tu ti yen-ke* 中國 內閣制度的沿革, (Shanghai, 1933).

[14] *Li tai chi-kuan piao*, 18, (ts'e 3) 479–493.

[15] Kao I-han 高一涵, *Chung-kuo yü shih chi-tu te yen-ke* 中國御史制度的沿革, (Shanghai, 1933) 29–31.

[16] *Ming shih,* 73, (ts'e 25) 1b–2a.

[17] Ibid., 2ab.

[18] *Chung-kuo li-tai cheng-chih te-shih,* 76–78; Kao I-han, *Chung-kuo yü shih chi-tu te yen-ke,* 47–61; *Ming shih,* 74, (ts'e 26) 11a–13a.

[19] *Ming shih,* 75, (ts'e 26) 9a–16b; *Hsü wen-hsien t'ung-k'ao, bo* (WYWK 1), 3343-3345; *Li tai chi-kuan piao,* 52 (ts'e 6) 1467–1472; *Chung-kuo li-tai cheng-chih te-shih,* 87–89; Ku Chieh-kang 顧頡剛 and Shih nien-tsu 史念祖, *Chung-kuo chiang-yü yen-ke shih* 中國疆域 沿革史, (Shanghai, 1938) 244–260.

[20] *Ming shih,* 73, (ts'e 25) 1b; *Hsü wen-hsien t'ung k'ao, 54,* (WYWK 1), 3288–3289; *Li tai chi-kuan piao,* 50, (ts'e 6) 1410–1413; *Toyo rekishi daijiten,* 4, 302; *Chung-kuo li-tai cheng-chih te shih,* 90–92; *Chung-kuo yü shih chi-tu te yen-ke,* 45–46.

[21] Chang Yang-hao 張養浩, *Mu-min chung-kao* 牧民忠告, 1, (TSCCCP 0,888), 12–13.

[22] *Ming shih,* 281, (ts'e 93) 1a.

[23] The History of the Ming dynasty after the time of the Yung-lo emperor records three revolts led by princes of the imperial family: the first was led by Kao Hsü 高煦 in 1426; the second by Chen Fan 寘鐇 in 1510; and the last by Ch'en Hao 宸濠 in 1519. Each of these revolts was suppressed within a month.

[24] *Chou Li,* T'ien-kuan 天官 chapter.

[25] *Ming t'ung-chien,* 16, (ts'e 2) 26b.

[26] *Ming t'ung-chien,* 7, (ts'e 1) 44a.

[27] Wang Ao 王鏊, *Chen-tse ch'ang-yü* 震澤長語, from *Chen-tse hsien-sheng p'ieh-chi* 震澤先生 別集, (no date or place of edition) (ts'e 15) 19ab; *Ming shih,* 89, (ts'e 32) 5a–6b.

[28] Wang Shih-chen 王世貞, *Chin-i-chih* 錦衣志, *(SCIS),* (ts'e 15) 19ab; *Ming shih,* 89, (ts'e 32) 13b, 14a.

[29] *Ming shih,* 95, (ts'e 34) 15ab.

[30] *Ming hui-yao,* 64, II, 1244, 1245.

[31] *Ming hui-yao,* 64, II, 1235, 1248; *Ming shu,* 73, (ts'e 14) 1478.

[32] *Ming shih,* 93, (ts'e 34) 6ab; *Ming hui-yao,* 64, II, 1237.

[33] *Ming hui-yao,* 64, II, 1245, 1246.

[34] *Ming hui-yao,* 64, II, 1244.

[35] Fu Wei-lin 傅維麟 (circa 1670) *Ming shu* 明書, 73, (ts'e 14) 1479; *Ming hui-yao,* 64, II, 1249; *Ming t'ung-chien,* 39, (ts'e 4) 15a.

[36] *Ming hui-yao,* 64, II, 1239.

[37] *Ming shu,* 73, (ts'e 14) 1484–1485.

[38] *Ming shih,* 95, (ts'e 34) 13a.

[39] *Hsü wen-hsien t'ung-k'ao,* 136, II, 4025.

CHAPTER THREE

The Army

THE WEI-SO SYSTEM

Like the emperors of the T'ang dynasty in its glorious days, the founder of the Ming dynasty kept a powerful army organized on a military system, known as the wei-so system 衛所制, which was similar to the fu-ping system 府兵制 of the T'ang dynasty. Under the wei-so system, a military district established within a prefecture was called "so" 所 and had one thousand one hundred and twenty-eight soldiers. A military district covering two prefectures was known as a "wei" 衛 and had about five thousand six hundred soldiers.

These military districts were distributed according to the importance of the various localities. Groups of military districts were often combined under the command of a Tu chih-hui shih 都指揮使, who was the highest military authority of the locality. All the wei-so of the whole empire, in turn, were under the Wu-chün tu-tu fu 五軍都督府, which had charge of all the military registers of the country. The Wu-chün tu-tu fu, however, did not enjoy full command of the troops for in time of war it was confined to the tactical direction of the army, the real commanding power remaining in the hands of the Board of War. In a word, the Board of War reserved to itself control of mobilizaton and strategic direction of the army; the Wu-chün tu-tu fu merely carried out the orders of the Board of War and led the army in battle.

The *Ming-shih-kao* 明史稿 tells us that the political intention of the founder of the dynasty in establishing the wei-so system was to maintain a strong army while avoiding close bonds between the commanding officers and the soldiers. The soldiers ordinarily were trained in their military districts. In time of war, troops were mobilized from all over the empire on orders from the Board of War and commanders were chosen from the Wu-chün tu-tu fu to lead them. As soon as the war was over, all the troops returned to their respective districts and the commanders lost their military commands. This system largely obviated troubles of the kind which had so often been caused under the T'ang and the Sung dynasties by military commanders who had great numbers of soldiers directly under their personal control.[1]

The wei-so system in the early Ming period was a great success, because of the t'un-t'ien 屯田 system with which it was combined. At one time the soldiers numbered over a million and the Hung-wu emperor, well aware of the difficulties of supplying such a number of men, adopted this ancient method of military settlements. In time of peace each soldier was given forty to fifty mou of land. Those who could afford it supplied their own equipment; otherwise it was supplied by the government. Thus the empire was assured a strong force, without burdening the people heavily for its support.

Conditions were favorable for the initiation of the system, for many of the farming areas had been laid waste toward the end of the Yüan period. A certain historian tells us that when the first Ming emperor took over the rule of the country, the provinces of Shantung and Honan were quite thinly populated.[2] The employment of soldiers to cultivate the land, therefore, served both to repopulate devastated areas and to increase food production. The *Ming shih* relates that seventy per cent of the soldiers stationed along the borders took up farming, while only thirty per cent of them were employed as guards. In the interior of the country, only twenty per cent were needed to guard the cities and the remaining eighty per cent occupied themselves with farming.[3] The rather more than one million soldiers were able to produce over five million piculs of grain, which sufficed not only to support great numbers of the troops but also to pay the salaries of the officers. For this reason the emperor could boast of maintaining his soldiers without asking the people to contribute a single grain of rice.[4]

Another important source of revenue for the support of the army was the government sale of salt to merchants. This system, known as k'ai-chung 開中, was instituted in 1370, as a supplement to the system of military settlements on the borders, where, because of low quality, the soil was not producing the expected quantity of grain. The government entered into contracts with merchants for the transport of grain to the borders. In payment for this, the government issued tickets or vouchers for salt to these merchants, who could then draw salt from the different salt-producing areas and sell it to the people. The merchants found this trade profitable and the number engaged in it was great. In order to avoid the inconvenience of transporting grain to the borders, certain merchants devised an ingenious method that served their purpose admirably. Laborers were employed to cultivate lands along the borders and the products were delivered to the local government under a system known as shang-t'un 商屯, or merchant settlements. The system was highly satisfactory both to the government and to the merchants, and for a time it flourished greatly. The merchant settlements were of great use to the government not only financially but as means for the distribution of population and the cultivation of barren land. Moreover, the denser the population along the borders the better it served as a defense against invasion by the neighboring tribes.

The wei-so system had its permanent organization. The number of soldiers had to be kept up and even the place of garrison duty was fixed permanently for every soldier.[5] At the start of the wei-so system the founder of the dynasty had picked out from among the people a certain number for service as soldiers. They were distributed to different wei-so, either along the borders or within the province, and were regarded as a class distinct from the ordinary civilians. They had their own register, which was kept by the Tu-tu fu, whereas the ordinary civilians were registered by the Board of Revenue. In a word, the wei-so system not only bound its soldiers to military service for life but also made such service hereditary in their families. For this reason, the soldiers of the wei-so were not permitted to remain single; every soldier had to set up a family. The younger generation were obliged to take the place of older members of the family when these died or retired. If, as sometimes happened, a family had no son to take his father's place the government still urged the obligation and summoned distant relatives, from far-off districts if necessary, to take up this family duty.

The *Ming shih* gives four sources for the original recruitment of the wei-so soldiers. First, there were those who had followed the founder of the dynasty in his conquest of the Mongol empire. Secondly, there were the soldiers of the Yüan government and the war-lords who had surrendered to the Ming forces. The original soldiers of the dynasty belonged to these two classes. The third source was the punitive enlistment of prisoners or political offenders. Finally, the fourth and the most common method of recruitment was direct conscription.

In the early Ming period one male member of every household was conscripted into the army. As soon as he was enrolled in the register of the Tu-tu fu, he and his descendants were permanently obliged to serve as soldiers. This regulation was very strictly observed and it was not easy to secure exemption.[6] To compensate the family for the loss of one member, another male member was ordinarily exempted from *corvée*.

As we have mentioned above, the Wu-chün tu-tu fu kept the register of the wei-so throughout the empire, but did not control the army and had no power to mobilize it. This power rested with the president of the Board of War.

This had not always been so. In the early days when the military class was highly honored, the rank of general in the Wu-chun tu-tu fu was given to meritorious ministers. But when these respected leaders had to lead an army out to fight they often took with them a civilian official as adviser, and these civil officials in time became so influential that they took over the command from the military leaders, leaving to the latter only the obligation of leading the army in battle. Ultimately these civilian officials were organized as the Board of War. In 1449, for instance, when Teng Mao ch'i 鄧茂七 revolted in Fukien, Ch'en Mao 陳懋, duke of Ning-yang 寧陽, led the army that was sent to fight the rebels. The real authority, however, was in the hands of the president of the Board of War, who was sent as commander-in-chief. The *Li-tai chih-kuan piao* 歷代職官表 tells us that after the reign of the emperors Ying-tsung 英宗 (1436–1449 and 1457–1464) and Hsien-tsung (1465–1487), owing to the disciplinary deterioration of the wei-so troops, the management of military affairs was wholly controlled by the Board of War. Military officials now could no longer act independently and had to submit to the orders of the board. They could not even keep their old external dignity. When a brigade general received orders from the Board of War, he was now made to kneel down, and even officers of higher rank became humble servants of the board.[7]

The Tu chih-hui shih 都指揮使 originally was the supreme commander of the wei-so troops in the province. In time of war it was the rule for the government to send officers from the Tu-tu fu or personalities of high rank as Tsung-ping-kuan 總兵官, or brigade generals, to direct the war. As soon as the war was over the Tsung-ping-kuan were dismissed. In the early days of the Ming dynasty, because of constant trouble along the border, the Tsung-ping-kuan were often left in command indefinitely. Eventually the more important localities in various provinces followed this example and since the Tsung-ping-kuan ranked above the Tu chih-hui shih, they became supreme commanders of the wei-so troops in the province.

The system kept on evolving. After some time the Tsung-ping-kuan were superseded by the Hsün-fu 巡撫, who had charge not only of military affairs but also of civil administration. After the Ching-tai reign (1450–1456) a Tsung-tu chün-wu 總督軍務, or Tsung-chih 總制, or Tsung-li 總理 was established to direct the military affairs of several provinces. In some localities this office was created only temporarily; in others it became a permanent appointment. Since its authority extended over several provinces, it was naturally superior to the Hsün-fu. Towards the end of the dynasty when rebellions were raging all over the empire and the Manchus were invading the Northeast, important officials, such as the president of the Board of War, were frequently sent to supervise military affairs. They were then given the title of Ching-lüeh 經略. Later still, a Tu-shih 督師 was appointed from among the Grand Secretaries to serve the same purpose, with power superior to that of the Ching-lüeh. Thus, authority within the military class took on a pyramid form that helped to increase the growing confusion among the subjects of the empire. In this, unscrupulous minor officials saw no doubt a great opportunity which they could turn to their own advantage.

THE CHING-WEI

The *Ming shih* mentions that in 1393 the nei-wei 內衛 (i.e. wei within the two capitals, Peking and Nanking; they are also known as ching-wei 京衛) and the wai-wei 外衛 (i.e. all wei other than the nei-wei) taken together, amounted to three hundred and twenty-nine wei.[8] The wai-wei were the wei-so stationed outside the capital whose organization we have described above.

In the capital there were two other wei: the ch'in chün wei 親軍衛 and the ching-wei 京衛. The ch'in chün wei, the emperor's body-guards and custodians of the imperial city of Peking, were independent of the Tu-tu fu. The chin-i wei, mentioned above, belonged to this group. In the Hung-wu reign there were thirteen ch'in chün wei. When the Yung-lo emperor came to power, he increased the number to twenty-two. Finally in the Hsüan-te reign four more wei were added and the number of the ch'in chün wei was fixed at twenty-six. From the time of the Yung-lo emperor onwards, they were closely associated with the eunuchs, a point we shall deal with in a later chapter.

The ching-wei were instituted by the founder of the dynasty to protect the imperial capital. They were trained by special officials appointed by the Hung-wu emperor and were directly under the command of the Wu-chün tu-tu fu. In contradistinction the wai-wei, which were stationed in the provinces, were also known as nei-wei.

In early Ming days there were in all forty-eight wei in the capital. During the reign of the Yung-lo emperor the number of the ching-wei was increased to seventy-two. This augmented number included some wai-wei that had been summoned from different provinces. The wai-wei summoned to the capital were sometimes known as pan-chün 班軍.

In 1415, by order of the Yung-lo emperor the ching-chün was organized into the San-ta-ying 三大營, or the Three Great Regiments: the Wu-chün-ying 五軍營, the San-ch'ien-ying 三千營, and the Shen-chi-ying 神機營. The creation of the San-ta-ying seems to have been a slow and piecemeal process, spread over the reign of the Yung-lo emperor. We are told that the Wu-chün-ying was organized temporarily while the monarch was on an expedition to Mongolia. Since it proved successful it was retained as a permanent organization. It consisted of infantry and was divided into five divisions, hence the name Wu-chün-ying, or the five regiments. The San-ch'ien-ying was instituted at about the same time. It is said that during one of his expeditions to Mongolia the Yung-lo emperor took three thousand Mongol cavalry who had surrendered to him and organized them into the San-ch'ien-ying. The Shen-chi-ying was a regiment of artillery. At the beginning of the Yung-lo reign, expeditions were sent to Annam and it is said that firearms were introduced into China from Annam at this period.[9]

The ching-chün had its heyday during the Yung-lo reign, rising to a strength of about a million. In the six wars waged against the Mongols between 1403 and 1435, it was regarded as the main force, but under the Cheng-t'ung 正統 emperor (1436–1449) it began to deteriorate and in 1449, in the disastrous battle of Tu-mu p'u 土木堡 (not far from Peking) the ching-wei was all but annihilated. "In those days the main forces of the capital all perished; less than ten thousand exhausted soldiers survived. The people were panic-stricken and no one knew what to do," the *Ming shih* tells us.[10] The Cheng-t'ung emperor himself fell into the hands of the Mongols and was carried away into captivity. In Peking an emergency government was set up to defend the capital from enemy attacks and the brother of the emperor was declared his successor with the style Ching-tai 景泰 emperor (1450–1456).

In 1452, Yü Ch'ien 于謙 (1398–1457), president of the Board of War, seeing the necessity of reforming the army, picked out a hundred and fifty thousand of the best soldiers from the San-ta-ying and formed them into ten regiments known as the Shih-t'uan-ying 十團營. The rest he formed into a single large regiment called Lao-ying 老營 for the defense of the imperial city. During this interlude the army system went through substantial changes, but the Cheng-t'ung emperor, having returned from captivity, regained the throne under the new style Tien-shun 天順 and quickly abolished the Shih-t'uan-ying system set up by Yü Ch'ien and restored the San-ta-ying system.

In 1465, one hundred and forty thousand of the best soldiers were picked from the ching-wei to form the Shih-erh-t'uan-ying 十二團營, or the Twelve Regiments. This organization was dissolved in the following year, 1466; but in 1467 it was restored under the name Hsüan-feng 選鋒. The rest of the ching-wei were retained for various employments and were known as Lao-chia ping 老家兵. The Shih-erh-t'uan-ying were organized in three divisions: Wu-chün 五軍, San-ch'ien 三千, and Shen-chi 神機.

When the Cheng-te emperor came to the throne in 1506, the Shih-erh-t'uan-ying had only a little over sixty thousand five hundred soldiers fit for service. Tens of thousands of soldiers from the border towns, therefore, were taken in to fill the depleted ranks, the new arrivals being known as the Wai szu-chia-chün 外四家軍. The Two Military Camps, the Tung kuan-t'ing 東官廳 and the Hsi kuan-t'ing 西官廳, were set up to train soldiers who had been carefully chosen from among the T'uan-ying. This picked force was thenceforth known as the Hsüan-feng, while the T'uan-ying had to be satisfied with the title of Lao-chia.

The year 1534 saw another reform in the army. Both the Two Military Camps and the Shih-erh-t'uan-ying were abolished. The original San-ta-ying system was restored, but the name San-ch'ien-ying was changed into Shen-shu-ying 神樞營. The soldiers who had hitherto belonged to the Shih-erh-t'uan-ying and the Two Military Camps were now put under the command of the Wu-chün-ying. The newly organized Shen-chi-ying and Shen-shu-ying had to draft soldiers from around the capital, and from Shantung, Shansi, Honan, and other places. Externally the San-ta-ying system seemed to have been restored to its original form; yet there was an essential difference: the profession of soldiering was no longer hereditary, soldiers being hired whenever needed. Furthermore, the newly constituted Jung-cheng fu 戎政府 took over the power of the Wu-chun tu-tu fu, which up to this time had had charge of the military registry.

Mercenary Army

Up to 1449, the Ching-chün was reputed to be the best fighting force of the empire. Between the Yung-lo and Hsüan-te reigns six expeditions were sent to Mongolia and three to Annam (Indo-China) and in each of these expeditions the Ching-chün played an important part. The decline dates from the battle fought in 1449, against the Mongols in Tu-mu p'u in which the whole army was almost completely destroyed. In spite of the ingenious efforts of Yü Ch'ien, the army never again reached its old standard. After the reversal of Yü Ch'ien's attempts at reform the deterioration became more noticeable. By the end of the Hung-chih reign, less than one hundred and fifty years after the foundation of the dynasty, the Ching-chün had lost its military vitality and in the eyes of contemporaries was no longer fit for war. Thus an official who lived near the end of the 15th century, having recorded that the Ching-chün were often sent to help to defend the borders against enemy attacks, suggested that they should not be employed in this way since their laxity and arrogance made them unreliable.[11] Later, in 1504, when the Mongols invaded Ta-t'ung, one of the ministers pointed out that the Ching-chün were timid and unfit for fighting. This, he said, was the fault of their superiors who, instead of giving their soldiers a good training, had employed them in manual labor.[12] Another of the ministers spoke still more sarcastically. "The Ching-chün are known for their cowardice," he said. "Therefore, even the fact that they are privileged to garrison the capital does not mean that they are capable of sustaining the morale of the people, and to employ them even in the lightest fighting would undoubtedly bring disgrace upon the throne; for as soon as they are brought face to face with the enemy, they immediately turn away and take to flight. Hence they are mocked by the enemy and, in consequence, have even caused the armies of the border to lose spirit."[13]

Conditions in the provinces were similar to those in the capital, for the Wei-chün too were unable to avoid deterioration. According to the observation of Wang Ch'iung 王瓊 who lived in the beginning of the 16th century, many of the Wei-chün force deserted, being unable to bear the hardships of army life. He gives the following explanation of this phenomenon. In the rebellions that broke out everywhere at the end of the Yüan dynasty, the people lost their property and were forced to move from place to place. Unable to find any other means of earning a living they were content to enlist in the army. In the early days of the Ming, the Hung-wu emperor imposed such strict military discipline that no one dared to desert. Later, however, the government began to lose control over the officers and the latter seized the opportunity to oppress their men. Under these circumstances the soldiers naturally tried to abandon their posts and return to their native villages.[14]

Yet even as early as the Hung-wu period soldiers were frequently reported to have abandoned their posts. Thus, in the thirteenth year of the Hung-wu reign (1380) the emperor issued an edict to the ministers of the Tu-tu fu stating that of late the soldiers of the wei-so had been deserting. He attributed this to lack of sympathy on the part of the officers. Accordingly, the officers were made responsible for the soldiers under their command and were liable to a reduction of salary in proportion to the number of soldiers they lost.[15] This solution was not sound. In a later chapter we shall see the damage it caused.

By 1436 it was clear that the wei-so was in difficulties and the Cheng-t'ung emperor had to send seventeen censors to restore the system to its original form. The edict given to the censors pointed out the abuses that were regarded as the main causes for the deterioration of the system. "Military organization is indispensable for the welfare of a country. But as years go on organization can degenerate into routine and then abuses of all sorts creep in. Soldiers have managed to block out their names from the military records and innocent people have been pressed into the army by fraud. . . . All these things have been caused by the corruption of the wei-so officers, the ministers of the government, and the Li-chia 里甲. Since they are in conspiracy, it was not easy to unmask them; hence they go on undisturbed. Their victims have to suffer in silence since no one will speak for them. In consequence, the number of soldiers in the army keeps on decreasing and innocent civilians become victims of the abuses."[16]

In 1434 an edict was published by the Hsüan-te emperor stating that brave and loyal subjects residing along the borders who were willing to volunteer to fight against the enemy might present themselves to the local government for approval. The compilers of the *Hsü wen-hsien t'ung-k'ao* regarded the publication of this edict as an important event in the military history of the Ming dynasty, since "this was the origin of the system of mercenary soldiers." The occasion of this edict was the Mongol invasion of China under the leadership of Adai 阿台. The very fact that the government had to hire mercenaries seems to show that the wei-so system was no longer as well organized as before. No wonder then that the above-mentioned compilers of the *Hsü wen-hsien t'ung-k'ao* lamented the fact that "it is easy for military affairs to become corrupt, but it is difficult to restore them to order. Little more than ten years elapsed between the end of the Yung-lo and the end of the Hsüan-te reigns, yet already it had become very difficult to institute a reform."[17]

The *Shih-lu* of the Hsüan-te emperor gives the following explanation of the number of missing soldiers. In the year 1433 the Board of War petitioned for the reaffirmation of the law for the replacing of missing soldiers. According to the custom of the time, the Board of War issued to the wei-so certain documents called K'an-ho 勘合 in which the number of missing soldiers and other details were filled in by the wei-so. These then sent their own officers to the native places of these missing soldiers, to draft their relatives for military service. When the orders had been carried out the officers returned and reported to their respective regiments, and the Board of War never made further inquiries about these reports. This last was the weak point in the scheme, and the officers soon took advantage of it. The names of the native places of the soldiers were often falsified and ordinary civilians were drafted as soldiers. Often, moreover, the K'an-ho that had been given out were not returned. Officers who had been sent to get replacements suffered no penalty for delay. The consequence was that such officers would stay away sometimes for as long as twenty to thirty years, or for good. Some of them set up their families on foreign soil; others retired to their own native places. These practices became so common that the threats of local authorities were insufficient to check them.[18]

Another cause for the decline of the wei-so system was the diversion of soldiers from military tasks to the non-military task of transporting grain to the capital. In the days of the Hung-wu emperor, the capital was in Nanking where farming products were abundant all around, and the provision of sufficient grain for both the government and the people presented no problem. But as soon as the Yung-lo emperor moved the capital to Peking in 1421, the problem of food transportation became acute. The soil in northern China was poor and could not support the enormous numbers of inhabitants who had moved to the northern provinces after the movement of the capital. Thus the capital and the provinces had to depend on the southern provinces for their supplies. Moreover, the salaries of government officials were still largely paid in piculs of rice, which naturally increased the government's need for grain. At first, grain paid to the government as taxes was delivered to the capital by the people themselves. But it quickly became clear that this system imposed an intolerable burden on the people, for the long journeys required of them often encroached on the time needed for cultivating their land. Accordingly, the people were instructed to deliver the grain to Huai-an 淮安 and Kua-chou 瓜州 in what is now Kiangsu province. The soldiers of the wei-so were then employed to transport it to the capital through the Grand Canal. The *Ming shih* tells us that this innovation caused the decline of the army in the southeast.[19]

The ruin of the wei-so system was naturally a very grave, indeed almost a fatal, blow to the policy of military settlement. The soldiers, being no longer able to support themselves by military service alone, were reduced to the status of mere laborers and quickly lost all aptitude for war. A month after the disaster of Tu-mu p'u (1449) fifteen censors were sent to recruit soldiers from among the people around the capital and from Shantung, Shansi, and Honan.[20] The capital must have been in a weak state to face Mongol attacks, for the Ching-wei-chün had been almost exterminated and the government had to rely on hired soldiers for its defense. In the provinces, too, hired soldiers were employed to protect the people from the bandits.

The *Ming hui-yao* gives another fact under the same date: "In the ninth month of the 14th year of the Cheng-t'ung emperor's reign, an order was given to the authorities of various localities to enlist soldiers. The local authorities were to be responsible for their training and they were to be employed in the defense of their own localities."[21] This order seems to have been intended to obviate one weakness of the wei-so system, the removal of soldiers from their native places to far-off regions where they found it very hard to get accustomed to the climate. The fact that it had proved necessary to enlist civilians into the army shows that wei-so soldiers were no longer sufficient either in number or in quality.

The decline of the self-sufficient military settlements left the army dependent on the people for its support, and additional taxes, in consequence, frequently had to be levied. The quality of the hired soldiers, however, was not high. In 1555, the President of the Board of War reported that the soldiers that had enlisted since the invasion of Yen-ta Han (Alda/—Alta (n)/Qan) 俺答汗 in 1550, were little better than an undisciplined mob.[22] Eight years later one of the generals, when proposing a reform of the army, suggested that full details of the enlisted soldiers from different provinces should be collected, so that the aged and men of bad character might be excluded from military services.[23] From his statement one can safely infer that the army must have been a very mixed batch.

In the later years of the dynasty, when rebellions were breaking out all over the empire, an ever greater number of soldiers was needed to maintain order. The levying of taxes became almost impossible since the people were so impoverished that they had nothing with which to pay. Under these circumstances the government had to allow the generals to provide for their own troops. Thus, the Hung-wu emperor's wise policy of precluding the leaders of the army from permanent control of permanent bodies of troops was set aside. The soldiers now received orders only from their own leaders and the government could no longer control them. The "war-lord state" of the T'ang dynasty had reappeared, a state of affairs which the Hung-wu emperor had feared so greatly and had tried with such foresight and energy to prevent.

FIREARMS

In the early days of the Ming dynasty the army equipment in general still followed the pattern of ancient Chinese tradition. Bows and arrows, swords and knives, were still commonly used in battle. Firearms, however, were coming into use. Their invention can be dated back to two centuries before the rise of the Ming. As early as 1132, the Sung government had been employing firearms to repel the invasion of the Juchen people who later founded the Chin dynasty. After the fall of the Northern Sung the Juchens inherited the secret of firearm manufacturing and improved greatly on what they had learned. Thus, we are told that the Chin dynasty used firearms in defending their capital Pien-liang 汴梁, Honan province, against the Mongol invaders. A historian tells us of the use of a ball-shaped weapon known as chen-t'ien lei 震天雷. This consisted of an iron container filled with gunpowder. When ignited, it exploded with a sound like thunder which could be heard miles away and the area of destruction covered half a *mou*. Even iron armor could not resist the heat and melted away. Another weapon used by the Chin was a sort of blunderbuss which emitted a projectile that exploded at a distance of several yards. The Mongol soldiers were awe-struck in face of these two deadly weapons.[24]

Then, in 1272 an Arab by the name of Isma'il 伊斯瑪晉 presented to the Mongol court a big cannon of which he himself was given charge in an invasion of Hsiang-yang. This weapon, said to weigh 150 catties and to cause an explosion like thunder, smashed everything that might happen to be in the way. It rendered great service to the Mongols and caused the fall of the city of Hsiang-yang, thus winning the name Hsiang-yang p'ao 襄陽砲.[25]

In the days of the Hung-wu emperor cannon were employed in warfare. Probably these were made in imitation of the Mongol gun, but in the Yung-lo emperor's reign a new type of cannon, the blunderbuss designed to shoot iron arrows and known as the shen-chi ch'iang-p'ao 神機槍砲, was introduced into China. According to Ch'iu Chun 邱濬 (1420–1495), after the suppression of a revolt in southern Annam, the Chinese soldiers got these weapons from the natives. Ch'iu, however, does not tell us the exact date of their introduction.[26]

The *Chen chi* 陣紀, a book on military affairs written at the end of the 16th century, says that the blunderbuss came from a foreign country and was an excellent weapon by the standards of the China of those days.[27] From this description we may say with certainty that European firearms were introduced into China before the Wan-li period, probably with the coming of the Portuguese at the beginning of the 16th century.

Writing of firearms in China, Père Jean Baptiste du Halde (1674–1743), a French Jesuit who compiled a history of China from the notes he had received from the early missionaries in China, commented:

"Although the use of gunpowder was ancient in China, the use of firearms is rather recent. People hardly employed gunpowder, after its invention, except for fire-works, in which the Chinese excel. At the gates of Nanking, however, there were then three or four mortars, short in size had extra strong, quite ancient by their look, showing they [the Chinese] and some knowledge of firearms. Nevertheless, they seem to have been ignorant of the use of them; for they [these mortars] were shown there only as objects of curiosity. They also possessed some stone-throwing guns on their naval vessels, but they lacked the skill to use them."[28]

The *Ming shih* states that after the introduction of firearms in the Yung-lo reign, the emperor ordered the institution of a special regiment known as the Shen-chi-ying 神機營 to study the use of firearms. Cannon and guns were made of brass, copper, and iron. In 1412, by order of the Yung-lo emperor five cannon were set up on the mountains along the borders just outside Peking. Ten years later one of the ministers petitioned the monarch to have other cannon set up in Shansi and other places. From that time onward, firearms of various types were produced and were used in warfare with effective results.[29] We are told that the method of manufacturing firearms was kept a secret and that they were made only in the capital.

With the coming of Europeans to the Far East, the ancient Chinese method of warfare underwent some changes. In 1520, a censor reported to the emperor that two years previously the Fo-lang-chi 佛郎機 (Portuguese) had appeared in Canton and had fired cannon that terrified the city. Portuguese who came to the city ignored the city regulations; others who went to visit the capital would not submit to the orders of the authorities. He attributed this to their firearms which had made the Chinese afraid of them.[30] In 1523, the Portuguese launched an attack in the Hsin-hui district 新會縣, in Kuangtung province. After some desperate fighting the Chinese gained the victory, capturing two ships and forty-two Portuguese, killing thirty-five others. Among the booty were firearms which were named Fo-lang-chi, after their former possessors.[31] Now, the Chinese could examine closely these deadly weapons which they dreaded so much. Their secrets were discovered and some of the ministers felt that they too could and ought to produce firearms modeled on these which they had captured from the Portuguese. Accordingly, in 1524, permission was obtained from the emperor to bring workmen from Kuangtung to Nanking for this purpose: possibly the close contact of the Kuangtung people with foreigners had given them a better understanding of foreign things.[32]

In 1529, the Chia-ching emperor gave an order for the casting of three hundred cannon, to be distributed along the border provinces. In the following year one of the censors suggested a more widespread use of cannon for defense purposes, arguing that, in spite of large garrisons in the border towns, the defense was inefficient owing to the lack of powerful weapons with which to halt the advance of invaders. The two types of blunderbusses (Fo-lang-chi ch'ung 佛郎機銃) were, he said, the ideal weapons for this purpose: the smaller type weighed only twenty catties and could shoot a distance of 600 paces; the larger type weighed seventy catties and could shoot five to six li. He estimated that three soldiers armed with one of the small blunderbusses would be enough to guard a tower and that ten soldiers with three of the large blunderbusses could defend a fort. Thus, the garrisons could be reduced considerably and their efficiency increased. In this way, he said, nine tenths of the soldiers could be employed in cultivating the land for their own support instead of depending on the government for provisions.[33]

The manufacture of firearms must have strengthened the empire very greatly. In 1532 an order was issued to the Board of Works to produce a larger number of blunderbusses for distribution to the soldiers of the Twelve Regiments. Four years later (1536) 2,500 blunderbusses made of brass and steel were distributed to the soldiers along the Shensi border. In the following year the same soldiers were given 3,800 iron blunderbusses and 3,000 brass cannon, known as hsüan-feng p'ao 旋風砲.[34]

When Mao Yüan-i 茅元儀 (d. c. 1625), produced the *Wu-pi chih* 武備志, a treatise on military affairs, he was able to give a long list of firearms used in his days. Some of these were weapons belonging to the ancient Chinese tradition of the Sung or Yüan period. On the other hand, it is obvious that the list contains firearms of the latest European type. The compiler of the *Ming shih,* which dealt with the military system of the Ming dynasty, declared that he did not hesitate to mention in full detail the different types of firearms, since he believed that up to the Ming period firearms were not commonly seen.

In fact, the types of firearms used in the Ming armies in the 15th century were quite different from those used in the second part of the 16th. Ch'iu Chün, who lived in the 15th century, tells us that in his time cannon were made of brass or iron and in the shape of a quiver, or arrow container. The side of the tube was filled with gunpowder and stones were loaded through the muzzle. When the fuse was lit the stones shot forth with such force that the destruction was tremendous. He then described the so-called shen-chi hou-chang 神機火槍 (probably introduced from Annam during the Yung-lo period) as an instrument that projected iron arrowheads to a distance of a hundred steps. Chiu, however, noted the great weakness of these weapons; namely, they could fire only one shot at a time. Often in battle the enemy would hide until they heard the explosion and then charge out suddenly. This would cause great confusion among the soldiers, since they were not ready to fire a second shot. He therefore suggested that soldiers should be divided into groups of five. In each group one or two who were skillful should take charge of the shooting and the rest should help to reload the weapons after they had been fired.[35] From this we can see that artillery of this period, though greatly improved, was still imperfect.

Let us turn now to the description of firearms given by writers after the middle of the 16th century. T'ang Shun-chih 唐順之 (1507–1560) says that though in the early days of the dynasty only the shen-chi huo-chang was known, a variety of firearms began to appear in the Chia-ching period. Among these new types he mentions the niao-tsui ch'ung鳥嘴銃, the newest and reputedly the most deadly of weapons. The barrel was made of brass or iron and was mounted on a wooden stock. The round bullets shot from it were mortal both to human beings and to horses. On the barrel there were front and back sights which enabled the operator to aim at the object he wanted to hit. As soon as the aim was fixed he lit the fuse and held the barrel firmly with both hands. T'ang hints that this weapon was introduced into China by the Japanese pirates who were then ravaging the coasts of the empire. If this is true, it is quite certain that these pirates must have learned the use of this gun from the Portuguese.[36]

Mao Yüan-i next describes the Fo-lang-chi p'ao as a weapon five to six feet long, made in two very different sizes. The large Fo-lang-chi weighed over a thousand catties; the small ones only one hundred and fifty catties. They were made of brass with long barrels and big breeches. A large hole was opened in the breech and five cartridges could be shoved in one by one. The weapons were mounted on wooden stands which allowed them to turn freely in any direction. Mao states explicitly that these firearms were of European origin, but that the Chinese had adapted and modified them into different types. They were especially useful in sea battles or in the defense of cities.[37]

Firearms became an important part of the equipment of a Chinese army after the first half of the 16th century and the Japanese seem to have learned their use from the Portuguese at about the same time. A writer in 1556, included the following passage in a book in which he gives the story of the invasion of Hai-yen 海鹽 in Chekiang province, by Japanese pirates: "The following day (i.e. the 25th day of the fourth month in the 35th year of the Chia-ching reign) the enemy brought out a chang-chun (cannon) made of brass and when our soldiers saw it they began to prepare their Fo-lang-chi for the attack. Before the enemy could do anything we had started to fire at them and the place echoed as if with thunder."[38] It is interesting to note that the author calls the cannon a chang-chün 將軍, i.e. a general. This was the name given by the Chinese of that time to the Fo-lang-chi cannon, presumably because their great power made them as terrifying to the enemy as good generals at the head of the armies. Indeed, cannon were almost deified during the reign of the T'ien-chi emperor, when ministers were sent to offer sacrifice to them and they were given the title of Ta-chang-chün.[39] The *Ming shih* tells us that the chang-chün were classified into five categories according to size.[40]

According to the *Ming hui-tien,* at the beginning of the Hung-wu reign two factories, the Chün-ch'i chü 軍器局 and the An-p'ei chü 鞍轡局, were established in Nanking for the manufacture of arms. When the Yung-lo emperor moved the capital to Peking two factories of the same name were established there. Later on, under the Hsüan-te emperor, the K'uei-chia ch'ang 盔甲廠 and the Wang-kung ch'ang 王恭廠 were established for the same purpose. Chün-chi chü were founded in the provinces and the wei-so by the Hung-wu emperor in 1387. Soldiers no longer fit for active military service were sent to them to learn how to make armor and weapons. If they were stationed along the borders, the equipment they produced was often kept for local use. Some of the arms produced by the wei-so of the interior provinces, however, were sent to the capital where they were kept for the use of the troops stationed there.[41] A factory known as Ping-chang chü 兵仗局 was founded in Nanking during the Hung-wu reign, and later on a similar factory was founded in Peking under the Yung-lo emperor. The main purpose of these two factories seems to have been to supply the imperial guards, although sometimes they also manufactured for the needs of the provinces.[42]

We are told that the Chun-chi chü and the An-p'ei chü started with a combined total of over 9,200 workers, and the Ping-ch'ang chü with at least 1,700.[43] The amount of military equipment produced must have been large. In 1558 the number of naio-tsui ch'ung alone was 10,000.[44] Military equipment sent to the capital from the provinces was kept in government stores and about the middle of the Chia-ching reign a special office was established to inspect this stored equipment. Any items that were found below standard were returned to the place of origin and new articles were demanded. Censors were sent occasionally to the provinces to inspect the military equipment, and the military settlements had to send in reports concerning their military stores.

By the end of the 16th century it was admitted by almost all that firearms were the most powerful weapons available, whether for defense or for attack.[45] The coming of the Jesuits to China had opened new horizons to Chinese scholars by showing them that China was not the only country with a high civilization and that even from barbarians there was always something to learn. Many of the wonders described by these missionaries sounded like fables, but when these tales of wonders were accompanied by facts, there was no alternative to conviction. This new knowledge arrived shortly after the end of the Wan-li reign when the country was still suffering from the effects of that emperor's extravagances. Natural disasters were happening everywhere and popular uprisings were being reported to the court every day. The Manchus were pressing hard along the eastern borders, the government was bankrupt, and the invasion of Korea by the Japanese under Hideyoshi (1592–1593, 1597–1598) and the defeat of the Chinese troops by the Manchus (1619), had brought the empire to a very low ebb. Far-sighted officials saw the need of reform in many government institutions, and especially in the army.

The strongest reform party came from the group that had been most influenced by European thought. Their close friendship with the missionaries had enabled them to acquire a great deal of information about the West. They admired the scientific achievements of the Europeans and received with open arms whatever new knowledge they could get from the foreigners. Hsü Kuang-ch'i 徐光啓 (1562–1633) and Li Chih-tsao 李之藻 (1569–1630) were the leading spirits of this movement. Fortunately we still have much of the writings of these men and are thus able to investigate their part in the adaptation of European science to Chinese needs. Here, however, we limit ourselves to their share in the introduction of European firearms.

In a memorial to the throne dated 1621, Li Chih-tsao pointed out that the time had come for using these firearms against the enemy, since "they are *soldiers* that need no provisions or horses." His memorial shows that, fully aware of the government's lack of money and of man power, he emphasized the fact that each of the guns employed would be equivalent to "several thousand well-trained soldiers."[46] The help of experts, he went on, was needed both for the manufacture and for the use of these firearms. Since the Chinese lacked the necessary experience, he suggested that Portuguese should be invited from Macao. Li's proposal was a daring one at a time when foreigners were not respected. Nevertheless he was convinced that there was no better way to save the empire from a Manchu invasion.

The battle of 1619 had cost the Chinese the lives of over 300 military leaders and not less than 45,000 soldiers. The year 1622, saw the Chinese troops fleeing from Liao-t'ung. Nearly all the territories around Shan-hai-kuan were lost to the Manchus. When the Ch'ung-chen emperor came to the throne in 1628 he was eager to recover the lost territories. Not realizing how unhealthy the state of the empire was, he expected great achievements. Hsü Kuang-ch'i in his diary records the following forecast as made by the Ch'ung-chen emperor: "The enemy are indeed very insolent and we must inflict such heavy blows on them that not even a wheel of their wagons shall return to their head-quarters. But from what I can see, I say that the time has not yet come for us to take this step. As soon as the enemy has been driven away from the border, we will spend six months regrouping our troops and then we shall be able to launch out. First then, we shall recover Ta-ning 大寧; once this is achieved, our capital will be quite certain that things will remain quiet for a whole year. We will then make our plans for the recovery of our lost territories in the East."[47]

From Hsü Kuang-ch'i's diary one can see that the forces of the Manchus must have been overwhelming. Hsü, accordingly, was unwilling to make unnecessary sacrifices. His idea was to stay upon the defensive rather than to launch an attack on the enemy when the latter were still strong. He advised the emperor that the science of war had changed greatly since the days of old. Whereas in former times it was almost impossible to protect a city unless one took the offensive, now one could guard the city and win the victories over the enemy by using firearms. He recalled how the renowned general Yüan Ch'ung-huan 袁崇煥 had successfully kept the Manchus out of the Ning-yüan 寧遠 city solely through the use of firearms. Hence he suggested that the government should take care to produce more firearms.[48]

Père du Halde has an interesting account of the presentation of three cannon to the T'ien-ch'i emperor by the Portuugese: "It was in the year 1621 that the city of Macao presented to the emperor three cannon, together with men to operate them. A test was performed in Peking in the presence of the mandarins who were surprised at first and then dismayed when they saw that having fired one of the pieces the recoil killed a Portuguese and three Chinese who did not withdraw quickly enough."

"The cannon were brought to the frontier of the empire, at the border of the Tartars [Manchus] who, having come with their troops close to the Great Wall were so terrified by the damage they did when they were fired at that they took to flight and no longer dared to come near again."[49]

The instructions given by the Portuguese to the Chinese soldiers on the use of firearms must have produced great changes in the method of warfare. Hsü Kuang-ch'i recalls that before 1626 the Manchus were afraid only of the niao-t'ung; after that they were frightened by the cannon also. For this reason a special mission was sent to Macao in 1629 to buy more cannon. The Portuguese presented ten pieces to the court and sent Gonsales Texeira Correira as captain and some other gunners. The Jesuit Father João Rodrigues Tçuzzu

陸若漢 (1561–1634) accompanied them to Peking and served as their interpreter.[50] When they arrived in Cho-chou 涿州 towards the end of the year it was reported that the Manchus were approaching the city. There was panic among the inhabitants and some of the military officers fled from the city. The Portuguese set up their cannon on the city wall and waited fifteen days for the invaders. The Manchus were informed of what was being done and, fearing the weapon, retired to Liang-hsiang 良鄉.[51]

Accordingly, Hsü Kuang-ch'i was highly enthusiastic about extensive employment of these firearms. He insisted strongly that the weapons and the training of the army should be completely after the European pattern. He stressed the quality rather than quantity of the soldiers and urged the government to pay them higher salaries. Furthermore, he realized that to be good gunners, men must have had good training in warfare. He had been informed that the Portuguese had attained their skill in gunnery through frequent conflict with the Dutch, then their bitter rivals in the East. He thought, therefore, that it would be a good idea to obtain a number of these fighters from Macao to train the Chinese soldiers and to let them look after the manufacturing of firearms. "They are the only ones who know how to manage the cannon, to instruct others in the management of them, and to manufacture them," he wrote to the emperor. He even insisted that the preparation of gunpowder and the making of the cannon balls must be done by the Europeans, though they might employ a few Chinese assistants.[52]

With regard to the manufacture of firearms, Hsü Kuang-ch'i said that it was not easy to obtain experienced artisans among the people of northern China. In a memorial to the throne dated 1630 Hsü stated that he had made a great effort to employ experienced artisans at high salaries but had been able to find only twenty-odd men. In another place he said that in spite of all his efforts he had been unable to find more than a few men, and even these he had had to instruct with great patience before he could make them follow his plans. Hence he was eager to get artisans from Kuangtung, since the people there, having closer contact with Macao, naturally had had greater opportunities of learning from the Portuguese. We are told that the military authorities in Kuangtung had in fact once borrowed from Macao twenty guns of different sizes in order to produce others like them and Hsü's statement had thus produced 300 pieces. Father Rodrigues confirms that artisans were numerous in Kuangtung and that the quality of iron was excellent and the price low.[53]

Another reason why Hsü Kuang-ch'i preferred to have the firearms manufactured in the provinces was that in the capital the prices of metal and coal, and even the wages of the artisans, were higher than in the provinces. Hence he suggested that the big niao-ch'ung should be made in Kuangtung and Fukien while other firearms might be produced in Wu-hu and in the provinces north and south of the Yangtze River, "because," he said, "these are the places where one can find copper, iron, and coal in abundance; thus they will save us half the price [that they would cost if we manufactured them in the capital]."[54] However, he pointed out that the making of firearms was a most important task and that great secrecy should be maintained especially in the capital where spies were everywhere.[55]

In the third year of the Ch'ung-chen reign (1630) great attention was paid in the capital to the manufacture of firearms. In one of his memorials to the throne Hsü said that out of the 107 guns that were to be made fifty had already been finished, and he expected to have them all completed within fifteen days. He went on to say that since "such powerful weapons were greatly needed by all cities and on the borders, it would be no harm to have plenty of them."[56] Though at this time the financial situation was bad, Hsü insisted on carrying out his plan. "With regard to the expenses," he wrote to the emperor, "your servant knows that they are huge. Yet if we want to have fine wrought iron, we have to use a good deal of material; if we wish to produce our weapons to the exact measurement, we have to pay good prices. Moreover, material and foodstuffs are both expensive, and since all the factories are working at the same time, there is a shortage of artisans. Prices are twice what they were last year. It is to be feared that if an effort is made to cut down the expense the quality of the articles produced will be below standard. For these reasons some officials have suggested of late that the articles should be produced in Shansi, where iron is produced, where raw materials are easy to obtain, and the price of coal is low."[57]

Even in the early years of the Ch'ung-chen reign, the budget for military equipment was too great for the resources of the Board of Works. Hsü, therefore, suggested the use of raw materials stored by the government and, if necessary, the collection of old equipment that had been destroyed in battle. Help might be contributed both by government officials and by the people. If necessary, fines might be imposed on corrupt officials to fill the war chest.[58] Clearly, Hsü spared no effort to augment the fighting power of the army.

The *T'ien-kung kai-wu* 天工開物 tells us that firearms were made either from wrought copper or from a mixture of equal parts of wrought and cast copper. Big cannon were made of iron.[59] From Hsü Kuang-ch'i's description it appears that they could be produced either by casting or by forging.[60] With regard to the cost for the manufacturing of these firearms it is interesting to note that the renowned general T'an Lun 譚綸 (1520–1577) stated in 1567 that a big Fo-lang-chi cannon made of copper cost twenty taels of silver and that the smaller size cost about fifteen taels. Iron cannon of the same sizes cost a little less than half as much as the copper cannon.[61] In 1630 Hsü Kuang-ch'i reported to the emperor that it would cost one thousand taels of silver to make a hundred small guns.[62] Unskilful soldiers often burst the cannon with great loss of life, especially if the cannon were recast from copper. Hsü, therefore, was opposed to recasting cannon from old material. He insisted on using new material and said that the copper of the old firearms should be used for making coins.[63]

To judge from government documents of the Ch'ung-chen period and contemporary accounts, firearms of all kinds seem by then to have been introduced into China. During the revolt of Shang K'o-hsi 尚可喜 and Keng Chung-ming 耿仲明 in Shantung (1632), big cannon weighing two to three thousand catties were used to check the invasion of Teng-chou 登州.[64] Muskets made of bamboo were also used against the enemy during the same revolt. Since we are informed that these had been kept in store by the government, they cannot have been newly made, and had probably been produced a score of years earlier.[65] As early as 1567 T'an Lun recounted his experiences in producing wooden cannon modeled on the Fo-lang-chi. These cannon, he says, were made of hard wood; they were seven feet long and one foot four inches in 'diameter, and were closely bound with six iron rings. He boasts that each cannon could be fired seven or eight times without damage to its frame. If an accident did occur, at least there was no danger of serious injury to the bystanders.[66]

The introduction and extensive use of firearms naturally involved a vast consumption of gunpowder. It was said that at the battle of Liao-tung in 1626 seventeen thousand Manchus were killed by cannon balls: the founder of the Manchu dynasty himself is said to have been seriously injured by a cannon ball and to have died as a consequence of the wound.[67] When the author of the *T'ien-kung kai-wu* comes to his treatise on gunpowder, he remarks ironically that not a few of his contemporaries had tried to make their way into government service by pretending to deep understanding of firearms and gunpowder. Though in fact inexperienced in such matters, they had had the audacity to write books on firearms, often adding several pages dealing with gunpowder.[68]

Again, the *T'ien-kung kai-wu*, having mentioned that sulphur and saltpetre must be mixed in order to obtain an explosion, goes on to say that though there was an abundance of saltpetre in the land of the northern barbarians, they lacked sulphur. This explains the strict ban on the export of sulphur to those places.[69] As early as the beginning of the 16th century, Hu Sung 胡松 had mentioned that the Manchus, since their advance into Liao-tung, had obtained good quantities of iron from the Chinese and even had Chinese mechanics working for them. What they still lacked was saltpetre. This they tried to get from the market of Lin-ch'ing 臨清, in Shantung, through Chinese agents.[70]

We are also told that in 1598 an order was issued by the Wan-li emperor forbidding the private production and marketing of sulphur and saltpetre. The purpose of this order was to prevent not the Manchus but the Japanese from getting a supply of saltpetre. It seems to have been a common practice for the Chinese along the coast to sell saltpetre to the Japanese at a high price, and a writer of the time suggested that the production of saltpetre should be made a government monopoly.[71]

In the *P'ing-p'an chi* 平叛記, a chronological account of K'ung Yu-te's rebellion in 1622–23 by Mao Pin 毛霦 who lived in the K'ang-hsi period, there is a full account of the preparation of gunpowder for different types of firearms, with a detailed instruction on the proportion of ingredients to be used. This instruction seems to have been given to prevent inexperienced soldiers from endangering their own lives or damaging the guns.[72] It would have been hard to blame the soldiers for their lack of experience in the management of firearms, especially the soldiers, mentioned just now by Mao Pin, who were relief troops from Szechuan, and had perhaps never managed any guns till then. Their ignorance should not surprise us for it is known that, as late as 1632, the soldiers in Shansi, though stationed so close to the capital, did not know how to use firearms.[73]

Even the higher authorities were exceedingly ill informed about the use of gunpowder. An edict of the Ch'ung-chen emperor dated 1630, asked why foreign cannon, expensive as they were, could not hold more gunpowder. In answer to this Hsü Kuang-ch'i had to explain that the amount of gunpowder had to be proportioned to the size of the cannon ball and that the cannon ball, in turn, had to conform to the type and size of cannon.[74] Hsü's experience gave him good reason to distrust his countrymen in the production of firearms.

In writing to the emperor he insisted frequently that the production of gunpowder and ammunition should be entrusted to foreigners from the West with Chinese artisans merely as their assistants.[75]

From the Wan-li reign onwards mention of the production of gunpowder becomes more and more common. In the autumn of 1605 a group of soldiers went to the ammunition factory to draw some gunpowder, but found that it had solidified owing to prolonged storage. They started to break it with hatchets. It exploded, killing countless soldiers and civilians at distances up to a hundred paces.[76] In 1626 lightning struck the ammunition factory causing so great an explosion that the bright day was darkened by the debris. Very numerous casualties were reported [77] Finally, the *Huai-tsung shih-lu* records that between the years 1638 and 1640, there were four explosions caused by gunpowder. The first, in the summer of 1638, killed over ten thousand. The disaster was so serious that five thousand taels of silver were distributed in relief to unfortunate victims by order of the emperor.[78] This long tale of disaster implies that the production of gunpowder was common in this period.

NOTES

[1] *Ming shih,* 90, (ts'e 32) 1a, 2b; Wang Hung-hsü 王鴻緒, *Ming-shih-kao* 明史稿, (Ching-shen t'ang 敬慎堂 edition) 86, (ts'e 22); *Yu seng-po tao huang-chuan,* 103–105; *Chung-kuo li-tai ch'eng-chih tei-shih,* 98–99.

[2] Ku Yen-wu 顧炎武, *Jih-chih lu chi-shih* 日知錄集釋, (Ch'ung-wen shu-chü 崇文書局 edition) (Hupei, 1872) 109, (ts'e 6) 6a-7a.

[3] *Ming shih,* 77, (ts'e 27) 8ab.

[4] *Hsü wen-hsien t'ung-k'ao,* 122, (ts'e 2) 3, 889.

[5] Wu Han 吳晗, *Tu shih cha-chi* 讀史劄記, (Peking, 1956) 92.

[6] In the biography of T'ang To 唐鐸 (*Ming shih,* chapter 138) there is mention of a certain Ch'en Chih 陳質 whose father died on garrison. In conformity with the law, Ch'en was summoned to fill his father's place. Ch'en, being a scholar, petitioned for an exemption on the grounds that he wanted to finish his studies. The president of the Board of War was reluctant to grant the permission. Ultimately, the Hung-wu emperor exempted him, giving as his reason that it was easier to find a soldier within the empire than a scholar. The *Ming shih* then goes on to say that this was a "special favor" of the emperor. Cf. also the biography of Ch'en Hsiu 陳修 (ibid).

[7] *Li-tai chi-kuan piao,* 12, (ts'e 2) 319–320.

[8] *Ming shih,* 90, (ts'e 32 TWSC).

[9] *Ming shih,* 89, (ts'e 32) 1b-3a.

[10] Ibid., 170, (ts'e 56) 2b-3a.

[11] *Ming shih,* 180, (ts'e 59) 27a.

[12] Ibid., 181, (ts'e 60) 8a.

[13] *Ibid.*, 183, (ts'e 60) 15b.

[14] *Tu shih cha-chi*, 112.

[15] *Tu shih cha-chi*, 118 where the *Ming-tai-tsu shih-lu*, chuan 131 is quoted.

[16] *Tu shih cha-chi*, 121 where the *Ming Ying-tsung shih-lu*, chuan 22 is quoted.

[17] *Hsü Wen-hsien t'ung-k'ao*, 122 (WYWK ts'e 2), 3894.

[18] *Tu shih cha-chi*, 119 where the *Ming Hsüan-tsung shih-lu* chuan 99 is quoted.

The Law of Replacing Missing Soldiers was instituted primarily to remedy this defect. It did not achieve its aim. On the contrary, it caused great confusion to the people and in consequence led to many abuses. Early in the Cheng-t'ung reign (in the 1430's) Yang Shih-chi 楊士奇 pointed out the main disadvantage of this law. Since it forced members of deserters' families to fill the vacancies left by their absconding relatives, southerners often had to go north and northerners to go south. Many perished from hardships of the long journey and those who survived had to experience the rigors of climate which was entirely new to them. We are told that at about this same time the censors who were engaged in enforcing this law went around the provinces making illegal arrests. In Kiangsi a censor actually forced the headman of a certain village to arrest innocent members of, it is said, two hundred families. When the Law of Replacing Missing Soldiers was first promulgated, it was the practice to summon members of deserters' families to fill the vacancies immediately. Later the system was changed into one of yearly replacement.

Two records were made of each soldier: one to be kept in the Board of War, the other, in the locality where the soldier was recruited. A censor was appointed for a three-year term to supervise the records. In general, if the censor was an upright man the system worked smoothly. But if he was not he could be a cause of great hardship, for such a censor might stubbornly insist on the recruitment of the requisite number of soldiers and the officials working under him would find that the only way of carrying out his orders was to seize people at random. When this happened no clear record was ever made of what had been done. Accordingly, as time went on, the records became ever more confused and unscrupulous sub-officials could do with them what they pleased. Often men who were registered under the Board of War were able to escape military service through bribery while civilians were forced to take their places. The greedier the officials and sub-officials were the greater was the burden on the people. Thus, the Law of Replacing Missing Soldiers did little good; in spite of its rigidity it failed to stop the soldiers from deserting.

[19] *Ming shih*, 90, (ts'e 32) 3ab.

[20] *Ming t'ung-chien*, 24, (ts'e 3) 13a.

[21] *Ming hui-yao* 明會要, 59, (ts'e 2, Chung-hua shu-chü ed. Shanghai, 1956) 1136.

[22] *Ming hui-yao*, 59, (ts'e 2) 1139.

[23] *Ibid.*

[24] *Hsü wen-hsien t'ung-k'ao*, 134, (ts'e 2) 3992 b.

[25] *Ibid.*, 3992c–3993a.

[26] *Hsi-yüan wen-chien lu*, 73, (ts'e 29) 15b; L. Carrington Goodrich and Feng Chia-sheng 馮家昇, "The Early Development of Firearms in China," *Isis*, Vol. 36, Pt. 2, No. 104, 1946, pp. 114–123; L. Carrington Goodrich, "motes on a Few Early Chinese Bombards," *Ibid.*, Vol. 35, Pt. 3, No. 101, 1944, p. 211; Kung Hua-lung 龔化龍, "Ming Ch'ing p'ao-shu hsi-hua k'ao-lüeh" 明清砲術西化考略, *Lo Chia yüeh-k'an* 璐珈月刊, 2.7; Kuroda Genji 黑田源次, "Shinki kaho ron" 神機火砲論, *Manshu gakuhō* 滿洲學報, 4; Mikami Tsugio 三上次男, "Min shutei ju shi nen mei no aru taiho ni tsuite" 明崇禎十四年銘の ある大砲就にシて, *Rekishigaku Kenkyu* 歷史學研究, 6, (1938) 5. 101; *Hsü wen-hsien t'ung-k'ao*, 134, (ts'e 2) 3994c.

[27] Ho Liang-ch'en 何良臣, *Chen chi* 陣紀, 2, (TSCCCP), (ts'e 0, 961) 30.

[28] Jean Baptiste du Halde, S.J.: *Description geographique, historique, chronologique, politique, et physique de l'empire de la Chine*, (Paris, 1735), 2, 47.

[29] *Ming shih*, 92, (ts'e 33) 10b–11a.

[30] *Ming shih*, 325, (ts'e 110) 19b; cf. Paul Pelliot, "Le Hoya et le Sayyid Husain de l'histoire de Ming", *T'oung-Pao*, 38, 1948, 199–207. Pelliot proves clearly from unofficial documents that European firearms were introduced into China before 1510. For the Portuguese Embassy to China 1520 cf. J. M. Braga: *China Landfall* 1513, (Macau, 1955 75, note 119.

[31] *Ming shih*, 325, (ts'e 110) 20ab. The Portuguese seem to put this event under the last year of the Ch'eng-te emperor (1521) whereas the Chinese historians give the date as 1523, i.e. the second year of the Chia-cheng emperor's reign. Among the prisoners captured by the Chinese, a certain Pieh tu-lu su-shih-li 別都盧疎世利 was mentioned by name. Probably he was the man recorded in the Portuguese document as Bartolomeu Soares and mentioned first among those killed in the fighting. Cf. Manuel Teixeira, *Macau e a sua Diocese* (Macau, 1940) 1, 18.

[32] *Hsü Wen-hsien t'ung-k'ao*, 134, (ts'e 2) 3996c.

[33] Ibid.

[34] Ibid., 3997a.

[35] Ibid., 3995b.

[36] *Ching-ch'uan hsien-sheng wai-chi* 荊川先生外集, 2, (Ssu-pu ts'ung-k'an smaller ed. ts'e 2) 381.

[37] *Hsü wen-hsien t'ung-k'ao*, 134, (ts'e 2) 3997a.

[38] Ts'ai Chiu-te 采九德, *Wo pien shih lüeh* 倭變事略, 4, (TSCCCP ts'e 3975), 73.

[39] *Ming shih*, 93, (ts'e 33), 12a.

[40] Ibid.

[41] *Ming hui-tien*, 193, (WYWK, ts'e 35), 3879, 3907–3908.

[42] Ibid., 3880, 3882–3885.

[43] Ibid., 3880.

[44] Ibid., 3903.

[45] Among the Confucian scholars most strongly opposed to everything foreign, was Liu Tsung-chou 劉宗周 (1578–1645). In 1642 Adam Schall was recommended by one of the censors as instructor of the army in the use of firearms. In an interview with the emperor, Liu said, "Throughout the T'ang and Sung dynasty, no one ever heard of the use of firearms in battles. But since this invention one depends entirely on it. This is a great mistake!" When the emperor heard of this he said, "But I still consider the firearms a powerful weapon for our empire." Liu answered, "T'ang Jo-wang 湯若望 (Adam Schall) is a mere foreigner, what talent can he possess? The fact that he occupied the Shou-shan Academy 首善書院 and transformed it into an observatory shows that he ignores the respect the foreigners owe to the Middle Kingdom according to the teaching of the *Spring and Autumn*. I beg of Your Majesty therefore, to send him away lest he mislead others." *Huai-tsung shih-lu*, (Taipei, 1967) chuan 15, p. 18a.

[46] *Tseng-ting Hsü wen-ting-kung chi* 增訂徐文定公集, (Shanghai, 1909) 3, (ts'e 2) 42a–44b.

[47] Ibid., 3, (ts'e 2) 8a.

[48] Ibid., 3, (ts'e 2) 7ab.

[49] J. B. du Halde, *Description geographique, historique, chronologique, politique, et physique de l'empire de la China*, 2, 47; Pao Ju-chi 包汝楫 (floruit 1620) in his book *Nan-chung chi-wen* 南中紀聞 has an interesting account of this mission: "The niao-ch'ung of the Hsi-yang country can reach a distance of 600 paces. The gun makes no noise when fired, but the projectile explodes as soon as it hits the body of a human being and always causes death. In the beginning of the T'ien-ch'i reign thirty men of that [Hsi-yang] country were summoned to Peking to instruct the soldiers in the use of these firearms. In 1624 they were dismissed [to Macao]. I saw them in Hang-chou. They were as black as ink and their hair was less than an inch long and curled like [the spiral] of the shell-fish: even the

beards on their cheeks were like that. They reminded me of the image of Bodhidharma 達摩 which we often see. The knives they used had thin and sharp edges made of very fine steel [literally: iron that had been refined a thousand times], and so were very flexible. The small guns that they used to shoot flying birds caused explosions in the air after the firing. Their shooting was exceedingly accurate. *Nan-chung chi-wen*, (TSCCCP, ts'e 3114), 19.

[50] Fang Hao 方豪, op. cit. 93–94 where chuan 17 of the *Ch'ung-chen chang-pien* 崇禎長編 was quoted.

[51] *Tseng-ting Hsü wen-ting-kung chi*, 3, (ts'e 2) 20b–21a.

[52] *Tseng-ting Hsü wen-ting-kung chi*, 3, (ts'e 2) 11b, 20ab, 22b–23a, 33a, 38b.

[53] Ibid., 27a, 28b, 20b, 21a.

[54] Ibid., 9b–10a.

[55] Ibid., 17a.

[56] Ibid., 22a.

[57] Ibid., 30b, 31a.

[58] Ibid., 23ab, 28ab.

[59] *T'ien-kung kai-wu* 天工開物, 2, (KHCPTS 國學基本叢書), 157.

[60] *Tseng-ting Hsü wen-ting-kung chi*, C, (ts'e 2) 12a.

[61] *Ming-ch'en tsou-i* 明臣奏議, (TSCCCP), 27, (ts'e 0919) 493.

[62] *Tseng-ting Hsü wen-ting-kung chi*, 3, (ts'e 2) 27a.

[63] Ibid., 17ab.

[64] Mao Pin 毛霦, *P'ing-p'an chi* 平叛記, (*Yin-li-tsai-ssu-t'ang ts'ung-shu* 殷禮在斯堂叢書), (ts'e 4) 13b.

[65] Ibid., 30a.

[66] *Ming-ch'en tsou-i*, 27, (ts'e 0919) 493; cf. also Chao Shih-cheng 趙士楨, *Shen-ch'i p'u huo wen* 神器譜或問, (*Hsüan-lan-t'ang ts'ung-shu* 玄覽堂叢書), (ts'e 86) 10b, 11ab. Chao was skeptical about the practicability of wooden and bamboo guns.

[67] *Hsi-yüan wen-chien lu*, 73, (ts'e 29) 15b.

[68] *T'ien-kung kai-wu*, 2, 258.

[69] Ibid., 2, 259.

[70] *Hsi-yüan wen-chien lu*, 73, (ts'e 29) 12.

[71] *Hsü wen-hsien t'ung-k'ao*, 134, (ts'e 2) 3998a.

[72] *P'ing-p'an chi*, (ts'e 4) 16b–17ab; cf. also Chu Kuo-chen 朱國楨, *Yung-chuang hsiao-p'in* 湧幢小品, (Shanghai, 1959) I, 265, where description is given on how to refine saltpetre.

[73] Tai Li 戴笠, *Huai-ling liu-k'ou shih-chung lu* 懷陵流寇始終錄, (other title: *K'ou-shih pien-nien* 寇事編年), (HLTTS second series), (ts'e 6) 6a; cf. ibid. 3 (ts'e 5) 6a where the author mentions the use of firearms by the soldiers of Shansi. Is there a contradiction in the two narrations? Or, did the author mean that, in general, the Shansi soldiers did not know how to manage firearms? The above-mentioned passage seems to indicate that the second sense is the true one. The soldiers, it says, used cannon to fight against the rebels, but during the operation the cannon burst and confusion began to spread among the soldiers. The rebels noticed this and, taking advantage of the confusion, pushed forward, and scattered the soldiers.

[74] *Tseng-ting Hsu wen-ting-kung chi*, 1b, (ts'e 1) 30b.

[75] Ibid., 3, (ts'e 2) 1 b.

[76] *Ming t'ung-chien*, 73, (ts'e 9) 10b.

[77] Ibid., 80, (ts'e 10) 9b.

[78] *Huai-tsung Ch'ung-chen shih-lu* 懷宗崇禎實錄, (KSSLTSK photographic reprint), (ts'e 11) 7b, 10b; (ts'e 12) 5b. The scholar Liu Hsien-t'ing 劉獻廷 (1648–1695) mentions in his book *Kuang-yang tsa-chi* 廣陽雜記, (*Kung-shun t'ang ts'ung-shu* 功順堂叢書), 1, (ts'e 18) 16b a great explosion in the old arsenal of the capital. According to him innumerable people were injured and great numbers of houses were destroyed. He then quotes the words of a certain Ting Ta-nien 丁大年 on how gunpowder was kept in the arsenal: "From the very time of the Hung-wu emperor it had been the tradition of the Ming government to store gunpowder underground. First they dug a hole thirty feet deep and filled it with gunpowder. On top of this they laid slabs of stone, and across these wood. The whole was then covered with earth." Further on, Liu tells us that after the explosion in 1642 another eight gunpowder store pits were made.

CHAPTER FOUR

The People

GENTRY

Among the subjects of the Ming dynasty the first place belonged to the gentry, who were practically identical with the landlord class. Almost all of them were associated in one way or another with the government, some because they were retired government officials, some because they had once been in the service of the government and were trying to re-enter it, and some because their position gave them influence in government affairs though they had never held office.

The gentry enjoyed great privileges from the government. First, they ranked as the intelligentsia and so had control of the educational system. Throughout the Ming dynasty most of the candidates for the Imperial Academy or higher government educational institutions came from families of the gentry class. Secondly, placed as they were between the government and the people, they were often the only source from which government officials could get advice on matters of local administration. This gave them considerable indirect influence over government policy. On the other hand, the people looked on them as their leaders and often chose them as chairmen of school committees, or public-works or relief commissions, for their monopoly of learning marked them out as the only possible spokesmen for the people whether in words or in writing.

The gentry, though they formed a ruling class, did not form a caste. Landlords with no official government rank might be classed as gentry. Books were already circulating widely in the days of the

Ming dynasty and many of these landlords were eager to introduce their children to the classics in the hope that some day they might pass the examinations and thus be elevated to the ruling official class.

Many landlords were eager to obtain government office not so much for the honor of such service as for the chance it gave of augmenting their possessions. Indeed the honor involved in government office was a perilous one for it derived from closeness of contact with the emperor. Now, all knew well that they were always at the mercy of the emperor and that losing his favor might entail the loss of property or life, or of both. This was why, in Chinese tradition, government officials never assumed office with great eagerness and never wanted to spend their whole lives in the service of the emperor. The conventional symbol of political life was a bird tiring of flight and returning to its nest. While in office, officials tried, by showering acts of kindness and other favors on their relatives, friends, and fellow countrymen, to ensure that they might retire respected and loved by all and in this way secure their property. As soon as an official had accomplished his purpose, he usually retired to his native place where, far from the emperor, he might enjoy all the produce of his farm without being himself a farmer.

Once secure in the possession and enjoyment of their property the landlords rested satisfied. They shunned the risks involved in interference in politics and had no desire to see governmental and social reforms, for they knew that if the exercise of imperial authority were changed their own manner of living would also suffer change. However, they did wish to have members of their families in government service so that they might have their influence to rely on in protecting themselves and their possessions against powerful aggressors. Moreover, if their relatives were employed in government service, especially at court, they themselves might attain such influence that they would be dreaded even by local prefects. The existence of such influence was the reason why local prefects frequently had to seek the cooperation of the landlord class. Ordinarily, when a newly appointed local prefect reached the scene of his future labors, his first act was to visit the gentry of the place. He did what he could to show them good will and, in return, asked for their support. Historical examples can be cited of local prefects failing because their lack of tact had caused the local gentry to combine to secure their dismissal.[1]

When the founder of the dynasty ascended the throne, he expressed his conviction that there ought to be a distinction between the landlord class and the commoners. In an edict of 1377, we read:

"There is a distinction of class between those who are in government service and the common people. It is the duty of the common people to serve their superiors by their labor. But, if, having first honored scholars and gentlemen, we then demand labor from their families, there will be no distinction between gentlemen and common people. We deem this an improper way of encouraging students, or of treating scholars. Henceforth, the families of all the government officials, if they possess any farms, shall pay the land tax, but shall be exempt from *corvée*. Let this be enforced as law."[2]

Two years later, a second edict was issued by the same monarch exempting the families of all retired government officials from *corvée*.[3] Still later, according to the *Ta-ming hui-tien* 大明會典, two members of the family of each licentiate were exempted.[4]

The officials were also granted a reduction in land taxes. Thus we read in 1521 of the enactment of a law by which court officials were granted various tax reductions according to their rank. From the first to the third rank they received exemption up to four ch'ing, from the fourth to the fifth rank up to three ch'ing, from sixth to seventh rank up to two ch'ing; and from eighth to ninth rank up to one ch'ing. During the Chia-ching reign this law was modified but it still favored the officials.[5] Students, we are told, if unable to pay land taxes, could petition the government for exemption.[6]

Even in social relations the landlord class enjoyed a position superior to that of the common people. An edict of 1379, stated: "Retired officials who are living in their native land should observe family etiquette when they are dealing with their clan; but at banquets, special tables must be set for them and they must not sit below those who have never been government officials. When there is a meeting of retired officials, they are to make a distinction according to the rank of each and, if some happen to be equal in rank, then they must make a distinction according to seniority. When they meet people of other clans who have never been employed in the government, they are not to return salutes. Commoners who come to visit them must treat them as government officials. If commoners dare to insult them, they are to be punished according to the law. Let this be enforced as law."[7]

Furthermore, we are told that at weddings and funerals special reception rooms, known as ta-pin-t'ang 大賓堂 (i.e. halls for distinguished guests), were prepared for the landlord class. When the landlords went out, they were always carried in sedan chairs and usually these were preceded by bearers carrying large ornamental fans and umbrellas. In some places the local prefects used to send their attendants to attend them. Even licentiates when out of doors always had a servant to walk before them with a paper umbrella.[8]

Although the standard of living of the landlords was higher than that of the common people, the scholar Chang Ying 張英 (1637–1708) says in his time it was common to find middle-class landlords beset by financial problems, for they lived extravagantly and often exceeded their means. "Nowadays," Chang Ying says, "members of the land-lord families dress elegantly and ride proudly on horseback. They frequently have feasts with dances and music. They easily spend several tens of silver taels on a fur coat. As for food, they do not hesitate to spend several silver taels on a single meal. In our village grain has been cheap for over a decade. In consequence, the price of over ten piculs of grain will not suffice one of these landlords for the preparation of a banquet, nor the sale price of over one hundred piculs of grain for the purchase of a coat."[9]

Landlords residing in the cities had a still higher standard of living and, in addition to their expenditure on food and clothes, incurred heavy expenses in their social life. Moreover, they burdened the peasantry in the manner common to absentee landlords of all ages and all countries. Their incomes often depended solely on rents from their farms yet they left the task of collecting the rents to their servants, who frequently treated this as an opportunity for exploiting the farmers, especially if their masters were persons of influence.

Landlords who resided in the villages usually took some interest in agriculture. Much or most of their land was leased to tenant farmers, but they also developed part of their own farms through hired farm laborers. Village life was simpler than life in the cities. The essential things of daily life could be obtained from the farm and there was usually better understanding between the landlords and the tenants who resided in the same village. The Shen-shih nung-shu 沈氏農書, written in the Ch'ung-chen period, gives some detailed accounts of the way in which a conscientious landlord should treat his tenants, specifying the various kinds of food to be served to farm workers in the different seasons of the year and constantly reminding landlords to be generous with their tenants.[10]

Chang Li-hsiang 張履祥 (1611–1674), who supplements the in-formation given in the Shen-shih nung-shu, gives us a still better idea of the life of the tenant farmers of his days. "In my village, T'ung-hsiang 桐鄉 (Chekiang)," he says, "the best farmers can cultivate at most ten mou of land. Hence those who possess a great deal of land usually lease their land to tenant farmers. Again, because of the large population, it is not easy to buy land, and the poor are forced to rent it. . . . The tenants work hard throughout the year, and here am I, sitting in comfort and receiving half of the harvest of the tenants as rent. In a plentiful year, even after the land tax and *corvée* tax have been paid, there still remains (in the landlord's hands) two thirds of the rent, which is quite a large sum. Yet many landlords do not seem to be satisfied with this and allow their servants to make all kinds of illegal demands. By what right do they do such things?"

Chang goes on to advise his landlord readers of their obligations: "In general, one should pay occasional visits to one's own farm in order to examine the quality of the land and know its measurements, and one should have a plan of the fields with all the details marked on it. On the day when a tenant rents a farm, the landlord should visit the family of the farmer and should also make the acquaintance of his neighbors. He should observe whether his tenant is a hard worker or a lazy one. He ought to know the number of persons in his tenant's household. He should try to choose a diligent and honest tenant who has a large household in which the members are of one mind. On the day when he receives the rent he should be generous and understanding. Abuses committed by his servants must always be checked. The landlord must be ready to advise and help if his tenants suffer disasters, or if there are lawsuits, deaths, orphans or poverty in the family of any of his tenants. Thus through mutual understanding a landlord and his tenants should treat one another as if they were of the same family. . . ."[11] Unfortunately, relations between landlords and their tenants, in practice, seemed to be quite unlike this: "Of late I have noticed that landlords belonging to rich and influential families dwell in deep seclusion and seldom go out. They never set foot on their own farms and cannot even recognize their own tenants. They leave their business in the hands of their servants, who sometimes sell their masters' farms, or secretly appropriate the rent and confuse their masters by passing off cultivated fields as uncultivated, or dismiss honest tenants in order to lease the land to unscrupulous farmers. These and other corrupt practices account for the disappearance of properties and the falsification of records; eventually they bring about the ruin of the landlord's family. Other landlords, relying on their influence, exploit the people, now trying to deny them their proper wages, now trying to appropriate their money or their wives and children, and even trying to have them cast into prison. It is terrifying to reflect that the treatment they now give to their people will some day return upon themselves."[12]

The *Ming shih* records many abuses committed by the landlords. Many of them, relying on the protection of relatives in official positions, did what they pleased on their estates. They gave shelter to runaway slaves and kept numerous servants whom they employed to exploit the people. Sometimes they took the law into their own hands and poor farmers would often suffer in silence, knowing that it would be futile to accuse them before the magistrates. Even Yang Shih-ch'i 楊士奇 (1365–1444) and Chang Chü-cheng 張居正 (1525–1582), with their reputation of being good ministers, could not prevent members of their families from falling into such abuses. Yang Shih-ch'i, we are told, died of grief because his son was accused of many serious crimes both by the people and by the ministers at court. Of Chang Chu-cheng we read that the oppression of the people by members of his family was one of the reasons for his posthumous disgrace.[13] An anonymous author has left us a small volume describing the selfishness and atrocities of the renowned littérateur Tung Ch'i-ch'ang 董其昌 (1555–1636). The author, a sympathizer with the people, may have exaggerated here and there, but there can be no doubt that his account is substantially accurate.[14]

The scholar Hsü Hsüeh-mu 徐學謨, who lived in the middle of the 16th century, says of the landlords of his time that when they were in government service they favored whomsoever they pleased and took revenge on all whom they did not like. Even in retirement, they were still dreaded by all because they retained the power of doing good or evil to the people.

As a good father of a family, Hsü admonishes the members of his household to guard themselves against the evil customs which seem to have been common among the great families of his days. First of all, he warns them against usury. Lending money to the needy and demanding interest on it he considered legitimate, provided that the interest did not exceed three per cent. He disapproved severely of the contemporary practice of demanding four per cent, five per cent, or even higher rates. Often the borrowers were obliged to sign a document stating that they had borrowed a certain sum, whereas in fact they had received only seventy to eighty per cent of this. When the day of repayment came, they had to pay back the amount stated in the bond. Many such unfortunate victims had to sell their belongings, or even their children, in order to avoid imprisonment.

Another abuse pointed out by Hsü was the formation of a conspiracy between vagabonds and the members of a landlord's family, whether these were in government service or not. Conspiracies of this kind often sprang up when the father of a family was absent from his

native place, or had lost contact with the outside world. The vagabonds offered their service to such families without the knowledge of
the father. As soon as they were accepted, they were given more or
less responsible posts: one might be given a capital sum to do business
with, another might be appointed as revenue collector, and so on.
Relying on the influence of the landlord's family they would then
proceed to oppress the people. One not uncommon practice of these
licensed vagabonds was to gather in front of the governor's office to
find out what was happening there. If a lawsuit was being tried they
often sided with one of the two parties, hoping to reap much profit
from him. In such cases they always tried to secure the cooperation
of the sub-officials. Worse than their personal misdemeanors was their
habit of extending to others—robbers and bandits, pickpockets,
monks of dubious character whom even the monasteries would not
admit—the protection under which they themselves felt so secure.

Finally, Hsü warns his family very seriously against gambling
parties in the home. The Ming code forbade gambling for money.
"Whoever gambles with money or the equivalent shall receive 80
strokes of the baton. The money with which they gambled as well as
the gambling instruments shall be confiscated. The proprietor of the
gambling house shall suffer the same penalty. But if they be government officials, let their penalty be double that of the commoners," says
the code. Rich landlords, however, often ignored this law and held
gambling parties in secret chambers of their houses. Young men of good
families were often lured into joining them and were kept gambling day
and night until they had squandered all their property. The families of
these unfortunates were naturally indignant, but through fear of the
landlords dared not bring the guilty parties before the magistrate.[15]

The gentry, belonging to the privileged class, enjoyed the best of
everything. Even those who had high reputations for integrity
possessed a great deal of property and erected magnificent buildings
on the best sites in the cities. We are told that many of them accomplished this without spending much money, for their former pupils
and the lower officials to whom they had shown favor provided them
with all that was needed. They intermarried with influential families
and tried to link themselves with renowned persons of their wives'
clans. They were always ready to help scholars in their financial
troubles in the hope of getting a rich return.[16]

FARMERS

The bulk of the common people were farmers. Agriculture and the
cultivation of silk had been regarded as the principal resources of the

country from time immemorial. In the early days of the dynasty the founder paid special attention to agriculture. He himself, coming from a family of farmers, was naturally interested in the cultivation of the land. Even apart from his personal inclinations, he thought that the prosperity of the empire could be built only on agriculture. He was convinced that if the people could support themselves by producing enough from the farms there would be no need to worry about the economic condition of the country. For this reason he was not in favor of taxing the people heavily. Once, when writing to the Board of Revenue, he asserted firmly that the taxes for the whole country had been fixed at the proper levels, and that the government would always have sufficient revenue if it could learn to use money frugally. Hence there was no need to overtax the people.[17]

In the early days of his reign the Hung-wu emperor realized that, owing to repeated military losses at the end of the Yüan dynasty, many of the provinces were but sparsely populated. In order to remedy this he did all he could to encourage the people to cultivate the land. About the middle of his reign an edict was published to the effect that those who brought waste land under cultivation might keep it as their property and would never be taxed. The response of the people was enthusiastic: we are told that in the early days of the dynasty the area of cultivated land rose to 8,804,623 ch'ing and 68 mou.[18] The *Ming shih* says that during the reigns of the first four emperors (1368–1435) the country attained great prosperity simply because the land was not laid waste and the people were not idle. Grain was so abundant that it rotted in the granaries.[19]

From the first, great care was taken by the Hung-wu emperor to distribute land to small farmers. It seems to have been his policy to favor the poor, whom he tried to help to support themselves and their families. For instance, in 1370 an order was given that some land of Honan and Anhui (then part of Nan-chih) should be distributed to young farmers who had reached manhood: to preclude the absorption of this land by unscrupulous landlords it was announced that the title to it was not transferable. In northern China, where the farms around cities had been laid waste, volunteers from among the people were employed to cultivate them. Each volunteer was given fifteen mou on which to cultivate grain and two more mou for the growing of vegetables.[20]

The gentry class possessed a great deal of land, but most of them were accustomed to reside in cities, entrusting their farms to agents or tenants. Members of the gentry who lived in the country usually ran their own farms. A separate rural group was formed by those who cultivated land belonging to the government or to the relatives of the emperors.

In general, the life of a farmer was not an easy one. The earlier emperors of the Ming dynasty seem to have realized this, for they tried to lighten the burden of excessive taxes and unnecessary *corvée*. Thus the Hung-wu emperor, we are told, having once brought his heir with him on a tour, took the opportunity of showing him the life of the farmers. Having shown him the dwellings, diet, and the domestic utensils of these simple people, he turned to him and said: "Now, you see the hard life of these people. They hardly ever leave their fields, and their hands are always on the plow. They work hard throughout the year, and hardly ever take any rest. They live in crude straw huts, their clothes are made of rough cloth, and their food consists of unrefined rice and vegetables. Nevertheless, the government depends chiefly on them for revenue. I wish therefore that in your daily life you shall remember the hardships of the farmers. When you exact anything from them, be reasonable and use what you received from them with great care, so that they may not have to suffer from hunger and cold."[21] Again, one day the same monarch, seeing a gaily clad official, asked him how much he had spent on his clothes and was told 500 strings of cash. "Five hundred strings of cash!" the emperor said. "That is the annual expenditure of an ordinary farmer with a household of several members. And here you spent it on one garment! Does not this seem extravagant to you?"[22]

As a secondary occupation the farmers took up the cultivation of silk. In the beginning of his reign the Hung-wu emperor tried to encourage the growing of mulberry trees, imposing a fine of one bolt of silk on those who disobeyed this order. Towards the end of his life he ordered every household to plant in one year two hundred jujube trees and mulberry trees, and to bring the number up to six hundred trees by the third year.[23]

Under the Ming dynasty the production of silk was widespread in all provinces and especially in the provinces to the south of the Yangtze River. Chekiang in particular was illustrious for the quality and quantity of its silk. After Chekiang came Nan Chih-li 南直隸 (now Kiangsu and Anhui) and Kuangtung, then Szechuan in the west. Lu-an fu 潞安府 in Shansi was also well known in north China for its silk. The local gazette of Wu-kiang hsien 吳江縣 says that silk weaving in this prefecture began between 1425 and 1435. At first skilled weavers had to be employed from the province, but by the beginning of the 16th century the natives had become expert and for a distance of forty to fifty li along Sheng-tse 盛澤 and Huang-ch'i

黃溪 silk was the sole industry. Those who had the capital employed weavers; the poor did the work themselves. Women devoted their time solely to silk manufacturing and children over the age of ten worked in the factories day and night.[24]

The silk industry was one of the greatest of all industries in the Ming period. It was one of the chief attractions for traders from neighboring countries and in the later days of the dynasty even from Europe. Technique improved greatly and connoisseurs today still admire the beautiful designs and harmonious colors of Ming silk.

In order to meet the demand silk was produced on a great scale. Mulberry trees were grown everywhere for the sake of the leaves, which are the food of silkworms. A contemporary writer in present Kiangsu estimated that a mou of good land would yield 160 catties of mulberry leaves yearly, at the cost of about two taels of silver yearly and with a profit of about four taels.[25] Naturally the farmers, especially to the south of the Yangtze, devoted themselves readily to this profitable type of cultivation. In Hu-chou 湖州 particularly, silk cultivation was the chief support of the people. The father of the scholar Mao K'un 茅坤 (1512–1601), for instance, was said to possess over ten thousand mulberry trees.[26] The local gazette of Hu-chou mentions that the great majority of the inhabitants in the islands of Tai-hu 太湖 cultivated silkworms: mulberry trees were planted everywhere; from their early days girls were trained in silkworm cultivation; during the third and fourth month of the year the inhabitants were so busy that they often cut off normal social relations with their neighbors.[27]

There were government silk factories in both Nanking and Peking. In each of these places there were two factories, one exclusively for the supply of the imperial family and the other for official purposes such as donations to nobles, meritorious officials, and foreign ambassadors. There were also factories in Su-chou, Chekiang, Fukien, and Shansi, the annual production of which was determined by the court. Extravagant monarchs were not always content with these fixed quantities and made extraordinary demands, to the detriment of the people. Thus, in the year 1460, the Emperor Ying-tsung demanded an extra seven thousand bolts of silk from five prefectures in present Kiangsu and Chekiang. In 1506, under the Cheng-te emperor, seventeen thousand bolts of silk were ordered from the prefectures of Nan Chih-li and Chekiang. Towards the end of the dynasty these demands kept on increasing and we are told that under the Wan-li emperor as many as one hundred and fifty thousand bolts of silk were sometimes ordered within a single year.[28]

In the silk factories work was divided among the workers according to each one's skill. The *Wan-li hui-tien* 萬曆會典 gives the distribution of duties among 1,317 workers, split into ten independent groups. The author of the *T'ien-kung k'ai-wu* describes the manufacturing of the imperial garments as "done by different departments and not exclusively completed by one group." This shows clearly that industrial production had made some progress towards the division of labor since earlier days when a single craftsman carried through the whole process.[29]

Silk production, however important, was not the sole textile industry. The manufacture of cotton cloth was one of the chief activities of the common people. Silk was the dress of the rich, cotton was the common cloth of the poor. Cotton plants were introduced into China under the T'ang dynasty, by foreign traders. At first the cultivation of the plant was confined to the southern region of Indo-China, then part of China, and to Kuangtung and Kuangsi. By the time of the Sung dynasty it had reached Fukien. Still later, during the reign of Khubilai Khan, cotton growing became quite common in the Yangtze valley. The slowness of its spread to north China seems to have been due to delay in introducing the methods of weaving. Tradition tells us that a certain old lady known as Huang tao-p'o 黃道婆 came to Sung-kiang 松江 from Hainan Island and taught the people how to weave.[30]

During the Ming period the cultivation of cotton was common in the Yangtze valley, especially where the soil was too poor for rice-growing. Cotton planting became the main occupation of people living on such land and cotton cloth produced in Shang-hai was known all over the country. The real weaving center in the Ming period, however, was Sung-kiang. The local gazette of this place says that weaving was common among villagers as well as among the inhabitants of the city. As soon as they had sold their finished goods they bought more cotton from the market in order to produce more cloth. They wasted no time and in general a weaver was able to produce one bolt of cloth a day. Some of them even worked throughout the night,[31] and not a few made fortunes by weaving. The scholar Chang Han 張瀚 (fl. 1570) recalls how his family grew wealthy through cotton weaving. "At the end of the Cheng-hua 成化 reign (1465–1487), my grandfather Yi-an 毅庵 decided to give up his wine business," he says. "He bought a weaving machine, a really fine one which enabled him to weave cloth of all kinds. As soon as he finished a piece it was sold immediately at a profit of one fifth of the price. He was able to add a new machine to his factory every fortnight and the number gradually went up to over twenty. Our house was always full of dealers trying to obtain more cloth from us, but their demands could never be satisfied, for there was not enough to supply them all. From then onwards our family was very prosperous, the family property amounting to several tens of thousands of silver taels."[32]

Contemporary statistics disclose the amount of cloth that was transported to the capital towards the end of the dynasty. Among the prefectures in Kiang-nan, Sung-kiang sent the largest total, 123,860 bolts. Hua-t'ing 華亭 sent only half as much as Sung-kiang, and Shang-hai and Ch'ing-p'u less still. The fame of Sung-kiang did not depend solely on the quantity produced; the quality of its cotton also was well known throughout the empire. During the Cheng-hua reign, we are told, the people of this locality used to make presents to the eunuchs and court ladies. This became known to the emperor and orders were sent to the governor of the place for similar cloth. Designs of many kinds, including the dragon and phoenix, were demanded and they were to be in many colors. The sub-officials seized the opportunity for profit for themselves and the price of some varieties of cloth rose to nearly a hundred silver taels a bolt. When the Hung-chih emperor came to the throne he discontinued these extravagant demands.[33]

Industry had been developing at a remarkable pace ever since the time of the Sung dynasty. Many varieties of silk were recognized— chin 錦 brocade, ling 綾 damask, lo 羅 gauze, ch'ou 紬 satin, sha 紗 thin silk, shih 絁 coarse silk—and each of these varieties could be sub-divided. A list of some of these precious articles can still be found in the *Po-wu yao lan* 博物要覽 .[34]

CRAFTSMEN

In the early days of Mongol rule this development continued. Marco Polo bears witness to the wonderful products of Cambaluc (Peking) or of the various provinces of the Yüan empire. The fact that under the Mongol rule foreign traders were welcomed to China goes far to explain the rapid progress of industry. The Mongols, moreover, always took great interest in having skillful workers in their service. A contemporary witness says that these nomads had no artisans until they conquered some Mohammedans. D'Hosson, in his history of the Mongols, describes the fall of Mewschahidjan, where only the four hundred artisans and a small number of children were spared from death, the rest of the inhabitants all perishing by the sword.[35]

During the reign of Khubilai Khan, foreigners, and especially skillful workers, were welcome at court and helped in many ways to build up the industry of the day. After the death of the great Khan, however, the Mongol empire was in continual decline and industrial production declined with it.

When the founder of the Ming dynasty came to the throne he labored hard to stabilize the living standard of the people. Under his protection industry began to flourish once more and the number of craftsmen in the empire rose to over 230,000. They were divided into two groups, tso-chiang 坐匠 and shu-pan 輪班. The tso-chiang worked for the government ten days every month; the shu-pan were exempted from such service on the payment of six ch'ien each month. This system gave a certain advantage to more skillful workers who by paying could win exemption from work for the government and so could devote their whole time, or part at least, to their own enterprises, a factor that accounts for the progress of skilled work in the Ming period.[36] Contemporary writers give us a glimpse of the prosperity of this period, and the number of foreign merchants in the country was evidence of the flourishing state of imports and exports.[37]

The metal, lacquer, and paper industries ranked next to silk and cotton. It is said that glass making was encouraged by Cheng Ho who is credited with introducing some professional glass-makers encountered on his voyages in the Indian Ocean.

Speaking of the Chinese craftsmen of his time, Father Matteo Ricci remarked: "Most of the mechanical arts flourish among them. They have raw materials of all sorts and they are endowed by nature with a talent for trading, both of which are potent factors in bringing about a high development of the mechanical arts." However, he observed that the Chinese craftsmen did not strive to enhance the price of their products by perfecting their workmanship. This was no doubt true, for the common people, usually not rich and living as sparingly as they could, were satisfied with less perfect articles if they could get them cheaply. The well-to-do class, however, was willing to pay for the best craftsmanship and this was always available. We shall see more of this when we come to the arts under the Ming dynasty.[38]

Handicrafts were firmly established from the beginning of the dynasty. The *Chin-ling shih-chi* 金陵世紀, published in 1569, gives us a picture of the streets of Nanking as they were in the early days of the Ming dynasty. The names of many streets or lanes seem to indicate that shops engaged in the same business used to be grouped together. This was common in the old days and one still finds it today in many places. In the *Chin-ling shih-chi* account of Nanking we read such street names as Chien-tzu hsiang 剪子巷, lane of scissors (shops); Yu-fang hsiang 油房巷, lane of oil manufactories; Shou-p'a hsiang 手帕巷, lane of handkerchief (shops); Kan-yu hsiang 乾魚巷, lane of dried fish (shops). There were three silk streets, Chih-chin i, erh, san fang 織錦 一, 二, 三坊. These are cited merely as illustration. In all, about forty lanes had trade names.[39]

From the description in the *Chin-ling shih-chi* it is clear that each of these streets and lanes of different crafts was close to, if it did not contain, the residence of some high court official. Thus, among the streets and lanes described in the above-mentioned book, there was the Ta Kung fang 大功坊 of the great general Hsü Ta 徐達 (1332–1385), and the Tu-hsien fang 都憲坊 where Wu Wen-tu 吳文度, president of the Board of Revenue under the Cheng-hua reign, used to live. Then there were the K'o-ti chüan fang 科第傳坊, Shang-shu fang 尚書坊, T'ai-pao shang-shu fang 太保尚書坊, Hui-yüan fang 會元坊, Chi-ti fang 及第坊, etc., all streets named after distinguished persons of the time and containing the mansions in which they lived.[40]

The craftsmen seem, in general, to have enjoyed much freedom and to have gone about their daily work with great diligence. The Hung-wu emperor himself was said to have enjoyed visiting such people incognito. The scholar Chou Hui 周暉 has left us a delightful story of a censor and the blacksmiths: "The censor Li Yin-hung 李飲虹, who resided to the south of the Yin-hung Bridge, had to pass T'ieh-tso fang 鐵作坊 whenever he went to his office. Since the blacksmiths were busy at work, most of them did not rise from their seats to pay him due honor. Yin-hung resented this and mentioned it to the censor of the central city. The latter, on hearing the story, immediately summoned one of the blacksmiths from the street, questioned him, and imposed a punishment for his offense. The unfortunate man's companions, greatly upset by this news, went to the censor to make a declaration. 'The fact that we remain sitting while his Excellency is passing by is not a novelty invented by us,' they said. 'Years ago when President Ni (倪尚書) was living among us in the same street, he himself told us not to rise for him lest it should interfere with our work. We did not know that his Excellency Li would insist otherwise. We feel that we were perhaps spoiled by President Ni. The punishment now imposed on our fellow worker serves as a warning to us and in the future we shall try observe the order!' When the censor of the central city heard this he turned to censor Li and said, 'What they have said is enough to make me blush!' "[41]

Unlike the farmers, the craftsmen had no land to till and they were not tied to any particular place, but could go wherever they could find work to do. Where industries flourished, there the craftsmen would come in flocks. Thus, great numbers of craftsmen were found in Ching-te-chen 景德鎮, center of the porcelain industry under both the Ming and the Ch'ing dynasties, but very few were natives of the prefecture. The Yao-chow fu 饒州府 gazette tells us that most of these craftsmen came from Tu-ch'ang 都昌, also in Kiangsi province.[42]

It is to be noted that the number of government porcelain factories in the reign of the Hung-wu emperor was twenty; in the Hsüan-te reign this number rose to fifty-eight. Besides the government factories there were others which were operated by private owners. A government official of the Cheng-hua period (1465–1487) has left us a poem written during his visit to Ching-te-chen. The glowing sky inspired his poetic ardor: "Like a glowing cloud arising from a crimson city, it is transformed into a piece of beautiful silk; or like the sun arising from a violet sea its brilliant rays spread all over." Nearly a century later, a scholar who happened to be in this town remarked that it was the center of porcelain factories and that the inhabitants were considered the most prosperous people of the whole province. Day and night noise came from the factories and after dark the sky was so brilliantly lit that it was impossible to sleep. Jokingly, he named the place "the town that thunders and lightens throughout the four seasons."[43]

According to one author Ching-te-chen in the Ming period had a population of nearly a million and had about three thousand porcelain factories, government and private. He gives no references for his estimate, but judging from the account of the *Ching-te-chen t'ao lu* and the writing of Wang Shih-mou 王世懋 (1536–1588) he may have been right.[44]

The K'ang-hsi (Ch'ing) emperor once said that the total expenditure on all palaces in his day did not equal the expenditure on a single palace under the Ming. His statement gives us a good idea of Ming extravagance, and certainly allows us to infer safely that the amount of porcelain used in the Ming imperial household must have been immense. We cannot, however, accept his statement at its face value, for it implies that the expenditure of the court of K'ang-hsi in thirty-six years was less than that of the Ming in one year. This is surely an exaggeration. There is, however, no doubt that the early Manchu emperors lived far less extravagantly than the Ming emperors. Yet in the Chien-lung (early Ch'ing) period, we are told, Ching-te-chen had several hundred thousand inhabitants including several tens of thousands of craftsmen. The private porcelain factories numbered two to three hundred. We do not know exactly how many government factories there were, but there were some: the *Ching-te-chen t'ao lu* 景德鎮陶錄 mentions that in the Lung-ch'ing and Wan-li reigns (1567–1619) in addition to a certain number of the government factories there were private ones that took in orders from the government. That the number of these private factories must have been large is clear from the quantities of porcelain ordered by the emperors. In 1436, for instance, the private factories of Fou-liang 浮梁 in Kiangsi delivered 50,000 pieces, and towards the end of the Cheng-te emperor's reign (1506–1521) an order was given for the delivery of over 300,000, including pieces ordered by the Hung-chih emperor but never delivered to the court. After this last date, it was not uncommon for emperors to order well over 100,000 pieces. Production for the court was but part, probably a small part, of the total output, for we are told that the Ching-te-chen products were well known all over the empire and in foreign countries as well. All this helps us to form a general estimate of the great number of craftsmen in this mountainous locality.[45]

The silk factories produced many different types of silk and craftsmen were usually employed for their special skill in working on one or other of these types. The craftsmen often had their fixed employers and received their wages, according to the custom of the places, by the month or by the day. In Su-chou, for instance, they were paid by the day. If they were absent for any reason, the employer could call upon the services of jobbing craftsmen, of whom there were always some waiting around in the public places. "Unemployed craftsmen could be found waiting on the bridge at an early hour of the day," wrote Fan Lien 范濂 (1540–?). "Silk craftsmen waited on the Flower Bridge; weavers on the Kuang-hua Bridge 廣化橋, and the weavers of silk, known as ch'e-chiang 車匠, in Lien-ch'i fang 濂溪坊. They stood there in groups of tens and hundreds looking eagerly for employment. They gathered together like vagabonds and they dispersed after their breakfast. If the work of the factories was cut down, they immediately lost their means of support."[46]

Thus, the industries of the Ming dynasty were well developed. In some big factories the craftsmen numbered from some hundreds to a thousand or even more. Moreover, the social standing of these craftsmen was by no means always low. Wu Ming-kuan 吳明官 of Hui-chou, for example, who was said to have made his fortune from his porcelain factories, enjoyed so much fame that he was regarded by the gentry as an equal; and the craftsman Hsü Kao 徐呆 was promoted during the Chia-ching reign to the office of president of the Board of Works. We are told that his promotion was due to his skill as an architect.[47]

MERCHANTS

Finally, let us take a glimpse at the commerce of the day. In spite of the Chinese tradition of regarding the merchant class as the last and the least of the four professions (the other three being scholars, farmers, and craftsmen), merchants had always played an important role in the economic history of the empire. From the first, the founder of the Ming dynasty was particularly hostile to the merchant class, despising them as unproductive and fearing their wealth. This is well illustrated by the history of Shen Hsiu 沈秀 better known as Wan-san 萬三 a merchant, a native of Wu-hsing 吳興, and an extremely wealthy man. On one occasion he offered to feed the army of the founder of the dynasty; later, with his own money, he helped to build one third of the wall around the capital. The wealth and influence of this man so roused the emperor's suspicion that only the intercession of the empress could save his life. He was, however, sent into exile in Yünnan where he ended his days.[48] Moreover, the imperial hostility was not reserved for such great magnates: if even a simple member of a farmer's family became a merchant the whole family was deprived of the privilege of wearing silk.[49]

However, the emperor's prejudice against the merchant class did not diminish the number of traders. Commerce was on a greater scale than in previous centuries and was ever on the increase, for the growing industries naturally needed the cooperation of the merchants and the poor soil in some of the provinces, and overpopulation in others forced many to leave home and seek their fortune in trade. This was especially true of Shansi, of Anhui and Kiangsu (these two provinces were then known as Nan-chih) and of Fukien. Hsieh Chao-che 謝肇淛 (c. 1610), writing of his contemporaries, remarks that the inhabitants of Hsin-an 新安 (Anhui) and Fu-t'ang 福唐 (Fukien) had had to leave their native land because of overpopulation and to seek their livelihood elsewhere, often traveling to remote and almost uninhabited countries where the lack of arable land forced them to invent various new means of gaining a living.[50]

The *Tu p'ien hsin-shu* 杜騙新書, a book written in the Ming dynasty and dealing with the frauds of the day in the business world, gives us a good description of the activities of the merchants. According to this book it was quite common for merchants to travel from place to place: thus, merchants of Hui-chou would keep their stores in

Su-chou, and merchants in a prefecture would move to the capital city to do more trade. It seems to have been quite common for the merchants of one province to bring their goods to another province in search of better markets. Some would travel to different provinces and bring back goods to be sold in their native towns. Others would bring the products of their own province to a second province and then bring the local products of that province to sell them in a third. Thus, constantly traveling, they piled up their profits. Towards the end of the dynasty the scholar Ho Ch'iao-yüan 何喬遠 (1588–1632) confirms that throughout the empire one found traveling traders everywhere.[51]

That commerce was flourishing in the middle of the 16th century may be seen from the *I-t'ung lu-ch'eng t'u-chih* 一統路程圖志, published in 1570. The preface reveals the author's purpose in writing. In his young days, he had to leave his too densely populated native land (present Anhui) and go with his father and elder brother, trading from province to province. Later, when he had given up trade and settled in Su-chou, he remembered all the hardships he had experienced in his journeys and decided to write a guide book for the benefit of other travellers. In Su-chou he was able to meet merchants from all over the empire and to collect from them minute details of different parts of their journeys. The book was in eight chuan and had cost him twenty-seven years of patient toil. In the end he was able to claim for his book the practical virtues that it contained the distances of all places and the topography of all of the mountains and rivers and that it did not neglect the state of public peace and order in the different localities. The writing of such a book implies that the author had come into contact with traders from all over the empire and that these in turn had described their experiences. From this and from the accounts of contemporaries one can see that merchants of those days must have been very active.[52]

Commercial activity along the coast of China was of a different type. There the merchants were more interested in foreign than in domestic trade. From ancient times, the coast dwellers had had much commercial contact with neighboring countries. In the Sung period Chao Ju-kua 趙汝适 had written the Chu-fan-chih 諸蕃志, which still remains an important document for those who wish to study communications between the Chinese and overseas countries under the Sung dynasty. Commerce between China and its neighboring countries became more common after Cheng Ho's expedition. "Our government has set up the Shih-po-ssu 市舶司 to look after the tributary foreigners," said the author of the *Ch'ou-hai t'u-pien* 籌海

圖編. "The one in Kuangtung looks after Chan-ch'eng 占城, Siam and neighboring countries; for Liu-ch'iu 琉球 alone, there is the Fukien Shih-po-ssu, and for Japan alone the Chekiang Shih-po-ssu."[53] It is to be noticed that what were known as tributary envoys were often groups of merchants whose main purpose in coming to China was to obtain native products. However, they had to disguise their purpose under a pretense of coming to pay homage to the emperor, since it was forbidden in those days to come solely for trade.

The people found that dealing with foreigners was always far more profitable than dealing with their fellow countrymen. In Fukien, for instance, at a time before the second half of the 16th century, a small town called Mei-ling 梅嶺 in Chao-an 詔安 was said to have had over a thousand families, most of them with the surnames Lin 林, T'ien 田, or Fu 傅. The men of this place did not till the land, yet they always managed to feast sumptuously; the women neither cultivated silkworms nor engaged in weaving, yet the cloth they wore was always of the best quality. Their only occupations, we are told, were "supporting the foreigners and robbery."[54] The truth seems to be that they traded with foreign countries. This was the period when the Japanese pirates were raging and devastating the coast. The government had forbidden trade with any foreign country, and to defy this prohibition would have been considered rebellious and might even have been considered robbery.

Compared with the life of a farmer, that of the trader was easy. The trader did not have to till the land nor was he tied down to one place. He was free from the land tax and need not worry about drought or flood. With some experience and a little labor, traders often made fortunes within a short time. Hence it is not surprising that so many became traders. Some were even ready to risk their lives for material gain. Even some of the gentry, though their social position forbade them to engage in so abject an occupation, were ready to lend their money to adventures, on the understanding that they would share in the profits. Not infrequently they would provide their slaves or servants with capital and encourage them to trade abroad. This was true even as early as the Cheng-hua and Hung-chih reigns (1465–1505).[55] In 1547 a group of merchants from Fukien who were selling silk and other products were caught by a typhoon. Their ship drifted to Korea and under the protection of the king of Korea they eventually reached Liao-tung. When the governor was informed of what had happened, he immediately reported the whole matter to the court. The emperor, annoyed to hear that these lawbreakers had fallen so disgracefully into the hands of foreigners, ordered that the case be investigated and that severe measures be taken against the culprits.[56]

The coming of the Europeans to the Far East increased the demand for Chinese products and so gave the merchants along the coast a wide field of activity. The people of Chia-teng-li 嘉登里 in Fukien, for instance, tripled their profits by dealing with the Dutch, and we are told that the people of Kuangtung flocked to Macao to do business with the Portuguese. Chu Wan 朱紈 (1494-1549), governor of Fukien, attempted at one time to stop the foreign trade. Not only the common people but, still more, the gentry felt the blow. Their protests and their complaints to the court eventually brought about the governor's removal from office. Later he was thrown into prison and committed suicide. After that, foreign trade went on unchecked and was ever on the increase, the numbers of Chinese merchants going abroad becoming greater every day. Chang Hsieh 張燮 (c. 1600) summed up the conditions of the time briefly but clearly: "The Shih-po-ssu originated under the T'ang and Sung dynasties. As a rule, we used to find foreigners coming to China for trade and it must be admitted that there never was a time in which so many Chinese went abroad for trade as they go in our day." After the 16th century the Chinese government was more or less forced to give some recognition to the legitimacy of trading with foreigners. "In the East Ocean such countries as the Luzon and the Sulu islands, and in the West, Siam and its neighbors and Cochin-Annam, are all our subjects. They have been loyal to us and therefore their trading vessels are not forbidden to come to China."[57]

SLAVES

To complete the picture of society under the Ming dynasty something must be added on the subject of slavery. According to the Ta-Ming lü 大明律 or Code of the Great Ming (dynasty), said to have been composed by order of the Hung-wu emperor, the common people were forbidden to keep slaves that they might learn to be diligent in their daily work and not rely on slaves. The families of government officials were allowed to keep them. In the early days of the dynasty the chief source of slaves was the capture of prisoners in war. All captives were either enlisted in the army as soldiers or distributed as slaves to meritorious officials. Political prisoners and offenders against the law provided a second source. Thus, in the year 1372, an edict was issued by the Hung-wu emperor forbidding the Mongols to marry among themselves, on penalty of enslavement to the government. When the Yung-lo emperor came to the throne an edict was issued to the effect that all military officials who had followed him in battle were to return to their families all the young men they had captured. The object of this edict was to reverse the bad policy of the Hung-wu emperor, who, as the *Hsü wen-hsien t'ung-k'ao* tells us, habitually presented as slaves to his well-deserving ministers all young men captured in battle. However, the Yung-lo emperor himself did not own an unblemished record. Shortly after usurping the throne from his nephew, he enslaved the families of all the ministers who had helped his nephew in his attempt to resist the usurpation—an inhuman act which had to be reversed by the Yung-lo emperor's successor.[58]

At various times in the history of the dynasty the emperors seem to have occupied themselves with the very problems raised by the selling of innocent people as slaves. In 1372, the Hung-wu emperor ordered the general release of all innocent people who had been enslaved during the anxious days towards the end of the Mongol regime. Fourteen years later the same emperor ordered his officials to buy back children in Honan province who had been sold as slaves by their parents because of a famine in that locality. Again, in 1466, a censor reported to the throne that in Su-chou and Honan people were selling children "in great numbers and at a very low price." We are told that even foreign merchants and monks were buying them. The Cheng-hua emperor ordered one of his ministers to buy back these children at the expense of the imperial treasury. Instructions were given to the gate-keepers on the borders not to allow foreign monks to take Chinese children away with them.[59]

The Ta-Ming lü did not lay down clearly the legitimacy of the buying and selling of slaves. Sometimes it seems to have allowed it as a privilege to the gentry; at other times it seems to hint that even the common people were permitted to buy and sell slaves.[60] Whatever the law may have been, there was no doubt that in practice the people did keep slaves. The law allowed common people to employ servants only, and to get around this, in the bond they avoided the word "slave" and put instead the words "adopted son" or "adopted daughter" or simply referred to the slaves as employed servants.[61] The selling of children occurred more frequently in time of famine or war. In 1594, for instance, during a great famine in T'eng-hsien 滕縣, Shantung, some farmers were willing to give away their young daughters to be concubines or slaves of the rich for as little as one ch'ien of silver, or a hundred copper coins, or one picul of rice. Others, so starved that they could hardly walk and were barely conscious of what they were doing, gave away their wives and children in exchange for a meal.[62] Under these circumstances the local government could do nothing to relieve the distress of the people; still less could it forbid them to sell their wives and children.

As for the government officials and gentry class, since they had the privilege of buying and selling slaves, it was quite common for them to possess them in great numbers. One of the accusations made by the Hung-wu emperor against his general Lan Yü 藍玉 was that he possessed several hundred slaves. Ku Yen-wu says that as soon as anyone was appointed to a position in the government, numbers of the people, sometimes a thousand or more, offered to serve him and were willing to be regarded as slaves. Some of these slaves received important posts and gained such influence over their masters that these fell almost completely under the control of their own slaves.[63] Many of these so-called slaves were really poor farmers who, unable to satisfy the demands of the local government, surrendered their farms to the gentry class in order to win their protection. Often, relying on the influence of their masters, they went around oppressing the poor till these, taught by the example of their new oppressors, surrendered themselves in turn to the gentry. Once secure in the protection of their masters, they too would take up the oppression of the innocent. One writer tells us that in a single prefecture or village the number of slaves might amount to two to three tenths of the whole population.[64]

The work of the slaves varied according to the occupations of their masters and was not always fixed. The gentry residing in the country would often employ them on their farms. Those living in the city not infrequently employed slaves to trade for them. Mou Chang-chi 繆昌期 (1562–1626) wrote of a certain scholar in Hsiu-ling 休寧 (present Anhui) who, after years of study, gave up his profession and went to help his father in commerce. He had large numbers of slaves who went all over the empire as salesmen. They did as they were told and the scholar's capital kept on increasing.[65]

The slaves of government officials or of the gentry who had retired from public office were often a source of trouble to the people, especially if their masters were men of low character. The slaves would serve as thugs for such masters, and not even the local authority could check them. The Min-ch'ao Tung-huan shih-shih 民抄董宦事實, written by an anonymous author, relates vividly the atrocities committed by the slaves of the renowned artist Tung Ch'i-chang 董其昌 (1555–1638).[66] Hence conscientious gentry often warned their descendants to beware of keeping slaves. Fan Li-pen

范立本 said that one who wanted to keep slaves should get them through a third party who could assure the legality of the sale and that he should make sure that the slaves were men of simplicity and honesty whose place of origin could be traced. The scholar Chang Ying 張英 was of the opinion that the number of slaves in the family should be kept as small as possible. Let them be well trained, he said, and one will get better results from a few than from the indiscriminate employment of many. The greater the number of slaves, he went on, the greater confusion there will be. For, first of all, rather than assume responsibility they will try to shift it to their fellows. Then, it will not be easy to look after them all equally well, or to attend to the instruction of all with equal care. Thus, numerous slaves will be of no advantage to the family, and they may well cause it a great deal of trouble.[67]

The code of the Ming dynasty was a great improvement on that of the T'ang dynasty as regards the treatment of slaves. Under the T'ang code slaves were treated as a species of domestic animal. For instance, one of the T'ang laws stated that, as in buying beasts of burden, so in buying a slave, if after three days the new purchase was discovered to be suffering from an old disease, the contract of sale was revocable.[68] A commentator on the Ming code says that slaves of the T'ang dynasty were in the same category as the animals, for they were under the absolute jurisdiction of their masters. If they were killed by a free citizen the law imposed no definite sanction on the killer. Under the Ming dynasty, however, this was not so. The law assumed the protection of the slaves as well as of the free citizens. "That is why," this commentator says, "the keeping of slaves among the people has become rarer and rarer in our day." In fact, however, the practice seemed to have become more common, at least among the gentry to the south of the Yangtze. This tradition continued up to the first years of the Ch'ing dynasty. A modern writer has given us some interesting accounts of this subject in an article entitled "Ming-chi nu-pien k'ao" 明季奴變考.[69]

In the Ming period, as throughout Chinese history, slaves enjoyed no social standing. They were considered inferior to the free citizens and were forbidden to intermarry with them. Their descendants, even if they were men of talent and passed the official examinations, were still regarded as sons of slaves and were generally looked down upon by the society of the day. The domestic precepts of the Yüan family (袁氏家範叢書), written shortly after the Yung-lo period, threw a lurid light on the treatment that slaves could receive from their masters: "If we keep slaves in the family and expect them to render us service, let us not forget to look after their food and clothing. Of late, I have noticed that the gentry, though sparing no efforts to make their own lives comfortable, so cut down the food of their slaves that throughout the year they hardly ever have a full meal. On extremely cold days, some have not even the clothes needed to protect them from the bitter wind. If they happen to displease their masters in their work they are beaten mercilessly. Worse still, they are ordered about in the most inhuman manner. What an inconsiderate world this is!"[70]

This injustice eventually led to a revolt of the slaves against their masters. After 1644, when the whole country was in tumult, the slaves took advantage of the confusion to rise. Everywhere in the south of the Yangtze valley the gentry were killed and their property was looted. The slaves demanded above all that their masters should give them back the bonds by which they had been sold as slaves. In the days of their prosperity, the gentry had tried to enslave all who came to them for protection, not foreseeing that these same people might one day cause their ruin.

Notes

[1] Wu Han 吳晗 and Fei Hsiao-t'ung 費孝通, Huang-ch'üan yü shen-ch'üan 皇權與紳權, (Shanghai, 1946) 49–50.

[2] T'ai-tsu kao-huang-ti shih-lu 太祖高皇帝實錄, (KPL photographic reprints) 111, (ts'e 17) 7a.

[3] Ibid., 126, (ts'e 18) 2b.

[4] Ta-ming hui-tien, 78, (ts'e 17) 1817.

[5] Huang-ming t'ai-hsüeh chih 皇明太學志, 2. This is quoted from Huang-chüan yü shen-chüan, p. 64.

[6] Ku Kung-hsieh 顧公燮, Hsiao-hsia hsien-chi tse-ch'ao 消夏閑記摘鈔, (Han-fan-lou pi-chi 涵芬樓秘笈 ed. by the Commercial Press) (Shanghai 1916–1921 (ts'e 15) B. 2b.

[7] T'ai-tsu kao-huang-ti shih-lu, 12b, (ts'e 18) 2b.

[8] Hsiao-hsia hsien-chi tse-ch'ao, (ts'e 14) A. 5b, 6a.

[9] Chang Ying 張英, Heng-ch'an so-yen 恆產瑣言, (Chin-te ts'ung-shu 進德叢書) (Shanghai) 3b.

[10] Anonymous, Shen-shih nung-shu 沈氏農書, (Hsüeh-hai lei-pien 學海類編 edited by Ts'ao Jung 曹溶 1613–1680), (ts'e 104) 20a–19b, 22ab.

[11] Chang Li-hsiang 張履祥, Pu nung-shu 補農書, (T'ung-hsüeh-chai ts'ung-shu 通學齋叢書) (ts'e 40) B. 9b, 10a.

[12] Ibid., 10a.

[13] Ming shih, 148, (ts'e 19) 3b; 213, (ts'e 26) 10a.

[14] Anonymous, Min-ch'ao Tung-huan shih-shih 民抄董宦事實, (CKNLWHLSTS), (ts'e 35).

[15] Hsü Hsüeh-mu 徐學謨 (1522–1593), *Kuei-yu-yüan kao* 歸有園稿, (1612 ed.) 12, (ts'e 5) 9b, 11b–14a; cf. also Ch'en Lung-cheng 陳龍正 (1585–1645), *Chi-t'ing wai shu* 幾亭外書, (1631 ed.) 4, (ts'e 3) 86ab.

[16] *Hsiao-hsia hsien-chi tse-ch'ao*, (ts'e 15) B. 5b–6b.

[17] *Erh-shih-erh-shih cha-chi*, 33, (ts'e 3,551) 693.

[18] *Jih-chih-lu*, 10, (ts'e 4) 48; Ch'i Po-yü 祁伯裕, *Nan-ching tu-ch'a-yüan chi* 南京都察院志, (Tien-ch'i 天啓 (1621–1627) edition) 25, (ts'e 13) 45ab.

[19] *Ming shih*, (HFL) 77, (ts'e 27) 1a; 78; 78, 3ab.

[20] *Ming hui-tien*, B. 53, 982.

[21] *Ming-shih chi-shih pen-mo*, 14 A. 65.

[22] Ibid., 14 A. 86.

[23] Wei Chieh 衞杰, *Nung-sang ts'ui-pien* 農桑萃編, (Shanghai, 1956), I, 20.

[24] *Wu-kiang hsien-chih* 吳江縣志, 38. This passage is quoted from: Fu Yi-ling 傅衣凌, *Ming Ch'ing shih-tai shang-jen chi shang-yeh tzu-pen* 明清時代商人及商業資本, (Peking, 1956) 16.

[25] Hsü Hsien-chung 徐獻忠, *Wu-hsing chang-ku* 吳興掌故, mentioned in the *Hu-chou-fu chih* 湖州府志, 29. This passage is quoted in *Ming Ch'ing shih-tai shang-jen chi shang-yeh tzu-pen*, 7.

[26] T'ang Shun-chih 唐順之 (1507–1560), *Ching-ch'uan hsien-sheng wen-chi* 荆川先生文集, (*Szu-pu ts'ung-k'an* 四部叢刊 edition reprinted in a reduced scale) (ts'e 2) 301.

[27] *Su-chou-fu chih* 蘇州府志, 3. The passage is quoted in *Ming Ch'ing shih-tai shang-jen chi shang-yeh tzu-pen*, 94.

[28] *Ming shih*, 82, (ts'e 29) 9a–10b.

[29] *Ming hui-tien*, 189, (ts'e 34) 3836; *T'ien-kung k'ai-wu*, A. 38.

[30] Chao I 趙翼, *Kai yü-ts'ung kao* 陔餘叢考, 30, (Shanghai, 1957) 640–643; cf. also: *Kuang ch'ün-fang-p'u* 廣羣芳譜, 12, (*Wan-yu-wen-k'u* 2nd series) (ts'e 3) 284–293.

[31] *Ming Ch'ing shih-tai shang-jen chi shang-yeh tzu-pen*, 7, 8, 10, where the author quotes from different sources.

[32] Ibid., 29. Here the author quotes from the *Sung-ch'uang meng-yü* 松窗夢語, by Chang Han 張瀚, 6.

[33] *Tso-lin tsa-tsu*, A. 30–31.

[34] Ku Ying-t'ai 谷應泰, *Po-wu yao lan* 博物要覽, 12, (Shanghai, 1941) 104–106.

[35] P'eng Ta-ya 彭大雅 and Hsü T'ing 徐霆, *Hei-t'a shih lüeh* 黑韃事略, (TSCCCP), (ts'e 3177) 13; d'Hosson, *Histoire des Mongols*, translated by Feng Ch'eng-chün 馮承鈞, (Shanghai, 1936) I, 122; cf. idem I, 102, 130.

[36] *Ming hui-tien*, 189, (ts'e 34) 3795 ff.; *Ming shih*, 78, (ts'e 27) 15ab.

[37] *Ming Ch'ing shih-tai shang-jen chi shang-yeh tzu-pen*; Chang Hsieh 張燮, *Tung-hsi-yang k'ao* 東西洋考.

[38] *China in the 16th Century: The Journals of Matthew Ricci, 1583–1610*, (translated by Louis J. Gallagher, S.J.) (New York 1953) 19.

[39] Ch'en Yi 陳沂, *Chin-ling shih-chi* 金陵世紀, 2, (Lung-ch'ing edition, 1569) (ts'e 2) 13a–16b. Of the streets and lanes mentioned in the book, eight were named after edibles: Yu-fang hsiang 油房巷 or lane of oil factories; Kan-yü hsiang 乾魚巷 or lane of dry-fish dealers; No-mi hsiang 糯米巷 or lane of glutinous-rice dealers; Hsien-yü hsiang 鮮魚巷 or lane of fresh-fish dealers; Ts'ai-hang 菜行 or vegetable market: Kuo-tzu hang 果子行 or fruit market; Ch'uan Kuang tsa-huo mi tou chu hang 川廣雜貨米豆諸行 or markets for rice, beans and products from Szechuan and Kuangtung; Sheng-yao p'u hang 生藥舖行 or lane of herb stores; Nineteen were named after common utensils: Chien-tzu hsiang 剪子巷 or lane of scissor dealers; Hu-tou hsiang 斛斗巷 or lane of bushels and peck dealers; Pan-hsiang 板巷 or lane of plank dealers; Wa-tzu hsiang 瓦子巷 or lane of tile

dealers; An-pe'i fang 鞍轡坊 or street of saddle and bridle dealers; Yin-tso fang 銀作坊 or street of silver-smiths; T'ung-tso fang 銅作坊 or street of copper smiths; T'ieh-tso fang 鐵作坊 or street of blacksmiths; Yen-liao fang 顏料坊 or street of paints; Hua-p'u lang 花舖廊 or lane of flower dealers; Ku-p'u lang 鼓舖廊 or lane of drum dealers; An-tzu p'u-lang 鞍子舖廊 or lane of saddle dealers; Chih p'u-lang 紙舖廊 or lane of paper dealers; Hsi p'u-lang 錫舖廊 or lane of lead dealers; Hsian-ya p'u-lang 象牙舖廊 or lane of ivory dealers; Hiang-la p'u-lang 香蠟舖廊 or lane of incense and candle dealers; Chu mu p'u-lang 竹木舖廊 or lane of bamboo and timber dealers; Piao pei p'u-lang 表背舖廊 or lane of shops for mounting scrolls and pictures. Twelve were connected with clothes; Shou-p'a hsiang 手帕巷 or lane of handkerchief dealers; San hsiang 繖巷 or lane of umbrella dealers; Yang-p'i hsiang 羊皮巷 or lane of sheep skin dealers; Chih-chin yi fang 織錦一坊 or first lane of silk factories; Chih-chin erh fang 織錦二坊 or second street of silk factories; Chih-chin san fang 織錦三坊 or third lane of silk factories; Chan-chiang fang 氈匠坊 or lane of blanket makers; P'i-tso fang 皮作坊 or street of leather dealers; Mao-erh hang 帽兒行 or hat factories; Pao-t'ou p'u-lang 包頭舖廊 or lane of head-dress dealers; Ma p'u-lang 麻舖廊 or lane of hemp dealers; Ts'ao-mao p'u lang 草帽舖廊 or lane of straw hat dealers. Finally, three of the lanes were named after weapons: T'ou-k'uei hsiang 頭盔巷 or lane of helmet dealers; Kung-chiang fang 弓匠坊 or lane of bow making dealers; and Ch'ien-chiang fang 箭匠坊 or lane of arrow making dealers.

40 *Chin-ling shih-chi*, 2, (ts e 2) 13a–16b.

41 Chou Hui 周暉, *Chin-ling so-shih* 金陵瑣事, 1, (Wan-li edition) (ts'e 1) 16b–17a

42 *Ming Ch'ing shih-tai shang-jen chi shang-yeh tzu-pen*, 13, where the *Yao-chou-fu chih* is quoted. Cf. also Lan P'u 藍浦, *Ching-te-chen t'ao lu* 景德鎮陶錄 8, (*Mei-shu ts'ung-shu* 美術叢書, Shanghai, 1947) (ts'e 9) 162, 176. Shen Huai-ch'ing 沈懷清 who lived in the beginning of the Ch'ing dynasty said that Ching-te-chen produced good porcelain but not good craftsmen. The good craftsmen came from other places.

43 *Ching-te-chen t'ao lu*, 8, (ts'e 9) 162–176; Wang Shih-mou 王世懋 (1536–1588), *Erh yu wei t'an chai-lu* 二酉委譚摘錄, (TSCCCP), (ts'e 2923) 14–15.

44 *Chung-kuo t'ung-shih chien-pien* 中國通史簡編, edited by Fan Wen-lan 范文瀾, (Shanghai, 1947) 547.

45 Inaba Iwakichi 稻葉岩吉, *Ch'ing-ch'ao ch'üan-shih* 清朝全史 tr. by Tan Tao 但燾, (Shanghai, 1924) I, 94–95; Chu Yen 朱琰, *T'ao-shuo* 陶說, 1, (*Kuo-hsüeh chi-pen ts'ung-shu* 國學基本叢書) (Shanghai, 1935) 13–14; *Ching-te-chen t'ao lu*, 8, (ts'e 9) 161; *Ming shih*, 82, (ts'e 29) 11ab.

46 *Ming Ch'ing shih-tai shang-jen chi shang-yeh tzu-pen*, 12, where the author quotes from *Yun-chien chü mu ch'ao* 雲間據目抄, by Fan Lien 范濂.

47 *T'ao-an meng-yi*, 5, 53; Hsü Ch'ung-hsi 許重熙, *Chia-cheng i-lai chu-lüeh* 嘉靖以來注略, (late Ming edition) 5, (ts'e 3) 13b; cf. also *Erh-shih-erh-shih cha-chi*, 34, (ts'e 6) 25ab.

48 Mao Ch'i-ling 毛奇齡 (1623–1716), *Sheng-chao t'ung-shih shih-i chi* 勝朝彤史拾遺記, in the *Hsi-ho wen-chi* 西河文集, (Wan-yu wen-k'u edition, second series), 1, (ts'e 7) 1603.

49 Ling Yang-tsao 凌揚藻, *Li-shuo pien* 蠡勺編, (TSCCCP), 16, (ts'e 0227) 264.

50 Hsieh Chao-che 謝肇淛, *Wu tsa-tsu* 五雜組, (Japanese edition, 1795) 4, (ts'e 2) 35ab.

51 *Tu p'ien hsin-shu* 杜騙新書 (Ming edition) 1, (ts'e 1) 9a, 13ab, 16b; 2, (ts'e 1) 9a, 13ab, 14a; Ho Ch'iao-yüan 何喬遠, *Ching-shan ch'üan-chi* 鏡山全集, (Shen-liu tu-shu-t'ang edition 深柳讀書堂 printed in the late Ming dynasty) 24, (ts'e 12) 17a.

52 Huang Pien 黃汴, *I-t'ung lu-ch'eng t'u-chih* 一統路程圖志, (1570 edition) 1, (ts'e 1) 1.

53 Cheng Jo-tseng 鄭若曾, *Ch'ou-hai t'u-p'ien* 籌海圖編, chuan 25 quoted by the *Ming Ch'ing shih-tai shang-jen chi shang-yeh tzu-pen*, 133.

54 Cheng Chieh 鄭杰, *Ch'ien-t'ai wo tsuan* 虔臺倭纂 B., quoted by the *Ming Ch'ing shih-tai shang-jen chi shang-yeh tzu-pen*, 111.

55 *Ming Ch'ing shih-tai shang-jen chi shang-yeh tzu-pen*, 108–109 where the *Ming Shih-tsung chia-cheng shih-lu* was quoted, chuan 38, 54, 154, 166, 189; *Tung-hsi-yang k'ao*, 7, 89;

Ch'en Jen-hsi 陳仁錫 (c. 1625) in his *Huang-Ming shih-fa-lu* 皇明世法錄, (Late Ming edition) 75, (ts'e 48) 43a quoted the following law: "Influential families, whosoever they may be, if they dare to supply undesirable persons with capital so that these may prepare goods for trade abroad although they themselves take no part in these trades, and if they try to share their profit, let them be sent to exile and incorporated into the Wei-so army as soldiers, and let all their goods be confiscated."

⁵⁶ Pu Shih-ch'ang 卜世昌, *Huang-Ming t'ung-chi shu i* 皇明通紀述遺, (Wan-li edition 10, (ts'e 5) 17ab.

⁵⁷ *Ming Ch'ing shih-tai shang-jen chi shang-yeh tzu-pen*, 109–114, where different sources are quoted. Cf. also *Ming shih*, 205, (ts'e 68) 1a–3b the biography of Chu Wan 朱紈.

⁵⁸ Hsüeh Yün-sheng 薛允升, *T'ang Ming lü ho-pien* 唐明律合編, (WYWK 2nd series), 12, (ts'e 2) 240; *Hsü wen-hsien t'ung-k'ao*, 14, (ts'e 2) 2899–2900.

⁵⁹ *Hsü wen-hsien t'ung-k'ao*, 14, (ts'e 2) 2899, 2900.

⁶⁰ *T'ang-Ming lü ho p'ien*, 12, (ts'e 2) 204.

⁶¹ Ibid., 22, (ts'e 4) 508; *Hsü wen-hsien t'ung-k'ao*, 14 (ts'e 2) 2900b.

⁶² Fung Ying-ching 馮應京, *Ching-shih shih-yung pien hsü-chi* 經世實用編續集, (Ming edition) 17, (*Li* section 3 利集三) 23ab.

⁶³ *Jih-chih-lu chi-shih* 日知錄集釋, 13, (ts'e 5) 67–68.

⁶⁴ *Hsiao-hsia hsien-chi tse-ch'ao*, A (ts'e 1) 6ab.

⁶⁵ *Ming Ch'ing shih-tai shang-jen chi shang-yeh tzu pen*, 81, where the passage was taken from the *Ch'ien-k'un cheng-ch'i chi* 乾坤正氣集, an anthology compiled by P'an Kuang-en 潘光恩, *chüan* 316.

⁶⁶ Anonymous, *Min-ch'ao Tung-huan shih-shih* 民抄董宦事實, (CKNLW-LSTS), (ts'e 35).

⁶⁷ Fan Li-pen 范立本, *Chih-chia chieh-yao* 治家節要. Manuscript copied in the Edo period now in possession of the Naikaku bunko, Tokyo, Japan, no number of pages; *Ts'ung-hsün-chai yü*, A. 3b.

⁶⁸ *T'ang Ming lü ho-pien*, 26, (ts'e 5) 589.

⁶⁹ Hsieh Kuo-chen 謝國楨, *Ming-ch'ing chih chi tang-she yün-tung k'ao* 明清之際黨社運動考, (Shanghai, 1934) Appendix I, 257–289.

⁷⁰ Anonymous, *Yen-t'ang chien-wen tsa-chi* 研堂見聞雜記, (*T'ung-shih* 痛史 edition) 20b; *Ming-Ch'ing chih chi tang-she yün-tung k'ao*, 274; Yüan Hao 袁顥, *Yüan-shih chia-fan ts'ung-shu* 袁氏家範叢書, (Ming Edition) 2, (ts'e 2) 25ab.

CHAPTER FIVE

Culture and Religion

SCHOLARSHIP, LITERATURE AND THE "EIGHT-LEGGED ESSAYS"

Even before he had overthrown the Mongol empire, the founder of the Ming dynasty realized that he could not entrust the government of the country to the generals who were then fighting so loyally and bravely for him, and that he would need the help of the scholars, the literati. It had long been a tradition of the country to employ scholars, usually Confucians, to govern the people. These scholars, though often poor in temporal possessions, were rich in learning and wisdom. The dictum of the founder of the Sung dynasty that the prime minister should be chosen from among the scholars had become a Chinese proverb. A scholar had to possess encyclopedic knowledge and was expected to know how to apply that knowledge to diverse problems as they arose. Above all, he was expected to excel in knowing how to govern the people according to the Confucian principles which had dominated Chinese society for so many centuries, so that at a moment's notice he might render great service to the emperor and to his fellow men.

From the beginning of his military career the founder of the Ming dynasty tried to gather around him eminent scholars and he had the good fortune to discover men of high character and of great talent such as Liu Chi 劉基 (1311–1375) and Sung Lien 宋濂 (1310–1381), both of whom were men of great learning. Liu Chi in particular was a gifted organizer.

The employment of literati had, however, its awkward side. Chinese scholars were often artists of some sort—poets or calligraphers or painters—and possessed the artistic temperament, and often the sharp tongue, proper to artists. They could be ironical if they wished, and frequently said bitter things under the cloak of a double meaning. The story about Chang Shih-ch'eng mentioned above is said to have been told to the Hung-wu emperor and to have aroused his suspicion of scholars. During his reign he started a number of literary inquisitions and not a few of his ministers perished in them.[1]

The emperor's unfriendly attitude naturally filled the scholars with terror and made them seek to keep away from the court. We are told, for example, that the great poet Yang Wei-chen 楊維楨 (1296–1370) was invited to the capital to compile several books on ritual and on music but resigned after he had made a stay of scarcely three months. Chao I says that the scholars' reluctance to take up posts in the government was due to the severe policy adopted by the Hung-wu emperor toward his ministers in his effort to correct the laissez-faire attitude of the Yüan government.[2] One result of this policy was that many eminent scholars tried to hide themselves or to find pretexts for being left alone. The situation became embarrassing, for the emperor needed thousands of scholars for the government of the empire. At one time he had to use threats to persuade some of the scholars to submit to the government and offer their services. He also tried to solve his problem by choosing non-scholars—members of the gentry class, village elders, and plebeians of talent—for various government posts. The number of such non-scholar officeholders amounted at one time to as many as three thousand seven hundred.[3] Ultimately a more fundamental solution had to be adopted. The dynasty was a new one, and naturally had a new spirit quite different from anything that had been known before. Old traditions would not always serve its purposes. The Hung-wu emperor therefore decided to train men after his own ideal.

Three years before the Hung-wu emperor ascended the throne (1365) he had already conceived the idea of founding an educational institute for the training of new officials. In the very year of his accession he founded an academy, the Kuo-tzu hsüeh 國子學, which later became the Kuo-tzu chien 國子監, or Imperial Academy. Promising young men were chosen from all over the country to study there, and enjoyed full support from the government and the personal interest of the emperor himself. The Nan-yung chih 南雝志 records a conversation between the emperor and his ministers which shows that the emperor was preoccupied with the care of his students. "I am too ready to do honor to the students, but I do not know if they realize this," the emperor said. "However, they have long been in the Academy. Send them home to visit their parents and let each of them bring with him four bolts of cloth to them as a gift from us. If they are married men let them bring their wives to the capital upon their return and we will supply them with money and grain for a month. We wish to try to make them happy. Let the ministers be generous with them." The empress assumed the obligation of supporting the wives of the students, thus relieving the latter from domestic cares so that they might devote their time to study. For this purpose she established in the Academy more than twenty storehouses filled with grain.[4]

The men who came to study in the Imperial Academy could be divided into two groups: students sent by the government, and students coming from among the common people. The former group were chiefly the sons and relatives of central government officials and of the headmen of the aborigines or students from abroad. This group was small compared to the second group, for the nobles did not always depend on the school in order to obtain governmental positions. Their number decreased towards the end of the Hung-wu reign, owing probably to the killing off of the more powerful families. Until 1371 the students for the Kuo-tzu hsüeh were chosen directly from among the people. Later they were supplied by local schools throughout the empire, an indication that educational institutions were gradually spreading.

In the Kuo-tzu chien the students were taught by eminent scholars appointed by the government. Great stress was laid on moral as well as on intellectual training. Monthly and annual examinations were held and those who passed the annual examinations were appointed to offices in the government. Those who failed were kept in the Academy for further studies. The students in general had a broad program. Besides the classics they had also to study history and political science. As early as 1372, we are told, the Hung-wu emperor used to send the students to different government offices to learn government administration. Later on they were frequently sent to survey the farming districts of the country, and to inspect the land-tax reports of different provinces. At times they were empowered to direct river conservation works, or to inspect government records. Hence, when they were appointed to a government office they generally were men of learning and experience.

In all the other schools, however, the program of study was quite different and a new institution was perhaps responsible for it. In the first year of Hung-wu (1368), the emperor, upon the advice of his learned minister Liu Chi, instituted a new system of examinations, known later as the "eight-legged essays" 八股文, for entry into government service and made it compulsory in all the schools. This system, which consisted in the exclusive and mechanical study of the Four Books and the Five Classics, survived, with one early and brief interruption, for over five hundred years, not being abolished till 1902.

On passing the examinations in the "eight-legged essays," the students received government posts, however little they might know about public administration—and they usually knew very little indeed. Recognizing this anomaly, the emperor suspended the examinations in 1373. In that year an edict was issued to the prime minister stating that the monarch had expected to obtain through the examination system men of learning thoroughly acquainted with the classics and of the highest integrity. "But," the edict continued, "most of the students passed by our ministers in recent days were young scholars. In their writings they appear as men of talent. Nevertheless, if one tries to employ them they are found unfit for the offices assigned to them." For nearly nine years after this, candidates for government posts were recommended by local officials who were told to base their choice of men primarily on integrity and only secondarily on literary knowledge.

In 1382, however, the examination system was revived. Apparently the recommendation system did not produce good results; it did not prove easy either to eliminate corruption among the local officials or to obtain sufficiently large numbers of candidates for the different government positions. The examination system therefore was restored. Yet the candidates recruited on the restored system did not gain the full confidence of the emperor. He praised them, indeed, but he still regarded them as men of no experience and ordered that they should undergo further training in political affairs.[5]

Throughout the time of these changes, the Hung-wu emperor was forming the pattern according to which his scholars were to be trained. Being an absolute monarch, he demanded complete obedience from his subjects and sought, by a skillful combination of favors and threats, to prevent them from interfering with government policy. The imperial precepts, the ta-kao 大誥, which he himself had composed, were taught in the schools and even made the subject of public examinations, thus ensuring that in the end the imperial will should dominate everything.

Not unnaturally the emperor felt a certain paternal affection for those engaged in the study of precepts which he personally had drawn up. We are told that in 1370, over 193,400 instructors in and students of the ta-kao came from all over the empire to visit His Majesty. This pleased the emperor immensely. He spoke to his visitors, gave them a gift of money, and sent them home.

Knowing that if he was to command the obedience of these student-candidates he must first make them submissive to their immediate superiors, the emperor was stern in dealing with insubordination. In 1394, a certain student was beheaded for having criticized his teacher, and the emperor ordered that his head be hung up on a long pole in front of the Academy to serve as a warning to others. The students learned the lesson and no longer dared speak their minds in public. However, there was no way of putting a stop to underground activities. Anonymous writings criticizing the teachers kept on circulating to the last year of the Hung-wu emperor. In 1398, a severe warning was issued to the effect that all who dared to continue publishing anonymous letters criticizing the teachers would incur capital punishment and that their families would be banished to a malarial district. Scholars who had failed in their public examinations were similarly forbidden to criticize their examiners. They were ordered to resign themselves to their fate instead of making violent speeches against the examiners or demanding justice by beating the drum set in front of the government office for this purpose.[6]

Scholarship in the Ming period seems to have made greater progress in the South than in the North. The most important reason for this was the development of the Yangtze valley and the southern provinces. Moreover, the unsettled political situation in the latter part of the T'ang period and foreign invasions under the Sung dynasty had disrupted society in the North. A great number of the northern gentry and well-to-do people had migrated to the South where life was more stable, and the development of farming and industry had raised the standard of living and given the inhabitants greater leisure to cultivate intellectual needs and enjoyments. Most of the prime ministers under the T'ang dynasty had come from northern families; but after the first half of the Sung dynasty most of them seem to have come from the South. Under the Ming dynasty more than two thirds of the prime ministers were from the South.[7] In 1425, the Hung-hsi 洪熙 emperor noticed that the scholars of northern China were greatly inferior to those of the South. On the advice of his minister it was then decided that in the public examination forty per cent of the candidates should be chosen from scholars of the North and the remaining sixty per cent from those of the South.[8]

As we mentioned above, the "eight-legged essays" were a compulsory subject in the schools. Since they were also covered in the public examinations, nearly all scholars spent a great deal of time studying them. The scholar Huang Tsung-hsi says that if prose did not particularly flourish in the Ming period, this was because of the proccupation of the scholars with study of the "eight-legged essays."[9] There is much truth in Huang's remark. The history of literature under the Ming dynasty records many great writers in both prose and poetry at the beginning of the period. Their success was due to a genuine delight in study, unmixed with thoughts of obtaining government posts. Their work was creative and they were not tied to any particular form. Then came a long period of peace, which seems to have provided little stimulus to the imagination of the scholars; the literature of the time remained stagnant. When at last some scholars saw the need for a renaissance, they advocated a revival of literature after the pattern of the Ch'in, Han, and T'ang periods. Later still it became the fashion to follow the Sung pattern. Thus, all writers were confined to imitating models; none of them showed ability to create anything that could be called their own. Even one of the best prose writers of the dynasty, Kuei Yu-kuang 歸有光 (1506–1571), was criticized for having intermixed the style of the "eight-legged essays" with his own style.[10]

While the orthodox classical style remained thus sterile, drama and the novel had their golden age in the Ming period. Drama had long been developing and had reached its zenith under the Yüan dynasty. It continued to flourish in the Ming period and the Hung-wu emperor himself is said to have had a high regard for the *P'i-p'a chi* 琵琶記 written by Kao Ming 高明 (1310–1380). Several of his sons and grandsons were themselves playwrights and musicians. We are told that when princes were sent to live in the provinces early in the Hung-wu reign they were often given books of dramas and poetry—up to as many as one thousand seven hundred volumes.[11] The fact that ten thousand natives of Ch'ing-yang 青陽 alone took up the profession of acting shows clearly in what a flourishing state the drama was.[12] The *T'ao-an meng-i* 陶菴夢憶, written in the late Ming period, gives us delightful reminiscences of its author's experience of drama and the stage. All this indicates that the stage was popular among the people.

Drama under the Yüan dynasty was distinguished for its simplicity and naturalness. The Ming drama, however, became elaborate and elegant, especially in the later half of the period when, having become chiefly an enjoyment of the literary class, it threw off the rigid rules of the Yüan dramas and became more flexible. The Ming drama reached its zenith in the Wan-li period. The K'un-ch'ü 崑曲 had by that time spread from its birthplace near Su-chou throughout the whole empire and it retained its influence till the middle of the Ch'ing period.[13]

Mention must be made of the Shih-ch'ü 時曲 songs composed by the common people, which the literary class despised as vulgar. A scholar of the Wan-li period says that these popular songs flourished along the Huai River and Kiang-nan. They were not what the learned class knew as poems or dramatic songs, but rather "indecent narrations composed more or less in rhyme." They eventually became so popular that throughout both the South and the North all learned to sing them and took pleasure in listening to them. They were later compiled and published in book form and circulated among the common people.[14]

The development of popular literature in the Ming period, especially in the second half, can be attributed to several causes. First, economically the country was prosperous. Both industry and commerce were making great progress. The popular standard of living had risen notably, especially in the South, and in consequence the people now had more leisure for artistic enjoyment. Too, the printing of books was becoming common in the Ming period. Publishers were established by the government, or by the princes in various provinces. Scholars sometimes published their own books. But most books were published by the bookdealers, whose lists included the classics as well as popular literature in the vulgar tongue. Of the many provinces and localities in which books were published, the most highly praised were Su-chou, Chekiang and Fukien. Su-chou was known for the high quality of its publications and Fukien for the large quantity, while Chekiang combined quality and quantity. The Chia-ching and Wan-li periods were the greatest age for publication in the whole Ming period.

But the most important cause of the development of dramas and novels in the vernacular was the opposition to the revival of old literary styles offered by some scholars. Among these Li Chih 李贄 (1527-1602) was perhaps the most daring. He strongly opposed the views of those who advocated the imitation of old masters. "Every generation produces its own literature. Why should stress be laid on the old classics?" he argued. "After all, are not the *Hsi-hsiang chi* 西廂記 and *Shui-hu chuan* 水滸傳 as good literature as the old classics?" The three Yüan brothers (Tsung-tao 宗道, Hung-tao 宏道 and Chung-tao 中道), who came immediately after Li, took the same line. Yüan Hung-tao (1568–1610) contended that in the classics what then appeared archaic was originally written in the language of the people. Those who lived in a later period had no reason to follow the dead dialects of the past. Rather, they should make use of modern language to develop their own literature.[15]

Two admirers of the Yüan brothers who tried to imitate their intellectual independence were Chung Hsing 鍾惺 (1574–1625) and T'an Yüan-ch'un 譚元春 (1586–1631). Both succeeded in achieving fame, especially for their anthologies, complete with critical annotations, of ancient and T'ang poems. These anthologies, known as Shih-kuei 詩歸, were so popular among the scholars that "nearly everyone tried to have a copy in his home and treasured them as if they were revised by Confucius himself." Orthodox scholars, however, regarded their writings as bad omens foreshadowing the fall of the Ming empire.[16] Later ages have described these two as belonging to the school of Ching-ling 竟陵派, the present Hupei, birthplace of both Chung and T'an, and the three Yüan brothers as belonging to the school of Kung-an 公安派, their birthplace, also in modern Hupei province.

Novels in the vernacular had their origin in the preaching of the Buddhist priests and in storytelling, two activities which flourished in the period of the southern Sung dynasty—the former may even date back to the T'ang dynasty. At first, the so-called novels existed in a crude form as manuscript stories prepared by storytellers for their own use. Eventually some of these stories were collected and, after rearrangement and refinement by literary men, became famous long novels or short stories. Many of the novels and short stories of the Ming period can be traced back to Sung dynasty origins. Recent discoveries and studies have provided abundant material and the systematic study of the genesis of such fictional works has become a science.[17]

Among the long novels, three were regarded as masterpieces: Shui-hu chuan 水滸傳, Hsi-yu chi 西遊記 and Chin-p'ing mei 金瓶梅. All three were written between the Chia-ching and Wan-li reigns. The Shui-hu chuan narrates a cycle of brigand stories based very lightly on the history of the Sung dynasty. Though vigorous efforts have been made to discover the author of this great book, no definite conclusion has been arrived at. There can be no doubt, however, that the final form, published in the 16th century, was the result of prolonged re-shaping by scholars. This novel exerted great influence on society in the late Ming period. Renowned scholars—Wen Cheng-ming 文徵明 (1470–1559) for instance—took pleasure in listening to it;

contemporary writers frequently mentioned it; and the *T'ao-an meng-i* gives us some idea of how great an influence it had on the life of the common people. The circumstances in which these bandit heroes of the book lived were remarkably like those of the late Ming period, when the government was riddled with corruption and selfishness. If these heroes had succeeded in obtaining a better life by revolt against the authorities, could not their Ming-period successors imitate their example?[18]

The *Hsi-yu chi*, by Wu Ch'eng-en 吳承恩 (c. 1500–1580) was based on the account given by the famous Buddhist monk Hsüan Tsang 玄奘 of his pilgrimage to India in the earlier part of the T'ang period. However, it is in no way historical, being an imaginative creation from beginning to end. A contemporary of Wu's remarked that though the *Hsi-yu chi* seems to contain many nonsensical flights of the imagination, these are in reality allegories of the human soul and its faculties.[19] Some critics, developing this remark, like to compare this book to the *Pilgrim's Progress* of John Bunyan. The author certainly tried to reconcile Confucianism, Buddhism, and Taoism, though without trying to expound his synthesis.

The *Chin p'ing mei* has nothing in common with the *Shui-hu chuan* or the *Hsi-yu chi*. Though the story is ostensibly laid in the Sung period, it is in fact a realistic novel describing the society of the Wan-li period, and satirizing the gentry and the corruption of government officials. Like the authors of many other well-known books, the author of the *Chin-p'ing mei* is unknown to us. Whoever he may have been, he certainly had a deep knowledge of human nature and was well able to express himself and to give us a clear idea of how the people lived in his day. The book's indulgence in sensuality has led many to describe it as a pornographic novel. Moreover, the author neglected to give his readers any ideal. He stripped bare the cruelties and darkness of his time, seemed to despair of a better future and ended in full Buddhistic pessimism.[20]

The flowering of the long novel in the Chia-ching and Wan-li period helped greatly towards the development of the short story. Many short stories, dating in their original more or less crude form from the Sung and Yüan dynasties, were polished in this period and transmuted into readable form. By the time of the T'ien-ch'i and Ch'ung-chen reigns (i.e. the last Ming reigns), short stories had become still more popular and were being published in ever greater abundance. Among the best known collections were the *San-yen* 三言 and *Erh-p'ai* 二拍. Feng Meng-lung 馮夢龍 (1574–1645), the author of the *San-yen*, was a talented and prolific writer and an earnest advocate of literature in the vernacular. The *San-yen* consists of three sets of short stories, *Yü-shih ming-yen* 喻世明言, *Ching-shih t'ung-yen* 警世通言 and *Hsing-shih heng-yen* 醒世恆言, each in forty chuan. Many of the stories were refashioned by the author from the Sung or Yüan originals, but some were his own creations. In the preface of one of his books he reveals clearly the importance of literature in the vernacular. The majority of the people, he argues, are not learned, hence books observing the classical norms are of no use to them, whereas a storyteller will capture the mind of his audience with his stories. He can make them laugh or cry, love or hate. He can make the coward brave and the sensual chaste. Thus, according to Feng Meng-lung, vernacular literature can exert great influence over the people and therefore should not be neglected.[21]

The *Erh-p'ai*, i.e. *P'ai-an ching-ch'i* 拍案驚奇 by Ling Meng-ch'u 凌濛初 (1580–1644) consists of a first and a second series, each series containing forty short stories divided into forty chuan. Although Feng Meng-lung was a great advocate of vernacular literature, the *Erh-p'ai* unlike the *San-yen*, is not a re-writing of old stories, but an original work, even though some of the stories may have been based on old legends. In his preface Ling states that it was his friend Feng Meng-lung's books that had induced him to write and he claims for his stories a certain pedagogic purpose as against those by some writers of his day which were "either absurd and therefore incredible, or so obscene as to offend the listeners." However, Ling's own stories are at times open to similar censure. Modern critics who have tried to explain this laxity can only say that moral standards had fallen since the Chia-ching and Wan-li periods. The laissez-faire spirit of the government and the liberty enjoyed by the people only helped to foster irresponsibility in the writings of the day.[22]

In dealing with books we must not omit mention of one of the greatest achievements of the Ming period, the production of the *Yung-lo ta-tien* 永樂大典, which ranks among the largest encyclopedias ever produced in any part of the world. This enormous work was compiled between the years 1403 and 1407 by order of the Yung-lo emperor. Five general directors and twenty sub-directors worked on it with the help of a huge staff of over two thousand scholars. The whole vast work consisted of 22,900 chuan in 11,100 volumes. The table of contents alone filled sixty chuan. It was the ambition of the emperor to include in this collection writings on all branches of study from the earliest possible date in Chinese history. The arrangement followed the Hung-wu Syllabary of Rhymes, *Hung-wu cheng yün* 洪武正韻, rather than any scientific order. Under each rhyme at least a few passages from ancient writings were given; sometimes a whole book was transcribed. In this way a large number of rare books which were no longer to be found after the time of the Ming dynasty were preserved. Unhappily, because of the cost of the block cutting, the encyclopedia was never printed.[23]

ARTS

Art too flourished in the Ming period. "If we should venture to characterize in a few words the art of the Ming period," writes a modern critic, "we should designate it as an art with growing Baroque tendencies, tendencies which had made themselves felt already in the days of Mongol rule. Classicist counter-currents were not missing, yet they do not seem to have been decisive. The Baroque spirit is to be found most distinctly in the applied arts. From now on and in increasing measure, they changed into a display of color and ornamentation."[24]

As in the previous centuries, the schools of painting were divided into the Northern and Southern, the Wen-jen hua 文人畫 (Painting of the Literati) being almost identical with the Southern School. The difference, however, was founded on a social rather than on a geographical cleavage and was almost wholly confined to landscape painting. Among the masters two in particular exerted great influence in the Ming period and even in the Ch'ing period: Tai Chin 戴進 (c. 1446) and Shen Chou 沈周 (1427-1509). Tai Chin, a native of Ch'ien-t'ang 錢塘, was considered the leader of the Che School, named after the province of Chekiang. Shen Chou, a native of Ch'ang-chou 長洲, was ultimately recognized as the greatest master of the Wu School, Wu being an alternative name for the modern Kiangsu province. The literati tended to produce paintings of an intellectual type, but the worldly court demanded purely decorative paintings. Minute details were stressed in this court style and the coloring was bright, but the artists, striving to flatter the senses, neglected the spiritual side of their art. The intellectual painters, though avoiding the weaknesses of the court painters, were justly accused of being too slavish in their imitation of the old masters, especially towards the end of the dynasty. Such artists as Tung Ch'i-ch'ang 董其昌 (1554-1636) and his followers were clearly open to this objection. Nevertheless it should not be forgotten that the Ming period produced many good and some great painters.

Ceramics ranked high among the arts of the Ming period. Porcelain was widely used among the people rather than stoneware or pottery, and instead of monochrome glazes the porcelain articles frequently bore painted or enameled decoration, particularly in the 16th century when the decoration became ever more elaborate and detailed. Ware of imperial quality was highly refined and the decorations were treated pictorially. Both the quality of the ware and the craftsmanship became more highly developed as the dynasty went on and for centuries such porcelain was regarded in the West as the typical form of Chinese art. From the hand of one of the first missionaries we have the following passage: " . . . The finest specimens of porcelain are made from clay found in the province of Kiam [Kiangsi] and these are shipped not only to every part of China but even to the remotest corners of Europe, where they are highly prized by those who appreciate elegance at their banquets rather than pompous display."[25] Towards the middle of the seventeenth century numerous curio shops in Europe sold a large variety of articles from the Far East. There was one wellknown shop of this kind in Lisbon and another in Amsterdam. In France, Portuguese used to be found in the market place of Saint-Germain, dealing in objects of all kinds brought from the Far East. The poet Paul Scarron (1610–1660), in describing a visit to Saint-Germain, mentions, among other things, Chinese porcelain, and has left us the following account in verse:

"Bring me to the Portuguese,
There we shall see something new,
The merchandise from China.
There we shall see gray amber,
Beautiful works of varnish
And of fine porcelain
From this magestic country
Or, rather, from this paradise."[26]

Work in bronze and copper was among the artistic glories of the Ming period. In 1427, by order of the Hsüan-te emperor, a foundry was established in which sixty-four skillful craftsmen were employed to cast bronze or copper vessels of all kinds, after Shang and Chou dynasty models. However, the old forms were not necessarily imitated closely; often they were more or less modified to meet the taste of the time. The casting of incense burners, known as lu 爐, was particularly successful—usually they were called hsüan-lu 宣爐, i.e. incense burners cast in the Hsüan-te reign (1426–1435). Even in our own days, vessels cast in imitation of this type still bear the name hsüan-lu and the bottoms of the vessels are not infrequently marked in relief with the words "Ta Ming Hsüan-te nien chi 大明宣德年製," "Made in the Hsüan-te reign-period of the Great Ming."

In Chekiang and Kiang-nan there were famous silversmiths whose craftsmanship was known throughout the empire.[27]

Although cloisonné, known as fa-lang 珐瑯 or fa-lan 發藍, had been made in the days of the preceding dynasty, its popularity dates from the Ming period. The art flourished particularly during the Ch'ing-t'ai reign (1450–1457) and became known as Ch'ing-t'ai lan 景泰藍. The color scheme of the Ming cloisonné is particularly rich, a splendid azure blue, opaque turquoise, dull crimson, and grass green being the predominant tones. The decorations are usually flowers, generally the peony, lotus and chrysanthemum. The records speak in particular of a certain artist, a native of Yünnan resident in the capital, who won fame in this art.[28]

The art of lacquer work attained a notable degree of perfection during the Ming period. The products of Su-chou, Hui-chou, and Lu-ling (in Kiangsi) were particularly celebrated and a lacquer factory was established by the government in Peking, and towards the end of the 16th century Huang Ch'eng 黃成, a well-known craftsman from Hui-chou, wrote a treatise entitled *Hsiu-shih lu* 髤飾錄 in which he explained the process in detail. Lacquered objects in general can be divided into two kinds: the painted, hua ch'i 花漆, and the carved, tiao ch'i 雕漆. Some of the more elaborate pieces are encrusted with semi-precious stones and have gilt metal mounts.[29]

Architecture has never held a great place in the history of Chinese art. As Sir Banister Fletcher puts it, while the Chinese reveled in the beauty of nature, they had little feeling for architectural design, which they held merely subservient to human needs.[30] Furthermore, the government could build only by using man power, but according to Chinese tradition an excessive use of man power was regarded as a form of cruelty. At a time when even emperors were governed by ritual (unless they were tyrants), the ideal emperor, however rich, preserved restraint and never abandoned his frugal way of life.

Despite this austere tradition the Ming emperors did in fact build many palaces and temples, especially after the first half of the 16th century. Indeed, the extravagant building of the Chia-ching and Wan-li emperors was one of the causes of the bankruptcy which eventually led to the fall of the empire. This may be a sad blot on the record of the Ming dynasty, but it added one of the most splendid chapters to the history of Chinese architecture.

To go back to the early period of the empire, the Hung-wu emperor, when he came to the throne, built a new capital at Nanking, encircling the 96 square li with a wall. Later he built a second wall nearly double the length of the first. Nanking was one of the largest cities in the East in those days and the emperor adorned it with beautiful palaces.

In 1421, the capital was moved by order of the Yung-lo emperor to Peking, the Cambaluc of the Mongols, which he substantially rebuilt. In the reign of the Chia-ching emperor in the first half of the 16th century Peking was rebuilt once more. Some of the palaces and temples built at that time (especially the one known as the Temple of Heaven) still rank among the artistic glories of Peking. The solid foundations of the walls were made of bricks baked in Lin-ch'ing 臨清, Shantung. The timber was taken from the Nan 楠 tree, a fine-grained tree grown in West China. The Peking of the Ming dynasty had a circumference of forty-five li, with the imperial palaces as its center. The main streets led from the gates of the city and ran parallel from south to north with small lanes running from east to west.

Among the most renowned religious buildings of the age were the porcelain pagoda in Nanking and the Chin-kang t'a 金剛塔 of the Chen-chüeh szu 眞覺寺, commonly known as Wu-t'a szu 五塔寺, near the suburbs of Peking. The majesty and dignity of tombs of the Ming emperors still arouse admiration: their designers are to be praised not only for their architectural excellence but also for the skill with which they utilized the natural surroundings to inspire awe and reverence in all who visit them.

RELIGION

Having conquered the Mongol regime, the founder of the Ming dynasty tried to restore the old Chinese tradition which had been so badly distorted by the Mongols. In religion, the Hung-wu emperor made an effort to revive the native Buddhist sects in opposition to Lamaist Buddhism which had been greatly favored by the Mongols from the reign of Khubilai Khan onward and had become very powerful in China. The new emperor had himself been a Buddhist monk and was naturally favorable to this religion. On the other hand, he realized that it was necessary for the government to control both Buddhism and Taoism. At the beginning of his reign a new office was established to take charge of both religions, and Buddhist and Taoist priests of high repute and well versed in their religion were appointed to this office. We are told that the emperor himself wrote a commentary on the *Tao-te ching* 道德經, the sacred script of Taoism, in order to guide the followers of that religion. He also honored the head of the Taoists with the title of Cheng-i chen-jen 正一眞人. Buddhist scriptures were reprinted by imperial order and copies were distributed to many monasteries. Buddhistic practices were permitted to all.[31]

Most of the emperors of the Ming dynasty seem to have taken great interest in both Buddhism and Taoism. Indeed, as we shall see in a later chapter, one of the causes of the fall of the dynasty was the extravagant expenditure of the emperors on these two religions, and the Yung-lo emperor, a great believer in both Buddhism and Taoism, was rumored to have died of poison contained in an elixir which he had taken from the hands of some Taoist priests.[32] Both Buddhism and Taoism flourished under the emperor Ying-tsung 英宗 (1436–1449 and 1457–1464). The Ch'eng-hua emperor (1465–1487) was always a devoted believer in Buddhism and, intermittently, in Taoism. In the capital, Buddhist and Taoist temples, which are said to have numbered 639 before 1481, kept on multiplying until an uninterrupted chain of temples was visible from the summit of the West Hills.[33] This rapid multiplication of temples implied of course an increase of monks. We know that in the twelfth year of the Ch'eng-hua emperor (1476) a hundred thousand monks were ordained and that ten years later another two hundred thousand were added. By the end of that emperor's reign the total number—including those ordained before 1476—must have been over five hundred thousand. An official calculated that the amount of rice they consumed would have supplied the capital for a whole year.[34]

Of the Cheng-te emperor we are told that he was devoted to Buddhism and that he was said to have learned Sanskrit.[35] His conduct, however, suggests that his religious interests were founded on curiosity rather than on devotion.

The ardently Taoist Chia-ching emperor, who succeeded the Cheng-te emperor, reversed his predecessor's religious policy. Perhaps because of the influence of Taoist priests, Buddhism was severely discouraged in the capital during his reign, and Taoism was highly favored. He seems to have had a very clear motive in adhering to this religion. His predecessors may have embraced Buddhism purely out of curiosity or through a vague belief in the future life. The Chia-ching emperor, however, had a definite ambition to be numbered among the immortals. Like Wu-ti of the Han dynasty he mourned the fact that even the all-powerful emperor must some day share the fate of his subjects. None could promise immortality more confidently than the Taoists, whose writings contain many secret ways of preserving life forever. These promises appealed greatly to the emperor and he set about making himself immortal. Père du Halde writes of this monarch as follows: "The behavior of this prince, from the beginning of his reign had given a favorable impression of the wisdom of his government: however, the end did not correspond to such a good commencement." He then gives the reason for the emperor's failure:

"What people blame in this prince is his passion for poetry and the credulity with which he adopted the superstitious ideas of the monks, and had [men] sent throughout the provinces in search of the elixir of immortality which the Taoist sect promises."[36]

This was true. The emperor's zeal for the Taoist ceremonies and alchemy brought about first the neglect of government and eventually the end of his own life.[37] Du Halde tells us that, in the eighteenth year of his reign, the emperor wished to abdicate in favor of his son that he might devote all his time to religion. It would perhaps have been better if he had abdicated, for during the last twenty-five years of his reign, he left the work of the government in the hands of the notorious Yen Sung, who nearly wrecked the empire. These were the years in which the Mongols under Yen-ta Han (Alda = Alta—(n) Qan) were attacking the empire from the north and the Japanese pirates were raging all along the Chinese coast; in the palace religious functions went on day and night, sometimes continuing for months without interruption.

The years went by. The Chia-ching emperor's passion for immortality grew ever stronger. He had completely forgotten his obligations as a ruler. Those who pretended to know the secret of long life, or who helped to compose essays and poems in praise of the immortals could win his friendship. Rapid promotion could be expected once the favor of the monarch was secured through these methods. Yen Sung, the most fortunate of all, wrote beautiful essays and poems for the emperor in praise of the immortals and thus pleased him immensely. As a reward, he was promoted to the position of Grand Secretary, an office which he held for over twenty years. Others too won high posts in unconventional ways. A certain official who had finished his term of office presented to the emperor some unfamiliar medicine alleging that it helped to prolong life: he was at once made president of the Board of Ceremonies.[38] Another presented a book on the life of the Taoist immortal Pai Yü-ch'an 白玉蟾 and was thenceforth highly esteemed by the emperor.[39] In 1544 the Taoist priest T'ao Chung-wen 陶仲文 was made president of the Board of Ceremonies, holding at the same time the titles of Shao-shih 少師 or Junior Preceptor, Shao-fu 少傅 or Junior Tutor, and Shao-pao 少保 or Junior Guardian—a collection of honors such as had never before been bestowed on any minister since the beginning of the dynasty. A year later, this same priest was offered the title of count. When he refused the offer, posthumous honors were conferred upon his ancestors up to the third generation and his son was made a student of the Imperial Academy.[40]

Rumors of good omens were freely invented to please the ears of the infatuated emperor. Every day good tidings or symbolic curiosities would arrive in the palace and the Son of Heaven received them with exceeding joy. One day he would be presented with wheat plants bearing three or four stems each. On the next day a turtle of five colors would be brought. On a third day the appearance of white cranes flying across the sky at the time of the sacrifice would be reported. All these things, he was told, were signs that he was one dear to the immortals. Day in and day out extraordinary presents continued to arrive at the palace and the donors always received high praise and substantial rewards. As if all this were not enough, the emperor himself would send censors to the four corners of the empire to look for magicians and magic charms and spells and infallible recipes for long life.[41]

Eventually, the emperor had the happiness of finding himself in personal contact with the extraordinary. As he was sitting one evening in the palace courtyard, he suddenly came upon a peach behind an awning. Some of the bystanders promptly declared that they had seen the peach fall from Heaven. The emperor, greatly pleased, concluded that the peach was a gift from Heaven and decreed a sacrifice of thanksgiving. Next day he found another peach. His joy was increased by the report that the preceding night a white rabbit had given birth to two young ones. Later he was informed that the same thing had happened to an old deer. Upon hearing of this good news all the court officials wrote to congratulate the emperor, and he answered each of them in his own hand.[42]

For all ministers who took their duties seriously, the extravagant behavior of the emperor was a source of great grief. They did their best to remind him of his obligations and to disabuse him of his belief in fantastic events, blaming the eunuchs for starting all the trouble and demanding that they be severely punished.[43] The emperor, however, refused to listen and their petitions were ignored. Chou I 周怡 (1506–1565) and Hai Jui 海瑞 (1514–1587) had the courage to point out to the emperor his mistakes, but this merely

enraged him: in a furious fit of temper, he condemned the former to
be beaten publicly at court and to serve a term of five years in prison.
He condemned the latter to death. Hai Jui was set free, however,
when the emperor was on his deathbed.[44] Even princes and members
of the imperial family who dared to admonish him did not escape
punishment for lese-majesty. Prince Cheng 鄭王 was kept in confine-
ment for eighteen years for having opposed the emperor's Taoist
ceremonies. The emperor's own son-in-law excused himself from
writing essays in praise of the immortals. This so displeased his
father-in-law that he was degraded and reduced to the rank of a
commoner.[45] The *Ming shih* says that towards the end of the Chia-
ching emperor's reign the country was restless both within and
without. In his devotion to Taoism he had emptied the government
treasuries and the financial stability that had lasted for over a century
began to weaken.[46]

During the Wan-li reign, which began six years after the death of
the Chia-ching emperor, Buddhism triumphed and was to remain
pre-eminent till the end of the dynasty. We are told by the eunuch
Liu Jo-yü 劉若愚 that there was in the imperial city a Han-ching
ch'ang 漢經廠 where the court ladies learned Buddhist scriptures.
On the emperor's birthday and on other feasts during the year,
religious ceremonies were held in this place. The longhaired court
ladies used to don the vestments and perform the functions of
Buddhist monks. In the Wan-li period (1572–1619), the emperor
used to select honest and pious women, learned in Buddhist scriptures,
to train some of the court ladies to perform ceremonies, offer incense,
and pray in front of the altar.[47] The same author tells us that many
of the eunuchs believed deeply in the future life. Great numbers of
them were devotees of Buddhism and made certain that when they
died they would be buried in Buddhist monasteries.[48] They were also
patrons of the monks and contributed to the building of Buddhist
temples. Gradually, however, under the influence of this patronage,
the temples lost their religious character and turned into centers of
political intrigue. The eunuchs used to frequent the temples they had
built; all who wanted a chance of asking favors from any particular
eunuch had only to bribe the official monk of the appropriate temple
and they could be sure of obtaining an interview. For similar reasons
even high government officials tried to win the friendship of the
official monks.[49]

Lamaism, despite its close association with the ousted Mongols,
never completely lost its hold under the Ming regime. As early as the
Yung-lo reign, the emperor established relations with Tibetan monks.

The Ch'eng-hua emperor especially gave them an enthusiastic welcome and invited them to come from Tibet and Mongolia. The secret spells which these monks claimed to possess pleased him immensely. During the Cheng-te reign Tibetan monks came in large numbers and their abbots were given the title of Kuo-shih 國師, "imperial teacher." The emperor learned the Buddhist scriptures in their alien language and not infrequently he dressed himself in the robes of a Tibetan monk and performed religious ceremonies in the inner temple of the palace.[50] After the death of this emperor Lamaism became less popular. Nevertheless, Tibetan monks maintained their connection with China throughout the Chia-ching and Wan-li periods.

The educated class was deeply affected by religion throughout the whole Ming period. The ministers were doubtless influenced by the favorable attitude of the emperors; but this was not the whole story. The intellectual class as a whole was strongly attracted toward Buddhism, which put forward a coherent system of philosophy, something which Confucianism seemed unable to do. In consequence, we often find scholars numbering Buddhist monks among their friends. The great scholar Sung Lien 宋濂 (1310–1381) boasted an intimate knowledge of the Buddhistic scriptures, which he had studied since his youth.[51] Even the great philosopher Wang Shou-jen 王守仁 (1472–1528) gave some time to intense studies of Buddhism and Taoism. The following autobiographical note by a supercilious critic testifies to the customs of those days: "In my youth," this eyewitness wrote, "when I saw people hanging up pictures of Buddha or of Lao-tzu, I used to reprove them for their superstition. I was quite convinced that an intellectual with a well-balanced mind would certainly abhor such practices. Later when I was employed in the office of a censor I once happened to be in the home of the prime minister. I noticed a solemn-looking building at the east of the bed chamber and they told me that it was the temple of Buddha. That left me astonished. Shortly afterwards I noticed hanging high up in the parlor of Mr. Shih-shou 石首 a picture of Kuan-yin 觀音. Unable to control myself I burst out laughing."[52]

Many eunuchs and court ladies were also strongly attached to the Buddhist religion. They firmly believed in the Buddhist doctrine of cause and effect and so were led to belief in the transmigration of the soul. The eunuch Liu Jo-yü 劉若愚 says that adherence to the Buddhist doctrine of cause and effect was so strong among his colleagues that many of them became Buddhists and these invariably had their graves built in monastic grounds.[53] Hence, many of the eunuchs lavished a great part of their wealth on the building of monasteries, notably such notorious eunuchs as Wang Chen 王振 and Wei Chung-hsien 魏忠賢. Apparently these men, realizing the enormity of their crimes, tried to expiate them by monastery building in the hope of escaping eternal punishment in the afterlife.

Among the people Buddhism seems to have had a stronger appeal than Taoism. Hsieh Chao-che 謝肇淛 (c. 1600), says that in his days Buddhist monasteries were more numerous than schools and the recitation of prayers was more popular than singing. High and low, he says, rejoiced equally in the discussion of Buddhistic doctrines and the worship of Buddhist deities. He tried to analyze this popularity and found two main reasons for it. The aged, knowing that their days in this world were numbered and believing in the doctrine of transmigration of souls, sought to expiate their sins, which they knew had been many. The more intellectual people were attracted by the subtlety of the Buddhistic philosophy of human life and life hereafter, and in the end their intellectual curiosity led them to embrace the Buddhist religion.[54]

Father Ricci, who was in China about the time of Hsieh Chao-che, says in his diary that in his time the number of Buddhist priests amounted to two or three millions. They lived in numerous cloisters of temples which were supported by alms and by revenues formerly established for that purpose. Some of them also supported themselves by personal labor.[55] The fact that so many could find support proves that their religion must have had a great number of believers. A scholar who lived towards the end of the dynasty says that in his day the government itself had become dependent on the income of the temples for funds: the income of the temple of T'ai Shan, for instance, served to pay the salaries of the government officials of Shantung province. This same scholar tells us that in the 1560's in Sui-p'ing hsien 邃平縣, Honan province, the governor of the prefecture forbade the people to go on pilgrimages outside their district. However, declaring that he had no intention of interfering with their worship, he ordered that devotional statues should be set up in certain Taoist and Buddhist temples to meet the wishes of the people. Within a year the collections made in those temples amounted to ten thousand taels of silver. And the scholar concludes in amazement: "though the government exhorted the people year after year to pay their taxes, the people were reluctant to do their duty; but when it came to making offerings for the temples a single word was enough to arouse their enthusiasm!"[56]

Doctrinally, Buddhism remained stagnant, with none of the intellectual vitality it had shown under the T'ang and Sung dynasties. A number of distinguished monks arose from the Ch'an sect 禪宗 the most flourishing of all the sects, towards the end of the dynasty, when the monasteries had begun to shake off their dependence on government control. Among the best known of these was Yün-ch'i Chu-hung 雲棲株宏 (1535–1615), who had been a Confucian scholar before he became a Buddhist monk and had the reputation of being a talented writer. The talent won him the respect of many scholars, and he remained on good terms with them to the end of his life. It was characteristic of him and of his time that he tried to reconcile Buddhism with both Confucianism and Taoism. "The three religions, greatly as they may differ in status, come from the same family," Chu-hung wrote to a friend. "Though of one family, they differ as grandfather, father and son. . . . So in a tree, we distinguish its roots, its branches and its leaves and must not confuse the branches and leaves with its roots."[57]

Taoism had flourished under the Sung, Chin and Yüan dynasties. Under the Ming dynasty it maintained its external splendor only with difficulty, and there was no development of its teaching. Several sects existed side by side. The Ch'üan-chen chiao 全眞教 was the most influential sect in northern China; the Cheng i chiao 正一教 was widespread in the South. The Ch'üan-chen chiao differed greatly from ordinary Taoism, discarding belief in the immortality of the body and other characteristic Taoistic doctrines, and seeking to borrow both ideas and terminology from Buddhism and even to reconcile the two religions. The branch of Cheng-i chiao that was known as "orthodox" because of its claim to direct descent from its Han-period founder, Chang Tao-ling 張道陵, had its headquarters in Kiangsi. The leader of the "orthodox" bore the title Chang t'ien-shih 張天師 and enjoyed the patronage of the emperors. The holders of this post were frequently summoned to the capital by the emperors to perform religious functions, especially in time of calamities. Father Ricci gives the following illuminating description of the Chang t'ien-shih of his time: "Their leader spends most of his time in Peking. He is a recognized favorite of the king and is even admitted into the most sacred chambers of the palace for ceremonies of exorcism, if perchance suspicion arises that these places are infested with evil spirits. He is carried through the streets in an open palanquin, wears the paraphernalia of the highest magistrates, and receives a fat annual stipend from the crown. One of our neophytes informs us that the present-day prelates of this sect are so ignorant that they do not even know the unholy hymns and rites of their own order. . . ."[58]

Four years before the fall of the Ming dynasty (1640) the Ch'ung-chen emperor participated frequently in Buddhist and Taoist sacrifices, hoping to avert the calamities that had begun to prey on his mind. In the following year Chang t'ien-shih was summoned to the capital to pray for snow and the chief eunuch was sent specially to escort him. He came; he prayed; no snow fell; he was dismissed. Not long afterwards he was summoned again. Taking this repeated summons as a great honor, he proceeded with much display through the provinces and spent six months on the journey to the capital. On his arrival he was impeached by the minister of the Board of Ceremonies as a "man of the world." He was accused of having failed in his prayers for snow and for rain, of having lied by claiming he had produced rain, and finally of having wasted money from the government treasury.[59]

The people, and even the intellectuals, mingled many superstitious beliefs with their religion. Such things as omens, fortune-telling, and the interpretation of dreams had great influence on the daily life of the people. Ricci said of the China of his day: "No superstition is so common in the entire kingdom as that which pertains to the observance of certain days and hours as being good or bad, lucky or unlucky in which to act or to refrain from acting; because the result of everything they do is supposed to depend upon a measurement of time." He also said: "The imposture has assumed such a semblance of truth among the people that two calendars are edited every year, written by the astrologers of the crown and published by public authority. These almanacs are said to be sold in such great quantities that every house has a supply of them."[60]

The book publishers liked to get well-known scholars to compile for them encyclopedic handbooks in which everything from astrology and medicine to jokes could be found. In the Naigaku Library 內閣文庫, Tokyo, one still can see the Wan-pao ch'üan shu 萬寶全書 compiled by the scholar Ai Nan-ying 艾南英 (c. 1630) and the Wan-yung cheng-tsung pu-ch'iu-jen ch'üan-pien 萬用正宗不求人全篇 compiled in 1607, by Lung-yang tzu 龍陽子. They supply a good deal of information on the society of the time and are of great help in the study of this subject. The inclusion of much superstition in books of this kind shows that the people really believed in it. To return once more to the diary of Father Ricci: "It happens not infrequently that if one is about to build he will put off the work for days and days, or those intending to go on a journey will defer their departure so as not to be in the least at variance with the time prescribed for such things by the divining mountebanks. Even the elements cannot turn them aside from this superstition. If the appointed day should bring a downpour of rain or contrary winds for a voyage, they would never be deterred from beginning an undertaking on the day and at the exact time designated beforehand as being propitious for a successful issue."[61]

Fortunetelling and geomancy were commonly practiced by all, from the emperors to the most ignorant peasants of the empire. The intellectuals used these means for discovering their chances of promotion in government offices. The common people used them to gauge their future prosperity. Contemporary writings were full of anecdotes about this. Father Ricci in his *Chi-jen shih-p'ien* 畸人十篇 tells us of a certain sixty-year-old scholar of whom it had been foretold that he would die very shortly. He believed this and came to bid Father Ricci farewell, but in fact he lived for over two decades more, in spite of the prophecy.[62] Hsieh Chao-che says that some of the fortunetellers and geomancers he had met were men of great reputation; yet the things they foretold never came to pass. He condemns them as quite untrustworthy and unreliable; yet even he could not help falling into superstitious practices in his daily life.[63]

Islam was introduced into China by the Arabs, and as early as the time of the T'ang dynasty it became one of the religions of the Chinese, though probably it then had comparatively few followers. Under Mongol rule the Mohammedans spread all over the empire. From contemporary records we know that there were mosques in Canton, Ch'üan-chou, Hang-chou, Hsi-an and Kun-ming. In Hang-chou there was a Mohammedan cemetery and in Kun-ming there were two mosques built by Seyyid Edjell Sham edin Omar 賽典赤瞻思丁 (1211–1279), who had been sent by Khubilai Khan to administer the province of Yünnan. We are told that both he and his descendants greatly influenced the natives of the place, especially by introducing Chinese culture.[64]

When the Hung-wu emperor came to the throne, his policy towards Mohammedanism was determined not so much by its religious character as by his judgment on the loyalty and the usefulness of the Mohammedans to himself. From the beginning of his reign he prohibited the P'u 蒲 family from taking part in the examinations for government offices. This was due to the monarch's distaste for the disloyalty of P'u Shou-keng 蒲壽庚 to the Sung dynasty. This man, a Mohammedan of foreign blood, had been employed by the Sung government as overseer at the customs of Ch'üan-chou, Fukien. In time, he surrendered to the Mongols and had the nobles of the Sung dynasty murdered in cold blood.[65] The Hung-wu emperor's disapproval of the P'u family was not, however, extended indiscriminately to their co-religionists. Thus we are told that in 1369 eleven Mohammedan astronomers, headed by a certain Cheng Ali 鄭阿里, were summoned to the capital to reform the calendar. Under subsequent emperors, Mohammedans were employed in the government. Of these the best known was Cheng Ho 鄭和, a Mohammedan of foreign origin.[66]

In the days of Ricci, we are told: "The Saracens are everywhere in evidence, and, except for a few of them, they are always looked upon as outsiders. Owing to their rapid propagation, they had become so numerous that thousands of families of them are scattered about in nearly every province and are to be found in nearly every sizable city."[67] Indeed, they were so well known to the people that their very way of cooking was imitated. The *Chü-chia pi-yung* 居家必用, a vade-mecum for the people of the time, recommended several ways of preparing Mohammedan dishes.[68]

The Mohammedans within the Ming empire were tenacious in their beliefs though they did not make any effort to propagate them. They did not eat pork—a startling singularity in China. Wherever they were numerous they built their own mosque at great expense, maintained their own graveyards and had their own ritual. These religious peculiarities rendered them offensive to the people at large. The *Chin-ling so-shih hsü-chi* 金陵瑣事續集 describes the customs observed at Mohammedan funerals: they wore white headdresses and white clothes and girdled themselves with a white cloth. All who participated in the ceremony, even government officials and licentiates, had to observe these customs. It happened once that when the empress died and the people had to mourn her as tradition demanded, one of the Mohammedans, following the custom of his religion, wore white. He was severely reprimanded by the magistrate for observing a foreign custom in the mourning for the empress and was even considered to have disobeyed the imperial precepts. Apparently this magistrate's action was instigated by a complaint from the people, who found this Mohammedan practice intolerable and so brought charges against the culprit. We are told that the people rejoiced greatly at the measures taken by the magistrate to humiliate the Mohammedan.[69]

The Mohammedans for their part often resented the remarks and acts of the pagans against their religion and, sometimes unable to restrain their resentment, resorted to violence. During the reign of the Ching-t'ai emperor (1450–1456) the Buddhist temple Lung-fu szu 隆福寺 was built in Peking. On the inauguration day, when the people were allowed to visit the temple, a Mohammedan came with an axe and killed two monks and wounded several others. He was arrested and brought before the magistrate. On being questioned he said that his motive for killing and wounding the Buddhist monks was purely religious. The explanation was that in the temple there was a new chest under which was a carved picture representing a number of Mohammedans turning the wheels of the revolving chest where Buddhist manuscripts were kept. This irritated the Mohammedan to the point of murderous violence.[70]

The ill-will of the people toward the Mohammedan faith strengthened the unity of the believers. The tumult of 1588, was a good example of this. Outside the Hsüan-wu Gate 宣武門, Peking, there was a colony of Mohammedans who for generations had been butchers of cattle. For reasons unknown to us, a censor tried to prohibit them from this trade. The Mohammedans protested so violently that eventually the court ministers had to step in and pacify them.[71]

On the frontier and in distant provinces where Mohammedanism was strong, it always constituted a source of anxiety for the government. In 1436, five hundred Mohammedans were moved from Kansu and Liang-chou 涼州[72]—seemingly because they were growing too strong there. Several writers of the time point out that the difficulty in governing Shensi arose partly from the presence there of the great numbers of Mohammedans. "Between Feng-hsien 鳳縣 and Mien-hsien 沔縣 there have always been great numbers of Mohammedans. Among them there are men of dubious character who are on the watch for some disturbance during which they may be able to induce others to rise. Heaven knows, this lethal trouble may keep on growing and we think it is the duty of those who govern to foresee and to provide for the safety of the community."[73] In the beginning of the Ch'ung-chen reign (1628) when revolts began to break out, Shensi was one of the first provinces to rise. One of the more notorious leaders was nicknamed Lao hui-hui 老狃狃, "the old Mohammedan," and was reputed to be a Mohammedan. His real name is said to have been Ma Kuang-yü 馬光玉 or Ma Shou-ying 馬守應, and Ma was a common surname among the Mohammedans. The arch-rebel Li Tzu-cheng 李自成 himself was suspected of being a Mohammedan. Charles Boulger in his history of China attributed the success of Li Tzu-ch'eng in his campaigns to the fact that he formed an alliance with the Mohammedans.[74]

The earliest trace of Christianity in China dates back to the time of the T'ang dynasty when the Nestorians first appeared in Hsi-an (or Ch'ang-an) in the year A.D. 635. The mission, led by A-lo-pen 阿羅本, a Syrian, settled in that city, then capital of the great T'ang dynasty. Soon a Syrian monastery was built there with a community of twenty-one monks. After the persecution of Buddhism and other foreign religions by the Emperor Wu-tsung (A.D. 845), the Nestorian missions seemed to have disappeared from the empire until the 13th century, although small groups continued to exist in north China under both the Liao and the Chin. Under the rule of the Mongols, Nestorian missions became prominent in China. Monasteries are known to have existed in widely separated places—in Kansu and Ta-t'ung, in Chen-kiang and Hang-chou, in Wen-chou and Yang-chou, and in Fukien and Yünnan. Peking, then known as Cambaluc, being the capital of the Great Khan, was the center of their activities.

The Franciscans were the first Roman Catholics to come to China. John de Monte Corvino, of the Friars Minor, was sent by Nicholas IV as Nuncio to the Mongol court in the year 1289. In 1307 an arch-bishopric was established in Peking. In the same year seven friars were consecrated bishops by Clement V and were sent to China to assist Monte Corvino, who was then archbishop of Peking. Soon after this a bishopric was founded in Ch'üan-chou, Fukien. The mission of the Friars Minor lasted for less than a century (1289–1370) and it came to an end soon after the establishment of the Ming dynasty. From then onward a desolate silence of two hundred years shrouded the Christian Church till the coming of the Jesuit missionaries.

In the 16th century the sea route to China was rediscovered and about the middle of that century the Portuguese settled in Macao. Missionaries began to move from India into Japan in the footsteps of the great Saint Francis Xavier; but China was still closed to foreigners. Despite all difficulties Xavier had tried to get in, but his attempt failed, and he died in 1552 in the small island of Shang-ch'uan 上川 within easy reach of the coast of Kuangtung. His vision was to be realized twenty years later by one of his fellow Jesuits, Matteo Ricci.

Matteo Ricci, a native of Italy, began his missionary life in Goa but was soon sent to Macao, where he studied the Chinese language in preparation for entering China. Not quite thirty years of age but fully equipped with all appropriate learning, especially in mathe-matics and astronomy, he engaged in lengthy negotiations and was ultimately permitted to reside in Chao-ch'ing 肇慶 in southern China. He soon saw how vast the country was and how difficult it would be to make converts. After careful study of the structure of Chinese society he became convinced that conversion would have to start from the imperial court and work down to the common people. This method of evangelization seemed strange to the Christians of his day, but to him it was obvious that it was the right way to set about the work he had at heart. It took him twenty years and much patience to succeed in his dreams.

His adaptation to Chinese culture and tradition was rapid. In order to gain recognition among the educated class he adopted the dress of the scholars of the time. Instead of preaching to crowds he sought discussions at private meetings. He mastered the Chinese classics so thoroughly that he was able to quote from them with facility and to write in elegant style books explaining the Christian point of view.

As soon as he had been accepted by the scholars he made use of his scientific knowledge to secure their attention and eventually brought many of them to the faith. He personally had the consolation of receiving into the Church a notable number of converts, including several such men of dignity as Hsü Kuang-ch'i 徐光啓, and Li Chih tsao 李之藻.

The interest taken by scholars and by many government officials in the Catholic religion accounted for its rapid propagation. The *Ming shih* tells us that "from government officials to the ordinary people, all showed respect to him (i.e. Ricci) and all tried to make his acquaintance." "Now, throughout the whole empire there is no one who does not know Mr. Li Hsi-t'ai 利西泰," a contemporary of Ricci's said.[75] The motives behind the friendship offered to Ricci differed from man to man. The greedy took him for an alchemist and approached him in order to learn the secret of transforming cheap metals into precious ones. The seekers after the truth, on the other hand, found in his sayings abundant material for thought. Still more common were those who came to seek knowledge of the universe. All, however, admired his personal integrity.

By 1614, four years after Ricci's death, Jesuit missionaries were working in nine provinces.* By the end of the Ming dynasty they had extended into thirteen of the fifteen provinces (the exceptions were Yünnan and Kueichou). The Chinese Christians of the empire numbered about 150,000.[76]

---

* Here the word "provinces" is used in a loose sense. Strictly speaking the Ming empire was divided into two capitals: Nanking and Peking, or Nan chih-li 南直隸 and Pei chih-li 北直隸, and thirteen Pu-cheng-ssu 布政司. Often they are referred to briefly as the liang-ching shih-san ssu 兩京十三司.

As we have seen, Buddhism became quite independent of government control at the end of the Ming period. Considerable numbers of monks who enjoyed a reputation for learning took up the task of expounding their doctrine, thus attracting many of the intellectuals. The majority, however, were more or less ignorant and highly superstitious. For them, the priesthood was merely a profession, one which probably offered greater security than most other professions. The renowned Ts'ang-hsüeh fa-shih 蒼雪法師 (1588–1656), writing in 1641 to one of his disciples, said that it was common to see monks who had died of overeating but unknown to see one who had died of starvation.[77] And Chu Kuo-chen 朱國楨 told of an abbot who had come from a region north of the Yangtze accompanied by over twenty disciples. They were enthusiastically received by the people, both rich and poor all made offerings to them. However, only those who were exceptionally generous got a few lines from the brush of the abbot. This monk was said to have collected several thousand taels of silver.[78] The scholars were repelled by such worldly behavior and on comparing Christianity with Buddhism they concluded that Christianity was closer to Confucianism and that its moral teaching was solid, unlike the Buddhist doctrine which appeared subtle but was not firmly founded.[79]

The conflict between Christianity and Buddhism developed into an acrimonious controversy between the two parties. The Christian apologists were led by Ricci and Hsü Kuang-ch'i, and the Buddhists by Yü Ch'un-hsi 虞淳熙 (c. 1588) and the Buddhist monk Chu-hung 株宏. Both parties received support from Confucian scholars and Chu-hung even suspected that a certain letter addressed to him by Ricci had in fact been written by Chinese scholars. This same monk expressed his anxieties as follows: " . . . But if their teaching should grow to such an extent that our intellectuals were drawn to it, I should not spare this feeble body of mine, nor should I restrain my tongue from defending our belief. Meanwhile, however, I regard their preaching as the singing of fishermen or shepherds, nay, even as the buzzing of a mosquito or the croak of a frog."[80]

The controversy between the two religions led to the publication of a large number of treatises in defense of their beliefs. The Catholics, who until then had written practically nothing in Chinese, now began to publish a great deal on apologetics. Two books by Ricci (*T'ien-chu shih-yi* 天主實義 and the *Chi-jen shih-pien* 畸人十篇) won high reputation and were so well written that nearly two centuries later both were included in the *Ssu-k'u ch'üan-shu* 四庫全書 compiled by order of the Chien-lung emperor.

In 1616 Hsü Kuang-ch'i presented a memorial to the throne giving a summary of the teachings of the Catholic faith. This came at a time when a minister of the Board of Ceremonies had just presented an unfavorable report to the Wan-li emperor and tried to persuade that monarch to expel all the missionaries. In his memorial Hsü sought to show the reasonableness of the Christian faith in contrast with the Buddhist and Taoist systems. He pointed out that Christianity was close to the teaching of Confucius but utterly at variance with Buddhism and Taoism. This, he said, was the reason why the Buddhists and Taoists could not tolerate the missionaries. Accordingly he suggested that the missionaries should meet outstanding Buddhist and Taoist priests in a public disputation, with Confucian scholars as judges. "If Your Majesty," he went on, "would but serve the Heavenly Lord in the place of Buddhism and Taoism, and accept the services of these foreign missionaries, the guidance of the people and the government of the empire would undoubtedly become even better than they were in the T'ang and Yü period of the Three Dynasties. . . ."[81] However, the Wan-li emperor, preoccupied with his own affairs inside the palace and at no time a man of action, merely acknowledged the good intention of his minister, without any sign of either approval or disapproval.

During the Ch'ung-chen period, Hsü Kuang-ch'i tried hard to convert the emperor to Christianity and at one time seemed near to success. We are told that the emperor came to the point of ordering the destruction of all the idols in the palace, but was frightened out of this resolution by the death of one of his sons. The dying prince was said to have seen an apparition of the Chiu-lien-hua niang-niang 九蓮花娘娘 reprehending the emperor for having destroyed the idols.[82] Notwithstanding this check, the monarch still remained favorable to Christianity. When Father Trigault returned from Europe he brought back with him as a gift from the Duke of Bavaria a magnificent album depicting the life of Christ, which was presented to the emperor with an explanation of the pictures written in Chinese by Adam Schall. The monarch was greatly pleased and he showed the album to the empress and the court ladies. Several of these court ladies were baptized shortly afterward, including three who later bore the title of empress. The Christian names of these Christian empresses were Agatha, Helen & Theodora. By 1640 fifty court ladies, forty eunuchs and one hundred and forty nobles had been baptized. We are told that the princesses led a retiring life, devoting much time to making objects for sacred use, and clothes for the poor and for the missionaries.[83]

After the advance of the Manchus in 1644 the Ming princes had to retreat towards the South where they set up their courts. Prince Kuei 桂王 set up his court in Chao-ch'ing 肇慶, not far from Canton, in 1648, taking Yung-li 永曆 as the title of his reign. Through the zeal of the eunuch P'ang T'ien-shou 龐天壽 (known to the Europeans as Achilles Pang) Prince Kuei was well disposed to Catholicism, and several of the court ministers and court ladies were converted to the faith. About this time a son was born to the Yung-li emperor and was baptized by Father Koffler. He was given the baptismal name of Constantine and the missionaries had great hopes that, in case this child should some day recover the lost territories of his ancestors, he might be a Constantine of China who would lead his people to Christianity. But the Ming dynasty ended with the Yung-li emperor and the hopes of the missionaries were never realized.

NOTES

[1] *Erh-shih-erh-shih cha-chi*, 32, (ts'e 6) 6b–8a.

[2] *Erh-shih-erh-shih cha-chi*, 32, (ts'e 6) 8ab; The *Ming shih*, 285, (ts'e 94) 3a relates a significant anecdote about Yang Wei-cheng. When Yang, then over seventy, was first summoned to the court, he declined the invitation saying, "How could an old woman whose days are numbered, try to think of marriage?" Soon the summons was repeated. This time he agreed to go on the condition that the monarch should not force him to do what was impossible.

[3] *Ming shih*, 285. (ts'e 94) 10b. 71 (ts'e 24) 3b.

[4] Huang Tso 黃佐 (1490–1566). *Nan-yung chih* 南雍志, (Ming edition) 1, (ts'e 1) 20b; *Ming shih*, 69, (ts'e 24) 2b.

[5] *Ming shih*, 70, (ts'e 24) 1a–4b; Hsü Hsüeh-chu 徐學聚, *Kuo-ch'ao tien-hui* 國朝典彙, (1634 edition) 128, (ts'e 45) 4b, 5a, 6a.

[6] *Kuo-ch'ao tien-hui*, 128, (ts'e 45) 14a; *Nan-yung chih*, 2, (ts'e 2) 17a; 1, (ts'e 1) 53ab; Pu Shih-chang 卜世昌, *Huang-Ming t'ung-chi shu-i* 皇明通紀述遺, (Wan-li edition) 3, (ts'e 2) 37a; (ts'e 1) 25b; Chang Jui-ch'ao 張瑞朝, *Huang-Ming kung-chü k'ao* 皇明貢舉考, (Ming edition), 1, (ts'e 1) 40a.

[7] Ch'ien Mu 錢穆, *Kuo-shih ta-kang* 國史大綱, (Shanghai 1930) B. 510.

[8] *Kuo-ch'ao tien-hui*, 128, (ts'e 45) 15ab.

[9] Huang Tsung-hsi 黃宗羲, *Nan-lei wen-ting* 南雷文定, (TSCCCP), 1st series, 1, (ts'e 2,463) 1; Liu Ta-chieh 劉大杰, *Chung-kuo wen-hsüeh fa-chan shih* 中國文學發展史, (Shanghai 1958) C. 103–104.

[10] Sung P'ei-wei 宋佩韋, *Ming wen-hsüeh-shih* 明文學史, (Shanghai 1934) 1–6. Cf. also note 9.

[11] *Chung-kuo wen-hsüeh fa-chan shih*, 3, 102–103.

[12] *Huan li man-chi* 宦歷漫紀, 2, (ts'e 1) 9b–20b.

[13] Aoki Masaru 青木正兒, *Chukoku Kinsei gikyoku shi* 中國近世戲曲史, (translated by Wang Ku-lu 王古魯) (Peking, 1958) I, 165–171.

[14] Cheng Chen-to 鄭振鐸, *Chung-kuo wen-hsüeh yen-chiu* 中國文學研究, (Peking, 1957) 3, 1019–1023. The quotation is taken from *Ku ch'ü tsa-yen* 顧曲雜言 by Shen Te-fu 沈德符 (1578–1642). This was perhaps the type of literature that honest families abhorred and referred to as "indecent poems and love-songs" which might have a bad influence on the young, especially on women, and should therefore, never be looked at. Cf. Fan Li-pen 范立本, *Chih-chia chieh-yao* 治家節要, (Edo mss, now kept in the Naikaku bunko, Tokyo) B. under the chapter "Chih-shu" 置書. When Lü K'un 呂坤 (1536–1616), was hsün-fu 巡撫 of Shansi he issued the following admonition to the people: "The people like to listen to fashionable melodies and new songs, which contain indecent words and offensive tunes and are harmful to morality. These therefore should be strictly forbidden. Learned scholars and poets who are able to produce songs of educational and moral value based on popular melodies will receive one peck of rice for each song they compose. . . ." Lü went on to promise rewards to those who would write songs or novels that would serve to teach the people good morality. The language need not be classical and should be made as simple and clear as possible so that both women and children might understand. The songs and novels should be sincere and direct so as to touch the hearts of the people. Each book should contain over thirty paragraphs. The writer of the prize-winning book would receive five piculs of rice, and if he was willing to train more than twenty candidates to carry out the teaching contained in his book, he would be given ten piculs of rice and other special gifts. Cf. *Ching-shih shih-yung-pien*, 17, (*li chi* 利集 3) 23ab. All this shows how influential this popular literature must have been.

[15] Yüan Hung-tao 袁宏道, *Yüan Chung-lang ch'uan-chi* 袁中郎全集, (Shanghai, 1935) under *Yüan Chung-lang wen-ch'ao* 袁中郎文鈔, 6–7; cf. Ch'ien Ch'ien-i 錢謙益 (1582–1664) *Lieh-ch'ao shih-chi hsiao-chuan* 列朝詩集小傳, (Shanghai, 1957) 2, 705–706; 566–569; Cheng Chen-to 鄭振鐸, *Ch'a-t'u-pen Chung-kuo wen-hsüeh-shih* 插圖本中國文學史, (Peking 1957) 4. 942–948.

[16] *Lieh-ch'ao shih-chi hsiao-chuan*, 570–574. Cf Chu Tung-jun 朱東潤, *Chung-kuo wen-hsüeh p'i-p'ing-shih ta-kang* 中國文學批評史大綱, (Shanghai, 1947) 269, where the *Ming-shih-tsung* 明詩綜 is quoted; *Jih-chih-lu chi-shih*, 18, (ts'e 6) 122–123.

[17] Ch'en Ju-heng 陳汝衡, *Shuo-shu shih-hua* 說書史話, (Peking, 1958); Ch'en Ju-heng 陳汝衡, *Shuo-shu hsiao-shih* 說書小史, (Shanghai, 1936); *Ch'a-t'u-pen Chung-kuo wen-hsüeh shih*, (Peking, 1957); Cheng Chen-to 鄭振鐸 *Chung-kuo wen-hsüeh yen-chiu* 中國文學研究, (Peking, 1957); Kuo Chen-i 郭箴一, *Chung-kuo hsiao-shuo shih* 中國小說史, (Shanghai, 1939).

[18] Cf. Chapter 12 and Appendix below. The *Shui-hu chuan* was translated by Pearl Buck as *All Men Are Brothers*. There is another translation of the *Sui-hu chuan* by J. H. Jackson with the title *Water Margin* in two volumes (Shanghai, 1937).

[19] *Wu-tsa-tsu*, 15, (ts'e 8) 35b–36a. The *Hsi-yu-chi* was partly translated by Arthur Waley under the title *Monkey*, (London, 1944).

[20] There is a German translation of the *Chin-p'ing-mei* which has been re-translated into English by Bernard Miall and Frans Kuhn (1940) with an introduction by Arthur Waley (cf. Thesaurus of Book Digests, New York 1949, p. 132). Herbert A. Giles in his *History of Chinese Literature*, (New York, 1931) p. 309 wrote of the *Chin-p'ing-mei*: "Altogether the book is objectionable, and would require a translator with the nerve of a Burton."

[21] *Chung-kuo wen-hsüeh fa-chan shih*, 3, 232.

[22] *Chung-kuo wen-hsüeh yen-chiu*, 1, 409–410; *Chung-kuo wen-hsüeh fa-chan shih*, 3, 236–237.

[23] *Huang-ming t'ung-chi*, 5, (ts'e 3) 3b, 22a. We quote the figures given in this book for the number of chuan and volumes in the *ta-tien*. Other authorities give different figures, Cf. *Kuo Ch'üeh*, (Shanghai, 1958 ed.) 14, (ts'e 1) 998; *Ming t'ung-chien*, 15, (ts'e 2) 3b; 62, (ts'e 7) 20a. The original set was taken from Nanking to Peking in 1421. When a fire broke out in 1557 it was saved, but the narrow escape prompted the decision to make one duplicate set which was completed in 1567. The original was destroyed at the collapse of the Ming and one tenth of the duplicate, during the Yung-cheng reign, was transferred to the Han-lin college where it remained till 1900, when the Boxers set fire to the college

library which adjoined the British Legation. The collection was in great part destroyed in the fire. Herbert A. Giles in his *History of Chinese Literature,* (New York and London, 1931) p. 296 has an interesting footnote in which he says that just when he had finished writing on the *Yung-lo ta-tien,* (23rd June, 1900) the Han-lin College was completely destroyed. The author's son who went through the siege of Peking says in a letter that when it was too late an attempt was made to save the *Yung-lo ta-tien.* However, he was able to secure a volume of the collection for himself. The *Eminent Chinese of the Ch'ing Period* tells us (Vol. I, 198) that "At present only some 370 volumes are known, 41 of these (two of them loaned) being in the Library of Congress." For further reference cf. Mou Ts'uan-sun 繆荃孫 (1844–1919), *Yung-lo ta-tien k'ao* 永樂大典考, (*Lien-yün-i ts'ung-shu* 連筠簃叢書); Kuo Po-kung 郭伯恭, "*Yung-lo ta-tien tsuan-hsiu k'ao*" 永樂大典纂修考, *Li-shih chi-k'an* 歷史集刊, 3, (1937) 275–320; Yüan T'ung-li 袁同禮, *Yung-lo ta-tien hsien-ts'un chuan-mu piao* 永樂大典現存卷目表, (Peking, 1929); "Yung-lo ta-tien chuan-hao" 永樂大典專號, Peking, *T'u-shu-kuan yüeh-k'an* 圖書舘月刊, 2, 3–4; Li Chin-hua 李晉華, *Ming-tai le-chuan-shu k'ao* 明代勅撰書考, (Peking, 1932); Higuchi Tatsu-tarō 樋口龍太郎, "Ei-raku dai-ten o kataru" 永樂大典を語る, *Sho motsu tenbo* 書物展望, 8, 1; Kanda Kiichiro 神田喜一郎, "Ei-raku dai-ten kan-suru ni-san shiryo" 永樂大典關する二三史料, *Rekishi to chi-ri* 歷史と地理, 21, 2; "Iwa-sake bunko konyu no Ei-raku dai-ten" 岩崎文庫購入の永樂大典, *Shi-bun* 斯文, 1, 1; Yüan T'ung-li 袁同禮, "Kuan yü Yung-lo ta-tien chih wen-hsien" 關於永樂大典之文獻, *Peiping t'u-shu-kuan kuan-k'an* 北平圖書舘舘刊 7.1; Chao Wan-li 趙萬里, "Kuan ts'ang yung-lo ta-tien ti-yao" 舘藏永樂大典提要 *Peiping t'u-shu-kuan kuan-k'an* 2.3.4 combined issue.

24 William Cohn, *Chinese Painting,* (London, 1951), 87

25 *China in the 16th Century,* 14–15.

26 H. Belevitch-Stankevitch: *Le Gout Chinois en France au Temps de Louis XIV,* (Paris, 1910) 86.

27 Omura Seigai 大村西崖, *Chung-kuo mei-shu shih* 中國美術史, (tr. by Ch'en Pin-ho 陳彬龢) (Shanghai, 1928) 210–211, 216; *Hsüan-te ting-i p'u chi hsüan-lu po-lun* 宣德鼎彝譜及宣爐博論, compiled by Lü Chen 呂震 on imperial order (*Mei-shu ts'ung-shu* 美術叢書 Shanghai, 1946) Vol. 7; George Soulie de Morant, *A History of Chinese Art from Ancient Times to the Present Day,* (tr. by G. C. Wheeler), (New York), 221–222.

28 Omura Seigai, op. cit., 216; G. S. de Morant, op. cit., 222–224; Leigh Ashton and Basil Gray, *Chinese Art,* (London) 277, 278.

29 Omura Seigai, op. cit., 211–212; Kato Shige Shi 加藤繁, *Shina Keizaishi Kaisetsu* 支那經濟史概說, (Tokyo, 1944) 67–69; Leigh Ashton and Basil Gray, op. cit., 277.

30 Banister Fletcher, *A History of Architecture,* (London 1938) 913.

31 *Hsü wen-hsien t'ung-k'ao,* 61, (ts'e 1) 3,363; Huang Ju-liang 黃汝良, *Yeh-chi meng sou* 野紀矇搜, (Ming edition) 2, (ts'e 1) 19ab.

32 Wang Ch'ung-wu 王崇武, "Ming Ch'eng-tsu yü fang-shih" 明成祖與方士, CKSH-CCSCK, 8, (January, 1949) 1, 12–19; cf. also "Ming Ch'eng-tsu yü fu-chiao 明成祖與佛教", by the same author, (CKSHCCSCK), 8, (January, 1949), 1, 1–11.

33 *Hsien-tsung ch'un-huang-ti shih-lu* 憲宗純皇帝實錄, (KPL photographic reprint) 260, (ts'e 183) 4a.

34 Cheng Hsiao 鄭曉, *Chin-yen lei-pien* 今言類編, (*Sheng-ch'ao i-shih* second series 勝朝遺事續編 ed. by Wu Mi-kuang 吳彌光 1883), 4, (ts'e 14) 90b.

35 Mao Ch'i-ling 毛奇齡 (1623–1716), *Wu-tsung wai-chi* 武宗外紀, compiled in the *Hsi-ho wen-chi* 西河文集, (*Wan-yu wen k'u* 萬有文庫 2nd series) (ts'e 8) 1679.

36 J. B. du Halde S.J.: *Description geographique, historique, chronologique, et physique de l'empire de la Chine,* 1, 518.

37 *Tsui-wei lu,* 12, (ts'e 5) 43b, 49ab, 50b, 51a, 52ab; 57b, 58b, 59a, 61b, 62b, 63b, 66b, 68ab, 69a, 72b, 75b, 80a, 81a.

38 Lü Pi 呂毖, *Ming-ch'ao hsiao-shih* 明朝小史, (*Hsüan-lan-t'ang ts'ung-shu* 玄覽堂叢書, Nanking, 1947), 12, (ts'e 91) 11a.

[39] *Tsui-wei lu,* 12, (ts'e 5) 74b.

[40] Ibid., 12, (ts'e 5) 47a, 72b; *Ming-ch'ao hsiao-shih,* 12, (ts'e 91) 13ab.

[41] *Tsui-wei lu,* 12, (ts'e 5) 43b, 63b, 64a, 76b; 81b, 82a, 83a; *Chia-ching i-lai chu-lüeh,* 5, (ts'e 3) 15a.

[42] *Ming-ch'ao hsiao-shih,* 12, (ts'e 91) 11b, 12a.

[43] *Hsi-yüan wen-chien lu,* 105, (ts'e 40) 4a, 16a.

[44] Chou I 周怡, *No-chai tsou-i* 訥齋奏議, (TSCCCP), (ts'e 0,907) 22, 23. 25, 26; *Ming shih,* 226, (ts'e 75) 1a-7a.

[45] *Tsui-wei lu,* 12, (ts'e 5) 63b, 64a.

[46] *Ming shih,* 18, (ts'e 5) 13ab.

[47] *Cho-chung chih,* 17, (ts'e 3,967) 121.

[48] Ibid., 22, (ts'e 3,967) 195.

[49] Lu Jung 陸容 (1436-1494), *Shu-yüan tsa-chi* 菽園雜記, (TSCCCP), 5, (ts'e 0,320) 54.

[50] *Wu-tsung wai-chi,* (ts'e 8) 1680.

[51] The second letter of Ch'ien-yen yüan-ch'ang 千巖元長 to Sung Lien in the *Tzu-lin ch'ih-tu* 緇林尺牘, compiled by Cheng Chi-sun 鄭績孫, (Shanghai, 1934) 44a-45a.

[52] Li Shao-wen 李紹文, *Huang-ming shih-shuo hsin-yü* 皇明世說新語, (1754, Japanese edition) 8, (ts'e 8) 28a.

[53] Liu Jo yü 劉若愚, *Cho-chung chih* 酌中志, (TSCCCP), 22, (ts'e 3967) 195.

[54] *Wu tsa-tsu,* 8, (ts'e 4) 32ab.

[55] *China in the 16th Century,* 100.

[56] Yü Yen 余寅, *Huan li man-chi* 宦歷漫紀 (T'ien-chi (1621-1627) edition), 2, (ts'e 1) 13ab.

[57] *Tsu-lin ch'ih-tu,* 51b.

[58] *China in the 16th Century,* 104.

[59] Sun Ch'eng-tse 孫承澤 (1592-1676), *Ssu-ling chin-cheng chi* 思陵勤政紀, (TSCCCP), (ts'e 3,972) 15

[60] *China in the 16th Century,* 82-83. The *Huang-ming shih-shuo hsin-yü,* 8, (ts'e 8) 8a mentions a certain government official who collected almanacs to the number of one thousand and handed them to the dealers to be sold to the people. We are told that these almanacs were distributed by government offices to the local gentry during the winter. This seems to have been the custom of the time. However, one must not confuse the almanacs (*li-jih* 曆日) with books on astronomy (*t'ien-wen shu* 天文書). The possession of the latter was considered illegal and might involve heavy penalties. A writer who lived in the last period of the Ming dynasty informs us that a certain head of the imperial observatory was sent into exile for having secretly transcribed a copy of the books of astronomy. This writer warned the gentry class to be careful not to lend such books to anyone—it was then quite common for people of this class to possess such books obtained from illegal sources. Cf. Hsü Hsüeh-mo 徐學謨, *Shih-miao chih-yü-lu* 世廟識餘錄, (1608 edition) 2, (ts'e 1) 9a, 10a.

[61] *China in the 16th Century,* 83.

[62] Li Ma-tou 利瑪竇 (Matteo Ricci), *Chi-jen shih-pien* 畸人十篇, (Hong Kong, 1904) 59-64.

[63] *Wu tsa-tsu,* 6, (ts'e 3).

[64] *Chung-hsi chiao-t'ung-shih,* 3, 118-131; *Yüan-shih, ch'uan* 125; *Hsin Yüan-shih, ch'uan* 155; A. E. Moule, *The Chinese People,* (London) 317.

[65] Ch'en Mou-jen 陳懋仁, *Ch'üan-nan tsa-chih* 泉南雜志, (TSCCCP), (ts'e 3) 20-21; As to the nationality of P'u Shou-keng, Kuwabara Jitsuzō 桑原隲藏 was of the opinion that he was of Arab descent, Fang Hao 方豪 held that he came from a noble family of Chan-ch'eng 占城 (Cambodia), cf. Kuwabara, *P'u Shou-keng chih shih-chi* 蒲壽庚之事蹟, (tr. by Ch'en Yü-ch'ing 陳裕菁) (Shanghai, 1929) 111-148; *Chung-hsi chiao-t'ung-shih,* 2, 241-243.

⁶⁶ *Huang-Ming t'ung-chi shu-i*, 2, (ts'e 1) 7a; Ch'en Lien 陳璉, *Ch'in-hsüan chi* 琴軒集, (K'ang-hsi ed.) 25, (ts'e 9) 15a; Hsia Kuang-nan 夏光南, *Yüan tai Yünnan shih-ti ts'ung-k'ao* 元代雲南史地叢考, (Shanghai, 1935) 50–51; 201–204; T'an Ch'ien 談遷 (1594–1657) says in his *Kuo-ch'üeh* 國榷, (Transcriptian from the copy of Tung-fang wen-hua hui 東方文化會, Peking, now in Toyo bunko 東洋文庫, Tokyo, Japan), that in 1381 one hundred and eighty soldiers went under the leadership of a certain Mohammedan, T'ang Ha-san (Hasan) 唐哈散 to hunt for tigers in Ch'ang-te 常德 (Hunan). T'ang, a renowned tiger-hunter, was summoned for this work by the emperor (ts'e 8) 38a. Ten years later (1391), T'ang Ha-san was given the same commission but was sent to Kiang-pei 江北 (ts'e 10) 3b.

⁶⁷ *China in the 16th Century*, 107,

⁶⁸ Huang Hsi-hsien 黃希賢, *Chü-chia pi-yung* 居家必用, (Ming ed) 6, (ts'e 6) 15b–16b.

⁶⁹ *China in the 16th Century*, 107; *Shang-ching i-lan*, B 23a; *Chin-ling so-shih hsü-chi*, (contained in the *Chin-ling chi-shih* mentioned above) A, 43ab.

⁷⁰ *Huang-Ming shih-shuo hsin-yü*, 8, (ts'e 8) 13a,

⁷¹ *Huang-Ming t'ung-chi hsü-pien*, 9, 9b, 10a.

⁷² *Ming t'ung-chien*, 22 (ts'e 2) 42b.

⁷³ Hu Wen-huan 胡文煥, *Hua i feng-tu chih* 華夷風土志, (Ming edition) 2, 1ab; Cheng Ta-yü 鄭大郁, *Ching-kuo hsiung-lüeh* 經國雄略, (ts'e 5) 6b, 1a, where the author quotes from the *Shen-si i* 陝西議 of Ch'en Wo-tzu 陳臥子 i.e. Ch'en Tzu-lung 陳子龍 (1608–1647), who probably quoted the passage from *Hua-yi feng-tu chih*.

⁷⁴ Tai Li 戴笠, *Huai-ling liu-k'ou shih-chung lu* 懷陵流寇始終錄, (other title: *K'ou-shih pien-nien* 寇事編年), (HLTTS second series), (ts'e 5–12), 4, (ts'e 5) 12a; Demitrius Charles Boulger, *A Short History of China* (London, 1900) 116; cf. also Tazaka Kyogi 田坂興義, "Ri Jisei wa kaiyoto ka" 李自成は回教徒か, *Tōhōgaku hō* 東方學報, 12, 2; Mao Ch'i-ling 毛奇齡 (1623–1716), *Hou chien lu* 後鑒錄, (*Sheng-ch'ao i shih* 勝朝遺事), 5, (ts'e 18) 80b; T'an Ch'ien 談遷, *Tsao-lin tsa-tsu* 棗林雜俎, (*Pi-chi hsiao-shuo ta-kuan* second series) (ts'e 88) 3b,

⁷⁵ *Chung-hsi chiao-t'ung shih*, 5, 118; *Ming shih*.

⁷⁶ Pasquale M. d'Elia, S.J., *The Catholic Missions in China*, (Shanghai, 1934) 42.

⁷⁷ Ch'en Yüan 陳垣, *Ming-chi Tien Ch'ien fo-chiao k'ao* 明季滇黔佛教考, (Peking, 1959) 66–67.

⁷⁸ Chu Kuo-cheng 朱國楨 (1557–1632), *Yung-chuang hsiao-pin* 湧幢小品, (PCHSTK), 32, (ts'e 109) 12a.

⁷⁹ *Wu tsa-tsu*, (Shanghai, 1959 edition) A. 120.

⁸⁰ *Tzu-lin ch'ih-tu*, 50b.

⁸¹ Huang Pai-lu 黃伯祿, *Cheng-chiao feng pao* 正教奉褒, (Shanghai, 1904) 11b.

⁸² Wen Ping 文秉 (1609–1669), *Lieh-huang hsiao-chih* 烈皇小識, (*Ming-ch'i pi-shih*, first series) (Shanghai, 1938), 6, (ts'e 1) 123.

⁸³ *Cheng-chiao feng-pao*, 10a–20b; Louis Pfister, S.J., *Notices Biographiques et Bibliographiques sur les Jésuites de l'Ancienne Mission de Chine 1552-1773*, (Shanghai, 1932) I, 164–165.

CHAPTER SIX

Economics

FISCAL ADMINISTRATION

The scholar Hsieh Chao-che surveyed the Mongol invasion and found it a terrible calamity in which the Chinese people either perished by the sword or were led to slavery. He concluded his tale of sorrow with the sad reflection that though a country, however prosperous, can be ruined in a trice, the stabilization of a country after a calamity is anything but an easy task.[1]

Nearly all the founders of dynasties grasped this principle, and on coming to power they devoted their energies to stabilizing the living conditions of the people. The achievement of stability was always followed by a period of prosperity and increasing population. The abandonment of concern for stability was often one of the first indications of the decline of a dynasty. Hence the importance of the study of the economics and financial administration in the history of a dynasty.

When the Hung-wu emperor ascended the throne his first object was to correct the abuses that had flourished under the Mongol government. "Unlike the selfish individual," he would say, "the virtuous man, when he is in a governing position, has before him the ideal of doing what is right. This leads him to act for the good of the country, whereas the selfish man seeks only his own good even at the expense of the welfare of others." For this reason he was always on guard lest his ministers should try to induce him to make unreasonable demands on the people.[2] From the beginning of his reign he tried to reduce the taxes, but the time had long passed when the government could be run at small expense.

The ineptitude of the financial administration had grown steadily more obvious under the Yüan dynasty. This weakness did not indeed originate with the Yüan: it can be traced back even as far as the late T'ang period, but it was especially characteristic of the Yüan dynasty. The Mongol conquests had given the conquerors a vast empire, the administration of which was a perpetual problem. In China alone the territory was immense. The number of soldiers and government officials employed must have been huge; yet the population was not large nor were the people well-off. Little wonder that Marco Polo wrote: "Cublay, the Grand Khan who now reigneth, having heard much of the immense wealth that was in the island [Chipangu, or Japan], formed a plan to get possession of it."[3] We can gain some understanding of the difficulties the Great Khan labored under if we remember that he had to employ ministers such as Ahmad and Lu Shih-yung 盧世榮, who were so unfavorably criticized by Chinese scholars.

The difficulties that had puzzled the Great Khan became overwhelming under his incompetent successors. When the first Ming took over the government he found an empire in financial chaos.

It gives us the measure of the Hung-wu emperor that, despite all difficulties, he succeeded in reorganizing the financial system and thereby laid a solid foundation for his dynasty. By instituting military settlements (see Chapter 3) he solved the problem of maintaining his soldiers and part of the problem presented by the officials' salaries. The "Yellow Records" and the "Fish Scale Records" were established to eliminate the evasion of land taxes. By vigilance and severe punishment he curbed the excesses of corrupt officials. By the end of his reign he had eliminated most of the abuses that had flourished under the Mongol government.

Improvement of financial administration, however, offered little hope of success. The source of the difficulty lay in the established practice of slavishly following old traditions without any understanding of how to adapt them to changing circumstances. If in certain periods the country enjoyed great prosperity this was usually due to the exceptional ability of certain individuals. Prosperity often died away as soon as these experts retired or died. If at times it lingered for a while, this was due chiefly to the maintenance of their policy. With the rise of new obstacles to which these experts' policy was not applicable, prosperity soon waned. The prevailing lack of initiative becomes easy to understand if we remember that the appointment of ministers of the Hu pu 戶部, or Board of Revenue, was regulated by success in examinations in the classics and had no relation to training in the science of economics. Furthermore, these ministers, being Confucians, were usually conservative, enamored of old traditions, and suspicious of novelties.

Among the sources of government revenue the most important throughout succeeding centuries were the land taxes. This was inevitable, since China was primarily a farming country. The rest of the taxes—salt, wine, and tea taxes, customs, etc.—were lumped together as tsa shui 雜稅, or miscellaneous taxes, a title which implied comparative unimportance. In fact, however, they often became of great importance to the government in the later periods of the various dynasties, and especially toward the end of these dynasties, when governments invariably found themselves in severe financial straits. After the revolt of An Lu-shan 安祿山 (killed in A.D. 757), for example, many of the provinces were controlled by military leaders, and the government, deprived of most of the land taxes, had to rely almost completely on miscellaneous taxes. Similarly, under the Sung dynasty (especially towards its end), the rapidly increasing expenditure could not be met from the almost stable land taxes and the miscellaneous taxes became an indispensable source of imperial revenue.

CURRENCY

Before we deal with the revenue of the Ming government it is necessary to make a brief review of the monetary system of the time. Towards the end of the Yüan period when the government was unable to make ends meet, paper money was issued in great quantities. The resulting inflation deprived the paper money of all its value. Copper coins, therefore were minted but their value was never standardized and this proved a serious obstacle to their circulation. Moreover, the quality of these coins was poor and they broke easily.[4]

In order to remedy the inflation introduced by the Mongol government, the Hung-wu emperor decided to reform the monetary system. Even before he ascended the throne he established a mint in Nanking. Later, mints were established in all the provinces and coins of different values were minted. These new coins and those of previous dynasties were used indifferently by the people. By 1374, we hear of the government's issuing paper money once more. The *Ming shih* says that the merchants normally used paper money, finding coins inconvenient.[5] Probably, however, this was not the chief reason for the reissuing of paper money: the same *Ming shih* narrates that "in those days (i.e. before 1374), government officials demanded copper from the people, who had to destroy their utensils and vessels to meet these demands. They resented this."[6] It was probably this shortage of copper that forced the government to issue paper money in 1375. Paper money was used in all business transactions involving more than a hundred coins. It was forbidden to use silver and gold as media of exchange, though the people were allowed to buy paper money with them. For business taxes it was decreed that thirty per cent was to be paid in copper coins and the rest in paper money. Worn-out notes were returned to the government treasury, where new ones were issued.

By 1390, the value of the paper money had fallen greatly. In Chekiang a note of one kuan 貫 was worth only two hundred and fifty copper coins, exactly one fourth of its original value.[7] In spite of the Hung-wu emperor's efforts to stabilize the currency, inflation continued. South of the Yangtze valley the people were said to prefer copper coins to notes, and in 1393, the note of one kuan was worth only one hundred and sixty coins there. New notes were worth fifty per cent more than old ones owing to the merchants' preference for new notes. The tax collectors took advantage of this confusion to make profits for themselves, demanding new notes from the taxpayers but handing in old notes to the treasury. In 1394, it was decided to abolish the use of copper coins. A decree was issued ordering the people to bring all their copper coins to the treasury, where paper money would be issued to them instead. This imperial order, however, produced practically no result. In some provinces, the merchants, having lost all confidence in the currency, tried to fix the price of their goods in terms of silver and gold.[8]

Thus, throughout the Hung-wu reign the monetary system was in an unhappy state. Subsequent emperors tried to maintain the use of paper money. During the Yung-lo reign, a censor diagnosed the cause of the inflation, rightly pointing out that the fundamental mistake lay in the fact that the government had overissued paper money and was not able to redeem its own notes. In accordance with his advice salt-consuming families were asked to pay for their purchases in notes, for it was thought that in this way the government would get back a large number of the depreciated notes. During the Hsüan-te reign the government ordered that an increase of certain taxes should be paid in paper money. All these efforts, however, served only to multiply confusion.

By the 1430's the value of the paper money had fallen to a thousandth of its original value, the lowest point ever reached. The people had clearly lost all confidence in it and nothing remained for the government but to relax the ban on using silver as a medium for business transactions. It should be noted that silver had never been regarded as an important medium by previous dynasties or by earlier Ming emperors. From the 1430's onward, however, it played an important role in the monetary history of China and it may fairly be said that the elevation of silver to an important monetary role was a major event in Ming history. Thenceforth silver was widely employed both by the government and by the people. In the 16th century Wang Shih-cheng 王世貞 (1526-1590) did not hesitate to say that silver was the best of all media for business transactions: it was not bulky, it was durable, and it was not easy to counterfeit.[9]

The *Ming shih* tells us that paper money practically went out of use at the beginning of the Chia-ching reign.[10] By then silver was the principal medium employed among the people. It is probable that when Matteo Ricci came to China at the end of the 16th century paper money was no longer in circulation. In his diary he mentions no form of currency other than copper coins and silver.[11]

Even the minting of coins seems to have met with great difficulties throughout the Ming period. From the beginning of the dynasty the people along the seacoast carried on very active trade with the neighboring countries. Java, for instance, used Chinese coins of different dynasties, and Ceylon is said to have traded again and again with Chinese coins.[12] This explains, in part at least, the shortage of copper coins in China at this period. The Hung-wu emperor, seeing this, forbade the export of coins and of various metals. Under the Yung-lo emperor large quantities of coin were used in horse trading along the borders. In the Northwest alone several tens of millions of coins were lost to China in this way. When appearing at court, ambassadors from Liu Ch'iu 琉球 (the Pescadores), Japan, etc., always asked for coins. In 1459, the T'ien-shun 天順 emperor had to refuse a request of this kind made by the ambassadors of Liu Ch'iu.[13]

REVENUE

The chief source of government income was, as we have said, the land tax. Under the Ming dynasty the area used for farming was far larger than it had been under the Yüan dynasty.

In general, the farms were divided into two classes: kuan-t'ien 官田 or farms owned by the government, and the min-t'ien 民田 or farms in private ownership. The kuan-t'ien were subdivided into four groups: first, there were the kuan-t'ien in Su-chou and Sung-kiang. It is said that when the Hung-wu emperor conquered Chang Shih-ch'eng 張士誠 he confiscated not only all farms belonging to Chang's government but also the farms belonging to well-to-do families who had assisted Chang in his resistance. In 1432 an official estimated that in his locality only one-fifteenth of the land belonged to the farmers; the rest belonged to the government.[14] By 1502 the area of land owned by the government throughout the empire was equal to one-seventh of the area owned by the people. Unscrupulous speculators conspired with the officials and eventually took possession of this government land. Tenants too, taking advantage of the carelessness of the government, secretly transferred government land to their own names and then sold it to the rich. Towards the end of the dynasty a grand secretary was able to say that in Kiang-nan six- or seven-tenths of the well-to-do owned only a hundred mou of land, and three- or four-tenths owned as much as a thousand mou. One or two out of one hundred possessed ten thousand mou of land.[15]

The other three types of government-owned land were land owned by the imperial house, land owned by the princes, and land owned by the nobles, who usually were relatives of empresses or deserving ministers. These farms were either cultivated by hired farm laborers or rented to farmers. Such farms caused a great deal of trouble to the people, as we shall see in detail in later chapters.

The people held their titles to their land either by hereditary possession—i.e. land cultivated by farmers and inherited by their descendants—or by gift from the government, which made them owners of the land on which they had labored. This second way of possessing land was very common among small farmers in the early days of the dynasty when the population was thin and much land lay idle.

Having himself come from a peasant family, the Hung-wu emperor knew only too well how much the farmers had to suffer from the gentry and the wealthy. Many of the latter, relying on their influence with the magistrates, not only encroached without scruple on the land of the farmers but even contrived, by bribing sub-officials, to transfer the burden of taxation to the small farmers they had wronged. The method was simple: the total amount of tax to be paid in their district was divided into small sums and added to the assessment of small farmers. Thus the government got the income it expected, but the small farmers alone paid. Often they were surprised to have to pay such heavy taxes but they paid because they had to pay, without any clear idea of how they were being victimized.

To prevent such abuses the Hung-wu emperor instituted two very important systems, the huang-ts'e 黃冊, or "Yellow Records," and the yü-lin t'u-ts'e 魚鱗圖冊, or "Fish Scale Records," which served to guarantee both the government's income from land taxes and the people's enjoyment of their property.

The emperor is said to have labored for more than twenty years on the immense task of making an accurate census of the population and of the cultivated land of the whole empire. For centuries the making of such a census had been a common ambition, but hitherto no one had succeeded in carrying it out. The Hung-wu emperor, however, threw all his energies into the task and by the end of his reign had achieved his purpose, thus winning high and well-deserved praise from later generations.[16]

The "Yellow Records," sometimes known as fu-i-ts'e 賦役冊 or "records for the levying of taxes and corvée," were among the most valuable of the administrative instruments at the government's disposal. They recorded the domicile of every inhabitant of the empire and were invariably made the basis for the levying of taxes or corvée. The li 里, or village, was taken as the unit in compiling these records. Each li consisted of a hundred and ten families, and the record of each li was compiled in a single volume. Each family, with all its members and its property, was listed in great detail. Every ten years new records were made and the government levied taxes and corvée according to the increase or decrease of the number of individuals or the amount of property in each family. In order to prevent abuses, five copies were made of every volume of records. One copy was kept by the li-chang 里長, or village elder, one was sent to the Board of Revenue, and the other three were kept in the archives of the province, the district, and the prefecture.[17]

The "Fish Scale Records" were diagrams of the lands registered in the yellow records. All the land boundaries within a locality were indicated accurately and the dimensions of these lands, the names of the owners, and the quality of the soil were carefully noted. They differed from the "Yellow Records" in that the latter dealt primarily with families and individuals and took the li as the territorial unit, whereas the "Fish Scale Records" dealt primarily with farms and took the land centering upon a city or suburb as its unit. Their odd name was derived from the fact that the fields as recorded on the diagrams looked like fish scales. They were especially helpful in settling disputes about the measurements and boundaries of lands.[18]

The "Yellow Records" were first put to use in 1381. Six years later (1387) the "Fish Scale Records" were instituted as a check on rich men who were trying to evade taxes by omitting to report the full amount of land they possessed.[19] The Hung-wu emperor's vigilance ensured that the officials were very energetic in carrying out their duties, and while this efficiency lasted the two systems worked very well. But the negligence of later emperors, especially those of the later half of the dynasty, permitted officials and sub-officials to indulge in corruption of all kinds. Like many other excellent institutions devised by the founder of the dynasty, the system of records soon became unworkable, for when abuses arose there was no one to check them.

The land taxes were collected twice a year, in the summer and in the autumn. In general, they were paid in rice, wheat, silk, coins and notes. In the autumn collection wheat was not demanded. In 1393, the cultivated land throughout the country amounted to 8,507,623 ch'ing and 86 mou.[20] No later period of the dynasty was able to exceed this area. Although the Hung-wu emperor before he ascended the throne had fixed the land taxes at one-tenth of total production, the incidence of the tax was not fully determined. As we have seen elsewhere, the land taxes in Su-chou and Sung-kiang were especially heavy.

Ever since the time of the Sung dynasty, farming had been very prosperous in the South and it was particularly prosperous under the Ming dynasty. Even after the transference of the capital to Peking in 1421, during the reign of the Yung-lo emperor, the government still depended on the South for its revenue.

One of the most important causes of the development of farming was water conservancy. The Hung-wu emperor paid special attention to the irrigation of farms all over the empire. Thus in 1394, a number of students from the Kuo-tzu-chien were sent to all the provinces to help in developing irrigation and 40,987 ponds and dikes were dug in various places. In the last year of Hung-wu (1398), 130,000 ch'ing along the Hung Creek (in modern Kiangsu and Anhui) were drained.[21] Most of this development was confined to the South. As late as 1619 a censor reported that "the people of the North do not know the advantage of water conservancy. In consequence, after one year of production, the land which they have cultivated becomes barren and they have to give it up and go elsewhere in the second year. Finally, in the third year there is neither a farm nor a man left in the place." With the permission of the government, therefore, this censor built up a splendid irrigation system from which the northerners benefited greatly.[22]

Linked with the system of land taxes was a *corvée*, which was strictly exacted from the people. Under this service were grouped a large variety of administrative and economic services as well as manual labor. Thus the duties of the liang-chang 糧長, or "tax collector," and the li-chia 里甲, or "village headman," the supplying of horses for the government postal system, the cutting of firewood for the government, the repairing of roads, the drainage of rivers, and many other highly diverse tasks, all ranked as *corvée*. This meant that, in addition to cultivating the land, the farmers had to find time for all these public works. Later, in the 16th century when the I-t'iao-pien fa 一條鞭法 was instituted, the people were exempted from *corvée* but had to pay instead an additional tax so that the government might hire laborers to do the work.[23]

Among the public services demanded by the government, those of the liang-chang and li-chang were perhaps the most important. In the early Hung-wu days when the monarch exempted the landlord class from all other minor public tasks he did not exempt them from these two, for he knew that only members of rich and influential families could fill such posts satisfactorily. The landlord class, however, came to regard both posts as excessive burdens and there was always a tendency to evade them. In later days, when government officials were corrupt, the landlords often succeeded in evading these offices by means of bribes.[24]

Originally, the post of liang-chang was not unpopular. The founder of the Ming dynasty instituted it as a means of maintaining close contact with the people and took care to make it attractive. Distrusting government officials, he wished to receive directly from the people themselves reports on their own lives. Accordingly liang-chang were appointed to collect all the land taxes (paid in kind in those days) and transport them to the capital, Nanking. As this office was important and the responsibility great, the Hung-wu emperor usually chose members of rich and honest families for the task. The liang-chang enjoyed many privileges including that of audience with the emperor. At their audience they would report on the living conditions of the people in their own districts and other matters concerning civil administration. The monarch would listen carefully and ask questions. At the end of the audience the emperor would give them an exhortation and dismiss them with kindness. In this way the Hung-wu emperor was able to get much information about his subjects and his ministers.[25]

Under these favorable circumstances, the office of the liang-chang was aspired to by all. Not only did it give the holder of the office great prestige in his village; if he happened to find favor with the emperor, he might even be appointed a government official.[26]

The li-chia system grew out of the "Yellow Records" system. Originally in 1381 each li consisted of a hundred and ten families. In 1395 it was reduced to one hundred families. These families, again, were grouped in tens to form a chia 甲. A li-chang was appointed as head of each li, and a chia-shou 甲首 as head of each chia. Their duties were to see that the people paid their taxes in due time, to keep order in their localities, to promote knowledge of agriculture, to reward the virtuous, and to warn and punish the bad. Thus, these offices, that of the li-chang in particular, involved to some extent the functions of a civil servant, of a judge, and of a teacher. The term of office of both the li-chang and chia-shou was one year, and each family had to take its turn in regular rotation.[27]

The liang-chang, li-chang, and chia-shou worked in close cooperation in the collection of taxes. Every year in the seventh month every liang-chang traveled to the capital, then Nanking, where he obtained a k'an-ho 勘合, or identification document, from the Board of Revenue. Armed with this he returned to his own district and gave orders to the li-chang to collect land taxes. The li-chang passed on these orders to the chia-shou. When the collection had been completed, it was the duty of the liang-chang to deliver it personally to the government in the capital.

In the later days of the dynasty we sometimes find that the liang-chang's office had been abolished and the vacancy filled by the li-chang. This was an intelligible change. The liang-chang was often a stranger to much of the extensive territory subject to his care and so was unable to check carefully the taxes paid by different individuals. The li-chang, on the other hand, were always natives of the places where they were in charge and did not find it difficult to find out what was going on. Furthermore, since the territories entrusted to the liang-chang were large, it was practically impossible for them to attend to the collection of the often very complex variety of taxes. For the li-chang, the task was easier, since they had less extensive territories to look after and consequently far smaller amounts of tax to collect.

Two points were common to the liang-chang and the li-chang: originally both were appointed from well-to-do families with large households and many acres and both had the duty of collecting land taxes. In other ways the two offices differed widely. The li-chang, a far less important functionary than the liang-chang, received his office as a regular *corvée* assignment whereas the liang-chang's appointment lay outside the ordinary *corvée* routine. The li-chang held office for only one year, and then only every tenth year. The office of liang-chang might be imposed for several years or even for several generations. Furthermore, the duties of the liang-chang were confined to the collection of land taxes; the li-chang had many other assignments.[28]

From the beginning of the 16th century onward the collection of taxes became ever more complicated. Poor farmers who were unable to pay their land taxes often abandoned their land and ran away. As the liang-changs' duties became more difficult to perform, their number was increased, in some places to as many as ten. The problem was not solved until the Chia-ching period (1522–1566) when a new system, known as the I-t'iao-pien fa, was instituted and put into practice. Under this system both the old land taxes paid in kind and the *corvée* gave way to a fixed annual payment in silver. From then onward public works were carried out not by the forced labor of the people but by workmen specially employed by the government. Taxes were levied according to the amount of land each household possessed and not according to the number of persons. This was of great advantage to the poor, who possessed either no land at all or at most a very small patch. One consequence of the change of system was that the collection of land taxes was now carried out by government officials directly. The functions of the liang-chang gradually lost their importance; for, though the office still survived in name, the system from which that importance had derived was no longer the same. Indeed, a liang-chang of the later Ming period was no longer forced to serve personally and could easily commute his service into a money payment.[29]

After the land taxes, the most important source of government income was the salt monopoly. Along the coast salt was produced from sea water; in the interior it was obtained from lakes or wells. The government sold salt to the merchants, who in turn sold it to the people. The salt market was divided into regions and salt produced in one region might not be sold in another. Violators of this law were punished as smugglers. During the Yung-lo reign salt was sold directly to the people in an effort to get back some of the inflated paper money, but later the old middleman system was restored.

Salt rakers, known as yen-ting 鹽丁 or tsao-ting 竈丁, were employed by the government for work in the pits. Each had to deliver to the government a fixed annual quota of salt, in return for which the government paid him a salary. The government then purchased from the salt rakers any salt produced in addition to the quota. All the salt was sold to the merchants, who paid a tax of one twentieth of the price at which they bought the salt and later sold the salt to the public.

The *Hsü wen-hsien t'ung-k'ao* says that the profits of the government salt monopoly were huge and that the revenue derived from it was employed mainly for the upkeep of the troops on the borders, or for relief in times of drought or famine. On exceptional occasions even the salaries of the imperial kinsmen were paid from this source. Sometimes when the government was in need of special articles, salt was given in exchange for them. Thus, in the year 1438 there was a shortage of horses on the Ning-hsia 寧夏 border and permission was granted to trade salt for horses. A hundred yin 引 of salt (each yin being four hundred catties) was offered for a first-class horse and eighty yin for a horse of fairly good quality. Time and again we read also of salt being given in exchange for paper for printing money notes, for iron, cloth, etc.[30]

The tea monopoly came next to the salt monopoly in importance and was exercised in a very similar fashion. In the early years of the Hung-wu emperor, those who possessed tea plantations were taxed one-tenth of their product by the government. When the leaves of the tea plant had been picked the owners could sell them to the government at a fixed price and they were then kept in government stores. Dealers who wished to do business directly with the cultivators had first to obtain from the government a document empowering them to apply to the tea plantations for what they wanted.

From the beginning of the Hung-wu reign the emperor realized how important it was to have good horses for military purposes. Accordingly he tried to develop systematic horse breeding for the government among the people of both northern and southern China. This scheme failed completely, for all these people were completely lacking in the necessary experience and the climate and geography of the interior were altogether unsuitable. Beyond the borders however, it was a different story. There, the climate and the surroundings were ideal, and, more important still, the nomads had for centuries been famous horse breeders. It was the excellence of their horses that had enabled them to win so many victories over the Chinese. If the Chinese could only get horses from them, they would not only have a supply of high-quality horses but would also be able to eliminate the menace of these neighboring tribes. The monarch soon found a means of attaining this end. The nomads, so the *Ming shih* tells us, were fond of butter but had to take tea with it to avoid some physical inconvenience—presumably indigestion. Whether this is true or not, there is no doubt that they drank large quantities of tea, and for tea they were dependent on China. The government was at pains to secure a complete monopoly of the export of tea so that it might trade with the border tribes for horses. Markets were set up in Liao-tung, along the Mongol borders, and in Kansu, Shensi and Szechuan. One hundred and twenty catties of tea were given in exchange for an outstanding horse, seventy catties for a horse of medium quality and fifty for an inferior horse. We are told that by the end of the Hung-wu reign over half a million catties of tea had been used to purchase thirteen thousand five hundred horses.[31]

Commerce was taxed at a rate of about thirty per cent under the Ming dynasty and tax offices were set up in thoroughfares and at city gates. These taxes were paid either in kind or in money, but in the later days of the dynasty chiefly in silver. To begin with, the taxes were simple enough, but as time went on they began to increase and to multiply. Eventually, we are told, the capital and the provincial markets had in all over 400 tax offices. Nearly everything, except agricultural implements and books, was taxed.[32] In 1429, a new tax was levied on ships passing between Nanking and Peking. Most of the stations taxed only the ships, but a few of them taxed the freight also.

EXPENDITURES

Probably the heaviest item of government expenditure was the salaries of officials and imperial relatives. In the early days of the Hung-wu period, when money was scarce, salaries were paid in the form of land. Later rice was given as payment to all the officials: eighty-seven piculs of rice monthly to officials of the first rank and decreasing amounts to lesser officials according to their rank, the lowest officials receiving five piculs of rice monthly. Even under the Hung-wu emperor officials were sometimes paid in paper money. The value of money being still high in his days, a thousand coins or a bill of equivalent value was given in lieu of one picul of rice. Later, when paper money had depreciated considerably, ten such bills were treated as the equivalent of a picul of rice. In the year 1471, the Board of Revenue, because of the lack of paper money, decided to pay salaries in the form of cloth. A bolt of cloth was made equal to two hundred paper bills of a face value of a thousand coins each. By this time, however, each bill was in reality worth only two to three coins, though the Board of Revenue gave only ten such bills in lieu of a picul of rice. The *Ming shih* says that never before in Chinese history had government (real) salaries been so low as under the Ming dynasty.[33]

When the Hung-wu emperor founded his empire he wished to show favor to his family and kinsfolk but he was determined not to entrust to them any share in the administration of the government. He therefore set up a system under which each of the imperial kindred received a pension according to his rank. Thus, in 1376, it was decreed that the annual pension of each of the sons of the emperor was to be 50,000 piculs of rice in addition to gifts of all kinds, including paper money, silk cloth, salt, and, moreover, tea. If these princes wished to build they were supplied with labor and materials. At first when the imperial family was not numerous, this did not seem to involve any problem. But, towards the end of his reign even the first Ming emperor began to see that his pension system was impracticable, for the salaries of the government officials were continually increasing and his kinsmen were becoming numerous. He found it necessary, therefore, to revise the system, cutting the pensions of his sons from 50,000 piculs of rice each to 10,000 piculs and making a considerable reduction in the scale of gifts.

By the middle of the 16th century the descendants of the Hung-wu emperor numbered nearly thirty thousand[34] and the government revenue could not cope with the rapid increase of the imperial clan. In 1562, for instance, the quantity of grain supplied to the capital was four million piculs annually while the pensions for the imperial relatives amounted to eight million five hundred and thirty thousand piculs. In Shansi alone the pension for imperial relatives amounted to two million twelve hundred thousand piculs of rice, while the actual amount of rice in the province was only one million five hundred and twelve thousand piculs.[35] The government therefore had to limit the immediate payment of pensions, promising full payment at an indefinite date.

In time, the support of soldiers became another heavy drain on the revenue. As we have already seen, in the early days of the Ming dynasty the system of military settlements enabled the government to maintain a large army at a low cost. These were instituted throughout the empire and some of the soldiers were employed in cultivating the land. In many places the soldiers were able not only to support themselves but even to provide a surplus for the payment of the salaries of government officials. Along the borders where the population was thin the merchant settlement system was instituted and taxes levied in kind; e.g. rice, wheat, cloth, and hay were sent to the soldiers to make up the deficits of the merchant settlements. By these means the government was able to maintain a strong army without great expense. These systems worked admirably for a time, but by the end of the first half of the dynasty, circumstances had changed, the systems themselves had been altered in many ways, and the time was ripe for a major reorganization.

When Li Min 李敏 became president of the Board of Revenue towards the end of the 15th century, a new system was instituted. As an administrator in Shansi, Li had observed the burden imposed on taxpayers by the obligation of transporting the taxes in kind from Shantung and Honan. The journey was long and the expenses heavy and he realized how difficult it was for the people to carry out this duty. As soon as he became president of the Board of Revenue he commuted these taxes into payments of silver. From then on taxes were paid directly to the local government in silver. The silver collected was sent to the borders as pay for the soldiers.[36] Li Min's innovation seems to have been beneficial, and it certainly was a great convenience to the people.

Li's successor, Yeh Ch'i 葉淇, whom the *Ming shih* describes as an honest and talented man of high character, changed the system of merchant settlements. We have seen that the merchants cultivated the land along the borders and handed over their produce to the government in exchange for salt. For many reasons (which we shall see later) this system became unworkable. The merchants found it very difficult to obtain the promised salt from the government, and they had to wait sometimes even for two to three generations. Naturally they became discouraged and enthusiasm for the merchant settlement system waned. Yeh Ch'i presumably saw the difficulty. Wishing to serve both the interests of the government and the convenience of the people, he asked the merchants to pay taxes in silver, which was to be sent to the soldiers along the border. The rate is said to have been in favor of the government, but the merchants were willing to pay a little more since salt was released to them immediately. In the biography of Yeh Ch'i we are told that his innovation increased the revenue by over one million taels of silver, which in those days was a considerable sum of money.[37]

Yet another heavy drain on the revenue was the expense of the imperial household. The Hung-wu emperor, understanding the people's difficulties, never made exorbitant demands upon them for his own gratification, but his descendants were less considerate. Ultimately their extravagant way of living even brought about the bankruptcy of the empire and the revolt of the people, as we shall see in due course. Imperial donations formed another important item of imperial expenditure. For emperors to make donations to their subjects was nothing new in Chinese history; it was only natural for them to reward the virtuous and to punish the wicked, thus showing their benignity and their care for justice. However, the donations of the Ming emperors seem to have passed all reason. When discussing the functions of the Board of Ceremonies the *Ming hui-tien* gives a list of occasions when donations were demanded. The list is subdivided into donations to officials residing in the capital, donations to officials residing outside the capital, donations to imperial relatives, donations to chiefs of various tribes in the provinces, and donations to foreigners. The occasions were legion. On the accession of a new emperor all the officials in the capital and some soldiers and others received gifts. If tributary messengers happened to be on hand for the occasion, they too partook of the imperial munificence. These gifts included silver, silk, ordinary cloth, paper money, and foodstuffs. The amount received by individuals ranged from sixty taels of silver to a paper note of one hundred kuan 貫 (one kuan equaling 400 copper coins) and three catties of dried fish. Among other great occasions for donations were the compilation of the *Shih-lu* 實錄 or *Acta Imperatorum,* the first lecture on the classics attended by the emperor, the nomination of the prince heir, seasonal festivities, and the offering of sacrifice by the emperor.

Donations were presented to foreigners, sometimes through the benevolence of the emperor, sometimes at the request of the foreigners themselves, and sometimes on the recommendation of the Board of Ceremonies. Donations normally took the form of quantities of silk. Beneficiaries living in certain tributary countries in which Chinese culture prevailed—Korea, for instance—often received Chinese books and musical instruments. Mongols sometimes received Tibetan Buddhist scriptures. Those who brought tribute to the emperor received gifts which varied in value according to the value of the tribute. Even ambassadors received gifts in this way. Before they left the capital the tribute-bearers were allowed to hold a market for three days in the Hui-t'ung-kuan 會同館, or guest house, to sell any goods they had brought with them from their native lands. Often such sales were exempted from taxation. The tribute-bearers were also permitted to buy limited amounts of Chinese native products to bring home. Seemingly these privileges were highly profitable. Time and again foreign traders wishing to enjoy them came disguised as ambassadors, a stratagem that usually met with success.[38]

Donations, which went on unceasingly throughout the year, inevitably absorbed huge amounts of money. By the end of the

Ching-t'ai period (1450–1456), according to Wang Ch'i 王圻 (fl. 1565), the imperial donations had almost emptied the ten caves used for storing gold in the imperial treasury. In 1581, on the occasion of the birth of a princess, the Wan-li emperor, perhaps the most extravagant of all the Ming emperors, demanded two hundred thousand taels of silver each from the t'ai-ts'ang 太倉 and the Kuang-lu-ssu 光祿寺 for the purpose of making donations to his subjects. Seven years later, in 1588, two hundred thousand taels of silver were again demanded from the t'ai-ts'ang. These raids on the public funds were the result, we are told, of the exhaustion of the imperial treasury owing to the incessant donations. On both occasions the officials did what they could to check the emperor's unreasonable demands, but to no avail.[39]

We end this chapter with a consideration of relief work in the Ming period, a subject highly pertinent to any discussion of the finances of the government. From the very beginning of the dynasty relief work was taken seriously by the emperors. In 1385 the Hung-wu emperor issued a decree to the effect that if officials failed to report calamities occurring in the districts they governed, the gentry of those places might send to the government joint reports setting forth the facts. The government then would take severe measures against the officials responsible. In 1393 an order was issued to all magistrates throughout the empire that in case of famine they were to give relief to the people without delay, even before reporting to the imperial government. In 1426, shortly after the accession of the Hsüan-te emperor, a famine occurred in Lung-ping 隆平 (in modern Hopei province). When the Board of Revenue petitioned for permission to lend wheat to those in need, the emperor replied "Why try to lend it? Can you not give it free?" This imperial wish was carried out.[40]

Relief can be divided into two categories: relief of sufferings caused by natural calamities such as fire, floods caused by excessive rain or the breaking of dikes, famine, drought, locusts, and plagues; and relief of suffering caused by human perversity—chiefly banditry and war. In addition to such exceptional sufferers, there were the poor who had nowhere to go and for whom the government had to build places of refuge. As early as 1372, the Hung-wu emperor ordered that asylums known as yang-chi-yüan 養濟院 be built throughout the empire.[41] In the year 1457, the emperor Ying-tsung ordered the building of two such asylums in Ta-hsing 大興 and Wan-p'ing 宛平 (in modern Hopei province). In 1466, upon the petition of the president of the Board of Ceremonies, the poor of the capital who were registered under the Board of Revenue were put into the yang-chi-yüan, which had been built in Peking for them only. Those who were registered under the Board of Military Affairs or were not registered under either board were put in the Fan-kan 旛竿 and La-chu 蠟燭 temples. According to a report made by the Board of Revenue for the year 1480, the number of destitute in Ta-hsing and Wan-p'ing was over 7,490 and the amount of grain provided for them was over 26,900 piculs.[42]

The *Ming shih* gives the rule for distributing rice to the people in want, and states that in the beginning of the dynasty six bushels of rice were given to each adult. Children over five years of age received three bushels. Children of five and under received no rice. In his biography, the Hung-wu emperor is said to have issued in 1386 an order that all poor widows, widowers, and orphans who were unable to earn their living should each receive six piculs of rice yearly. The aged poor were given five bushels of rice, three catties of wine, and five catties of meat monthly, when over eighty, and were to receive in addition one bolt of cloth and one catty of cotton yearly when over ninety. Those who owned farms were not to receive rice.[43] In the reign of the Yung-lo emperor the amount given in relief was curtailed. When a flood occurred in Su-chou and Sung-kiang in 1404, relief was given to the destitute as follows: to adults a bushel of rice; to children aged six to fourteen one-sixth of a bushel, to children under six nothing. In 1550, when the Mongols invaded Shansi, the capital was inundated with refugees and the emperor ordered the distribution of relief. Each of the poor received a mat and a sheng 升 (one tenth of a bushel) of rice.[44]

In addition to its relief work the government had to face the problem of buying back children who had been sold during famines or other calamities, for the law forbidding the sale and purchase of innocent people as slaves had never been scrupulously observed, least of all in time of famine. The *Hsü wen-hsien t'ung-k'ao* records several instances. Thus, in 1386, the Hung-wu emperor ordered the ransoming of children who had been sold by their parents during a famine in Honan province. In the eighteenth year of the Yung-lo reign (1420), a great flood devastated several provinces along the Yangtze River. Many of the people, and even many soldiers, having lost everything they possessed, were unable to support their families and as a last resort sold their children. When the Yung-lo emperor heard what was happening, he ordered the local magistrates to ransom the children and restore them to their parents.[45] However, not all such tragedies ended so happily. In places where most of the population were in need it was hard to find anyone willing even to take in the children free, much less to buy them. Under such circumstances parents were forced to abandon their own children and it was difficult for the government to find any way of coping with the problem. In 1529 an order was issued to the effect that whoever was willing to take in one of these abandoned children would be given a sheng of rice per day.[46]

Since calamities were numerous in the Ming period the sum spent by the government on relief work must have been immense. Indeed if it had had to draw on the treasury for all that it needed for this purpose the whole system might have broken down. Thanks, however, to the founder of the dynasty, the provident store system, known as yü-pei ts'ang 預備倉, had been instituted by the government and organized partly by the government and partly by the people themselves. We are told by the *Ming hui-tien* that, at the beginning of his reign, the Hung-wu emperor ordered all the provinces to have provident stores built, four in each province. It was the duty of the local magistrates to fill them with grain, and elders of good moral standing were appointed to take charge of them. Whenever a famine occurred, grain from the appropriate store was used to relieve the needs of the sufferers. In 1490 it was laid down that magistrates should store fifteen thousand piculs of rice in every ten li. Similarly, to meet the needs of soldiers in time of famine, each chien-hu-so 千戶所 was to store fifteen hundred piculs of rice, and every pai-hu-so 百戶所 three hundred piculs.[47]

The people were also encouraged to contribute grain to the provident stores. Those who did so received a testimonial of honor, and might be employed as sub-officials, or even as minor officeholders in the government. Furthermore, the local magistrates were allowed to use certain types of taxes for buying grain to be kept in the provident stores.

In the year 1529, permission was given to the provinces to establish provident stores organized by the people themselves. In certain chosen localities the people were divided for this purpose into groups of twenty to thirty families, with a man of honest family and of good personal moral standing at the head of each group. Meetings were held twice a month. Each family made a donation of rice according to its status, well-to-do families giving four bushels, middle-class families two bushels, and lower class families one bushel. In time of famine all the stores were opened and put at the disposal of the people. The well-to-do, whose need was of course merely temporary, might borrow from the stores on condition of paying back in kind.

The middle and lower classes, however, received what they needed without any obligation of repayment.[48]

Various other means were used by the government to collect the food or money needed in time of calamity. Thus goods confiscated by the government were sold at the end of each year and the money so gained was used as a fund for the provident stores. In 1450 the government demanded rice from the merchants in several of the prefectures in Chih-li in exchange for salt, and this rice, we are told, was kept for relief purposes. This was not an innovation. From the earliest days of the dynasty the merchants from time to time had had to give rice in exchange for salt, partly for the support of the soldiers on the borders and partly for relief. The government moreover tried in every way to help the poor in times of calamity, and exhorted the well-to-do classes to exempt the poor from payment of rent and to lend grain. The government itself used to allow the people to fish in lakes and to hunt or collect firewood in places which were ordinarily forbidden to them.[49]

NOTES

[1] *Wu tsa-tsu,* 4, (ts'e 2) 33a–34b.

[2] *Jih-chih-lu chi-shih,* 12, (ts'e 5) 9–10,

[3] *Travels of Maro Polo,* 2, 255.

[4] Wu Han, *Tu-shih cha-chi,* 303; cf. T'an Ch'ien 談遷 *Kuo ch'üeh,* Transcription now in Toyo Bunko (ts'e 13) 94b.

[5] *Ming Shih,* 81, (ts'e 28) 1b.

[6] Ibid.

[7] *Ming ta-tsu shih-lu,* 205. This is quoted from *Tu-shih cha-chi,* 305,

[8] *Tu-shih cha-chi,* 305–306.

[9] *Tu-shih cha-chi,* 301; *Chung-kuo kuo-pi shih,* B, 462; *Kuo ch'üeh,* (ts'e 7) 28b,

[10] *Ming Shih,* 81, (ts'e 28) 5b,

[11] *China in the 16th Century,* 14,

[12] Ma Huan 馬歡, *Ying-yai sheng-lan* 瀛涯勝覽, (*Chi-lu hui-pien* 紀錄彙編, photographic-reproduction by the Commercial Press), 63 (ts'e 20) 6a; 7a; 14a.

[13] *Hsü wen-hsien t'ung-k'ao,* 11, (ts'e 2) 2868.

[14] Ibid , 2, (ts'e 2) 2788.

[15] Ibid , 2, (ts'e 2) 2791; *Ming Shih,* 251, (ts'e 83) 10a.

[16] Wu Han 吳晗, *Chu Yüan-chang chuan* 朱元璋傳, (1949, Kirin) 138.

[17] Liang Fang-chung 梁方仲, "*I-t'iao-pien fa*" 一條鞭法, *Chung-kuo chin-tai ching-chi-shih yen-chiu chi-k'an* 中國近代經濟史研究集刊, 4, (May 1936) 1, 9.

[18] Ibid.

[19] Liang Fang-chung 梁方仲, "*Ming-tai huang-ts'e k'ao*" 明代黃冊考, *Ling-nan hsüeh-pao* 嶺南學報, 10, (June 1950) 2, 145–172.

[20] *Hsü wen-hsien t'ung-k'ao*, 2, (ts'e 2) 2787.

[21] *Ming hui-yao*, 53, (ts'e 2) 994. One chang 丈 is equivalent to ten Chinese feet. One Chinese foot (ch'ih 尺) equals 0.3581 metres.

[22] Ibid., 999.

[23] Liang Fang-chung 梁方仲, "*I-t'iao-pien fa*" 一條鞭法, *Chung-kuo-chin-tai ching-chi-shih yen-chiu chi-k'an* 中國近代經濟史研究集刊, 4, (May 1936) 1, 21–22.

[24] Ibid., 10–15.

[25] Liang Fang-chung 梁方仲, "*Ming-tai liang-chang chih-tu*" 明代糧長制度, *Chung-kuo she-hui ching-chi-shih chi-k'an* 中國社會經濟史集刊, 7, (July, 1946) 2. 107–133.

[26] Liang Fang-chung 梁方仲, *Ming-tai liang-chang chih-tu* 明代糧長制度, (Shanghai, 1957) 1–6.

[27] Chu Tzu-shuang 朱子爽, *Chung-kuo hsien-chih shih-kang* 中國縣制史綱, (Chungking, 1942) pp. 54–55.

[28] *Ming-tai liang-chang chih-tu*, 86–88.

[29] The authorities are not in agreement on the date of the origin of this system. According to Shimizu Taiji's long investigation, the system was first mentioned in 1529 in Kuangtung Province, although not yet under the name of *I-t'iao-pien*. This name was given by P'ang Shang-p'eng 龐尚鵬 in the last year of the Chia-ching reign (1566), and it became common throughout the empire in the 9th year of Wan-li (1581), cf. Shimizu Taiji, *Chukoku kinsei shakai keizaishi* 中國近世社會經濟史, (Tokyo, 1950); Id, "Ichi to ben ho" 一條鞭法, *Kuwabara hakase kanreki kinen tōyōshi ronsō* 桑原博士還曆記念東洋史論叢, (Kyoto, 1931). For the origin of the title "*I-t'iao-pien fa*" cf. Liang Fang-chung, "*I-t'iao-pien fa*", 21–22.

[30] *Hsü wen-hsien t'ung-k'ao*, 20, (ts'e 2) 2960, 2961, 2963.

[31] *Ming shih*, 80, (ts'e 28) 28a; *Ming hui-yao*, 62, (ts'e 2) 1207–1208. The *Huang-ming t'ung-chi shu i*, 2, (ts'e 1) 26a, mentions a report of the Board of Revenue which said that in 1372 there were 477 places where a certain kind of tea known as pa ch'a 巴茶 was cultivated in Szechuan, and that these places were owned by 315 tea cultivators. It was estimated that if the government imposed a tax in kind of one tenth on the total crop, the yield would come to about 9,280 catties annually. This tax was approved by the emperor and we are told that tea was stored by the government who used it to exchange horses with the tribes along the border.

[32] *Ming shih*, 81, (ts'e 28) 15b, 16a

[33] *Ming shih*, 82, (ts'e 29) 15a–16b; *Erh-shih-erh shih cha-chi*, 32, (ts'e 6) 12ab.

[34] *Ming hui-tien*, 4, (ts'e 1) 61, 62. Cheng Hsiao 鄭曉, who also was a contemporary, gave the number as nearly 50,000, and Lu Chi 陸楫, went so far as to put it near 100,000. However, we prefer the figure we quote, since it is mentioned by several government officials in official reports.

[35] *Hsü wen-hsien t'ung-k'ao*, 53, (ts'e 2) 3376.

[36] *Ming shih*, 85, (ts'e 61) 1b–2a.

[37] *Ming shih*, 85, (ts'e 61) 3ab. Historians often blamed Yeh Ch'i for his innovation, arguing that it led the merchants to rest satisfied with paying taxes in silver and so to give up the merchant settlements. In consequence, they said, the land along the borders was not cultivated, food became scarce and the transportation of food difficult, cost of living soared. Yeh Ch'i was made responsible for all this. Some in an effort to analyse his motives said that Yeh, a native of Huai-an 淮安 (in modern Kiangsu province), a kinsman or a friend of most of the salt merchants, wished to favor them. Cf. *Hsü wen-hsien t'ung-k'ao*, 20, (ts'e 2) 2664; *Ming shih*, 80, (ts'e 28) 9; *Yeh-chi meng-sou*, 8, (ts'e 4) 11b, 12a. Hsü Ch'ung-hsi 許重熙, author of the *Chia-ching i-lai chu-lüeh* 嘉靖以來注略, 2, (ts'e 1) 3ab, did not mention Yeh Ch'i by name, but he certainly regarded the decay of the merchant settlement system as disastrous to the defense of the border. After that change, he said, a picul of rice cost five silver taels. The *Ming hui-yao* quotes from the *T'ung-chien kang-mu san-pien*

fa-ming 通鑑綱目三編發明, one of the very few authorities who tried to justify the action of Yeh Ch'i. The defense seems reasonable. The author says first that the Ming government's neglect of the cultivation of the land along the border was the main cause of the failure of the merchant settlement system. Next, he blames the greedy nobles who tried to monopolize the sale of salt and so caused serious losses to the merchants, who seeing that the merchant settlements were no longer profitable naturally gave them up. Hence Yeh Ch'i was not to blame. In fact his innovation was designed a substitute for an already vanishing system. His intention was to maintain the interest of the merchants and thus indirectly to increase the amount of taxes. In this he succeeded, for, the merchants did support his system and the government did increase its revenue as a result. (Cf. *Ming hui-yao*, 50, (ts'e 2) 1053–1054).

[38] *Ming hui-tien*, 110–113, (ts'e 21, 22) 2351–2390.

[39] *Hsü wen-hsien t'ung-k'ao*, 30, (ts'e 1) 3083, 3087.

[40] Ibid., 32, (ts'e 1) 3122.

[41] *Ming hui-yao*, 51, (ts'e 2) 959.

[42] Ibid., 51, (ts'e 2) 960; *Ming shih*, 78, (ts'e 27) 18a.

[43] *Ming shih*, 78, (ts'e 27) 18a.

[44] *Ming hui-tien*, 17, (ts'e 5) 468, 471.

[45] *Hsü wen-hsien t'ung k'ao*, 32, (ts'e 1) 3121.

[46] Ibid., 32, (ts'e 1) 3120, *Ming shih*, 78, (ts'e 27) 18a.

[47] *Ming hui-tien*, 22, (ts'e 6) 606, 608.

[48] Ibid., 22, (ts'e 6) 607, 609, 610.

[49] *Hsü wen-hsien t'ung k'ao*, 32, (ts'e 2) 3122; *Ming shih*, 78, (ts'e 27) 17b, 18a.

CHAPTER SEVEN

Government

IMPERIAL ADMINISTRATION

The author of the *Huang-ming t'ung-chi* describes a temple in Nanking dedicated to the emperors of all the dynasties: every year a sacrifice was offered to these emperors conjointly, and a cup of wine was offered before the tablet of each emperor. When the Hung-wu emperor, the author says, saw the tablet of the founder of the Han dynasty during a visit to this temple, he went to it and spoke smilingly. "Mr. Liu," said he, "I notice that all others here already had some influence when they set out to conquer the empire. You and I are exceptions. We possessed not an inch of ground but had to rely on our own swords. The conquest we made was certainly more difficult than that of any of the others." He then ordered three cups of wine to be set in front of the tablet of Han kao-tsu and this order remained in force from then onwards.[1]

As this story shows clearly, the Hung-wu emperor had great admiration for the founder of the Han dynasty, and the scholar Chao I pointed to several occasions on which the Hung-wu emperor deliberately followed the example of Han kao-tsu.[2] Nevertheless the Hung-wu emperor also saw the weaknesses of the Han dynasty and sought to guard his own dynasty against any repetition of them.

Although of peasant origin, the Hung-wu emperor acquired considerable learning. Guided by the old Chinese saying that the present is a reflection of the past, he took great interest in the study of history and was able to discuss historical questions intelligently with his ministers. On one occasion when speaking of two historical figures, he preferred King Chuang of Ch'u 楚莊王 to Duke Wu of Wei 魏武侯 because the former had been troubled to see his ministers less good than himself, whereas the latter rejoiced in the same circumstances. This ancedote illustrates not only the emperor's knowledge of history but also his opinion of his ministers.[3]

He used history as "a mirror" in which to examine the establishment of governmental institutions. It was this practical study of history that led him to preclude, from the very beginning of his reign, all interference by dowagers and their relatives in affairs of state. He left a strict order to his successors that empresses and imperial concubines should be chosen from the common people and that, though their relatives should be given honors, they were not, under any circumstances, to be given any power in the government. The palace ladies too were forbidden to interfere in matters of government and care was to be taken to segregate them from the outside world. Even the more insidious problem of the eunuchs was foreseen by the Hung-wu emperor who confined them to strictly domestic matters and did not allow them even to discuss politics or to communicate with court ministers. If the eunuchs came in fact to control the government in later periods, this was the fault not of the Hung-wu emperor but of his descendants who neglected his precepts.

The Hung-wu emperor's historical studies also taught him that the Sung dynasty had been weakened by its distrust of the military men and its employment of scholars in their place. Yet he himself had little confidence in his generals and he believed that security was to be found only by strengthening his own family. All his twenty-six sons, except the prince-heir, were given territories in the provinces and some of them, especially those whose territories lay along the frontier, were given strong armies. Although these princes were forbidden to interfere in the policy of the government, in their own territories they lived like little kings.

When establishing his sons as provincial princes, the emperor secretly believed that he was safeguarding the position of his grandson, for with all his sons far away from the capital there would be less danger of an ambitious prince's claiming the throne. This hope, however, was to prove fallacious. Not long after the Hung-wu emperor's death one of the princes revolted against his emperor-nephew, usurped his throne and set himself up as the Yung-lo emperor.[4]

Taught by his own successful treason, the new emperor recognized the danger of leaving too much power in the hands of the princes. Accordingly he stripped them of all military influence and imposed strict precepts on them, forbidding them to leave their territory without explicit leave of the emperor, even for such pious purposes as visiting the ancestral tombs. This restriction was so all embracing that they were not allowed to come to the rescue even of the emperor's own person from imminent danger unless he himself had so ordered them.[5]

The Yung-lo emperor, being a warrior, was able to maintain the foreign policy of his father. Under his rule Annam was absorbed into the empire and Cheng Ho's expeditions brought back to subjection a number of small tributary countries in the South Seas. The emperor in person led several campaigns against the Mongol invaders, and died on his way back from one of these expeditions. His vigorous policy died with him. His successors attached little importance to foreign affairs and this eventually led to the deterioration of the army. Annam regained its independence (1427) twenty years after its subjection, and in the north the Mongols quickly regained their strength. In 1449 a Mongol army defeated and captured the emperor Ying-tsung. Later, under the Chia-ching emperor, the capital itself nearly fell into the hands of the Mongols. At that same time the Japanese pirates were raging along the coast—a front so extensive that it was scarcely within the power of the government to guard it. Next, the Japanese under the leadership of Hideyoshi set out to conquer China. Both financially and militarily the Chinese suffered severely and it might have gone hard with the Ming dynasty had not Hideyoshi died in 1598. After his death the Japanese withdrew from Korea and the Chinese empire was relieved of this menace. But by this time there had begun to the north of Korea the rise of a tribe, descended from the Chin dynasty, which was to set up the Ch'ing dynasty in China in the middle of the 17th century. This tribe very rapidly extended its power as far as Shan-hai-kuan. Like an aged invalid exhausted by disease, the Ming government no longer had the vitality to face this last enemy and the helpless empire yielded to its conqueror.

Such, in brief, is the history of foreign relations under the Ming dynasty. Now, let us try to form a picture of the internal policy of the dynasty.

When the Yung-lo emperor usurped the throne of his nephew he was fully aware that many of the ministers disapproved of his action and were therefore unfriendly toward him. For this reason he preferred to entrust to the eunuchs a large share of the business of government, despite his father's severe prohibition against employing eunuchs for such purposes. In the first part of the reign of the emperor Ying-tsung (1436–1449), then the Cheng-tung emperor, the evil influence of the eunuchs began to make itself felt. It was the chief eunuch Wang Chen who persuaded that emperor to embark on the ill-fated expedition against the Mongols which led to the captivity of the emperor himself and the disastrous defeat of the Chinese army. After some negotiation the emperor had the good fortune to be brought home alive and eventually to regain the throne, changing the style of his interrupted reign to T'ien-shun. Yet he returned only to witness the revolt of the eunuch Ts'ao Chi-hsiang 曹吉祥. His successor, the Ch'eng-hua emperor, was no better as a ruler than his father had been. During his reign the power of the government was in the hands of the eunuchs and their party, with Wang Chih 汪直 as their leader. A reform took place in the succeeding reign, that of the Hung-chih emperor who was a more conscientious ruler. But he was succeeded in turn by the extravagant and pleasure-seeking Cheng-te emperor, whose neglect of government allowed the notorious eunuch Liu Chin 劉瑾 to usurp the power of the throne. This unlawful despot even took into his own hands the punishment of government officials, and once, on suspicion that some of the ministers had denounced him in an anonymous letter, obliged over three hundred of them to kneel before the imperial palace for half a day before sending them to prison.[6]

The decline of the empire became more obvious in the second half of the Ming period. Most of the emperors lived in retirement and supreme power fell sometimes into the hands of the all-powerful officials, sometimes into the hands of the eunuchs. To complicate matters still further there was strife among the ministers, much to the profit of the eunuchs. This unhappy state of things lasted till the end of the dynasty.

When the Chia-ching emperor succeeded his cousin on the throne at the beginning of the 16th century he showed himself a youth of talent and energy. These qualities never deserted him, and throughout his long reign (1522–1566), he was able to keep the eunuchs in check. Unfortunately soon after his accession to the throne he became, as we have seen, extravagantly attached to the Taoist religion, spent most of his time in religious ceremonies and made the quest of immortality the ruling passion of his life. Gradually the power of the government fell into the hands of the Grand Secretary Yen Sung 嚴嵩 a shrewd but unscrupulous man, under whom the administration deteriorated sadly. Only on his death bed did the emperor realize his own mistakes but by then it was too late to repair them. His successor's reign was too short to allow of any real reform and by the time the Wan-li emperor came to the throne in 1573, at the age of ten, the country was already in a precarious condition. The little boy emperor had the good fortune to have had a very capable tutor and Grand Secretary, Chang Chü-cheng 張居正, to guide and assist him. Under Chang's influence the country became prosperous once more; but after his death in 1582, the Wan-li emperor himself took the government into his own hands and showed himself probably the greediest and most selfish of all the emperors of the Ming dynasty. The eunuchs, quick to take advantage of the emperor's manifold weaknesses, offered their services, promising to help him to become rich. While they went around the country exacting from both rich and poor all that they could get, the emperor stayed in his palace refusing to interview any of his ministers, or to listen to their advice. Taxes of all kinds were levied and the country suffered almost complete financial exhaustion. Harmful though it was, the power of the eunuchs grew unchecked throughout the Wan-li emperor's reign and reached its zenith in the reign of the T'ien-ch'i emperor who succeeded him after a brief interval. The reign of this monarch lasted only seven years but they were years of disaster, characterized by the complete control of the government by the chief eunuch Wei Chung-hsien 魏忠賢 and his faction. To counteract the baleful influence of the eunuchs and to secure the triumph of justice, government officials and scholars all over the empire banded together in a movement known as the Tung-lin 東林 Party from the name of an ancient hall in which it was known to have started. Unfortunately dissension sprang up among the scholars and they fought among themselves, much to the delight of the eunuchs. Thus, when the Ch'ung-chen emperor succeeded his brother in 1628, the country was in a state of utter chaos. The Manchus, so strong that they were no longer subject to the Ming government, were advancing steadily towards Shan-hai-kuan, a strategic point in the empire. Within the empire revolts occurred everywhere. Officials of talent and integrity found no favor with the emperor and the wicked were in control of all government affairs. Corruption became so common among the ministers that the emperor, suspicious by nature, would not trust any of them. Most of the confidential posts were given to the eunuchs, who, when the time came, did not hesitate to betray their master and the once glorious empire which he represented.

Why did this great empire fall? Where did the main weakness lie? In the system? In the concentration of authority? In the abuse of power? Or, did the cause of fall lie in the very prosperity of the empire and the corruption that waxed strong under the protection of prosperity and apparent security?

It is clear that the Hung-wu emperor laid a solid foundation for the dynasty. He had conquered all his rivals and restored order in the country. He had built up a large army along the borders to prevent future invasions. He had so curbed the power of the military officials that they were under the control of the government. He had reorganized the system of administration and revived the economic prosperity of the country. He showed outstanding vigilance in repressing corruption among the officials and abuses among the landlords. These were remarkable achievements. The Ch'ing dynasty when it succeeded the Ming, derived much of its administrative system from the institutions of the Hung-wu emperor. The decline of the Ming dynasty, therefore, cannot be attributed to the system of administration established by its founder. In so far as the decline was due to administrative weaknesses, these are to be found in the abuses and the negligence of later rulers and their ministers, not in the system as it was originally set up. The changing methods of employing officials give a good example of how incompetent execution ruined an admirable system. The Hung-wu emperor used to give high positions to the Kuo-tzu-chien students, who were both well trained academically and well trained in the business of government administration. After the time of the Hung-wu emperor the tendency was to give preference to licentiates and in time this became the fixed practice. Under the emperor Ying-tsung all the Grand Secretaries were appointed from among the licentiates.[7] Scholars aiming at high government position spent most of their time in the exclusive study of the eight-legged essays, since this was the only way to obtain the licentiate. Ch'iu Chün (1418–1495) was horrified to find that scholars who had passed the examinations were ignorant of the titles of the dynastic histories, and that they were not able to enumerate the dynasties in order or to give the correct formation of different characters. Ku Yen-wu 顧炎武 speaks of the superficiality of the scholars of his time, saying that, though scholars, they did not necessarily possess a solid knowledge of the classics. To gain the licentiate they had only to memorize an extensive selection of essays and try to put them down on paper at the examinations. Often they owed their passes to mere luck.[8]

In a little book entitled *Ming-yi tai fang lu* 明夷待訪錄, written in 1662, the scholar Huang Tsung-hsi 黃宗羲 discussed various problems that beset a government institution, diligently applying his well-thought out political philosophy to the political institutions of the

Ming government. Time and again his views may seem idealistic, yet they are in general sound and firmly based on historical facts. Huang Tsung-hsi's political thought is that of a man of originality. He stressed the importance of the condition of the people and used to say that good is distinguished from bad not by the prosperity or decline of a dynasty but rather by the happiness or suffering of the people. To him the emperor and his ministers, as rulers, were men strictly bound to care for the welfare of the people. Between the emperor and his ministers there was a difference of dignity, but not of grade. "The empire is so extensive," he said, "that no one man can govern alone, hence the ruling power must be shared with others." Similarly an official in an administrative position in the government was in reality working not for the person of the emperor or for his family, but rather for the welfare of the people.[9]

Having explained this principle, Huang Tsung-hsi applies it to an analysis of the history of the Ming government. The great mistake of the Ming dynasty was committed, he held, when the founder himself abolished the office of Prime Minister. Since the days of the Ch'in dynasty the prime minister had stood at the head of all the government officials and had acted in the name of the emperor. It was his duty not only to assist the emperor but also to check him if ever he tended to act wrongly. When the Hung-wu emperor abolished the office of the Prime Minister in 1380 he absorbed these powers. The emperor became absolute head of the government and all the ministers were directly subject to him. This in turn led to dictator-ship: the emperor could confidently say *l'état c'est moi*, without fear of contradiction from any of his ministers. He could now look down on them and make them tremble before him. The officials were crushed, the power they had once exercised passed to their master, and they became mere instruments of the emperor instead of collaborators. The emperor was no longer forced to think of the good of the people, and the people were enslaved under the arbitrary rule of an individual and his family.

Such were the unfortunate consequences of the abolition of the office of Prime Minister in 1380. The Six Boards of the government, formerly subject to the Prime Minister, were put directly under the authority of the emperor. Huang Tsung-hsi regarded this as a cardinal error. In ancient times, he says, the throne was not hereditary: each emperor handed on his power to another virtuous man. Later the practice of leaving the throne to a prince heir was introduced, but a prime minister (whose office was not hereditary) was appointed to assist him. If the emperor was not virtuous, at least a good prime minister could be appointed to help him. To do away with the office of the Prime Minister was to introduce a terrible risk; if a man of bad character became emperor no one now was in a position to check him.

However, so long as the Hung-wu emperor remained in power, the machine of government ran smoothly if ruthlessly. He was a man endowed with sagacity and common sense and based most of his actions on his own experience. His success, moreover, was won by personal hard work. His remarkable achievement in strengthening the government where it was weak and eliminating undersirable practices and persons had involved immense labor and this labor was shared with no one.

The emperor had subordinates in large numbers, but he would have no collaborators. A new dynasty, coming to power by force in a time of tumult, could not tolerate the possible rivalry of great military lieutenants. Yet the emperor both disliked and distrusted the scholars. His only resource was to strengthen his own family. He had twenty-six sons, and most of these he entrusted with military power and sent them off to guard the frontier of the empire. Yet this did not solve all his problems. He needed more men to help him rule a vast country and he had to turn perforce to the scholars who, much as he disliked them, were strongly favored by Chinese tradition. His plan, therefore, was to get rid of most of the military men who had followed him so faithfully in the early days of his career and to keep the indispensable scholars in a state of abject dependence. Toward the end of his reign there was hardly anyone left in the court who could be called a real expert in warfare. The ministers were kept directly under his authority and were frequently beaten in public—some of them dying as a result of such beating. We are told that officials going to court in the morning used to say farewell to their families as if they did not expect to return alive. If they came home safely the whole family would rejoice and congratulate one another. Such was their fear of the emperor.[10]

The first few successors of the Hung-wu emperor carried out their duties conscientiously and ruled as wisely as their abilities allowed. They frequently consulted their ministers on matters of government, though always reserving the decision to themselves. However, as time went on, the emperors began to take less interest in government and to lose that contact with the empire at large which had been one of the chief strengths of the Hung-wu emperor. Being unfamiliar with the outside world they tended to evade their duties and to leave everything in the hands of their ministers, especially the Grand Secretary. Under the Hsüan-te emperor, for the first time the Grand

Secretary was authorized to read all memorials to the throne and to attach to each of them a slip of paper giving a brief summary of the contents. The emperor would then read through these summaries and make his decisions, consulting his ministers if necessary. Later still, even this perfunctory inspection was abandoned by the emperors, and decisions were often made by the chief eunuchs to whom authority was supposed to have been delegated by the emperors.[11]

Several emperors became so negligent that for long periods they would not even interview any of their ministers. A barrier had grown up between the emperor and his ministers and to break through it the help of the eunuchs was necessary. The eunuchs, who could move freely on either side of the barriers, knew exactly what was happening both in court and inside the palace and were able to use this knowledge to influence the emperors. Very few of the Ming emperors managed to keep themselves free from the bad influence of the eunuchs. Ambitious ministers anxious to increase their power did not hesitate to seek the cooperation of the eunuchs, even at the expense of their own dignity and integrity. This naturally put the eunuchs in a very strong position, and they maintained their power to the very end of the dynasty.[12]

The concentration of authority in the person of the emperor helped to weaken the power of the government. The ministers bowed to the imperial will, right or wrong. Officials who wished to be obeyed often found that they had to rely on the authority of the emperor. Although in the latter part of the Ming dynasty the Grand Secretary exercised power equal to that formerly held by the Prime Minister, legally he was merely an official of the fifth rank. Even a capable minister like Chang Chü-cheng, who had set the country on its feet once more, could not avoid severe criticism from his colleagues. The main accusation against him was that he had made himself Prime Minister, which was strictly against the orders of the founder of the dynasty. Hence he was considered a usurper of imperial power. Soon after his death he was stripped of all the honors bestowed on him by the emperors and his property was confiscated. In the seventeen years of the reign of the Ch'ung-chen emperor almost fifty Grand Secretaries were in and out of office as the imperial whim decreed. By many the ancient maxim 'ming-che pao-shen' 明哲保身, 'a wise man protects his own body', was regarded as the safest principle. As was only natural, they remained passive and silent in all that regarded government administration, though they might be active in taking bribes. When the end came the emperor was left complaining that his ministers had betrayed him, not realizing that this was due to defects in the organization of government.[13]

Like the emperors of most of the dynasties, the emperors of the Ming dynasty, with the exception of the founder and the Yung-lo emperor, were men of little ambition. This is easy to understand. The founder of a dynasty had to win the throne by conquest and then to devote all his energies and his vigilance to building up the empire and solidifying the power of his house. For his descendants things were quite different. They were born in the imperial palace and had everything provided for them. They lived isolated from society and had no clear idea of the life of the people. Hence it was almost impossible for them to rule without the help of capable ministers. More than half of the Ming emperors came to the throne before the age of twenty, some of them, for instance, Cheng-te, Wan-li and the T'ien-chi emperors seem never to have come fully to the age of discretion. They were the prodigal sons who eventually squandered the substance of their forefathers. Their lives of pleasure undoubtedly shortened their reigns. Of the sixteen emperors of the Ming dynasty only the founder lived to the age of seventy-one. The Yung-lo emperor died at sixty-six, the Chia-ching emperor at sixty and the Wan-li emperor at fifty-eight. The rest died at an average age of thirty-five.[14] The early emperors of the Manchu dynasty seem to have been aware of this weakness in their predecessors, for they tried to retain hunting as their chief pastime in order to keep themselves and their soldiers fit for military affairs. Unfortunately this good custom was abandoned, or at least not seriously maintained, after the Ch'ien-lung period.

The causes of the decline and fall of the Ming dynasty are many. The immediate causes were the revolt of the people and the aggression of the Manchus. But the remote causes can be traced back to the very beginning of the dynasty. Since human affairs develop slowly and gradually, it would be impossible to lay down a year from which definite decline may be dated. We must go through the history of the Ming dynasty from its beginning and examine some of the significant events that eventually led to the downfall of the empire. When the Ming dynasty was founded everything looked so splendid that its weaknesses passed unnoticed. But as time went on, the splendor began to fade and the weaknesses showed forth clearly. The decline was occasionally checked by more conscientious emperors and capable ministers, and the empire was able to linger a little longer. But the hour came when only the wicked and the incapable were left to govern the country. When this happened the people believed that

Heaven had withdrawn its mandate from the imperial house and that they were no longer subject to the emperor's authority.

DECLINE OF AUTHORITY:
USURPATION OF POWER AND CORRUPTION

The severity of the Hung-wu emperor toward his ministers, cruel though it seemed at times, helped greatly towards the reform of the government. Throughout the reign, ministerial corruption and incapacity were, to a large extent, kept at bay. The emperor himself took great interest in the people and tried to maintain close contact with them by mixing with them personally and by frequent communication with the liang-chang. The early emperors of the dynasty seem to have maintained good relations with the people by always taking an interest in their living conditions. Of the Hsüan-te emperor the story was told that one day an old woman appeared before him to accuse her daughter-in-law of failure in filial piety. What had happened was that the old lady had waked up one night and asked for a drink. The untimely request was unwelcome to her daughter-in-law, who therefore offered cold broth. The old woman took this as a mortal insult and made haste to bring the case before the emperor. The emperor, having ordered both the accuser and the accused to be brought before him for trial, was able to reconcile the parties and dismiss the case.[15] An old minister, reminiscing in later and less happy times, described the unforgotten days when the Yung-lo, Hung-hsi and Hsüan-te emperors used to grant interviews to their ministers after the court had been dismissed. One by one they were permitted to express their views freely on government affairs. But, he continued, since the Cheng-t'ung reign, when the imperial power was usurped by the chief eunuch Wang Chen 王振, the ministers have lost the privilege of interviews with the emperor: even if they are sometimes granted an audience they are usually afraid to say much for fear of Wang Chen.[16]

Another reason for the excellence of the government in early Ming days was the perfect control of state affairs exercised by the emperors. They had the good fortune to have able ministers to assist them and they wisely left them to do their work. The three Yangs, who served four emperors in the office of Grand Secretary, had a long record in the government. Yang Shih-ch'i 楊士琦 (1365–1444), retained his post for forty-three years, Yang Jung 楊榮 (1371–1440) for thirty-seven years, and Yang Pu 楊溥 (1372–1446) for twenty-two years. In the court many ministers of long experience gave able assistance to their masters. The Hung-wu emperor had abolished the office of the prime minister, but eventually the office of the Grand Secretary took its place. Although no one ever dared to call the Grand Secretaries by the name of prime minister, the power they exercised was in reality the power of the prime minister. This, however, did not happen until the Hsüan-te reign. During the Yung-lo reign they had indeed been summoned to participate in important affairs in the government, but they remained in the fifth rank and had no greater power than the other officials and served merely as the emperor's secretaries.

Once the emperors had assumed sole control of the government there was an obvious danger that they would often rule according to their own arbitrary preferences. Capable as the Hung-wu emperor was, even he was not able to avoid this defect. The Yung-lo emperor, sanguinary as a usurper of the throne, was inevitably prone to excesses. Almost immediately after seizing the throne he ordered an inexcusable slaughter of all who had opposed him in his struggle with his nephew. Even their families, relatives and friends did not escape punishment. During his reign thousands perished through the tyranny of the emperor.[17] His successors, too, the Hung-hsi and Hsüan-te emperors, also committed notable acts of cruelty.[18]

The Ming emperors after the Yung-lo reign were men of ordinary, or less than ordinary, ability. Apart from the Hung-chih 弘治 emperor (1488–1505), whom Chinese historians considered a reformer, not one of them may be said to have achieved anything noteworthy. They came to the throne so young and inexperienced that the authority of the government often fell into the hands either of all-powerful ministers or of the eunuchs. The government was badly neglected from the Chia-ching reign (1522–1566) onward. The emperors retired to their palaces and were happy to be left alone with their own families. The early tradition of the dynasty prescribed that the emperor should appear at court every day to interview his subjects and discuss problems of importance. Both the Chia-ching emperor and his grandson, the Wan-li emperor (1572–1619), became so wrapped up in their personal interests that they could spare hardly any time for holding court in the later halves of their reigns. In consequence there was very little communication between the sovereign and his subjects. Sometimes the emperor did not even know all his court officials, and the latter hardly ever had any chance of speaking to their master. Nearly all government affairs were transmitted to the emperor for his decision: but he, knowing little about the outer world, very often had to depend on others to make decisions. Frequently, therefore, the emperor had no policy of his own and let his favorites act for him. These favorites were often chosen from among the eunuchs, with whom the emperor had close relations. Moreover, since the eunuchs were often the intermediaries through whom government business reached the emperor, they could easily interfere in government affairs. If a eunuch happened to be an astute and ambitious man, he could make use of such opportunities to gain power, or at least could use his influence to enrich himself. Court officials often had to depend on the eunuchs to gain the emperor's favor for they themselves had no easy access to the imperial ear.

The Chia-ching emperor exercised close vigilance over the eunuchs and never gave much real power to them. He made the mistake, however, of choosing Yen Sung 嚴嵩 (1480–1568), as a Grand Secretary. This unscrupulous man remained in office for over twenty years and acquired great riches and great power. Under him the government reached a very low ebb. When he found that he was too old to rule alone he brought in his son Yen Shih-fan 嚴世蕃 to share the government with him. Shih-fan was a clever politician and was more corrupt than his father. It was said that the decisions he made on government affairs were often in accord with those of the Chia-ching emperor, and for this reason his father relied on him entirely. He very soon won for himself in the capital the title of "little prime minister."[19]

The public scandals of which Yen Sung was the center soon aroused strong opposition among a group of loyal officials who banded themselves into a party in order to gain strength from unity. They had no easy task. Yen Sung having entered through bribery and craft, had succeeded in overthrowing his predecessor Hsia Yen 夏言 (1482–1558). Gradually he had consolidated his power and, since he enjoyed full protection from the emperor, he seemed to be entrenched almost immovably in power. However, his rivals ultimately gained the emperor's ear and Yen Sung, was dismissed. The immediate outcome of this struggle was satisfactory but the example of party strife proved an unhappy development that carried on into the early years of the Ch'ing dynasty. From this time onward factions within the government flourished ever more widely. The first factions were formed only to overthrow undesirable members of the government; soon, however, they were being employed as means of seizing power for one's own party. Thus, after the fall of Yen Sung, his rival Hsü Chieh 徐階 (1503–1583) took his place. Not long afterwards Hsü Chieh was overthrown by Kao Kung 高拱 (1512–

1578), and at the beginning of the Wan-li reign, Kao Kung in turn was overthrown by Chang Chü-cheng 張居正. Later in the Wan-li reign there was strife between the eunuchs and the court officials, the emperor favoring now one party, now the other, through zeal not so much for the good of the country as for his own selfish interests. Eventually this spirit of faction spread to the provinces. Retired government officials who were still influential at court tried to manipulate government policy from a distance. Even students became absorbed in politics. From the beginning of the seventeenth century onward, there were four great parties: Tung-lin 東林 (present Kiangsu), Ch'i 齊 (Shantung), Ch'u 楚 (modern Hunan and Hupei) Che 浙 (Chekiang).[20] These four parties fought a bitter four-sided fight until ultimately the Tung-lin triumphed. Even that was not the end: discord among its members split the Tung-lin, while the defeated parties were lying in wait for an opportunity to regain their power. About this time, there emerged a eunuch sufficiently gifted to be able to take advantage of these quarrels and seize control of the government. A desperate struggle then broke out between the eunuchs and the Tung-lin.

This struggle was more than a mere party squabble. It was a war fought for a principle, a war between the just and the wicked, a war between honesty and corruption. The Tung-lin Party, despite its factious past, was formed of solidly trained Confucian scholars. The eunuchs and their followers (who included some scholars) were opportunists whose sole aims were power and riches. They were under the leadership of Wei Chung-hsien 魏忠賢, who did not scruple to destroy by most cruel tortures anyone who opposed him. Within five years, most of the great leaders of the Tung-lin Party had died at his hands and most of the rest were in exile or in forced retirement.

It would have taxed the abilities of a second Hung-wu emperor to solve the problems involved in this dangerous situation. Certainly, no solution was to be expected from the T'ien-ch'i 天啓 emperor (1621–1627), an immature young man with very little interest in politics, who occupied himself day and night with carpentry, the chosen hobby in which his soul rejoiced. The eunuchs saw his weakness and did everything to encourage him to devote himself exclusively to his toys. A contemporary wrote of this emperor that, when he had made a beginning with some piece of carpentry, he would at first feel exceedingly happy, but, after a while, he would get tired of the task and abandon it. Then after an interval, he would often resume the interrupted task. He wasted a great deal of material for his own amusement, without any knowledge of its value. Whenever important documents requiring replies were received, the eunuchs would wait until the young monarch was absorbed in his carpentry. Then they would come and read the documents to him. He would continue his work and when the reading was over, would say, "Go ahead and do what you think best. I have understood all about it."[21]

When the Ch'ung-chen 崇禎 emperor (1628–1644) succeeded his brother in 1628, his first act was to suppress the party of Wei Chung-hsien. The empire was, as he knew, practically exhausted after the Wei Chung-hsien reign of terror, so, being a well-intentioned ruler, he tried hard to re-establish a sound government. Unfortunately he lacked experience and, taught perhaps by the last few years of his brother's reign, he was not ready to trust anyone with power. He dreaded the thought that the factions might revive and took precautions to prevent it. This was in itself wise; but his suspicions that his ministers would prove disloyal led him to think that the wisest course for him was to undertake the direction of the empire single-handed. His attempt to carry out this lonely and probably impossible task developed in him a strong strain of stubbornness. Historians were amazed at the number of grand secretaries he appointed—fifty in all during a reign of seventeen years. His suspicions of his ministers gave corrupt officials a chance to do as they liked. Loyal officials were freely dismissed when their outspoken honest criticism aroused the suspicions of the monarch, whereas the wicked took care to gain his confidence by a pretence of honesty and timidity. Thus behind the emperor's back bribery and corruption of all kinds flourished as luxuriantly as ever.

A new war against the Manchus along the border increased the confusion into which the government had fallen. Government officials saw clearly that in order to support a strong army they must have money, but the only way they could find of getting money was to lay heavier taxes on the people. The heavier the taxes the more numerous the insurrections.[22] Officials appreciated the dilemma which faced them, but could devise no solution.

Early in 1630 the president of the Board of War reported to the emperor that the revolts were being caused by the corruption and the cruelty of the local rulers and petitioned the monarch to punish the culprits. The emperor would not accept this advice. Distrustful as ever, he kept on changing ministers. Even capable officials could do little to help such a government. Indeed, the emperor's suspicious frame of mind blinded him to the capabilities of his ministers. Frequently he relied solely on his personal judgement in weighing their merits, and the consequence was favoritism towards some and prejudice against others. One of the ministers, in a memorial to the throne, called the attention of the emperor especially to this point, telling him that his unbalanced judgment had given officials reason to complain. This plain speaking threw the emperor into a rage, but the minister succeeded in calming him by citing various proofs in justification of his bold memorial.[23]

From the start the emperor knew that he could not govern the whole country by himself and that he would have to seek the cooperation of others. Being unwilling to entrust important government positions to his ministers, he turned perforce to the eunuchs. He had not forgotten the enormities of the Wei Chung-hsien regime, but he had no other choice. At the same time, he revived the practice of using the Chin-i-wei 錦衣衛 or palace-guards as imperial spies. Once more prisons gaped open for the court officials.[24] Under such restrictions no one dared to say very much, unless he was ready to sacrifice his freedom or his life.[25] The emperor's impatience grew till he often failed to consider whether or not his commands were practicable. The case of the censor Huang Shu 黃澍 was typical. He was ordered to bring relief to the poor in Honan province. Some time afterwards the emperor heard that he was still lingering in the capital. Immediately he summoned Huang Shu to court, and demanded the reason for this delay. The dry and timid answer of the censor was that he had no soldiers to accompany him on his journey. The monarch was surprised to hear such a reply and, in all simplicity, asked why he wanted the soldiers. Seemingly he thought it an easy task to bring a hundred thousand silver taels a long distance through a bandit-infested countryside. Ultimately he agreed to give his minister three thousand soldiers, and, in a tone of reproach, ordered him to begin his journey within three days.[26]

In 1638, owing to the emperor's folly, the renowned general Hung Ch'eng-ch'ou 洪承疇 (1593–1665) was removed from his office as President of the Board of War and two other officials were degraded. They had been given orders to put an end to the revolts within five months.[27] Three months later a note came from the emperor saying that since the general had asked an extension of a year to suppress the revolts, he wanted to know whether the word year meant that same winter or something else. Undoubtedly he failed to appreciate the real efforts being made by his general and expected him to accomplish his task within the appointed time, whatever the military situation.[28] No wonder so many of the generals suffered great defeats. Hardly had they begun their preparations when an imperial order would come urging them to launch an attack. A year before the fall of the

Ming dynasty the general Sun Ch'uan-t'ing 孫傳庭, who was famous for his strict military discipline, was directing an operation against rebels in the province of Shansi, which for some time past had been suffering from famine. The general issued an order to the well-to-do of the place to contribute to the support of the army. Those who resented his order sent complaints to the court accusing him of delaying and so wasting the money and supplies allotted for military purposes. Many of the court officials, well aware of the emperor's impatient longing for a victory, tried to please him by agreeing that Sun should push on with his army immediately. They even threatened the general, saying that if he should delay any longer an imperial order for his imprisonment might be issued. Sun, who had previously been a prisoner for a long time, knew what this would mean. Sighing he said: "I have no desire to face a judge once more." He led his army to the battlefield, where he lost his life after a desperate fight with the rebels.[29]

The employment of eunuchs as supervisors of government officials was an unhappy device. Originally the well-intentioned emperor thought that by it he would ensure having men whom he could trust to report to him the activities of the officials. He conceived this fatal idea in 1633, when one of the eunuchs reported to him the corruption of a provincial governor in Anhui. The emperor was so pleased that thereafter when complaints were brought against the eunuchs he always came to their defence. Soon, eunuchs were being sent as supervisors to all the important military districts, where in fact they interfered with the work of officials and gave a great deal of trouble to the poor. In 1640, after strong protests by the officials, the emperor recalled a number of them, but a month before the fall of Peking (1644), he again sent them to supervise all the military districts. Their greed and their abuse of power again caused the ministers of the Board of War to complain of the shortage of supplies and the lack of a central authority, but the monarch refused to reconsider his decision.[30]

By the end of the Ch'ung-chen reign the emperor had lost practically all his loyal officials owing to his distrust. It is said that one day in the first month of the seventeenth and last year of his reign (1644), he granted to his Grand Secretaries an audience during which the Grand Secretaries reported unanimously that the treasuries of the different boards had been all exhausted and that revenues from the provinces were not coming in. Since money had to be found for the support of the soldiers, they suggested as a last resort that it should be taken from the imperial treasuries. The emperor remained silent for a while, with tears pouring down his cheeks. Incredible as it may seem, he had to confess that even the imperial treasuries were empty. He then gave orders to the Board of War to give generous rewards to those who volunteered to fight against the rebels whether they were military officials who had been dismissed because of their misbehavior or brave warriors from among the people. But the disillusioned Board of War did no more than suggest the restoration of a dismissed military man.[31]

We have referred many times to the evil wrought by the eunuchs. Throughout the dynasty they had great influence on the emperors; in several periods they controlled the policy of the government; they ended by betraying the dynasty. Many historians have delivered the severe judgment that the eunuchs of the Ming period were as noxious as their predecessors in the Eastern Han and the T'ang periods.[32]

The trouble started when the emperors grew mistrustful of their ministers. The eunuchs were quick to perceive this weakness in the minds of the emperors and, by a hypocritical display of loyalty, secured for themselves the direction of many undertakings. The founder of the dynasty had been shrewd enough to avoid this mistake: throughout his reign he never trusted the eunuchs with any task of importance.[33] He had laid down the prescription that the eunuchs should not be granted a rank higher than the fourth grade and that their salaries should consist of one picul of rice monthly each.[34] Under his successor, his grandson, the Chien-wen 建文 emperor (1399–1402), this severe attitude towards the eunuchs was maintained, and when Yen-wang revolted against his emperor-nephew, many of the eunuchs went over to his side and revealed all the secrets of their master. Yen-wang treated this disloyalty as an act of loyalty and ever afterwards employed eunuchs with all confidence.[35]

When Yen-wang became the Yung-lo emperor he saw that his position was precarious, for many of the officials surrounding him were still faithful to his nephew whose throne he had usurped. This strengthened his tendency to look upon the eunuchs as his helpers and he did not hesitate to turn to them for service. He confided his secrets to them and they became his spies. In the year 1421, after the transference of the capital to Peking, the Yung-lo emperor established the Tung-ch'ang 東廠 [36] as the headquarters of the secret police, and put eunuchs in charge of it. The emperor's prime purpose in establishing these secret police was to prevent revolts in the new capital. Before establishing the Tung-ch'ang, he had employed palace guards to spy for him all over Peking, but he was afraid that the officers of the guard might lack the necessary vigilance and act carelessly. The eunuchs seemed to be more completely dependent on him and as his servants in the palace day and night they knew better how to carry out his will. The influence of the eunuchs developed therefore very rapidly, and they soon got out of control.[37] The Tung-ch'ang lasted till the fall of the dynasty. It was to become a place of terror where innocent people lost their lives and loyal ministers were cruelly slaughtered—in short, a place where crimes of every kind were committed with impunity.

The Tung-ch'ang was directly under the control of the emperor and kept everyone, except the emperor himself, under its watchful eyes. Since the organization was a most important one, the emperors always chose for it men whom they could trust. Every day they went around the capital in disguise, visiting government offices, listening to trials in the law courts, and finding out what the various officials were doing. On their return to the palace they reported to the chief eunuch, who had charge of the whole organization. In addition to their main task of espionage they had to report on the market prices of different food-stuffs—rice, beans, oil and flour etc.[38] Naturally, in so large a city as Peking, a thousand spies or so were not enough. The eunuchs, therefore, hired idlers as assistants. These undesirables were only too willing to undertake their dishonorable duties and prowled around the city like famished wolves looking for prey. When they detected misdeeds they immediately reported them to the eunuchs who then sent guards to make the arrest. These guards carried no identifying marks of any kind and wherever they went always looked for bribes. If these bribes were paid according to demand, the victims were left unmolested; otherwise they were liable to undergo tortures which were always more severe than official punishments.[39]

An official of the Board of Punishments in the Ch'ung-chen period has left the following account of his own experiences:

"When I was first appointed to the Board of Punishments, I was told that the Tung-ch'ang reached the height of injustice in criminal cases. When the officials arrested robbers they always punished them with most cruel torments. They sought out the wealthiest of their victims for purposes of extortion. Once they had satisfied themselves with loot, they presented these cases to the Tung-ch'ang which, in turn, sent reports, usually full of fictitious details, to the emperor. Within less than four days the cases were sent to the Board of Punishments for consideration. A little over ten days was again needed to concoct similar faked reports. Finally, less than four days later the officials of the Tung-ch'ang and those of the Board of Punishments came together to pronounce the sentences. Once there was a robber, who, on going to the place of execution, sighed and murmured, 'I have never been a robber. Why accuse me of being one!' One day at the Board of Punishments I met one of the judges and advised him to re-examine wrongfully decided cases, but he answered me sorrowfully, 'I have not the courage to do it.' I asked for an explanation and he said sadly, 'There may be some honest officials within the empire who are not moved by bribery, but there are no such sub-officials. If I were to re-examine now the cases that have already been judged by the Tung-ch'ang, some day they might under some pretext, try to involve us in crime (e.g. in their sub-officials' acceptance of bribes). And then we should all perish both officials and sub-officials. Why should we act so imprudently and get ourselves into trouble?"[40]

Besides the Tung-ch'ang the Yung-lo emperor also revived the Chin-i-wei or palace guards (cf. chapter 2). The two organizations were directly under the control of the monarch and were of very much the same nature. There was, however, this difference between them, that the Tung-ch'ang had been instituted precisely because the Yung-lo emperor had lost his full confidence in the Chin-i-wei. Eventually, in 1477 under the Ch'eng-hua emperor, a Hsi-ch'ang 西廠 was instituted which combined the functions of the two earlier organizations, and in addition had the duty of watching over the misbehavior of the Chin-i-wei.[41] We are told that the Hsi-ch'ang was instituted especially to watch over officials who had become so corrupt that ordinary means were no longer able to prevent them from receiving bribes. Unhappily the eunuchs in charge of this new organization abused their power and thus did great harm to the government.[42] Later on, in the period when all power was in the hands of the chief eunuch Liu Chin 劉瑾, the Nei-hsing-ch'ang 內行廠 was established to watch over the three above-mentioned organizations.[43] This did not necessarily mean that the power of the ch'ang was always superior to the wei, for the distribution of power depended ultimately on the favor of the emperor. In fact, however, throughout the second half of the Ming period, the eunuchs enjoyed practically unbroken favor: hence we can safely say that the power of the ch'ang predominated.

It should not be thought that the ch'ang and wei were constant rivals. On the contrary, they worked closely together, for they realized that they often needed each other's help. An interesting paragraph in the *Ming shih* gives us a clear idea of the collaboration of these two organizations:

"The ch'ang often obtained information from inside (the palace) about the sentences at a trial. If there was opposition from outside (the court), the wei sent their guards of the Eastern and Western Department to spy and arrest the opponents, and the Northern Department took charge of their trials. As soon as they had made out a case in their own favor, they transmitted it to the public court. Even people arrested by the Tung-ch'ang had to be sent to the wei for re-trial before the Board of Punishments could pronounce sentence. Consequently at the time when the ch'ang was in power the wei submitted to it. On the other hand, if the influence of the ch'ang diminished, then the wei rose and took the upper hand. One example of this was the case of Lu Ping 陸炳 (commander of the Chin-i-wei), who was able to spy out the secret misdeeds of the chief eunuchs Li Pin 李彬 and Ma Kuang 馬廣 of the Tung-ch'ang and (ultimately) to cause their death, all because he had the good will of the Grand Secretary Yen Sung 嚴嵩. Later, however, the influence of the eunuchs became stronger than that of the grand secretary, and the wei in consequence declined in favor. This led the officials of the wei to seek the patronage of the ch'ang and to become its slaves.[44]

Under the Yung-lo emperor, the eunuchs began to consolidate their power. Instead of attending to their domestic duties around the palace, many of them were sent as special envoys to various regions of the empire, and even to distant lands. The most renowned of them was Cheng Ho 鄭和 (circa 1400), who went as a special envoy to the South Seas, making seven great expeditions with fifty or more large junks and twenty-seven thousand men between 1405 and 1422. Once he penetrated as far as Africa.[45]

The eunuchs now participated not only in political affairs, but even in military affairs. It had been easy for a capable monarch such as the Yung-lo emperor to keep command of the situation and to make the eunuchs submit to his authority. But he had been followed by a line of successors of greatly inferior talent whose control over these troublesome subjects was by no means sure. Moreover, many of the eunuchs, taking advantage of their masters' youth, tried to enmesh them in worldly pleasures so that while the emperors were enjoying themselves, they themselves could do what they pleased with the government. Thus in nearly every reign we find one or more eunuch, trying constantly to interfere in government affairs—Wang Chen 王振 and Ts'ao Chi-hsiang 曹吉祥 in the Cheng-t'ung T'ien-shun reign, Wang Chih 汪直 in the Ch'eng-hua reign, Liu Chin 劉瑾 in the Cheng-te reign, and still later, the notorious Wei Chung-hsien

魏忠賢 in the T'ien-ch'i reign. Ultimately they became so influential that their authority almost equalled that of the emperor.

A government official exclaimed in sorrow: "In recent years ancient traditions have been ignored and harmful innovations are being introduced daily. Imperial authority comes through the hands of these people (the eunuchs). For internal government they are trusted as prime ministers, and for external affairs they are employed as generals. The frontier provinces rely on them as their governors. Actors and artisans look to them (for advice) to produce fanciful works (to please the emperor). Abbots and priests rely on their influence that they may frequent the palace. Under their protection, neither the Chen-kuo 鎮國 nor the Yung-ch'ang 永昌 temple is afraid of giving offence to the public. And there are innumerable misgivings, beyond all imagination, over what they are doing out of sight or hearing."[46]

The Chia-ching emperor had a reputation for severity in dealing with the eunuchs and in his reign they were more cautious about their behaviour. Yet, about the middle of his reign one of them was able to boast that although in the old days when Chang Ts'ung 張璁 was the Grand Secretary they had to bow to him when they saw him entering the court, and later, when his successor Hsia Yen 夏言 entered they had at least glanced at him, now when Yen Sung 嚴嵩 came to his office he used to fold his hands and salute them before going in to the emperor for an audience.[47] Even so early as the Ch'eng-hua reign, the emperor had been warned by one of his officials that it had almost become a tradition for the government officials of his time to seek promotion through the eunuchs; once promoted they had to rely on them for protection; official ranks were being bought and sold like merchandise.[48]

Under these circumstances the eunuchs naturally had no high regard for the officials and sometimes committed shocking atrocities against them. In 1568 a eunuch was punished by one of the censors for extorting money from the people. Infuriated by this humiliation of one of themselves, over a hundred eunuchs gathered at a gate through which the censor was to pass. When they saw him coming, they rushed up and scourged him viciously. All the ministers were horrified at this act of barbarism but they were helpless to do anything about it. One day in 1602, according to a report made to the Wan-li emperor, when Ao Wen-chen 敖文禎, a Hanlin scholar and Vice-president of the Board of Rites, was being carried in a sedan chair near the Hsüan-wu Gate 宣武門, three eunuchs on horseback came galloping toward him. In some way the ornamental fans carried before his sedan chair frightened the horses. This greatly irritated the eunuchs and they ordered the fans to be destroyed and then started to belabor Ao's attendants. Ao himself had to take refuge near the gate, but the eunuchs came after him and ill-treated him brutally. When this was reported to the palace guards, they immediately sent men to restore order; but this only helped to involve the guards in a quarrel, and even they were not spared from violence. Five years later came a more serious and tragic incident involving the district magistrate of T'ai-hsing 泰興 from present Kiangsu province. This unfortunate man had just finished an audience with the emperor and was about to leave the city when several eunuchs came after him, demanding a donation. He refused. Instantly violence was used and the magistrate was attacked and seriously injured. He was then brought to a nearby house where he died from the effects of the beating.[49]

While the influence of the eunuchs caused fear among the people in general, the high positions they held aroused the emulous admiration of some. Poor ambitious commoners especially saw in these eunuch-held offices the easiest and quickest way to honor and riches. Were not Liu Chin 劉瑾 and Wei Chung-hsien 魏忠賢 ignoramuses in their early days? Yet, as soon as they became eunuchs, their fortunes prospered. Fathers of poor families who did not know what to do with their numerous offspring now began to see how they could secure a future for their children, and even for themselves: many of them castrated their sons and presented them to court to be employed as eunuchs. This abuse was by no means new—it went back to the beginning of the dynasty—but, in earlier days the penalties had been very severe. Not only those who castrated their children but even relatives or neighbours who had neglected to report such castrations were liable to the death sentence. Despite the severity of the punishment, however, the abuse was never entirely stamped out. In the early Ch'eng-hua days poor parents of large families in the Ho-chien 河間 prefecture used to castrate their sons two months after they were born, and those who, on growing up as eunuchs, found favor with the emperor were able to obtain official rank for their families. Such families became in time so rich that they were said to rival the high government officials in the abundance of their lands and slaves. Their example proved contagious. Eventually it was reported that every year the Board of Ceremonies was admitting several thousand eunuchs into the palace. The numbers presented became so great that usually a few thousand had to be rejected, but this did not discourage the abuse, and the castration of boys went on. Many of the children died of course from the operation, since the method employed was crude and there was very little attention to cleanliness.[50] In the year 1492 an order was issued by the Board of Ceremonies re-enforcing the earlier prohibition. Those who dared to have their children castrated and those who performed the operation were to be executed and their families and any neighbours who knew of a case and failed to report it were to be sent into exile. Even the elders of the village were not to be spared if they tolerated such crimes.[51]

Nevertheless the emperors themselves were partly responsible for this abuse in as much as it was their demand for eunuchs that encouraged the people to perform this illegal and unnatural operation.

About the year 1500, a minister of the court in his memorial to the throne warned the emperor about his unreasonable desires: here are now several tens of thousands of them (eunuchs) in the imperial city and this number is by no means small. Yet, Your Majesty has ordered the Board of Ceremonies to present another five hundred castrated boys under fifteen years of age. In what service will Your Majesty employ them? It is human nature to long for riches and honor. If the farmers with the encouragement of others are wont to castrate their sons in the hope that they will be employed in the palace, how much more often will they do it when they see an order demanding castrated boys. I am afraid the damage will be irreparable.[52]

Again we have the record of the T'ien-ch'i emperor who in the year 1621 demanded four thousand two hundred castrated boys.[53] By this time it was obvious that the whole government was practically dominated by the influence of the eunuchs. The more their numbers increased, the stronger became the party which they had organized to carry on a political war against their enemies. It is not surprising then that the number of eunuchs increased.[54]

As we have seen, the emperor not only represented the government but also controlled it. If the eunuchs were to take over the power of the government they would have to win control of the emperor. Could they find a way of so identifying their will with that of the emperor that what they did could be said to be exactly what the emperor wished to do? The eunuchs seemed to have succeeded in establishing such an identity of wills. In the presence of the emperor they always pretended to be his most faithful subjects, and always tried to do what pleased him most. Eventually they succeeded in distracting his attention from government affairs, so that while he was preoccupied with trifles they could do whatever they pleased with the government. This was the method employed by Liu Chin.

We are told that he used to appear for an audience with the Cheng-te emperor on important government affairs at a time when the latter was absorbed in his numerous hobbies. These untimely visits naturally annoyed the emperor, who, in order to get rid of his inopportune visitor, would say: "Have I not entrusted my business to you? And here you are coming to trouble me again! Clear out of my sight as quickly as possible!" Liu repeated this trick several times and always received the same treatment. After a while he no longer reported to the emperor, but made all imperial decisions as he wished, often without the emperor's knowing anything about them.[55] Such, too, was the method employed by Wei Chung-hsien with the T'ien-ch'i emperor, as we have said in an earlier chapter. Often the emperors fell completely under the eunuchs' power.

Once the eunuchs had succeeded in gaining control of political matters, it was not hard for them to interfere in financial matters also. In the palace they were put in charge of all the imperial treasuries—a trust which they found lucrative. All items in these treasuries were catalogued it is true, but the lists were practically never checked. Shortly after his accession the Chia-ching emperor wished to inspect one of these treasuries in which his predecessors had stored many valuable articles; but the chief eunuch persuaded him not to take this trouble, saying that if he was really interested in knowing about the items, there were catalogues from which he could learn all the details. Later on his colleagues asked the chief eunuch for an explanation of what had happened. With ready cunning he answered that he thought that this treasury was apt to tempt anyone to covetousness; hence he had thought it wise to hide it from His Majesty lest it might so tempt him.[56] This sage answer was of course a mere subterfuge by which the chief eunuch prevented the emperor from checking up on his misbehavior. A scholar who lived in the Wan-li reign said boldly that stealing was the chief accomplishment of the eunuchs. Sometimes when they had looted a storehouse so thoroughly that the gaps had become conspicuous they would pretend carelessness and have the whole storehouse burned to the ground. The case was then referred to the emperor, who usually ruled that the fire had been unintentional and imposed only a slight penalty on the culprit. In 1566 one of the storehouses was gutted and the eunuch in charge reported that over one hundred and eighty-eight thousand catties of incense had perished in the fire. However, not long afterwards, his fellow-eunuchs accused him of having stolen the incense and then set fire to the storehouse. The emperor immediately ordered the case to be investigated and it was discovered that the accused man had appropriated the incense and set fire to cheap goods substituted for it. The discovery of this fraud was abnormal— the result of a quarrel among the eunuchs. Ordinarily such a case would have passed unnoticed.[57]

During the Wan-li reign the eunuchs had recourse to two economic expedients, the promotion of mining and the exploitation of commercial taxes.

The first of these was at best ill judged; the second was openly unjust; both helped to hasten the fall of the Ming dynasty. Attempts to promote mining can be traced back to the earlier days of the dynasty. In the very first Ming reign, it was suggested to the Hung-wu emperor that he should open the silver mines of Shantung and Shensi. He ignored this advice, judging that the profits would not justify the expense of labor. His argument was that these silver mines would profit the government very little whereas they would do a great deal of harm to the people. He probably knew that, in the general exhaustion produced by the Mongol regime, even the vigorous new government was still too weak financially to start great enterprises. Silver mines were worked in the Chekiang and Fukien provinces in his reign, but he was not in favor of opening any new mines. Several gold and silver mines were opened in various provinces during the Yung-lo emperor's reign, but some of these failed miserably, probably owing to lack of knowledge of mining. Thus, at one time the Yung-lo emperor sent several eunuchs to supervise the mining of gold in Hei-shan 黑山. Six thousand miners, having labored for three months, produced only eight ounces of gold.[58] The caution of the Hung-wu emperor had been justified and many of the new mines were shut down. The Ch'eng-hua emperor, following the advice of his eunuchs, ordered the opening of twenty-one gold mines in twelve districts of Hunan. It was estimated that over half a million miners were employed and many of these died of hardship. Yet all there was to show at the end of a year was fifty-three ounces of gold. The motive of the Chia-ching emperor in mining, however, seems to have been religious rather than economic, for he cherished the superstitious belief that the discovery of mines revealed the favor of heaven to the emperor. The *Ming shih* tells us that, in order to comply with the wishes of the emperor, both the government and the people sought throughout the provinces for mines. Naturally many of his subjects saw in this quest a magnificent opportunity for enriching themselves. Some of these seized the chance to rob the mines of Chekiang and Kiangsi; their turbulence extended to the present Kiangsu and Anhui and this led to riots throughout all four provinces.[59]

In 1584, after the death of the Grand Secretary Chang Chü-cheng, the Wan-li emperor, who till then had left everything to his capable minister, took over personal control of the government. Soon his court began to fill with undesirable characters, many of whom tried to persuade him of the advantages of mining. The emperor was quite ready to yield to their suasions, but a group of faithful government officials opposed the project so strongly that the emperor, still a young man, reluctantly gave in to their weighty advice. Twelve years later, in 1596, the project of mining was again suggested to the emperor, and this time he made up his mind to carry out his long cherished desire, despite repeated strong opposition. In that very year eunuchs were sent to several provinces to supervise mining. Far-sighted officials saw in this the seed of much trouble, but no one could dissuade the Son of Heaven.[60] Suddenly minerals were said to have been discovered everywhere and petitions for the opening of mines came from all over the empire. One province presented simultaneously petitions for the opening of thirty-one mines. This multiplication of mines led to the employment of an enormous army of miners. In the Yün-yang 郧陽 prefecture alone (the present Hupei province), there were over a hundred thousand miners within an area of about sixty square miles. Two thousand men were employed to work in Wen-chia tung 文家洞 and, after three months' labor, ore was found in sixteen places, but it was not certain that silver could be extracted from it.[61]

And what was the result of all this expense of labor? In 1605, the eunuch Wang Hu 王虎 who had charge of mining in the Chen-ting 眞定, Pao-ting 保定 and Chi-men 薊門 prefectures in the present Hopei province, reported to the throne that from 1596 to 1604, the mines in his area had yielded five hundred and fifty taels of gold and ninety-two thousand six hundred and forty-two taels of silver. In addition, one hundred and nineteen catties of lapis lazuli had been mined. Labor and mining equipment had cost over one hundred thousand silver taels, far more than the profit yielded by these mines.[62] The eunuchs who had been so enthusiastic about the mining and had painted such glowing pictures of the profit of the mines now found it embarrassing to return to the palace empty-handed. Since, there was of course no question of their making up the loss from their own pockets, they had to find some way of transferring the burden to the pockets of others. They discovered a solution; in such matters the eunuchs were highly skilled. They appointed rich men as overseers of the mines, and forced the poor to act as miners. The rich men, being farmers, had no experience of mining and could not expect to succeed. As overseers, they were given the duty of supplying the miners with equipment and, worse still, paying the salaries of the miners and the guards of the mines. The poor were given no choice: they had to leave their farms and work for the government. Yet, though their land lay fallow in their absence, they were still expected to pay their taxes. The organization of these mines was deplorable. Food was short and living conditions were poor; many of the forced miners died of disease, or from accidents, and those who survived often received no pay. There were perpetual tumults and perpetual fights among the miners.[61]

Meanwhile eunuchs who enjoyed the title of Supervisor of Mines were travelling around the country to exploit the people. Some well-to-do families were accused of having stolen from the mines, and their properties were seized. Others who possessed fertile farms or great mansions were subjected to barefaced extortion. If they dared to refuse, miners were sent forthwith to dig up their farms and destroy their mansions on the pretext that there were precious ores underneath them. Even graveyards were not spared. Tombs were often opened and the bones of the dead scattered—heinous acts in the eyes of the people. Worst of all, the Supervisors of Mines usurped civil authority, ordering the arrests of innocent people and imposing penalties on them in whatever way they pleased. Women were insulted and violated, and if the local government officials tried to defend their own people, they were accused of interfering with the orders of the emperor.[64] These atrocities of the eunuchs eventually ruined innumerable families, both rich and poor. Many were driven to despair. The timid tried to end their lives with their own hands. Strong-willed men went mad. Others offered stubborn resistance to the aggressors, and when they had been scattered by armed force, retired to the mountains where they lost all fear of the soldiers and became bandits.

Eunuchs who went as tax-collectors to different provinces, being strangers, often had to depend on the natives of those provinces for information and many native ne'er-do-wells offered their services, helping to make great profits. Frequently such men obtained official positions from the eunuchs through bribery, and under the protection of the eunuchs went around exploiting the people more audaciously than ever. The *Ming shih* relates that they set up numerous customs stations along both land and water routes. They laid hands on merchants and confiscated their goods, searching even their personal belongings. They also made their way into small villages and imposed taxes on such common necessities as rice, salt, chickens and pigs. Their atrocities sometimes became all the more intolerable in that they followed one another in quick succession. Yet when such cases were reported to the emperor, he always came to the defence of his favorites, for he was interested in nothing but wealth, and the eunuchs, well aware of his greed, often presented part of their loot to him under euphemistic labels. They pretended, moreover, to show their affection for the emperor by sending him stolen articles of special value, such as furs and horses. The emperor used to receive these gifts with great pleasure and with high praise for the donors' talents.[65] In 1600, some of the eunuchs remitted to the imperial treasury annual taxes amounting to nearly a million silver taels together with an uncounted number of jewels. Seemingly this was made known throughout the empire, for it is said that the example of these eunuchs aroused enthusiasm for profit-seeking throughout the whole country. A typical example of the contagious spread of this by the eunuchs is offered by the history of a certain man from Anhui who was reported to have gone around exploiting the people under pretext of mining and tax collecting. That this man was under the protection of the eunuchs is beyond all doubt. Time and again, we are told, he returned to his native town and never failed to infuriate the censor by visiting his court, summoning the officials of the court and acting as if he were their equal. The infuriated censor reported the case to the emperor. The emperor listened to the complaint but never mentioned it again.[66]

The eunuchs were abhorred by the government officials and the people alike. The Supervisory Censor to the Board of Punishments, Kuo Shang-pin 郭尙賓, did not hesitate to tell the emperor that "the people of Kuangtung province are wont to see in a government official the image of His Majesty, but when they look at the face of a eunuch, they see in him the image of Yama!" He also compared them to wild beasts that "sharpen their teeth looking for the best prey to devour."[65] Kuo, who was a native of Kuangtung, knew his people well and watched over their interests with great zeal. In 1614 he reported to the Wan-li emperor that criminals from different provinces had gathered in Kuangtung, and were being employed by the eunuchs. These desperadoes tried to induce the notorious eunuch Kao Ts'ai 高寀 to go to Kuangtung, where, since the death of the eunuch Li Feng 李鳳 some years previously, no one had been appointed to succeed him as tax collector. The vacancy was temporarily filled by Kao Ts'ai, who was then tax collector in the province of Fukien and was still residing in that province. The invitations of the racketeers seem to have attracted him, for he was contemplating moving his residence to Kuangtung. Kuo was fully aware of Kao's unpopularity in Fukien, where his atrocities had recently raised a tumult, and the people were plotting to kill him. This plot failed. Kao got wind of it, and one day, secretly, brought two hundred armed men with him to the office of the magistrate and took him by surprise. He kept the magistrate as a hostage, and commanded him to order the people to cease plotting against him. The people, fearing that something might happen to their magistrate, reluctantly abandoned their plot. Nevertheless, fear that some day he might be murdered by the people of Fukien may have contributed to his decision to change his place of residence. In addition, the Fu-chow magistrate, brooding, no doubt, on his experiences of captivity, memorialized the throne requesting Kao Ts'ai's removal to Kuangtung. When the people of Kuangtung heard of this proposal they were alarmed. Kao had been in Fukien for over a decade and they knew him for the scoundrel he was. Accordingly Kuo Shang-pin sent up several memorials to the throne on behalf of the people, reminding the emperor of the damage Kao Ts'ai might cause in Kuangtung and telling him that the people of that province might arise in self-defence. He also accused the magistrate of Fukien of selfishness and lack of consideration in recommending so notorious and undesirable a character for Kuangtung.[68]

Among other accusations Kuo Shang-pin brought was a serious charge which he described as deserving severe punishment, namely, that Kao had built two large boats with the intention of communicating with the Japanese pirates. This accusation was probably inaccurate. Kao's real intention was to establish commercial relations with the Dutch. The author of the *Tung-hsi yang k'ao* 東西洋考, a contemporary of Kao Ts'ai's, tells us that by about the year 1600 there were already commercial relations between the merchants of Fukien and the Dutch. One of the Chinese merchants actually advised the Dutch to seize the Pescardores Islands as a base for business with the mainland of China. The Dutch followed his advice and took the Islands. Next a good-will envoy was sent to Kao Ts'ai bringing him a present of thirty thousand taels of silver and requesting in return the favor of being allowed to do business with Fukien. The greedy eunuch was delighted with the gift and, on the pretext that the Dutch were brave and far better armed than the Chinese, was ready to accede to their request. The Fukien authorities, however, objected strongly and the Dutch request was refused.[69] Nevertheless, communications between the eunuchs and the foreigners went on secretly. Meanwhile the Portuguese, who had already settled in Macao, were doing business with the Chinese. Gradually they built houses and cities in the Macao peninsula and very soon they became independent of Chinese authority. It was reported that the leaders of these foreigners had bribed the eunuchs, and, under their protection, had behaved badly in their dealings with the native people.[70]

Besides the office of tax collector the eunuchs were frequently given other commissions, such as buying pearls from Kuangtung, silk from Hang-chou, and porcelain from Kiangsi. Several of the emperors of the Ming dynasty seem to have had a passion for pearls. In 1499, a commission was sent to Kuangtung to get pearls from the sea, and met with striking success. In all, they obtained pearls valued at twenty eight thousand taels of silver at a cost of only a little over ten thousand taels. During the Chia-ching reign orders were frequently sent to buy pearls and to get them from the sea in Kuangtung. In 1557, the emperor actually demanded a fantastic total of eight hundred thousand pearls. Six years later the Board of Revenue was ordered to spend over twenty seven thousand taels of gold to purchase eighty-one thousand eight hundred pearls, diamonds and precious stones of all kinds.[71] These commissions to buy pearls and to obtain them from the sea were normally given to government officials, but under the Wan-li emperor the eunuchs were employed almost exclusively to carry out such orders. The task of obtaining pearls from the sea seems to have been a perilous one. We are told that in 1526, over fifty people lost their lives in the sea in this way. "O water, why dost thou produce pearls so that I must work like this?" sang a poet, in the person of one of these laborers. "I do not grudge the sacrifice of my life for pearls; for, I feel better off than my eastern neighbor who had to sell all his children in order to pay his taxes!" However, the misery of the poor worried the emperor very little.[70]

In the year 1598, a eunuch was sent to Kuangtung to obtain pearls, but after seven years of labor had to report failure. He was recalled to the palace but the laborers whom he had employed lost their livelihood. Several hundred of them then gathered in a few big boats and went forth on the high seas to live as pirates. This was not the only, not perhaps the most serious, consequence of this eunuch's mission. His very coming had improverished the treasury of the province. Since he had come as a resident imperial envoy, the local authorities had to build him a residence and supply him with everything needed for his comfort. Even his followers, who usually numbered from one to two hundred, had to be looked after. Thus, such a mission which robbed the province of its treasure, turned the laborers into pirates and brought no pearls to the emperor, was of benefit to no one except the eunuch and his followers.[73]

While such irregularities were flourishing outside the capital, the officials at the court were watching developments with deep concern. The wealth of taxes and of luxuries coming into the imperial treasuries made it appear that the empire was enjoying great prosperity; but the officials were not blind to the suffering of the people. The complaints of the merchants and the universal popular revolts showed that the political and economic condition of the country was unsound. The officials therefore submitted memorials to the emperor, warning him of the crisis and petitioning that all the eunuchs should be recalled to the capital. One official in particular exposed the ills of the time with the lucidity of despair. He said that since the despatch of the eunuchs to the provinces, nearly everything had become taxable. He recalled how many there were who, relying on the influence of the eunuchs, secretly exploited the people. Worse still were those who pretended to be government officials and robbed in public without anyone's daring to check them. This illegal way of taxing the people was more oppressive, he said, than the official raising of taxes by the government. If the taxes had been raised officially it would have been done according to law and the amount would have been fixed and known to the public; whereas the eunuchs and their followers gave free vent to their personal pleasure. Since they claimed to have come directly from the emperor, neither the provincial governors nor the local migistrates dared to question them. If complaints were presented to His Majesty, the emperor would take this as an attempt by the accuser to hinder the carrying out of the imperial command. Hence the people were left to suffer without defence. After all this oppression, the taxes really profited the imperial treasury only very slightly. The real benefits went into the pockets of the oppressors of the people. They always took twice as much as they presented to their superiors, yet it was the superiors who received the blame. The ambition of the eunuchs, he ended, increased every day with every new means of exploiting the people; if this went on unchecked the day might come when revolt would break out everywhere.[74]

This was the general opinion of the officials, but there was very little hope that the emperor would listen to them. In 1602, the Wan-li emperor suddenly took ill. Fearing that his end was approaching, he sent for the Grand Secretary and ordered, as his last wish, that all the mining and extraordinary taxes should be discontinued. This was an unexpected boon and the court officials felt that at last a great relief had come. Without a moment's delay the President of the Board of Civil Office and the Censor promulgated the imperial edict throughout all the provinces. Unhappily, by the next day the monarch was on his way to a speedy recovery. He at once repented his repentance and revoked his edict. The sacrifice was too much for his selfish and avaricious heart.[75] A modern writer has humorously surmised that the Wan-li emperor, whom he calls the greediest of all the Ming emperors, inherited his greed from his mother, who was the daughter of a small farmer in Shansi. Whether or not we agree with him, it is undeniable that this emperor's whole life was dominated by the love of gain. In the words of the *Ming shih* "his love for profit came from congenital instinct". Historians have had no hesitation in saying that the seeds of the fall of the Ming dynasty were planted during his reign.[76]

NOTES

[1] Ch'en Chien 陳建, *Huang-ming t'ung-chi* 皇明通紀, (Japanese edition) 2, (ts'e 1) 60b.

[2] *Erh-shih erh-shih cha-chi*, 32, (ts'e 6) 6b, 7a.

[3] *Yeh-chi meng-sou*, 2, (ts'e 1) 3a.

[4] The *Hsü wen-hsien t'ung-k'ao*, 208, (ts'e 2) 4455 tells the story of a certain Yeh Chu-sheng 葉居升 who had warned the emperor of the excessive power of the princes. This warning displeased the emperor and Yeh was arrested and died in prison. After that, no one dared to moot such a point before the emperor.

[5] During the Ming period, four such family tragedies occurred in the imperial house. Prince Yen 燕王, the only rebel prince to succeed, usurped the throne of his nephew and became the third emperor of the dynasty under the style Yung-lo 永樂 emperor. The other three princely rebellions occurred in 1426, 1510 and 1519. They caused little damage and were suppressed almost as soon as they had started.

[6] *Ming-shih chi-shih pen-mo*, 43, (ts'e 2) 55–56.

[7] *Hsü wen-hsien t'ung-k'ao*, 36, (ts'e 1) 3168; 47, (ts'e 1) 3216, 3217; *Ming-shih*, 70, (ts'e 24) 10b.

[8] *Kuo-shih ta-kang*, 487; *Jih-chi-lu chi-shih*, 16, (ts'e 6) 46, 47.

[9] *Ming-yi tai-fang-lu*, 3–4.

[10] *Erh-shih-erh-shih cha-chi*, 32, (ts'e 6) 9b.

[11] *Li-tai chi-kuan piao*, 4, (ts'e 1) 89–91.

[12] *Ming-shih* 229, (ts'e 76) 1a–19b.

[13] *Ming-shih*, 24, (ts'e 6) 11a.

[14] Liang Ting-tsang 梁廷燦, *Li-tai ming-jen sheng-tsu nien-piao* 歷代名人生卒年表, (Shanghai, 1933) second part, *Li-tai ti-wang sheng-tsu nien-piao* 歷代帝王生卒年表, 14–15.

[15] *Chao-tai chi lüeh*, 6, (ts'e 6) 29a.

[16] *Yeh-chi mang-shou*, 5, (ts'e 3) 13b, 14a.

[17] *Ming-shih chi-shih pen-mo*, 18, (ts'e 1) 60–61.

[18] Ibid., 28, (ts'e 1) 49–69.

[19] Ch'a Chi-tso 查繼佐, *Tsui-wei lu* 罪惟錄, (photographic reprint by the Commercial Press) (Shanghai, 1928) 12, (ts'e 5) 21a.

[20] Hsieh Kuo-chen 謝國楨, *Ming Ch'ing chih chi tang she yün-tung k'ao* 明淸之際黨社運動考, (Shanghai, 1934) 14–71.

[21] Liu Jo-yü 劉若愚, *Cho-chung chih* 酌中志, (TSCCCP), 14, (ts'e 3, 967) 75.

[22] Sun Ch'eng-tse 孫承澤 (1592–1676), *Ch'un-ming meng-yü-lu* 春明夢餘錄, (*Ku-hsiang-chai hsiu-chen shih-chung* 古香齋袖珍十種 series, late 19th century edition), 24, (ts'e 7) 39a.

[23] Li Ch'ing 李淸, supplement to the *San-yüan pi-chi* 三垣筆記, (Kiangsu, 19th century edition) (ts'e 4) A. 26b.

[24] *Tsui-wei lu*, 16, (ts'e 7) 3b.

[25] *Huai-tsung Ch'ung-chen shih-lu* 懷宗崇禎實錄, (KPL photographic reprints), 10, (ts'e 499) 4b, 5a; *San-yüan pi-chi* A. 21b.

[26] Supplement to the *San-yüan pi-chi*, (ts'e 4) A. 26b.

[27] Kuan-ko shan-jen 管葛山人 (i.e., P'ang Sun-i 彭孫貽), *P'ing-k'ou chih* 平寇志, (Peiping 1931) 3, (ts'e 1) 6a.

[28] Tai Li 戴笠, *Huai-ling liu-k'ou shih-chung lu* 懷陵流寇始終錄 (other title: *K'ou-shih pien-nien* 寇事編年); (*Hsüan-lan-t'ang ts'ung-shu hsü-chi* 玄覽堂叢書續集, Nanking, 1947) 11, (ts'e 9) 11a.

[29] *K'ou-shih pien-nien*, 16, (ts'e 11) 14a; *Ming-shih chi-shih pen-mo*, 78, (ts'e 2) 69–71.

[30] Wen Ping 文秉 (1609–1669), *Lieh-huang hsiao-chih* 烈皇小識, (*Ming-chi pai-shih ch'u-hsü pien* 明季稗史初續編, first series, published by the Commercial Press) 3, (ts'e 1) 9a; *K'ou-shih pien-nien*, 13, (ts'e 9) 5b; *Huai-tsung Ch'ung-chen shih-lu*, 17, (tse'e 500) 5ab.

[31] *K'ou-shih pien-nien*, 17, (ts'e 11) 1a.

[32] *Ming-shih*, 304, (ts'e 101) 2a; *Erh-shih erh-shih cha-chi*, 35, (ts'e 6) 32b.

[33] Hsü Hsüeh-chü 徐學聚 in his *Kuo-chao tien-hui* 國朝典彙, 33, (ts'e 19, ed. in 1934) mentions an embassy consisting of two eunuchs, Erh Nieh 而聶 and Ch'ing T'ung 慶童 sent by the founder of the dynasty to some tribes along the Shensi borders to get horses by barter. Hsü describes this as the first commission ever given to the eunuchs in the Ming period. Did the Hung-wu emperor violate his own order by sending them? Probably not. The names of both eunuchs seem to indicate foreign origin and it is probable that they were Mongols and knew the language of these tribes. It seems likely that the emperor, unable to find ministers equipped for this commission, had no alternative to sending these eunuchs. It is interesting to note that many of the eunuchs in the palace at that time were foreigners. In 1384, the King of Annam presented thirty Annamite eunuchs to the Hung-wu emperor. Seven years later (1391), the same Hung-wu emperor demanded two hundred eunuchs from Korea. Cf. Tan Chien 談遷, *Kuo Ch'üeh* 國榷, (ms kept in the Tōyō bunko, Tokyo) (ts'e 8) 94a; (ts'e 10) 2b.

[34] *Kuo-ch'ao tien-hui*, 32, (ts'e 19) 3a; *Kuo-ch'üeh*, (ts'e 6) 48b.

[35] *Ming-shih*, 304, (ts'e 101) 1b.

[36] The *Shih-lu* of the Yung-lo emperor omits all mention of this event. The *Hui-tien*, however, quotes from Wan An's 萬安 (floruit 1480) memorial to the throne a passage giving the institution of the *Tung-ch'ang*, in the eighteenth year of the Yung-lo emperor. Cf. *Kuo-ch'ao tien-hui*, 33, (ts'e 19) 11b; *Kuo-ch'üeh*, (ts'e 16) 15b.

[37] *Ming t'ung-chien*, 17, (ts'e 2) 15b, 16a.

[38] *Cho-chung chih*, 16, (ts'e 3, 967) 104.

[39] *Ming-shih*, 95, (ts'e 34).

[40] *San-yüan pi-chi*, (ts'e 1) A. 3b.

[41] *Ming-shih*, 95, (ts'e 34).

[42] *Yeh-chi meng-shao*, 6, (ts'e 3) 24b, 25a; 7, (ts'e 4) 2b, 5ab.

[43] *Ming-shih*, 95, (ts'e 34) 4a.

[44] Ibid., 96, (ts'e 34) 12b.

[45] Paul Pelliot, "Les grand voyages maritimes chinois au debut du XVe siècle", *T'oung Pao*, 30, (1930) 237–452.

[46] *Hsi-yüan wen-chien lu*, 101, (ts'e 38) 1ab.

[47] *Erh-shih erh-shih cha-chi*, 35, (ts'e 6) 32b.

[48] *Ming-shih*, 180, (ts'e 59) 14a. The *Yeh-chi meng-sou*, 7, (ts'e 4) 12a, says that during the Ch'eng-hua period when the eunuch Wang Chih was in power, even higher court officials were afraid of the eunuchs (grand secretaries) and tried to flatter them. Whence the popular saying: "The three *Ko-lao* (grand secretaries) are made of paper and the presidents of the Six Boards are statues molded from clay" 紙糊三閣老, 泥塑六尚書. The same book, 7, (ts'e 4) 5ab tells of a certain censor who had become a favorite of Wang Chih and used to pay him frequent visits. It happened that the president of the Board of Civil Office and other ministers also wished to visit the eunuch and begged the censor to introduce them. Before the interview they asked the censor whether it was necessary to kneel before the eunuch and the answer was: "It is unheard for the ministers of the Six Boards to bend their knees before any officials." The day of the visit came and the censor went in first to interview the eunuch. His colleagues remained outside but succeeded in peeping in. They were amused to see the lofty censor kneeling before the eunuch and kowtowing to him. Later, they went in and did as they had seen him do. On coming out the censor began to laugh at their undignified behaviour, but one of them said, "We saw somebody who did this and we only imitated him".

[49] *Chia-ching i-lai chu-lüeh*, 6, (ts'e 4) 11b, 12a; *Ming-ch'en tsou-i* 明臣奏議, (TSCCCP), 33, (ts'e 0921) 642; *Ming-shih ch'ao-lüeh*, (ts'e 1) 20a; *Chia-ching i-lai chu-lüeh*, 10, (ts'e 7) 28a.

[50] *Hsi-yüan wen-chien lu*, 101, (ts'e 38) 2b; 102, (ts'e 39) 24b.

[51] *Tien-ku chi-wen*, 16, (ts'e 134) 6a.

[52] *Hsi-yüan wen-chien lu*, 101, (ts'e 38) 2ab. Shen Te-fu says that it was quite common for the people around the capital to castrate their children in order to be able to present them to the court as eunuchs. However, sometimes these castrated children were rejected and usually grew up to be beggars or robbers. Shen himself experienced their depredations during one of his trips. Several score of these wretched men hid under ruined walls. When travellers on horseback or in carriages were passing by the weaker eunuchs would come out to beg while the stronger ones would demand money with threats. If the journey-makers happened to be travelling in small groups, these eunuch-bandits used violence to rob them. The local authorities knew well what was happening but did nothing to stop it. As a result tradesmen often suffered great losses. Cf. *Yeh-hu-pien* 野獲編 (Shanghai, 1959) 6, A. 178–179.

[53] *Tsui-wei-lu*, 16, (ts'e 7) 4b. The author of the *Chia-ching i-lai chu-lüeh*, 10, (ts'e 7) 7b, says that in 1598 the court took in four thousand and five hundred castrated men as eunuchs.

[54] The *Ming t'ung-chien* describes an event (78 (ts'e 9) 47b) which illustrates the extent to which the eunuchs abused their power. It was the custom of the president of the Board of Works to supply winter clothes to the eunuchs every other year. In 1623 more than a thousand of the eunuchs went to the president while it was still summer to demand winter clothes. On being refused they rushed into the president's office and destroyed his official chair, a mark of disrespect for the office he held, and did not go away till they overwhelmed him with monstrous insults. Huang Tsung-so 黃尊素 (1585–1626), father of the renowned scholar Huang Tsung-hsi 黃宗羲, was an eye-witness of the abuses of the eunuchs and has left an account of an atrocity which occurred in 1624. Wan Ching 萬燝, minister of the Board of Works, had criticized the eunuch Wei Chung-hsien before the throne. The eunuch, exceedingly annoyed, issued an order in the name of the emperor to have Wan beaten publicly in the court. Eunuchs were sent to Wan's residence. They gave him harsh blows, and carried him away half dead. "A meeting at which I was also present was held by the Grand Secretary concerning the public court beating of Wan," Huang Tsun-so says. "Several hundred eunuchs gathered in the office of the Grand Secretary. They

shook their fists and pulled their trousers up to their thighs and kept on shouting and denouncing. The Grand Secretary was dumbfounded. His face went red, but he was not able to utter a word to stop them. Then in a rage I roared out: 'The Nei-ko is a solemn place, even the chief eunuch is not permitted to enter without the order of the emperor. Who are you who dare to intrude? You are disgracing His Majesty, and the imperial ancestors! (When they heard this) they gradually dispersed." *Shuo-lüeh* 說略, (*Hsien-fen-lou pi-chi* 涵芬樓祕笈, second series; Shanghai, 1917), (ts'e 5) 30a; cf. also *Ming-t'ung-chien*, 79, (ts'e 10) 3ab.

[55] *Hsi-yüan wen-chien lu*, 101, (ts'e 36) 22a.

[56] *Ming-ch'ao hsiao-shih*, 12, (ts'e 91) 12ab.

[57] Shen Te-fu 沈德符 (1578–1642), *Yeh-hu-pien* 野獲編, (ed. by Yao Tsu-en 姚祖恩) (Chekiang, 1827), 6, (ts'e 6) 30ab; *Tsui-wei lu*, 12, (ts'e 5) 82b.

[58] *Ming-shih*, 159, (ts'e 54) 16b.

[59] *Ming-shih*, 81, (ts'e 28) 12b; Chu Kuo-chen 朱國楨 (1557–1632), *Yung-chuang hsiao-pin* 湧憧小品, (PCHSTK), (ts'e 92).

[60] *Ming-shih*, 81, (ts'e 28) 12b–13b.

[61] *Ming-ch'en tsou-i*, 32, (ts'e 0,920) 606; *Hsi-yuan wen-chien lu*, 92, (ts'e 35) 31b.

[62] *Ming-shih ch'ao-lüeh*, (ts'e 1) 11a.

[63] *Hsi-yüan wen-chien lu*, 92, (ts'e 35) 3 b; *Ming-shih*, 81, (ts'e 28) 13b–14a.

[64] *Ming-shih chi-shih pen-mo*, 65, (ts'e 3, 926) 73–86; *Ming-shih*, 81, (ts'e 28) 13ab.

[65] *Ming-shih*, 81, (ts'e 28) 12b–13b.

[66] *Tsui-wei lu*, 14, (ts'e 6) 28b, 29a.

[67] Kuo Shang-pin 郭尚賓, *Kuo chi-kan shu-kao* 郭給諫疏稿, (TSCCCP), 1, (ts'e 0, 908) 34.

[68] Ibid., 1, (ts'e 0, 908) 28–30; 2, (ts'e 0, 908) 38; *Erh-shih erh-shih cha-chi*, 35, (ts'e 6) 27b–28b; Chou Shun-ch'ang 周順昌 (1584–1626), *Chou-chung chieh-kung chin-yü lu* 周忠介公爐餘錄, (TSCCCP), 1, (ts'e 2, 165) 1–7.

[69] *Kuo ch'i-kan shu-kao*, 2, (ts'e 0, 908) 37–39; Chang Hsieh 張燮, *Tung-hsi-yang k'ao* 東西洋考, (TSCCCP), 6, (ts'e 3, 260) 84–86.

[70] *Ming-shih ch'ao-lüeh*, (ts'e 1) 2a; *Tsui-wei lu*, 14, (ts'e 6) 26ab.

[71] *Ming-shih*, 82, (ts'e 29) 8b–9a; *Tsui-wei lu*, 12, (ts'e 5) 69a, 78b; cf. also 81b. 84b.

[72] Wu Yen 吳炎 and P'an Sheng-chang 潘檉章, *Wu P'an chin-yüeh-fu* 吳潘今樂府, (*Yin-li tsai-ssu-t'ang ts'ung-shu* 殷禮在斯堂叢書 ed. by Lo Chen-yü 羅振玉) (Shanghai, 1928) ts'e 2) A. 11a; b. 12b; *Ming-shih*, 82, (ts'e 29) 8b–9a.

[73] *Kuo ch'i-kan shu-kao*, 1, (ts'e 0, 908) 4–6; The author of the *Tu p'ien hsin-shu* 3 (ts'e 2) 51ab describes the abuses of the eunuchs, briefly and clearly: "Often the Court listened to the suggestion of greedy ministers and eunuchs were sent all over the country to collect (commercial) taxes under pretext of protecting the farmers by keeping the merchants in check. In reality where commercial taxes are heavy, goods must be sold at a higher price. Since the purchasers have to pay more for the goods they are burdened by the system. On the other hand, where commerce does not flourish, goods inevitably suffer depreciation. The consequent lowering of the selling price of such goods naturally affects those who sell them. Although only the merchants were taxed, the system insensibly forced all the people to endure higher expenses. Thus such occult demands are worse than public increases of land taxes. Moreover, if the court got one (silver tael) from these commercial taxes, the eunuchs would pocket ten, the tax collectors a hundred, and the soldiers a thousand. It all comes down to this, that the people are losing hundreds and thousands in order to allow the court to receive one silver tael, a very insignificant gain indeed, but a great loss to the people. . . ."

[74] Yeh Yung sheng 葉永盛, *Yü-ch'eng tsou-shu* 玉城奏疏, (TSCCCP), ts'e 0, 911) 8–9.

[75] *Ming-shih chi-shih pen-mo*, 65, B. 81.

[76] Chu Tung-jun 朱東潤, *Chang Chü-cheng ta-chuan* 張居正大傳, (Shanghai, 1945) 320; *Ming-shih*, 81, (ts'e 28) 14a.

CHAPTER EIGHT

The Army

DISCIPLINE

After the Hung-wu period the wei-so system went slowly through a series of changes. The *Ming shih* summarizes these changes as follows: "Wen-huang (i.e. the Yung-lo emperor), after transferring the capital to Peking, continued to follow the tradition of T'ai-tsu; but, when he employed eunuchs to command the army, one saw the beginning of the change. After Hung-hsi (1425) and Hsüan-te 宣德 (1426–1435) the country was so habituated to peace that there soon came the disaster of T'u-mu 土木 (where the emperor Ying-tsung 英宗 was captured by the Mongols in 1449). Then came the reigns of the four emperors, Hsien-tsung 憲宗, Hsiao-tsung 孝宗, Wu-tsung 武宗, and Shih-tsung 世宗. Under them the military system suffered frequent alterations and the military power deteriorated more than ever. . . . Finally towards the end of the dynasty, the military records were, for a long time, left unchecked, and the number of soldiers kept on diminishing. With the rise of the rebels, the empire collapsed at once: the eunuchs surrendered at the city gates and the palace guards dispersed under the city walls, thus bringing the dynasty to an end."[1]

In the early days the Hung-wu emperor was careful, as we said above, to keep the army up to strength, especially along the borders. But by 1528, it was reported that the twelve divisions in the capital, originally numbering over a hundred and seven thousand soldiers, had been reduced to about fifty-four thousand four hundred. Similarly, the number of horses in the army was reduced from the original hundred and fifty thousand two hundred to about nineteen thousand three hundred.[2] When the Mongols attacked the capital in 1550, all that the President of the Board of War could muster was about fifty to sixty thousand soldiers, and even these had to be forced to fight. Valor had been lost.[3] Towards the end of the reign of the Chia-ching emperor, the governor of Yen-sui 延綏, Shensi Province, reported a decrease in soldiers and horses in the military districts of Yen-sui, Ning-hsia and Kansu Province. He attributed this to the corruption of the local authorities who, in order to justify the drawing of large sums of money, were accustomed to exaggerate expenses and to dress up insignificant incidents as serious. In their reports they recorded greater numbers of soldiers than had actually gone into battle, and withheld urgent information and dealt with matters of minor importance, drew excessive sums from the public funds for their travels, or took what was not their due.[4]

The scholar Cheng Hsiao 鄭曉 (1499–1566) tells us that in the year 1557, four successive Presidents of the Board of War were dismissed within six months, apparently because of incompetence. Chang Tsan 張瓚, a later President, remained in office longer than his predecessors. He was a capable man, but, being corrupt, weakened government policy in dealing with the problems of the borders.[5] Corruption was rife in the military class toward the last century or so of the Ming dynasty and the corruption of the officers was responsible for the decrease in the number of soldiers.

The early Ming emperors were vigilant to prevent the military class from abusing its powers. In an edict of 1382, the Hung-wu emperor strictly forbade commanders of troops to employ soldiers on construction work or for personal services. The Yung-lo emperor, following the example of his father, issued an edict in 1404, stressing the same point.[6] But later emperors came to ignore the warning of their predecessors. Troops summoned to protect the capital were employed by the emperors themselves and by the nobles for construction. In 1496, the President of the Board of War complained that between one and two thousand soldiers in the capital were employed in manual labor and such work often went on for years. Many of the soldiers deserted, being unable to bear the hardships involved in the forced work.

When the Mongols invaded Hsüan-fu 宣府 towards the end of the Chia-ching reign, it was decided to mobilize a hundred and twenty thousand troops to defend the capital. In fact, hardly thirty thousand could be mobilized. The blame for this fell on the nobles who had diverted the best soldiers to manual labor, leaving the second-rate to fill the ranks of the guards. According to the records of the Board of Revenue, a hundred and twenty thousand were still drawing salaries, but no such number could be found.[7]

The officers in the provinces were no better than their superiors in the capital. They too had no hesitation in employing soldiers for their personal service. In 1630, an official reported to the throne that it was a common practice among military officers to employ soldiers for labor of all sorts. In T'ung-chou 通州 the practice was universal: government officials were numerous there and nearly every official had soldiers working as laborers. Those who worked under their own officers remained with their units. Others were set to work for officials other than their own officers; these often left their units with no intention of returning. If by chance there was an inspection in the army, the officer thought up a variety of excuses to explain away the gaps in their ranks and, if necessary, brought in strangers to fill the vacant places temporarily. The Board of War made no serious attempt to check the number of soldiers that an officer commanded, or even to ascertain whether a commander was alive or dead. It merely transcribed lists of names from old records and sent these to the emperor. The emperor, knowing nothing except what he saw in the lists, and usually impressed by the well filled rolls, rested satisfied.[8]

It may be asked why military officers so easily allowed their soldiers to leave their posts to work for non-military departments. The answer is the obvious one: the soldiers usually obtained the consent of the officers through bribery—a transaction known to their contemporaries as mai-hsien 賣閒, an expressive term meaning "the selling of leisure." On payment of about two hundred coins monthly a soldier was exempted from drill and other military obligations and was free to do what he pleased. If he was willing to pay another three hundred coins or so per month, he could use a military horse for his own purposes.[9] This happened in the old T'ung-chou division around the year 1631. We are told that the salary for each old soldier in that region was eight pecks (10 pints) of rice or the equivalent of five or six ch'ien, mace, of silver per month, whereas the newly trained soldiers in the same place each received one silver tael and five ch'ien monthly—three times more than the former.[10]

The soldiers' readiness to work is still more easily explained. They had to work or to starve. In early Ming days when the military settlements were still flourishing, the soldiers in general produced from the farms sufficient amounts to supply their own needs and even a surplus for the payment of the officers. After the Cheng-te reign (1506–1521), owing to the lack of grain, money was paid instead of farm produce. Moreover, these salaries were not paid in full. If a picul of rice cost one silver tael, only six-tenths of a silver tael was given to each soldier. Thus his pay would buy only six pecks of rice instead of the full picul that was his due.[11] This abuse seems to have persisted till the end of the dynasty. In 1630, an official reported to the throne that the soldiers were receiving eight pecks of rice monthly instead of a full picul. Since they could not survive on this meagre dole, they had to turn elsewhere for a living. This official also pointed out that although government offices did not pay much for soldiers' off-time work, at least the soldiers had free time in which to take up extra work which enabled them to live. If they were to give full-time service to the army they would get only a few pecks of rice per month, which would be unjust to the soldiers.[12]

The worst military abuse of all was the appropriation of the soldiers' pay by the officers. Yeh Hsiang-kao 葉向高 (1559–1627) says that many of the military men in the capital came from merchant families. To obtain their commissions they paid heavy bribes to the eunuchs and the influential officials. As soon as they had received an appointment they lost no time in reimbursing themselves by exacting from the soldiers illegal payments of all kinds. In consequence the soldiers were often forced to desert.[13]

With such selfish and corrupt officers it is evident that strict military discipline cannot have been well maintained, and, once good discipline had vanished it would have been in vain to look for a good army. Early in 1389 the founder of the dynasty had given orders to the Board of War and to the Wu-chün tu-tu-fu to punish severely any officers who did not fulfil their duties faithfully. Officers who taught their sons how to sing songs instead of teaching them how to use the bow or to ride a horse were to have their tongues cut out. Chess players and football players were to have their arms or feet cut off. Officers who dared to engage in business were sent into exile. Apparently, not many took these orders seriously when they were first issued: they were soon undeceived. Sun Ch'eng-tse 孫承澤 tells us of a certain official whose son was caught playing a flute and singing songs. The unhappy father's upper lip and the tip of his nose were cut off. Another officer lost his leg, because he had been caught playing football with one of the guards. The Hung-wu emperor's strictness in this matter appears to have produced many good generals.[14]

By the latter part of the Yung-lo emperor's reign, the standard of military discipline had declined considerably despite the vigilance of the emperor. The *Ming shih* attributes this decline to the appointment of eunuchs to army commands. The following warning contained in an imperial order sent in 1419 to the Wu-chün tu-tu-fu and to the Board of War is clear evidence of this deterioration: "Recently the number of troops has decreased and weapons are being poorly serviced. Officials have tried to deceive each other, and there has been much intrigue. . . ." In a fit of temper, the monarch proceeded: "Do they want to sell the court and endanger the empire?" Finally, he commanded all to make quick amends, even threatening capital punishment if obedience were not forthcoming.[15]

Beyond all doubt, the eunuchs were responsible, to a great extent, for the decline of military discipline. Practically all of them came from low social levels and had never been trained in military affairs. The disaster of T'u-mu 土木 in 1449, for instance, was caused by the eunuch Wang Chen 王振. This notorious man succeeded, despite widespread opposition, in persuading the emperor Ying-tsung to lead his army in person against the Mongols.

The *Ming shih* has an interesting account of what followed: " . . . when they reached Hsüan-fu there came a great storm and it rained very heavily. Again some of the officials tried to persuade the monarch to return. Wang Chen was exceedingly angry. Chu Yung 朱勇, Duke of Ch'eng-kuo 成國公, and some others happened to arrive to report on certain affairs and they were made to enter on their knees. The Presidents of the Boards, T'ang Ych 唐坴 and Huang Tso 黃佐, having offended Wang Chen, were ordered to kneel on the grass. . . ."[16]

During the Chia-ching reign military discipline reached a very low level. Most of the military leaders had inherited their posts and knew very little about warfare. They commonly employed the soldiers for their personal service and drew salaries under fictitious names.[17]

Honest ministers at various times tried to reform the army. All failed. Under the Wan-li emperor the capable Chang Chü-cheng made a last attempt. He too failed. The reform movement initiated by him persisted to the end of the dynasty, but the evil had already gone so far that the earnestness of a few ministers could not prevail against the bad will of so many.[18]

The decline in the number of soldiers had a disastrous effect on the military settlements. In 1631, it was reported to the Ch'ung-chen emperor that the produce of the military settlements in Kansu, which had been six hundred thousand piculs yearly in the Hung-wu and Yung-lo days, had fallen to less than a hundred and thirty thousand piculs. In Ning-hsia 寧夏 the fall was from one hundred and eighty-eight thousand piculs yearly to one hundred and forty thousand, and in Yen-sui from sixty thousand to less than fifty thousand.[19] The deterioration of the military settlement had already become apparent as early as the Cheng-te days (1506–1521), when many of the soldiers in the settlements either deserted or died of disease. In addition, the border territories were often left uncultivated on account of the frequent Mongol invasions. Thus, the army lost a large part of its means of self support and had to turn to the imperial granaries for the necessary supplies. By the time of the Lung-ch'ing emperor (1567–1572), the number of deserters had become so great that the lands along the borders were turning into deserts.[20]

Another source of weakness was the appropriation by the army officers of lands attached to the military settlements. According to the findings of the Japanese scholar Shimizu Taiji 清水泰次, this was due to two causes. First, the inflation of paper money had lowered the real salaries of the military officials; to compensate them for their losses, the government allowed them to occupy lands that were attached to the military settlements. Secondly, once the military profession had become hereditary, the officers inevitably tended to occupy such lands as private property.[21] This abuse cropped up as early as the Yung-lo period, but it did not become serious until after the reign of Ying-tsung. In addition, the lands of the military settlements were often occupied by nobles, eunuchs, landlords, and even monasteries. The *Ming shih* and many of the contemporary documents cite an abundance of instances. In a note we refer to a few of the many sources.[22]

By the Ch'ung-chen period, the army had fallen into an appalling state. Many of the soldiers had deserted and the officers had to depend on mercenaries. The caution given by the Hung-wu emperor against allowing military leaders to possess permanent armies could no longer be observed; for, if the leaders were to put down the rebels, they often had to remain with their soldiers for years at a time. Eventually they came to regard such troops as their own, and the soldiers looked on them as their sole commanders. Thus Mao Wen-lung 毛文龍, having occupied a small island opposite the mainland of Manchuria at the beginning of the Ch'ung-chen reign, lived there quite independently as a warlord.

In 1642, when the dynasty was nearing its end, a censor tried to pinpoint the trouble of the time. The fundamental cause, he said, was the excessive multiplication of officers: then it was a grave error to have too many hsün-fu 巡府 (provincial governors in charge of civil administration) and hsün-fang 巡方 (officials responsible for the maintenance of public order). In his day there were four hsün-fu and two hsün-fang in Hu-kuang Province: each confined his interest to his own territory, and their strength was divided.[23]

Not only were these officials selfish; they were also ignorant beyond belief. When Yang Ssu-ch'ang 楊嗣昌 took over the command of the troops in present Hunan, one of his friends, a governor of the district of Tai-hu, was given a military post. This man was naive enough to believe that he could persuade the rebels to surrender and even wanted to go to meet them in the mountains. While he was pondering this fantastic plan, the rebels were approaching Hunan. When they arrived, he, having no idea of how to deal with them, ordered his soldiers to remove the cannon from the top of the city walls and place them in front of his office so that, after the fall of the city, he might carry on street fighting. This same man is said to have written a book on "secret merits" 陰隲 and to have shown it to the people: it gave them a sage warning not to kill birds. Another official, we are told, got quite a reputation for demanding bribes. His military reputation was impressive: when the attacks of the rebels became formidable, his only resource was to gather Buddhist monks to recite prayers that he personally might be spared.[24]

Sometimes, either because of jealousy or because of quarrels among themselves, the officers laid accusations against one another before the throne or high authorities. Often these cases became so confused that the judges could not come to any decision. This naturally hindered military activity, to the advantage of the enemy. Thus, in 1633, the governor of Shansi, Hsü Ting-ch'en 許鼎臣, impeached a battalion-commander, Liu Kuang-tso 劉光祚, for having received bribes and for having conspired with the rebels. Orders came from the emperor that the accused man should be removed from office and punished according to the law. But not long afterwards the eunuch Liu Yün-chung 劉允中 who was then supervising troops in Shansi, reported to the emperor that Liu Kuang-tso had shown great bravery in the siege of a city. Next, in a separate memorial, the eunuch accused Hsü Ting-ch'en of frequent interference in military operations. The emperor was greatly puzzled by these reports. "On the one hand," he said, "there is strong evidence that Liu Kuang-tso has been conspiring with the rebels. Yet, on the other hand, there is the eunuch's report, attributing the recapture of a city to Liu Kuang-tso's merits. How can there be such a contradiction?" He accordingly suspended judgment and ordered the censor to investigate the case thoroughly.[25]

In consequence of such false reports, many good generals were dismissed, imprisoned, or, not infrequently, executed. The renowned

General Hsiung T'ing-pi 熊廷弼 suffered in this way. In 1620, while awaiting sentence after dismissal, he had the courage to tell the emperor that for a long time the court had had no real news from the frontier other than the "courier news".

Whenever the ministers were informed that the enemy forces were less active, orders were issued urging the army to carry out a full-scale offensive. The ministers' idea was that by delaying, the army would lose its spirit, and revenue would be wasted. When the army in carrying out these orders suffered great defeats, the ministers all became depressed and, realizing that the disaster had been the result of their ill-considered interference, took refuge in a policy of silence and no longer dared even to mention fighting the enemy. Hsiung's judgment was that, since it was not easy for the court ministers to obtain true news from the army, it would be far better for them to leave the affairs of different regions to local authorities. Interference with them could only increase the confusion.[26]

When a rebellion broke out in Shansi at the beginning of the Ch'ung-chen period the government did not know what measures to take. Some favored the use of force to suppress the bandits; others thought it might be better to bring the rebels to submission by persuasion and lenience. For a time it seemed as if the second policy would prevail. One of its strongest advocates was the governor of Shensi, Yang Ho 楊鶴, a timid character, a pacifist rather than a soldier. According to him, the majority of the rebels were soldiers from the borders who had revolted because the government had not paid their salaries for four years. Since the soil of Shensi was far from fertile, a few years' drought had made agriculture impossible. Yang Ho may not have been a hero, but this observation was certainly accurate, and he was facing facts when he said that under these circumstances the soldiers could do nothing but revolt. He added a second argument based on the time when one of the Mongolian tribes revolted in the Ch'eng-hua reign. It had cost the government a great outlay of both men and money to suppress the revolt. In his own day, the physical resources of the country were nearly exhausted and he thought the struggle beyond its power. After all, the Manchus had been making trouble in the northeastern part of the empire for over a decade, and no one seemed to have been able to check them. Where could one find the resources and manpower to wage war against the rebels? Besides, the forces of these rebels seemed to be irresistible, and it was impossible to guard every place.[27]

Yang Ho's analysis of contemporary difficulties was factual and his reluctance to use force against the rebels was defensible. Nevertheless he is to be blamed for the insufficiency of his efforts to alleviate the sufferings of the people. He was too intelligent not to recognize that suffering, but his attempts to cope with it were superficial. He was inclined to be too lenient towards the rebels, as may be seen from his own account to the throne:

"Your servant agreed with the magistrate of the district, Chou Jih-ch'iang 周日强, that those who had surrendered should be treated with civility. Accordingly, an imperial monument (龍亭) was set up on the city wall and the rebels were ordered to prostrate themselves before it. They all cried thrice 'Long live the emperor!' and were then admitted into the city. They were then ordered to carry the imperial monument, with two yellow banners preceding it. On one of these banners was written: 'Long live the emperor!' and on the other: 'Let there be peace!' The monument and the banners were installed in your servant's office, where your servant led the civil and military officials, the people and their elders in performing the ceremonies of the five bows and the three prostrations. Then the students of the prefecture read the edict of Your Majesty. The rebels all knelt down and, while listening to the reading, repeatedly struck their heads on the ground in salutation.

"The ceremonies being over, your servant gave orders to some of the officials to lead the rebels to the temple of Kuan-ti 關帝, where incense was burnt and oaths were taken. Your servant was there in person. The rebels came, surrounding your servant's sedan chair, and your servant allowed himself to be carried by them to show that peace was now reigning. Then the elders of the people were told not to be afraid. After that, the people in the prefecture celebrated the occasion with exceeding joy. They all praised the awe-inspiring virtue of Your Majesty which was responsible for the submission of the wicked. . . ."[28]

Among the military officers there was a group of men of undetermined status who occupied a place between the government and the rebels. Officially they were in government service, but they were not fully under its control and frequently had secret communication with the rebels. Being very well aware of the corruption of the court ministers, they were unwilling to submit fully to their commands lest they should lose their freedom and find themselves at the mercy of both the government and the rebels despite their tried skill as soldiers. The court ministers often had to yield to their audacious demands for fear that they might revolt. The rebels, in turn, found that the only way of avoiding unendurable pressure from government troops was to bribe these men into inaction.

Of this class of men, perhaps the most famous was Tso Liang-yü 左良玉. Tso Liang-yü, a genuine soldier who in his youth had won fame for bravery, held the rank of tsung-ping-kuan 總兵官 in the imperial army. Toward the end of the Ch'ung-chen period, knowing what the government was, he had no confidence in it and his campaign against the rebels seems to have been waged rather for the defense of his own position than for the security of the empire. The historian Tai T'ien-yu 戴田有 has left an interesting account of this soldier of fortune. When he passed through T'ung-ch'eng 桐城 he had with him an army of over twenty thousand, formed into a long line extending many li. For three days he and his troops stayed in a suburb of the city. Some of the local gentry went to interview him, and he did his best to make them understand what he was doing. Ten per cent of the rebels, he said, had surrendered to the government, two or three tenths of them had been captured, and nearly half had lost their lives in battle. The number of rebels, nevertheless, kept on multiplying on account of famine and bad government administration. If the rebels won a battle they pressed on; if they suffered defeat they scattered money on the ground to tempt the greedy soldiers, and so escaped. When Tso was asked whether all military officers received bribes from the rebels, he frankly admitted that all did: there was no exception. But, seeking apparently to excuse himself, he said that he himself received money with his left hand but cut off the heads of the rebels with his right. Finally, when asked whether there was any hope of completely suppressing the revolts, he answered that it would not be very difficult to do so. The real trouble, he said, was that the military class did not wish to see the rebels completely destroyed, for they well knew that as soon as they had put an end to the revolts they would be removed from their posts by those who envied them, and that they might even have to face more serious consequences.[29]

These remarks of Tso Liang-yü's may be said to have mirrored his own life. Towards the last few years of the Ch'ung-chen period, the rebels grew so strong that his forces could no longer meet them on equal terms and he suffered repeated defeats. Eventually many of his own soldiers deserted him and he was forced to incorporate into his army rebels who had surrendered to the government. The *Tsui-wei-lu* 罪惟錄 tells us that in 1642, though Tso was still able to maintain an army of two hundred thousand, their morale was very low, for they had not been trained to strict military discipline. As a result the people lost confidence in Tso and preferred to entrust the defence of their cities to their own guards rather than depend on his half-bandit soldiers. Tso indeed could no longer face the challenge of the rebels, because his troops were not fully equipped and resources were wanting. It was said that only one-tenth of his two hundred thousand soldiers were maintained by the government, the rest had to support themselves by robbing the people.

When the arch-rebel Li Tzu-ch'eng was approaching Hsiang-yang, Tso ordered the withdrawal to the south of the boats built in Fan-ch'eng 樊城 for rice transport. The people of Hsiang-yang on learning of this were enraged and set fire to all his boats. Undeterred, the stubborn general ordered his soldiers to seize the merchants' boats for the transportation of his own family and his troops to Wu-ch'ang. The people of Hsiang-yang, in a frenzy of despair, decided to abandon the city to the rebels. In revenge for their cruel desertion by the government, they went to meet the rebels, bringing with them offerings of cattle and wine, as symbols of total submission. Meanwhile Tso had withdrawn to Wu-ch'ang where he tried to obtain from Prince Ch'u 楚王 a hundred thousand men, besides horses and resources. The avaricious prince, however, refused to yield to such extravagant demands, and Tso, disappointed and resentful, ordered his soldiers to sack the city. By now the rebels, under the leadership of Li Tzu-ch'eng, were approaching Wu-ch'ang, so Tso, realizing his own weakness, fled eastward, taking with him the army of Hupei. Many of the cities were thus left defenceless and the people had to organize themselves in bands for their own protection.[30]

FUNDS

After the ruin of the military and merchant settlements, it became more difficult every day to support the soldiers. When Yen-ta Han (Alda[—Alta (n)] Qan) invaded the capital about the middle of the Chia-ching reign, taxes had to be increased in order to meet the expenses of the army.[31] In an official report compiled about the middle of the Wan-li period we find it stated that around the years 1480 to 1520, military expenditure in the border districts had been about four hundred and thirty thousand silver taels a year. But in the course of the Chia-ching reign (1522–1566), the amount rose to one million and eleven hundred thousand yearly. Under the Lung-ch'ing reign it went up to over two million and three hundred thousand taels. By the middle of the Wan-li period the sum had risen to three million or eight hundred thousand. Even this huge sum does not seem to have sufficed, for the Board of War made an attempt to borrow money from the Court of the Imperial Stud. The precedent thus established was followed by other boards, and before long half of the four million silver taels stored in the court treasury had been dissipated. A minister accordingly complained to the emperor that this money had been reserved in the treasury since the Chia-ching and Lung-ch'ing periods for the purpose of buying horses as need arose. Since the money was being borrowed with no serious intention of repayment, the whole fund would soon be exhausted. How then would the imperial city defend itself should the Mongols launch an attack?[32]

Not all the soldiers seem to have benefited from the increased taxation. In 1606 the Supervising Censor of the Board of Revenue reported that there had been frequent famines in the Hsüan-fu and Ta-t'ung prefectures, and that for four months there had been a scarcity of food supplies in Chi-hsien 薊縣. The soldiers were suffering from malnutrition and many of the horses had starved to death. In Liao-tung the situation was no better. A soldier's pay was only four ch'ien (less than half of a silver tael) per month, and the soldiers often had to wait three or four months for this meagre sum. In spring and summer, the seasons of high prices, a ch'ien would buy only a few pints of grain and the soldiers often found it necessary to borrow money from usurers or to pawn their clothes if they were to survive. Then when winter came, many of them perished from cold and starvation.[33]

Shortly after the accession of the Ch'ung-chen emperor, the Vice-President of the Board of War had an audience during which he was able to give the new emperor a clear account of the difficulties of the time. Since the end of the Wan-li period, he said, taxes had increased to six million silver taels yearly owing to the cost of the war with the Manchus. The soldiers were suffering severe hardship chiefly because the impoverished Board of War had to withhold their pay, sometimes for as long as five or six months. Indeed, in Yen-sui, the soldiers had not received their pay for two and a half years.[34]

Early in the Ch'ung-chen period, the imperial treasuries, not yet exhausted, were often employed to supply the needs of the troops. Some of this money, however, was foolishly squandered. We are told that to celebrate the accession of the Ch'ung-chen emperor, two and a half million silver taels were spent on banquets for the soldiers, each of whom also received two silver taels. Mao Wen-lung 毛文龍, who was then holding a small island opposite the mainland of Manchuria, received three hundred thousand silver taels, because he claimed to have fifteen thousand soldiers, although in reality he had only a few thousand.[35]

In 1629, it was foreseen that the revenue from ordinary taxes would not suffice to cover military expenditure. Accordingly, a tax increase of three li 釐 (a li is one thousandth of a tael) was imposed on every mou of land. Eight years later (1635), Yang Ssu-ch'ang 楊嗣昌 petitioned for an increase of another two million eight hundred thousand silver taels. The emperor was fully aware of the burden that extra taxation would lay upon the people, but he could conceive of no alternative. "Without soldiers we are deprived of the means of suppressing the rebels, and without increased taxes there will be no supplies for the soldiers. We regret that we have to burden our people for one year . . ." said the edict. Two years later the rebels were still waging war, so taxes amounting yearly to another seven million three hundred thousand silver taels were levied. It was estimated that in the twenty-two years between the end of the Wan-li period (1620), and the fall of the dynasty (1644), taxation had risen by over sixteen million seven hundred thousand silver taels.[36]

In 1632, Hung Ch'eng-ch'ou 洪承疇 was in command of the army fighting the rebels. Seeing the difficulties involved in feeding and equipping his large army, he suggested to the emperor that two hundred thousand silver taels of the revenue of Shensi be employed partly to support the army that was engaging the rebels, and partly to help the soldiers to set up farms. This plan for reviving military settlements came too late. The rebels were devastating villages and farms everywhere, and since the troops had to be constantly on the move, they had no time for farming.[37]

The rebels kept on multiplying and it became impossible for the government to increase the number of soldiers in proportion to the need. Besides, every increase in the number of soldiers meant a heavier financial burden on the government. In 1636, the Governor-General of Shensi reported that the prefectures and districts of his province were all financially exhausted. Gradually the number of soldiers began to decrease, but the number of rebels daily increased. The soldiers often went hungry and suffered every kind of misery, whereas the rebels were always well fed and moved about at their ease.[38] By 1639, the military revenue was so low that an official in Shensi suggested the dispatch of court ministers to every corner of the empire to look for the money and grain needed to supply the troops.[39]

By the latter half of the Ch'ung-chen reign, the emperor was no longer able to support the army from the imperial treasury. A eunuch who saw the difficulties of the situation proposed that every court minister should make a personal contribution toward the war fund.

Beginning with the Grand Secretary they all contributed. Early in 1628 and 1629, the court ministers had voluntarily proposed the same plan, but the emperor had haughtily rejected their offer, saying that if they were really sincere and loyal in serving the country, they would reform all the abuses—a far more valuable service than the contribution of part of their salaries. Now, however, he gave silent approval.[40] So low had he fallen that he yielded to the necessity of borrowing from his relatives, from the ministers, and even from the eunuchs.[41]

In 1644, when Ta-t'ung was lost to the rebels, the emperor convoked an emergency council, but by this time all the ministers had lost courage and they hardly uttered a word. The emperor was deeply disappointed. When financial help was being discussed, an official proposed selling examination degrees to the students. Formerly the President of the Board of War, knowing that the imperial treasuries were exhausted, had proposed the selling of pardons to murderers and bandits, promising the emperor that by this means he could obtain several tens of thousands of silver taels in Kiang-nan alone. The emperor rebuked the minister severely for his dishonesty and, in a rage, ordered his imprisonment. Later, however, he pardoned him and restored him to his former office as President of the Board of War.[42]

It would be difficult to prove that the emperor was ignorant of the threat of woe. Early in his reign he had already been warned by his ministers. One of them, in 1632, told him that the number employed in the Ching-ying exceeded one thousand, including fortune-tellers, merchants, sub-officials and clerks. They had got their jobs through a variety of pretences. The officials had admitted many of them either through personal partiality or through sheer ignorance. What wonder then if the military forces had deteriorated so seriously?[43]

The emperor regarded the levying of taxes as justifiable since the upkeep of the soldiers was necessary for the protection of the people. Apparently he did not fully realize that times had changed and that many of his subjects were no longer loyal to him. Even those who were still loyal had little reason to believe that they would help the emperor much by paying heavy taxes; for a great part of the sums raised by the government for training new soldiers went into the pockets of the officials. "Where are the soldiers and horses that Your Majesty ordered to be trained? The tu-fu of Chi chou 薊州 received orders to train forty-five thousand soldiers, but so far he has only twenty-five thousand. And the tu-fu of Pao-ting 保定 has only two thousand five hundred though he was ordered to train thirty thousand. . . ." Such was the situation that the Grand Secretary had to report to the Ch'ung-chen emperor. He added that over-zealous officials in order to obtain the prescribed amount of taxes put heavy pressure on the people, thus driving them to such despair that they went willingly over to the side of the rebels.[44]

By the last year of the Ch'ung-chen reign (1644), the financial position of the government had become desperate. A minister of the Board of Revenue suggested the revival of paper money, saying that if the government could issue three hundred million kuan 貫 yearly at one tael of silver per kuan, a total of three hundred million taels of silver would be obtained. Accordingly a printing-house was founded and day and night paper money was produced. An appeal was made for merchants to sell this paper money to the people, but the merchants declined. The plan fell through because the people had lost confidence in the government.[45]

MERCENARIES

In the Wan-li period most of the soldiers were mercenaries, the wei-so soldiers having declined considerably in number and in quality. Even earlier, the scholar Ch'en Chien, who lived in the Chia-ching period, had a very low opinion of them. "The total number of the wei-so army is still over nine hundred thousand," he said. "The garrison of the northwest numbers about three hundred thousand and is of some use, but the remaining six hundred thousand, stationed in the two capitals or in the provinces, burden the country and are the source of many troubles. They start riots and try to revolt whenever the authorities are slow in paying them. They have even dared to kill government officials and rob and burn the houses of the people. The court is helpless and has to suffer them in silence. Nowadays much of our revenue is spent on the maintenance of these soldiers who are not only useless but are a cause of endless anxiety to the country. The old proverb says 'soldiers are raised to protect the people'. But now, whenever there is a rumor of war there is actually fear (among the authorities) that the army may be injured. Accordingly, village guards and mercenaries are employed to deal with the bandits. In a word, civilians are used to protect the soldiers. Alas, it would be better if we had no soldiers at all!"[46]

As a rule, the mercenary soldiers of the Ming dynasty were also of low quality. They were enlisted from among the poor, the vagabonds, and in the later period even from among the bandits. They never received much military training; hence their discipline was never good. Their pay was low and their equipment poor. Yet the government had no choice but to depend on them. A memorial submitted by a censor in 1620 gives us some idea of the troops in the capital—perhaps the best in the country. "The capital, the most important place in the country, depends solely on one Ching-ying 京營", he said. "Nominally the Ching-ying consists of one hundred and twenty thousand soldiers; but half of those listed in the records are no longer there, and those that still remain are vagabonds. It would be impossible to depend on them for the defence of the capital if war should break out. It is said that (the authorities) dare not reform them lest the attempt at reform should lead to a riot. They dare not train them since this might cause the same disaster. . . ."[47] The censor's mistrust of the military rolls was well grounded. Early in that same year General Hsiung T'ing-pi 熊廷弼 reported to the emperor that though soldiers were said to have been sent to him by the Board of War, in truth only a list of soldiers' names had arrived, never the soldiers. Elsewhere we are told of over seventeen thousand four hundred new soldiers who were recruited and sent as garrisons to Chen-kiang 鎮江 and Ch'ing-ho 清河: they all deserted.[48]

As time went on the old homogeneous army gave way to a bizarre collection of highly diverse groups. Among the mercenary soldiers there was a band of miners, known as mao-hu-lu ping 毛葫蘆兵, who were citizen soldiers from Sung-shan 嵩山, Honan province. Their leaders were called nao-chüeh 腦角. These and the yen-ping 鹽兵, who originally were workers from the salt pits, were employed in times of emergency. Both groups contained many bad characters and both were audacious and hard to control.[49] Then there were soldiers who had been summoned from the Liao-tung border under their own officials, to fight against the rebels. These borderland troops were feared by the rebels, who, not understanding their language, found them hard to bribe. They had their own customs and their food and drink were quite different from those of the ordinary Chinese. They would not take orders from the Chinese officials, and we are told that their behavior was no better than that of the rebels.[50] Finally, there were Chinese soldiers from different provinces. Shensi, the birth-place of so many notorious rebel leaders, also produced many soldiers. Perhaps the poor quality of the soil compelled many of its inhabitants to seek a life of adventure. There was naturally a certain camaraderie between the Shensi rebels and the native soldiers of Shensi. This was strengthened by the frequent discovery that rebels and soldiers had been boys together in the same village. Among the native soldiers many, we are told, came from the prefecture of Hsiang-fu 祥符, Honan province. Their discipline was good and they were, therefore, easy to control, but they lacked courage.[51]

Since few soldiers at this period were true professionals, military inefficiency was almost inevitable. Indeed, many soldiers had earlier been bandits and had thus acquired an independent spirit and a taste for booty. The author of the *San-yüan pi-chi* tells us that the soldiers sent to suppress the rebels often deserted on the way. Vagabonds were then enrolled to take their places. The officers seized the opportunity to appropriate the salaries of the absent soldiers, and the vagabonds made haste to plunder the populace. The military leaders were so skilful in drawing up false reports that officials were often deceived by them. We are told that at time of defeat they could create such confusion either on the field or in their reports, that the defeat looked like a victory.[52]

Because of lack of support from the government, the burden of providing for the soldiers fell on the shoulders of the commanding officers. Under such circumstances it is hard to see how they could have both remained honest and maintained great forces. One commander indeed does seem to have attempted to preserve his honor. In 1636, General Hung Ch'eng-ch'ou, then fighting against the rebels in Shensi, had eight thousand soldiers under him. For a whole month they had received nothing from the government and this in the season when food prices were at their highest in Sian. The soldiers sent up a clamor for their pay. The general at first tried kind words, but they kept on insisting, and he could only tell them frankly that they were free to remain in the army or to leave it. Many, we are told, deserted.[53]

Such frankness was rare. Most of the military leaders, if they failed to obtain supplies from the central government, had no scruple about demanding what they needed from the local government, and the local government could meet these demands only at the expense of the people. Sun Ch'eng-tse recalled how, when he was prefect of a certain prefecture, orders would arrive from military commanders, some demanding grain and hay, others mules and sacks, or cauldrons and horses. The unfortunate prefect had to make immediate delivery under threat of court-martial. Having no other resources, he was often forced to spend taxes collected for other purposes.[54] In 1634, the censor who had been appointed to visit Shensi wrote of a military officer who had come with his soldiers to Ch'ing-chien 清澗, and exacted four days' supply from the local governor. Later this officer moved to Yen-an and for over ten days allowed his soldiers to molest the inhabitants while paying no attention to the rebels. His negligence almost caused a revolt among the people.[55]

In those days the people used to say that the rebels were like broad-toothed combs which slip easily through the hair, whereas the soldiers were fine combs which go through the hair slowly and thoroughly. Thus the people feared the army more than the rebels. Many recorded instances point to habitual misconduct among the soldiery. Here is one instance given by the censor Wang-sun Fu 王孫莆. When the rebels took Chang-ch'iu 張秋 in Shantung, they remained there for only two days. Later government troops came and stayed for thirty-seven days, during which time they dug up the ground and split the walls open, examining every nook and cranny to find where the people had hidden their goods. On the day of their triumphant return to the capital, in addition to what the officials had taken by cart, every soldier brought his own personal loot. Within a day or two of their arrival in the capital, the silk stores near Cheng-yang Gate 正陽門 were sold out, and soldiers dressed in the finest silk robes could be seen walking proudly through the streets of the capital. How had these soldiers got their money, Wang-sun Fu asked, if not by looting the people? Worse still, on their way to the capital, they had kidnapped a number of male and female citizens. For fear of outraging public opinion in the capital, they kept the women in a suburb for a time, smuggling them into the city a little later. Many of these women were afterwards sold to brothels.[56]

An eye-witness describes the distress caused in many districts in Szechuan province by the comings and goings of soldiers and rebels in the troubled years when the rebels were invading the northern and eastern parts of the province. The rebels, he said, though cruel, did not take from the people things of small value. The soldiers rivalled the rebels in such acts of major savagery as killing, robbing, kidnapping, and torturing the innocent, and surpassed them in petty cruelty, even taking from the poor their old clothes and their worthless little treasures.[57] Another eye-witness says that in a certain village the people killed all their cocks lest their crowing should attract the attention of the soldiers and start them looting.[58]

Many of the soldiers entered into secret communication with the rebels. The Board of War stated, in 1636, that soldiers were frequently seen concealing their emblems on the battlefield in order to carry on conversations with the enemy. Sometimes these treasonable conversations turned into tearful reunions when the soldiers found in the rebels fellow townsmen and old friends. A historian has left us an account which helps to explain such ludicrous scenes:

"The soldiers on the border of Shensi were countrymen of the rebels and so were never earnest in battle. The Szechuan soldiers were greedy for loot and often allowed the rebels to get away, provided they deposited on the road the money and clothes they had looted or the people they had kidnapped.

"When the rebels met troops from Shensi, they generally winked at them and asked whether they desired to fight a peaceful battle or a real one. The troops, being afraid of the enemy and loath to fight, would answer nonchalantly, 'We want a peaceful battle.' They were then given bribes. If they insisted on receiving a token of victory to be brought back as a means of winning the honor due to victors, they were given some of the innocent people whom the rebels had captured. (On their return to their base the soldiers would behead these unfortunate prisoners and present the heads in support of their mendacious reports of sanguinary defeats inflicted on the enemy.) This worse than barbarous practice explains how reports of government victories and the actual number of rebels multiplied simultaneously.[59]

The killing of innocent people to bolster claims to victory and thus gain credit was a notorious and long established tradition. In 1512 the Board of War announced a generous reward for all who should kill rebels. Those who succeeded in killing rebel leaders were promised high government rank. The soldiers at once became eager to obtain enemy heads, and the rebels, realizing this, adopted the practice of driving captured non-combatants into the front line on the field of battle. These helpless victims were slaughtered to the great satisfaction of the soldiers. Victory after victory was reported to the Court, but the number of rebels never seemed to diminish.[60] In the days of the Chia-ching emperor a scholar pointed out the evils of this mercenary head-hunting:

"Consider!" he said. "The farmers labored to support the soldiers but the soldiers were unable to protect the farmers and instead of fighting the enemy they cut off the farmers' heads in order to claim a victory. Then the officers, wishing to cover up their own incapacity, cut off the heads of the soldiers who were killed in battle in order to make false reports of victory. Thus, not only did the farmers nourish bitter feelings against the soldiers, but the soldiers themselves had reason to murmur against their officers."[61] As early as 1583, we read of an official of the Board of War severely criticizing the corruption of the border troops. He accused them of having gathered the corpses of starved people in order to fake the number of the enemy they had killed on the battlefield. Sometimes, they even enticed innocent civilians to wild places and butchered them for the same purpose.[62]

Again, we are told that in 1618, in a quarrel between the Manchus and a certain tribe, the Manchus killed several hundred tribesmen and carried off their leaders. When the local Chinese military commander was informed of this incident, he immediately came in secret and cut off the heads of one hundred and sixty-five corpses, and returned with them to report a great victory over the Manchus![63] From this it seems clear that in the Wan-li days, a commander who wanted to gain merit of the first class had to present the heads of a hundred and sixty-five enemies killed on the battlefield. But, in the account left by a historian of the Ch'ung-chen period, it is stated explicitly that the military tradition required one hundred and twenty heads of the enemy in order to gain merit of the first class. We read elsewhere of a commander who killed thirty-five innocent civilians in order to make up the number of one hundred and twenty.[64]

In 1633, when the rebels learned that the government troops were approaching, they fled from Liao-chou. Later, when the troops came into the city, civilians were slaughtered by military officers to provide the heads needed for reports of victory. One of the officers, however, refused to copy the evil example of his colleagues and was highly praised by the people of Shansi.[65] As this account clearly implies, during the last years of the Ch'ung-chen period, the abominable practice had become common among the military class. The rebels, well aware of this fact, often kept large numbers of captured civilians. When they suffered defeat, they forthwith released these unfortunates to be slaughtered by the conscienceless soldiers. Thus the soldiers deceived their officers and the officers deceived the eunuchs. The eunuchs sent the welcome reports to the court and the court knowing nothing directly, gladly believed these reports of what seemed to be the genuine victories of an invincible celestial army.[66]

The practice of presenting the heads of noncombatants was always an atrocious one. It became in addition ridiculous when women's heads were substituted for those of soldiers. The origin of this monstrous aberration is not clear. Possibly there were times when men were not easy to find and so the soldiers fell to killing women; possibly the cause was that women offered less formidable resistance to the assaults of the murderers. In 1631, when the rebels were devastating many districts of Shensi, there was a general only twenty li away from them, but fear kept him from launching an offensive. When he was urged by the people to fight, he reluctantly acquiesced. Before long he announced a victory over the enemy and the massacre of fifty rebels; but when the heads were brought forth to be examined it was said that they were the heads of women.[67]

In time fraudulent production of severed heads became common, almost universal in the empire. Thus in Liao-tung during the war against the Manchus when the eunuch Tsao Hua-ch'un 曹化淳 was supervisor of the army, it was said that anyone who brought him the head of an enemy was given a large silver ingot of fifty taels (元寶). According to the information of the Board of War, the Manchus themselves had round faces with small mouths, but many of their soldiers came from Liao-tung and did not differ in features from the Chinese. Innocent people were often killed and their heads were presented as those of Liao-tung enemies. Sometimes these heads were beaten with a wet sandal to remove the marks of the headdresses on the forehead. Then when they had been steamed a little to make them look bigger and wider, were passed off as heads of the Manchus.[68] If Manchu soldiers were captured, they were confined within four high walls but were allowed to keep their own mode of dress and were given the food they were accustomed to. When next the Chinese troops were defeated by the Manchus, they would behead these prisoners, and bring forth the heads as proofs of victory. If these heads were examined, they were of course always found to be indubitable Manchu heads and showed no trace of imprisonment. For such heads the soldiers never failed to receive their rewards.[69]

In 1632, after the rebels had fled to T'ai-hang-shan, a group of soldiers came after them. The commanding officer requested the local governor to report victory to the government, but the latter refused to do so. According to him, it was not permissible to claim a victory, unless the heads of the enemy were brought forth as proof. When the official heard this, he declared that that would present no difficulty. He went off and quickly returned with a thousand human heads. Over eighty of these were identified as the heads of students from neighboring districts.[70] It is certain that toward the end of the Ming dynasty all those who claimed victories over rebels had to present human heads in confirmation of their claim. The practice was, no doubt, imposed by the government as a precaution against the submission of false reports and it was not foreseen that it might give rise to fearsome abuses.

In the last four years of the Ch'ung-chen period, however, the emperor seems to have come to know what was happening. Towards the end of 1640, he issued an edict to the governor of Honan, reminding him that he was bound in duty and in honor to suppress the rebels. Thenceforth, he was told, it would be unnecessary to report victories with the number of enemy heads recorded, for these after all, added nothing to victory over the rebels.[71] Needless to say, this edict did no good; it was too late now to look for obedience from the military class.

NOTES

[1] *Ming-shih*, 89, (ts'e 32) 1ab.

[2] *Tien-ku chi-wen*, 17, (ts'e 134) 8ab.

[3] *Ming shih*, 89, (ts'e 32) 5b, 6a.

[4] *Tien-ku chi-wen*, 17, (ts'e 134) 21a–22a.

[5] Cheng Hsiao 鄭曉, *Chin yen lei-pien* 今言類編, (SCIS second series), 4, (ts'e 14) 5b.

[6] *Hsü wen-hsien t'ung-k'ao*, 122, (ts'e 2) 3,891–3,892.

[7] *Tien-ku chi-wen*, 17, (ts'e 134) 7ab.

[8] Fan Ching-wen 范景文, *Fan-wen-chung-kung wen-chi* 范文忠公文集, (TSCCCP), 3, (ts'e 2,455) 40; *Ming-chen tsou-i*, 35, (ts'e 0,921) 678.

[9] *Fan wen-chung-kung wen-chi*, 3, (ts'e 2,455) 40.

[10] Ibid., 3, (ts'e 2,455) 44.

[11] Hsieh Yü-ts'ai 解毓才, "Ming-tai wei-so chih-tu hsing-shuai k'ao" 明代衞所制度興衰考, *Shuo-wen yüeh-k'an* 說文月刊, 2, (Dec., 1942) 413.

[12] *Fan wen-chung kung wen-chi*, 3, (ts'e 2,455) 38.

[13] "Ming-tai wei-so chih-tu hsing-shuai k'ao" Ibid. 5.

[14] *Ch'un-ming meng-yu-lu*, 30, (ts'e 8) 19b.

[15] *Ming shih*, 89, (ts'e 32) 1a; *Chin-yen lei-pien*, 4, (ts'e 14) 7b.

[16] *Ming shih*, 304, (ts'e 101) 9a.

[17] Ibid., 89, (ts'e 32) 6ab.

[18] Ibid., 89, (ts'e 32) 8ab; *Tien-ku chi-wen*, 17, (ts'e 134) 19ab; *Ming-chen tsou-i*, 35, (ts'e 0921) 681–682.

[19] *K'ou-shih pien-nien*, 4, (ts'e 5) 5b.

[20] *Ming shih*, 77, (ts'e 27) 10b.

[21] Shimizu Taiji 清水泰次, "Ming-tai chun-t'un chih peng-k'uai" 明代軍屯之崩潰 (tr. by Fang Chi-sheng 方紀生). *Shih-ho pan-yüeh k'an* 食貨半月刊, 4, (1936) 10. 31–45.

[22] From e.g. *Ming shih*; *Ming shih-lu*; *Huang-ming ching-shih-wen pien* 皇明經世文編; "Ming-tai wei-so chih-tu hsing-shuai k'ao" Ibid. 419–421 cites several examples.

[23] *Ming-mo nung-min ch'i-i shih liao* 明末農民起義史料, (Peking 1952) 400–402.

[24] Tai T'ien-yu 戴田有, *Chieh i lu* 孑遺錄, (*Kuo-sui ts'ung-shu* 國粹叢書, 3rd series) (ts'e 45) (Shanghai 1909) 4a, 7b.

[25] *Ming-mo nung-mi ch'i-i shih-liao*, 34–45, 94–97; cf. also Cha To 查鐸, *I-chai tsou-shu* 毅齋奏疏, (TSCCCP), (ts'e 0907) 3.

[26] Kuan-ko shan-jen 管葛山人 i.e. P'eng Sun-i 彭孫貽, *Shan-chung wen-chien lu* 山中聞見錄, (*Yü-chien-chai ts'ung-shu* 玉簡齋叢書, edited by Lo Chen-yü 羅振玉) 2, (ts'e 4) (1910) 16b, 17a.

[27] *Ming-mo nung-min ch'i-i shih-liao,* 11, 12.

[28] Ibid , 1 , 13.

[29] *Chieh-i lu,* 5b.

[30] *Tsui-wei lu,* 31, (ts'e 57) 8 b; *K'ou-shih pien-nien,* 15, (ts'e 10) 20ab, 21a; cf. also Kao Tou-shu 高斗樞, *Shou Yün chi-lüeh* 守鄖紀略, (*T'ung-shih* series) (ts'e 30) 1b, 2a; Huang Tsung-hsi 黃宗義, *Nan-lei wen-ting* 南雷文定, first series, (TSCCCP), 5, (ts'e 2463) 83; Ch'en T'ien 陳田, *Ming-shih chi-shih* 明詩紀事, (*Kuo-hsüeh chi-pen ts'ung-shu* 國學基本叢書, 22, (ts'e 10) 3161.

[31] Cheng Ta-yü 鄭大郁, *Ching-kuo hsiung lüeh* 經國雄略, (late Ming edition) *T'un-tien k'ao* 屯田考, 2, (ts'e 12) 17b; *Ming shih,* 202, (ts'e 67) 11b.

[32] *Ch'un-ming meng-yu-lu,* 35, (ts'e 10) 14ab; 53 (ts'e 20) 6b–8b.

[33] *Hsi-yüan wen-chien lu,* 64, (ts'e 26) 1b–3a; *Shan-chung wen-chien lu,* 2, (ts'e 4) 12a.

[34] *Wang-hsiao-ssu-ma tsou-shu,* 52.

[35] Sun Ch'eng-tse 孫承澤, *Ssu-ling tien-li chi* 思陵典禮紀, (TSCCCP), 1, (ts'e 3,979) a; *Huai-tsung Ch'ung-chen shih-lu,* 1, (ts'e 498) 3ab, 5ab, 8.

[36] *Erh-shih erh-shih cha-chi,* 36, (ts'e 6) 35b, 36a.

[37] *P'ing-k'ou-chih,* 1, (ts'e 1) 7a.

[38] *K'ou-shih pien-nien,* 9, (ts'e 8) 25a; *Huai-tsung Ch'ung-chen shih-lu,* 10, (ts'e 497) 7b, 8a.

[39] *K'ou-shih pien-nien,* 12, (ts'e 9) 7a.

[40] *Huai-tsung Ch'ung-chen shih-lu,* 2, (ts'e 498) 3a; 3, (ts'e 498) 2b; 9, (ts'e 499) 7a.

[41] Ibid., 9, (ts'e 499) 11b; *K'ou-shih pien-nien,* 9, (ts'e 8) 24b.

[42] *K'ou-shih pien-nien,* 17, (ts'e 11) 11b.

[43] *Ch'ung-chen ts'un shih shu ch'ao* 崇禎存實疏鈔, 2a, (ts'e 3) 15b–16a

[44] *Ch'üan-chou-fu chih* 泉州府志, (edited since the Republic), 44, (ts'e 27) 87a–88a; c. *Ming shih,* 251, (ts'e 83) 22a–26a.

[45] *Ch'üan-chou-fu-chih,* 44, (ts'e 27) 86ab; *Ming shih,* 251, (ts'e 83) 24a. The *Ch'ung-chen chang-pien* (13–14) says that Chiang Ch'en 蔣臣, one of the ministers of the Board of Revenue, suggested the printing of five hundred million kuan notes at one silver tael per *kuan.* According to his estimation the silver then circulating throughout the empire amounted to two thousand five hundred million. By issuing five hundred million kuan notes the government would be able to buy in one fifth of the silver in a year: within five years it should be able to take in all the amount of silver of the country. With this government reserve of silver to back it the paper money would be stabilized.

[46] Ibid., 25, (ts'e 19) 38a–39a.

[47] Shen Kuo-yuan 沈國元, *Liang-ch'ao ts'ung-hsin lu* 兩朝從信錄, (late Ming edition) 1, (ts'e 1) 1gb, 18a. The Ching-ying was regarded as the cream of the army in the earlier years of the dynasty. In the Yung-lo and Hsüan-te period six expeditions were sent against the Mongols and three against Annam, and in each the Ching-ying played the most important role. After the Tu-mu disaster in 1449 it declined till by the Ch'eng-hua reign it had lost its vitality. The *Ming shih* time and again refers to it as proud, lazy and useless. It is also accused of cowardice and of infecting border officers with cowardice. Cf. Wu Han 吳晗, "Ming-tai ti chün ping" 明代的軍兵 in the *Tu-shih cha-chi* 讀史劄記, (Peking, 1956) 110–111.

[48] *Chia-ching i-lai chu-luch,* 11, (ts'e 8) 42b, 41ab; cf. also 45b.

[49] *K'ou-shih pien-nien,* 5, (ts'e 6) 12a.

[50] Ibid., 9, (ts'e 8) 10b, 18b.

[51] Ibid., 9, (ts'e 8) 10b; 5, (ts'e 6) 12a; for full descriptions of the soldiers of different provinces cf. Shih Chi-tsu 史繼祖, *Huang-ming ping-chih k'ao* 皇明兵制考, (Ming edition) ts'e 3) 46ab, 47a; Ling Yang-tsao 凌揚藻, *I-shao pien* 蠡勺編, (TSCCCP), 16, (ts'e 0,229) 266.

[52] *Supplement to the San-yüan pi-chi,* (ts'e 1) A. 17b; cf. also *Lou-shan-t'ang chi,* 11, (ts'e 2,168) 133–134.

[53] *K'ou-shih pien-nien,* 10, (ts'e 8) 3a.

[54] *Ch'un-ming meng-yü-lu,* 36, (ts'e 11) 56a–58a.

[55] *Ming-mo nung-min ch'i-i shih-liao,* 104–105.

[56] *Chi-yüan chi so chi,* 9, (ts'e 14) 44b.

[57] Ou-yang Chih 歐陽直, *Ou-yang-shih i-shu* 歐陽氏遺書, (manuscript copy, no date) 7b.

[58] *Lou-shan-t'ang chi,* 23, (ts'e 2,169) 301.

[59] *P'ing-k'ou chih,* 2, (ts'e 1) 13a.

[60] *Ming t'ung-chien,* 44, (ts'e 4) 5a.

[61] *Ming-mo nung-min ch'i-i shih-liao,* 119–122; Wang Wen-lu 王文祿, *Shu-tu* 書牘, (TSCCCP), 1, (ts'e 0,755) 97.

[62] *Tsui-wei lu,* 12, (ts'e 5) 71b.

[63] *Shan-chung wen-chien lu,* 2, (ts'e 4) 9b.

[64] *K'ou-shih pien-nien,* 4, (ts'e 5) 5b.

[65] Ibid., 6, (ts'e 6) 1a.

[66] Ibid., 8, (ts'e 7) 16b; 13 (ts'e 9) 8a.

[67] *Huai-tsung Ch'ung-chen shih-lu,* 0, (ts'e 498) 13b; *P'ing-k'ou-chih,* 1, (ts'e 1) 6a; The text of the *Tsui-wei lu,* (17, Ts'e 7, 8b) combines two incidents into one and gives 5,000 heads instead of 50 heads. This is obviously a copyist's error. Two novels written and published in the late period of the Ming dynasty mention this contemporory practice. The following passage is from the 17th chapter (ts'e 2, 5a) (Late Ming edition) of *Liao-hai tan-chung lu* 遼海丹忠錄, (author unknown): "If they (i.e. the soldiers) happened to meet the Tatars (i.e. the Manchus) on the way, they should not be too eager to cut off the heads (of the enemy) in battle, for this would hinder their pursuit of the enemy and thus ruin the tactical plan. Furthermore, they should not seek rewards by killing Liao-tung civilians and reporting falsely that they were Manchus. In this matter we can find out the truth very easily. The Manchus shave their heads and keep their queues from their boyhood. Though the Liao-tung people may be made to look like Manchus for a time by shaving their heads, still, if the heads are put into the water for half a day, one cannot fail to see the mark of the head-dresses. Hence their heads are not to be confused (with the heads of Manchus) . . ."

The *P'ing-lo-chuan* 平虜傳, (anonymous) says in the second chapter (ts'e 2, 45b–46a) (late Ming edition): "The Manchus, as a rule, never killed all of them (i.e. the prisoners they captured). They brought them to their camps and shaved their heads to make them like their own, so that if the Chinese troops pursued them they might drive their prisoners out to face the army. The Chinese soldiers for their part, as soon as they cut off the head of an enemy immediately claimed a reward for it. Ordinarily if they met bald-headed civilians they cut their heads off without hesitation in order to claim a reward. They did this much more readily if they captured them on the battle-field. They cared little whether they were genuine Manchus or otherwise and never spared them. The prisoners knew clearly that they could not escape, but thought that they might have a better chance if they cooperated with the Manchus. Hence they fought desperately for the enemy. The latter, then, would let their prisoners meet the army while they themselves followed behind. The troops were often deceived by this trick. Most of the enemy they killed were not genuine."

[68] *San-yüan pi-chi,* (ts'e 1) A. 9b.

[69] *Yung-chuang hsiao-p'in,* 30, (ts'e 108) 4ab.

[70] *K'ou-shih pien-nien,* 5, (ts'e 6) 12a.

[71] *P'ing-k'ou-chih,* 3, (ts'e 1) 16b; cf. also *Yeh-chi meng-sou,* 6, (ts'e 3) 26a–27b.

Emperor Ch'eng-tsu, the Yung-lo Emperor, who reigned from 1403 to 1424. This and subsequent illustrations reproduced from the Collections of the Library of Congress.

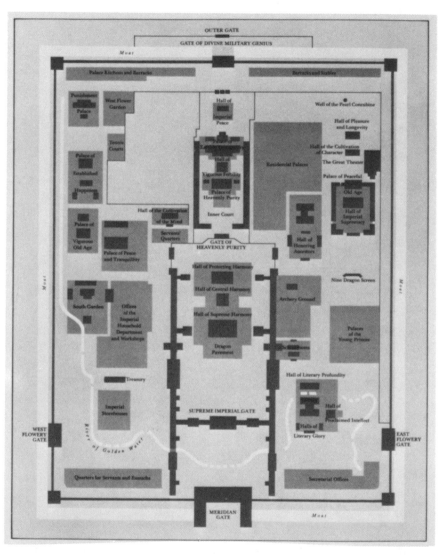

The Forbidden City, within the Imperial City, in northern Peking.

Emperor Ying-tsung, the Cheng-t'ung Emperor, who reigned from 1436 to 1449.

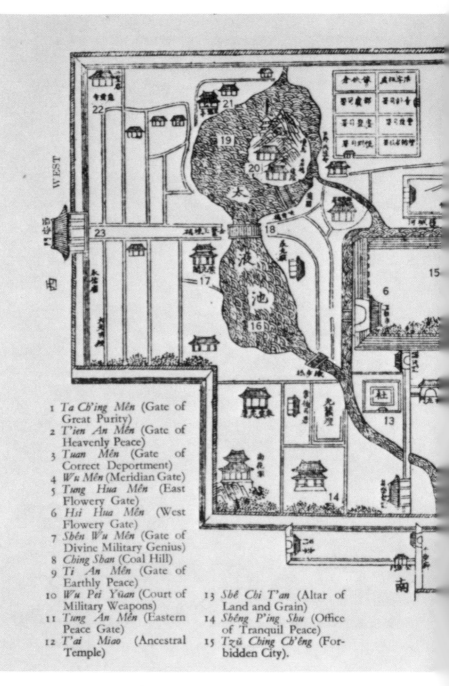

1 *Ta Ch'ing Mên* (Gate of Great Purity)
2 *T'ien An Mên* (Gate of Heavenly Peace)
3 *Tuan Mên* (Gate of Correct Deportment)
4 *Wu Mên* (Meridian Gate)
5 *Tung Hua Mên* (East Flowery Gate)
6 *Hsi Hua Mên* (West Flowery Gate)
7 *Shên Wu Mên* (Gate of Divine Military Genius)
8 *Ching Shan* (Coal Hill)
9 *Ti An Mên* (Gate of Earthly Peace)
10 *Wu Pei Yüan* (Court of Military Weapons)
11 *Tung An Mên* (Eastern Peace Gate)
12 *T'ai Miao* (Ancestral Temple)
13 *Shê Chi T'an* (Altar of Land and Grain)
14 *Shêng P'ing Shu* (Office of Tranquil Peace)
15 *Tzŭ Ching Ch'êng* (Forbidden City).

Old Chinese map of the Imperial City.

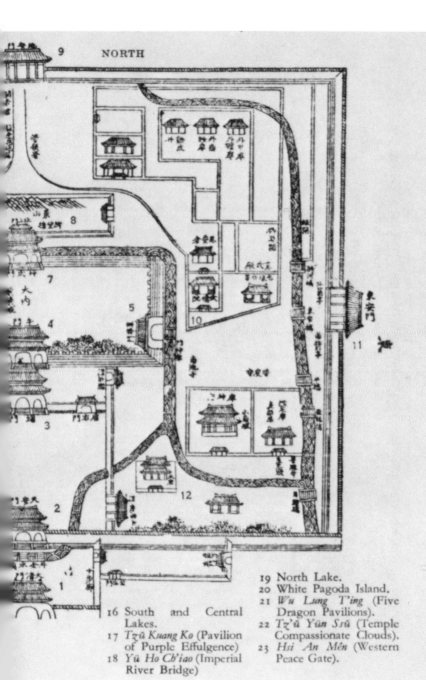

16 South and Central Lakes.

17 *Tzŭ Kuang Ko* (Pavilion of Purple Effulgence)

18 *Yü Ho Ch'iao* (Imperial River Bridge)

19 North Lake.

20 White Pagoda Island.

21 *Wu Lung T'ing* (Five Dragon Pavilions).

22 *Tz'ŭ Yün Ssŭ* (Temple Compassionate Clouds).

23 *Hsi An Mên* (Western Peace Gate).

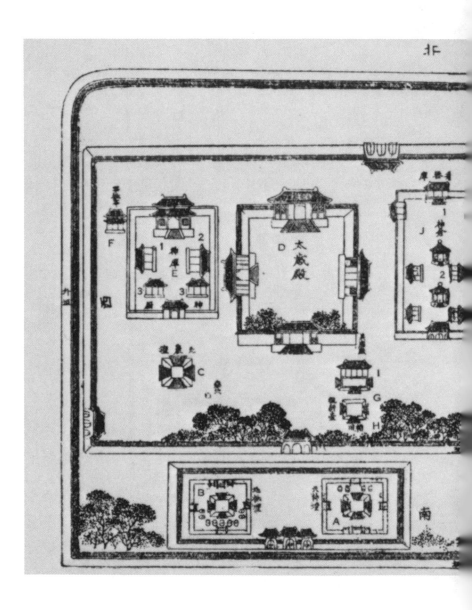

Old Chinese map of the Altar of Agriculture, Peking.

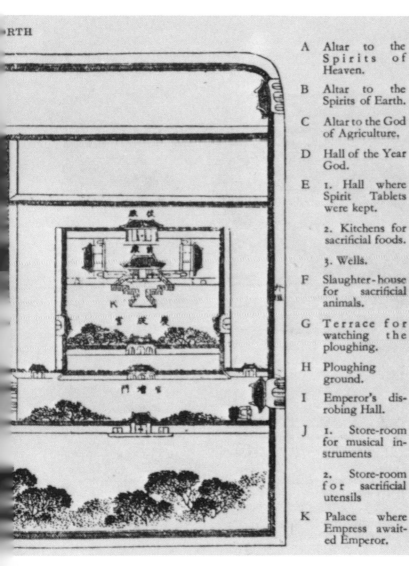

A   Altar to the Spirits of Heaven.

B   Altar to the Spirits of Earth.

C   Altar to the God of Agriculture,

D   Hall of the Year God.

E   1. Hall where Spirit Tablets were kept.

    2. Kitchens for sacrificial foods.

    3. Wells.

F   Slaughter-house for sacrificial animals.

G   Terrace for watching the ploughing.

H   Ploughing ground.

I   Emperor's dis-robing Hall.

J   1. Store-room for musical instruments

    2. Store-room for sacrificial utensils

K   Palace where Empress awaited Emperor.

The Temple of Heaven, in the Outer City (Peking): Top (north), the Hall of Prayer for Harvests; center, the Temple of the Ruler of the Universe; bottom (south), the Altar of Heaven. Photograph by Dmitri Kessel.

Above: The Hall of Prayer of Harvests—a circle in a square—northern part of the Temple of Heaven. Below: Entrance to the Hall of Prayer for Harvests.

Examination Halls, Peking. The halls were long rows of buildings divided into cubicles five feet square and ten feet high. Each candidate for a doctoral degree was confined in a cubicle for the duration of the written examinations, three days and two nights. Guards patrolled the lanes between the cells to be sure that there was no communication with the students.

Candidates for civil service positions await the results of competitive public examinations in Peking. Painting by the famed Ming artist Ch'ui Ying.

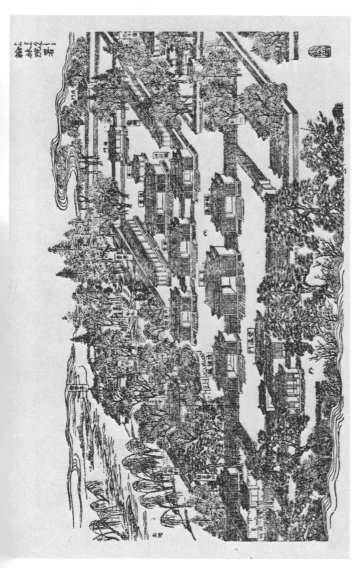

The Han-lin Academy, the prestigious academy for postdoctoral scholars who had passed the examination with great distinction. From a painting dating from the Ming Dynasty. The academy, in the southeastern part of the Imperial City, was founded in 1442, during the Cheng-t'ung reign. The academicians had several important duties: they supervised all literary productions, expounded on the classics before the emperor, composed prayers for ceremonial occasions, compiled histories and accounts and acts of the emperors, and kept topographical records.

Left: *Snow Scene,* by scholar-painter Weng Cheng-ming (1470–1559). Right: Detail of painting. Wen Cheng-ming taught at the Han-lin Academy.

Left: *Bird and Plum Blossoms,* by Ch'en Hung-shou (1599–1652), one of the dynasty's great painters.

Wisps of Smoke Among Bamboos at T'ai Hu, painting by Ming Dynasty artist T'ang Yin.

Above: The Valley of Thirteen Tombs, where the Ming emperors were buried. The tomb of the Yung-lo Emperor is in the distance. Photograph by Hedda Morrison. Below: Heroic marble statue, one of a guard of honor for dead emperors as they were borne into the burial valley.

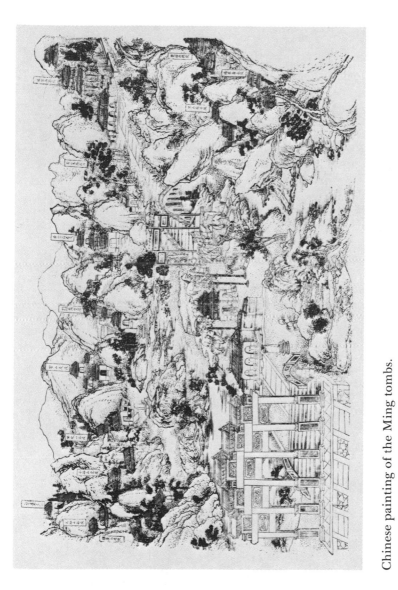

Chinese painting of the Ming tombs.

Emperor Shih-tsung, the Chia-ching Emperor, who reigned from 1522 to 1566.

CHAPTER NINE

Economics I

EMPEROR AND PEOPLE

In the year 1397, an order was issued by the Hung-wu emperor to the T'ung-cheng-ssu 通政司 (Transmission Office) giving it permission to report at the morning and evening court meetings both on civil and on important military affairs. The officials of the T'ung-cheng-ssu held important offices though they belonged to only the third and fourth degree of the official hierarchy of rank. Memorials to the throne throughout the empire went through this office before being presented to the emperor. The Hung-wu emperor used to say apropos of this office that government administration (in Chinese: *cheng* 政) is like water: it must not remain stagnant. This was his idea in founding this office—an idea expressed in the very name T'ung-cheng-ssu.[1]

The Hung-wu emperor attached great importance to the maintenance of close relations between the government and the people. We have already seen how, fearing that his ministers might fail in this respect, he tried to obtain information about the people through their own representatives. In this way, undesirable ministers were to a large extent eliminated and the foundation of the Ming imperial greatness was laid. The first emperor had given a good example and he expected his descendants to follow it. Shortly after his death, we are told, his grandson-successor fell into a habit of coming late to court. Very soon a censor gave him this counsel: "Our late emperor used to rise at cockcrow and make his appearance at court before dawn. Before sunrise he had seen all his subordinates. The benefits thus conferred on the administration of the government were manifest and the empire enjoyed great peace. Your Majesty who has now succeeded to the throne should follow closely in the footsteps of your grandfather by governing diligently. Your Majesty having grown accustomed to comfort, you delay your appearance at court till long after sunrise. Both ministers and guards grow tired of waiting and they suffer loss of time. What will people say when they hear, or later when they read in history that both superiors and subjects were negligent in their duties?" The young emperor, a well disposed man, had the humility and courage to admit and correct this fault.[2]

On the accession of the emperor Ying-tsung (1436) the afternoon court meeting was for the first time discontinued. His successor later tried to revive this tradition. He failed: both emperor and ministers had become accustomed to the new routine and regarded the revival of such old traditions as an unnecessary innovation.[3] Chao I, who made a study of this question, said that the emperors of the latter half of the Ming dynasty seldom interviewed their ministers. They lived in seclusion in their palaces and hardly ever appeared at court. The Wan-li emperor especially was notorious for this. For over twenty years in the latter part of his long reign he refused to grant any audiences at all to his ministers. Toward the middle of his reign a minister wrote to warn him that times had changed and that the country was not as peaceful as was imagined. He ended his warning with the remark that no one had ever heard of any empire remaining at peace while its ruler was neglecting his duty. His advice, however, was ignored by the emperor.[4]

The emperors' lack of interest in government affairs greatly encouraged corrupt ministers to indulge in open abuses. "Heaven is high and the emperor is far away" (天高皇帝遠) says an old Chinese proverb, i.e. one who is far from the court may do as he pleases. This was verified when the emperors of the late Ming period kept aloof from their ministers and so lost all their authority. A minister of the Chia-ching period wrote that in his day, with taxes becoming heavier every day, both soldiers and civilians were in great need. The emperor tried to shower benefits on the people but the people did not receive them and there was no means of reporting the sufferings of the people. An imperial edict ordered that help be given to the people but nothing was done. Another edict granted exemptions from taxes, but this led only to illegal exactions. The growth of corruption of every kind kept on increasing and officials paid attention to appearances rather than to reality.[5]

Since land taxes were the most important source of revenue, it might be thought that close relations between the government and the farmers were inevitable. Under the Hung-wu emperor such close relations existed. The emperor himself took great interest in the farmers and did his utmost to protect them from corrupt ministers. However, things changed after his death. The later emperors took very little notice of the people and left the way open for rapacious ministers to oppress the people. The life of the farmer under the Ming dynasty was not an easy one. Few farmers owned land. Normally their farms were rented from landlords and high rents were exacted— especially for farms owned by imperial relatives or eunuchs, and for those granted as rewards to ministers. The land taxes in Su-chou 蘇州 and Sung-kiang 松江 were known to be exceptionally high. According to one scholar, the Su-chou prefecture contained slightly less than one eighty-eighth of the farms of the whole country, yet the yield from the land there came to only a little less than a tenth of the total yield from the whole country. The taxes on the farms of the prefecture of Sung-kiang came to about 1,029,000 piculs of rice yearly.[6]

An old tradition explains why farm rents were so high in Kiang-nan. The Hung-wu emperor felt bitter resentment against the rich in this part of the country who had helped Chang Shih-ch'eng 張士誠 to put up a strong resistance against his forces in the earlier part of his struggle for power. When in time he came to the throne he sought revenge by confiscating the farms of the rich and demanding the same rate of rents as he found in the records of the rich families.[7] Whether this be true or not, he certainly seemed to nourish some resentment against the people of Kiang-nan. In the *Ta-ming hui-tien* we read that natives of Chekiang, Kiangsi, Su-chou and Sung-kiang were not admitted to offices in the Board of Revenue owing to the Hung-wu emperor's fear that the officials from these places might favor their own countrymen.[8]

FARMERS

In the early days of the dynasty it was found that many farms had gone out of cultivation in the preceding anarchy and it became a common practice for the government to transfer farmers from other districts to populate these man-made deserts. Thus, in the seventh year of the Hung-wu reign (1374), 140,000 inhabitants of Kiang-nan were sent to populate Feng-yang 鳳陽, the native country of the Hung-wu emperor. They were given cattle and grain to help them to cultivate the land and were told that any land they might cultivate would be regarded as their own property.[9] In the following year (1375), a minister who had been sent to inspect Han-chung reported that many of the people were living in the mountains. Apparently they had been so frightened by the heavy land-taxes and *corvée* that they had preferred to sacrifice their fertile farms and live tax-free in the mountains. When the emperor heard this he immediately ordered the local authority to reduce the land-taxes and impose lighter *corvée* on the people. Similarly when in the first year of the Hung-hsi reign (1424) it was reported to the emperor that the large number of empty farms was attributable either to the emigration of the people who could not sustain the heavy land-taxes and *corvée*, or to famine and plague, he at once took steps to remove all such difficulties. He instructed his ministers to alter any laws that were harmful to the people and to institute relief works for the destitute. Ministers who dared to delay the execution of these orders were threatened with severe penalties.[10]

The wise protection given by the early emperors to the farmers soon brought the country back to prosperity. In 1393, the area of cultivated lands amounted to 8,576,230 ch'ing.[11] Some of the farms belonged to the government, the rest were in private ownership, and the government kept careful records of both. Later, through negligence of the government, these records, the "Fish Scale Records" and the "Yellow Records", were allowed to fall into inaccuracy and many abuses began to creep in. By the Hung-chih period, only a century later, the area of cultivated land had shrunk to 4,290,300 ch'ing and 75 mou. A later estimate, made in the 22nd year of the Chia-ching reign (1543), gives almost the same area—4,360,563 ch'ing and a little more than 60 mou.[12] An official of the Chia-ching period explored the causes of the shrinkage of the large area of cultivated land in the Hung-wu period to less than half that area in the Hung-chih period. It was attributable, he said, to the donation of farms to princes, bandit devastation, errors in the records, and false returns made by dishonest landlords who wished to evade the payment of taxes. Finally extravagant donations by the emperors to officials and monasteries were among the causes of the decrease in revenue from farming areas.[13]

In the early days of his reign the Hung-wu emperor paid government officials in land, not in money. Very soon, however, he adopted the salary system, having apparently recognized the disadvantage of having land in the possession of government officials. Land, however, was frequently donated to nobles and deserving ministers. Soon, moreover, abuses crept in and covetous petitions for more land began to arrive from nobles and ministers. This abuse arose as early as the Hung-hsi (1425) and Hsüan-te (1426–35) periods when ministers of no great deserts did not blush to make such requests. Sometimes favorite eunuchs also dared to make such requests, and the weaker emperors often consented to their demands. Greed often led nobles and ministers to appropriate government and private land, and to cover up their crimes they sometimes accused the people of having occupied government farms. In 1440, the emperor Ying-tsung ordered that a record be made of the pasture land belonging to the nobles: all appropriated land was to be returned to the people.[14] In 1444, an edict was issued forbidding the nobles to make requests for farms within the capital, where, it was pointed out, the area available was strictly limited. In 1458, under the same emperor, another edict was issued threatening with heavy penalties any nobles who dared to appropriate farms belonging to the people: members of the families of errant nobles and any others who cooperated in this crime were to incur the penalty of exile for life.

Despite these imperial orders and others issued by later emperors the abuses continued and became even more serious. Thus, in 1467, the empress dowager's two brothers, Chou Shou 周壽, and Chou Yü 周俞, influenced by a set of scoundrels, petitioned successfully for large areas of farmland belonging to a host of small farmers. Chou Shou asked for the land of Ch'ing-tu 慶都, Ch'ing-yüan 清苑 and Ch'ing-ho 清河, over 5,400 ch'ing in all; Chou Yü asked for the land of Tung-kuang hsien 東光縣 in Ching-chou 景州, which amounted to over 1,900 ch'ing. Chou Yü moreover was ready to quarrel with the people of Chen-ting 眞定 and Wu-ch'iang 武强 over land. A minister of the Board of Punishments who was sent to investigate this case reported that since the early days of the dynasty, the emperors had permitted the people to cultivate the land of Chen-ting. Having put labor into it, they were permitted to possess the farms they cultivated. And to encourage farming these farmers were exempted from land taxes. It would therefore be unjust, he said, to rob the people of their means of livelihood.[15]

During the Hung-chih reign an attempt was made to halt the abuses and to remedy the situation. In the second year of the reign (1489), the farms of deceased eunuchs and some government land in the six prefectures of Peking were given to the people. Later, an ordinance was promulgated imposing the penalty of exile on those who offered land to the princes. However, in the later part of the Hung-chih reign this ordinance was no longer enforced and we are told that there was no lack of people who wished to offer their farms to the nobles. The nobles, for their part, kept on petitioning for more farms and the emperor frequently granted these requests. Four of the princes possessed between them over 7,000 ch'ing.[16]

Under the Cheng-te emperor the nobles kept on multiplying their requests for land—usually for land belonging to the people. The *Ming shih* says they asked for an "unlimited amount." This continued into the Chia-ching period, till 1560, when a censor was sent to investigate what had happened. As a result of his investigation more than 16,000 ch'ing of appropriated land was returned to the original owners.[17] The Wan-li emperor was fondly attached to his children and spoiled them by his excessive readiness to grant all their petitions. Prince Fu 福王, the *Ming shih* tells us, possessed in four provinces farms totalling 40,000 ch'ing.[18] Yet even this did not satisfy his avarice. On the pretext of visiting his farms he tried to seize still more land from the people, and, when they resisted, his eunuchs brutally slaughtered them. Some of the court officials, seeing in the silence of the emperor a sign of approval of the behavior of the prince, submitted a warning to the throne. Their arguments were: (a) Prince Fu's farms were to be found in several provinces. This was establishing a bad precedent which other princes might use later as an argument to induce the emperor to satisfy their greed for more land. (b) All the lands in these provinces had their rightful owners recorded in the official books of revenue. It was very bad policy to seize the property of the people simply to please the prince. (c) Although it was true that the emperor was nominally the possessor of the whole empire, this in fact meant only that he had the right to levy taxes on the land. The people had the right to live and needed to possess land for production. If their property was taken by violence, this would infallibly stir the people into rebellion.[19] These wise counsels did not please the emperor, but, feeling unable to resist the persistent admonitions of his ministers, he reluctantly agreed to cut Prince Fu's swollen land-holdings by half.[20]

Nor was Prince Fu's an isolated case. In 1605, the governor of Szechuan, K'ung Chen-i 孔貞一, declared that the princes possessed seventy per cent of the irrigated soil in Szechuan. Of the remaining thirty per cent, twenty per cent was owned by the military settlements, and only ten per cent was in the hands of the common farmers.[21]

The imperial house itself came to have its own estates. Such estates existed as early as the Hung-hsi period (1425), under the title kung-chuang 宮莊; but large scale development did not begin till the year 1461, when, after the revolt of the eunuch Ts'ao Chi-hsiang 曹吉祥, all his estates were confiscated to the imperial house. It was then that the term huang-chuang 皇莊 or 'imperial estates' first appeared in the history of the Ming dynasty. The farms originally given to Ts'ao Chi-hsiang amounted to one thousand ch'ing and thirteen mou, and he had gradually added to this by appropriating farms from the people. When these became imperial estates the eunuchs appropriated more land and, by the time of Chia-ching, the estates were almost ten times larger than the original ones of 1461. The author of the *Huang-Ming t'ung-chi* gives this as an illustration of the harm done to the people by the imperial estates and adds: "This is only one example: we can imagine the rest!"[22]

The Cheng-te emperor established seven imperial estates within a month of his accession. Later the number increased to over three hundred estates. The chief eunuch, Liu Chin, was, no doubt, behind the scheme. In the days of his power, about the year 1507, he made a habit of confiscating the lands of the people and turning them into imperial farms. The Chia-ching emperor (1522–1566), aware of the injustice thus done to the people, ordered the restoration of many of these confiscated lands to their rightful owners. It was officially reported at this time that the total area of imperial estates and farms owned by the nobles within the six prefectures of Peking amounted to over 200,919 ch'ing, of which over 20,229 ch'ing had been appropriated from the people. No wonder the grand secretary had to remind the emperor that half of the land in the capital belonged to the government and that the people had hardly anything from which to pay land-taxes, greatly to the detriment of the imperial revenue.[23]

The Chia-ching emperor tried hard to undo the wrongs done by the imperial relatives but the eunuchs kept on interfering with the carrying out of his orders and the good that he wished to do was only half done. The above-mentioned restoration of confiscated land was carried out in 1527. Five years later it was reported by some ministers that lands in the eight prefectures within the capital had been appropriated by the nobles, eunuchs, and other influential persons. These lands, which had been taken from small farmers, were turned into pasture or into imperial estates. The report went on to state that the people, having lost their property, were unable to make a living and had either to starve or to turn outlaws. The emperor sent special officials to investigate the case and the lands that had been seized were restored to their rightful owners.[24] For all the emperor's vigilance he did not find it easy to have his orders carried out. In the year 1529, the President of the Board of Revenue called his attention to the deterioration of the administration of military settlements around the capital. He attributed this deterioration to the action of the nobles, who, by putting pressure on the officials, rendered the administration powerless. It was judged necessary to appoint censors to look after the military settlements. The term of these censors was to last for three years.[25]

It is quite clear that the Chia-ching reform had little permanent effect, since the Ming history after this period is full of the abuses committed by the imperial family and the nobles. Towards the end of the dynasty, a certain writer said, "The emperor (in his dignity) should not possess a private treasury, much less private farms. But now, the area of estates attached to the Tz'u-ch'ing 慈慶, Tz'u-ning 慈寧 and Ch'ien-ch'ing 乾清 palaces amounts to 21,166 ch'ing and 25 mou. The rent collected is 55,814 silver taels. Further, he possesses more than seventy coal-pits from which a rent of one hundred and seventy silver taels is collected. There is too an orchard with over 6,000 trees from which he receives a rent of sixty-five silver taels. Finally, there are farms belonging to the princes, deserving ministers, and imperial relatives, and these total much more than the items we have just mentioned. Who would be able to tell the damage they will do to the treasuries of the country?"[26]

Prominent landlords took advantage of the confusion of government records to encroach on the farmers' holdings, either by force or by fraud. In 1480, an edict was issued forbidding powerful families to appropriate land belonging to the humble classes. It was said that most of the fertile lands along the borders of Ta-t'ung and Hsüan-fu had been filched by influential persons and that nearly half of the farms within the eight districts of the capital had been taken away from the poor farmers, who, having lost their means of living, were in great distress.[27] Often these farms were asked for by nobles or donated by emperors under the title of unoccupied farms. Thus, in the third year of the Cheng-te reign (1508), two imperial relatives received as a donation over 6,542 ch'ing of unoccupied land, which was in fact the property of small farmers. Hsia Yen, who lived in the Chia-ching reign, vigorously rejected the idea that there were unoccupied lands in his day. After all, he argued, one hundred and sixteen or seventeen years have passed since permission was given to the people to cultivate unoccupied land; the population is growing larger and larger every day and the lands are well occupied: it is not possible to find much of this unoccupied land for which the nobles keep petitioning.[28] This talk about unoccupied lands was simply a pretext which the nobles used to cover up their ill-doing. The following instance illustrates this admirably. On the death of

Prince Ching 景王 the Grand Secretary, Hsü Chieh, presented a memorial to the throne stating that Prince Ching had absorbed farms of private farmers amounting to several tens of thousand ch'ing; these farms should be restored to their owners. Permission for this restitution was granted and we are told that the people of Chu rejoiced exceedingly.[29]

The misappropriation of land by influential persons became a common practice in the 16th century. Hsiao Liang-kan 蕭良幹 (cir. 1570) says that in his days the most fertile soil was in the grip of the nobles and that half of the hereditary possessions of the common people had fallen into their hands. Swindlers went around looking for someone whom they could deceive. As soon as they found good farms they offered them to the powerful families pretending that these were unoccupied farms. Hsiao says that many poor farmers who had lost their property could be found in monasteries within the capital. Unable to find any other way to live, they were forced to become Buddhist monks or Taoist priests.[30]

Rich families on the other hand, were always eager to buy lands, since the traditional measure of riches was real property, above all, land, which was always a profitable possession. The author of the *Hsiao-hsia hsien-chi* 消夏閑記 tells us that in the middle of the Ming dynasty the prices given for farms were very high. Probably he was speaking of his native place, Su-chou, where the people were rich and the soil fertile. Land dealers went among probable purchasers looking for the highest bid. They did their business at dawn in secret chambers: hence the common saying: "Evening is the time when the farms are taken over" 黃昏正是奪田時, i.e. the transacted sale was made in the morning and possession was taken in the evening.[31] The very fact that the sale was made in a secret manner implies that in some way both parties were acting illegally. Hsü Hsüeh-mu 徐學謨 (1522–1593), who lived in this period, wrote in a letter to a magistrate friend as follows: "Some time ago I mentioned to you personally that the farm I had inherited amounted to over three hundred and sixty ch'ing: this was a fact. Recently, I have been told that my son has been lured into buying land to the amount of over eight hundred mou. My information is not certain, but I know the total area does not exceed 2,000 mou. Nevertheless, I have seen in the records of privileged exemptions which were sent to the Board of Revenue, that the amount of grain which I am supposed to receive from my farm is over 27,000 piculs, which would mean that the land I possess comes to over 9,000 mou. I am puzzled to know the source of this record and I am greatly disturbed by it. Can it be that some of my clansmen have contrived to put their farms under my name in order to get exemption from land-taxes? Now in Su-chou land-taxes are heavy and an official of the second rank is exempted from only two silver taels.[32] The concession granted to him is smaller than that granted to a hsiu-ts'ai in the north. How then can he share such a concession with others? It may be said that the President of a Board, having an obligation to maintain due state, must receive as much as 27,000 piculs from his land. To this I answer that should full payment be later demanded from me on my farms, it would mean that the higher the dignity the greater the disaster. To put it bluntly, the farms I possess are far from fertile and, nine out of ten years, produce hardly anything. If my descendants were to pay land-taxes (on the above-mentioned assessment) their families would be ruined. Hence I feel it necessary to explain my position clear and I sincerely hope you will investigate the case. Make it clear so as to render it easier for you to judge later on."[33] It was then quite common for families of government officials to transact illegal business without the knowledge of the latter, who might be living in the capital.

It was the duty of the li-chia to look after the welfare of their districts, but they boldly used their position to oppress the people. In Shantung for instance, the li-chia, posing as the friends of small farmers, would offer their services in paying land-taxes to the magistrates. Upon their return to the villages they would tell the people that the money used to pay land-taxes had been borrowed on condition of repayment with interest. The poor farmers were left without any choice: they had to pay. The money paid to the land-office might have been only five ch'ien but the li-chia would exact perhaps fifteen ch'ien. When such demands exceeded the capacity of the farmers, the only thing left for them to do was to abandon their farms and run away. The li-chia would then sequestrate the farms and install themselves as the owners, either cultivating the land themselves or letting it to tenants. Then when government officials came to survey the land the li-chia would refuse to pay taxes on these farms, saying that they belonged to farmers who had fled from the village. When surveys of uncultivated farms were being made they insisted that these farms, which they had in fact seized as private property, had their owners and consequently should not go to the government.[34]

The amalgamation of farms led to serious consequences. Hsieh Chao-che says that in Fukien influential families owned most of the farms of the province: nearly nine-tenths of the production of grain belonged to them—and so, "the rich became richer while the poor became poorer."[35] This inequality soon led to great trouble. The greedy rich tried unceasingly to extend their estates, yet strove in every way to evade taxes and *corvée*. Thus, in the second part of the emperor Ying-tsung's reign, the Marquis of Shou-ning 壽寧侯, not satisfied with a donation of several hundred *ch'ing* of land, wanted to absorb neighboring farming areas amounting to over one thousand ch'ing. Having succeeded at length in this, he sent in a petition for a reduction of land-taxes.[36] In the 13th year of the Chia-ching emperor (1534) a censor reported that influential personages in the prefectures of Su-chou and Sung-kiang had witheld tens of thousands of silver taels due from them in taxes. When pressure was exerted to make them pay, they at once put forward a great variety of excuses in the hope of evading their obligations.[37] Between 1567 and 1579 it was reported that over a million silver taels of land-taxes were still unpaid. This tax evasion was spread over many provinces, but the main centers of default were the prefectures of Su-chou and Sung-kiang, which, between them, owed over 700,000. The land-taxes demanded from these prefectures were very heavy, and this no doubt was one reason why payment was especially slow. But the fundamental cause of default, there and elsewhere, was that influential men, relying on their power, quite often refused to pay any taxes at all. The local authorities having no control over such potentates, turned their attention to the poor farmers and tried to force them to make up as much as possible of the deficit.[38]

There do not seem to have been any fixed rules to ensure a uniform levying of land-taxes. Each place worked out its own system. The scholar Chang Hsüan 張萱 who lived in the Wan-li period says that it was common in his time to divide the farms into three classes, good, mediocre and poor, to which there corresponded three rates of land-taxation. The authorities, he says, failed to see that the farms allocated to one of these classes might differ in productivity from locality to locality. He takes as typical examples the farms in Hsin-chi 新集, Chang-p'ing 長平, and Ning-chi 寗集. In Hsin-chi one peck of grain sown in a mou of land yielded three piculs and the land-tax was about two pints of grain per mou. In Chang-ping and Ning-chi one peck of grain would yield only one picul, five pecks, yet the land-tax demanded for these farms was no less than three pints of grain per mou. Because of the paucity of production the farmers tried to sow more grain to obtain bigger crops. To do this they had to cultivate larger areas of land, though this involved the payment of still more taxes. This, in turn, led to great differences between the prices of grain in these three places. In Hsin-chi, which was comparatively free from this evil, grain produced from poor soil sold at one tael and five ch'ien per picul and grain from good soil at above two taels per picul; whereas in Chang-p'ing and Ning-chi the best grain (i.e. from good soil) sold at only one tael per picul and grain of low quality at only three to four ch'ien. As Chang points out, the price of the best grain in Ning-chi was lower than that of grain produced from the poor soil of Hsin-chi. The local authorities however took little of this into account when imposing taxes on the good soil in Hsin-chi or on the poor soil of Chang-p'ing and Ning-chi.[39]

Corvée was demanded from the farmers because they possessed land. The greater their possessions the heavier the *corvée*. Landless artisans and rich merchants who possessed no land were exempt from *corvée*. Naturally, many farmers, finding life impossible, abandoned their farms and sought new ways of earning a living.[40]

In Shensi, by no means a rich province, the taxes were high. In 1616 Lung Yü-ch'i 龍遇奇, hsün-fu of that province, reported to the emperor on the difficulties of the people. First, he pointed out, Shensi, being near the border, was seldom visited by merchants. The taxes therefore depended solely on the farmers and artisans. Secondly, despite the poverty of the province, the people were made to pay heavy taxes: the neighboring provinces of Shansi and Szechuan paid only a little over ten thousand taels of silver and even Honan which ranked as a large province paid little more than 60,000; but Shensi had to pay 100,000. Even if a reduction were granted, it would still have to pay more than any of the other three provinces. Moreover, he pointed out, the people of Shensi had also to contribute to the support of the soldiers along the borders, which might rightly be described as extra taxation. Since the resources of the people were limited, they could not keep on paying both kinds of tax. They could pay one or the other, but not both. As an illustration Lung cited the year 1590, when the people paid a total of 1,500,000 silver taels in taxes. In addition to this they were supposed to contribute 2,040,000 silver taels for the support of soldiers along the borders. It was beyond their power to pay both sums.[41]

From the Wan-li period onward increases of land taxes became common. The greediness of the emperor and his eunuchs on the one hand, and the unsettled situation of the empire on the other, kept on draining the wealth of the country. Among those most affected were the poor farmers. The eunuch Wang Sheng 王昇 first introduced an extraordinary tax known as chien-yin 監銀 and then increased the land taxes from one fen (one tenth of a ch'ien) to three fen per mou. The farmers had to pay taxes both to the Board of Revenue and to the chien-yin. In 1611, the prefectures around the capital suffered severely from floods. Chou Yung-ch'un 周永春, then acting as chi-shih-chung, took the opportunity to petition the emperor to spare the people this burdensome obligation. "In a plentiful year one might expect them to obey the law and fulfil their obligation," he said. "But now, when nothing is coming from the soil, what are they going to pay the taxes with? Formerly they might have tried to sell their children; but now the families are all scattered and there is nothing left to sell. Formerly they might have mortgaged or sold their houses, but now these have all been ruined by the flood. In the old days perhaps they could have borrowed from the rich, but now the rich have become poor and the poor have had to run away." The poor waited eagerly for some show of imperial kindness, but the callous emperor was not moved by the pitiable plight of his subjects. We are told that the minister's report was kept in the palace and that no decision was made on it.[41] Nine years later (1620) a censor brought the question up again. If tumults were produced by the misery of the people, he said, then tumults must be near at hand. By then the land taxes for the support of the Liao-tung soldiers had increased from seven to nine li 釐 (one li being one-tenth of a fen) but the emperor still seemed unconcerned about the increase. To use the words of the censor: "A petition is submitted for an increase of land-taxes and His Majesty approves of it that same evening. Does His Majesty not realize that the people are as much under his care as the wealth of the empire?"[43]

By the time of the Ch'ung-chen emperor the condition of the people had become still worse. The testimony of Lin Yü-chi 林欲楫, President of the Board of Ceremonies, depicts a scene of desolation. "The vitality of the people of Kiang-nan is now exhausted. As I went across the Yangtze towards the North, from Hao 濠, Hsü 徐, Ch'ing 青 and Ch'i 齊 to the imperial domains, I saw everywhere a scene of desolation. The people moved about aimlessly, having lost all interest in farming and all knowledge of the system of irrigation."[44] This sad picture is not surprising if one keeps in mind how bad things then were throughout the empire. Fang Kung-chao, supervising censor of the military settlements, said that the *corvée* duties were becoming too heavy for the people. The rate of land-tax per mou was said to be one hundred and seventy to eighty coins—high enough in all conscience—but payment for *corvée* could be as much as three to four hundred coins. Those who were unable to meet these demands had only one resource if they were to avoid spending their days in prison:

they had to offer their farms to the rich in the hope of being protected by their patrons.[45]

A study made by a modern scholar shows that before the second quarter of the 15th century the maximum rent for government-owned farms was from four pecks to more than two piculs per mou, and the minimum was one peck of rice per mou. In the Hung-wu period, government-owned farms were rented for five pints per mou and privately owned farms paid only three pints. The 15th century farmers therefore were paying from three times to more than ten times more than their predecessors. And this was not the end. As time went on, land-taxes became ever heavier till, in the last years of the dynasty, they were an unbearable burden.[46] Ku Yen-wu tells us that although the men of Sung-kiang prefecture cultivated the land and the women wove the silk, they were not able to earn enough to pay their taxes. Many of them sold their children, but even this did not help very much, so they fled to avoid imprisonment. Ku also tells us that the autumn harvest in Su-chou yielded, at most, about three piculs of rice per mou: some land yielded less than two piculs. The tax varied from one picul and two or three pints to eight or nine pecks, so after payment of rent and taxes, the farmers had no more than a few pecks of rice per mou for themselves.[47]

Such was the condition of the tenant farmers. Those who possessed their own land were better off. They paid taxes but they had no rent to pay. Very few small farmers, however, possessed their own land. In Wu-hsien 吳縣, for instance, it was estimated that only one ninth did so, the rest being tenant farmers.[48] Peasant proprietors had been numerous in earlier times, but most of them had lost their farms to the imperial relatives, eunuchs, officials or landlords, by confiscation, force or fraud. In 1489, the President of the Board of Revenue stated that within the imperial city five farms totaling 12,800 ch'ing were possessed by imperial relatives. The 332 farms belonging to officials were said to amount to 33,000 ching. During the reign of the Wan-li emperor the princes possessed about 40,000 ch'ing of land in Honan, Shantung and Hu-kuang provinces.[49] Such examples can be cited in abundance from the *Ming shih* and contemporary documents.

Perhaps the most important cause of the failure of the "Fish Scale Records" and the "Yellow Records" was the negligence of the officials and sub-officials, probably deliberate negligence indulged in for the sake of self-enrichment. The results were very serious for the government, since without the records it was impossible to levy taxes efficiently. In 1633, for instance, the President of the Board of Revenue reported that the records of taxes and *corvée* were in such disorder that it was impossible to know the exact extent of the farm lands or the number of the population and that it was in consequence difficult to levy taxes.[50] Once the "Fish Scale" system and the "Yellow Record" had become unreliable, abuses naturally began to spring up.

First, there was widespread evasion of tax-paying, especially among the landlords. Then these same landlords began to encroach on the farms of small farmers either by force or by fraud. Towards the end of the Chia-ching period such encroachment had become so common that according to a supervising censor the landlord class owned a great part of the land of China. The landlords were so powerful, he said, that the small farmers could find no alternative to selling all their property and becoming laborers.[51] Another contemporary witness tells no more than the truth when he says that in his day the most fertile soil was in the hands either of the nobles or of influential persons: half of the hereditary property of the people had been usurped by them. Scoundrels who wished to curry favor with the influential landlords sought their protection by getting for them the farms of small holders on the pretext that these farms were unoccupied, or that they were government farms that had been exempted from taxation. This writer saw little hope for the future, for the people had been reduced to such wretchedness that they had lost all feeling for honesty.[52]

In the last year of the Ch'ung-chen period, report after report reached the court announcing that many cities had fallen into the hands of the rebels. Not only did the people fail to resist; many of them went over to the side of the enemy. The supervising censor of the Board of War, having investigated the causes of this ominous state of affairs, came to the conclusion that it was due to the inequality between the poor and the rich. Not only had the landlords monopolized the farms that paid high rent, they were also usurers and shrank from no form of exploitation of the people. Thus the rich kept on multiplying their wealth while the poor became more miserable every day. The greediness of the landlords created discontent among the people. When the rebels attacked towns and cities the landlords usually suffered more than others; but it was only in a time of crisis that they became aware of their own folly.[53]

Towards the end of the dynasty in particular, the injustice of the landlords became notorious, probably because the government officials had abandoned their duty of watching out for abuses. Far from protecting the common folk, they themselves were corrupt and often conspired with exploiting landlords. Wu Ying-chi 吳應箕

(1594–1645), describes the living conditions in his native place during those days. Kuei-ch'ih 貴池, he says, was a place where farms were scarce and the soil poor. Since the production of grain was insufficient to support the people of the place throughout the year, food supplies had to be brought from other provinces both by land and by water. The rich, taking advantage of the needs of the people, demanded higher prices for grain. Moreover, not satisfied with high rent and high prices, they tried to rob the people by fraudulent manipulation of the units of measurement. The rent for a mou of land was two piculs of rice; but when the payment of rent was due they manipulated the standards, making the picul weigh two hundred and twenty catties instead of the regular 120 catties; then when the time came for selling grain to the people they made the picul weigh only ninety catties. Money also was used as a means for exploiting the poor. The coin used by the people to buy food contained only eighty to ninety per cent of silver, but the landlords demanded money that was a hundred per cent pure, and if the poor could not produce this they were ordered to pay more. Often the computation of the silver content was made arbitrarily by the landlords.[54]

Not only were the landlords cruel to the people; they also showed no love for the country and were interested exclusively in their own families and possessions. In 1644, the Board of War reported that many of the landlord class had surrendered to the rebels. Some of them induced the people to give up their cities or towns, arguing that if resistance were offered all the people of the place would be massacred by the rebels, but that they would be spared if they gave themselves up without a siege. Often, the landlords had made plans to surrender their cities long before the approach of the rebels.[55] We are told that in 1643, when the Manchus invaded Lai-yang 萊陽 the men who opened the gates of the city to them belonged to the landlord class.[56]

The people, already oppressed by the landlords, had also to bear the ruthlessness of government officials and sub-officials. In all matters concerning the payment of taxes, the law was carried out to the letter and the officials were ready to use savage torture to enforce payment. A scholar of the Chia-ching period describes an instrument of torture invented by a certain official of the Salt-Control Department. It consisted of bamboo poles, weighing over four catties and fitted with nails resembling the teeth of a saw. The victim was struck with this gruesome instrument and at every blow the blood gushed forth so violently that the clothes of the official who administered the punishment soon became red all down the front. This torture used to go on for hours, and at the end of the day the courtyard had to be washed thoroughly to rid it of the blood and the smell.[57] Over half a century later the author of the *San-yüan pi-chi* had no better report to give of the officials. When he passed through Yin-hsien 恩縣 in Shantung, he noticed that the courtyards there were often covered with the blood of unfortunates who had had to undergo cruel torture because of their inability to pay taxes.[58]

As if the ordinary taxes were not enough, illegal demands were made by government officials or members of the military class either to cover deficits in the ordinary taxes or because there was no other way of raising public funds. In the last years of the dynasty when great quantities of rice and beans were needed to supply the army, rich families were told to do the purchasing and they were ordered to have their purchases transported to Tientsin. Thus the rich families had to prepare means of transportation in addition to satisfying all the illegal demands of government sub-officials. At first their task did not seem altogether uninviting; contracts were made and it was laid down that the rich families were to do the purchasing as agents of government. But payment in full soon became uncertain and it was always in arrear.[59]

Side by side with the decline of the farming system went a gradual decline of the liang-chang, which eventually became a burden on the people. When the Yung-lo Emperor transferred the capital to Peking in 1421, the liang-chang continued to bring taxes to Nanking and so lost the privilege of interviews with the emperor. Later, when the government relaxed its vigilance over its officials, the liang-chang often took advantage of their position to oppress the people and went so far as to appropriate the land-taxes due to the government. Then, about half way through the Ming period when the government found itself unable to manage with the ordinary land-taxes and had to levy more, many farmers abandoned their farms and ran away and the liang-chang had to make good the loss of revenue. The rich thereupon paid their way out of this no longer profitable office and members of the middle class were appointed in their stead.[60]

Writing in the Chia-ching period, Wang Wen-lu sternly criticized the defects of this system in his day. The office of liang-chang, he says, was imposed on rich men owning ten thousand mou of land and on comparatively poor men whose land was measured in tens of mou. But the rich could easily purchase complete, or at least partial, immunity from this office, and their duties were transferred to those who had not the means to purchase such immunity. Thus, the rich became more prosperous as the poor sank deeper and deeper into misery.[61]

The same author says that the rich who possessed thousands of ch'ing of land were exceedingly happy on the day when they received rents from their tenants, or when the rice they received was heaped as high as in the market place. They also felt great joy on getting a good price for their rice. But as soon as they learned that they had been appointed to the offices of li-chang or liang-chang, they at once became dejected and tried by every means to evade their duties. "Therefore", he says, "I used to say to them mockingly: 'It will not be difficult to evade these duties. All you have to do is petition the Court to abolish the offices of liang-chang and li-chang; for it would be very unkind to wish to have yourselves exempted from these offices—you who possess great numbers of farms—and to leave such burdens to be borne by poor men without possessions of any kind. Their services, remember, are not for one year only, but for ten years. And these unfortunate men will suffer the breaking up of their families and the death of their dear ones. This they will have to suffer alone, without anyone to whom they can look for assistance. . . .' "[62]

In the last years of the dynasty the offices of liang-chang and li-chang became an intolerable burden. It was said that if a family possessing a thousand taels of gold became liang-chang for a single year, some of its members would have to become beggars. If a family with ten or more strong sons became liang-chang for a year, the household would be impoverished and its members would have dispersed by the end of its term of office. Thus everyone tried to evade this baneful office which was more dreaded than exile. Government officials, unable to find a fundamental solution to the problem of its increasing odiousness, sought to modify the suffering it caused by reducing the term of office from ten years to one. Even then, few held the office of liang-chang without involving their families in ruin.[63] Thus, we hear of a certain prefect who, having quarrelled with the former president of a certain board, assigned seven of his enemy's sons to the office of liang-chang. The unfortunate family was unable to bear this terrible burden. The members of the family ran away and the family broke up.[64]

By the beginning of the Lung-ch'ing reign (1567–1572), court ministers were including in their reports to the throne warnings against the abuses of *corvée*. In the early days of the dynasty *corvée* was imposed in proportion to the number of males in each family. Later, this was changed and *corvée* was imposed in proportion to the amount of land a family possessed, and it became such a burden that many sacrificed their property rather than carry out the duties it involved.[65] Wang Wen-lu tells us that in his village on the death of a certain farmer, the owner of over three hundred mou of land, his two sons had to sell all their father's land to pay off the *corvée* tax. Even when they had sold every inch of the land, *corvée* assignments were still being imposed on them. They now had nothing with which to pay the tax and were forced to run away. The same scholar tells us of a certain licentiate, the owner of about fifty mou of land, who lost every mou after his appointment to the office of li-chang.[66] In the Ch'ung-chen period assignments of *corvée* became so numerous that they amounted to more than the land taxes—sometimes to twice as much. Thus, in one account, we read that for each mou of land the farmers paid in land taxes about a hundred and seventy to a hundred and eighty coins, but in *corvée* tax three to four hundred coins. It is not surprising, therefore, to learn that people voluntarily combined their lands under the protection of the landlords in order to evade taxes.[67]

So many of the people ran away from their homes that in many places farms were left uncultivated. Eye-witnesses have left us a substantial number of accounts of rich soil turning into desert because of lack of human labor. In a letter to a friend, Wu Ying-chi described one of the most pathetic cases he had ever seen:

" . . . Twenty miles from Kuang-chou 光州 (the modern Heng-chou hsien 潢州縣, Honan province) there is a place called Huang-tzu kang 黃子岡 where we stayed overnight at the government residence. . . . What we now saw was very different from what we had experienced in Kuang-chou. That morning, having left the city gates, I travelled for sixty li. The weather was serene. Within a distance of forty li we could see nothing but yellow reeds and dry grass. I then noticed that we had been walking over farming fields, the boundaries of which were still discernible, but the farms had been neglected for so long that there was no sign left of rice or wheat plantations. I asked my sedan-chair carrier, 'Are all the farms around here as badly neglected as these?' 'About eighty to ninety per cent are like these,' he said. 'In Hsi-hsien 息縣 conditions are better, but even there nearly forty to fifty percent of the farms are like these.' I was quite astonished to hear this.

"On arriving at the rest house, I met an old man and several of the sub-officials. I summoned them and asked them whether the farms I had come across on my journey were free from taxes. Several of them answered together: 'How could they be free of taxes, since they were formerly fertile lands?' I, therefore, asked why they did not try to cultivate them. The answer was that there were no cattle left in the place. Most of them had been stolen and sold in other places, so that no one cared to rent these farms. Furthermore, the government of this district was known for its severity in exacting horses and labor from the people. When a man was assigned to some fixed duty and found the burden too heavy, he first sold his cow, then abandoned his farm, and a little later absconded. When he had gone, his land was left uncultivated but the land tax was still attached to it. His family then was summoned to pay the tax and if they failed to do so, the people of the li had to pay it for him. Sometimes, however, the relatives of the refugee were forced to settle the debt. For a rich family, it was possible to pay what was owed, but the poor usually left the neighborhood, abandoning all their property. This was why the villages were all empty and the farms were left uncultivated.

"Next I asked why the people did not sell their property to others instead of running away. But they replied: 'Your Excellency knows well that *corvée* is a burden precisely upon those who possess land. At this minute, there are many who wish to abandon their land but cannot do so. For what would happen if someone were willing to buy the property? As soon as he got possession of the land, he would forthwith be subjected to a land tax: would he be ready to pay it? This is the reason why so many have preferred to run away. Their land has been allowed to lie idle and, in time, it has become as bad as you see it now.'

"I next wanted to know whether anyone had reported all these facts to the governor of the prefecture. To this they answered, 'The governors are usually provincial graduates or licentiates. They are disappointed with their posts and think of nothing but bribes. They know well that there is corruption of every kind in the government office but they cannot prevent it. To ward off the censure of their superiors they try to collect the full amount of taxes, sparing no means, not even the daily torturing of the people. They care very little if the farmers and their families run away or if the farms are left uncultivated. Anyone who tries to explain these things to them is immediately condemned to a flogging. Hence, although the people are suffering and murmuring, no one dares say anything in public.'

"Finally, I wanted to know whether this was a place through which government officials must pass. They said yes: the provincial governor and the district governors all passed there. I was interested to know whether these officials had asked for an explanation of the desolation in the district. But they told me that none of them had ever asked. I sighed deeply and uncontrollably. Whereupon the sub-officials and the old man all knelt down and said through their tears: 'Your Excellency has asked what our officials do not wish to know!' 'What the rulers of this place ignored,' they went on, 'Your Excellency, though a stranger, has been informed about in full detail. If some day Your Excellency should happen to be in a position to do something for us, please remember our neighborhood.' Upon hearing this, I could no longer restrain myself: I also burst into tears.''[68]

These peasants' remarks about the sub-officials reveal a great deal about the difficulties that many higher officials had to face. As governors of different districts they were expected to carry out certain duties. Normally, what the Court was interested in was the result of their work rather than the methods by which they did it. This was especially true of the Ch'ung-chen emperor, who was always suspicious of his ministers. The officials knew that if they did not fulfil his insistent demands, they would be liable to punishment. Hence, they ruthlessly resorted to dishonest means and false reports, and even to open cruelty. In 1640, the Board of War quoted the findings of a certain official who had witnessed the intense sufferings of the people. According to this man, the population of the area between the capital and the Yellow River had fallen seriously. Conditions had become so bad that cannibalism was common among the people, but the government officials were afraid to report this lest they be held responsible for it. They were, moreover, being vehemently pressed by higher authorities to suppress bandits in their districts and they did not scruple to victimize the poor in their efforts to make a show of zeal for the cause—for example by imposing savage penalties on petty thieves. Thus when a number of so-called bandits were arrested in Shen-chou 深州, one man was accused of having stolen three pints of chaff from his grandfather; another of having stolen two pints of rice from his aunt. For these and similar petty misdemeanors, the members of this unhappy group were convicted as bandits and as a punishment were tied to a heated metal stake: before they reached the government office half of them were dead. The official suggested less pressure on the local officials in order to save the people from such unjust treatment.[69]

During the Ch'ung-chen reign the people suffered at the hands not only of officials and sub-officials, but also of soldiers and bandits. Often the villages became battle-grounds and the people lost all their possessions. An official, reporting in 1634, told the emperor that in the capital itself those who had formerly been known as rich could no longer afford to prepare a full meal and that refugees from all over the empire were wandering aimlessly through the streets of Peking.

Nine years later (1643), a censor, describing what he had seen during a visitation in the provinces, said that in Kiang-nan and present Anhui, for a distance of several thousand li, there was nothing to be seen but ruined cities and towns; if by chance the walls of a city had had not been destroyed, they were the only things left standing. Weeds grew in profusion along the roads, and in the villages no domestic animals were to be found. There were no farmers to be seen anywhere.[70]

Natural disasters—flood, drought, locusts, and famine, the result of human negligence, came one after the other. Many of these disasters could have been avoided had the officials in charge of public works been more conscientious in such duties as looking after the irrigation of the fields, and the draining of rivers and lakes. The Yellow River now began to give more trouble than it had for centuries. A modern scholar who has studied the history of the Yellow River says that it began to cause anxiety in the Sung dynasty (960–1278), and maintained its threat throughout the centuries that followed. His explanation is that, by the time of the Sung dynasty, Chinese civilization had already begun to deteriorate in the north, and the floods were, he holds, the consequence of the decline of human effort.[71]

In the Ming period, the Yellow River burst its northern bank fourteen times and its southern bank five times.[72] From the *Tsui-wei lu* we learn that during the Chia-ching reign it repeatedly caused terrible damage. In 1526, it burst its banks in Shantung and the floods spread over a radius of more than 30 miles. It is said that ninety-eight thousand laborers were employed to repair the damage, but they labored in vain. During the disaster in 1534, a hundred and forty thousand men were enrolled as laborers. Finally, in 1558, over two hundred and fifty miles of the river silted up and the water escaped in six directions.[73]

Toward the end of the Wan-li period (1605), a hundred and seventy miles of the river was drained. According to the Director General of the Yellow River (Ho-tao tsung-tu 河道總督) this cost eight hundred thousand silver taels and the labor of five hundred thousand men.[74] The Director General's report, however, may have exaggerated, for the memorial of another minister mentions only four hundred thousand silver taels and two hundred thousand laborers.[75]

Under the same Wan-li emperor, we are told, floods occurred frequently in Kiangsi, a province containing many low-lying districts near the Yangtze River. Nearly every year there were reports of floods in different parts of Kiangsi. The most serious of these floods, one which occurred around the year 1597, is described as follows in an official report:

" . . . the Nan-ch'ang 南昌, Chi-lin 吉林, and other districts near the Yangtze were all flooded. Banks burst and were washed away. Sometimes several members of the same family perished in the waters; houses, farms, animals and property were, of course, destroyed. Later, although the flood had subsided, water from the lakes lingered for months. Thus the autumn crops were delayed and there was no hope of a harvest. No one had ever experienced such desolation as this. . . ."[76]

During the Ch'ung-chen reign flood control was even more grievously neglected. The scholar Lu Shih-i 陸世儀 (circa 1630) says:

"What the fields (i.e. rice paddies) need is a good irrigation system. Let us prescind from other provinces and take only the province of Southern Chih-li (the modern Kiangsu and Anhui) 南直 as an example. This province has been known as the 'marsh country' from time immemorial. Recently, year after year, this province has suffered from drought and the three rivers and the lake have all dried up. Accordingly, when it rains for a while, there is a great flood, and when there is a drought the scorched lands stretch for thousands of li in such a state that the inhabitants south of the Yangtze River despair of the autumn harvest. . . ."[77]

In consequence of the failure to improve the irrigation system, the farmers suffered seriously in times of drought, especially in the northern part of the country where the crops were harvested only once a year. The Ch'ung-chen reign was exceptionally unfortunate in this matter: droughts were frequently reported from Shansi, Honan, and above all Shensi. In 1631, for instance, Yu-lin 榆林 prefecture was said to have been suffering from drought for four years. In Kansu it did not rain during the whole year of 1633, and when winter came it did not even bring snow. It was hoped that the spring of 1634 would bring some desperately needed rain, but none came. In that year, 1634, Shansi, Honan, Kiangsi and Yünnan all suffered from drought. The worst years of all were those of 1639 and 1640, when both capitals, Nanking and Peking, and Honan, Shantung, Shansi, Shensi, and Chekiang provinces were all reported to have suffered seriously from the lack of rain. In the following year

(1641), a drought occurred in present Kiangsu and many perished from famine.[78]

Then there were the locusts, which came, no one seemed to know from where, and ate up the crops within a few days. Locusts seemed to arrive chiefly in the years of drought. In the records of the Ch'ung-chen reign we frequently read of locusts appearing everywhere.[79] According to Wu Ying-chi, locusts were almost unknown south of the Yangtze before the Wan-li period. They had appeared only once and the people, acting under the directions of a certain local magistrate, had been able to get rid of them without much difficulty. But after the year 1638, all districts in Kiangnan were infested with them.[80]

The *Ming shih* records many natural calamities after the Chia-ching period, although the list is probably not exhaustive. In the Chia-ching reign, natural calamities of different kinds occurred eight times. In the forty-eight years of the Wan-li reign natural calamities were recorded no less than thirty-four times. These covered most of the provinces and sometimes many provinces suffered in the same year. In the seven years of the T'ien-ch'i reign calamities occurred seven times, and in the fourteen years of Ch'ung-chen fourteen times.[81]

The destruction of the crops brought famine. When food became scarce prices became outrageous, even astronomical. It is instructive to observe the price of rice, which had fallen steadily in the earlier years of the dynasty. In 1376, a picul of rice cost one silver tael, soaring sometimes to almost incredible heights in the years of disaster, but in 1386, it fell to half the amount of 1376. In 1443, it fell again to one fourth of a silver tael. In 1469, it rose to nearly three fourths of a silver tael. During the 1530's a picul of rice cost between three-fourths to one silver tael. But in 1631, one peck (one tenth of a picul) cost two-fifths of a silver tael (i.e. a picul cost four silver taels). At one time in Shantung the price of a picul of rice rose to twenty-four silver taels and in Honan it once rose to one hundred and fifty.[82]

In these circumstances, the rich could perhaps survive for a time by selling their treasures, but the poor, having nothing to sell, either died of starvation or took perforce to robbing their rich neighbors. During the famine of 1594, the people were reduced to eating the bark of trees and the seeds of grass. When this did not satisfy their hunger they even tried to eat the excrement of wild geese. The situation became not only tragic but also alarming, and an official had it represented in a painting and presented the picture to the Wan-li emperor in an attempt to touch that ruler's hard heart. Similarly, a censor sent a sample of the excrement of wild geese to the monarch in order to arouse his pity for the poor who were reduced to seeking nourishment from that filth.[83] Père du Halde records a famine of the Wan-li period:

"L'année dix-neuvième ilay eut une si grande stérilité dans la Province de Cham si (Shansi), qu'on ne peut compter le nombre de ceux qui y moururent de faim. On fit creuser en divers endroits environ soixant grandes fosses, qui contenoient chacune un millier de cadavres, et c'est pourquoi on les appelloit Van gin kang (萬人岡 —A.C.)

"Une femme voyant jetter dans une des ces fosses son mari, qui étoit mort de faim, s'y jetta aussi toute vivante. On l'en retira par ordre du Mandarin, mais inutilement, car ne pouvant survivre à la perte qu'elle venoit de faire, elle mourut trois jours apres."[84]

In many places cannibalism became so common in the time of famine, especially during the last years of the dynasty, that the historical documents reek of it. In 1640, for instance, after a battle in P'u-chou 濮州 in Shantung Province, in which rebel deaths were reported as five thousand, as soon as the dead rebels' heads had been cut off, their corpses were instantly cut up by hungry people for food. In Shansi there were markets for human flesh. Hunger often deprived the people of all human feelings: the author of the *K'ou-shih pien-mien* 寇事編年 mentions two cases of mothers killing and eating their young daughters. The same author also tells of a man in Shansi who killed his parents, roasted their bodies, and ate them.[85]

These tragic happenings were not confined to the northern part of the country. They occurred even in the south, where farm products had formerly been abundant. Yeh Shao-yüan 葉紹袁 gives the following eye-witness account of destitution and cannibalism in Su-chou:

"Formerly, when I was told of cannibalism in Shantung and Honan, I was inclined to be sceptical. But now this practice occurs frequently inside and outside the city of Su-chou. In spite of severe penalties imposed by the authorities for this offence, it is often committed. In the streets there are numerous beggars, very thin and worn. Moreover, since the new year, it has been cold and it has rained frequently. The spring has nearly come to an end, but the cold still persists. After the full moon of the second month, it rained continuously for over ten days. The people are dying in great numbers through lack of food. I have seen with my own eyes several tens of (starved) corpses being buried daily in the property of the prince. When the price of rice rises to over ninety coins a pint, what wonder if they have nothing to eat! Most of the residences in the city are empty and they are falling into ruins. Fertile farms and beautiful estates are for sale but there is no one to buy them. Formerly the city of Su-chou was prosperous and its people tended to be extravagant. It is natural that after a period of prosperity a period of depression should follow; but I never dreamed that I should have to witness these misfortunes in the days of my life.''[86]

Famine had drained away the strength of many and when epidemics broke out the people had no resistance. In the last years of the Ch'ung-chen period plagues were frequently reported in different places. The most violent of all was one that struck Peking in 1641; many of the inhabitants died and the whole capital was thrown into panic. Two years later another plague broke out in the spring and lasted for several months. About ten thousand people are said to have died daily when it was at its height. Sometimes large families of several tens of members were wiped out overnight. The head of the Taoist priests, Chang T'ien-shih 張天師, was summoned to Peking to propitiate the evil spirit, but to no purpose. The people were terrified and rumors soon spread that evil spirits were going around the capital. To drive away the evil spirits the people beat brass and iron instruments day and night so that the whole city was in a state of bedlam.[87]

Surrounded by these disasters, the more conscientious ministers could see little hope for the future, but they did what they could to bring relief to the people and to reduce the tension. The most obvious way of doing this was to provide immediate relief by sending money and food to the famine areas; but the organization was so poor that such relief was often delayed and the number of the starving was so great that the relief fund was often exhausted before help could reach a tithe of them. If some did receive help it lasted for only a very short time. The government treasuries were nearly empty; the thought of huge sums required for effective relief could only dishearten the emperors. The relief missions, therefore, were earnests of good will rather than attempts to render assistance. Thus the edict issued by the Wan-li emperor at the time of the great famine of 1594, for instance, may show that even this the most indolent of Ming emperors had his moments of humanity; it certainly shows his improvidence and the poor organization of his relief work:

" . . . We have repeatedly sent orders for the dispatch of relief to the people, but we do not know if our ministers have followed our instructions, or if our people have received benefit from this relief. This is a time of empty treasuries, public and private. We do not known whether there is any convenient means of bringing quick relief to our people, other than help from our imperial treasury and the tributary rice. Again, we do not know if our ministers have accommodated the miners and bandits and restored them to their own farms, or if they have prepared their men in case the bandits should launch an attack. . . ."[88]

Relief work in the Ch'ung-chen days must have been very difficult, for the number of sufferers kept on multiplying and the treasuries continued to be empty. In the first years of the reign a hundred thousand silver taels, at a time, were frequently sent to the provinces for relief. Later, the amount gradually decreased. The government was on the brink of bankruptcy at the very time when the people were in greatest need of help. Nevertheless we are told that relief centers were set up in the capital in 1641, and that congee was given to hungry people numbering several hundred thousand.[89]

But relief work was only a palliative. Fundamentally, what was needed was a solution of the economic problems. During the Wan-li reign an official wrote to the emperor pointing out the need of immediate reform: " . . . it is not that your servants do not want to wait, but that the empire is in such a critical state that it is impossible to wait any longer. Now Your Majesty still has the power to remedy the crisis before it goes beyond control. Your Majesty should issue an edict, and order will be restored. But if Your Majesty waits until the situation has gone beyond control, it is to be feared that the mobs will gain power, and once they are entrenched, it will be impossible to do anything."[90] The Wan-li emperor, however, was so wrapped up in his own interests that he gave no heed to the advice of his minister.

The minister's prediction came true and it was well for the Wan-li emperor that he did not live to see it. His descendants, less fortunate, were to witness the predicted disasters. A month after his death in 1620, his successor received a report from a minister who was then collecting revenue for the upkeep of the soldiers. "When I was in Ying-t'ien 應天 (Nanking)," this man wrote, "I was told that people to the north of the Huai river had resorted to eating grass roots and the bark of trees and that even these were no longer to be found. I was also told that in small villages members of families would fight one another for bean-stalks and wheat-stalks. Having crossed the Yangtze and gone north, I saw everywhere hungry mobs seizing rice and robbing government stores. I kept on assuring myself that such monstrous behavior was the result of last year's drought; but the situation south of the Yangtze remains a mystery to me. There, there had never been either drought or flood, yet the region is full of confusion. On reaching Chen-kiang 鎮江 one is shocked to find that a peck of rice costs a hundred coins! As one proceeds to Su-chou and Sung-kiang the price of rice increases to one hundred and thirty or forty coins per peck. Merchant ships now no longer appear at the customs, and rice shops are about to give up business. The people are reduced to a penniless state. They gather together and look for well-to-do families on whom to lay their hands. They try to post up manifestos by the roadside and to set fire to great houses. Fortunately the authorities have been able to take timely precautions and the wrongdoers have been suppressed. . . ." This minister, however, could suggest no solution for this heart-rending state of affairs. The Manchus were then raging along the border and all he could suggest was that the new tax levied for defence should be continued. He did attempt to analyse the incidence of the tax: "A demand comes from Liao-tung; we then make a demand upon the local government. The local government makes demands upon the people." He was unable to make out upon whom the people made their demands. This, he said, was a point worth considering![91]

The Ch'ung-chen emperor seems to have made an effort to re-establish economic stability in the country, but his effort came too late. In the latter half of his reign he frequently exempted the people from paying land taxes, aware, no doubt, of their extreme poverty, and recognizing that it was foolish to press them to pay taxes when they had nothing with which to pay. Such irrational demands subjected the people to further hardship at the hands of government officials and sub-officials. It is uncertain, however, whether the emperor's orders were carried out. A passage from the *Huai-tsung shih-lu* suggests that the people did not benefit from this exemption from land taxes, because of the corruption of the officials and sub-officials. In 1642, it says, an edict was issued exempting the people of the capital province from all land taxes due since 1638, and a sentence was inserted into the decree forbidding government officials to tax indiscriminately. The people cheered upon hearing this good news. Clearly, the officials till then must have been exploiting the people by taxing them for their own profit.[92]

It is not clear what course the government followed in exempting the different districts from land taxes. Most probably, all depended on the arbitrary decisions of the emperor. Sometimes he refused to grant any exemptions from land taxes. At other times he exempted certain districts from certain portions of these taxes. Again, in some districts, not only were land taxes cancelled but relief was sent to the people. Sometimes, too, wheat was accepted in payment of land taxes instead of money. Even the payment of tributary goods was partly or totally remitted in various provinces. Finally, in some districts the people were granted only permission to delay the payment of land taxes.[93]

In the year 1636, a minister of the Board of War suggested a plan for settling destitute people in abandoned cities and districts. He proposed that the families be organized according to the li-chia system, that they be given farming cattle and grain seed, and that their farms be exempted from taxation for three years.[94] Apparently, this suggestion was not carried out; if it was carried out it certainly did no good. The explanation for this failure is plain to be seen in a report of the Board of Revenue in 1634. There were, this report says, many abandoned farms in northern Chih-li, Honan, Shansi and Shensi. Some of these had been military settlements and others had been owned by civilians. There was also uncultivated land which had never been developed by human labor. All that was needed was to get volunteers from among the people to develop this land into farming districts. But the people were loath to cooperate because they knew that, as soon as the land had been cultivated, government officials would levy taxes on it. They were doubtful about their promised profits; but they were certain that once they had been made to pay land taxes they would never escape from this obligation, whatever might happen later.[95]

The people were equally loath to commit themselves to the occupation of abandoned farms. They feared that after all their labor the owners of the farms might return to claim their property. Even if this did not happen, they feared that the families of the former possessors might claim the farms. More threatening still, there was always the danger that the village headman or some influential landlords might cast covetous eyes on these rich farms and try to take them by force.[96]

These fears were by no means ill-founded. Huang Tsung-hsi, writing of the farming conditions of this time, says that at first much of the uncultivated land was enthusiastically developed by the people. But when that time came to pay the tax they were appalled to learn that they had to pay heavier taxes on these new farms than on farms that had already been cultivated. In fear and disappointment they began to abandon the land they had brought under cultivation. Government officials, seeing that their plans were failing, grew angry and tried to compel owners of established farms to pay the land taxes of their fugitive neighbors. Such injustice greatly irritated the people, many of whom ran away, having found these new burdens more than they could bear.[97]

The capital, which nearly always had an appearance of prosperity, attracted many poor people who, while not resigned to die of hunger, were unwilling to become outlaws. A late Ming writer says that there were more beggars than businessmen in the capital. Any money they got by begging was gambled away, and when they had lost all their money they gambled away their clothes. When winter came these unfortunates died by the thousand; yet, mysteriously enough, great crowds of beggars still remained.[98]

Vagrancy posed a perennial problem throughout the Ming dynasty. When it originated is not clear. The scholar Wang Fu-chih 王夫之 (1619–1692) says that up to the Sung dynasty vagrants were unknown to history. He assigns their emergence to the Yüan period, when, as a result of Mongol misrule, the rich waxed proud and the poor became at once lazy and recalcitrant. The authorities knew this but did nothing about it. When vagrancy first appeared, they did not try to banish it by distributing relief. When the vagrants had become a problem they made no attempt to pacify them.

Be this as it may, the problem of vagrancy had certainly become really serious by the Ch'eng-hua period (1465–1478). At first it was simply a problem of vagrancy but eventually it turned into a problem of rebellion. It continued to develop and no one could find an adequate solution.[99]

Earlier efforts to deal with vagrancy had met with success. Thus we are told that in the year 1402, in Peking alone over a hundred and thirty thousand six hundred vagrant families were restored to their original occupations. The same sources relate that in 1406, relief was given to the people of the southern part of Kiang-nan province and that over twelve hundred and two thousand nine hundred, 1,202,900, vagrant families were restored to their homes. Two years later, in 1408, vagrants were invited to take up farming with a promise of exemption from taxation and *corvée* for three years.[100]

The scholar Cheng Hsiao 鄭曉 (1499–1566) says that during the Chia-ching reign the southern part of Kiangsi, where that province adjoined Hu-kuang, Fukien and Kuangtung, was a center for rebels, and that the Yün-yang 郧陽 prefecture, in the present Hupei province, having easy communication with Shensi, Szechuan, and Honan provinces, was a place where vagrants found it easy to gather for mischief. Hence, special officials were appointed to watch over these two places.[101] That the Yün-yang prefecture had been a center of vagrants as early as the Hung-wu emperor's time we know from the narrative of a late Ming historian. In the beginning of the Hung-wu reign, this historian says, Teng Yü 鄧愈, duke of Shen-kuo 申國公, having conquered An-lu 安陸 and Hsiang-yang 襄陽, marched his army to Yün-yang and drove away all the vagrants. The place was then closed to all and no one dared enter. During the Yung-lo and Hsüan-te reigns, however, vagrants began to reappear there and by 1437 they must have been numerous, for the governor of Han-chung had begun to feel uneasy about them. In a report to the emperor Ying-tsung he said that unless the vagrants were dispersed as soon as possible they might cause trouble. The emperor, however, did not attach much importance to this warning. Believing that the vagrants were merely poor men who had been driven by hunger and cold to settle in Yun-yang, he thought that it would be cruel to use violence against them and so he sent a censor rather than an army to pacify them. Several of the leaders were sent into exile and a few of the vagrants made a pretence of submission, but as soon as the censor had left they resumed their independence. They numbered nearly a million, and the territory they occupied extended to several thousand square li.[102]

The negligence of the authorities led to a revolt of several tens of of thousands of these Yün-yang vagrants under the leadership of Liu Ch'ien-chin 劉千斤. They fought desperately against the government troops, keeping up the fight, it is said, till nearly ten thousand of their number had been killed. Ultimately, their leaders were captured and the rebels dispersed. Four years later, in 1470, another rising was incited by the followers of Liu Ch'ien-chin, who were still active in the locality. It was a year of drought, and farmers who had lost their crops drifted to the mountains to join the rebels, bringing their numbers to an estimated total of over nine hundred thousand. They held out against the government troops for two years and it is said that when they were finally defeated, the number of those who surrendered was four thousand. After the suppression of the rebellion, the soldiers searched all the mountains and valleys of Hupei and they are said to have found over one million one hundred and fifty thousand vagrants. Only one tenth of this number had any desire to return to their native places; the rest preferred to remain in Hupei. Accordingly, the government gave them land in proportion to the number of families and soon several new prefectures were established in the places where they had settled.[103] We are inclined to doubt the accuracy of this historian's estimates of the number of vagrants. Nevertheless, since several prefectures were created for their accommodation, they must have been very numerous indeed.

In 1571, a censor received a special commission from the Lung-ch'ing emperor to arrest vagrants who had made their way by stealth from all over the empire to the Capital. We are not told their number, but it must have been large, since they had attracted the attention of officials.[104] An eye-witness account from about this time tells us that vagrants had congregated in monasteries in all parts of the capital, where they did no work—neither sewing nor weaving, nor trade of any kind. In addition, the streets were crowded with Taoist and Buddhist monks, and fortune-tellers. Our eye-witness viewed all this with alarm: the vagrants seemed to be infecting the inhabitants of the capital with their bad example and sooner or later, he thought, disasters would be caused by these wanderers.[105]

Towards the end of the Ch'ung-chen period there were so many vagrants all over the country that no reliable estimate of their number could be made. Writing in 1635, an official warned the emperor that, unless something were done at once to relieve the distress of the people, a day might come when every part of the country would be crowded with soldiers and empty of civilians, all civilians having joined the rebels.[106] In that same year a censor had already reported that the rebels were being enthusiastically welcomed by the people wherever they passed. In some places the people longed for the coming of the rebels and felt disappointed if they did not appear. It was asserted that the poor people of Feng-yang had made a journey of several hundred miles in order to meet the rebels and persuade them to come to their native place. They revealed military secrets to the rebels and gave them lists of local rich families, for they had made up their minds to suffer no more from the cruel government officials and had chosen rather to be killed as rebels than to die from hunger and injustice.[107]

Bandits presented no less serious a problem than vagrants in the later part of the Ming period. It was not, indeed, a completely distinct problem; many of the bandits were vagrants. But not all vagrants became bandits and not all bandits had been forced into banditry by fear of starvation. In the year 1572, Kao Kung 高拱 wrote to the Lung-ch'ing emperor that many of the so-called bandits were adventurers who gambled and squandered money in illegal ways, formed gangs, and often quarrelled among themselves.[108] Their lawless lives, often unchecked by any authority, became an ideal for many poor people who, attracted by the idle way of life, gladly joined the gangs. The bandits, for their part, were pleased to find partners whose help would undoubtedly increase their influence. Kao Kung therefore felt uneasy for the future safety of the country, though at the time when he wrote, public order, despite multiplying ills, still seemed secure. The *Shang-ch'eng i-lan* 商程一覽, published during the Lung-ch'ing period as a guide-book for business men, kept on warning its readers to be wary of bandits.[109]

Contemporary scholars when writing about the people in the second half of the Ming period did not conceal the fact that they were becoming poorer every day and that poverty had forced many to set themselves up as highwaymen. These writers unanimously agreed that it was the duty of the government to start a reform. It was notorious that, owing to the negligence of the government, local officials had the people at their mercy and could impose illegal demands upon them at will. The military class encroached unchecked on the farms of the people, and the government land-records inevitably fell into disorder. The "Fish Scale Records" and the "Yellow Records", once the government's chief weapons in protecting the poor against unjust aggressors, became of merely historical interest. Rich landlords were delighted to find that they could easily avoid paying land taxes by bribing government officials, but the poor were often taxed heavily and subjected to a disproportionate share of *corvée*. On top of all this, inexorable demands of every kind arrived continually from the court. Toward the end of the dynasty when the Manchus were making trouble in the northeast and the rebels in the provinces, taxation for the upkeep of the soldiers kept on increasing. Meanwhile the imperial relatives, who were strictly forbidden to work for their living and could hardly obtain enough from the government to support themselves and their families, were trying to exact tribute from the people even by force.

Farming was in a permanently depressed state in the later Ming years. Hsü Chen-ming 徐貞明 explained this by saying that in the south the provinces were too thickly populated, while in the north-west the land was uncultivated because of lack of manpower. A more potent cause, perhaps, was negligence in maintaining and improving the irrigation system: farms turned into deserts in dry years, and into lakes when the rains were heavy.[110] Wet or dry, the farmers could never hope for a year of prosperity. Unable to make ends meet, they had to borrow to pay their taxes and to support their families, often accumulating debts without any hope of paying them off. Eventually they had to sell their belongings and even their own children, and thus ended up with broken families and no possessions. Men who could think for themselves realized that farming had become a tragic blind alley, and chose rather to become merchants, travelling from place to place and so escaping from the merciless faces of the land-tax collectors. Those who remained to labor on their farms, strove as best they could to earn a living. Contemporary writers when describing the life of the farmer frequently use the phrase: 'the people are poor and there are many suits among them.'—a clear indication that they had lost contentment and were not resigned to injustice inflicted upon them.

Since the Chia-ching reign the empire had been suffering from invasions—in the south by Japanese pirates, in the north first by the Mongols, and then by the Manchus. It was obvious to contemporaries that these foreign invaders could not have penetrated into the interior without help from inside. The scholar Cheng Hsiao confirms this. "The poor and the rebellious north of the Yangtze join the pirates for their own profit; the rich of the south have secret communications with them. The former take advantage of the invaders' presence to loot and thus cause great harm to the villages. The latter are more to be dreaded, for they are very cunning, supplying the enemy with provisions and revealing military secrets to them."[111] Such conditions could but encourage the hungry mobs who preferred risking their lives in violent action to suffering the slow horror of starvation.

In the year 1539, the Grand Secretary Ku Ting-ch'en 顧鼎臣 reported to the throne that of late wanderers from all over the empire had been coming secretly to the capital. These new-comers tried to find out all that was happening in different government offices and by bribery established secret communications with officials and members of their families. With the help of these suborned officials they falsified documents and engaged in every variety of illegal business.[112] Years later, an eye-witness commented on the same situation: "In former days when the country was not so thickly populated," he wrote, "a single man could have a hundred mou of land and so there were no idle citizens. Nowadays, with a population that must be more than ten times what it was in ancient times, one finds many who are doing nothing at all. Take the capital alone: there one finds eunuchs, court ladies, prostitutes, Buddhist and Taoist priests, amounting in all to not fewer than a hundred thousand. The imperial relatives, who reside in the provinces, may possess no eunuchs, but they keep great numbers of Buddhist and Taoist priests and their followers. In the cities, far and near, there are great numbers of prostitutes. The man-servants and maid-servants of noble families live like princes and princesses. Even bandits and wastrels are more numerous than ordinary civilians. 'A farmer produces for ten,' was the ancient saying. But now, I say, a farmer has to produce for more than ten!''[113]

The fact that people were flocking to the capital and big cities is a clear indication of their discontent with rural life. The worst of it was that they came as wanderers, and so had to depend on someone else for support. Failing this either they were reduced to beggary or they resorted to illegal activities, and in the great cities there was never a lack of dissolute people with whom they might consort. It is easy to see why conscientious ministers worried about them.

SETTLEMENTS

The military settlements, as we have seen, were vital to the government and the whole economic constitution of the Ming empire. Their decline was, beyond all doubt, a fatal blow to that empire. Without the military settlements, the army, instead of being self-supporting, had to rely on the government for its upkeep and this in turn laid a burden on the government which was ultimately to prove too heavy for it. The *Ming shih* attributes the decline of the military settlements to the period after the Cheng-t'ung reign. However, it may be traced back to an even earlier period. As early as 1429, Fan Chi 范濟 had pointed out to the Hsüan-te emperor how unwise it was to burden the soldiers with such non-military labors as horse raising, hay collecting, wood-cutting, and charcoal burning. Such mis-employment, he said, would help to destroy the good system instituted by the founder of the dynasty by which seventy per cent of the soldiers were employed on garrison duties and the remaining thirty per cent in cultivating the soil.[114]

The abuse of employing soldiers for private services, which we have described at length above, eventually had serious consequences. In the days of the Yung-lo emperor the men on active service numbered 190,000 and their food and pay were supplied by 40,000 soldiers working productively in military settlements. Even those on active service were permitted to cultivate land along the borders. Thus there was always an abundance for the soldiers and the government was under no necessity of providing for them.[115] But the employment of soldiers for other work took them away from the farms of the military settlements and many who could not suffer the hardships involved in the new work deserted and took refuge in other places. Often the military farms were left uncultivated or fell into the hands of military officials who treated them as private possessions. Things got worse when, after the Cheng-t'ung period, conflicts between the government and the tribes not infrequently rendered the cultivation of land along the border impossible. Production in the military settlement farms decreased till it could barely support the soldiers, and their pay had to be drawn from government treasuries. In the Wan-li period the total area of the military settlements, though still 644,000 ch'ing, had fallen by over 249,000 ch'ing since the Hung-wu period. The scholar Wang Ch'i 王圻 (chin-shih 1565), quoting a dictum of the President of the Board of Ceremonies, wrote: "Nominally they are military settlements, but the reality does not correspond to the implications of the name. In the farming season people do their work carelessly, and when the crops are reaped they are misappropriated (by whoever can lay hands on them). Those put in charge of these settlements, in general, live leisurely lives in cities; never do they dream of setting foot on the farms. Those sent to inspect the farms show too much confidence in the records. Never do they find out what has really happened in the granaries. Alas, these corrupt practices are still going on and one does not know where they will end!"[116]

That the misappropriation of military settlements by Ming nobles and military officials was common may be seen from abundant references in the writings of their contemporaries. In 1430, for instance, a censor reported that many of the military settlements in Ta-t'ung prefecture were being misappropriated by influential persons. A minister who was sent to investigate was able to restore nearly two thousand ch'ing of land to the soldiers. During the reign of emperor Ying-tsung, ministers had to be sent on several occasions to regain possession of military settlements that had been misappropriated either by military officials or by influential dignitaries. The imposition, in the 13th year of the Hung-chih emperor (1500), of a severe penalty on all who dared to appropriate land from the military settlements shows that the warnings of previous emperors had been disregarded by men of influence.[117] A censor in the Wan-li reign reported that it was common in his time for nobles, eunuchs and officials to appropriate farms belonging to the military settlements. No sooner had these been restored to the government by imperial order than they were again reoccupied by the same people. Local authorities might have full knowledge of the facts but they did not dare to inquire into such cases.

The *Ming shih* says that the founder of the dynasty strictly forbade the purchase of farms belonging to the military settlements and even forbade the sub-letting of such farms. But in later times government officials became careless, the records of the military settlements were neglected, and the lands were occupied even by the soldiers themselves. After all this it was not easy to check what properties were missing. Censors were sent every year to make an inspection, but they were interested solely in the land-taxes and hardly ever inquired about the area of the farms.[118] The usurpers of the land were thus left unmolested and could employ soldiers to cultivate these farms, which by right should have been supporting the soldiers.

Even those who worked in the settlements under their officers often suffered great injustice. In the biography of Liu Ta-hsia 劉大夏 (1436–1516), we have an account of an audience during which the Hung-chih emperor (1488–1505) showed himself unable to understand how the soldiers could suffer from poverty; they received monthly salaries and after mobilization daily pay as well. Apparently he did not know that these salaries often disappeared into the pockets of the officers. Wang Ao 王鏊 (1450–1524) could have undeceived him: speaking of the soldiers of his time he said that although they worked hard they did not share the products of the settlements; they were supposed to receive monthly salaries, yet their families never received anything. Later still, in the Lung-ch'ing period (1567–1572), we are told that soldiers on the borders, regardless of what they received from the military settlement, were given only half of their month's salary.[119]

The soldiers were driven to despair by the injustice of the nobles and military officers and they seem to have received little sympathy from the government. Heavy land-taxes were piled on top of the insatiable extortion of the officers till military life became intolerable. Many soldiers changed their profession and became laborers or merchants; others sought to return to their native land under any pretext and often succeeded in this by bribing their immediate superiors. Many farms along the border were in consequence left uncultivated. A further reason for the depopulation of the border regions is given by Hsieh Chao-che. Many of the people living along the border became accustomed to taking refuge with the tribes, he says, partly because they were familiar with the languages and customs of the tribes, but still more because they could not support the heavy taxes and heavy *corvée* that were imposed on them.[120]

Cheng Ta-yü, whose *Ching-kuo hsiung-lüeh* has been quoted earlier in this book, says that in Hu-kuang province, where an area of six thousand square *li* was known as fertile country, the cultivated land had fallen by the last years of the dynasty to only one-tenth of the former area. Similarly, in Honan the area of cultivated land was reported to have fallen to three-tenths. In Huai-yüan 懷遠 prefecture the farming area, which had once measured 5,275 ch'ing, had fallen to less than 2,135 ch'ing. Cheng seems to have attributed the fall to the long continuance of peace during which people grew accustomed to an extravagant life, ceased to find any attraction in labor on the land, and preferred to become merchants or to find some other profession that would enable them to travel to different parts of the country. In another book written by the same author there is a chapter entitled t'ao-i 逃移 or 'shirking one's responsibility by emigrating', in which he exhorts his readers to remember the loneliness and helplessness of an emigrant. He confirms his argument by the common saying that a man who leaves his native land loses all prestige. Hence, he says, a man should strive to remain in his own country and to be contented with his own affairs: he should not emigrate without taking thought lest he have regrets in the future. Cheng ends, however, with a cautious sentence, saying that if pressure from magistrates forces a man to take flight then it must be said that the magistrates are at fault.[121]

Side by side with the deterioration of the military settlements there had also been great changes in the wei-so system. The army could no longer support itself and the merchant settlements, which had formerly been such a help to the troops along the borders, were also in rapid decline.

We described in an earlier chapter how merchants who delivered grain to the army on the borders were given in exchange tickets for salt. Soon, however, the amount of salt produced was not enough to meet the claims of all the merchants. Furthermore, since the second part of the 15th century the frequent Mongol invasions had rendered cultivation difficult. While farming was thus becoming less profitable, sub-officials were constantly intensifying their demands on the farmers. Inevitably land began to go out of cultivation not only in this region but also in the interior, along the northern part of Southern Chih-li province.[122]

At the beginning of the Ch'eng-hua reign (1465–1487), a rich merchant succeeded in obtaining a monopoly of all the salt in present Kiangsu despite the strenuous opposition of the President of the Board of Revenue. From then onward it became all too common for influential people to secure monopolies of salt sales. The small salt merchants, angered by this injustice, turned to buying salt illegally from salt producers. We are told that in the Chia-ching days (1522–1566), even palace guards took up this illegal trade in salt, and acquired hundreds of large junks which sailed along the rivers selling salt as they went along. Sometimes they transported salt by pack-horse, and no one dared to question them, much less to lay hands on them.[123]

The year 1492, saw the end of the merchant settlements: the President of the Board of Revenue declared that, thereafter, money was to be used in the trading of salt between the government and the merchants. Since, from that time onward, money was sent to the borders by the government for the army salaries, the merchants could see no point in maintaining their settlements. They withdrew therefore from the borders. The disappearance of the merchant settlements deprived the border territories of the necessary capital, and farming declined rapidly. Food supplies had to be brought from long distances and the price of foodstuffs inevitably rose.[124] Thus the change introduced in 1492 brought farming to a standstill along the borders, and deprived the army of adequate supplies. Then too, the Board of Revenue was often dilatory in forwarding the money for the salaries of the troops on the borders and the government found it easy to divert this money to other purposes. Towards the end of the dynasty, when the Manchus were crossing the borders in force, the only means left of supporting a strong army was to levy heavy taxes on the people.

TAXATION

Commerce flourished in the earlier part of the Ming period. In Nanking and Peking the shops were often classified as nan-p'u 南舖 and pei-p'u 北舖 according to the types of goods they sold, for northern foodstuff merchants often had shops in Nanking and southern silk and salt dealers often had shops in Peking. Such flourishing trade was able to bear increasingly heavy taxation. During the Hsüan-te period (1426–1435) tax stations were set up in thirty-three prefectures and provinces where commerce was thriving, and we are told that the amount of taxes collected was five times greater than in the early days of the dynasty. During the Cheng-te reign (1506–1521) commercial taxes within the nine gates of Peking were several times greater than in the Hung-chih period (1488–1505). Seemingly trade was so prosperous that the merchants were always prepared to fulfil their obligations.[125]

Unfortunately, the abuses of government officials and nobles began to inject confusion into the system of taxation. The early Ming emperors had foreseen this danger and their timely warnings served to check abuses. Under the Wan-li emperor (1573–1620), however, taxes of all kinds were levied by the eunuchs with the emperor's silent approval. The *Hsü wen-hsien t'ung k'ao* says that because of this emperor's insatiable craving for wealth the people were reduced to such dire poverty that tumults started everywhere.[126]

In 1596, since it was apparent that the ordinary taxes would not suffice to finance the government, eunuchs were sent to nearly all the provinces to collect more taxes. New titles were created for the levying of new taxes; and the heavier the taxes became, the more detailed were the regulations laid down for collecting them. Let us take as a concrete example Ho-hsi-wu 河西務 which is located beside the Grand Canal in the Wu-ch'ing 武清 district, present Hopei province. Ever since the days of the Yüan dynasty it had been recognized as an important center of communications and hundreds of cargo boats went through it every day. A customs house was established there to tax all cargo ships. As soon as a ship arrived it had to pay a double tax: one according to the size of the ship, and the other according to the quantity and quality of the goods. The same goods were subject to further taxation when they were brought to or from the shops. Then, if they were sent to a more distant place, another tax had to be paid at the destination. In short, within a hundred miles, three sets of custom dues had to be paid. When the merchants paid a tax they either suffered a diminution of their profits, or, as was more commonly done, shifted the burden of the taxes to their customers.[127]

Chang Hsüan 張萱, department director of the Board of Revenue who lived in the Wan-li period, has left us a detailed description of the difficulties encountered at the customs station of Hu-shu-kuan 滸墅關, one of the most important customs stations of those days. In a letter to his superior, he writes:

"I took up office this year on the 20th of the second month. The 20th of the fifth month exactly completed a quarter (the first period). We collected strings of cash to the value of only a little over 13,500 silver taels. In the second quarter, from the 21st of the fifth month to the 20th of the eighth month (the second period) we collected only a little over 11,520 taels. From the 21st of the eighth month to the 20th of the eleventh month (the third period) we collected only something over 14,040 taels. That means that in the three periods of my office I have been able to send in only a little over 39,060 taels. How does this compare with the taxes collected in earlier times?

"According to my calculations there has been a great drop. According to some tradesmen, for years most of the cargo boats have come in or gone out in the third month of spring and in the ninth month of autumn. They seldom come or go in the other months of the year. Shortly after I took up office there came the first quarter or the first period, and the strings of cash I collected amounted to a sum so small as to be truly surprising. Still, I then thought, this was but by chance; the sums collected might differ from year to year or from season to season. I thought that perhaps by the ninth month, in autumn, the cargo boats might have gathered here and that the sum we should then collect might help to cover up the deficit of the preceding period. But now the ninth month is over and by comparison with the past month or so the number of cargo boats is small and it is growing smaller. After the tenth month there will not be many cargo boats. Fortunately it is not very cold at the end of the year; the rivers therefore may not be frozen and we can still hope that the number of cargo boats will increase. The lock of the canal between Chen-kiang and Ching-k'ou is blocked, owing to the shallowness of the river, and cargo boats that used to come from the north have changed their course to Meng-ho where they take the sea route and so no longer pass through our place. At the beginning of the year, tradesmen as a rule do not travel. By the 20th of the second month I shall have completed one year's service and I am afraid that the collection in the fourth period may not be comparable with that made in the third. If that happens it will mean that my full year of service will not have helped to increase the revenue but will have witnessed a decrease. There is obviously a deficit in the customs duties. Where then will the government obtain its revenue? We all know that Hu-shu is a well-known customs station and that San-wu 三吳 (comprising southern Kiangsu and northern Chekiang) is a country famous for its wealth and a place of concourse for tradesmen. Yet I have been able neither to increase the amount of taxes nor to collect the proper sum. Somehow I feel I am not doing my duty. . . .

"Most of our tradesmen come mainly from four provinces, namely, Hu-kuang, Kiangsi, Chekiang and San-chih. Since the beginning of the century these four provinces have never been known to suffer from natural calamities simultaneously as they are suffering now. Except for the transport of rice and wheat from Kiangsi and Hu-kuang to San-wu, the entry of goods has stopped. Since last autumn even these two provinces have ceased to sell grain. Rice and wheat ships are no longer sailing—if there chance to be one or two they are government ships carrying rice to be sold cheaply for relief purposes. Since these are, of course, exempt from taxation, it is impossible to impose duties on them. Then, consider the creek of Fu-shan 福山, which is under my jurisdiction. This creek is frequented by cargo boats of Nan-t'ung chou 南通州 and officials are sent every month to collect taxes, which once amounted to not less than several tens of thousands of silver taels. But Nan-t'ung chou has long since stopped selling grain and for six months not a single boat has come. . . . In other customs stations the taxes on goods not subject to fixed taxes are adjusted in such a way that if they appear to be too heavy they may be reduced, and vice versa. In our station, however, tax is levied only on the boats and only by size. This is all regulated in such a way that the rates are known to all. It would be impossible to effect an increase of one cent over what is laid down in the regulations. Hence one boat less means one string less of cash to the revenue and nothing can be done to expand it.

"Next, the Hu-shu station differs from other stations in this, that it is surrounded by creeks which are interwoven like a net. (It is situated near Tai-hu, consequently it opens out in all directions.) From San-shan-cha 三山閘 in Ch'ang-chou-fu 常州府 to Pai-chang-ho 百丈河 there are one hundred creeks; from Chu-t'ang-kang 竹塘港 in Ch'ang-shu 常熟 to Lu-chih 角直 there are twenty-three creeks; from Hsiao-chen-kang 小眞港 in Sung-kiang-fu to Kiang-yin-hsien 江陰縣 there are ten creeks, and in Sung kiang there is also Hsieh-chia-ch'iao 薛家橋 between which and Hua-tu-ch'iao 花瀆橋 there are nine creeks. Boats pass through all these creeks and commonly evade the paying of taxes. Formerly guards were stationed on these creeks with freedom of action while on duty and so the smugglers had to restrain themselves. Last year, while Ts'ao Chu-shih 曹主事 was in office, Hsü Ching-lüeh 徐經略 was appointed to patrol. He arrested some smugglers, and in retaliation for this, Hsü was falsely accused and was dismissed from office. His fate frightened a number of the officials and they ceased to send guards on patrol.

"Then, each creek is under the protection of an influential family and is controlled by a group of scoundrels who give open protection to smugglers. In former years when cargo boats were numerous the loss seemed insignificant; but now, when the number of boats is decreasing and the taxes are showing a deficit, how can we stand by with folded arms and see these smugglers' frauds? We have had the misfortune of suffering excessive rain which has caused floods everywhere. From the fourth to the tenth month, between P'i-ling 毘陵

and Chia Hu 嘉湖 (i.e. Chia-hsing 嘉興 and Hu-chou 湖州) the canal was as usual, but the flood is now so great that one can hardly see the shore or make out the beasts grazing on the land. In these circumstances it is not possible to take precautions against smugglers who hoist full sail and press along; even guards can do very little. Thus hardly thirty or forty per cent of the boats stop at the station to pay duties. What wonder then that the customs are yielding less and less every day.

"A more surprising development has occurred at the junction of Kiang-yin 江陰, Ch'ang-shu 常熟 and Wu-hsi 無錫, where there are two creeks, Huang-chuang 黃庄 and Ch'en-shih 陳市. Formerly these were used only by farmers but of late the unreasonable demands made by special customs stations set up in Hu-shu by the eunuchs have forced the people to take to these passages, using small boats. Recently the eunuchs sent men to patrol these places and some offenders were arrested, including a certain Chao Huan 趙煥 whose profession was to protect smugglers. Huan was drowned before he was handed over to the eunuchs. His wife Chin and his son Hsi-yen, at the instigation of local scoundrels, brought the case to the Hsün-fu and had tablets erected throughout the three cities forbidding guards to set foot on those places (Huang-chung and Ch'en-shih). As a result the law-breakers, relying on the influence of some powerful officials (although they dare not use these officials' names but rather lay stress on the tablets and the example of Chin) have erected stations and set up banners in Huang-chuang and Ch'en-shih. They try to attract the cargo boats to themselves and help them to smuggle; at the same time they set up counters in order to collect (from the tradesmen) as if they had a real customs station. An estimate of their daily income shows that it must be quite close to what we collect. . . .

"It is my duty as an official to levy taxes from the merchants who carry on business with the common people. The common people no longer exist. How then, can we expect to have merchants? From the fifth month to the present day the number of cargo boats coming in and going out has been falling every day, and they carry grain only. Most of these grain-sellers have obtained their grain by selling their children or whatever possessions they had in order to ward off starvation a little longer. Either they share a boat or each one manages his own, carrying in it no more than a few tens of hu 斛 (bushels) of rice. When you look at them you see emaciated old men or pale half-starved persons. Even to see them can cause one to shed tears. How then, can one have the heart to demand taxes from them?"[128]

Chang Hsüan's tale of woe throws light on several aspects of the customs-station system in the Wan-li period. First, many of the customs had not a fixed rate for merchandise and the officials might increase or reduce the duties they levied. Secondly, side by side with the regular customs stations there were independent stations set up at will, under the protection of the emperor himself, by the eunuchs, and levying taxes from merchants. Then, influential families acting through bands of scoundrels helped smugglers in return for a protection fee. Because of the great influence these families enjoyed in their localities, government officials seldom dared to interfere with them. It is easy to see how grievously all this harassed merchants and how strong the temptation was for them to evade taxes, or, failing this, to leave the locality. This explains why Chang had to complain that cargo boats were coming in ever smaller numbers or were not coming at all. The natural calamities that occurred so frequently in the reign of Wan-li helped still further to discourage commercial transactions.

Towards the end of the Ch'ung-chen reign (1640) customs taxation was officially increased. Already, at the beginning of his reign, the Ch'ung-chen emperor had increased it to one ch'ien per silver tael. Now he added two more ch'ien per tael. The increase, however, was not uniform; in some places it amounted to only half of the increase imposed at the beginning of his reign, and in other places there was no increase at all. The government was in dire straits and had to use every possible means to collect money. But as the *Ming t'ung-chien* says, the raising of 200,000 silver taels exhausted the financial vitality of the people.[129]

The scholar Huang Tsun-so 黃尊素 (1584–1626) tells us of a magistrate in Hua-t'ing 華亭 who, wishing to exempt the farmers from an increase of land-tax, taxed the merchants to make good the loss thus incurred. This system was put into practice in both Kuang-tung and Kuangsi provinces: merchants and hawkers and brokers were all taxed. But the system was so harmful to the merchant class that it soon aroused criticism and had to be discontinued.[130] The decline of the tax system had a disastrous effect on the income of the government. With the Japanese and Manchu invasions in the northeast and the outbursts of rebellion in the heart of the country, money was needed in larger quantities than ever before. With a declining income, the government was in a hopeless position. The end was near.

Notes

[1] *Ming hui-yao*, 12, (ts'e 1) 185; *Li-tai chi-kuan piao*, 21, (ts'e 3) 580–582.

[2] *Ming hui-yao*, 12, (ts'e 1) 185.

[3] The *Ming hui-yao*, 12, (ts'e 1) 187–18 gives an interesting account of the court in 1491. In the eighth month of that year, the fourth year after the Hung-chih emperor's accession to the throne, the afternoon court meeting was revived on the petition of some zealous ministers. Two months later the President of the Board of Civil Office and a number of the high ministers accused themselves before the monarch of having been late for the afternoon court meeting. Accordingly an imperial edict was issued that read: "You often reminded me to take great interest in the administration of the government. Now that I have revived that afternoon court meeting I am surprised to find you so negligent. Since you have all admitted your fault, I shall not press the case!"

[4] *Ming-ch'en tsou-i*, 32, (ts'e 0,920) 599–56 ; cf. the remark of Hung Liang-chi 洪亮吉 (1746–1809), on the Wan-li emperor in the *Li-tai shih shih cheng chih lun* 歷代史事政治論, (Shanghai, 1904) 282, (ts'e 22) 2b.

[5] *Ming-ch'en tsou-i*, 21, (0,918) 383.

[6] *Jih-chih lu chi-shih*, 10, (ts'e 6) 8a.

[7] *Ming shih*, 78, (ts'e 27) 4a; *Ming-ch'en tsou-i*, 32, (ts'e 0,920) 591; cf. also XIII, 9.

[8] *Ta-ming hui-tien*, 5, (ts'e 2) 9b; *Jih-chih lu chi-shih*, 8, (ts'e 5) 20a.

[9] *Huang-Ming t'ung-chi*, 3, (ts'e 3) 13b.

[10] *Huang-Ming t'ung-chi shu-i*, 2, (ts'e 1) 38b; *Huang-Ming t'ung-chi*, 5, (ts'e 3) 60b.

[11] *Ming shih*, 77, (ts'e 27) 6ab.

[12] *Nan-ching tu-ch'a-yüan chih*, 25, (ts'e 13) 45ab.

[13] *Tsui-wei lu*, 9, (ts'e 14) 1a; *I-t'iao-pien-fa*, 10–15.

[14] *Hsü wen-hsien t'ung-k'ao*, 6, I, 2834.

[15] *Huang-Ming t'ung-chi*, 8, (ts'e 4) 7b, 9ab; *Ming shih*, 183, (ts'e 60) 5b; 6a; 180, (ts'e 59) 7ab.

[16] *Hsü wen-hsien t'ung-k'ao*, 6, I, 2835.

[17] Ibid., 6, I, 2837.

[18] *Ming shih*, 77, (ts'e 27) 13b.

[19] *Ming shih ch'ao-lüeh*, (ts'e 1) 16ab; *Kuo chi-chien shu-kao*, 1, (ts'e 0,908) 21–23; 60–63; Fang Ta-chen 方大鎮, *Ning-t'an chü tsou-i* 寧澹居奏議, (TCFSCTIS), (ts'e 3) 22ab.

[20] *Ming shih*, 77, (ts'e 27) 13b.

[21] *Ming-shih ch'ao-lüeh*, (ts'e 1) 14b.

[22] *Huang-Ming t'ung-chi*, 7, (ts'e 4) 57a.

[23] *Huang-Ming chia-lung wen chien chi*, 1, (ts'e 1) 28b; *Huang-Ming t'ung-chi hsü-pien*, 1, (ts'e 1) 22a; *Chia-ching i-lai chu-lüeh*, 1, (ts'e 1) 8b, 9a.

[24] *Ming t'ung-chien*, 53, (ts'e 4) 31b, 32a.

[25] *Kuo-ch'ao tien-hui*, 156, (ts'e 52) 15b.

[26] Chu Huai-wu 朱懷吾, *Chao-tai chi lüeh* 昭代紀略, (1626 ed.) 6, (ts'e 6) 48b.

[27] *Hsü wen-hsien t'ung-k'ao*, 2, I, 2790a; 2791b.

[28] *Kuo-ch'üeh*, 47, (ts'e 3) 2910; *Ming shu*, 67, (ts'e 3941) 1365–1366.

[29] *Ming t'ung-chien*, 63, (ts'e 7) 25a.

[30] *Cho-chai shih-i*, 13–15.

[31] *Hsiao-hsia hsien-chi tse-ch'ao*, C. (ts'e 8) 6ab.

[32] The original text of Hsü Hsüeh-mu is not clear; it reads:" . . . 二品之所免，僅二兩銀耳，尚不比北方一秀才，其恩豈能旁及 . . ."

[33] *Kuei-yu-yüan k'ao wen-pien* 文編, 16, (ts'e 6) 20b–21b.

[34] *Ching-shih shih-yung-pien hsü-chi*, B. (ts'e 16) 37ab.

[35] *Wu-tsa-tsu*, (Shanghai, 1959) 4, A. 116.

[36] *Ming shu*, 67, (ts'e 3941) 1364–1365.

[37] *Chia-ching shih-lu*, 1st month of the eleventh year.

[38] *Huang-Ming t'ung-chi hsü-pien*, 7.

[39] Chang Hsüan 張萱, *Hsi-yüan wen-ts'un* 西園文存, (1664 ed.) 26, (ts'e 11) 4a–5a, "Po-lo hsien-chih fang-yü shuo" 博羅縣志方輿說.

[40] *Tien-ku chi-wen*, 18, (ts'e 2817) 300.

[41] *Ming t'ung-chien*, 75, (ts'e 9) 25b.

[42] *Ming-shih ch'ao-lüeh, Hsien-huang-ti pen-chi*, 3, (ts'e 1) 45b, 46a.

[43] *Ming-shih ch'ao-lüeh, Hsien-huang-ti pen-chi*, 4, (ts'e 1) 36b.

[44] *Kuo-ch'üeh*, 92, (ts'e 6) 5618.

[45] *Ch'un-ming meng-yü-lu*, 36.

[46] Hsü Hung-hsiao 許宏烋, "Ming-tai t'u-ti cheng-li chih k'ao-ch'a" 明代土地整理之考察, *Shih-huo pan-yüeh-k'an* 食貨半月刊, 3, (April, 1936) 10. 45.

[47] *Jih-chih lu chi-shih*, 10, (ts'e 6) 9ab, 18a.

[48] Ibid., 10, (ts'e 6) 18a.

[49] *Ming shih*, 77, (ts'e 27) 13b.

[50] *Huai-tsung Ch'ung-chen shih-lu*, 6, (ts'e 498) 7a.

[51] *Shih-tsung Su-huang-ti shih-lu* 世宗肅皇帝實錄, (KPL photographic reprints), 545, (ts'e 336) 6a–7a.

[52] Hsiao Liang-kan 蕭良幹, *Cho-chai shih-i* 拙齋十議, (TSCCCP), (ts'e 0,756) 13–15.

[53] *Ch'ung-chen ch'ang-pien*, 2, (ts'e 14) 7ab; cf. also *P'ing-k'ou-chih*, 8, (ts'e 2) 6a.

[54] Wu Ying-chi 吳應箕, (1594–1645), *Lou-shan-t'ang chi* 樓山堂集, (TSCCCP), 12, (ts'e 2,170) 135–136; 13, (ts'e 2,170) 152–153.

[55] *Ming-mo nung-min ch'i-i shih-liao*, 429–430.

[56] *Shan-chung wen-chien lu*, 6, (ts'e 4) 10a.

[57] Wang Wen-lu 王文祿, *Ts'e-shu* 策樞, (TSCCCP), 3, (ts'e 0,756) 50–51.

[58] *San-yüan pi-chi*, A. 70.

[59] *Fan-wen-chung-kung tsou-shu*, 2, (ts'e 2,455) 32.

[60] Supplement to the *San-yüan pi-chi*, (ts'e 3) C. 11ab; Liang Fang-chung 梁方仲, *Ming-tai liang-chang chih-du* 明代糧長制度, (Shanghai, 1957) 1–6.

[61] *Ts'e-shu*, 3, (ts'e 0,756) 58.

[62] Wang Wen-lu 王文祿, *Shu-tu* 書牘, (TSCCCP), 2, (ts'e 0,755) 50–51.

[63] *Yung-chuang hsiao-pin*, 2, (ts'e 98) 3a.

[64] Ibid., 13, (ts'e 102) 9a; cf. also *Ming-ch'en tsou-i*, 39, (ts'e 0,922) 758–759.

[65] *Tien-ku chi-wen*, 18, (ts'e 134) 2ab.

[66] *Shu-tu*, 2. (0.755) 8 58–59.

[67] Fang K'ung-chao 方孔炤, *Ch'u-yao hsiao-yen* 欽堯小言, (TCFSCTIS), (ts'e 5) 2b; cf. also *Chun-ming meng-yü lu*, 36, (ts'e 11) 6a.

[68] *Lou-shan-t'ang-chi*, 14, (ts'e 2,170) 159–160.

[69] *Ming-mo nung-min ch'i-i shih-liao*, 274–275.

[70] *Huai-tsung ch'ung-chen shih-lu*, 7, (ts'e 499) 1ab; 16, (ts'e 500) 4b.

[71] *Kuo-shih ta-kang*, 524–535.

[72] Ibid., 529.

[73] *Tsui-wei lu*, 9, (ts'e 14).

[74] *Ming shih ch'ao-lüeh*, 2, (ts'e 1) 14a.

[75] *Ming-ch'en tsou-i*, 33, (ts'e 0,921) 648–649.

[76] Wang Chia-chen 王家楨, *Yü-ch'eng tsou-shu* 玉城奏疏, (TSCCCP), (ts'e 0,911) 2–3.

[77] Lu Shih-i 陸世儀, *Li-ts'ai-i* 理財議, (*Hsüen-lan t'ang ts'ung-shu* 玄覽堂叢書) (ts'e 117) b–2a.

[78] *K'ou-shih pien-nien*, 4, (ts'e 5) 6a; 7, (ts'e 6) 6b; 12, (ts'e 9) 12a; 13, (ts'e 9) 24a; 14, (ts'e 10) 14b; *Huai-tsung ch'ung-chen shih-lu*, 7, (tse' 499) 4a, 6a, 17b; 13, (ts'e 500) 3b; 14, (ts'e 500) 14b; *P'ing-k'ou-chih* 3, (ts'e 1) 18b.

[79] *Huai-tsung ch'ung-chen shih-lu*, 11, (ts'e 499) 8a; 13, (ts'e 500) 10a; 14, (ts'e 500) 5b; *P'ing-k'ou-chih* 3, (ts'e 1) 18b.

[80] Wu Ying-chi 吳應箕, *Liu-tu chien-wen lu* 留都見聞錄, (*Kuei-ch'ih hsien-che i-shu* 貴池先哲遺書 by Liu Shih-heng 劉世衍, (Anhui, 1920) (ts'e 13) 13b.

[81] *Ming-shih pen-chi* 明史本紀, (photographic reprints of the 1777 Chien-lung ed. published by the Palace Museum of Peiping in 4 ts'e, Peiping, 1922).

[82] Shimizu Taiji 清水泰次 *Tōyō bunka shi dai-kei* 東洋文化史大系, (Tokyo, 1934) 5. 123; cf. also *Liu-tu chien-wen lu*, 13b; *Shan chung wen-chien lu* 2, (ts'e 4) 11b; Yeh Shao-yüan 葉紹袁, *Ch'i-chen chi-wen lu* 啓禎記聞錄, (*T'ung-shih* 痛史 ed.), 2, (ts'e 18) 7b.

[83] *Ming shih*, 30, (ts'e 8) 30b; *Tsui-wei lu*, 14, (ts'e 6) 21ab.

[84] J. B. du Halde, Op. cit., I. 522; Hsü Ch'ang-chih 徐昌治, *Chao-tai fang-mu* 昭代芳摹, (1636 ed.), 29, (ts'e 10) 32b.

[85] *K'ou-shih pien-nien*, 13, (ts'e 9) 21b; 9, (ts'e 8) 11b, 13a; 6, (ts'e 6) 8b; *Huai-tsung ch'ung-chen shih-lu*, 7, (ts'e 499) 5a.

[86] *Ch'i chen chi-wen lu*, 2, (ts'e 18) 10b.

[87] *Huai-tsung ch'ung-chen shih-lu*, 14, (ts'e 500) 6a; 16, (ts'e 500) 11a; Li Hsün-chih 李遜之, *Ch'ung-chen ch'ao chi-shih* 崇禎朝記事, (*Ch'ang-chou hsien-che i-shu* 常州先哲遺書, ed. by Sheng Hsüan-huai 盛宣懷) (Kiangsu, late 19th century ed.), 4, (ts'e 4) 20b.

[88] *Ming-shih ch'ao-lüeh*, 2, (ts'e 1).

[89] *K'ou-shih pien-mien*, 6, (ts'e 6) 3b, 8a; *Huai-tsung ch'ung-chen shih-lu*, 7, (ts'e 499) 4b, 5a; 10, (ts'e 499) 2b; 13, (ts'e 500) 1b, 2b, 3a, 4a, 6a, 7b, 8b; 14, (14 ts'e 500) 2b, 3a; 15, (ts'e 500) 2b, 12b.

[90] *Ming-shih ch'ao-lüeh*, 3, (ts'e 1) 2b.

[91] Shen Kuo-yüan 沈國元, *Liang-ch'ao ts'ung-hsin lu* 兩朝從信錄, (Late Ming edition) 1 (ts'e 1) 40b, 41a; *Chao-tai fang-mu*, 32, (ts'e 11) 15a.

[92] *Huai-tsung ch'ung-chen shih-lu*, 15, (ts'e 500) 2b.

[93] Ibid., 8, (ts'e 499) 3b, 6a, 7b; 9, (ts'e 499) 7a; 11, (ts'e 499) 1b; 13, (ts'e 400) 3a, 8a; 14, (ts'e 500) 8b; 15, (ts'e 500) 4a, 5b, 6b; 16, (ts'e 500) 11a.

[94] *K'ou-shih pien-nien*, 9, (ts'e 8) 25b.

[95] *Ch'un-ming meng-yü lu*, 36, (ts'e 11) 13b, 14a.

[96] Ibid.

[97] Huang Tsung-hsi 黃宗羲 (1610–1695), *Nan-lei wen-ting*, third series 南雷文定三集, (TSCCCP), 2, (ts'e 2,466) 24.

[98] *Wu-tsa-tsu*, 3, (ts'e 2) 9a; (ts'e 3) 17ab.

[99] Wang Fu-chih 王夫之, *E-meng* 噩夢 (Peking, 1956) 40.

[100] *Kuo Ch'üeh*, (ts'e 12) 69b; (ts'e 13) 59ab, 94b.

[101] *Chin-yen lei-pien*, 4, (ts'e 1) 7a.

[102] Chu Kuo-cheng 朱國楨, *Ta-shih-chi* 大事記, (Wan-li edition) 20, (ts'e 29) 1ab.

[103] *Tsui-wei lu*, 31, (ts'e 56) 17ab; *Ming shih*, 77, (ts'e 27) 3a; *Hsü t'ung-tien* 續通典, 10, (Wan-yu wen-k'u ed.) 1, 1167; *Ming-shih chi-shih pen-mo*, 38, (ts'e 2) 1–6; *Kuo-shih chi-wen*, 10, (ts'e 8) 42b, 43a.

[104] *Tien-ku chi-wen*, 18, (ts'e 134) 18ab.

[105] *Cho-chai shih-i*, 13–15.

[105] *Huai-tsung ch'ung-chen shih-lu*, 8, (ts'e 499) 4b.

[107] *Ch'un-ming meng-yü lu*, 36, (ts'e 11) 54–56.

[108] *Ming ch'en tsou-i*, 29, (ts'e 0,919) 526.

[109] Here are some of the quotations: "From Chia-hsing to Sung-kiang there are boats that leave in the afternoon, but they stop sailing by night because the place is infested with bandits." (ts'e 2) B. 40a; "From Peking to Hsü-chou there are often bandits on horseback (ts'e 1) A. 2b, 3a; (in Huai-an) salt rakers are themselves bandits. For this reason one should not travel by night. Moreover, one should be wary of the boatmen, for they are men of dubious character." (ts'e 2) B. 54ab. It seems that the salt rakers were active in the Huai region from Yang-chou to Shantung. The same author tells us that they often pretended to be salt smugglers but in reality were bandits. They would carry off travellers and demand ransom for them. Cf. (ts'e 2) B. 7b, 8a. In Kiangsi, we are told, bandits appeared frequently in P'o-yang lake. They differed from the bandits of the Yangtze river in that the latter were satisfied with their loot while the former often killed the passengers after robbing them. Cf. (ts'e 2) B. 44b, 45a. Then from Kuei-lin to Wu-chou the river was infested by aborigine bandits. Cf. (ts'e 1) A. 16b.

[110] Hsü Chen-ming 徐貞明, *Lu-shui k'e-t'an* 潞水客談, (TSCCCP), (ts'e 3,020).

[111] Cheng Hsiao 鄭曉, *Cheng tuan-chien-kung wen-chi* 鄭瑞簡公文集, (Wan-li edition) 3, (ts'e 2) 10ab, Cf. also *Wo-pien shih-lüeh*, 1, (ts'e 3975) 5–6; *Ching-kuo hsiung-lüeh*, 1, (ts'e 8) 27b, 28a.

[112] *Kuo-ch'ao tien-hui*, 133, (ts'e 46) 7a

[113] *Wu-tsa-tsu*, 8, (ts'e 4) 29ab.

[114] *Hsü wen-hsien t'ung-k'ao*, 5, I, 2821; cf. also *Ming-ch'en tsou-i*, 3, (ts'e 0,913) 52 when Sun Yüan-cheng 孫原貞 mentioned the same situation in the year 1454.

[115] *Ming shih*, 77, (ts'e 27) 9b, 10a.

[116] *Ming shih*, 77, (ts'e 27) 9b; *Hsü wen-hsien t'ung-k'ao*, 5, I, 2827a.

[117] *Ming shih*, 155, (ts'e 53) 15b; 177, (ts'e 58) 7a.

[118] *Ming shu*, 67, (ts'e 3,941) 1361–1362; *Ching-kuo hsiung-lüeh*, 2, (ts'e 12) 33a.

[119] *Ming shih*, 177, (ts'e 58) 7a; 182, (ts'e 60) 17a; Wang Ao 王鏊, *Wang wen-k'o-kung wen-chi* 王文恪公文集, 19. (This is quoted from *Tu shih tsa-chi*, 113; *Hsü wen-hsien t'ung-k'ao*, 0, I, 2823 c.

[120] *Tu shih tsa-chi*, 112–114, where many illustrations are given from diverse sources; *Wu-tsa-tsu*, (Shanghai, 1959) 4, A, 117. It is interesting to note the comparison given in the *Ching-kuo hsiung-lüeh, t'un-cheng k'ao* 屯政考 2, (ts'e 12) 32b–33a, between the production of grain by the military settlements in the Hung-wu and Yung-lo periods and toward the end of the dynasty.

	Hung-wu, Yung-lo period	*End of Ming dynasty*
Liao-tung	700,000 piculs	170,000 piculs
Kansu (present)	600,000 ,,	130,000 ,,
Ning-hsia	180,000 ,,	149,002 ,,
Yen-sui	60,000 ,,	50,000 ,,
Chi-chou	110,000 ,,	50,000 ,,
Shansi	100,000 ,,	28,000 ,,

The author of the book does not explain the decreases. Presumably the farms had either been laid waste or been misappropriated by influential persons.

[121] *Ching-kuo hsiung-lüeh, t'un-cheng k'ao* 屯政考, 2, (ts'e 12) 27ab, 28a; Cheng Ta-yu 鄭大郁, *Ching-shih t'o-yin* 警世鐸音, Edo edition, no number of pages, chuan 4.

[122] *Chia-ching i-lai chu-lüeh*, 2, (ts'e 1) 3ab.

[123] *Hsü wen-hsien t'ung-k'ao*, 20, I, 2962.

[124] *Ming shih*, 80, (ts'e 28) 9a.

[125] *Hsü wen-hsien t'ung-k'ao*, 18, I, 2931c and 2934b.

[126] Ibid., 18, I, 2934b.

[127] *Ch'un-ming meng-yü-lu*, 30, (ts'e 10) 39ab.

[128] Chang Hsüan 張萱, *Hsi-yüan ts'un-kao* 西園存稿, (1664 edition) 23, (ts'e 14) 33ab.

[129] *Ming t'ung-chien*, 87, (ts'e 11) 13b, 14a.

[130] *Shuo-lüeh* 說畧, (*Hsien-fen-lou pi-chi* 涵芬樓祕笈 edition, 2nd series) (ts'e 5) 27ab.

CHAPTER TEN

Economics II

IMPERIAL TREASURIES

"Having had a first view of Peking, it would be unfair to the Royal Capital and perhaps to the curiosity of the reader to pass by without a few words about it, . . ." wrote one of the missionaries in the time of the Wan-li emperor. "The size of the city" he continued, "the planning of its houses, the structure of the public buildings and its fortifications are far inferior to those of Nanking, but in population, in the number of soldiers and of government magistrates, it is superior. . . . The royal residence is not so wide as the palace at Nankin, but the grace and beauty of its architecture are emphasized by its slender lines. Because of the absence of the kings, Nanking is gradually falling into decay, like a spiritless body, while Peking is growing more and more attractive because of their presence." But unfortunately, although "there is an abundance of everything in Peking, most of which is brought into the city",[1] to live in Peking in those days, it seems, was not easy except for the well-to-do. In spite of this, the people of Peking, like the inhabitants of other great cities, were extravagant, spending lavishly on banquets and ceremonies. Even the common people wore ostentatious dress and ornaments and the rich were of course far worse. An eye-witness tells us that the eunuchs and nobles of the capital kept huge fat white cats, weighing several tens of catties each, which knew nothing about catching mice and served only as pets for their masters. Pet dogs with thin golden hair and short legs were also fashionable. These waddling little animals—-they were smaller than the cats—never even learnt to bark at thieves.[2]

Nanking, though less prosperous than Peking since the removal of the Ming court to the north, was still recognized as the second capital of the empire and remained one of the great cities of China. The scholar Ku Ch'i-yüan 顧起元 (1565–1628), who had lived there for many years, said that since taking up residence there he had observed a rapid increase in the population. Unfortunately the increase in production did not match the increase in population proportionately and to make things worse the people became ever more extravagant as time went on. The poor were greatly affected by these changes and sensed the uncertainty of the future. Ku observed that things would improve if the government set a good example of frugality.[3] Presumably he was thinking of the extravagant life of the Wan-li emperor during whose reign the financial condition of the whole empire was going from bad to worse.

Among all the Ming emperors only the Hung-wu and Ch'ung-chen emperors, the first and the last emperors of the dynasty, can fairly be described as frugal. All the rest inclined towards extravagance. The Hung-wu emperor was frugal because he came from the farmer class, and frugality is one of the farmer's virtues. If the Ch'ung-chen emperor was thrifty (as indeed he was), he was so by necessity. The imperial treasuries had been exhausted by his predecessors and he had no choice but to adapt himself to circumstances and be frugal. The Hung-wu emperor's policy was "to keep the wealth of the country in the people," i.e. the government interfered with the people as little as possible and let all have a chance to produce wealth. This theory was a very ancient one. In *The Great Learning* we read: "Hence, the accumulation of wealth is the way to scatter the people; and letting it be scattered among them is the way to collect the people."[4] It is not easy to put this theory into practice; it demands in the government men of great self-denial with deep devotion to the common good.

Several reasons may be given for the extravagance of the Ming emperors. First of all, they were brought up in the palace in the company of eunuchs and court ladies whose knowledge of the outer world was very limited. The eunuchs moreover were often men of low character, ignorant, selfish and deceitful. Then, most of the emperors came to the throne as mere boys with no experience of government. Their contacts with court ministers were superficial and they found administration and politics tedious. The restricted palace life was more attractive: the emperors lived in peace; everyone sought to please them; the tender attentions of eunuchs and court ladies persuaded them that their lives lacked nothing, there was always much amusement to be had. Eventually the emperors were led to give all their affection and all their trust to these complacent courtiers and to follow their suggestions in all things. Some of the emperors seem to have found a fascination in religion. The charms and spells of Tibetan Buddhist monks and the immortality offered by Taoist priests were novelties that helped to relieve the unrecognized yet very real monotony of court life. Anything that captured the minds of the emperors was welcomed with great enthusiasm. Money was no problem. All they had to do was to keep making demands on the people about whose lives they knew nothing and so, inevitably, cared nothing.

A historian of the late Ming period traced the financial decline of the dynasty to the Cheng-t'ung reign. The stresses and strains of the first Ming half-century were over and from 1425 to 1435 the empire knew peace both within and without. The number of imperial relatives and military officials was still small; government expenditure therefore was moderate and there was always a surplus in the government treasury. Then came the Mongol invasions, affecting at first only the Kansu borders but gradually spreading to other provinces. Within the empire now one spot and now another became infested with bandits. To meet these growing threats the government had to keep up a great army and this involved so great an increase in expenses that the treasury began to empty. In the Ching-t'ai reign it was reported that the government was suffering from perpetual financial troubles even in time of peace. In time of war the situation was of course much worse. Unable to find a fundamental solution, the government often resorted to abuses such as levying excessive taxes and selling government offices and ranks of honor.[5]

There was yet another reason for the financial exhaustion of the government: the extravagance of emperor after emperor had emptied the treasuries and thus deprived the government of what should have been a reserve fund large enough to meet any emergency. These treasuries were divided into three main classes. Ten treasuries, known as the nei-k'u 內庫, were reserved for the use of the imperial household and when full contained precious goods of every kind sent from the four corners of the empire and the tribute received from foreign countries—silver, gold, and other articles of great value. Next there were the wai-k'u 外庫 which were kept in the provinces for local expenditure. In the early days of the dynasty most of the taxes were paid in kind, not in money. The taxes levied on gold and silver mines, however, were paid with money which went to the ch'eng-yün k'u 承運庫, the imperial treasury specially designed for the storing of gold, silver, jewels, and other articles of value. In the earlier reigns, if the land taxes were paid in money, as sometimes happened, this money was collected and sent not to the ch'eng-yün k'u but to Nanking to be used in paying the salaries of military officials and in supporting the army in times of border conflicts. The Cheng-t'ung emperor made a new regulation ordering that the million silver taels, which was the sum collected thus annually in commutation for grain, was to be transported to the capital and deposited in the ch'eng-yün k'u. This money, known as chin-hua yin 金花銀, was still used for paying the salaries of the military officials; but these came to only a little over a hundred thousand silver taels, and the imperial treasury appropriated the huge sum, almost nine hundred thousand silver taels, that was left over.[6] In the days of plenty these various treasuries contained what seemed an inexhaustible supply of treasure. An eminent scholar of the 16th century said that the goods stored in the imperial treasury used to fill ten caves.

The later emperors, however, soon showed that the treasuries were exhaustible. The Cheng-hua emperor had dissipated a huge part of the accumulated wealth in building temples, subsidizing religious ceremonies, purchasing precious stones, and other extravagances.[7] Then came the Cheng-te emperor, who like a spendthrift son devoted himself to squandering his inheritance, while his notorious eunuch Liu Chin was proving himself a virtuoso in the art of treasury-looting. The Cheng-te emperor's successor, the Chia-ching emperor, allowed his zeal for the Taoistic religion to turn him into a still more extravagant spender. Throughout his reign court expenditure was double the amount allowed by his predecessor, and when the Lung-ch'ing emperor (1567–1572) succeeded his father he was alarmed to hear from the Board of Administration that the imperial treasuries were almost exhausted. He did what he could by ordering more sparing court expenditure.[8]

Despite the economy practised in the five years of the Lung-ch'ing emperor's reign, the finances were still in a very unhealthy state at the beginning of the Wan-li reign. The imperial treasuries were nearly empty and money had to be borrowed from the provinces or from various government departments. The capable minister Chang Chü-cheng, however, succeeded in weathering the financial crisis and the country was once more on the way to prosperity when Chang died leaving his task of economic restoration well begun, indeed, but only half done. The Wan-li emperor, anything but a capable ruler, quickly abandoned the wise policy of his late minister. His many vices eventually undid Chang Chü-cheng's work and by the end of his reign the whole empire was in a state of chaos. Chao I had no hesitation in pointing to the Wan-li emperor as the real cause of the fall of the Ming dynasty.[9]

It is probably not an exaggeration to say that the greater part of the money in all the treasuries went into the pockets of the eunuchs. Their depredations have been described in previous chapters. Much money also was spent on building. Two modern writers have compiled a useful book from official documents listing chronologically the architectural works under the Ming emperors.[10]

The *Hsü wen-hsien t'ung-k'ao* gives us a brief summary of these Ming dynasty building operations.

The works of construction in the early Ming period were so numerous and varied that a great army of workers had to be employed on them. The program included the building of the two capitals, of the ancestors' temples, of imperial palaces, and of palaces of princes. All this, of course, involved endless timber cutting and brick-making. Then too, cities were being built or rebuilt and numerous drainage dams were constructed. All these projects were being carried out simultaneously and though the great initial effort continued into the Hung-hsi and Hsüan-te periods, the sacrificial altars to Heaven and Earth and the granaries had not even then been constructed. Between the Cheng-t'ung and T'ien-shun reigns the three halls (Feng-t'ien 奉天, Hua-kai 華蓋, Chin-shen 謹身), the two palaces (Ch'ien-ch'ing 乾清, K'un-ning 坤寧), the Nan-nei 南內 and the imperial villas were built one after the other. They were indeed magnificent. Then came the Hung-chih reign when the soldiers of the ching-ying were assigned to the work of construction. Military officials were forbidden to employ soldiers as laborers as they pleased—and with good reason: sometimes the task in hand would require only five thousand men but they would petition for ten or twenty thousand without any records that could be checked.

In the reign of Wu-tsung 武宗 (i.e. the Cheng-te emperor) there was the (re)building of the Ch'ien-ch'ing palace, and especially the T'ai-so hall 太素殿, which was originally simple in style, but was then transformed into a most elaborate edifice. This work cost over twenty million silver taels,[11] and the labor of over three thousand laborers. In addition, there was the building of the following halls: Ning-ts'ui 凝翠, Chao-ho 昭和, Ch'ung-chih 崇智 and Kuang-chi 光霽 and the renovation of the Office of the Imperial Stables 御馬監, the Chung-ku-ssu 鐘鼓司, the Nan-ch'eng 南城, the Pao-fang 豹房, the Hsin-fang 新房 and the great arsenal 火藥庫. As if all this were not enough, officials of the Board of Works hastened to curry favor with the favorites of the emperor and the eunuchs by using public funds to refurnish their farms, ancestral halls, and grave-yards, or various temples and monasteries in which they took an interest.

The building program became still more complicated under Shih-tsung 世宗 (i.e. the Chia-ching emperor). Before the fifteenth year of his reign (i.e. before 1536), despite the stress he laid on frugality, the sum spent on building up to that time had amounted to six or seven million. Expenses had risen. Later, this sum was to be multiplied by more than ten. Fasting chambers and sacrificial halls were frequently built. There were twenty to thirty factories and the number of laborers amounted to tens of thousands. The financial resources eventually fell short of the needs and the emperor had to seek help from his subjects. Even this did not bring in enough and recourse was had to the sale of government offices to the public. In causing trouble to the people and in dissipating money this emperor surpassed Wu-tsung.

Later, the Wan-li emperor occupied himself with the manufacturing of silk and the expenditure exceeded the whole imperial budget several times. Further, with the levying of taxes and the opening of mines, the people could enjoy no peace. Then came the eunuchs' attempt to usurp the imperial power. They built for themselves mansions and mausolea in open disregard of the limited rights of their rank. Commemorative monuments and temples were built for them throughout the empire. After more than two centuries of such rule the people were exhausted.[12]

By the early part of the Chia-ching period, several palaces had burnt down. About the year 1540, therefore, several palaces were built within a period of only a little over four years at a cost of about sixty-seven thousand silver taels. A historian tells us that in the first fifteen years of the Chia-ching reign (1522–1536), the money spent on building came to six or seven million silver taels. Between 1536 and the end of the reign in 1566, the expenditure on building went up to over ten times what it had been in the earlier period. Buildings of all sorts were being put up simultaneously. Over seventy thousand of the soldiers in the capital were working as laborers. There were 20 to 30 factories for the production of building material in the capital alone. The professional laborers employed daily were estimated at about 94,700 with an annual wage bill of over 1,870,000 silver taels. Of the most essential building materials, bricks alone from Su-chou and Lin-ch'ing cost over one million silver taels and timber from Hu-kuang province cost seven hundred thousand.[13]

In the fifth month of the nineteenth year of the Chia-ching reign (1540) the President of the Board of Works reported that in recent years a great deal had been spent on buildings. The total building expenses amounted to nearly six million four hundred thousand silver taels. The treasuries were exhausted and the only resource was to sell government offices. Even this was no great help, for several months passed and it was found that barely ten thousand silver taels had been collected in this way. A month after this melancholy discovery, the President of the Board of Revenue warned the monarch of his extravagance. The building of the Tz'u-ning palace 慈寧宮, he said, cost only four hundred and eighty thousand silver taels. But when, later on, the Tz'u-ch'ing palace 慈慶宮 was built, the expenses went up to over seven hundred and ten thousand. Still later palaces had cost more than seven hundred and sixty thousand.[14] We are told that many of the ministers, eager to please the emperor, were inclined to be lavish with money. Princes residing in the provinces sought to please the monarch by sending him money and great balks of timber, which, indeed, pleased His Majesty immensely. The princes' generosity was not purely altruistic: it was not to be supposed that the emperor would suffer himself to be out-done by his subjects in generosity.[15]

Two of the main palaces were destroyed by fire (1596) in the Wan-li reign, and it took two years to reconstruct them. The minister charged with this great operation was able to accomplish his task at a cost of only seven hundred thousand—nine hundred thousand silver taels less than had been expected. The secret of his success is said to have been his constant care to exclude interference by the eunuchs— an interesting index of the normal scale of the eunuchs' raids on the treasuries.[16]

The Wan-li emperor loved his children inordinately and spared no one and nothing in his efforts to please them. He wished to build a prince's palace in Honan province at an estimated cost of eight hundred and twenty thousand silver taels. An official of the Board of Works however offered such strong opposition that the cost was cut down to two hundred and fifty thousand.[17] Again in 1627, the building of three palaces cost nearly six million silver taels. Most of the laborers employed were farmers. When summoned by officials they had to leave their homes and their work, and for months and sometimes even for years, they had to toil for their selfish monarch. Yet at home they still had to pay land taxes. As we have seen already, even the soldiers whose duty it was to guard the capital were diverted to work on buildings. Sometimes the guards so employed would number almost twenty thousand. The work might last for months or for years, and the guards naturally neglected their real duties and often had hardly any military training. Gradually they lost the spirit of discipline and became soldiers only in name. In 1550, when Yen-ta Han (Alda/-Alta (n)/Qan) attacked the capital, the President of the Board of War had only fifty to sixty thousand men under him and these were so reluctant to leave the city that force had to be used. Once outside they were ordered to march towards the enemy but they all began to groan and refused to advance. This caused great alarm and the commanding officers turned to one another and grew pale, according to the official account.[18]

IMPERIAL KITCHEN

It belonged to the office of the Kuang-lu-ssu 光祿寺 or Court of Entertainment to look after the imperial kitchen and to provide the banquets given by the emperor to his ministers or to foreign envoys. The importance of this court may be gauged from the attitude of the Hsüan-te emperor. In the fifth year of his reign it was reported to him that ministers of the Court of Entertainment had secretly reduced the supplies provided for foreign envoys who happened to be in the capital. He at once sent a minister from the Board of Punishment to punish the culprit. Though he regarded eating and drinking as insignificant, yet, he said, if food and drink were withheld when properly demanded, ill feeling would be caused and great damage might thus be done.[19]

The *Ming hui-tien* gives the number of the kitchen staff in the Kuang-lu-ssu in the early days of the dynasty as 9,462. From 1435 onward the number oscillated. Under Ying-tsung over 4,700 were withdrawn from the staff, but we are not told of the original number. In the sixth year of the Cheng-te reign (1511) the number was fixed at 6,884 and in the first year of the Lung-ch'ing reign the number was further reduced to 3,400.[20] Clearly the wages paid to the kitchen staff of this court must have been enormous. The same *hui-tien* gives a detailed list of the foodstuffs and material needed by the court. A good deal of these foodstuffs came from the provinces, according as each province was outstanding in the production of this or that delicacy, and both the quantity and the quality were determined. Yet there seem to have been frequent shortages of supplies, necessitating purchases from merchants in the capital.

As the Court of Entertainment had constant dealings with the market, unpleasant incidents easily occurred. Clearly the founder of the dynasty realized this, for he issued an order to his Court that whenever it bought anything from the market for the imperial kitchen it was to pay ten coins more than the prevailing price.[21] In this, no doubt, the Hung-wu emperor wished to show benevolence to his people. But he must also have meant it as an example and a warning to the officials not to use their influence to rob the people. The Yung-lo emperor was equally careful to preclude abuses, but at the beginning of the Ch'eng-hua reign we find complaints beginning to come to the Board of Ceremonies about the extravagance and dissipation of the Court of Entertainment. The President of the Board of Ceremonies complained of the quadrupling of the expenses for game and meat which till then had cost thirty to forty thousand silver taels yearly. What the founder of the dynasty had foreseen now came to pass. When dealing with the merchants, the officials often used their position to take advantage of them, and the merchants felt that they were being robbed. Still more unfortunately, dishonest people were employed as buyers, and often, under the protection of the officials, tried to take for themselves what should have been the merchants' profits. An incident which illustrates this happened shortly after the Hsüan-te emperor came to the throne. The mayor of Nanking charged the Board of Works and the Board of Entertainment with buying from the people and deferring payment for three years. The emperor therefore issued an order that anything the government bought from the people should be paid for without delay. It is doubtful what effect this order had. Hsieh Chao-che says that it was a common practice in the Chia-ching period for the Board of Entertainment to buy from the merchants and not to pay them in due time. Often these debts were so large as to reduce the merchants to bankruptcy, but being in an inferior position, these merchants did not dare to sue their debtors.[22]

Nor were the officials satisfied with robbing the people; they also sought to loot the imperial purse. Yü Tzu-chün 余子俊 (1429–1489), one of the ministers in the Board of Revenue during the early days of the Ching-t'ai reign, pointed out to the emperor that the daily supply from the Kuang-lu-ssu to His Majesty was not as large as might have been expected. One great cause of the emptying of the imperial treasury lay in the conspiracy of ministers with lower officials and the kitchen staff for an enormous misappropriation of imperial funds.[23] Before the Chia-ching period the annual budget for the Court of Entertainment was two hundred and forty thousand silver taels, but the actual expenditure was usually only half of this sum. About the middle of the Chia-ching reign, however, the annual expenditure rose to three hundred and sixty thousand. This aroused the suspicion of the monarch: for twenty years the court had been frugal and the custom of giving frequent banquets had been discontinued; what then was the explanation of an expenditure of three hundred and sixty thousand silver taels? He therefore ordered an inquiry and after a careful check of the accounts, four sources of embezzlement were discovered. First, when orders came from the palace for articles, the only authorization was a mere unsealed document, yet no one dared to question its authenticity. Second, all who were employed in offices, whether in the imperial city or outside it, were normally allowed to draw daily wages for their subsistence so long as their work lasted. Many took advantage of this arrangement to draw wages for several offices concurrently or continued to draw wages even when their tasks were completed. Third, the guardians of the treasury did not exercise proper care and accounts were often left unchecked. Fourth, the *Ta-Ming hui-tien,* or Institutes of the Ming dynasty, required that, when articles were drawn from the Court of Entertainment for the imperial kitchen, special stamps issued by the eunuchs in charge of the emperor's table should be used on all the documents, and that the Court of Entertainment should keep account books to be checked monthly by a censor who was then to report to the emperor. When these four causes had been discovered, remedies were applied to check the abuses. The expenditure of the Court of Entertainment was cut by over twenty thousand silver taels within two months, and in the last years of the Chia-ching reign it fell to one hundred and seventy thousand yearly.[24]

The Wan-li emperor came to the throne in 1572, when he was only ten years of age, and reigned for forty-eight years, longer than any of his Ming predecessors or successors. In the early years of his reign he enjoyed the services of one of the greatest statesmen of the Ming period, the renowned Chang Chü-cheng who held the office of Grand Secretary for over ten years. The government flourished greatly under the management of Chang Chü-cheng. Along the borders the Mongols submitted to the imperial power and the Japanese pirates met final defeat. Internally Chang Chü-cheng reformed the government. He took steps to make all the officials assume responsibility; he surveyed the farming areas of the empire; he tried to eliminate the evasion of taxes among the rich. Even the imperial expenditure was checked under his vigilant eyes. We are told, for instance, that at the beginning of the Wan-li reign the expenditure of the Court of Entertainment was as low as one hundred and thirty or forty thousand silver taels yearly. By the time of his death in 1582, the economic condition had improved greatly.

On the death of Chang Chü-cheng the Wan-li emperor, then a young man of great promise of whom the ministers expected great things, took over direct control of the government. He was eager to assert himself for he had resented the government of Chang Chü-cheng, who, although never usurping the imperial title, had really ruled as a dictator. Very quickly the fatal weakness of Chang Chü-cheng's system of government began to show itself. The great Grand Secretary had indeed governed exceptionally well, but he had governed single-handed, allowing no one else to handle important government affairs. Thus he left no successor trained in the supreme direction of the state or ready to assume supreme responsibility. The best hope was that a second Chang Chü-cheng would emerge. This did not happen; so, once more all had to bow before the supreme will of the Son of Heaven, and once more all ministers were at the mercy of their master.

Of all the Ming emperors, the Wan-li emperor was probably the most extravagant. He was moreover obstinate and selfish, and always governed according to his personal likes and dislikes. Despite his early promise, he manifested very few noble qualities or gifts for government, and the older he grew the worse his government became. In the last twenty-five years of his reign he almost completely neglected his duties as a ruler, very much as his grandfather, the Chia-ching emperor had done. Association with eunuchs from boyhood had made him, like them, greedy for wealth and heedless of the suffering of others. The eunuchs took advantage of this to encourage him in multiform extravagance which soon emptied the imperial treasuries. The emperor's quest for pleasure was not to be checked, however, by so trifling an inconvenience as an empty treasury: hundreds of ingenious means were invented for overcoming this embarrassment.

A scholar who lived at the end of the Ming dynasty says that the Wan-li emperor's banquets were the most sumptuous ever given by an emperor of the Ming dynasty. The same scholar says that in the Wan-li reign the eunuchs were very rich and that they all used in turn to entertain the monarch at their own expense. There was even competition among them as to which of them had given the best banquet.[25]

In addition, the Court of Entertainment had to spend annually about three hundred thousand silver taels on the imperial kitchen. Much of this money went, of course, into the pockets of the eunuchs, who, when making purchases for the emperor, squeezed the merchants without fear of the consequences: their influence with the emperor had set them above the law. This abuse became so bad that ultimately many of the merchants found it necessary to flee the capital. Balked of their first victims the eunuchs turned on the rich and forced them to disgorge the money that had formerly been forced from the merchants. It was said that when the well-to-do received assignments they felt as if capital sentences had been pronounced on them. Heavy bribery was the only means by which they could evade the dreadful obligations imposed on them, and the officials took advantage of this to enrich themselves. The *Ming shih* tells us that these abuses went from bad to worse till in the T'ien-ch'i period merchants often delivered their goods to the government officials without receiving any payment at all.[26]

RELIGIOUS EXPENDITURES

In dealing with the finances of the Ming government, mention must be made of the Ming emperors' expenditure on religion. It is known to all students of Chinese history that one of the causes of the fall of the Yüan dynasty was excessive spending on religion. The amount of government money diverted to Lamaism and the monks greatly weakened the financial position of the government and eventually helped to bring it down. The Ming dynasty did not equal it in this respect. Nevertheless its excesses in spending on the externals of religion were far from negligible and were a perpetual drain on government funds. Since most of the emperors of the dynasty were interested either in Buddhism or in Taoism, the treasuries, reign after reign, had to pour forth huge sums of money for the building of temples. The bad effect therefore was not confined to any definite period, but continued to sap the financial strength of the government.

The Ming emperors' deep interest in Buddhism and Taoism went back to the very foundation of the dynasty, but in the earlier reigns this interest was a source of strength, not of weakness. The founder himself had been a Buddhist monk and knew well how easily people could take advantage of religion to advance their own interests. He, therefore, took great care to preclude this. The Yung-lo emperor issued rigid regulations for Buddhist and Taoist monks and their monasteries. The number of monks to be ordained for each district, prefecture and province was laid down in detail. Those who wished to be ordained had to pass an examination before they could obtain their certificates. These measures were designed not only to prevent the evasion of taxes but also to guard against wandering monks who might take advantage of their position to create trouble. The abuses began with the emperor Ying-tsung, who, under the influence of the eunuch Wang Chen 王振, spent several hundred thousand silver taels on building in the capital a temple on which over ten thousand laborers are said to have been employed. This was the greatest temple built at this time. It was far from being the only one. We are told that, during the reign of this monarch, over two hundred temples were built in and outside the capital. Buddhist and Taoist monks very soon increased to an astonishing number.[27]

According to the account of Chou Ch'en 周忱 (1381–1453), who lived in the first reign of the Ying-tsung emperor, great numbers of Buddhist and Taoist monks from Su-chou and Sung-kiang were to be found all over the empire and gave endless trouble to the government and to the people. "Those who are talented," Chou says, "are appointed abbots by recommendation; those who are new to monastic life go on pilgrimage and their spoor can be detected in well-known monasteries. Loafers from their native villages flock to them and offer their services, and the young men of good appearance receive the title of hsing-t'ung 行童, mature adults the title shan-yu 善友. They dress up as monks, complete with staff and alms-bowl. Sometimes they form groups and perform religious ceremonies; sometimes they go along the streets begging for alms. Most of the monks in Nanking, Peking and many other towns are natives of Su-chou and Sung-kiang. Thus, an abbot often has several score in his service and an ordinary monk may have three to five loafers under him. The number of Buddhist and Taoist monks keeps on increasing and the poor farmers suffer ever more from them."[28]

In the fifth month of the fifth year of Ch'eng-hua (1469), the number of monks was thirty-one thousand and in 1484, the number of temples in or near Peking rose to over a thousand. Not satisfied with having temples within easy reach of the imperial city, the emperor even ordered a temple built right beside it. Several hundred families had to be moved from the site of the new building and the imperial treasury had to disburse a hundred thousand silver taels. One of the ministers very sensibly pointed out to the emperor that only one altar was needed for offering sacrifice to heaven and earth, and only one temple for ancestors. "Why is it" he asked, "that we must have a thousand Buddhist temples?"[29]

The Ch'eng-hua emperor was not satisfied to have Chinese monks alone, he had to have exotic monks also from Tibet and Mongolia. As early as the Yung-lo reign, relations had been loosely established with Tibetan monks. At first they came merely as loyal subjects bringing tribute to their sovereign lord; very soon, however, they established trade posts along the borders. Their first embassy to Peking consisted of only a few individuals, but soon the envoys were numbered in tens and ultimately in hundreds. It was the fixed policy of the emperor that the imperial court should never allow itself to be outdone in generosity by its subjects, hence the largesse distributed to tributary embassies was always lavish. The Court of Entertainment was charged with supplying them with their daily needs and they often took advantage of this generosity by demanding more than their due. This went on through the Hsüan-te reign and we are told that up to the accession of Ying-tsung no attempt had been made to put a stop to this abuse.[30] The Tibetan monks won the special favor of the Ch'eng-hua emperor by their claim to possess secret spells, and they were greatly honored by him. They lived like princes. When they went out they were always carried in sedan chairs accompanied by bodyguards, and even government officials and nobles had to give way to them. They were summoned to the palace to recite prayers and perform ceremonies and on these occasions they received great banquets and splendid gifts. Since these monks sometimes numbered several thousand, it is not surprising to learn that the officials in charge of the treasuries were distressed by such extravagant expenditure.[31]

In the days of the Yung-lo emperor, the foreign monks were always sent back to their own lands after their audience with the emperor. But from the Ch'eng-hua period onward the emperors tried to keep them in the capital and gave them land and financial help to build temples and monasteries there. The Fan-ching ch'ang 番經廠, where Tibetan scriptures were studied, was within the boundaries of the imperial city, and in the palace itself there were three temples, the Ying-hua tien 英華殿, the Lung-te tien 隆德殿 and the Ch'in-an tien 欽安殿, which were in the charge of the eunuchs.[32] Up to the Chia-ching period there was a Ta-Shan-Fo temple 大善佛寺 in the palace; but in the latter part of his reign, the Chia-ching emperor ordered its destruction to make room for a palace he was building for the dowager empress. A hundred and sixty-nine gold and silver Buddhist statues and Buddhist relics—skulls, teeth, bones and the like—to a weight of over thirteen thousand catties were destroyed during the carrying out of this imperial command.[33]

The Hung-chih emperor (1488–1505), a conscientious ruler, made a great effort to rid the government of abuses. When he came to the throne his first move was to check the evil effects of certain Buddhist scandals which had occurred during his father's reign. However, he was unable to stop the activity of the eunuchs, who seemed to have no scruples about using public funds for the building of monasteries.[34] His successor, the Cheng-te emperor, was a great patron of the Tibetan monks. During his reign thousands of silver taels were spent on bringing the living Buddha to the capital and lavishing gifts on his followers. We are told that when a certain Tibetan monk asked for a donation of money to be spent on funeral services for his master, the Board of Ceremonies refused to consider the case since it was at variance with contemporary custom, but the emperor issued a special order and two thousand silver taels were granted.[35]

The *Ming shih* says that when the Chia-ching emperor (1522–1566) succeeded to the throne he cut down the expenditure of the imperial household to one tenth of what his predecessor had spent. Yet in the later part of his reign he outdid the extravagance of the Cheng-te emperor, at first in the building of houses of worship and then in furnishing them and providing them with ceremonial supplies.[36] The *Ming shih* tells us that in 1558, thirty thousand pieces of porcelain were ordered from Kiang-si for religious purposes. The yearly consumption of wax exceeded three hundred thousand catties, yet even this did not satisfy the emperor. He demanded ambergris (龍涎香) which was so rare that for over ten years none could be found. Ultimately, a limited amount was obtained in Macao, presumably from the Portuguese merchants.[37] The cost of the food consumed at each religious function was estimated at eighteen thousand silver taels—not a surprising figure if we remember the huge numbers of participants. At the function of the seventh moon in the 26th year of the Chia-ching reign (1547), for instance, there were over twenty-four thousand Taoist monks in the ceremony, which was so solemn that, out of respect, the punishment of criminals was suspended for twenty-three days, and the slaughter of animals for nine days.[38]

The Chia-ching emperor's enthusiasm for the Taoist religion enabled many to seek favors under the pretext of zeal for religion. Thus, in 1554, T'ao Chung-wen 陶仲文 appealed to the court to complete a bridge in Shantung. The work, he said, had been started by a certain Taoist priest, and during the draining of the river bed a complete set of "dragon bones" weighing a thousand catties had been discovered, and a sandy island several score feet long had appeared. "This no doubt is a sign of the propitious help of the gods and we must carry the work to an end. We therefore petition Your Majesty to be generous with us so that we may accomplish this great work." Tao's appeal was not made in vain: we are told that fourteen thousand silver taels were granted by order of the emperor.[39]

The Wan-li emperor was no less enthusiastic a patron of the Buddhist religion than the Chia-ching emperor had been of the Taoist. As we have seen something of this, it will suffice here to quote the following passage from a memorial submitted to the throne by a certain minister: "In and outside the capital the monasteries are all beautifully decorated and they are the gift of the imperial treasury. To spare the people heavy taxes would be a better thing than to give donations to far-away monasteries or for the performing of frequent religious functions, the results of which are quite uncertain."[40]

Another drain on the public funds resulted from the multiplication of unnecessary officials in the government. The *Tien-ku chi-wen* asserts that the number of military officers in the Ch'eng-hua period was four times what it had been in the Hung-wu reign and the number of officials in the Chin-i-wei was eight times greater than in the early days. The writer was greatly worried by this, since the population was declining while the expenses were increasing.[41] Towards the end of the Ch'eng-hua reign it was seen that a cut in government expenditure was called for, and the emperor dismissed over 560 officials, civil or military. Throughout the Ming period the government was constantly trying to reduce the number of unnecessary officials but these efforts produced little fruit and the reduction was always quite insignificant.[42]

PENSIONS AND RELIEF

The pensions of the imperial clansmen constituted another great problem for the government. As we have seen above, all the descendants of the Hung-wu emperor received pensions from the government. It was also the wish of the monarch that none of his decendants should take the examinations for government offices or engage in trade. We do not know exactly what his motive was in imposing these bans. Probably he did not wish to give to the clansmen any chance of meddling in government affairs and since they were all to receive pensions there would be no need for them to engage in trade. The course he had laid down was easy to follow in the days when the government had abundant means and the number of clansmen was still small. But by the time of the Wan-li emperor the government was hard pressed for money and the descendants of the Hung-wu emperor had multiplied till there were nearly two hundred thousand of them.[43] By then it had become clear that if the government continued to support the clansmen at the old rates, it would imperil its own financial stability: already it was spending more on the support of the imperial clansmen than on the salaries of government officials. "Such is the number of these descendants that even the palaces cannot hold all of them. They are supported by the local government regardless of their degree of relationship with the emperor. Whether for marriages or for funerals, their expenses are always drawn from the government. This continues month after month without end. . . ."[44] As one writer pointed out, the territories of the empire were limited but the number of imperial clansmen was growing limitlessly. At the beginning of the Hung-wu reign the only imperial clansman in Shansi was Prince Chin, whose yearly pension was 10,000 piculs of rice. But the number of imperial clansmen increased till, toward the end of the dynasty, the pensions in Shansi amounted to 870,000 piculs of rice. On the other hand the area of farming territory in Shansi was 410,000 ch'ing at the beginning of the dynasty, but by the 15th year of the Hung-chih emperor (1478) 30,000 ch'ing had gone out of cultivation. There was nothing that the government could do except to cut down the pensions, and even these reduced pensions could not always be paid.[45] Reasonable though the cuts were, the clansmen felt that their rights were not being respected, and being unable to live according to their state they were prone to create trouble. It was clear that the pension system did no good to any party. All suffered from it: the government, the people and the imperial clansmen themselves.

When the Portuguese Jesuit missionary Gabriel de Magaillans (Magalhães) came to China toward the end of the Ming dynasty he bore witness to the decline of the imperial clansmen:

" . . . and since the preceding family had ruled for two hundred and seventy-six years, they [the descedants] had multiplied and spread to such an extent, and as a result their income had become so small that many of them were obliged to exercise some manual arts in order to earn a living. When I entered this empire I saw one of them in the capital of Kiamsi [Kiangsi] province who was engaged in the trade of a locksmith. To distinguish himself from his fellow of the same profession he carried on his back the instrument of his profession, quite bright and varnished in red. Under the reign of the preceding family there was an infinite number of them [i.e. the descendants] spreading all over the empire. They, abusing the privileges of their birth, committed thousands of outrages and affronts to the poor people; but have all been exterminated to the last one of the family from whom they descended. . . ."[46]

Most of the imperial clansmen, being forbidden to trade or to take examinations for government positions, spent their lives in an idleness which gradually led to all kinds of disorders. Very few of them had any ambition to study. Those who could afford to enjoy themselves lived like kings, and those who were less prosperous tried hard to ward off hunger and cold. Poor though they were, their dignity as descendants of the first emperor was still respected by all, including government officials, and they often tried to take advantage of this fact in order to make money. Toward the end of the fifteenth century a renowned official, Ma Wen-sheng 馬文升 (1426–1510), made a report to the emperor on living conditions among the imperial clansmen. Most of them, he said, were gradually falling away from old traditions. There was a lack of discipline in their homes and they did not even appoint officials to look after the affairs of their palaces. Women were employed as porters instead of men, and the riff-raff of all classes of society frequented their palaces unchecked. Relatives who had authority over them were afraid to admonish them, although they clearly saw the disorder of their conduct. Government officials were still less ready to admonish them, for they too were afraid of being accused by them of insulting the emperor's kinsmen. Relying on the influence they enjoyed as imperial kinsmen, they did whatever they pleased. They kidnapped young girls, and, if they were resisted, murdered the innocent in cold blood. They fought savagely among themselves in bitter enmity. Some of them took in children, adopting them as their own. Others brought harlots into their palaces, or, despite their dignity, frequented brothels. Others of them spent all their time drinking and gambling in the market places, not only losing all their money but finding themselves obliged to borrow and disgracing themselves in the eyes of the public.[47]

In the last years of the dynasty the financial situation had become so difficult that the government was no longer able to support all the clansmen. It was decided therefore in 1621 that they should be allowed to take government examinations—not so much to allow them to show their talent for governing as to give them an opportunity to earn a living. Ordinarily, however, they obtained their appointments not by passing examinations but through the recommendations of princes or by bribery. We are told that those who offered substantial bribes generally obtained positions in the imperial patent office (中書舍人). Those who gave less were usually appointed district magistrates.[48] This system, however, did not last long: with the fall of the dynasty it disappeared.

Finally we must not forget to mention that huge sums from the government treasury were spent on relief. Though the reckless expenditure of the emperors had exhausted the treasury, the government could not easily evade the serious obligation of providing for the people in time of calamities. We have already dealt with the problem of relief in previous chapters. To recapitulate, this relief consisted in exempting the people from land taxes. In the happier days of the dynasty when there was an abundance of everything, the government had been able to tackle the problem, usually to good effect. It had been able not only to bring temporary relief to the sufferers but also to help to set them on their feet again. Thus during the famine of 1493, over half a million silver taels and two million piculs of grain were distributed in relief in Shantung alone. The number of lives saved was said to be above two million six hundred thousand. Similarly in Su-chou and Sung-kiang the people were exempted from nearly two million piculs of grain in land taxes because of floods.[49]

But in the later days of the dynasty things were very different. Mismanagement had emptied the treasuries; there were frequent natural calamities of all kinds in the provinces; wars raged along the borders almost unceasingly. There was so little in the treasuries that it was exceedingly difficult to grant relief. 1609 was a year in which most of the provinces suffered natural calamities of one kind or another. The disasters seem to have been serious, and reports came in continually to the court begging for help. Having nowhere else to turn for money, the Wan-li emperor had to order the Board of Revenue to borrow two hundred and fifty thousand silver taels from the Court of the Imperial Stud and one hundred and fifty thousand silver taels from the Board of Works for distribution in relief. Some provinces were ordered to use one third of the taxes for the same purpose.[50]

Toward the end of the Ming period relief work became almost impossible; yet the government had to do what it could, for there was great danger that it would lose the people. In 1631, a censor was sent to Yen-sui with a hundred thousand silver taels for distribution among the famine-stricken. He immediately sent a report to the Ch'ung-chen emperor stating that among the starving people there were hungry soldiers who had deserted from the army and were inciting the people to revolt. Many of the younger men, though underfed, were still fit to bear arms as bandits. In such circumstances, he said, a hundred thousand silver taels was not sufficient for distribution among the people of the nineteen districts of Yen-sui. This was the time when the rebels were becoming active and the imperial treasuries were exhausted. The government, lacking adequate means to solve the problems, tried to find excuses and suggested that contributions should be collected from Prince Chin, from government officials, and from the gentry and the well-to-do of the locality.[51]

Another huge expense at the end of the Ming period was the support of the army. What we have seen in chapter 8 is enough to give some idea of the difficulties the government had to face. The constant increase of the land taxes shows that the government could devise no better ways of raising funds. The President of the Board of Revenue, who had to bear the chief responsibility for the finances of the empire, had an appallingly difficult task. Chao Shih-ch'ing 趙世卿 wrote in 1603 that the right of levying taxes was frequently usurped by the eunuchs and that the taxes collected were often kept in the provinces for local use. The issuing of vouchers for salt by officials of the Salt Office interfered greatly with the collection of the revenue of the Board of Revenue. Money moreover was frequently borrowed by different governmental departments from the Board, which was thus always left short. On the other hand the expenditure on wars and other extraordinary items was astonishing. The suppression of revolts in Szechuan cost over two million silver taels and the war with Japan nearly six million. Court expenditure on ceremonial functions and the cost of purchases made for annual festivals amounted altogether to nine or ten million silver taels. Chao, having tried to give a factual description of the state of the government, ended: "The two lao-k'u 老庫 are at their lowest and in the tai-ts'ang 太倉 there is hardly enough for a year's expense. Transportation is held up. On the borders the soldiers are beginning to riot and everywhere within the empire the people are becoming restive. It is not easy to predict where all this will end."[52]

MONETARY SYSTEM

Silver came into official use as currency only after the Hsüan-te period (1426–1435). It was widely used in such official matters as the payment of taxes and the payment of government salaries, and the people used it when large sums had to be paid. But for ordinary transactions copper coins were undoubtedly the chief form of currency. In the early days of the dynasty when the emperors were trying to make paper money the main currency the use of copper coins was greatly discouraged. Indeed at one time during the Hung-wu reign the use of copper coins was forbidden altogether.[53]

Ultimately, however, inflation destroyed popular confidence in paper money and copper coins regained their place as the most popular medium of transaction.

Before the Wan-li period the purchasing power of copper coins was high and they had appreciated in terms of silver. During the Hung-wu reign, one silver tael was worth one thousand copper coins. A century later, in the Cheng-hua period (1465–1487), it was worth only eight hundred copper coins. In the Hung-chih, Cheng-te and Chia-ching reigns (1488–1566), the rate fell to seven hundred coins per silver tael.[54] The explanation for this was that the coins were never issued in very large quantities and the quality was always kept up to the standard. Indeed, the tendency was to increase the weight of copper rather than to decrease it: early in the Hung-wu reign each coin weighed one ch'ien; in 1390, two more fen 分 (i.e. twenty per cent of a ch'ien) was added to each coin; in the Chia-ching period each new coin weighed one ch'ien and three fen.

The government's reason for restricting the coinage of copper was its wish to maintain paper money as the chief medium of exchange. It should be noted that besides the coins issued by the Ming government, copper coins of previous dynasties were still in circulation with the approval of the government. However, despite the retention of the older coins and the minting of new ones the circulation decreased at a rate faster than could have been accounted for by accidental losses and normal wearing away. One reason for this was the use of Chinese coins in neighboring countries. We have seen that in the Chia-ching reign the internal rate of exchange was one silver tael to seven hundred copper coins; but in Japan at that time as few as 250 coins would buy a silver tael.[55] Currency smugglers were inevitably attracted by these terms. Another reason for the disappearance of coins was the practice among the well-to-do of hoarding coins. These people never dreamt of using capital for productive purposes and were satisfied to keep their money in a cellar.

Throughout the Ming dynasty the coinage caused constant worry to the government. First, there was the problem of ancient and new coins. Many of the ancient coins, having been handled throughout the centuries, were in poor condition. The people discriminated between worn and unworn coins, with much consequent confusion. During the T'ien-shun period (1457–1464), it was decreed that no discrimination was to be made between new and old coins, unless they were counterfeit or made of lead. A new system was tried in the Hung-chih reign (1488–1505), when it was reported that large numbers of the coins of the Hung-wu, Yung-lo and Hsüan-te periods were still stored in the treasury—kept back, probably, lest they should interfere with the circulation of the paper money. It was decided that these coins should be used in paying the salaries of government officials, and that in the exaction of taxes, half of the sum due should be demanded in copper coins of these periods and half in ancient coins. People who failed to produce the newer coins might pay in ancient coins but at a rate of two old to one new coin. This system did not work well and eventually it became necessary to accord the same value to old and new coins.[56]

In the Chia-ching reign the capital was flooded with counterfeit money and the government had to take action. In 1554, it was declared that the rate of exchange for copper coins issued by the Ming emperors and for the ancient coins in good condition was seven coins to one fen of silver. Less perfect coins were then classified into three categories, with rates of exchange at ten, fourteen or twenty-one to one fen of silver. It was forbidden to circulate coins of really bad quality in the market. Very stupidly, however, this classification was ignored in the payment of salaries of government officials. These were paid in coins of any quality, at a fixed rate of seven coins to one fen of silver. Understandably, the government officials often tried to force the people to accept coins of inferior quality at the rate at which they themselves had received them. This naturally caused alarm among the people. Furthermore, the complete rejection of bad coins (which had flooded the market) had caused great inconveniences and eventually the government had to yield to public opinion and permit their circulation. The rate of exchange was then fixed as follows: six thousand bad coins, three thousand pre-Ming coins, one thousand Hung-wu coins, or seven hundred Chia-ching coins to one silver tael. This soon led to the counterfeiting of Chia-ching coins since these had the best exchange rate.[57]

Then we are told that Nanking produced more coins than Peking, with a resulting difference in value. Toward the end of the Wan-li reign the rate of exchange in Nanking was ten coins to one fen of silver; in Peking it was six to one. During the T'ai-ch'ang period these values remained more or less the same. The Ch'ien-pi k'ao 錢幣考 however says that since the Wan-li reign the value of copper coins had been three times higher in the north than in the south.[58]

Variation in the quality of the coins was an important factor in the deterioration of the Ming monetary system. In the last years of the Chia-ching reign copper coins of diverse types were minted, some of them of very poor quality. The i-t'iao-kun 一條棍, described as light, varying in color and rough edged, seems to have been cheap to mint.

The hsüan-pien 鏇邊, so called because the edges were smoothed with a lathe, was originally a good coin. Later it was found that minting it had cost too much labor. Files, therefore, were substituted for lathes—with unhappy results. The laborers, wishing to spare their energies, put extra lead into the coins, which made their work easier indeed, but lowered the quality of the coins. Hsü Chieh 徐階 (1503–1583), who was then Grand Secretary, strongly opposed the i-t'iao-kun, saying that, since the introduction of these coins was likely to end in failure, it would be unwise to keep on minting them. He gave five reasons for his view that these new coins should be abandoned. Firstly, it cost the Boards of Revenue and of Works 28,000 silver taels yearly to mint the new coins which were not being well received by the people. Secondly, the poor quality of the coins made things easy for conterfeiters. Thirdly, if the emperor should make a donation to his minister in these coins, his generosity would not be appreciated since the gift would be of little value. Fourthly, if the government tried to pay in these new coins in business transactions the people would feel discontented since they would suffer loss. Finally, the new coins would cause great confusion in the monetary system and the government would lose prestige through its inability to control the situation. We are told that the Chia-ching emperor accepted the advice of his minister: the mint was ordered to discontinue producing new coins.[59]

Yet when the Lung-ch'ing emperor succeeded his father in 1567, the monetary system was still unstable. Accordingly a meeting of the court ministers was called, at which the Board of Revenue pointed out the causes for the deterioration of the monetary system. The flooding of the market with bad copper coins seems to have been one of the chief causes. The ancient coins had fallen out of popular use; the value of coins issued by the Ming emperors was fluctuating since there was a rumor that they were soon to be withdrawn; above all the abundance of counterfeit coins had driven the good coins from the market. The Grand Secretary, Kao Kung 高拱, put the blame on the government. Since it had no fixed policy, changes occurred frequently and the people were thus led to mistrust the government.[60]

The decline of the national economy had become apparent by the Wan-li reign. Until then the value of coins had been high and inflation had been avoided. But when the war with Japan started in 1597, the economic foundations of the empire began to shake. The minister Ho Ching 郝敬 suggested that large copper coins be minted with a face value of ten, thirty or fifty coins. Though this plan was never carried out it indicates the situation in which the government had found itself.[61]

The war with Japan sapped the financial strength of the Ming government. The Wan-li emperor, seeing the difficulties of the time, decided that copper coins should be minted in great quantities. The new coins, he held, would not only help to maintain the army and be of use to the merchants but would also serve for the payment of the salaries to government officials and for the making of donations to his subjects. Orders therefore were given for the mints throughout the country to produce coins. The furnaces used for this purpose in Peking alone were said to number over one hundred and twenty. The new copper coins were used only in Peking and, since their purchasing power was low, even government employees were unwilling to accept them (thirty per cent of these employees' salaries were supposed to be paid in copper coins and the rest in silver). Commodity prices began to rise. Copper, which had cost only seven silver taels per hundred catties at the beginning of the Wan-li reign, now cost fifteen silver taels. The government, therefore, was forced to reduce the production of coins and many of the mint craftsmen had to be dismissed. These craftsmen, unable to make an honest livelihood, turned to counterfeiting, and a very good job they made of it. The coins they produced were, we are told, very similar to the genuine coins, and, since they were able to sell them to money dealers below the official rate the market was soon flooded with these counterfeit coins.[62]

The forging of coins was perhaps the most serious cause of the ruin of the monetary system under the Ming dynasty. The emperors repeatedly published stern warnings against forgers but to no avail. That so many were ready to risk their lives rather than to give up this dangerous profession shows how profitable it must have been. Even a number of the imperial relatives could not resist the temptation to make easy money. They too began to mint counterfeit coins and the local officials dared not stop them. At the beginning of the Wan-li reign indeed, one of the imperial clansmen in Ch'ü-kiang 曲江 who had been caught forging coins was duly degraded to the rank of commoner and put under house arrest, and his assistants were thrown into prison. Yet, twenty-two years later a censor reported that the difficulties of the monetary system were due to the forging by the imperial clansmen, with whose machinations the officials found it embassassing to interfere.[63] The government itself recognized how difficult it was to suppress forgery and the only effective plan was to use first-rate materials and workmanship so as to render forging difficult—hence the saying: pu ai t'ung, pu hsi kung 不愛銅, 不惜工, i.e. spare no copper, spare no workmanship.

Unfortunately the copper coins minted after the Chia-ching period had generally been defective as we saw above when treating of the i-t'iao-kun. Forgers had been quick to see the opportunity this gave them to flood the market with counterfeit coins. A censor described these as light, thin, small and easy to break. They were inscribed but the inscriptions were hardly legible. Sometimes, indeed, these counterfeit coins were merely pieces of lead or·iron cut into the shape of coins so that they could be mixed with real coins. Their value, we are told, was three hundred coins to one ch'ien of silver.[64]

Severe penalties were ordained for all those who dared to forge coins, but no one seems to have been terrified by the threat. In the thirty-eighth year of the Wan-li reign the emperor issued a new order imposing punishment on those who knew what was going on and failed to report it; and giving high praise to government officials who had helped effectively to put down forgery. Wang Chi 王紀, hsün-fu of Pao-ting, regarded the emperor's action as unwise. He blamed the government for using inferior material in minting coins, thus at once lowering its own prestige and giving the forgers their chance to sell their counterfeit coins. Now when the national economy was depressed and the people were mostly poor, it was inadvisable, he held, to encourage the officials to act strongly in monetary matters. The more pressure the government put on the officials the more pressure would the officials put on the people, thus increasing the sufferings of those who were already in misery. Why then try to encourage the officials to do what was not necessary. He suggested that the government should buy copper from places where copper was abundant or build mints near copper mines or open mines where copper could be obtained in abundance.[65]

In the last two Ming reigns, the T'ien-ch'i and Ch'ung-chen, mints were established throughout the empire. The government's sole purpose was to obtain money to meet its overwhelming expenses. The profit from minting seems, in fact, to have been very great. In the years 1623 and 1624, for instance, the cost of minting copper coins in Nanking was 290,054 silver taels and the profit amounted to 128,606 silver taels and eight ch'ien. In the following year the cost was 143,441 silver taels and the profit 128,831 silver taels. However, this unbridled zeal for quantity was not combined with an equal interest in quality and very soon there was inflation. At first, we are told, each coin was supposed to weigh one ch'ien and three fen, but very soon, owing to the corruption of officials, the weight was reduced to about seven fen and the proportion of lead to copper was raised from thirty-seventy to fifty-fifty. In some places the coins contained only twenty or thirty per cent of copper, and were grey and so small and thin that they broke easily.[66]

In the Ch'ung-chen reign when the government could no longer support the army from its revenues, orders were given for the establishment of mints in garrison cities so that the government might be able to pay the salaries. In many places copper coins were minted for private use and there was no uniformity of size or type. The coins produced at this time were of poor quality. The *Ming shih* says that "a hundred coins piled up hardly measured an inch in thickness and when they were thrown on the floor they broke into pieces." The mints established all over the country gradually used up all available supplies of copper so that to obtain further supply of copper the government had to order that old coins and articles made of copper should be melted down. Copper and lead dealers had to get special licenses from the government and if they traded without these licenses they were to be punished severely. By this time, however, the forging of coins had got beyond control and many government mints had to close down because they could not compete with the counterfeiters. Severe penalties were imposed on forgers though without appreciable result. It is said that censors were appointed in the capital to supervise the money exchangers at the nine gates of the city. If one counterfeit coin was found the culprit was given thirty strokes; if two he was sentenced to a year's imprisonment; if three, he was exiled; if four, he received a capital sentence.[67]

The government's feverish attitude toward coin production seemed to some to be mistaken. Chang Shen-yen 張慎言, one of the ministers of the Board of Works, reminded the emperor in 1638 that a mere increase in the production of coins was not the immediate need of the time. The government, it was true, had made huge profits by minting, but the value of coins had depreciated so sharply that their purchasing power was only one-fourth of what it had been in the Wan-li reign. The vital problem lay, Chang said, in the production of grain, and it was the shortage of grain that had caused the rise of prices in all commodities. He recalled how in the old days a laborer who earned thirty coins per day was able to support his family, whereas at the time at which he was writing sixty coins would not suffice. The soldiers on the borders would find themselves short of money even if the government tripled their pay, yet it was impossible for the government to keep on increasing the army's pay. Chang therefore proposed that the soldiers be given farms so that they might increase agricultural production and that the people might be free from military oppression. The people should also be encouraged to cultivate the land. This, he argued, might prevent the people from joining the rebels and would help to increase production on the farms.[68] Chang's proposals sound well, but they show him to have been a theorist with little grasp of the needs of his time. The government by then was too weak to exercise full control over the soldiers, who were subject rather to their own officers than to the emperor, and the provincial towns and villages had been so devastated by battles that it was no longer possible for the people to live peacefully on their farms. The few who tried to do so were eventually discouraged by heavy land taxes or by the insatiable demands of the soldiers and rebels.

The imperial household during the last Ming reign was likened to that of a great but bankrupt family. The head of the family struggled hard to maintain the social standard of the whole family on his strained means. The Ch'ung-chen emperor tried to cut down all expenses and himself set an example of frugality. The time in which he was living was extremely difficult. The Manchus' strength had increased to an alarming degree and there were rebels everywhere in the empire. In the year 1635, the Board of Revenue reported that the taxes collected that year amounted to six million eight hundred thousand silver taels, but the expenditure had exceeded the revenue by a million.[69] In that same year rebels destroyed the imperial tombs in Fen-yang, and there was so little in the imperial treasury that all the court officials had to contribute to repair the damage. Thirty thousand precious pieces of silk with dragon designs still came yearly to the palace from Hang-chou, but because the appropriate bribes had not been given, the eunuchs refused to present the silk to the emperor and even quoted the emperor as saying that, since the silk was not of the quality he had demanded, all the pieces were to be sent back and better pieces made. A court minister who had witnessed this tragic folly told the Grand Secretary that though the silk might not be good enough for the emperor's own use, it could be used for presents which he was wont to give to all his subjects. The silk, he argued, had cost several hundred thousand silver taels to manufacture, and it had cost a good deal to transport it to the capital. The people who had supplied it should therefore be spared further expense. The Grand Secretary, however, disagreed, and the silk was sent back to be remade.[70] Such punctilio, however, helped very little to bolster the authority of the government and in the end it hastened the fall of the dynasty. In the year 1642 the expenditure of the Court of Entertainment was cut down to a little over twenty thousand silver taels. Two years later, when the arch-rebel Li Tzu-ch'eng conquered the capital he was surprised and disappointed to find in the treasuries only a hundred and seventeen thousand taels of gold and a hundred and thirty thousand of silver.[71]

NOTES

[1] *China in the Sixteenth Century*, 309, 310.

[2] *Li Chung-wen kung chi*, 6, (ts'e 8) 54b; *Wu-tsa-tsu*, 9, (ts'e 5) 19a.

[3] Ku Ch'i-yüan 顧起元, *Lan-chen ts'ao-t'ang wen-chi* 嬾眞草堂文集, (1618 edition) 9, (ts'e 6) 14b, 15a.

[4] *Ta Hsüeh* 大學 (The Great Learning), Chapter 10, verse 9, James Legge's translation in the *Four Books* (Shanghai, 1930) 338.

[5] *Ku-chin chih-ping lüeh*, 3, (ts'e 3) 117ab.

[6] The *Ku-chin chih-ping lüeh*, 3, (ts'e 3) 141b says that the Chin-hua yin started in 1436. The amount to be sent to the cheng-yün k'u was a million silver taels. Under the Wan-li emperor, however, another two hundred thousand was added to the chin-hua yin. Cf. also *Chia-ching i-lai chu-lüeh*, 10, (ts'e 7) 22a; *Hsü wen-hsien t'ung-k'ao*, 30, I, 3086.

[7] *Hsü wen-hsien t'ung k'ao*, 30, I, 3038.

[8] *Ming shih*, 79, (ts'e 27) 14b, 15a; *Hsü wen-hsien t'ung-k'ao*, 30, 1, 308 ; *Tsui-wei lu*, 13, (ts'e 6) 7b.

[9] *Erh-shih erh-shih cha-chi*, 30, (ts'e 6) 28ab.

[10] Shan Shih-yüan 單士元 and Wang Pi-wen 王璧文, *Ming-tai chien-chu ta-shih nien-piao* 明代建築大事年表, (Peiping, 1937).

[11] There must be a mistake in the *Hsü wen-hsien t'ung-k'ao* in this sum. It seems altogether too large. Chu Hsieh 朱偰 in his book *Ming-Ch'ing liang-tai kung-yüan chien-chih yen-ke t'u-k'ao* 明清兩代宮苑建置沿革圖考, (Shanghai, 1947) 15, gives the sum as over two hundred thousand.

[12] *Hsü wen-hsien t'ung-k'ao*, 16, 2, 2913-2917.

[13] *Kuo-ch'ao tien-hui*, 192, (ts'e 63) 20ab.

[14] *Chia-ching i-lai chu-lüeh*, 3, (ts'e 2) 17a; *Huang-Ming t'ung-chi shu-i*, 10, (ts'e 5) 60b, 65a.

[15] *Kuo ch'ao tien hui*, 19 , (ts'e 63) 20b; 194, (ts'e 64) 6a.

[16] Hsiang Meng-yüan 項夢原, *Tung-kuan chi-shih* 冬官紀事, (TSCCCP), (ts'e 15).

[17] *Ming-shih ch'ao-lüeh*, (ts'e 1) 36b.

[18] *Ming shih*, 89, (ts'e 32) 5b, 6a.

[19] *Ming hui-yao*, 38, I, 665-666.

[20] *Ming hui-tien*, 217, (ts'e 39) 4315; *Ming hui-yao*, 38, I. 666.

[21] *Ch'un-ming meng-yü-lu*, 27, (ts'e 8) 3ab.

[22] *Kuo-ch'üeh*, (ts'e 18) 222; Hsieh Chao-che 謝肇淛, *Hsiao-ts'ao-chai wen-chi* 小草齋文集, (Ming edition) 14, (ts'e 3) 4b.

[23] *Hsü wen-hsien t'ung-k'ao*, 30, I, 3083.

[24] *Ming shih*, 82, (ts'e 29) 4a; *Tien-ku chi-wen*, 17, (ts'e 134) 24b, 25a; *Ch'un-ming meng-yü-lu*, 27, (ts'e 8) 4ab.

[25] *Ch'un-ming meng-yü-lu*, 27, (ts'e 8) 5ab. The *Yeh-hu-pien*, (Shanghai, 1959 ed.) 1, A. 28, mentions a certain eunuch who sold a big house but got only enough to furnish the imperial court for one day. It is hard to see how the eunuchs could have gone on without theft from the imperial treasury or extortion from the people!

[26] *Ming shih*, 82, (ts'e 29) 4b.

[27] Shimizu Taiji 清水泰次, "Min dai ni okeru bukkyō no tori—shimari" 明代にけ於る 佛教の取締, *Shigaku zasshi* 史學雜誌, 40, (March 1929) 3, 263–310. *Tōyō bunka shi taikei* 東洋文化史大系, (Tokyo, 1938) 5. 45; Cf. also Wang Chung-wu 王崇武, "Ming Ch'eng-tsu vü fo-chiao" 明成祖與佛教, *Chung-kuo she-hui ching-chi-shih chi-k'an* 中國社會經濟史集刊, 8, (January, 1949) 1, 1–11; and "Ming Ch'eng-ts'u yü fang-shih" 明成祖與方士, Ibid., 12–19. In these two articles the author very ably discusses both the great interest the Yung-lo emperor had in Buddhism and his connection with the alchemists. In the first article especially, he tries to disprove official documents stating that the Yun-glo emperor was hostile to the Buddhist religion.

[28] *Hsi-yüan wen-chien lu*, 104, (ts'e 40) 22a.

[29] *Ming shih*, 182, (ts'e 60) 4a.

[30] *Wan-li yeh-hu-pien*, (Shanghai, 1959), 27, C. 684–685.

[31] *Hsien-tsung shun-huang-ti shih-lu*, 53, (ts'e 153) 8ab; *Ming shih*, 331, (ts'e 112) 1b–5b.

[32] *Cho-chung chih*, 17, (ts'e 3,967) 122.

[33] Shen Te-fu 沈德符 (1578–1642), *Supplement to the Yeh huo-pien* 野獲編補遺, (ed. by Yao Tsu-en 姚祖恩, Chekiang, 1827), 4, (ts'e 34) 16b–17b, 166–176; *Tien-ku chi-wen*, 17, (ts'e 134) 15a; Chou Te-p'u 鄒德溥, *Sheng-ch'ao t'ai-chiao lu* 聖朝泰交錄, (1634 ed.) B. 52ab; *Hsi-yüan wen-chien lu*, 105, (ts'e 40) 16b. Instead of "over thirteen thousand catties," it reads "no less than one thousand catties."

[34] Chang Ch'üan 張銓, *Kuo-shih chi wen* 國史紀聞, (1620 ed.) 11, (ts'e 9) 100ab.

[35] *Wu-tsung wei-chi*, (ts'e 8) 1680–1681.

[36] *Tsui-wei lu*, 27, (ts'e 12) 9b–12a.

[37] *Ming shih*, 82, (ts'e 11) 3a; *Tung-hsi-yang k'ao*, 12, (ts'e 3,261) 181; *Tien-ku chi-wen*, 18, (ts'e 134) 1a.

[38] *Tsui-wei-lu*, 12, (ts'e 5) 49ab; *Ming-ch'ao hsiao-shih*, (HLTTS), 12, (ts'e 91) 12b.

[39] *Kuo-ch'ao tien-hui*, 125, (ts'e 47) 15a.

[40] *Chia-ching i-lai chu-lüeh*, (ts'e 5) 42b, 43a.

[41] *Tien-ku chi-wen*, 17, (ts'e 134) 10.

[42] *Hsü-wen-hsien t'ung-k'ao*, 30, I, 3,084; *Ming hui-yao*, 44, II, 821–823. Huang Tsun-so has left an account of an interesting incident in the T'ien-chi period: The death of Kuang-tsung (i.e. the T'ai-ch'ang 泰昌 emperor) occurred almost immediately after that of Shen-tsung (i.e. the Wan-li emperor). When the next emperor (T'ien-chi) came to the throne he issued an edict re-employing all dismissed ministers, none of whom seem to have been left out. The Ching-t'ang 京堂 officials who originally numbered only twenty-six, increased to nearly one hundred within the period of one or two years. Even in Nanking the number was doubled. Petitions still kept coming in. The yamens had to share their salaries with them and they worked together. But half of these (dismissed ministers) were physically weak and deaf; they had lost the sense of time! . . . *Shuo-lüeh*, 10ab.

[43] *Ku-chin chih-p'ing lüeh*, 3, (ts'e 3) 126b, 127a. In 1627 one of the clansmen in Shansi reported to the throne that his pension had not been given to him for eight years. Cf. *Kuo-ch'üeh* (Shanghai, 1958), 93, (ts'e 6) 5666.

[44] Chang Ho-chung 張和仲, *Ch'ien pai nien yen* 千百年眼, chuan 12 (*Pi-chi hsiao-shuo ta-kuan* series 筆記小說大觀) published by the Chin-pu Book Company 進步書局; (Shanghai, no date) (ts'e 95), 14b–15a.

[45] *Ming-ch'ao hsiao-shih*, 12, (ts'e 91) 11b, 12a.

[46] Gabriel Magaillans (Magalhães), *Nouvelle relation de la Chine, contenant la description des particularites les plus considerables de ce grand empire,* (Paris, 1688).

[47] *Ch'un-ming meng-yü-lu,* 39, (ts'e 13) 75b, 76a.

[48] Sun Ch'eng-tse 孫承澤 (1592–1676), *Ssu-ling tien-li chi* 思陵典禮紀, (TSCCCP), 2, (ts'e 3,972) 28.

[49] *Ming hui-yao,* 54, II, 1027; *Ming t'ung-chien,* 37, (ts'e 4) 4b.

[50] *Ming hui-yao,* 54, II, 1032.

[51] *Hsü wen-hsien t'ung-k'ao,* 32, II, 3126.

[52] *Chia-ching i-lai chu-lüeh,* 10, (ts'e 7) 16b.

[53] Anonymous, *Ch'ien-pi k'ao* 錢幣考, (TSCCCP), B. (ts'e 0771) 90.

[54] *Chung-kuo huo-pi-shih,* 470.

[55] Ibid., 482 note 28 where the *Ch'ou-hai-t'u pien* 籌海圖編 is quoted.

[56] *Hsü wen-hsien t'ung-k'ao,* 11, I, 2870–2871.

[57] Ibid., 11, I, 2870 2071. Cf. also *Chung-kuo huo-pi-shih,* 476.

[58] *Chung-kuo huo-pi-shih,* 485; *Ch'ien-pi k'ao,* A. 44.

[59] *Ming hui-yao,* 55, II, 1042–1043; *Ming shu,* 81, (ts'e 3943) 1604–1641.

[60] *Ming shu,* 81, (ts'e 3943) 1641; *Ming hui-yao,* 55, II, 1043.

[61] *Chung-kuo huo-pi-shih,* 484.

[62] *Ming shu,* 81, (ts'e 3941) 1642; *Chung-kuo huo-pi-shih,* 471, 484.

[63] *Hsü wen-hsien t'ung-k'ao,* 11, I, 2874.

[64] *Ming shu,* 81, (ts'e 3943) 1639.

[65] *Hsü wen-hsien t'ung-k'ao,* 11, I, 2875.

[66] Ibid., 11, I, 2876, 2878; *Chung-kuo huo-pi-shih,* 486, 487.

[67] *Hsü wen-hsien t'ung-k'ao,* 11, I, 2878, 2879, 2880; *Chung-kuo huo-pi-shih,* 487–488; *Ming shih,* 81, (ts'e 98) 10a.

[68] *Hsü wen-hsien t'ung-k'ao,* 11, I, 2879. During the Ming period the average rate of exchange was about 600 to 610 coins to a tael of pure silver, After the accession of the Ch'ung-chen emperor, however, the value of coins kept on depreciating, By 1643 the rate of exchange had risen to more than two thousand coins to a silver tael. (Cf. Ibid. 2880.)

[69] *K'ou-shih pien-nien,* 8, (ts'e 7) 17a.

[70] Ibid., 8, (ts'e 7) 31b.

[71] *Ch'un-ming meng-yü lu,* 27, (ts'e 8) 5b, 6a; Ch'ien Hsing 錢軹 *Chia-shen chuan-hsin-lu* 甲申傳信錄, (CKNLWHLSTS, ed. by Sheng-chou kuo-kuang-she 神洲國光社, Shanghai, 1936), 6, (ts'e 12) 115.

CHAPTER ELEVEN

Ethics and Religion

Offices

The Chinese government had a tradition of selling official positions
when the level of the government treasuries was low, a tradition
going back as far as the time of Wu-ti of the Han dynasty. Rich
merchants, who otherwise might have had no hope of entering
government service, were always willing to pay highly for these
positions, which adorned their riches with power, and practically
guaranteed the future glory of their families. The sale of offices
seemed equally desirable to the government which found in it a
means of raising without delay large sums of money to relieve
temporary needs. Trouble started, however, when the government
began to make frequent use of this means of gain. Officials attached
to a corrupt government soon learnt how to augment their incomes
by taking bribes. Once this abuse had crept into the government
there was very little hope for the survival of sound ethics among the
officials.

When in the earliest days of the dynasty the Hung-wu emperor
founded schools throughout the empire, his chief purpose was the
training of good men for the government of the country. He was strict
in selecting only the best and all had to pass examinations before they
were given government posts. In this matter, the founder's influence
lasted long. Not till the first year of the Ching-t'ai reign (1450) do
we find a Ming government selling offices. The ominous change
came immediately after the Tu-mu incident when the Mongols were
threatening the capital. In the desperate search for defence funds it

was decreed that government positions were to be given to those who would contribute to the defence fund. Students who were willing to donate rice or horses were admitted to the Kuo-tzu-chien; commoners or members of the military class who contributed received titles; officials who had been dismissed for delinquency were to be reinstated on condition of contributing; those who were willing to contribute more than four thousand piculs of beans were to receive the hereditary title of chih-hui 指揮.[1]

The desperate crisis of 1450 may have seemed to justify the perilous innovation, but it soon became apparent that it had involved a permanent abandonment of the old strict principle. Three years later an edict was issued to the effect that students contributing a stated amount of rice for relief purposes would be admitted to the Kuo-tzu-chien. The amount was first fixed at eight hundred piculs. Later it was reduced to five hundred and finally to three hundred piculs. The government's action was criticized by certain ministers. One of them wrote to the emperor pointing out that the selling of offices happened only under a deteriorating government. If students who had neither virtue nor qualifications were allowed to enter the Imperial Academy what would be the result when, after a few years, they were appointed to govern? "It would be like sending out wolves and tigers to look after the flocks. How could one prevent them from devouring?" Fortunately, the emperor saw the point and this abuse was discontinued in due time.[2]

We are told that the Chia-ching emperor (1522–1566) was especially strict against abuses in admitting students into the Kuo-tzu-chien. But by the time of the Wan-li reign such abuses were rampant. An eye-witness tells us that not only students but even the illiterate sons of wealthy vulgarians could make their way into the Kuo-tzu-chien, provided they were willing to pay. Once admitted to the Kuo-tzu-chien, these louts were numbered among the intelligentsia. Our eye-witness says that such men occupied two thirds of the places in the academy. From other sources we know that they were counted in great numbers. As rich men they dressed well and were seen frequently on horse-back on their way to restaurants or to the houses of sing-song girls. Even local authorities did not dare to interfere with their lascivious conduct.[3] Since they judged everything by standards of external display, they believed, no doubt, that they were thus winning great honor for themselves and for their families, and this consideration alone must have led many to purchase undeserved academic distinction. The *Tu-pien hsin-shu* 杜騙新書 says that in Chien-ling fu 建寧府, Fukien, there was great enthusiasm for

the buying of academic degrees. It was, he says, a prefecture containing many vain and credulous rich men who were deceived easily
and often.[4]

According to a scholar of the late Ming period, it had become
traditional by his time for those who wanted to compete for the offices
of the Grand Secretariat to spend a great deal of money, for, as a rule,
they had to seek the support of well-to-do people. The same scholar
also tells us that the members of the Han-lin academy were ready to
say quite openly that this man or that had got his office by paying
so many scores of thousands of silver taels. The Grand Secretary
Shen Ch'üeh 沈淮, for instance, had obtained his office principally
through the help of a Mr. Yung of Tung-t'ing 洞庭 who had been
asked to contribute fifty thousand silver taels and had been promised
in return the rank of General of a Brigade 總戎. In addition to this
wealthy backer, dismissed military and civilian officials contributed
by the thousand in the hope that as soon as Shen Ch'üeh had taken
up office they might be restored to their former positions. The practice
of seeking such help became so common that often men renowned for
their integrity did not blush to adopt it.[5]

The profits to be made by selling minor offices proved highly
attractive to members of the government. Titles involving no official
responsibilities were also multiplied so that they might be sold. After
a time the multiplication of unnecessary offices could be noticed
everywhere. In the reign of the founder of the dynasty the number of
civilian and military officials in the empire was under thirty thousand.
By the time of the Ch'eng-te reign, the number had risen to a
hundred thousand. Two hundred and eleven palace guards were
thought sufficient in the Hung-wu period; toward the end of the
16th century there were over one thousand and seven hundred.[6] At
the beginning of the dynasty the creation of offices was ruled by the
needs of each locality, and the number of officials was in proportion
to the size of the locality. All these factors were carefully determined
and carefully considered. Later, these rules were neglected and the
number of officials multiplied to such an extent that many officials
seemed to have no clear idea of their offices. The memorial of Hsü
K'o 徐恪 to the Hung-chih emperor (1488–1505) gives examples of
this. In the seven prefectures of Honan province through which the
Hsin river 沁河 passed, the memorial says, new officials had been
appointed to drain the river and control the floods. Since then the
Yellow River had changed its course and had joined the Hsin river,
causing a flood. From K'ai-feng to Hsü-chou the flood was uncon-
trolled and no one seemed to worry about it. Hsü K'o asked, therefore,

what these supplementary flood-control officials were doing: they seemed to have an abundance of leisure. The coming of an official, he went on, involved the payment of a new salary and the building of one or more official residences, and the people had to pay for his maintenance. New officials brought their families and servants with them, and the servants had their own families. To support such a mob was an intolerable burden on the people.[7]

The sale of offices continued in the Chia-ching reign notwithstanding the emperor's strict prohibition. A contemporary official said that the greatest evil of the time was the corruption of ministers, especially of ministers of minor rank. He was convinced that they were nearly all corrupt—the exceptions amounted to only one or two per cent. Most of them had come to office through bribery. Government positions were sold like goods in the market: those who were willing to pay high usually obtained positions of higher rank; those who paid less had to be satisfied with minor posts. When the government decided to sell offices, he said, it may have had the benevolent intention of raising funds from the well-to-do class instead of levying higher taxes on the poor. It had not foreseen the danger that most of the buyers would be men of no education, whose selfishness would make them a menace to the people.[8]

In the later years of the Wan-li period the machinery of the government was so badly out of gear that no one could doubt that the end of the Ming dynasty was approaching. The emperor himself must be held responsible for a great part of the disorganization. While the selling of minor offices and titles flourished gaily, important offices in the government were left vacant because the emperor would not make the necessary appointments. Toward the end of 1607, the Grand Secretary Yeh Hsiang-kao 葉向高 (1559–1627), reported:

"To-day most of the important government offices are vacant and the situation is most lamentable. There is only one official in each court; some of these have asked for permission to resign on account of sickness, others because of criticism. Only three great officials now remain in office: Li Hua-lung 李化龍, President of the Board of War, Yang Tao-pin 楊道賓, Vice-President of the Board of Ceremonies, and Liu Yüan-lin 劉元霖, Vice-President of the Board of Works. Of these, Tao-pin has asked for leave, and Hua-lung is absent because of his health, so that in the capital one can find hardly a trace of an important official. Moreover, the President of the Board of Revenue, Chao Shih-ch'ing 趙世卿, is in such distress that he seems to have lost his interest in life, solely because he is unable to provide the salaries for the troops on the borders. The Board of Works finds it difficult to supply rewards for the foreigners. Both the Board of War and the Court of Entertainment, owing to lack of resources, have petitioned for leave to borrow from the Boards of Revenue and Works, and in their discouragement, they are beginning to find fault with each other. . . ."[9]

Nor was this an isolated case. Two years later, in 1609, the three Boards of Revenue, Ceremonies and Punishment were left vacant, and when the Grand Secretary sent in a petition to have officials appointed, the petition was pigeon-holed. Shortly afterwards the Wan-li emperor did make an effort to set things to rights, but he went only half way and his remedies were never happy. He often appointed officials of one board to take charge of the affairs of other boards. In 1613, except for the Board of War, there was only one official in each of the boards. The vacancies in the court of censors were left entirely unfilled. Officials of the Board of War were ordered to manage the affairs of the Board of Punishment as well as the affairs of their own Board. Later, the same duplication was imposed on the Board of Civil Office and the court of censors. With all this muddle, the officials could not fulfill their obligations conscientiously; neither their energy nor their experience had fitted them for such tasks. Naturally, this confusion at the top had a disastrous effect on the whole administration. We are told that the trials of prisoners were suspended because of vacancies in the Board of Punishment. Prisoners were left in jail and their families used to gather at the Ch'ang-an Gate 長安門 to claim justice. The situation became so bad that even business in the capital was affected. Even the office of the Grand Secretary, one of the most important, perhaps the most important of government offices, was no better treated than the others. Fang Ts'ung-che 方從哲 found himself the solitary custodian of the office, and when he petitioned for new appointments to fill the vacancies the emperor said that one man was enough. Fang was so discouraged that for forty days he refused to carry out his duties and did not return until after repeated requests from the emperor.[10]

As we have seen, the salaries of the government officials in the Ming dynasty were low. The Hung-wu emperor seems to have recognized that unless his ministers received a "living wage" it would be impossible to expect them to maintain their integrity. Shortly after ascending the throne he gave directions to the prime minister that when a scholar was appointed for the first time to government office it was necessary to cultivate his sense of honor, otherwise no good could be expected from his administration. He laid it down that scholars on their promotion to the governorships of prefectures were to receive ten silver taels and six bolts of cloth each. If the governor of a prefecture was reported to be a man of integrity, he would send a messenger to congratulate and reward him.[11] Unfortunately these wise customs were not observed by the later emperors, who scarcely gave a thought to how their subjects, or even their higher servants, lived. As early as 1432, the Grand Secretary Chang Ying 張瑛 saw that this constituted a serious problem. He petitioned the Hsüan-te emperor to increase the salaries of the officials below the seventh rank both in Nanking and in Peking.[12] Four years later, in the reign of Ying-tsung, it was stated in a report that in the day of the Hung-wu emperor the officials in the capital used to receive their full salaries, but that later, on account of heavy expenditure on construction, the salaries of government officials were often cut so drastically that the lower officials found it difficult to keep alive. The provincial censor of Kiangsi, for instance, who had been appointed to this office shortly after passing the metropolitan examination, had a salary of only a picul and a half of rice monthly. Finding it impossible to support his family on this, he had to borrow over thirty piculs of rice from his colleagues. In view of all this, the Vice-President of the court of censors submitted a petition for an increase of salaries for government officials under the seventh rank in Nanking and Peking.[13]

Towards the end of the 16th century even the tutor of the heir to the throne was treated no better. It had been the tradition of the emperors in the past to honor these tutors with a sumptuous banquet when the day's lectures were over. Moreover, in the past, tutors had normally received frequent presents from their imperial disciples. But in the latter part of the Wan-li period these customs were discontinued, and tutors had to bring their own meals to the palace. One of them described their situation with wry humor:

"When we first passed the licentiate examination, we used to receive fifty to sixty silver taels yearly for teaching boys, and often we also received presents from our pupils. But since becoming tutors to the imperial family we have received only thirty silver taels annually and we have to buy our own meals. Then, every morning throughout the whole year we have to get up at three o'clock and walk several miles to the palace to start lectures at daybreak. Such hardships prove that the life of a licentiate in his early days is far superior to the state he enjoys in his old age. . . . Again, one does not much mind going out on hot summer mornings, when the weather is pleasant, but on harsh winter mornings, when the cold wind is piercing, it is very trying to be on the road. Also, the late emperor's practice of making presents on feast days has been discontinued so that on the feast of tuan-wu 端午 we received not even a fan as a present. Truly, the example His Majesty gives to his heir is very rigorous and very frugal."[14]

The problem of salaries seems to have become still more serious by 1636. In that year, a Supervising Censor of the Board of Civil Offices advised the emperor that, unless adequate salaries were given to the government officials it would be hard to expect them to be honest. Besides, he argued, no matter how low the rank of an official might be, he had to live on a scale corresponding to his dignity and was expected to spend part of his salary in social activities. All this would have required a fitting income such as an official expects to obtain from the government. But the situation had become so bad that some of the officials did not receive their salaries for a whole year and anxiety and complaints were rife in their families. Naturally these officials were discontented with their positions.[15]

OFFICIALS

The early Jesuit missionaries noticed in the government officials a "violent ambition for rule and command", and a great passion for wealth. Père Magaillans describes an interesting interview between Father Ricci and a certain Mandarin:

" . . . This priest [Ricci] spoke to him [the mandarin] of our divine law and of the eternal happiness enjoyed after death by those who had followed it. Leave that out, replied the mandarin, leave aside these illusions. Your glory and your happiness as a stranger, is to reside in this kingdom and in this court. As for me, all my glory and happiness consists in this belt and this mandarin dress, all the rest are but fables and words carried away by the wind; they are things that people relate and that one does not see. What one can see are the governing and commanding of others; they are gold and silver, wives and concubines and a multitude of valets and servants; they are beautiful houses, great wealth, banquets and enjoyment; in a word, property, honor and glory are the consequences of the advantage of being a mandarin."[16]

Père Magaillans had much to say of the corruption of the officials, in whom he saw the image of the corrupt officials in ancient Rome.

Government business, he says, was transacted in terms of money: "All things there are put up for sale."

"If in the judgement of law-suits the mandarins acted in accordance with the law and according to the intention of their prince, China would be one of the happier and better governed among the countries of the world. But as much as they are exact in the observance of exterior formalities—as we said, so much are they hypocritical and cruel in their hearts. Their tricks and deceits are so numerous that one volume would not be enough to explain them. Suffice it here to give some idea and to say that it is quite rare to find a mandarin free from avarice and corruption. They do not consider justice or injustice at all, only who would give them more money or presents. And so be it property, honor or life, these insatiable and sanguinary judges have no regard for them and they dream of nothing more than the satisfaction of their sacrilegious avarice, like ferocious wolves. What we have mentioned up to now applies to all the Six supreme Tribunals. . . ."

What these missionaries witnessed with their own eyes and what they heard from the people, they recorded in their accounts, which were in general quite reliable. Magaillans did not hesitate to conclude that:

"There is no viceroy, visitor of provinces, or other similar official who at the end of three years of their office do not return home with six or seven hundred thousand or sometimes even a million escudos."

That this statement was not exaggerated is confirmed by a scholar, Wang Wen-lu, who lived not long before Magaillans' time. In his writings this man lamented the low morals of government officials in the later part of the Ming dynasty:

"In our days those employed in government service return home loaded with wealth. They fit themselves out with big farms and gardens, and they start constructions of all kinds. Everywhere they have pawn shops[17] and lending houses. They use their authority and influence without restraint. They luxuriate in sumptuous banquets, and even their servants wear silk and clothes of fine quality. . . ."[18]

From the Wan-li reign on, we come across numerous memorials to the throne dealing with the impeachment of the censors. The law of censors in the Ming dynasty was very severe on corrupt censors. Because of the importance of their office, the penalties imposed on them were three times heavier than those imposed on other officials; but corrupt censors who enjoyed the protection of eunuchs were immune from impeachment.[19] In 1583, it was reported to the Wan-li emperor that the censors appointed to visit the provinces used to receive innumerable personal letters with lists of secret recommendations even before their departure from the capital, and that on arrival in their provinces they found their offices already full of letters of recommendation. It is interesting to find Père Magaillans recording the same thing:

"The mandarins who compose the tribunal known as Tu cha yuen [都察院], are visitors or syndics of the court and of the whole empire. Its president is equal in dignity to the presidents of the Six supreme Tribunals. And so he is a mandarin of the second order. Its first assessor is of the third [order], the second is of the fourth [order], All the other mandarins who are in great number and of great authority, are of the seventh order. Their office is to watch continuously at the court and throughout the empire, to enforce the observance of the law and good customs; [to see] that the mandarins exercise their offices with justice and that people perform their duty. They punish light offences in their tribunal and inform the king about more serious ones. Every three years they make a general visitation, sending fourteen Visitors throughout the empire, one to each province. As soon as these Visitors enter their provinces, they become superiors to the viceroys, and to the mandarins, great and small. They try to discipline them with such majesty, authority and severity, that the fear they inspire in the mandarins has given rise to the common proverb among the Chinese: Lao xu kien mao [lao-shu chien mao 老鼠見貓], that is to say, the rat saw the cat. It is natural that they are afraid of them since they have the power to remove them from their office and ruin them. The visit accomplished, they return to the court, each one as a rule bring about more or less four or five hundred thousand escudos with them. These were given to them by the mandarins: those who are guilty give them more for fear that they might be accused before the king. Others give less so that no accusations might be invented against them. Upon their arrival they share the money which they had robbed with the first president and with the assessors. Following immediately they render an account of their visit to them and to the king. Ordinarily, they denounce only those mandarins whose injustice and tyranny are so public that it is impossible to conceal them or those whose virtue or poverty prevent them from making them presents. . . ."[20]

During the T'ien-ch'i reign a Court Censor, the renowned scholar Kao P'an-lung 高攀龍 (1562–1622), tried to impeach Ts'ui Ch'eng-hsiu 崔呈秀, one of the censors appointed to visit the provinces. This case was part of the Tung-lin party campaign against the party of the eunuch Wei Chung-hsien. Kao accused Ts'ui of releasing notorious robbers at a charge of three thousand silver taels per head and local criminals at a thousand silver taels per head. Ts'ui was also accused of having recommended corrupt officials for high offices in return for bribes, and of having ignored the claims of those who really deserved promotion, simply because they had nothing to offer him.[21]

By the time of the Ch'ung-chen emperor's accession, official morals were at such a low ebb that a Supervising Censor of the Board of Revenue could say in a frank report to the monarch:

" . . . Today what place is there that does not depend on the use of money, and what officials are there who do not long for money? And does Your Majesty know why the civil officials must long for money?"[22] Seemingly he was hinting at the lowness of the salaries of civil officials.

From the beginning of his reign, the Ch'ung-chen emperor was well informed about the corruption of the ministers. In the second year of his rule (1629), at an audience with his Grand Secretaries, he told them frankly that the Boards of War and of Civil Office were guilty of many abuses in the appointment of ministers. There was always, he said, bribery, before anyone was appointed to office. Hence before nomination poor candidates had to seek loans from their friends. Later when they had been appointed to an office, they had to busy themselves with paying back these loans. But how, the emperor asked, were they to pay back these loans, if not with money exacted from the people? In such circumstances, how could there be really good officials who loved their people? The emperor therefore exhorted his ministers to help in cleaning up these abuses by fulfilling their duties conscientiously, and to hold to principle rather than listen to the persuasions of others.[23]

The emperor's sage admonition came too late to produce satisfactory results. Even the Grand Secretaries were no freer than other officials from the taint of bribery. When Hsüeh Kuo-kuan 薛國觀 was dismissed from this office it was said that he had many cart-loads of belongings, most of which he had received from other officials in the form of bribes. Another Grand Secretary, Ch'en Yen 陳演, resigned shortly before the rebels approached Peking, with the intention of getting out of the city before the siege; but so cumbrous was his luggage, which consisted chiefly of things received as bribes, that he was not able to leave in time. When the rebels took the capital, Ch'en Yen was arrested and all his possessions were confiscated. Not long afterwards he was killed by the rebels.[24]

In discussing the causes of the fall of the Ming dynasty, Chao I blamed the empty talk of the scholars. In their early days, he says, the Manchus had no intention of conquering China. Had the Ch'ung-chen emperor made peace with them, he could have concentrated his army on suppressing the rebels instead of having to fight both Manchus and rebels. Chao tried to show that on several occasions the emperor seriously considered making peace with the Manchus, but gave up the attempt because of the opposition of scholars, who knew very little about the gravity of the situation.[25] Towards the end of the Ming dynasty there was, beyond all doubt, a spirit of hypocrisy among the government officials. Chang Chü-cheng, Grand Secretary from 1567 to 1582, had already noticed this defect creeping into the government. For years, he said, there had been much theorizing and little practical work in government affairs. Officials, on taking charge of a place, forthwith presented to the throne memorials discussing diverse problems and made many changes among lower officials. Their memorials were written in a flowery style that charmed many readers. Frequently, without further examination of the merits of the case, these readers would jump to the conclusion that the authors of the memorials must be talented officials, conscientious in the performance of their duties. Chang disapproved of such unfounded approbation and pointed out that, in reality, these officials had no original ideas of their own. They were new to their offices, and the localities of which they had charge were still unfamiliar to them, hence whatever they had to say was based on hearsay. Their eloquent writings left only vague impressions in the minds of their readers. In general they made not the slightest attempt to carry out what they had suggested; if they did here and there attempt action the results were never happy. When one of them proposed something, the others might agree for a time, but soon they were at variance. Finally, Chang stressed the importance of the spirit of simplicity and sincerity, which, he said, might help to restore the morale of the government.[26]

Toward the end of the dynasty, government offices became so commercialized that their primary purpose seemed to be to serve as milch cows for the officials. Many of these officials were so ignorant that they did not even know court etiquette. We are told that on the day of the T'ien-ch'i emperor's accession the ceremonies were all confusion because the master of ceremonies had no exact knowledge of what was to be done.[27] The Wan-li emperor's almost complete refusal to grant audiences to his ministers in his last years may have been responsible for this ignorance. Then too, the destruction of the three palaces by fire in 1597 cut down still further the opportunities for court functions. Nevertheless, the court officials cannot easily be excused for their ignorance of etiquette, for they were under obligation to understand their duties and all things connected with them.

Among the government officials of the time there was a very strong 'do nothing' spirit which is summed up in a familiar Chinese saying: 多一事不如少一事, "It is better to have one less problem than to have one more." Glaring problems were studiously ignored because officials had neither the energy nor the courage to face them. We are told that in 1635, in the northern provinces, the negligence of higher officials who should have prepared to fight against the rebels was such that no resistance at all was put up. As soon as the rebels had left Shensi for Shansi, the officials of Shensi immediately claimed victory as if they had driven them out. When the rebels left Shansi for Honan, the officials of Shansi copied the example of their colleagues in Shensi. When the rebels approached Honan, the governor was taken unawares and many districts fell into rebel hands.[28]

In the first year of the Ch'ung-chen reign (1628), there was rebel agitation everywhere. It was a most critical moment, one which demanded full cooperation between all government officials if the empire was to be saved. Had they been more conscientious in their duties, they might have snuffed out the revolt at the very beginning; but the 'do-nothing' spirit now dominant among the officials gave the rebels the chance they needed to consolidate their power. Toward the end of 1628, the bandits of Shensi, joined by deserting soldiers in the province, were doing great damage in neighboring districts. When this was reported to the dignitary who was both censor and governor of the province of Shensi, that asinine old gentleman ordered the reporter to be flogged for giving a false alarm and insisted that the alleged bandits were no more than hungry civilians who had turned to robbery because they had no food. His plan was to let them alone until the return of spring, when he was sure that they would all go back to work on their farms. His wishful dreams did not come true. The number of bandits gradually increased to over five thousand.[29]

Certain timid officials were loath to resort to violence and cherished the hope that the bandits could be won back to submission by kind persuasion. The most famous of these was Yang Ho 楊鶴, governor of Shensi, who sent agents to persuade the bandits to return to their homes, promising them safe conducts. The bandits, whose power was still weak, thought it prudent to yield to the suasions of the governor. Under the protection of the authorities they gave up burning houses and killing, but they kept on robbing from the people, who, seeing tacit consent in the silence of the authorities, dared not complain.[30]

Other officials were reluctant to report the troubles they were having with the bandits lest they themselves might be held responsible and in consequence be punished. They preferred therefore to settle everything quietly whenever possible. In 1636, when the city of Hsiang-yang 襄陽 was besieged by the rebels, the unhappy governor did not know what to do. One day a friendly message arrived from one of the rebel leaders. This aroused in the governor joyful thoughts of negotiating peace. He, therefore, sent two officers to escort the leader of the rebels to his office where a banquet was given in his honor. The celebration was protracted cheerfully and hopefully, till a late hour, but no sooner had the bandits left the city than they again devoted themselves earnestly to arson and pillage.[31]

Still, other officials thought that they would have fulfilled their obligations if they could safeguard the cities committed to their care. Hence, instead of taking the offensive, they chose to shut themselves up in the cities and guard them with heavy forces, leaving the rebels to do what they pleased outside the cities. The rebels naturally made use of the opportunity thus presented to consolidate their power in the countryside, after which they sought to weaken the resistance of the cities by cutting them off from supplies and external support. Once this was accomplished, all they had to do was to wait until disaffection had sprung up among the people of the cities. Then they struck. Usually this method proved highly effective.[32]

In 1628, at an audience with the Ch'ung-chen emperor, the Vice-President of the Board of War pointed out that, after two centuries of peace in the empire, the people commonly esteemed a civil career more highly than a military one. Even people from the borders felt greatly honored when they passed the licentiate examination, but very few valued the ranks of ch'ien-hu 千戶 and pai-hu 百戶 in the tribal government.[33] Higher officials, whose duty it was to maintain full communication with military men at the borders of the empire, were content to take charge of internal affairs only.

Hsia Yün-i 夏允彝 (1596–1645) blamed the higher government officials for the weakness of Chinese policy on the Manchurian border: "In the days when Chang Chü-cheng was at the head of the government, he was thoroughly familiar with military affairs on the borders", he said. "If a barbarian leader sent an agent to watch a certain place or to invade a certain portion of the border, Chang always found out beforehand, and was thus able to warn his officials on the border and they all used to follow his directions clearly. But since Chang there have been very few to compare with him. A certain governor of the border once told me that the Grand Secretary Yeh T'ai-shan 葉臺山 (i.e. Yeh Hsiang-kao 葉向高 1559–1627) was a man hard to equal. Whenever the officials from the borders wrote to him, he always answered them in his own hand. Those who came after him, however, used to answer by merely sending a card. Without co-operation between the officials in the central government and those far away on the borders, how could we expect to succeed? Still, this was not too bad. But when Chou Yi-hsing 周宜興 (i.e. Chou Yen-ju 周延儒) was head of the government, having once been accused of illegally supporting an official at the border, he answered the accusation by asserting emphatically that he never had any correspondence at all with officials of the borders. This assertion was equivalent to saying that the affairs of the borders had nothing to do with the office of the Grand Secretary. No wonder he later ended his career in disgrace. . . ."[34]

There were, on the other hand, officials who, though utterly ignorant of tactics, interfered with military matters. This was the fault of the Ch'ung-chen emperor, who often appointed civil officials to take charge of military affairs. These officials frequently hindered the free operation of military men and very often spoiled their plans. A year before the fall of the dynasty (1643), the governor of a certain district pointed out to the emperor that the ministers in charge of military affairs were boastful scholars who might have heard or read something about the art of war, but had never served in the army. Often, when they had to appear at the frontier they lost their nerve. Yet they were given full authority, even the military officers being subject to them. Such interference often led to the defeat of the armies.[35]

This is well exemplified by the case of Yang Ssu-ch'ang 楊嗣昌, a son of Yang Ho, of whom we have given an account in some detail. He had been attached to some military forces in his early days, but his knowledge of soldiering was very limited. Largely by luck, he eventually came to hold the office of Grand Secretary during the last years of the Ch'ung-chen reign. When the revolts that were to end the dynasty were breaking out everywhere, he offered to fight in person against the rebels and was given full command of the army.

We are told that he was vain and stubborn, inclined to be a trifler, and lacking in vision. Even while directing a campaign in the provinces he would organize excursions and spend most of his time with his friends feasting and writing poems. As a devout Buddhist and a great believer in geomancy, he was fond of visiting temples, mountains and hills, and he is said to have claimed that the fourth chapter of the Avataṁsaka-sutra 華嚴經 had a miraculous power of killing locusts in the fields and preventing drought. When directing operations he always wished to exercise full control of everything, with the result that strategic opportunities were often lost. Officers in the field were powerless to give final orders, and time was consumed in waiting for Yang's directions. Many of the court officials were disgusted by his self-important ineptitude, and in 1641, he was impeached by the supervising censor of the Board of Revenue. The accusations were that he had dissipated over three hundred thousand silver taels during his two years of command without result, that he had so neglected his duty of protecting the imperial clansmen that some of them had fallen into the hands of the rebels and been killed by them, and that he had retained the best troops around him to ensure his personal safety. The imperial decision, however, was given in favor of Yang and he continued to enjoy the protection of the emperor until the spring of 1641, when he ended his own life.[36]

Some officials were loyal servants of the emperor, men of unquestionable integrity who would have died rather than disgrace the empire. On the fall of the dynasty, many of these ended their own lives rather than surrender to their enemies. Yet even these men seem to have been moral cowards rather than heroes. An eye-witness wrote in 1643 that the officials at court were trying to deceive each other by ignoring the seriousness of the situation. The Ministers of the Board of War, who should have been making positive preparations to fight against the rebels, quieted their consciences by saying that they would be loyal to the empire, even to the point of sacrificing their own lives. The same eye-witness tells us that this attitude persisted among the officials until the end of the dynasty.[37] The P'ing-k'ou chih contains a typical example of this odd mixture of heroism and poltroonery. In 1634, the rebels besieged the district of Ch'ung-te 崇德 in Kansu Province. The state of the fortifications was no credit to the governor. Prolonged rain sufficed to crumble the city wall and the rebels were able to break in without much difficulty. Yet when they came to the discredited governor's office they found him in the hall defiantly arrayed in his all-red uniform. They pushed him from the platform and tried to make him kneel, but he shouted at them, "You dogs, how dare you insult the legitimate representative of the empire." The rebels then threatened him with their knives, but he only redoubled the violence of his reproaches. In the end, they dragged him outside the city and there quartered him.[38]

Such officials, with their slavish and unprofitable loyalty to the emperor, aroused the contemptuous loathing of the scholar Huang Tsung-hsi, who believed that they had completely misinterpreted the duties of a true government official. The officials, he said, had been enlisted to help the emperor in governing the country, a task which he could not carry out single-handed. They were obliged therefore not only to the service of the emperor but also to the promotion of the good of the people. His contemporaries seemed to have missed this point, regarding the people as the private possession of the emperor and themselves as responsible solely to the emperor. Their interest in the welfare of the people was in inverse proportion to their interest in the emperor. They knew only one thing: that they must live or die for their lord. In this Huang saw nothing but folly: the officials had made themselves slaves of the emperor, and an arbitrary monarch could take advantage of this lop-sided devotion to serve his own selfish purpose.[39]

If it is asked who was the first arbitrary Ming monarch to enslave his ministers, we may, perhaps, fairly reply that it was the founder of the dynasty!

SUB-OFFICIALS

In spite of the vigilance of the Hung-wu emperor the sub-officials of even the early Ming period seem to have been no better than those of the Yüan period. In 1410, when the Yung-lo emperor forbade the employment of sub-officials as censors, he gave the reason that sub-officials were devoted to self rather than to justice and tended to be severe rather than conciliatory. To employ such men as censors would lessen the dignity of the Court.[40]

A witness of the Chia-ching reign describes sub-officials as crafty and always ready to spread slander. Since their number was great the rumors they started spread far, and easily found credence. Some of the government departments in Nanking used them as spies and it became a popular saying that any minister who succeeded in having a sub-official punished by beating should be considered heroic. Unfortunately this proof of ministerial courage was not given over a period of several score of years.[41]

As the end of Ming dynasty approached, corruption increased among the sub-officials. Every scoundrel who could keep accounts and knew how to deal with superiors and the people, sought a post in the land-tax office and within a few years left that office, loaded with wealth. Their next move was to visit the capital and try to secure some official rank by offering a substantial sum of money. A contemporary writer testified that men whose reputation in their native place was bad were often found by those who met them in the capital to have changed suddenly into men of high dignity. As sub-officials they had extorted money from the people of their native place: now, having obtained rank in the capital, they wished to keep away from their fellow-countrymen lest they be prosecuted for what they had done.[42]

In 1641, three years before the fall of the dynasty, the Duke of Feng-ch'eng 豐城 wrote to the emperor:

"In spite of the institution of the *Fu-i ch'üan-shu* 賦役全書 or complete record of land-taxes and *corvée*, the accounts frequently seem to be in a state of confusion. Why is this? Half of the fraud in Chekiang and Chih-li has been caused by the sub-officials. The people are made to pay taxes year after year—a little shortage in their payment and they are not spared a beating. But the sub-officials are left to rob the people unchecked. Exemption from land-taxes is sometimes announced, but the people do not benefit by it; it serves only to provide a gratifying income for sub-officials. In spite of the penalties imposed by the Ministry of Finance and the vigilance of the administrators, these abuses persist and the items of taxes are so numerous that it is not easy to check everything thoroughly. In addition to the t'iao-pien 條鞭 taxes, there is also the tax levied for the upkeep of the soldiers in Liao-tung. And, in addition to this, there is a third tax for the training of new soldiers. Then, provincial expenses of many kinds are met from the land-taxes. Orders come from one authority after another and the sub-officials benefit greatly by the system from which they make their living. But, how much can the farms produce? Though the people work hard throughout the year, what they get is not enough to enable them to pay the taxes; yet they are expected to spare no energy to satisfy the sub-officials and their insatiable desires. The poor are made to suffer physically while the rich feel that the properties they own are merely a burden to themselves."[43]

Within the government the sub-officials with their wide experience could usually do as they pleased without fear of discovery. Thus, permanent deposits in public treasuries often tempted their cupidity. Sometimes they would steal from them or use some of the funds to start a business. If officials were sent to inspect the accounts, the sub-officials were shrewd enough to be able to throw dust in their eyes. As soon as the unwelcome inspectors had left they returned without difficulty to their old practice.[44]

They were as audacious in their contacts with their superiors as in their dealings with the ordinary people. Since the government officials were usually strangers from other places whose office did not last for more than a few years, the sub-officials had well founded confidence that with their superior knowledge of local affairs they could easily deceive any superior.

Relying on these advantages they often took into their own hands the transaction of government affairs. The author of the *San-yüan pi-chi* 三垣筆記 in one of his books gives an instance of this from his own experience:

"Shortly after I assumed office (in the Board of Punishment) a sub-official came to me one day with a book for my signature. I inquired what it was about. Another sub-official who stood by answered that this was the *Book of History*. In it were collected all the memorials from the Board of Punishment which were to be sent to the Han-lin Academy for the eventual compilation of the Shih-lu 實錄 (Veritable Records). I took the book to examine it and found that the original documents had been altered and added to. I asked the sub-official who handed me the book who was the author of these corrections and additions to the original documents. He looked at me in amazement, not knowing what to reply. The other sub-official having informed me that the man was deaf, I moved near him and shouted a few times into his ears. He then began to nod and said, 'Your humble servant is the author of all these.' I was astonished and said [to myself], 'What does he know [about correcting documents]?' It would be bad enough if he had corrected less important documents: but what if he had omitted [that which was important]! I therefore gave orders that I wished for the future to reserve to myself the task of copying and sending out these documents. Not long afterward, however, I went into exile on account of my outspokenness, and I am afraid that the sub-officials may have taken up their old practice once more."[45]

Because of the influence of the sub-officials, the local gentry who wished to evade taxes often bribed them.[46] Criminals frequently tried to seek their favor in order to regain freedom, and innocent people had to give them presents lest they be involved in court prosecutions.

In a word, the sub-officials had dealings with all classes of men, and often they inspired fear in the common people. Sometimes they even became intimate friends of bandits, as may be seen from a case reported in a recently published half-destroyed official document, dated 1640. This document, which exposes the negligence of a certain governor, points out the strange fact that wherever this governor went the districts he governed always seemed to become infested with bandits. The sub-officials were responsible for this, the document says. They were intimate friends of the outlaws and in order to secure full protection for these friends managed to deceive their incompetent superior. Having accomplished this easy task, they set free notorious leaders of the bandits and involved innocent people in crimes.[47]

The close organization that existed among the sub-officials helped, no doubt, to increase their audacity. Spread as they were through all government departments, they bound themselves together and acted with great uniformity, conspiring always for their own good. A writer of the late Ming period did not hesitate to declare them to be worse than the Manchus. The Manchus, he said, threatened from outside and it was not difficult to see their injustices. The menace of the sub-officials was hidden but it had spread through the whole empire and no one dared to complain against them. They started as insignificant clerks but because government officials had to depend on them for information, they eventually became so independent that they almost aspired to dominate the affairs of the government offices. If one of them chanced to be dismissed, he returned in a short time under a false name and continued his iniquities.[48] In an edict of the Shun-chih 順治 emperor (1644–1661), the first Manchu emperor to rule China, dated 1658, we read:

"The abuses of sub-officials have existed from time immemorial. Their craftiness and deceitfulness of character have been an enigma to many. The sub-officials of the Board of Civil Offices, in particular, are very wily. They have not only fostered corruption among the four divisions of the Board of Civil Office but have even linked up with the clerks of other Boards. They exchange among themselves all the incoming and outgoing documents, and thus prepare the way for their conspiracies. They try to conceal all these from outsiders so that they may be able to do what they please for their own profit. If perchance they are discovered, they produce ingenious skilful excuses by which they try to unload their responsibilities on one another. The result is that, even if they are impeached, it is not easy to cut off the sources of their abuses. . . ."[49]

This bad tradition existed throughout the Ch'ing dynasty and we frequently read in the *Tung-hua-lu* 東華錄 edicts by different emperors severely reprehending the abuses of the sub-officials.[50]

That the office of sub-officials was a very profitable one is evident from contemporary witnesses. Wu Ying-chi says that, whereas formerly it had cost only some tens of silver taels to buy this office from a sub-official, in his day the price had gone up to several hundred. His comment was that if so many people were willing to pay so much money for this office they must all have expected still more money in return. Some of these purchasers, as soon as they bought their offices, at once began to look around for fertile fields and comfortable houses. Their clothes were those of the rich and they were surrounded by servants. Where then, he asked, did they obtain the money? Was it not from the people?[51] Huang Tsung-hsi says that in the capital the more important sub-official offices were sold at several thousand silver taels each. Once bought, these offices were often retained in the family, passing from father to son and from brother to brother.[52]

Wu Ying-chi also tells us that many officials were dismissed from office because of compromising relations with dishonest sub-officials. The trouble often sprang from a corrupt sub-official's determination to win the good will of his superiors. If such a man had charge of government stores or some other offices giving him power over government property, he would gaily raid the public domain to make presents to the appropriate official. Once these presents had been accepted, the official was in the power of the sub-official and was no longer free to take action even if he surprised the sub-official in open corruption.[53]

The abuses of sub-officials persisted throughout the whole Ming period. The sub-officials have been compared by historians to millions of tigers and wolves kept among the people for their destruction. They have been blamed for the ruin of the country.[54] According to Ku Yen-wu the sub-officials employed in a single district often numbered several thousand. Not infrequently six or seven of them held the same office. It is hard to see how they could have earned a living if they did not try to create work for themselves.[55]

All through the Ch'ing dynasty the district of Shao-hsing of Chekiang Province was famous for the number of sub-officials it spewed all over the empire. This specialized fecundity had already attracted notice in the days of the Ming dynasty. The philosopher Ch'en Lung-cheng 陳龍正 (circa 1630), writing on the occasion of the appointment of his friend to the post of Governor of Shao-hsing,

earnestly exhorted him to do all he could to induce good behavior
in the elders of this district who were the fathers and elder brothers
of innumerable sub-officials spread throughout the country. Being a
philosopher he reasoned logically: good or bad government depended
solely on the Six Boards, and since the sub-officials were variously
employed in the Six Boards, they undoubtedly had great influence
in the government. But most of the sub-officials came from Shao-
hsing. Hence, Ch'en thought, by influencing the elders of that place
for good it should be possible to provide the government with good
sub-officials.[56] Ch'en, no doubt, exaggerated the importance of
Shao-hsing, but he could scarcely exaggerate the importance of good
sub-officials to good government.

IMPERIAL RELATIVES

Even when the empire was in rapid decline, the imperial relatives
in general seem to have shown no concern for the increasing difficulties of the government.

The last years of the Ch'ung-chen period witnessed the emperor's
desperate effort to save the empire from the Manchus and the rebels.
The treasuries of the empire being nearly exhausted, the levying of
taxes became more frequent; but the imperial clansmen, heedless of
the needs of the time and of the places where they dwelt, continued
to demand their due. In present Hunan their pension, formerly
eighty-thousand taels yearly, had increased to a hundred and fifty
thousand taels. The raids of the rebels had made the collection of
taxes impossible in many parts of the province, but the governor did
his best and succeeded in scraping together forty to fifty thousand
taels for them. This did not please the imperial clansmen. They
insisted on the full amount, which, they said, was theirs by right. The
treasurer of the province tried to explain the difficult circumstances:
he was subjected to intolerable infamy. The imperial clansmen
abused him in the most insulting language and tore his uniform to
shreds.[57] When the arch-rebel Chang Hsien-chung came to attack
the city of Wu-ch'ang there was very little left in the treasury to
support the army. Someone suggested that Prince Ch'u 楚王, who
had a million silver taels in cash, might perhaps at this critical hour
be willing to give some of his money for the good of the public, and
indeed for his own protection. He was, therefore, urged to lend his
money to the government for the defence of the city. The selfish and
senseless prince refused to listen and within less than a month the
rebels had taken the city, and many of the imperial clansmen in

present Hupei province went over to the rebels. Prince Ch'u was captured. The rebels sacked his palace and took away the million silver taels in hundreds of cartloads. Finally they took the Prince himself in a sedan chair and drowned him in a lake.[58] The historian who recounted this tells us that the people of present Hupei pitied the folly of Prince Ch'u. Perhaps insanity is a better word than folly to describe the behavior of Prince Ch'u, who, even if he could not read the signs of the times, should have been taught by the fate suffered by Prince Fu in Honan province only two years earlier.

The notorious Prince Fu scarcely needs description. According to a contemporary scholar, the Wan-li emperor had bequeathed him his treasures and whatever he had squeezed from the people under pretext of mining and commercial taxes, and he was considered the richest man of his time. In 1614, when he left the capital to take up residence in Honan, it was said that over one thousand two hundred boats were needed to carry his belongings.[59] In 1641, there was a famine in Honan. It became so serious that cannibalism was repeatedly reported but the avaricious prince ignored the sufferings of the people. At about the same time some troop reinforcements passed through Lo-yang; again the prince made no effort to help, an omission that caused a great deal of resentment among the soldiers. A gentleman of the city, aware of the tension, advised the prince to be more considerate and tactful, but failed to convince him. Not long afterwards a group of rebel soldiers from Shensi came through Lo-yang and the governor of the province secured their aid for the defence of the city. When this was reported to the court, the emperor ordered the arrest of the chief culprits among the rebellious soldiers. News of the emperor's order naturally threw the whole group into a state of panic. Meanwhile Prince Fu had contributed three thousand silver taels to give a feast to the soldiers (an uncharacteristic act of generosity, the motive of which does not concern us here); but the brigade general hid the money. The fears of the soldiers turned to rage and they decided to join the rebels, who were then under the leadership of Li Tzu-ch'eng. As the rebels approached Lo-yang, the soldiers offered to be their spies and the city fell after a siege of only one night. Prince Fu was captured by the rebels and was killed by them and his palace was consumed by fire.[60]

Early in 1641, an episode of a very different character was enacted in the city of K'ai-feng. This city was besieged by Li Tzu-ch'eng with a strong force. Prince Chou 周王 who, unlike Prince Ch'u and Prince Fu, was a man of sense, saw the danger that threatened him and his people. He thereupon generously contributed five hundred thousand silver taels to be used as rewards for brave citizens who defended the city. Fifty silver taels was the reward for anyone who killed a rebel. The families of those who were fatally wounded or killed on the battlefield were to receive a reward of fifty silver taels. The less seriously wounded were to receive twenty-five silver taels. This generous aid kept up the morale of the people and, we are told, both the civilians and soldiers showed great bravery in the fight against the rebels. A few victories were won and the rebels were forced to retire.

In the following year the rebels once more approached the gate of the city. By this time, Prince Chou had spent over one million taels on the defence of the city: his treasury was nearly exhausted and food was becoming scarce. Towards the end of the siege rice was sold at the price of pearls. The troops had to be supported by rich farmers. The well-to-do and the city elders bought all the grain they could find and willingly paid fabulous prices for it—as much as ten thousand coins a pint. In spite of all difficulties the city held out for nearly nine months before falling into the hands of the enemy. The credit for this brilliant defence was due to Prince Chou and his brave people.[61] The brave response to Prince Chou's courageous leadership is significant of what might have been if all the imperial clansmen had shown a like spirit of cooperation with the people and the government officials; they might well have saved the country from the destruction at the hands of the rebels. Even at this late hour, imperial leadership still meant much. Unfortunately nearly all of the imperial clansmen were selfish exploiters who hastened the fall of the empire which their ancestors had founded.

The Ming dynasty had the good fortune to be little troubled by empresses or their relatives. Very few of these tried to interfere in political affairs. The faults they had generally sprang from greed, wherein they were no different from hordes of imperial clansmen. Many of empresses came from middle-class families, which found it hard to restrain their desire for gain when their relatives were suddenly elevated to the highest rank. Duke Chou K'uei 周奎, father-in-law of the Ch'ung-chen emperor, and a few other relatives of the empress were especially notorious for avarice. They were known to be usurers who always demanded high rates of interest for their loans and did not scruple to seize farms from their debtors, and sometimes even kidnapped the children of the poor. In 1638, complaints reached the ears of the emperor. Accordingly he wrote to warn them of their abuses:

You who are related to the imperial family have the privilege of enjoying our favors. Take care to cultivate virtue and learn to be frugal that you may preserve your good name. If you show contempt for good behavior and take advantage of the people you will incur the anger of heaven and the hatred of the world. It is vain to beat one's breast, when it is already too late to repent. . . .[62]

The emperor frequently issued warnings which did not please the relatives of the empress. When the fifth son of the monarch fell seriously ill a rumor was spread that the prince had claimed to have had a vision in which the goddess Chiu-lien P'u-sa 九連菩薩[63] had uttered reproaches against the emperor for having ill-treated the empress's relatives, predicting that if he did not make amends all his sons would die young. When this was reported to the emperor he was greatly frightened. The historian who relates this says that the whole story was concocted by the eunuchs to frighten the emperor, who had never been to the room of the sick prince. The motive of this plot was to save the Marquis Wu-ch'ing 武清侯, brother of the empress, whom the emperor had ordered to be degraded and all of whose treasures were to be confiscated. The plot succeeded. The terrified emperor pardoned the Marquis.[64]

Duke Chou K'uei, i.e. the Ch'ung Chen emperor's father-in-law, was known as one of the richest of the empress's relatives. In the last days of the Ming dynasty, when the imperial treasuries were almost exhausted, the Ch'ung-chen emperor made a great effort to raise funds in a final attempt to defend the city against the rebels. All the government officials and even the eunuchs were asked to contribute as generously as their means allowed. A eunuch was sent to Duke Chou to plead this noble cause, but the avaricious Duke excused himself, saying that he had nothing to give. The eunuch renewed his plea with tears, but in vain. Convinced at last of the hard-heartedness of the Duke, he could not restrain his anger. Turning to him, he said sternly, "what more hope is there for the empire if even the relatives of the emperor behave like this?" Not long after Duke Chou sent word to the emperor that he was willing to contribute ten thousand silver taels. The emperor, however, tried to persuade him to contribute twenty thousand. The Duke wrote secretly to the empress for help and she, finding it hard to refuse her father, sent him five thousand silver taels. At the sight of this windfall the covetous Duke put two thousand taels from the empress's gift into his pocket and sent only three thousand to the emperor. He was not to enjoy his augmented fortune for long. The city quickly fell to the rebels and all his possessions were seized—fifty-two thousand silver taels in cash, it was said, and a collection of valuables estimated to be worth some hundreds of thousands. The rebels, however, were not satisfied even with this enormous haul for they suspected that he had hidden part of his fortune. He was cast into prison, where they tried by cruel torture to force him to disgorge. Overcome by the tortures he soon died.[65]

MORALITY AND RELIGION

The later half of the Ming dynasty saw a decline of morality among the people. In the days of the Hung-wu reign the emperor himself set an example of frugality, and all extravagance was abhorrent to him. His successors were utterly unlike him in this as in so many other respects, and the ever-growing luxury of their lives naturally influenced their subjects. Furthermore, the prosperity produced by the progress of commerce and industry led the noble and well-to-do classes to live sumptuously. The ordinary people aped their betters, disregarding the customs and traditions of their own state of life. "Wherever there is a second-hand clothes store", wrote a contemporary, "immediately the streets are full of men wearing silk. One can hardly distinguish the poor from the rich."[66] The scholar Li Pang-hua (1574–1644) says that civilians of the capital were outstanding in extravagance of life and often lived beyond the standard of their state of life. In weddings and funerals, he says, they sought to excel all comers in sumptuousness, and in their banquets they exceeded all limits. Prostitutes and actors mixed with the ordinary people. Buddhist priests did not avoid meeting members of the opposite sex who visited the temples. Gold and pearls had become the head ornaments of the poor, and the wives of ordinary civilians were found wearing the clothes of nobles. The morals of his time, he ends, had fallen low.[67]

The morals of the people were no better in the provinces than in the capital. We are told that in Chekiang in the time of the Wan-li emperor, men going to a funeral would bring with them women of dubious character and they would sing and dance to the funeral music. They did not even blush to induce mourners in mourning clothes to drink toasts with them. Others would get married even immediately after their father or mother had died. Scholars who could find no suitable opening for their talents became Buddhist priests or disguised themselves as hermits and went around beguiling people with their unorthodox doctrines. Even government officials and men of high society were attracted by this novelty and tried to make friends with these learned mountebanks. Chekiang must have been prosperous in those days, judging from the way in which people were able to spend money on amusements and superfluities. The same author tells us that actors were to be found everywhere. Many of these were natives of Ch'ing-yang 青陽 from which over ten thousand actors had spread out to perform plays in other provinces. Craftsmen went in for the production of curiosities knowing that these were the best source of profit. A fancy fan would sell for three silver taels.[68]

In Ch'ao-chou 潮州, Kuangtung province, gambling became very popular. The craze was started by a few important families in the Lung-ch'ing and Wan-li periods. It spread rapidly, for the value of copper coins was then fluctuating so violently that they were of little use in commerce and many people began to gamble largely because the coins were useful for nothing else. When Kuo Tzu-chang 郭子章 was governor of Ch'ao-chou, gambling had become so common that it was spreading from the market places to private houses. Gambling led to theft and robbery. Steps were then taken by the authorities to put down gambling but this proved a formidable task. As Kuo puts it, it was not difficult to deal with the common people, but the influential families, who were the main sources of all the trouble, were so powerful that even government officials dared not touch them and they were left alone to do what they pleased.[69]

Superstition was no doubt common throughout the Ming period but it became more obtrusive towards the end of the dynasty. Calamities of all kinds, natural and man-made, occurred everywhere. In their despair, the poor turned to the practices of superstition. Unscrupulous cheats were quick to see how to turn this popular weakness to their own advantage. Secret societies were organized under the pretext of public worship. Big crowds were to be seen everywhere beating gongs and chanting prayers. Charms were sold to the people and the secrets of the future were theirs, for a price. By the time the authorities noticed this danger it was too late to combat it, and it proved difficult to keep the mobs under control.[70]

The White Lotus sect, a perverted form of Buddhism which had flourished and done much harm in the Yüan period, seems to have resumed its activity from the Chia-ching period onward. About the year 1550, they were stirring up trouble along the Mongol border and they even attempted to stop the Mongols from making peace with the Chinese government, fearing that peace might work to their disadvantage. In 1564, they were active in the capital and Honan. Two years later they were so strong in the capital that an order was issued by the emperor to the governor of the capital to forbid Buddhist priests and nuns to preach in public, and the censors were told to search all the monasteries, both in the capital and outside it, for undesirable characters.[71] Under the Wan-li emperor in 1578, sixty-four rebels of the White Lotus sect were arrested and executed by Hsü Hsüeh-mu 徐學謨, then governor of the Yün-yang prefecture. In 1598, a censor reported danger from the sect, which, he said, had shown signs of restlessness. A government official at about the same period reported that the people of the eastern provinces were easily seduced to false religions. They refused to honor their parents, and did not venerate the deities. They met at night in mixed congregations of men and women and separated in the morning. They were everywhere, and were under the command of leaders who boldly predicted the future of their members and, rather than have their predictions proven false, were ready to sacrifice their own lives. This sect and others spread all over the empire.[72]

The year 1622 saw the uprising of Hsü Hung-ju 徐鴻儒 in Shantung. His followers numbered over one hundred thousand and we are told that the people worshipped him as a god and were willing to die for him. When he wanted to make a collection an order was given and all contributed with great enthusiasm. "Unlike the collection of taxes which they are reluctant to yield even to force," said a contemporary historian. "Important as is one's own life, he (Hsü Hung-ju) was able to make them regard it as something of no value. Desirable as are one's own possessions, he succeeded in persuading them to give them up without regrets. There is only one thing the ignorant people are looking for, and that is the promised power and riches!"[73]

Another reason why the religious spirit deteriorated so rapidly was because the monks whose duty it was to teach the people were too worldly. Riches and comfort can lead even a monk to forget his state of life, and the early emperors of the dynasty were vigilant and quick to check any abuses arising from such causes. In 1401, an edict was issued by the Chien-wen emperor to the Board of Ceremonies concerning the Buddhist monks. The emperor expressed his disappointment with the religious observance of the Buddhist monks who, having gained possession of a great deal of land, had forgotten their duty as monks. "When they come to possess an abundance of riches they will no doubt attract the attention of the authorities and in consequence will be molested by them. Furthermore, riches often becomes a temptation to them and brings them into disgrace, nay, even to violation of the law. When this happens not only do they

disgrace themselves but the religion they profess will suffer. . . ."
Accordingly their possession of land was greatly curtailed.[74]

Their insatiable desire for temporal goods caused the monks to
quarrel among themselves: there is abundant material on this point
in the history of the Ming dynasty. Such quarrels occurred in such
remote provinces as Yünnan (which was not fully developed in the
Ming dynasty) and much more in the wealthy cities.[75] Shen Te-fu
沈德符 (1578–1642) tells us that in Nanking and Peking whenever a
vacancy for abbotship of a monastery occurred, examinations were
held for a suitable candidate. The candidates came together and
wrote essays after the style of the "eight-legged essays", often in
flowery language, though the themes were taken from Buddhist
scriptures. They tried to imitate in all details the examinations for
government officials, which seemed to Shen ridiculous.[76] This
examination fever illustrates the immersion of the monks' hearts in
worldly affairs. Indeed, Hsieh Chao-che says that the monks of
Fen-yang drank wine, ate meat and married wives like any civilian
of the time. The only difference was that the monks were exempted
from *corvée*. The same things, he says, were happening in other parts
of the empire. Sometimes in a monastery of several hundred monks
only the door-keeper shaved his head in the manner of a Buddhist
monk; the rest kept their long hair so that they might visit government offices without being recognized. Others mixed with the
ordinary people and escaped being identified.[77] Fang Kung-chao
方孔炤 says that south of the Yangtze the people were superstitious
and liked to keep Buddhist priests and sorcerers. Accordingly Buddhist priests were innumerable there. They possessed large farms and
numerous disciples, paid no taxes, and did not work for their living.[78]
The T'ien-chu Temple 天竺寺 in Hang-chou was one of the famous
Buddhist places of pilgrimage, but its priests, we are told, were not
observers of the Buddhist canon. "The priests of this temple are,
without exception, drunkards. Outside the temple, there are many
butcher shops," wrote a writer of the time.[79]

By the Ch'ung-chen reign it had become obvious that religion had
lost its old significance for many. An official of the Board of Rites
wrote, "Of late new religions have been propagated in large numbers.
Loafers and scoundrels abandon farming to become Buddhist or
Taoist priests. When they have done this, they are no longer under
the census and are exempt from the payment of land taxes. Millions
are thus lost to the government in revenue." It is not then surprising
to read in official reports that among the bandits arrested in the
capital were a number of Buddhist priests. They had become so

materialistic that they often sought the help of others (many of these helpers were unscrupulous men) to intercede for them with the powerful and the rich. Their association with these undesirable intercessors often lowered their character. For this reason honest families repeatedly warned their descendants not to have frequent communications with Buddhist priests and nuns.[80]

EDUCATION

Education also was on the decline. The emperors who came after the Hung-wu period gradually attached more importance to the "eight-legged essays" examination system than to studies in the Imperial Academy. The Academy, in consequence, began to count for less. The prestige of teachers in the Imperial Academy soon declined and eminent scholars no longer aspired to such positions. Eventually even the quality of the students became a thing of no concern, and commoners found that they could go to the Imperial Academy. In later reigns the schools failed to maintain the standards set in the Hung-wu reign. In the second quarter of the 15th century great numbers of the government teaching positions were left vacant all through the empire. Provincial graduates (舉人) declined to apply for them. Only to aged senior licentiates (貢生) in poor circumstances did the teaching profession seem attractive and such elderly instructors could do very little because they no longer possessed the vigor it required. Scholarship suffered greatly.

The decline of scholarship led to the stultification of the examination system. So long as scholarship was held in high esteem, the students had regarded the examinations as opportunities for displaying their talents and their learning, and so had worked hard in preparation for them. But when scholarship lost its old glamor, many were content to pass their examinations by bribery. The usual channel was to bribe the local gentry. These, in turn, approached the examining officials who, in their anxiety to please the landlords, were often ready to grant their requests. Thus, the monthly and annual examinations became so casual that anyone could pass, if he was willing to resort to bribery.[81] The government in consequence often accepted candidates who were unfit for their posts, greatly to the detriment of public administration. The scholar Wang Wen-lu 王文祿 who lived in the first half of the 16th century, pointed out the evils of his day in his discussion of the defects of the examination system:

"If there are no genuine government officials," he said, "This is because we have no genuine metropolitan or provincial graduates

(進士, 舉人) and no genuine licentiates (貢生). This lack is due to the lack of genuine scholars. Since government officials come from among scholars, it follows that without genuine scholars there cannot be good government officials. The defect lies in this, that the seniors are too eager to see their juniors get into government offices. These young men are promoted from salaried licentiates (廩生) to senior licentiates (貢生), and if they happen to pass the examinations are appointed to government offices, their attitude toward all government affairs is one of insincerity. When they come together to talk, they unfailingly claim that they want to follow tradition. This spirit of pretence is opposed to sincerity and earnestness. If they entertain these thoughts in their minds, their minds will certainly be poisoned. If they try to put these thoughts into practice and use them as principles to guide their behavior, their characters will be ruined. Finally, if they try to apply them to political affairs, these will suffer great damage."[82]

Wu Ying-chi 吳應箕 (1594–1645), who came almost immediately after Wang Wen-lu, says that the morality of the students of his day was at a very low level, as a result of the corruption of the government officials. These officials, little concerned about the education of the young, used the examination system as a means of currying favor with the landed gentry of their districts. Success in the examinations was measured rather by the wealth and influence of the clan than by the talents of the students. Poor scholars who wished to obtain government offices borrowed in order to pay bribes. Those who could not find the necessary money became discouraged and in the long run gave up their hopes of an official career. The examiners did all they could to raise the price for different government positions, and emerged at the end of the examinations with their pockets full of money.[83] Thus in the year 1642, at the provincial examination in Honan, the market was thrown open to all who were willing to pay bribes: most of those who won successes had simply paid for them.

Examinations were quite as corrupt in the capital as in the provinces. In 1643, at the examination for Han-lin offices, there was great competition among the metropolitan graduates. The first and second places were offered to whoever could pay the highest prices. When the emperor learned what was going on, he turned to the eunuchs and said: "Competition among the new metropolitan graduates for Han-lin offices has caused all the money of the capital to disappear!"[84]

From the second half of the 16th century onward both the rich and the poor were willing, as we have seen, to sacrifice their time and money to obtain government positions. For a poor scholar especially, the sacrifice was great. He had, for instance, to gain recognition from the learned and the gentry of the locality. He had to dress elegantly and buy himself a horse and a carriage. He had to reward his inferiors generously, and to give frequent banquets to his friends and admirers. How could he get the money for all these expenses except by borrowing from relatives and friends? The higher the position the greater were the expenses. Often, as soon as a new official had received an appointment, his debtors appeared at his door. Knowing that his salary was small and that his only hope was to get money from the people, he would open an office for illegal transactions, and there was never any lack of people queuing up for favors. Bribes seem to have been the ordinary source of income for many officials. As a rule, higher court officials expected to receive bribes from provincial officials, and provincial officials expected them from the people. Once they had acquired this thirst for gain, there was very little that they would not do.[85]

The scholar Wang Shih-cheng (1526–1590) says that in his day poor scholars were not acceptable to government examiners but semi-illiterate young men of well-to-do families received honors. These *ersatz* scholars pretended to be men of learning and in conversation often quoted renowned contemporary scholars as if they were personal acquaintances. This was particularly common in T'ai-tsang 太倉 and Hsi-hsien 歙縣, where apparently, even the poor had to make a show of some kind if they were to be accepted by the government officials. The same Wang Shih-cheng recalled how, as a young man, recently successful in the metropolitan examination, he had been considered rather extravagant because he used to spend three hundred silver taels yearly. Some of his colleagues had not been able to spend even a hundred silver taels yearly. But as he grew older he noticed the younger generation becoming far more extravagant than he had ever been. The ordinary scholar was spending over six or seven hundred silver taels, most of it borrowed money. Even in remote provinces the scholars had gradually fallen away from their old tradition of restraint. Frequent celebrations had become the fashion among them and at every banquet they would call for sing-song girls to enliven the feast with music. They even dared to commit their scandalous doings to writing. The most shocking offenders were the scholars who discarded the ordinary decencies of mourning. They dressed up in gay clothes and went around to places of pleasure accompanied by their favorite friends, including lady friends, in no way embarrassed by the criticism of those who saw them.[86]

A report on education in Chekiang published in 1610, showed that the scholars of that province were as bad as their peers in other provinces. The ancient classics in which scholars had formerly specialized were no longer studied. They were interested only in the "eight-legged essays" through the study of which they hoped to pass the examinations. Even in this limited branch of learning they made no effort to be original but handed themselves over to rigid formalism. They formed factions and behaved in a shameless fashion, now flattering their superiors in the hope of obtaining favors from them, now fighting fiercely with their opponents and trying to avenge personal affronts. If one of them chanced to pass the examinations he felt that he had reached the goal of his ambitions. The typical scholar no longer hesitated to sacrifice his integrity for the sake of riches and power. Towards the end of the dynasty it was mournfully observed that people considered a scholar fond of study if he had worked hard for the government examinations. Very few gave themselves to the study of ethics; fewer still wrote books on learned subjects. Even the government examiners judged examination papers by elegance of style alone, paying hardly any heed to the thought.[87]

It is to be noted that the study of the *Four Books* for the public examinations was based on the commentaries of the Sung scholars, especially on that of Chu Hsi 朱熹 (1130–1200), the best known of them. This tradition went back to the Mongol regime and the Ming Government did no more than carry on the system. The editions of the *Four Books* and the *Five Classics* published by order of the Yung-lo emperor all had commentaries by the Sung scholars and were used as the standard works for the public examinations. Hence, in the earlier years of the dynasty, most of the scholars were faithful followers of Chu Hsi. The first break in Chu Hsi's hegemony came in the second half of the 16th century under Ch'en Hsien-chang 陳獻章 (1428–1500). Like most of the scholars of his time he started with the teachings of Chu Hsi, but was not satisfied with them. After some years of meditation he discovered his own system of philosophy which in the eyes of Huang Tsung-hsi was "precise and comprehensive".[88] His teachings encouraged meditation rather than the study of books and for this he was sometimes criticized as being Buddhist. Others saw in his teaching a similarity to those of Lu Chiu-yüan 陸九淵 (1140–1192), a celebrated rival of Chu Hsi. According to Chu Hsi, we have an obligation to perfect our nature by making ourselves free from ignorance of the truth. Hence the "investigation of things" (*ke-wu* 格物) is necessary. In a word, we must study the universe objectively. But, since life is too short for us to examine everything for ourselves, the writings of ancient sages are a great help; for these are the result of their studies and provide us with a short cut to the investigation of things. Lu Chiu-yüan disagreed with Chu on this point. Chu's teaching, he said, was inadequate. "If we depend on books to help us to improve our own nature, on what can the ancient sages have depended before books were written?" For him contemplation of the interior "ego" was sufficient: by meditation and reflection one would, without doubt, come to sudden enlightenment. This explanation contained too much of Ch'an philosophy (a Buddhist sect which was flourishing at the end of the Ming dynasty) for the taste of the Confucian scholars and was not well received by them.

Speaking of his own time, Chu I-tsun 朱彝尊 (1629-1709) says that scholars who were eager to pass the public examinations necessarily took up the study of the *Four Books,* with, of course, the commentary of Chu Hsi. The other Classics too had to be studied through the commentaries of Chu Hsi.[89] This regulation of studies in the hope of material gain naturally had a deplorable influence on the spirit of the time. Many, forgetting that the purpose of learning was to perfect oneself, treated knowledge and action as two different and disparate things. It seems likely that Wang Shou-jen 王守仁 (1472-1528) saw this danger, for he put forward a theory of knowledge similar in many ways to that of Lu Chiu-yüan. He had spent much of his youth in the study of Buddhist and Taoist canons but his mind was still questing for certainty as to the standard of truth. Then, one depressing night during his exile in Kuei-chou he was suddenly illumined by the thought that truth must be sought from within. Like Lu Chiu-yüan he held that his own nature was a sufficient source of wisdom and he held firmly that our conscience is the norm of good and evil. To remedy the evil of the time he proposed his theory of the correlation of knowledge to action. "Knowledge is the principal force of action and action is the result of knowledge. Knowledge is the beginning of action and action is the completion of knowledge. He who understands this knows that when he says 'I know,' this implies action also. In the same way, when he says, 'I do,' he knows that this implies also understanding. . . . But alas, people nowadays separate knowledge from action as two distinct objects. They presume that one must first obtain knowledge before one can act. They say: 'Let us first try to acquire knowledge. As soon as we come to possess it we will try to put it into action.' Thus they never come to act, nor do they ever come to know. This is by no means a light matter nor is the problem a new one. It is because I wish to remedy this defect that I now try to expound my theory of the correlation of knowledge to action."[90] This theory, no doubt, saves Wang Shou-jen from being criticized as a Buddhist of the Ch'an sect, with which elsewhere in his teaching he seems to have so much in common.

After the death of Wang Shou-jen his followers spread all over the empire, expounding the teachings of their master, though not always in an orthodox sense. Some of them went so far as to mix their teachings with Buddhism and temerarious doctrines (as, e.g. Li Chih did) so that their teaching no longer resembled that of the master, and the Yang-ming 陽明 (Wang Shou-jen is better known by this name) school was frequently denounced as heterodox. Nevertheless, it flourished throughout much of the Ming period and influenced later generations not only in China but also in Japan and Korea.

In the Wan-li period, we are told, even the commentaries of Chu Hsi were given up and instead ready-written "eight-legged essays" were published by bookstores as models for the students. The report from Chekiang which we have just quoted blamed unscrupulous scholars for yielding to their own itch for novelty and so leading others into unorthodox views.[91] Probably, however, their intellectual vagaries were due to their ignorance of the Sung scholars rather than to any wish to lead others astray. Their purpose in publishing was to get a good market, not to advance scholarship, and their readers were intent on passing examinations, and cared little for ideas. Ku Yen-wu says that all students in his days were on the look-out for short cuts through their studies. Instead of studying the *Four Books*, they picked out one or two hundred subjects from each Book and searched around for essays dealing with those subjects. They committed these essays to memory and transcribed them and hoped for the best.[92]

This unashamed superficiality was of course deeply resented by the few remaining genuine scholars. Those who considered themselves orthodox Confucianists hated all novelty and logically advocated a return to the old way of the Master. They, however, commanded little influence, for they were generally regarded as dry and exaggeratedly dogmatic. Another group of savants went to the other extreme. Embittered by the prevailing insincerity they wished to make themselves different from the rest and sought to destroy all established traditions. In the literary field, for instance, they reacted sharply against the unimaginative movement for a revival of the T'ang and Sung classics which had been going on since the Chia-ching reign. Among the best known of these intellectual innovators was the brilliant Li Chih 李贄 (1527–1602), a man of independent character and outstanding audacity, who had the courage to say openly what his contemporaries wished to say but dared not. This boldness won him widespread popularity and attracted many followers. The hypocrisy of the Confucian pseudo-scholars and the corruption of government officials provoked him to a contempt that was at times extreme. His sayings and his behavior shocked the educated class of his time. He was supposed to have said that Kuan Chung 管仲 was more virtuous than Confucius; that Feng Tao 馮道 (882–954) was a great loyal minister, and Cho Wen-chün 卓文君 (circa 100 B.C.) a wise woman. Li became a Buddhist and shaved his head after the manner of a Buddhist priest. It was said that when he preached in Buddhist monasteries, women admirers came flocking to listen to him, some even bringing their bedding with the intention of spending the night in the monastery.[93]

Li Chih was shrewd and he really understood the psychology of the people. He saw the importance of literature in the vernacular and had written commentaries on several such books. The best known of these was the *Shui-hu-chuan* 水滸傳 which was widely read in his day. In it he attacked corrupt officials mercilessly and sympathized with the heroes of the book. Thus when speaking of Li K'uei 李逵, he said, "Our Li K'uei is nothing but sincerity itself and there is no artificiality in him. Hence, when Yin T'ien-hsi 殷天錫 was found guilty of atrocity, he might as well have finished him with a lethal blow. Why try to get a safe-conduct from the higher authorities?" In another chapter he wrote, "A Buddhist priest, having read the passage saying that T'ao-hua shan 桃花山, Erh-lung shan 二龍山 and Pai-hu shan 白虎山 were infested with bandits, exclaimed, 'Truly there were many bandits in those days!' To this I answered that nowadays there are far more of them in the imperial court!" In a sarcastic vein he wrote, "Madame Ku 顧大嫂, though a woman, knew how to help those who were in need. But in our days, there are men in high government offices who try to run away as soon as they see some calamity befall the empire. Do you think they are worthy to become the maids of Madame Ku?" Finally, he had this to say of the scholars, "It is a common disease of the hsiu-t'sai 秀才 to become jealous of the virtuous. Would that we could now find a Lin Chiao-t'ou 林教頭 to slaughter every one of them!"[94]

This attitude toward his contemporaries won Li Chih great popularity among the common people and despite his eccentric behavior, he was respected by some of the great scholars of his time. However, the traditional scholars and government officials whom he had insulted, never forgave him for his irreverence. In 1602 he was accused before the Wan-li emperor of immorality and of having done great harm to the people by his prolific writings. He was arrested and was thrown into prison where he committed suicide. In 1625, over twenty years after his death, his writings were still popular among the people. The censor of Szechuan province received an order from the emperor to seek out the wooden printing blocks of his works and to have them burnt, and the bookstores were forbidden to sell any of his writings. Ku Yen-wu (1613–1682), however, records that even in his day Li Chih's writings were still popular among the scholars, who, defying the imperial warning, refused to give up their collections of Li writings.[95]

NOTES

[1] *Ku-chin chih-ping lüeh*, 20, (ts'e 15) 87b, 88a; *Ming-t'ung-chien*, 25, (ts'e 3) 15a.

[2] *Ming-t'ung-chien*, 26, (ts'e 3) 25a; *Hsü Wen-hsien t'ung-k'ao*, 43, I, 3190.

[3] *Wu-tsa-tsu*, 15, (ts'e 8) 44b; *Hsü-wen-hsien t'ung-k'ao*, 43, I. 3192.

[4] *Tu-pien hsin-shu*, 4, (ts'e 2) 6b.

[5] *Shuo-lüeh* 說略, (ts'e 5) 10a.

[6] *Tien-ku chi-wen*, 17, (ts'e 134) 10ab; *Chin-yen lei-pien*, (ts'e 13) A 107b, 105b; *Yung-chuang hsiao-pin*, 8, (t'se 100) 1b.

[8] *Hsü wen-hsien t'ung-k'ao*, 51, I, 3255.

[7] Yüan Chih 袁袠 (1502–1547), *Shih-wei* 世緯, (*Chih-pu-tsu chai ts'ung-shu* 知不足齋叢書 ed. by Pao T'ing-po 鮑廷博 (1728–1814), Anhui, 1776) B. 7a–9a.

[9] *Ming-shih ch'ao-lüeh*, (ts'e 1) 29b.

[10] *Tsui wei lu*, 14, (ts'e 6) 36b; *Kuo chi-kan ssu-kao*, 1, (ts'e 0,908) 19–20; *Erh-shih erh-shih cha-chi*, 35, (ts'e 3553) 731.

[11] *Ming-t'ung-chien*, 1, (ts'e 1) 6b; *Li-tai chi-kuan chih* 54 (ts'e 6) 1533.

[12] The *Kuo-ch'ao tien-hui*, (162, ts'e 58, 51) mentions two noteworthy facts from the Hsüan-te reign. In 1451 it was reported that Nanking government officials travelling to Peking on affairs of state had to pay their own travelling expenses. When the emperor heard of this he abolished the unreasonable practice on the twofold ground that (1) these ministers were travelling on government business and (2) the salaries of officials were lower in Nanking than in Peking.

[13] *Chin-yen lei-bien*, 3, (ts'e 14) 107b.

[14] *Yung-chuang hsiao-pin*, 1, (ts'e 98) 14a.

[15] *Ming-mo nung-min ch'i-i shih-liao*, 119–122.

[16] *Nouvelle relation de la Chine*, 214–215.

[17] Pawn shops in the Ming dynasty were known by innumerable names: chieh-k'u 解庫, tien-k'u 典庫, chieh-p'u 解鋪, tien-p'u 典鋪, chieh-tien-p'u 解典鋪, ch'ieh-tang-p'u 解當鋪, chieh-tang k'u 解當庫, tien-tang-p'u 典當鋪, tang-p'u 當鋪, chih-k'u 質庫, chih-p'u 質鋪, yin-tzu-p'u 印子鋪 etc. History and the documents of the time tell us very little about the organization of these pawn shops. However, contemporary miscellaneous writings and novels give glimpses of what they were like. In general, the capital varied from one to ten thousand silver taels. The number of men employed depended on the size of the shop. If there were three employees in one shop, one of them would be in charge of the treasury, one would look after storage and the third dealt with the customers. Pawn-broking was naturally the main business. In addition, they also went in for money-

lending, in this respect resembling the chieh-tien-k'u 解典鋪 of the Yüan dynasty. They also transacted various other kinds of business, including money changing and the buying and selling of military provisions. In 1607 the Honan province alone had two hundred and thirteen pawn shops, most of them owned by natives of Anhui. At that time the government was very short of funds and the taxing of pawn shops had been suggested as a means of raising money. Cf. *Chung-kuo huo-pi shih*, 2, 474.

[18] *Ts'e shu*, 3, (TSCCCP ts'e 0,756) 65–66.

[19] *Ming-tai chien-ch'a chih-tu kai-shu*, 6, (November, 1936) 2.

[20] *Ming-ch'en tsou-i*, 30, (TSCCCP ts'e 0,92) 541; *Nouvelle relation de la Chine*, 221–223.

[21] *Ch'un-ming meng-yü-lu*, 48, (ts'e 19)

[22] *Huai-tsung Ch'ung-chen shih-lu*, 1, (ts'e 498) 13a.

[23] *Ch'un-ming meng-yü lu*, 48, (ts'e 19) 54b.

[24] *Huai-tsung ch'ung-chen shih-lu*, t13, (ts'e 500) 6a; *Chia-shen chuan-hsin lu*, 4, (ts'e 12) 60–61.

[25] *Erh-shih erh-shih cha-chi*, 32, (ts'e 6) 32a.

[26] *Tien-ku chi-wen*, 12, (ts'e 134) 5b–6b; cf. also Fang Kung-chao 方孔炤, *Ch'u-yao hsiao-yen* 芻堯小言, (*T'ung-ch'eng fang-shih chi-tai i-shu*) (ts'e 5) 10ab.

[27] Sun Ch'eng-tse 孫承澤, *Ssu-ling tien-li chi* 思陵典禮紀, (TSCCCP), 1, (ts'e 3,972) 1.

[28] *Ts'e Shu*, 3, (ts'e 0,755) 54.

[29] *Huai-tsung ch'ung-chen shih-lu*, 1, (ts'e 498) 17b.

[30] Ibid., 3, (ts'e 498) 8a.

[31] *K'ou-shih pien-nien*, 9, (ts'e 8) 24a.

[32] Ibid , 6, (ts'e 6) 10a.

[33] Wang Chia-chen 王家禎, *Wang hsiao-ssu-ma tsou-shu* 王少司馬奏疏, (TSCCCP), 1, (ts'e 0,911) 50–52.

[34] Hsia Yün-i 夏允彝, *Hsing-Ts'un lu* 幸存錄, (*Ming-chi pai-shih ch'u-hsü pien*, first series) (ts'e 4) 4ab.

[35] *Huai-tsung ch'ung-chen shih-lu*, 3, (ts'e 498) 3b; Anonym. *Ch'ung-chen ch'ang-pien* 崇禎長編, (*T'ung-shih* 痛史 series, by Lo-t'ien chü shih 樂天居士, Shanghai, 1912) 1, 10b.

[36] *K'ou-shih pien-nien*, 13, (ts'e 9) 6ab; Ibid. 14, (ts'e 10) 6b; *Ming shih*, 252, (ts'e 83) 1a–6b; P'ang Tsun-ssu 彭遵泗, *Shu Pi* 蜀碧, (CKNLWHLSTS), 1, (ts'e 35) 12.

[37] *Ch'ung-chen ch'ao chi-shih*, 4, (ts'e 4) 25ab.

[38] *P'ing-k'ou chih*, 1, (ts'e 1) 17b.

[39] *Ming-i tai-fang lu*, 3–4.

[40] T'an Hsi-ssu 譚希思, *Huang-Ming ta-cheng tsuan-yao* 皇明大政纂要, (Wan-li edition), 14, (ts'e 5) 53b; *Kuo-shih chi-wen*, 5, (ts'e 5) 35a.

[41] *Chin-ling so-shih*, second series (ts'e 2) B. 51ab.

[42] *Chi-t'ing wai-shu*, 4, (ts'e 4) 38ab.

[43] *Kuo-ch'üeh*, (ts'e 81) 38b.

[44] *Ching-shih shih-yung pien*, 14, (Heng chi 2 亨集二) 22.

[45] *San-yüan pi-chi*, (ts'e 1) A. 7b, 18b; cf. also *Sung-ling wen-hsien*, 10, B. 9b, 10a of a similar case.

[46] Ch'üan Tsu-wang 全祖望 (1705–1755), *Chi-ch'i-t'ing chi wai-pien* 鮚埼亭集外編, *Ssu-pu ts'ung-k'an* 四部叢刊, photographic edition by the Commercial Press (Shanghai, 1929), 9, (ts'e 18) 8b, 9a.

[47] *Ming-tai nung-min ch'i-i shih-liao*, 279–280.

[48] *Ching-shih chi-ch'ieh shih-wu*, 8, (ts'e 4) 26a–27b.

[49] *Shih-i-ch'ao tung-hua lu* 十一朝東華錄, (Ts'un-ku-chai 存古齋 edition) (Shanghai, 1911) (ts'e 8) 7a–8a.

⁵⁰ Ibid., (ts'e 33) 22b–23a; (ts'e 29) 4b–7a.

⁵¹ *Lou-shan-t'ang chi*, 12, (ts'e 2168) 140–142. Ch'en Lung-cheng mentions a candidate in Ch'ü-i 句邑, who paid several tens of silver taels to obtain the office of sub-official. Even then, he was not admitted by his colleagues until banquets were given. Cf. *Chi-t'ing wai-shu*, 3, (ts'e 3) 7b.

⁵² *Ming-i tai-fang lu*, 30–31.

⁵³ Wang Hui-tsu 汪輝祖 (1730–1807), *Hsüeh-chih i-shuo* 學治臆說, (early 19th cent. ed., Kiangsu) A. 7ab.

⁵⁴ *Jih-chih-lu chi-shih*, 8, (ts'e 3) 79–80.

⁵⁵ *Jih-chih-lu chi-shih*, 8, (ts'e 3) 79–80.

⁵⁶ *Chung-kuo li-tai cheng-chih tei-shih*, 94–95.

⁵⁷ Fang Kung-chao 方孔炤, *Fu-chu kung-tu* 撫楚公牘, (TCFSCTIS), (ts'e 5) 7b, 8a, 30a.

⁵⁸ *Ming-shih chi-shih pen-mo*, 77, (ts'e 2) 50–51.

⁵⁹ *Wu-tsu-tsu*, 15, (ts'e 0) 14b.

⁶⁰ *K'ou-shih pien-nien*, 13, (ts'e 10) 23b; *Ming-shih chi-shih pen-mo*, 78, (ts'e 2) 59.

⁶¹ *K'ou-shih pien-nien*, 14, (ts'e 10) 4b; 15, (ts'e 10) 11b; *Ming-shih chi-shih pen-mo*, 78, (ts'e 2) 62–64; Po Yü 白愚, *Pien-wei shih-chin lu* 汴圍濕襟錄, (*Ching-t'o i-shih* series 荊駝逸史, Tao-kuang 道光 ed.) (ts'e 8) 36ab.

⁶² *Huai-tsung ch'ung-chen shih-lu*, 11, (ts'e 499) 11a.

⁶³ Chiu-lien P'u-sa was the goddess who was said to have appeared to the empress Hsiao-ting 孝定. The empress had a painting made of the goddess sitting on a nine-headed phoenix. (Cf. *Huai-tsung ch'ung-chen shih-lu*, 15, (ts'e 499) 6a; Gabriel De Magaillans, however, gives a different version of the story. The Wan-li emperor, he says, wanted to honor his mother with great distinction and so "declara solemnellement qu'elle estoit kieu lien pu sa, c'est-a-dire Deesse de neuf fleurs; & elle a des Temples dans tout l'Empire, ou elle est adoree sous ce titre, de meme que la courtisane Flore estoit honoree par les Romains comme Deesse de Fleurs. . . ." (*Nouvelle relation de la Chine*, pp. 265 266).

⁶⁴ *Huai-tsung ch'ung-chen shih-lu*, 13, (ts'e 499) 6a.

⁶⁵ *Ming-shih chi-shih pen-mo*, 79, B. 83.

⁶⁶ *Kuei-yu-yüan k'ao*, (wen-pien 文編) 12, (ts'e 5) 9b.

⁶⁷ Li Pang-hua 李邦華 (1574–1644), *Li Chung-wen kung wen-chi* 李忠文公文集, (1694 edition) 6, (ts'e 8) 54b. Cf. also *Ching-shih shih-yung pien* (supplement), 6, (ts'e 16) 19b, 20a.

⁶⁸ Yü Yin 余寅, *Huan li man chi* 宦歷漫紀, (T'ien-chi 天啓 edition), 2, (ts'e 1) 9b–20b.

⁶⁹ Kuo Tzu-chang 郭子章, *Yüeh-ts'ao* 粵艸, (Wan-li edition), 1, (ts'e 1) 8b, 9a.

⁷⁰ *Li Chung-wen kung wen-chi*, 6, (ts'e 8) 55b; *Huan li man chi*, 2, (ts'e 1) 9b–20b.

⁷¹ *Kuo-ch'ao tien-hui*, 13, (ts'e 9) 30a; 134, (ts'e 47) 31b; cf also *Huang-Ming t'ung-chi shu-i*, 10, (ts'e 5) 29ab; 11, (ts'e 5) 45b, 46a.

⁷² *Chia-ching i-lai chu-lüeh*, 7, (ts'e 4) 39b; 9, (ts'e 6) 35a; Yen Chi-heng 顏季亨, *Ching-shih chi-ch'ieh shih-wu* 經世急切時務, (1623 edition) 9, (ts'e 4) 23ab; *Ching-shih shih-yung pien* supplementary, 6, (ts'e 16) 18b, 19a.

⁷³ *Chao-tai fang-mo*, 33, (ts'e 12) 51ab.

⁷⁴ *Kuo-ch'ao tien-hui*, 134, (ts'e 47) 5b, 6a.

⁷⁵ *Ming-chi T'ien-Chien fo-chiao k'ao*, 65, 66.

⁷⁶ *Yeh-hu pien*, 27, (Shanghai, 1959) 3. 687–688.

⁷⁷ *Wu-tsa-tsu*, (Shanghai, 1959) A. 233.

⁷⁸ *Ch'u-yao hsiao-yen*, (ts'e 5) 9a.

⁷⁹ *Chi-t'ing wai-shu*, 2 (ts'e 2) 19b, 20a.

⁸⁰ *Ch'un-ming meng-yü lu*, 39, 67a; Ch'i Pai-yu, *Nan-ching tu-ch'a-yüan chih* 南京都察院志, 20, (ts'e 10) 13ab; Ch'en Yi-shan 陳怡山, *Hai-pin wai-shih* 海濱外史, (Han-fen lou pi-chi 涵芬樓祕笈 edition, 5th series) 2, 15, 16; *Chih-chia chieh-yao* B. under the title "Nai-wai".

⁸¹ *Ming Shih*, 69, (ts'e 24) 9a; *Ch'un-ming meng-yü-lu*, 55, (ts'e 21) 9ab.

⁸² *Ts'e shu*, (TSCCCP), 3, (ts e 0,756) 62–63.

⁸³ *Lou-shan-t'ang chi*, 10 (ts'e 2. 168) 121–124; 13, (ts'e 2, 169) 146–147. Cf. also *Chou chung-kai-kung chin-yu chi*, (TSCCCP), 2, (ts'e 2,165) 9; *Ku-chin chih ping lüeh*, 18, (ts'e 13) 93b, 94a.

⁸⁴ Li Hsün-chi 李遜之, *Ch'ung-chen ch'ao-chi-shih* 崇禎朝記事, (*Ch'ang-chou hsien-che i-shu* 常州先哲遺書 ed. by Sheng Hsüan-huai 盛宣懷, Kiangsu, late 19th century), 4, (ts'e 4) 5b; supplement to the *San-yüan pi-chi*, (ts'e 4) C. 5b, 6a. The *Chia-ching i-lai chu-lüeh*, 5, (ts'e 3) 17b mentions a case (1562) of a group of metropolitan graduates competing for the office of the Hanlin bachelor (庶吉士). The Grand Secretary had already selected fifty of them for the examination. The secret was made known to the emperor and by his order the examination was suspended.

⁸⁵ *Lou-shan-t'ang chi*, 9, (ts'e 2,168) 100–102. Wang Shih-mou in his book *"Shih-t'u hsüan-ching"* 仕途懸鏡, a kind of manual for beginners in public services, has this advice: "Incense, thin silk (絹) and official boots, are things one must prepare when making presents to one's superiors. It may be useful to add to these a few bolts of gauze and satin (紗, 紬). If the presents are not accepted, they do not amount to anything of great value and can always be disposed of in a useful way. On the other hand, if one were to offer substantial gifts and they were not accepted, one would find it difficult to make good use of them. Worse still, since they would be expensive, the amount of money borrowed to buy them would he considerable and the interest would increase proportionately." (Ch'ing edition 1 (ts'e 1) 9a). It seems that official boots (京靴) were commonly chosen as presents for those in government services. Ministers of integrity who might refuse other gifts, would accept, perhaps, this present. Cf. *Kuei-yao-yüan k'ao*, (wen-pien 文編), 17, (ts'e 6) 26a.

⁸⁶ *Huang Ming shih-hsüeh hsin-yu*, 7, (ts'e 7) 27b.

⁸⁷ *Liang-che hsüeh-cheng* 兩浙學政, (1610 ed.) 6a, 3b; *Huan li man chi*, 2, (ts'e 1) 6ab; *Wu-tsa-tsu*, 13, (ts'e 7) 0b, 10a.

⁸⁸ Huang Tsung-hsi 黃宗羲, *Ming-ju hsüeh-an* 明儒學案, (KHCPTS), A. 47.

⁸⁹ Chu I-tsun 朱彝尊, *P'u-shu-t'ing chi* 曝書亭集, (KHCPTS), 39, B. 586. "Tao-ch'uan-lu hsü" 道傳錄序.

⁹⁰ Wang Shou-jen 王守仁, *Wang wen-cheng-kung ch'üan-shu* 王文成公全書, (SPTK), 1, (ts'e 2) 7ab.

⁹¹ *Liang-che hsüeh-cheng*, 4ab.

⁹² *Jih-chih-lu chi-shih*, 16, (ts'e 6) 46.

⁹³ *Chi-t'ing wai-shu*, 1, (ts'e 1) 87b, 88a; *Jih-chih-lu chi-shih*, 18, (ts'e 6) 121–162; *Wu-tsa-tso*, 8, (ts'e 4) 41ab.

⁹⁴ *Chin-ling so-shih*, 2, (ts'e 1) 56; *Li chuo-wu hsien-sheng p'i-p'ing chung-i shui-hu-chuan* 李卓吾先生批評忠義水滸傳, (Published by Yung-hsing-t'ang 容興堂, Late Ming edition), 52, (ts'e 11) 14b, 15a; 57, (ts'e 12) 15b; 10, (ts'e 17) 17a; (ts'e 4) 15b; *Chia-ching i-lai chu-lüeh*, 11, (ts'e 8) 6a.

CHAPTER TWELVE

End of a Great Empire

CONDITIONS IN PROVINCES

In the year 1633, an edict was issued to the censorate stating that the reason for the recent growth in the number of the destitute and of bandits was the rapacity and cruelty of the officials. The greater the officials' success in getting what they wanted, the greater were the sufferings of the people. The emperor therefore ordered the censors to move around and to inquire carefully into the activities of corrupt officials.[1] This edict, issued in the 6th year of the Ch'ung-chen reign, shows that the monarch was fully aware of the difficulties of the time. At the end of that same year the President of the Board of Ceremonies reported to the Emperor that there had been a catastrophic decline in agriculture in the South. In the past, he said, the capital had depended on the South for four million piculs of grain; but the productive power of the farmers there had now been exhausted. "Having reached the region north of the Yangtze, your servant noticed that from the districts Hau 濠, Hsü 徐, Ch'ing 青, Ch'i 齊 to the capital, there exists complete desolation: the people move about aimlessly, the irrigation system and the farms are all neglected. . . ."[2] Warnings of this kind had been coming to the court continuously since the Wan-li reign, but very little attention had been paid to them. When the Ch'ung-chen emperor recognized the danger it was already too late.

A topographical survey compiled in the late Ming period revealed the restless state of the people. All were anxiously questioning the future of the empire. Thus one man, speaking of Northern Chih-li, said that since the place was so near to the borders they often suffered from invasion by the barbarians; worse still, the eunuchs possessed many of the farms there and often involved the people in serious trouble. In general, he said, many of the districts were poor and many of the people were unable to pay the land taxes; they were moreover difficult to govern since they were troublesome and the whole area was infested with bandits.[3]

Of Southern Chih-li the author of the survey tells us that several of the districts near Su-chou were frequently flooded and that the increase of taxes for the upkeep of the soldiers often imposed a very heavy burden on the people. Southern Chih-li had formerly been reckoned one of the most prosperous provinces of the empire, but by the end of the Ming period unreasonable demands for *corvée* had drained the people of their energy. Many of the prosperous cities on the coast and on the Yangtze River, Yang-chou and T'ung-chou for instance, had suffered severely from the ravages of Japanese pirates. Many of the saltrakers and miners, unable to make an honest living, had become bandits.[4]

The maritime southern provinces were subjected to the unceasing attacks of Japanese pirates. In Chekiang, the people of Hang-chou, Chia-hsing and Hu-chou were prosperous and lived luxuriously, but many poor farmers in mountainous districts, unable to pay their land-taxes, had grouped together as bandits. In Fukien and Kuangtung many adventurers had taken to the high seas as pirates. In Kuangtung especially the officials were corrupt because they were far away from the court and so were free to do as they pleased.[5] The people of Kiangsi had the reputation of being frugal and hard working, but from the end of the 15th century the imposition of ever heavier land taxes and *corvée* had been undermining the life of the the province. To escape these burdens robust young men began to abandon their farms and take to commerce. In order to gain freedom of movement they were ready even to desert their wives and children, and a fall in the moral standards of this province inevitably followed.[6] The provinces of Kuangsi, Kueichou and Yünnan seem to have been considered less important. There had always been conflicts between the Chinese and the aborigines in those distant parts of the empire, and time and again they had given endless trouble to the government.

Szechuan was a mountainous province well-known for its production of timber. Most of the construction work in the capital depended on Szechuan timber and the insatiable demands of the government became a heavy burden on both the merchants and the people. Barbarian tribes were numerous and their pugnacity constituted a perpetual menace to the province. Land taxes and *corvée* were heavy in all the big cities, particularly in Cheng-tu.[7]

A description left by a writer of the later Ming period shows the province of Hu-kuang as quite different from the Hunan and Hupei of the Ch'ing period. Apparently the saying "when Hu-kuang reaps its crops the whole empire will get a full supply" 湖廣熟, 天下足 had no application to the Hu-kuang of the Ming dynasty. The province is described as connected with the Yangtze River and the P'o-yang Lake, and full of marshes, with but little farming land. The inhabitants were fierce and easily roused and had hardly a thought of practising frugality. Since the province bordered nine other provinces, there was constant and heavy traffic through it and couriers became a serious problem. Furthermore, descendants of the imperial house increased to such an extent that it was difficult to support them all. Then, heavy land-taxes and *corvée* and demands from the court for local products aroused the people to resentment and even revolt. Great parts, for instance, of Ch'en-chou 辰州, were dominated by bandits, and the aborigines along the Kueichou borders were restless. Towns and cities near the Yangtze repeatedly suffered from floods, and many destitute farmers became highwaymen rather than die of hunger.[8]

In Honan province the most serious problem, perhaps, was the menace of the Yellow River. "The Yellow River has no respect at all for Chinese law and order," wrote Ricci, "It comes from a barbarous region and, as it were, seeking vengeance for the hatred the Chinese have for outsiders, it frequently ravages whole districts of the realm when it fills up with sand and changes its course at will. . . ."[9] Every year the government lavished great sums of money and a huge labor force on restraining its ravages, yet all too often the province suffered inundations that destroyed everything. This was one of the reasons for the poverty of many districts in the province. Another menace equally serious was the ever growing flood of the imperial clansmen. We have already glanced at the misdeeds of Prince Fu. Unaided, he could have upset the whole province; when the imperial clansmen added their frivolous enormities to his, the result was calamitous. In addition to all this, many mountainous districts in the province were notorious for miners-turned-bandit.[10]

Stubbornness was perhaps the most notable characteristic of the people of Shantung. They were also easily roused and if a leader could be found a big mob could be formed in a short time. In the words of a poet, there were one hundred and eight prefectures in Shantung and all without exception possessed battle-fields. The

Shantung of the late Ming period shared all the ills suffered by the neighboring provinces—the heavy burden of land-taxes and *corvée*, the Yellow River floods, the imperial clansmen, the swarms of bandits, the ex-miners in mountain districts and ex-saltrakers along the coast—and it suffered a still worse misfortune proper to itself. The north of the province adjoined the territories of the Manchus and so was exposed to frequent invasions. Lin-ch'ing and Te-chou, two prosperous cities in the north, exerted a strong attraction on the Manchus. Many of the people, especially the poor, were employed by the Manchus and seem to have been well treated by them. "They went with great enthusiasm to join the barbarians: The more they were killed by fire arms (of the soldiers—A.C.) the greater their number seemed to grow."[11]

Shansi was by no means a rich province. Being near the borders, it too suffered from the attack of the barbarians. The districts around the T'ai-hang mountain were overrun with bandits. Miners of Yü-chou 蔚州, soldiers from the military settlement in Lin-chin 臨晉 and destitute refugees from Lu-chou 潞州 had formed savage bands and subjected the people to perpetual spoliation. The taxes levied for the upkeep of the soldiers on the border were heavy. Above all, we are told that the imperial clansmen in Fen-chou 汾州 were numerous and, like the lawless wastrels they were, did endless harm to the people. One writer says that within a period of a few years the ninety prefectures of this province had nearly all been devastated by bandits and that the soldiers were on the verge of mutiny because they had not received their due. "Soldiers at the borders were crying out for their pay and even disobeyed the orders of their superiors."[12]

"Whoever is the governor of this place he has a heavy task; he has to be at once a shepherd and a military commander," as was truly said of the governor of Shensi province at the end of the Ming dynasty. This overburdened official, in addition to directing the whole administration of the province, had the very onerous duty of guarding the border of the province. The author of the *Hua-i feng-t'u chih* 華夷風土志 tells us that outside Yü-lin 榆林 one could see the nomads' tents stretching out mile after mile. At Ku-yüan 固原, despite the presence of a large garrison, a battle was lost to the nomads. Substantial premiums were promised to all who would enlist in the army, but less than a thousand applied. One reason given for this poor response was that natives of Shensi, being fine soldiers, were sent year after year to guard the capital, with consequent exhaustion of the manpower of the province. This, however, was not the whole explanation. The province could not support large numbers. The soil of Shensi was poor and produced little and what fertile farms there were had passed into the possession of the imperial clansmen. The government seems also to have worried over the presence of the Mohammedan colony. The Mohammedans were regarded as men of doubtful character and were said to have given shelter to undesirable citizens. "They are waiting for the opportunity to rise and they will induce others to follow them. Heaven forbid the development of this into a serious menace!"[13]

This bird's eye view of the last years of the Ming empire is a gloomy one. The authors cited here knew well how serious the situation was and agreed unanimously that the government alone could save the country. Hence they repeatedly called the attention of the government to the need for wise action if peace were to be preserved. "Those who have authority over others should preserve their integrity and be frugal. If they would but take greater interest in the welfare of their people they would have great success in their rule": " . . . Would that we had a good magistrate who would encourage the people to farm and to cultivate mulberries, or one who would lighten the people's burden of taxes and *corvée,* one who would institute the pao-chia system 保甲法 and prevent the lawless from doing harm; one who would enforce the laws and watch over the community. Let such a magistrate give no pardon to those who revolt against the law! This perhaps would help to quench the flame of injustice!" On the other hand they did not hesitate to mix with their admonitions threats of what might happen if the rulers failed to do their duty: " . . . It is the duty of the rulers to spare their people, that they may be able to support themselves and to help to support the soldiers on the borders. To do otherwise is to eat one's own flesh in order to satisfy one's hunger. This would beyond doubt cause one's instant death!"

REBELS AND BANDITS

The *Ming-shih* includes, rather unexpectedly perhaps, a set of biographies of rebels. Towards the end of this section, the compiler remarks: "Throughout the age there had always been trouble from bandits, but there had never been so many disturbances as those caused by Li Tzu-ch'eng 李自成 and Chang Hsien-chung at the end of the Ming dynasty." The compiler-in-chief points out that the insurrection of T'ang Sai-erh 唐賽兒 had broken out in the Yung-lo reign but had soon been suppressed, and that the rebels had become so dangerous in the days of the Cheng-te emperor as almost to ruin the empire, yet the government had survived. How then, he asks, can the Ming dynasty have ended with the Ch'ung-chen emperor who was so energetic and so full of hope for the future of the empire?[14] The compiler-in-chief was, no doubt, well aware of the causes of the fall of the dynasty. His question was rhetorical—a lament over the undeserved fate of the last emperor of the dynasty.

As we have already seen, from the beginning of the 16th century, the empire had been in rapid decline. The emperors' neglect of their duties allowed corruption to grow among their ministers and eunuchs. With Japanese pirates attacking continually along the coast and the Mongols along the borders, the defence of the empire was a constant drain on the public treasuries. Next came the most serious threat of all, the rise of the Manchus. This people started as a small tribe in a region along the northeast border of the empire. At first they were obedient to the emperors, but as their power waxed and the emperors' waned, they threw off their allegiance and became an ever more menacing threat to the very existence of Ming rule. From the end of the Wan-li period onward taxes had to be levied to support the army in Liao-tung and this burden soon became so heavy that the people found it difficult to bear. Added to this, the corruption of the government officials and insatiable demands of the soldiers had reduced the farmers to absolute destitution. The poor people of the empire, most of them honest and unwarlike citizens, bore their sufferings with surprising resignation, eating rough herbs, the bark of trees, and even earth, in their effort to keep alive. Many, however, were unwilling to starve without a struggle. They began by begging from the rich and the nobles. When begging failed, they resorted to violence. When trouble of this kind broke out anywhere, it usually involved the whole locality and the authorities could do very little to check angry mobs.

Honest scholars, unable to condone the selfishness and injustice of the rich and the nobles, or the cruelties of the officials, often sympathized with the poor.[15] This, no doubt, gave great encouragement to the disaffected poor, but it did not constitute a threat to the empire. No large-scale revolt or revolution could hope to succeed unless it could show by signs that the favor of heaven was gradually being withdrawn from the ruling dynasty. Supernatural revelation of some sort was needed to attract followers. Hence many rebellions started in that way.[16] The White Lotus insurrection, led by Hsü Hung-ju 徐鴻儒 in Shantung in 1622, was a serious revolt largely because it claimed the support of such signs. It took the government over a year to pacify the area of revolt, and even this pacification did not at all mean that the White Lotus movement had been entirely suppressed.

Hsü Hung-ju's followers scattered all over the empire and kept up their secret activities.[17]

The long Chia-ching reign (1522–1566) was, as we have already said, a period of rapid deterioration, owing to the negligence of the emperor. By the time of his death, signs of restlessness were discernible in the provinces. At the end of 1569, a revolt of bandits was reported in Shensi and in the spring of the following year these bandits moved to Szechuan. In the middle of the Wan-li reign famines occurred so frequently in the provinces that many of the starving were forced to revolt. Towards the end of the Wan-li period, Shantung, we are told, was infested with bandits.[18] At the beginning of the T'ien-ch'i period (1622) the White Lotus sect started a new insurrection which caused the government a great deal of anxiety. Two years later, an official, writing to the emperor, reported that in Fukien there had been a revolt. This revolt, he said, was due to a drought which had driven the price of food so high that even bare subsistence was beyond the reach of the people. All of Central China and the northwest, the same official said, were suffering the same fate: "The people are planning to rise and Heaven seems to be provoking them by droughts!"[19] Another minister told the emperor how times had changed. In former days, he said, even thieves did not dare to violate the law publicly, but now, serious crimes were being committed in the open: even an imperial treasury had been looted and government officials had been murdered.[20]

In the second year of the Ch'ung-chen reign (1629), banditry began to spread in Shensi province and prefectures were raided. In this matter Shensi might consider itself lucky. Many other provinces had had to endure this particular affliction much earlier. Nevertheless there were many reasons to explain why Shensi was the first province to revolt, and why so many of the leaders of the rebels came from there. Physically, Shensi is a dry cold region, particularly in the north. In Huai-yüan 懷遠, for example, snow begins to fall in September and spring does not come until April. Hence this and the neighboring regions are very poor agriculturally. Furthermore, since the north of the province is mountainous it is not easy to find water there. The wells have to be dug thirty feet or more and the irrigation of the farms is difficult. The soil in general is sandy and, therefore, produces indifferent crops. The local gazetteers say truly that the people of these places are poor and that their soil is mediocre.[21]

The people, depressed by poverty and lacking in enterprise, seem never to have developed a talent for business. Most of the trade in the Ming days was in the hands of merchants from other provinces, especially Shansi. Silk and cotton, for instance, were produced in Yen-an but the people did not make cloth out of them, nor did they weave rugs, although they produced wool. Even for domestic utensils the natives depended on merchants from other provinces. Thus these merchants were able to monopolize the market and many of them also became money-lenders, charging heavy interest on their loans.[22]

Shensi therefore was regarded by government officials as an exceedingly unattractive province, and many who were appointed to posts in the northern districts sought to excuse themselves from taking up office. Those who went willingly often regretted it and asked to be transferred. In the middle of the Ch'ung-chen reign, over thirty local offices were vacant at one time. As a result, civil administration was inefficient and very little was done to improve the condition of the people.[23]

We are told that their surroundings had made the people of Shensi daring and belligerent. They were gruff and unpolished.[24] They were, however, natural horsemen and many of them served in this capacity in the army or as couriers in the government postal service.

This last was the main outlet for such young men in Shensi as were not content to spend their lives scratching the barren earth. The decline of the postal service was a severe blow to the province and goes far to explain the origin of the revolt. A word then about the postal service in Ming times.

The government posts were organized primarily for the transmission of government messages and the transportation of military supplies. In the days of the Hung-wu monarch rich families used to be assigned to this office. Families possessing one hundred piculs of grain had to supply horses or boats for the posts, and people with less than five piculs of grain were assigned as couriers.[25] In the Hung-wu period the service was practically limited to the transmission of important military messages. High officials who had obtained the emperor's permission to retire were allowed to use the horses and boats; but only special imperial envoys were allowed to make regular use of the services of government posts. The Hsüan-te emperor repromulgated these rules for the use of the government posts. Apparently, abuses had been creeping in.[26]

Later, we are told that nearly all the officials in the capital or in the provinces were using the postal facilities freely in their travels. Permits known as k'an-ho 勘合 which formerly had rarely been issued could be obtained so easily that even laborers in local government offices could hope to get them.[27] Officials often borrowed these permits from each other and sometimes even sold them to third parties. Sub-officials and laborers in government offices saw in this an opportunity for enriching themselves at the expense of the people. They made this illegal trade in passes the basis for illegal demands of all kinds and, because the people were timid, forced them to suffer many injustices.[28]

When the *corvée* was commuted into a money payment, it seemed that the people would be relieved from the burden of supplying the government with personal services. In reality, the change only increased their burdens and their suffering. In Kuangtung, for example, the officials appropriated the *corvée* payments for themselves and forced the village headmen to supply horses and boats for the government posts. Service as couriers was still required of the people.[29]

Local strong men too sought to secure a share of the *corvée* payments by making contracts with local officials for supplying the necessary horses and couriers. One such man would contract to supply several horses for several tens of couriers, but often enough his sole interest lay in receiving his money and he would do nothing about fulfilling his part of the contract till a peremptory demand sent him scurrying around to hire horses and laborers. Some even ran away with the money, or spent it, borrowing at high interest when the contract had to be carried out.[30]

The less astute found in the postal service a source not of gain but of loss. In the year 1624, a censor reported to the T'ien-ch'i emperor that upon his arrival in Chung-mou 中牟, Honan province, more than ten of those who had the assignment of supplying post horses came to petition him for relief from this assignment. Some of them had been couriers for over ten years, others for twenty or thirty years. They admitted that they belonged to rich local families, but said that they had exhausted their fortunes in maintaining the government postal service. Now they had debts to pay, and if the father of the family failed to meet such obligations his sons became liable. There was no way of relinquishing these assignments, and no way of gaining exemption from paying the debts deriving from the assignments.[31]

Some sections of the government posts used sea routes. These do not seem to have escaped the weaknesses that afflicted the land posts. From a report of the President of the Board of War we learn that it was customary for the people of Te-chou 德州 in Shantung to supply what was needed to the government post services. Many officials took advantage of this custom to demand extraordinary favors from the local government. As time went on the abuses became more serious. Sometimes the demand for couriers was so great that the local government had to force merchants and travellers to come to the rescue. Officials in charge of government transportation would approach these merchants and travellers in the middle of their journeys and demand money from them. Some unfortunates having nothing to offer, would hand over the clothes they were wearing in order to gain freedom. Others, finding no way to escape, committed suicide by throwing themselves into the water. It was said that the soldiers carried more smuggled goods than legitimate cargo in these transport ships.[32]

Shortly after the Ch'ung-chen emperor's accession, he received reports from two of his ministers on the abuses of the government system. One of these ministers, Liu Mou 劉懋, a supervising censor of the Board of War, suggested a contraction of the government postal system, saying that by this means the government treasury would save hundreds of thousands of silver taels each year. The emperor thought this advice most reasonable: an addition of several hundred thousand taels to the treasury each year would mean a great deal to the hard pressed government. Accordingly, in 1629, orders were given for a reduction. The post was cut by thirty per cent, at an annual saving of six hundred thousand silver taels.[33]

This reduction, however beneficial to the treasury, brought calamity to many. Poor people in Shansi and Shensi who had worked as couriers found themselves unemployed. Their old salaries may have been very scanty, but they had been something. Now the ex-couriers were absolutely destitute. Then, at this very time, repeated famines occurred in these two provinces and the price of rice went up to a thousand coins per peck. When the emperor heard of this he sent a hundred thousand silver taels for the relief of the people. Several of the ministers, aware of the desperate situation, advised the emperor to restore the government post system to its old size, but the emperor, with fatal obstinacy refused to accept their counsel.[34]

From the end of the T'ien-ch'i period, Shensi had repeatedly suffered from famines. In 1627, when the people of Ch'eng-hsien 澄縣 were in a state of semi-starvation the magistrate was still demanding taxes. Infuriated by this, many tax-payers and even some tax collectors burst into the town under the leadership of Wang Erh 王二 and murdered the magistrate.[35] Government troops were sent to suppress the revolt but they were defeated largely because of their unfamiliarity with the locality.[36] Soon deserting soldiers began to join the growing rebel bands. In the following year (1628), a revolt broke out in Fu-ku 府谷 prefecture, under the leadership of Kao Ying-hsiang 高迎祥. After a time Wang Erh joined forces with Kao to form an armed group of five to six thousand rebels.[37]

Meanwhile five thousand "brave" soldiers had been summoned from Shansi by the emperor to defend the capital. Upon their arrival, they were sent to guard T'ung-chou 通州, but on the very next day they were moved to Ch'ang-p'ing 昌平, and on the third day they received orders to leave for Liang-hsiang 良鄉. According to the army custom of those days, the soldiers were not paid until the second day after taking up quarters in a given place. The Shansi soldiers therefore had lost three days' pay through the fumbling of the higher command and in a sudden outburst of rage they started to pillage the civilian populace. Later, their commander was arrested and was accused of negligence in maintaining military discipline. The soldiers knew that this man was being made a scapegoat. Regarding his arrest as an act of intolerable injustice, they deserted in a body. For a time they maintained themselves as an independent band of trouble-makers in Shantung, but eventually joined Kao Ying-hsiang, and kept on the move between Shensi and Honan.[38]

Such rebels are referred to as liu-k'ou 流寇, a term which implies that these outlaws were bandits who never stayed for long in one locality but continued to move from place to place. They acted in this manner partly to avoid pursuit by government troops, especially at the beginning of the revolt when their forces were far weaker than those of the government, partly to make sure of an abundant supply of food.

We are told that many of the leaders of the rebels had formerly belonged to the forces then guarding the borders of the empire. In order not to endanger their families in the interior of China, these men disguised themselves and assumed false names. Often, when one of them was killed his immediate successor would assume the same false name, thus making it very difficult for the government troops to identify the leaders of the rebels.[39]

Among the rebels there were foreign bandits from across the borders who had never been Chinese subjects. Also there were Mohammedans, native bandits, miners, and destitute people of all kinds. According to the confession of Yang-ho, many of the native bandits had come from among the soldiers sent to reinforce the army of Liao-tung towards the end of the Wan-li reign and during the T'ien-ch'i reign. They had found life on the frontier unbearable and had deserted to return to their native places. Unable to find a living at home, they had then gathered together and set up as highwaymen.[40] Gradually, as they passed from place to place, they were joined by hungry mobs and eventually formed large bandit groups.

The Mohammedans, who had settled in Kansu, Szechuan, Shensi and Shansi, were always known for their belligerent spirit. At Tse-chou 澤州 and Lu-an 潞安 in Shansi, for instance, Mohammedan revolts had been occurring for several decades before the Ch'ung-chen reign.[41] Toward the end of 1628, there were reports of unrest among certain Shensi Mohammedans living near the borders of Kansu and Szechuan. Several local famines having occurred, locally born soldiers were induced to revolt, and many districts in Shensi were rapidly devastated by the rebels who were fully equipped with armor and horses.[42] In 1631 a censor reported the presence of several tens of thousands of Mohammedan rebels between Lo-ch'uan 雒川 and I-ch'uan 宜川.[43] Among the great leaders of the rebels there was one bearing the nickname Lao Hui-hui 老狪狪 or "Old Mohammedan (Dog)." Even the arch-rebel Li Tzu-ch'eng was suspected of being a Mohammedan.[44]

The revolt of the miners can be traced back to the Chia-ching reign. The *Tsui-wei lu* twice mentions the suppression of miners in Shansi under that monarch, in 1557 and 1566.[45] In 1590, a court minister advised the Wan-li emperor to discontinue mining operations, "for," he said "to open mines one must gather many laborers and then because of the big crowd an effort is needed to prevent disorder. At this moment, the miners are gathering together in Shansi and Honan and the local magistrate is wondering how to disperse them."[46]

Towards the end of the Wan-li period (1617) a thousand miners came to Ling-pao prefecture 靈寶縣 and robbed the government treasury.[47] In present Anhui, we are told, miners who had turned bandits caused trouble for several decades. Although government officials knew of this they could not prevent it.[48] The *Hou-chien lu* 後鑒錄 gives an account of a certain Ch'en Chi-yü 陳際遇, a native of Honan, who, having failed in the government examination, took up work as a farmer and soon became acquainted with some neighboring miners. One of these miners one day claimed to have found a book from Heaven in a mine. Influenced by this tale, Ch'en joined him and they began to stir up the people. When the local government learned of what was happening, it acted without delay, and the miner and Ch'en's wife and children were arrested and later were all executed. Ch'en himself, however, and his followers escaped and started a revolt. When Li Tzu-ch'eng came to Honan Ch'en submitted to him.[49]

Among the rebels there were a certain number, called by the government I-jen 夷人 or "barbarians," who had never been subjects of the Ming government. These were also sometimes known as lo 虜 or hsi-jen 西人. In 1630, when the Governor of Shansi reported to the Ch'ung-chen emperor, he gave the following description of the situation in the northern part of this province and its Kansu boundary:

" . . . Many of the inhabitants of these parts of the province dwell in caves or strongholds. Toward the west, where the boundary reaches Hua-ma 花馬 and Ting-pien 定邊 (east of Kansu), the line runs very close to the barbarian homes known as the dens of thieves. Recently, on account of famine, the leaders of the bandits have frequently induced these border barbarians to go out to rob with the help of runaway soldiers."[50]

Many of the leaders of the rebels at the beginning of the Ch'ung-chen period came from the military class. Chang Hsien-chung and Li Tzu-ch'eng were the best known of these ex-officer bandits. The contrasting histories of revolt in Shensi and Shansi illustrate the effect produced by the presence of these trained leaders. In Shensi, where the leaders were amateurs, there was at this time no real unity among the different groups of rebels. Each group followed its leader wherever he led them. If the rebels won a battle they kept on advancing; if they were beaten, they retired to the mountains and waited for their chance to strike again. This made it difficult for government troops to find out with which group they were fighting or how many there were altogether. Yet in the end the lack of coherent organization proved fatal to the revolt. In Shansi conditions were quite different. The rebels under the leadership of Wang Tzu-yung 王自用 were organized into thirty-six divisions. Their movements were usually well planned and a constant supply of leaders was maintained in the later years of the revolt. Among the best known of these were Kao Ying-hsiang, the two ex-officers Chang Hsien-chung and Li Tzu-ch'eng, Lo Ju-ts'ai 羅汝才 and Lao Hui-hui. All of these had belonged originally to the thirty-six divisions of Shansi.[51]

Other leaders seem to have come from good families and some were even scholars. Li Yen 李巖 and Niu Chin-hsing 牛金星, for instance, were two scholars who became important advisers of Li Tzu-ch'eng in the later years of the revolt. Li Yen came from an especially distinguished family: his father was President of the Board of War.

The *P'ing-k'ou chih* tells of a certain man from Yü-lin in Shensi, a man famous both for his wealth and for his strong physique, who became a rebel. A censor noticed this man's beautiful estate and wanted to buy it as a villa, but the owner refused to sell. The censor greatly resented his refusal and tried to arraign him before the local magistrate on a criminal charge. The man, however, escaped with eighteen of his friends, and found it easy to gather a group of rebels, for there was famine in the province that year.[52] In 1635, after the defeat of the rebels at Huang-p'o 黃陂 and Hsiao-kan 孝感 in present Hupei, it was said that the leader of the rebels was a provincial graduate.[53] Even the notorious Tien-teng tzu 點燈子 was reputed to have once been a retiring scholar. We are told that he used to reside in a temple, where, during the day, he devoted his time to study and his nights to copying manuscripts (hence his nickname "Master Light-the-Lamp"). The rumor spread that he was studying books on tactics with the intention of starting a revolt. He tried to prove his innocence but no one would believe him. Fearing that the magistrate might apprehend him, he ran away, gathered a group of followers, and started a revolt.[54] From the year 1630 onward, the power of the rebels developed with astonishing speed. At first their strongholds were in the southwest of Shansi. But in 1631, they extended their operations to Honan and penetrated as far as the northern bank of the Yellow River. In the following year the northern part of Shansi and the northern bank of the Yellow River came under their sway. Finally, in 1633, they spread throughout the whole province of Shansi and reached the boundaries of the present Hupei province.

By 1632, the number of rebels had increased greatly and it was reported that there were twenty-four divisions in Shensi and thirty-eight in Honan and Shansi.[55] It is not easy to determine the exact number of the rebels, for they moved continually from place to place, and often an older group might be taken for a new. The rebels themselves left no records of their own numbers and the official estimates were not always reliable. When the government troops were defeated, they often exaggerated the size of the enemy forces to excuse their failure; when they gained a victory they exaggerated the number of the enemy in their reports to show their bravery. A modern writer has given the following rough estimate of the number of rebels: in 1633 there were about a hundred thousand; by the fall of the next year, there were five hundred thousand; in 1635, their numbers rose to over six hundred thousand: but in the following year they fell to a little over three hundred thousand.[56]

The author of the *P'ing-k'ou chih* informs us that the rebels held three main centers: the northern part of Shensi, the districts at the juncture of the four provinces of Shensi, Honan, Hu-kuang and Szechuan, and finally, the northern bank of the Yangtze-River. The territory they commanded in the northern part of Shensi extended from the north-eastern section of Shansi to western Kansu, whence they could move easily to Szechuan. Tung-ch'uan 東川 and Hsi-ch'uan 西川 in northern Shensi were especially known as rebel strongholds. These places were surrounded by a chain of mountains stretching for several hundred miles with deep streams and small winding paths, and government troops never dreamt of going into such difficult regions. There was probably reason for the rebels' choice of such places. Many of the people, shrinking from the brutality of the soldiers and the merciless government officials, had hidden themselves in these mountains to develop the land there and live in peace, and the rebels were able to share the products of the land with the farmers.[57]

In 1633, the President of the Board of War reported that for four years the rebels had occupied the northern part of Shensi as far as eastern Kansu, altogether a territory of over five hundred square miles. When they took a village, they killed the feeble and the aged and took away the young men and women, cutting their hair short, after the fashion of the rebels at that ime. Once these young people had lost their long hair they were considered rebels and even their families and relatives did not dare to communicate with them. Many of them were in consequence forced to join the rebels.[58]

In the extreme southern part of Shensi (Han-chung 漢中) the scene was very different. Volunteers came there from all around to join the rebels. Seemingly, their strongholds were so well sited that the poor of the four provinces of Shensi, Honan, Hu-kuang and Szechuan could reach them with great ease. The President of the Board of Revenue, Li Yü 李遇, himself a native of Han-chung, was able to report with clear knowledge on the situation of his native place in 1637:

" . . . Your servant's native place, Han-chung, is surrounded by great mountains and great marshes extending over a thousand *li* in all four directions. The rebels have gathered together in these places for the past few years. . . . The people come from everywhere to join them in Han-chung and altogether they number no less than one hundred thousand."[59]

The quick movements of the rebels made it almost impossible for the soldiers to pursue them. When moving they always divided into groups and could dodge into so many places that the soldiers found it almost impossible to cope with them. By these tactics the rebels confused the government troops but often succeeded in making their own small numbers seem very large.[60] Furthermore, the government troops suffered from the lack of cooperation. In general, each commander had charge of a certain region and was interested only in the problems of that region. He might be ready to fight if the rebels attacked his territory, but as soon as they went elsewhere he rested satisfied without any thought of pursuing them. Occasionally an isolated conscientious official might attempt pursuit but, hampered by want of cooperation, he was almost certain to fail. In 1637, for instance, the magistrate of Pao-ting 保定, while pursuing a group of rebels, was drawn into a mountainous region. The rebels, experienced in mountain climbing, moved with great ease. The soldiers who were not trained for such a task found it impossible to follow them. The food which the troops had brought with them was nearly consumed, and the soldiers' shoes were worn out, but the magistrate would not give up. He and his soldiers pushed on as far as the borders of Shansi and Honan, where the rebels again disappeared into the mountains. The magistrate and the soldiers had to recognize that further pursuit was beyond their powers, since the region was unknown to them and they could not find a guide. The magistrate therefore was forced to return, but he remained convinced that with proper cooperation from the authorities of the other provinces, he could have suppressed the rebels effectively.[61]

As early as 1634, an official had called the attention of the government to the strategic importance of Szechuan and warned the government to fortify the province quickly: "If the rebels can but get into the eastern part of Szechuan," he said, "it will be like giving the tiger a mountain range, or allowing a mouse to escape into a hole. You will not find it easy to get rid of them!"[62]

We do not know what measures the government took for the defence of Szechuan, but in that same year of 1634, it was reported that many of the people of Han-chung who had been kidnapped by the rebels had joined them in eastern and northern Szechuan. These kidnappings were carried out in hope of ransom. The rebels disappeared from the villages at the time of sowing, but when the crops were ready for the harvest they came out of hiding to rob the farmers. We are told that in the early days of the revolt the rebels did not invade towns and disliked killing. However, when they were opposed by civilians and soldiers they were greatly angered and began to kill savagely. Their looting increased and they tried to equip their forces as completely as their enemies. Eventually they accumulated weapons of all kinds and a great number of horses. They even had fire-arms.[63]

Firearms

It is to be noted that in the late Ming period the secret of success in war lay in superiority of fire-arms. When the Chinese first learnt from the Europeans the art of making fire-arms they kept it secret and were thus able to defend the territory outside Shan-hai-kuan against the Manchus. "The powerful cannon had its origin in the country of the red-haired barbarians," wrote a scholar of the late Ming period. "The barbarians of Hao-ching-ao 濠鏡澳 (i.e. the Portuguese of Macao—A.C.) in Kuangtung are able to make them. Heaven has favored us and has given us these barbarians of Ao to fortify our cities. Formerly very few of these cannon were sent to us from Kuangtung. The reason was that we had not made clear our attitude towards the barbarians, and the authorities in Kuangtung were slow to make a move. For the same reason the captain of the barbarians declined our requests. But now that the welfare of the borders is in such a state that cannon are more in demand, Your Majesty should issue an edict to inform the barbarians of Ao of your intention, and at the same time to instruct the governor of the two Kuang to pay the price accordingly. The more fire-arms we get, the better it will be for us and the security of our borders, which will no doubt be as well fortified as with a solid wall."[64] In his remarks about the Portuguese of Macao the writer seems to have been recalling the embassy of 1621. Fortunately Père Du Halde has left this interesting account giving further details about this embassy:

"It was in the year 1621 that the city of Macao presented to the emperor three cannon, together with men to operate them. A test was performed in Peking in the presence of the mandarins who were surprised at first and then dismayed when they saw that having fired one of the pieces the recoil killed a Portuguese and three Chinese who did not withdraw quickly enough.

"The cannon were brought to the frontier of the empire, at the border of the Tartars [Manchus] who, having come with [their] troops close to the Great Wall were so terrified by the damage they did when they were fired at that they took to flight and no longer dared to come near again."[65]

The art of firearm-making could not be kept secret for very long. The Manchus knew full well that if they wished to win the war the possession of abundant fire-arms was a *conditio sine qua non*. Hence they tried very hard to obtain such weapons and offered high rewards to those who could make them. The following account from *Chung-kuo hsiung-lüeh* shows how determined the founder of the Ch'ing dynasty was in his quest:

"The Barbarians of the East (i.e. the Manchus—A.C.) have attempted to produce fire-arms for the past ten years. Time and again they have defeated our forces and have taken away fire-arms big and small to the number of fifty to sixty thousand and several million catties of gun powder. They used them for practice and when they invaded Liao-yang 遼陽 again these were employed to defeat our army. Their defeat in Ning-yüan 寧遠 was solely due to the fact that their forces were fewer. Although they suffered a heavy blow still they have great stores of fire-arms and gunpowder. That old scoundrel (i.e. Nurhaci (1559–1626), founder of the Ch'ing dynasty —A.C.) has under him twenty thousand trained soldiers. He pretends to send them out for fire-wood-cutting or hunting but his real plan is hidden even from his wife and children. What is the secret that he is keeping. Who can tell? Perhaps he is now training his forces and waiting for a favorable time to strike. If someone tells me that he has no fire-arms I will answer that he must be looking for them day and night. And to obtain them he will use bribery or force or fraud or theft. We must face him now before he becomes too strong. . . ."[66]

The great effort made by the Manchus to find out the secret of fire-arm making was eventually successful. It could no longer be said of the barbarians that they had only bows and arrows. In 1640 the governor of Hsüan-fu and Ta-tung reported that the barbarians had forged sixty cannon. These must have been of considerable size, for the report said that they were not easy to carry around and that the barbarians would probably employ them for local use.[67]

While this struggle for superiority in fire-arms was going on between the government and the Manchus, the rebels did not over-look the importance of the new weapons. As early as 1633, five years after the rebel uprising, the eunuch Kao Ch'i-ch'ien 高起潛 reported in his memorial to the throne that the government troops did not dare to launch an attack on the rebels since the latter possessed great quantities of fire-arms. A stratagem similar to that of the Trojan horse nearly succeeded in Peking toward the end of the Ch'ung-chen reign. One day, it is said, several huge statues of Buddha were being carried into the imperial capital through the Chang-i Gate 彰義門. The guards examined them and found a cannon inside every statue.[68]

By this time the rebels were expert in the use of fire-arms. Chang Hsien-chung, for instance, possessed fire-arms of all kinds, which he had obtained from Annam.[69] In 1640, when the rebels attacked Shantung, the provincial governor reported that the enemy possessed a great number of fire-arms. During a fight in P'u-chou the government troops claimed to have captured two hundred and three cannon and over five hundred guns. In 1642, General Tso Liang-yü suffered a serious defeat at the hands of Li Tzu-ch'eng in which the latter's use of cannon was the decisive factor.[70] A letter written by Hsü Piao 徐標 (floruit 1630) says that the rebels he captured in Kao Yu 高郵 had fire-arms of outstanding quality. "What we possess cannot be compared with theirs and (I am told) that they produce fire-arms of this type in their quarters day and night."[71]

Horses

In the early days of the revolt when the rebels were still poorly equipped, they were afraid to face the government troops. But as time went on, they came to know the weakness of the soldiers and so feared them less. Later still, when their strength was established, they dared to challenge the army. The memorial of Hung Ch'eng-ch'ou shows that the rebels were well equipped. They had two horses for each fighting man, whereas only thirty per cent of the government soldiers were mounted.[72] The *Tsui-wei lu* describes the rebels' methods. When they conquered a place, their first thought was to seize the horses and mules. Rewards were given to those who could find them.[73] Both Li Tzu-ch'eng and Chang Hsien-chung were said to have good horses.[74] Of Li Tzu-ch'eng it is said that his troops used boats only when they crossed the Yellow River. At the other rivers they merely sat on their horses and swam them across. The number of horses was so great that it sometimes gave onlookers the impression that the water of the river was dammed by the hooves.[75]

In the days of the Hung-wu emperor, great stress was laid on breeding horses for military purposes, as we saw in an earlier chapter. Special envoys were sent frequently to neighboring countries to buy horses. Tributary states were encouraged to give horses rather than any other presents.[76] The government monopolized the export of tea in order to trade with the border tribes for horses. Markets were set up in Liao-tung on the Mongol borders, and in Kansu, Shensi and Szechuan. One hundred and twenty catties of tea were given in exchange for a fine horse. For a horse of medium quality seventy catties of tea were offered, and for an inferior horse, fifty catties. We are told that towards the end of the Hung-wu reign over half a million catties of tea were used to purchase thirteen thousand five hundred horses.[77]

The government also set aside pasture for horse raising. Along the borders and in some of the northern provinces, government horses were bred under the supervision of the T'ai-p'u ssu 太僕寺 or Court of the Imperial Stud. Also, as part of the *corvée*, the people were compelled to look after government horses. In general, government horses were bred in Shansi, Shensi, and Liao-tung. In Nanking, Peking, Shantung, and Honan, horses were bred by the people. During the Hung-wu reign, we are told, in Kiang-nan every eleven households, and north of the Yangtze every five households, were obliged to keep one horse for the government. Similarly, in many sections of the wei 衞 every group of five house-holds was put in charge of a horse. Pastures and stables were supplied by the government.[78] If the horse happened to die the households in charge of it had to replace it. In 1412 an order was given to the Board of War by the Yung-lo emperor to search out retired Mongol officials of good character who would teach the people how to breed good horses. In that same year an order was issued for the inspection of soldiers in charge of horses. If they had bred horses to the standard number, every hundred soldiers were given a reward of five ting of silver. If they failed to improve on the methods formerly in use, they were to be punished.[79] For a time these efforts were highly successful: by the Hsüan-te period (1426–1435) the number of horses in the empire was said to be twice what it had been in the Hung-wu period.[80] It was reported that, shortly before 1416, the ponies raised under the supervision of the Court of the Imperial Stud numbered 197,484.[81]

In this, as in so many other things, the Hung-wu emperor's arrangements worked admirably so long as they were observed. But in this, as in so many other things, they were soon neglected, with disastrous results. Pasture land which had been granted by the Hung-wu emperor for raising horses was appropriated by the military officials, and sometimes sold, or was seized by government officials. The Board of War decided to check such abuses and it was proposed to redistribute the pasture land among the people, each male receiving about one ch'ing and thirty-five mou of land on which government horses were to be bred. This scheme, by and large, was a failure. The dishonest made false reports in order to obtain more land. Sometimes men with only two or three horses obtained twenty to thirty ch'ing of land. Honest people reported the truth and often suffered in consequence. If, for instance, they reported that there were only one or two males in the family, they naturally received only one or two ch'ing of land, but they sometimes were bound to raise from three to five horses for the government.[82] Since the pasture allotted to them did not produce enough grass for so many horses they very often had to buy hay to make up the shortage. Villages which had originally received an equitable command to keep fifty government horses, had to keep the same number, even after a serious fall in the number of households. Conversely the villages which, in the beginning, had been assigned twenty horses, retained the same obligation, even if the number of households in the villages increased.[83] Then, the villagers' ignorance of horse-breeding often led to the death of horses entrusted to them, and they had to spend their own money on replacing the dead beasts.

When the time came for the people to deliver their horses to the government, the officials had a golden opportunity for exacting bribes. Those who did not give bribes might find their horses condemned by the government officials, after which they would have to borrow money to buy better horses and even these might not be accepted.[84] The horses that had been delivered to the government were left to the care of the soldiers. Since hay was not regularly supplied, the beasts naturally suffered malnutrition. Not infrequently the soldiers rented their horses to the postal service or influential officials appropriated them. These mis-applied horses were exposed to heat and cold and were not given proper food. Most of them either died or at least became useless for military purposes.[85]

During the Lung-ch'ing reign the rules for the supplying of horses were changed (1568). Instead of forcing the people to raise horses, the government declared itself satisfied to receive in South China an equivalent payment in money, and in North China a money payment of sixty per cent of the cost of the horses and the other forty per cent in horses.[86] These money payments were paid into the Court of the Imperial Stud. By the end of the Lung-ch'ing period the total sum thus collected was said to amount to over ten million silver taels.[87] This money soon attracted the covetous eyes of the emperors and of officials of different boards. During the Wan-li reign the Board of War borrowed nearly a million silver taels from the Court of the Imperial Stud for the payment of the soldiers, and the Court of Entertainment borrowed three hundred and eighty thousand silver taels for the expenses of the emperor's marriage. At one time, the Board of Revenue had actually borrowed over seven million silver taels. By the end of 1614, barely eighty thousand taels remained in the treasury of the Court of the Imperial Stud.[88]

While the rate of supply from within the empire was thus rapidly falling, the horse-trading markets along the borders were also becoming less productive. At about the middle of his reign, the

Yung-lo emperor, wishing to show special favor to foreigners, increased the amount of tea to be given in exchange for horses. Officials in Tiao-men 碉門 in Szechuan Province were said to have paid over eighty thousand catties of tea in exchange for seventy horses of low quality.[89] One of the reasons for the decline of the government horse trade was the smuggling of tea by merchants who wished to buy horses directly from the tribes. As the merchants got more horses and the government got fewer, dishonest officials tried to cheat the foreign traders by giving them tea of inferior quality. In revenge the foreign traders passed off third-rate horses on the officials.[90] In 1502, a censor reported that horse trading with foreign states along the Chinese borders, which had yielded ten thousand horses yearly up to the beginning of the 15th century was yielding less than a thousand by the end of that century.[91]

In the middle of the T'ien-ch'i reign (1621–1627) an official reported that government horses in the capital numbered only six thousand eight hundred.[92] In 1629, the President of the Court of the Imperial Stud in Northern Chih-li reported that the income of the office from the whole of Northern Chih-li Province amounted to nearly 420,950 silver taels, but that its expenditure exceeded 450,000 silver taels.[93] From then on the reserves in the treasuries fell lower every day, for horses were almost unobtainable except at high prices. Towards the end of the dynasty, when Fang K'ung-chao 方孔炤 wrote to the gentry of present Hunan, he could but utter the despairing cry: "Of late, the price of horses has become higher and higher and we lack money to buy them. What can we do?"[94]

CHANG HSIEN-CHUNG

Since most of the leaders of the rebels in the later Ch'ung-chen period had served under Kao Ying-hsiang in their early days, it was only to be expected that their way of life and methods of warfare would be essentially the same as his, and their constant movement had taught them to adapt themselves everywhere. As in all such irregular forces, the training and the spirit of the rebel forces depended on the leaders. It would be impossible to treat all of them here. We shall therefore single out two of the most influential, two men who loom large in Chinese history, Chang Hsien-chung and Li Tzu-ch'eng.

Chang Hsien-chung was a native of Shensi, born in 1606. In his early days he was a salesman. Later he abandoned trade and became a sub-official. It is said that he once committed a crime which almost cost him his life, but was saved by a government official. At the beginning of the Ch'ung-chen reign he joined Kao Ying-hsiang and remained with him until 1636, when Kao was captured by government troops and executed. In 1638, after suffering repeated defeats, he surrendered to the government, but in the following year he revolted again under the influence, it was said, of some scholars. From 1637 to 1641, his forces increased more rapidly than any other rebel group. At one time he commanded several hundred thousand men, and his field of activities covered several provinces. However, in the fall of 1641, he was defeated by the army of Tso Liang-yü and barely escaped with his life. Before the end of the year he had joined the rebels of Anhui and eventually succeeded in rebuilding strong forces. In 1643 he led them to Han-yang and Wu-ch'ang, where he looted the palace of Prince Ch'u, bringing away over a million silver taels. The prince and most of his family were slaughtered and Chang occupied the prince's palace and made himself king of Ta-hsi 大西. Three months later he was again badly defeated, but escaped to Chang-sha where he retained his royal title and began to build palaces. In 1644 he began to move toward Szechuan, capturing Cheng-tu and making it the capital of his kingdom.

This Chang Hsien-chung, a man of powerful physique, who was known to his companions as the "Yellow Tiger" among the leaders of the rebels, was reputed to be the man of great sagacity. His successes were due in part to his possession of a strong force, but his shrewdness may have counted more than his imposing numbers. He saw clearly how dissatisfied the people were with the government, and to win them to his side, wherever he went he always shared his loot with the poor, giving them alms and help of other kinds. When he came to Chang-sha he ordered all the people of the districts under his control to carry on their business and exempted them from taxes for three years.[95] This naturally attracted the people and made them exceedingly well disposed towards him.

His ingenious system of espionage was another source of strength and may have helped him more than mere force of arms. We are told that as soon as he had settled down in a new place he sent out batches of scouts to spy out the land to a distance of two hundred miles in all directions. At the end of every mile each group dispatched a messenger to report to Chang, so that no military movement of the slightest importance could be kept secret from him. Before a siege, spies disguised as Buddhist or Taoist monks, or as travellers and merchants, were sent into the city. As soon as they had made their entry they began to bribe the local criminals of the place to help the rebels. If Chang happened to capture people of good standing outside the city, he would carefully investigate the condition of their families, parents, wives and children, thus establishing a hold over the prisoners. Then he would send rebels disguised as servants to accompany them to the gate of the city, pretending that the prisoners and their 'servants' had escaped from captivity. Once they were inside, the rebels turned to helping the besiegers. Few cities succeeded in unmasking this treacherous deception.[96]

If government messengers were captured, their documents were taken by rebels who disguised themselves as messengers and used the documents to gain entry to the city to which the documents were addressed. Not infrequently they also falsified government documents. The author of the *Chieh-i-lu* 孑遺錄 says that many of the cities fell into the hands of the rebels through this means. Later, to prevent this deception, all government documents were marked with special signatures.[97] At times a group of rebels disguised as defeated government troops would seek admission to a city, on the plea that the enemy were pursuing them. The city, unaware of the deception, would admit them. By the time the truth was found out, it was already too late to save the city.[98]

It seems to have been common for the rebels to employ children for spying and propaganda. To frighten the timid and to convince them that the Ming dynasty was near its end they tried to provide weird portents such as turning the water in a city moat blood red, or making groups of children cry at night—a sign of mourning for the passing of the dynasty—or leaving bloody hand marks on doors throughout the city.[99] During a siege the rebels would play on the discontent and fear of the people by starting rumors. Sometimes children were made to sing the songs of the native districts of the government soldiers in order to arouse memories of their homes. The children were forced to sing such songs over a period of months, if necessary. Often these cunning tactics would throw a whole city into confusion till many were ready to welcome the rebels.[100] It is asserted that on the fall of a city, the rebels usually handed over their prisoners to be massacred by children and that if any of the children wilted they were killed by the rebels. After killing for a while, the children began to develop a taste for savagery. Subsequently, they were taught horsemanship and the art of warfare, and were organized into the hai-erh-chün 孩兒軍 or "Children's army."[101]

Chang Hsien-chung, having conquered Cheng-tu and set up an independent government there, wished to prevent criticism of himself and of his government. He therefore used to send out spies, many of them children, to mingle both with the rebels and with the people.

All murmuring against Chang's government was reported by the spies, and the careless speakers, and often those who lived in the same house with them, were executed. The reign of terror became so dreadful that members of the same family dared not talk to one another when they met in the streets.[102]

Rebel espionage terrified the people and cast them into a condition of great anxiety. "Our every movement is known by the rebels," Hsü Piao lamented. "Some of the spies are in the direct service of the rebels, others work for their (rebel) relatives. They supply them with news of all kinds or spy at the Yamen. Others receive great sums of money from the rebels and try to buy fire-arms and gun-powder for them. Government officials are surrounded by men who are working for the rebels from within and who are preparing the way for them. The authorities have no idea of what the rebels are doing, but the rebels know clearly every movement of the government. Officials charged with the suppression of the rebels are hindered by calumnies, and the maneuvers fixed upon for fighting the enemy are often abandoned or delayed. The people are thus constantly kept in great suffering, but the authorities do not seem to have awakened from their dreams. As soon as the rebels have consolidated their strength, revolts will break out suddenly and will bring about the ruin of the city and of its people. Government officials themselves will meet dreadful disasters. The spies alone will benefit by all this."[103] The same author speaks also of spies on water: "It is dreadful to see the eight-oared boats of the rebels, known as shui-shang-fei 水上飛 (flight above the water). They come in three or four times daily to obtain news from spies who communicate to them all the secrets of the city. A little carelessness in watching often causes great damage."[104]

In 1644, when Chang Hsien-chung and his forces were pushing on to Chungking, they met strong resistance. When he took the city he ordered a general massacre as a punishment for this stubbornness. We are told that over ten thousand men had their ears, noses and right arms cut off, and were then paraded in many places as a warning for those who refused to surrender.[105] The *Tsui-wei lu* tells that it was the practice of the rebels to spare only those who surrendered at the first demand. If the people of a city resisted, even for a day or two, a third or a fourth of them would be killed as soon as the city had fallen. If the city resisted for five to six days and then surrendered, the rebels massacred all indiscriminately.[106] This explains, perhaps, why so many places surrendered so quickly.

Li Tzu-ch'eng

Li Tzu-ch'eng also was a native of Shensi, and was born in the same year as Chang Hsien-chung. He belonged to the family of a rich farmer, and went to school until he was fourteen or fifteen, when he gave up his studies to devote his time to military arts. Shortly after his father's death he dissipated all the family's fortune. About the year 1626, he obtained the office of courier in the government postal service, but he committed a crime and had to escape to Kansu where he enlisted as a soldier. Being a skillful and brave fighter he was soon promoted to a minor rank, but after some time he quarrelled with an official, who was promptly killed by Li's soldiers. Li therefore judged it wise to gather his men for desertion *en masse*.

In 1631, Li Tzu-ch'eng was acting under the command of the notorious Kao Ying-hsiang, then the ringleader of the rebels. The fall of Kao in 1636 destroyed Li Tzu-ch'eng's influence and for a few years he lived in retirement. In 1639, when Chang Hsien-chung revolted in present Hupei, Li went to join him, but the meeting was not a happy one and Li went off to raise a force of his own. By 1640, he was at the head of a large and growing force. On the advice of the scholar Li Yen he sent out his men as propagandists promising not only exemption from taxes but even equal distribution of land. This latter promise was received with the utmost enthusiasm by the people of Honan, where the farmers had suffered more perhaps than elsewhere from the loss of their land to nobles and landlords. A contemporary writer tells us that about the year 1640, the province of Honan was prosperous apart from the plight of the nobles about which we have already seen something. Most of the landlords vied with one another in extending their possession of land and slaves. Some of them owned over a thousand ch'ing of land apiece, and the least prosperous of them not less than five hundred ch'ing.[107]

In 1643, Li Tzu-ch'eng, having conquered Huang-chou 黄州, exempted the people from taxes for three years.[108] This so pleased the people that many cities capitulated to him of their own accord. Wherever he went, he was always eager to expose the corruption of the Ming government, with special stress on the heavy taxation it imposed. His propaganda was so successful that government officials ultimately decided to learn something from it. When, after the fall of Peking (1644), Prince Fu succeeded to the throne in Nanking, one of the ministers presented to him a memorial, petitioning that the regions north of the Yangtze River, Honan and Shantung, be exempted from land taxes. "Let us not give our enemy any cause for belittling us," he said.[109]

Li Tzu-ch'eng's hostility towards the nobles and the rich was itself effective rebel propaganda. "I kill them," he said, "because they are the oppressors of the people." He showed his sympathy with the people by giving alms generously. This generosity and sympathy soon became known to the hungry and the helpless, and many travelled long distances to join him.

At the beginning of the revolt, Li Tzu-ch'eng was inclined to be cruel, and the people were so much afraid of him that they tried to organize a strong resistance to him. Later he saw his mistake and changed his whole attitude towards the people. He strictly forbade his soldiers to disturb the people of conquered cities unnecessarily, and he announced that his purpose was to deliver the people from their sufferings. When people learnt of this good will, their hostile attitude changed into friendliness and cooperation. In the last few years of the Ch'ung-chen period the people of many cities refused to fight for the government, preferring to surrender to the rebels.[110] We are told that in 1644, when puppet magistrates were sent by Li Tzu-ch'eng to several districts of Honan and Shansi, the people drove away their legitimate rulers and welcomed Li's nominees. The author of the *K'ou-shih pien-nien* in describing one of these incidents says that the people's enthusiasm was such that they nearly became frantic.[111]

Unlike Chang Hsien-chung, Li Tzu-ch'eng, we are told, lived a simple life, accompanied only by his wife and one concubine. In moments of leisure he pursued academic studies, and asked scholars to comment on the classics and history. When important decisions were to be made, he usually summoned his staff and sat in silence, listening carefully to the views of each. At the end of the meeting he quietly made his own decision, selecting the best opinions from those submitted.[112] Among the rebel leaders, Li was outstanding for his tactful dealing with his subjects and always shared the joys and sorrows of his subjects and treated them as his equals. Probably he owed these valuable characteristics to his genuine frankness and simplicity of life. After the fall of Peking, an eyewitness saw him entering the city in an ordinary uniform indistinguishable from that of the other rebel officers.[113] Thus, for many reasons, he was far better liked by his subjects than the notorious Chang Hsien-chung. In the last few years of the Ch'ung-chen period he was joined by many of the rebel leaders including erstwhile followers of Chang Hsien-chung.[114] Even certain government officers are said to have admired his good qualities so much that they offered him their services.[115] Government soldiers too fell under his influence. In 1643, his messengers brought several tens of thousands of silver taels to the soldiers in Yü-lin as a sign of friendship and a bid for their surrender.[116]

Li Tzu-ch'eng had a well organized army of about sixty thousand men, divided into five divisions. The largest division numbered one hundred regiments and the other four divisions had over thirty regiments each. In all, he had about two hundred and thirty regiments, each consisting of fifty cavalrymen, one hundred and fifty infantrymen, and thirty to forty servitors in charge of the horses and arms. His horses and mules numbered about twenty thousand.[117] His best men, who were between the ages of fifteen and forty, were allowed to bring their wives and servants with them, but if children were born, they were not permitted to keep them. Even in conquered cities his forces were commanded to live in tents, which were made of so many layers of cloth that not even bullets or arrows could penetrate them. His horses were well cared for and were used only on the battlefield. Each of Li's best soldiers kept a few horses and changed them frequently during a campaign in order to keep them in good condition.[118]

Li Tzu-ch'eng's spy service was no less efficient than Chang Hsien-chung's. His spies wore the distinguishing marks of all professions, and they were spread everywhere. He even tried to get scholars who were going to the capital for government examinations to spy for him. Often he helped these scholars to bribe their way through the examinations, and they, in gratitude, willingly rendered services in return to the rebels. Chao Chi-shih 趙吉士 says that it was astonishing to see how many spies would be present at the fall of a city. "No one knows where they come from!"[119] An eyewitness of the fall of Peking tells us that many of the cloth merchants and restaurant proprietors in the capital were from Shensi and Shansi, and that many of them spied for Li Tzu-ch'eng.[120]

One of the causes of Li Tzu-ch'eng's success at this period was his respect for scholars and his readiness to accept their services. Chang Hsien-chung, it is true, also employed scholars, but he had very little patience with them and was so stubborn that no one could advise him about anything. Among the scholars who were in Li Tzu-cheng's service was Li Yen (see above), who was said to have joined the rebels because he had been falsely accused by a corrupt magistrate. It was he who proposed to Li Tzu-ch'eng the exemption of the people from land taxes and the equal distribution of land. The *Ming shih* says that his propagandist folk songs influenced many to follow Li Tzu-ch'eng.[121]

Another scholar who helped Li Tzu-ch'eng to build up his new government was Niu Chin-hsing 牛金星, a provincial graduate from Honan, who eventually became both Li's chief adviser and his tutor.[122] In 1643, Yang Yung-yü 楊永裕, director of the Imperial Observatory, joined Li Tzu-ch'eng. We are told that he kept on trying to persuade Li to assume the title of emperor, but that Li always pretended unwillingness, although at heart he greatly approved the suggestion. Li commissioned to this man to write his official documents and public proclamations.[123]

This association with men of letters had a profound influence on Li Tzu-ch'eng, who in time became quite learned. The traditional scholarly theory of the ruler's mandate of heaven must have been much in his mind, for nearly all the scholars in his service hailed him as the chosen one. In his public proclamations, he began to denounce the Ch'ung-chen emperor as a despot who employed the eunuchs to rob the people and to accuse the government officials of corruption and of cruelty to the people. He himself assumed the mantle of savior of the people. "For ten generations my family have been honest farmers. (Unable to suffer the abuses of the government), I have marched with an army of justice in order to save my people, from their sufferings. . . ."[125] To gain the good will of the people he gave strict orders to the soldiers to respect the lives of the citizens. At the end of 1643, after the fall of Yü-lin, several hundred rebels were sent by Li Tzu-ch'eng to proclaim in innumerable localities that "anyone who kills a man will be considered to have killed my own father. If he insults a woman, I shall take this as an insult to my own mother!"[126]

From 1641, onward Li Tzu-ch'eng moved swiftly. In that year he conquered Lo-yang where Prince Fu was captured and killed. He next attacked K'ai-feng. Strong resistance forced him to withdraw for a time but he returned in the following year and inundated the whole city by breaking the dikes of the Yellow River. By 1643 all Honan was under his control. From Honan he moved on to Shansi where he conquered Ta-t'ung, Chu-yung and Hsüan-fu at the beginning of 1644. Two days after the capture of Hsüan-fu, Peking fell. The Ch'ung-chen emperor strove desperately to save the city but none of his subjects would cooperate with him. In despair he climbed a small hill near the palace and there hanged himself.

NOTES

¹ *Kuo ch'üeh*, (ts'e 75) number of page not given.

² Ibid.

³ Hu Wen-huan 胡文煥, *Hua-i feng-t'u chih* 華夷風土志, (late Ming editiAn) 1, (ts'e 1) 1a–17b.

⁴ Ibid., 1, (ts'e 1) 18b–35a; cf. also *Ch'ing-kuo hsiung-lüeh*, 3, (ts'e 9) 2b–3a. Here the author says that the districts near Su-chou had been suffering from floods since 1539. He attributed these disasters to the negligence of the local rulers who preferred seeing the people suffer to reporting disasters to high authorities. The floods turned fertile farms into barren land and the farmers were left homeless.

⁵ *Hua-i feng-t'u chih*, 2, 34b–46b; 3, 43a–53a; *Ch'ing-kuo hsiung-lüeh*, 3, (ts'e 5) 35a; *Hua-i feng-t'u chih* 3, 53a–67b; As early as 1570 we are told that bandits were numerous in Kuangtung. "Formerly Kuangtung was known for its prosperity" wrote Kao Kung 高拱 (1512–1587), then Grand Secretary, "but of late the people have become poor and the place is infested with bandits. One must admit that corrupt officials are the cause of this. From now on we must choose good officials for this post (the governorship). We must not appoint officials who are in exile to govern the place, lest they do injustice to the people. (Cf. *Chia-ching i-lai chu-lüeh*, 6, (ts'e 3) 26b–27a).

⁶ *Ku-chin chih-p'ing lüeh*, 24, (ts'e 18) 58ab.

⁷ *Hua-i feng-t'u chih*, 3, 22ab.

⁸ Ibid., 3, 1ab.

⁹ *China in the 16th Century*, 305.

¹⁰ *Hua-i feng-t'u chih*, 2, 20a–34b.

¹¹ Ibid., 1, (ts'e 1) 35a–49b; *Ch'ing-kuo hsiung-lüeh*, 1, (ts'e 4) 22b–33a; 1, (ts'e 3) 20a.

¹² *Hua-i feng-t'u chih*, 1, (ts'e 1) 49b–50a; *Ch'ing-kuo hsiung lüeh, Sheng fan k'ao*, 1, (ts'e 4) 40a–42a; Ch'eng Po-erh 程百二, *Fang-yü sheng-lüeh* 方輿勝略, (Wan-li edition) (ts'e 2) 1a.

¹³ *Hua-i feng-t'u chih*, 2, 1a–19b; *Ch'ing-kuo hsiung-lüeh, Sheng fan k'ao*, (ts'e 5) 6b–7a.

¹⁴ *Ming shih*, 309, (ts'e 103) 1a.

¹⁵ E.g. *Ming-jen shih-ch'ao* 明人詩鈔, (edited by Chu Yen 朱琰), First series, 4, (ts'e 4) 10ab; second series 14, (ts'e 8) 9b.

¹⁶ *Erh-shih erh-shih cha-chi*, 36, (ts'e 6) 39b–42b; *Ming-shih chi-shih pen-mo*, 70, 2, 73–75,

¹⁷ *Ming Ch'ing shih-liao chia-pien* 明清史料甲編, (ed. by the Palace Museum of Peiping) (Peiping, 1931) p. 713.

¹⁸ *Ming shih*, 20, (ts'e 6) 13a.

¹⁹ *Ming-ch'en tsou-i*, 38. (ts'e 0,922) 732–733.

²⁰ Ibid., 38 726–727.

²¹ *Mi-chih-hsien chih* 米脂縣志, compiled by Kao Chao-hsü 高照煦. (Shensi, 1907), 6, (ts'e 2) 2a; *Huai-yü-hsien chih* 懷遠縣志, compiled by Su Chi-chao 蘇其炤 and revised by Ho Ping-hsün 何丙勳, (Shensi, 1928) 2, (ts'e 2) 1a, 17b.

²² Li Wen-chih 李文治, *Wan-Ming min-pien* 晚明民變. (Shanghai, 1948) 13, notes 48, 49.

²³ Ibid, 13, notes 50–53.

²⁴ Ibid, 14, note 69.

²⁵ *Hsi-yüan wen-chien lu*, 72, (ts'e 28) 11a.

²⁶ *Tsui-wei lu*, 20, (ts'e 17) 6b, 7a.

²⁷ *Hsi-yüan wen-chien lu*, 72, (ts'e 28) 5b; *Wan-Ming min-pien*, 26.

²⁸ *Hsi-yüan wen-chien lu*, 72, (ts'e 28) 12b.

²⁹ Ibid., 14b.

³⁰ Ibid., 11a.

[31] Ibid., 16b; cf. also *Wan-Ming min-pien*, 25.

[32] *Chun-ming meng-yü-lu*, 42, (ts'e 15) 75a.

[33] *Wan-Ming min-pien*, 26; Tsou I 鄒漪, *Ming-chi-i-wen* 明季遺聞, (*Ming-chi pai-shi* second series) (ts'e 1) 1a.

[34] Ibid., (ts'e 1) 1a.

[35] *Lieh-huang hsio-chih*, 2, (ts'e 1) 4b.

[36] *Ch'ien-lung po-shui hsien-chih* 乾隆白水縣志, (Ch'ien-lung edition), 1, (ts'e 1) 11.

[37] *Ming shih*, 309, (ts'e 103) 1b–2a.

[38] *Chi-yüan chi so chi*, 9, (ts'e 14) 2a; *Lieh-huang hsiao-chih*, 2, (ts'e 1) 8a.

[39] *K'ou-shih pien-nien*, 1, (ts'e 5) 2a; 6, (ts'e 6) 28ab; *Tsui-wei lu*, 17, (ts'e 7) 8b.

[40] *Ming-mo nung-min ch'i-i shih-liao*, 27.

[41] *Wan-Ming min-pien*, 32.

[42] *K'ou-shih pien-nien*, 1, (ts'e 5) 1b, 2a.

[43] Ibid., 4, (ts'e 5) 3b.

[44] Cf., chapter 5, note 71 above.

[45] *Tsui-wei lu*, 12, (ts'e 5) 75b, 85b.

[46] *Ming-ch'en tsou-i*, (ts'e 0920) 567.

[47] *Tsui-wei lu*, 14, (ts'e 6) 41a.

[48] Cheng Ch'in 鄭欽 and Cheng Jui 鄭銳 *Po-chung t'ai-shu-ts'ao* 伯仲臺疏草, (TSCCCP), (ts'e 0,912) 6.

[49] *Hou-chien lu*, 8, (ts'e 18) 118ab.

[50] *Wan-Ming min-pien*, 28.

[51] Ibid., 33

[52] *P'ing-k'ou chih*, 1, (ts'e 1) 2a.

[53] *K'ou-shih pien-nien*, 8, (ts'e 7) 7a.

[54] Ibid., 3, (ts'e 5) 2a; *Chi-yüan chi so chi*, 9, (ts'e 14) 27a.

[55] *P'ing-k'ou chih*, 1, (ts'e 1) 9a.

[56] *Wan-Ming mi-pien*, 66; according to the *P'ing-k'ou chih*, 1, (ts'e 1) 17b the number of rebels in the fall of 1634 was a little over two hundred thousand.

[57] *K'ou-shih pien-nien*, 4, (ts'e 5) 21b; 11, (ts'e 9) 6b; 7, (ts'e 6) 2b; 5, (ts'e 6) 3b; 6, (ts'e 6) 14b.

[58] *Ming-mo nung-min ch'i-i shih-liao*, 72.

[59] *K'ou-shih pien-nien*, 10, (ts'e 8) 10a.

[60] *P'ing-k'ou chih*, 3, (ts'e 1) 6a.

[61] *Ming-mo nung-min ch'i-i shih-liao*, 103–106.

[62] Ibid., 108–109.

[63] Ku Shan-chen 顧山貞, *K'o T'ien shu* 客滇述, (T'ung-shih edition) (ts'e 29) 2b.

[64] *Wu-meng-yüan chi*, (ts'e 10) 59b, 60a.

[65] J. B. Du Halde, *Description geographique, historique, chronologique, politique, et physique de l'empire de la Chine*, 2. 47. From other sources we know that the Portuguese killed in this accident was João Correa whose epitaph was written by the scholar Ho Ch'iao-yüan 何喬遠 (floruit 1620) at the request of Father Nicolas Longobardi (1559–1654) cf. Ho Ch'iao-yüan, *Ching-shan ch'üan-chi* 鏡山全集, (late Ming edition) 66, (ts'e 30) 21b–22b; *Chung-hsi ch'iao-t'ung-shih*, 4. 91–92.

[66] *Ching-kuo hsiung-lüeh*, *Wu-pi k'ao* 武備考, 7, (ts'e 20) 3b, 4a.

[67] Pi Mao-k'ang 畢懋康, *Chün-ch'i t'u-shuo* 軍器圖說, (1638 edition) preface, *Kuo-ch'üeh* (ts'e 80) 81b.

[68] *Ch'ung-chen ts'un-shih shu-ch'ao* 崇禎存實疏鈔, (Shanghai, 1934) 6A (ts'e 11) 70a; *Chi-yüan chi so chi*, 1. 246.

[69] *Fu-chu shu k'ao*, 8b.

[70] *Ming-mo nung-min ch'i-i shih-liao*, 308–309; *K'ou-shih pien-nien*, 15, (ts'e 10) 10b.

[71] Hsü Piao 徐標, *Hsiao-chu erh yen* 小築邇言, (Ch'ung-chen edition) 24, (ts'e 16) 24a–25a.

[72] *K'ou-shih pien-nien*, 8, (ts'e 7) 24ab; *Ming-chi i-wen*, 3b.

[73] *Tsui-wei lu*, 31, (ts'e 57) 60a–63a.

[74] *Fu-chu shu-k'ao*, 8b.

[75] *K'ou-shih pien-nien*, 16, (ts'e 11) 12a.

[76] *Hsi-yüan wen-chien lu*, 70, (ts'e 27) 25b.

[77] *Ming hui-yao*, 2, 1207.

[78] *Hsi-yüan wen-chien lu*, 70, (ts'e 27) 7b The *Ming shih*, 92, (ts'e 33) 17b, the *Ming hui-yao*, 2. 1198 and the *Ching-kuo hsiung-lüeh, lu-shui k'ao* 2, (ts'e 11) 17a all agreed that in Kiang-nan eleven households were to keep one horse for the government. The *Hsi-yüan wen-chien lu* however, gives the number as ten. Perhaps the author had confused the Hung-wu emperor's law with a new law published by the Yung-lo emperor in 1417. Cf. *Ming hui-yao*, 2. 1199.

[79] *Kuo-ch'ao t'ien-hui*, 157, (ts'e 52) 3b.

[80] *Hsi-yüan wen-chien lu*, 70, (ts'e 27) 7b, 8a.

[81] Ibid., 70, (ts'e 27) 11a.

[82] Ibid., 70, (ts'e 27) 29b.

[83] Ibid., 70, (ts'e 27) 29b.

[84] Ibid., 71, (ts'e 28) 6a, 17b.

[85] Ibid., 71, (ts'e 28) 16ab, 14b; 70, (ts'e 27) 14b

[86] Ibid., 71, (ts'e 28) 19a; *Tien-ku chi-wen*, 18, (ts'e 134) 4b.

[87] *Hsi-yüan wen-chien lu*, 71, (ts'e 28) 19a.

[88] Ibid., 71, (ts'e 28) 19a; *Yung-chuang hsiao-pin*, 2, (ts'e 98) 13a. Ch'en Jen-hsi however, gives another version: "Since the Cheng-te reign the money for horses had accumulated to a sum of over ten million. Between 1590 and 1625 all this money was borrowed, over ten million by the Board of Revenues and over eignt hundred thousand by the Board of Works." Cf. *Wu-meng-yüan chi*, (ts'e 19) 64b.

[89] *Ming shih*, 80, (ts'e 28) 20b.

[90] *Ming hui-yao*, 62, 2. *1208*.

[91] Ibid.

[92] H*sui-wei lu*, 22, (ts'e 1g) 7ab.

[93] *Ch'un-meng meng-yu lu*, 53, (ts'e 29) 9b, 10a.

[94] *Fu chu k'ung-tu*, (TCFSCSIS), (ts'e 5) 30a.

[95] Wu Wei-yeh 吳偉業 (1609–1671), *Sui-k'ou chi-lüeh* 綏寇紀略, (TSCCCP), 10, (ts'e 3,991) 225.

[96] *K'ou-shih pien-nien*, 14, (ts'e 10) 11a.

[97] Ibid., 14, (ts'e 10) 3b; *Chieh-i-lu*, 3b.

[98] Li Fu-yung 李馥榮, *Yen-yü nang* 灧澦嚢, (Tao-kuang edition) 1, (ts'e 1) 28ab.

[99] Ibid., 2, (ts'e 2) 32a.

[100] *Supplement to the San-yüan pi-chi*, C. 14a.

[101] *Chi-yüan chi so chi*, 9, (ts'e 14) 47a.

[102] *Shu pi*, 54; Ou-yang Chih 歐陽直, *Ou-yang shih i-shu* 歐陽氏遺書, (Manuscript) 13b.

[103] *Hsiao-chu erh-yen*, 24, (ts'e 16) 28ab.

[104] Ibid., 24, (ts'e 16) 31a.

[105] *Ch'ung-chen-ch'ao chi-shih*, 4, 26a.

[106] *Tsui-wei lu*, 31, (ts'e 57) 61.

[107] Cheng Lien 鄭廉, *Yü pien chi-lüeh* 豫變紀略, (Published by P'eng Chia-ping 彭家屏, 1743), 3, (ts'e 3) 13b.

[108] Chi Liu-ch'i 計六奇, *Ming-chi pei lüeh* 明季北略, (Peking, late 19th century edition) 19, (ts'e 7) 21a.

[109] *Ming shih*, 274, (ts'e 90) 14a.

[110] *K'ou-shih pien-nien*, 15, (ts'e 10) 20b; *Ming-shih chi-shih pen-mo*, 79, 2. 78.

[111] *K'ou-shih pien-nien*, 17, (ts'e 11) 5b.

[112] Ibid., 16, (ts'e 11) 12a; *P'ing-k'ou chih*, 6, (ts'e 3) 10a.

[113] Ch'en Chi-sheng 陳濟生, *Tsai-sheng chi-lüeh* 再生紀略, (HLTTS), (ts'e 110) B 5; 5b, 7a.

[114] *K'ou-shih pien-nien*, 14, (ts'e 10) 15b, 15, (ts'e 10) 15b.

[115] Ibid., 16, (ts'e 11) 25b.

[116] Ibid., 16, (ts'e 11) 26a.

[117] *Chia-shen ch'uan-hsin lu*, 6, 108.

[118] *K'ou-shih pien-nien*, 16, (ts'e 11) 12a.

[119] *Chi-yüan chi so chi*, 9, (ts'e 14) 46b.

[120] *Tsai-sheng chi-lüeh*, A. 4a.

[121] *Ming shih*, 309, (ts'e 103) 11b.

[122] *P'ing-k'ou chih*, 6, (ts'e 3) 10a.

[123] *Chia-shen ch'uan-hsin lu*, 6, 108.

[124] Ibid., 6, 116.

[125] *P'ing-k'ou chih*, 6, (ts'e 3) 1b.

[126] *K'ou-shih pien-nien*, 16, (ts'e 11) 28a.

CHAPTER THIRTEEN

After the Fall of Peking

The Ming dynasty had fallen. The rebels were triumphant. The history of China had reached a turning point. It might have been expected that Li Tzu-ch'eng would complete his conquest and found a new dynasty that would last for some time. He had behind him a long tale of brilliant success. His armies were both loyal and powerful. His propaganda had been effective and many of the people were on his side. He himself certainly had seriously thought of seizing the vacant throne, and most of his contemporaries must have expected him to do so. Yet he failed. Within a few years all his hopes had vanished and his forces had disappeared.

The chief cause of Li Tzu-ch'eng's downfall was, probably, his failure to keep the glowing promises he had made to the people. Neither the exemption from taxes nor the equal distribution of land was ever put into practice. In his early days, the poor supported him in high hopes, and longed for the day when he would reform the abuses of the Ming government. But after the fall of Peking he attempted only a superficial reform of the government. He changed the names of certain departments and offices, but the machinery of government remained substantially as it had been under the Ming emperors. The people, noting the sad contrast between promise and performance, began to lose confidence in Li, and his public proclamations, once hailed in eagerness, lost most of their old effect. After his defeat by the Manchus, Li became highly irascible and began to act as a tyrant. We are told that, in 1644, during his retreat to Shansi, he was exceedingly cruel to the people wherever he went. Having arrived at Han-ch'eng 韓城, in Shensi province, in grievous financial straits he did not scruple during his twenty-five-day stay in that city to use barbarous means for exacting supplies from the people.[1] His reign of terror only provoked a popular rising, and strong opposition arose among the people everywhere. In the end he was to be killed not by a great leader with imperial ambition, but by disaffected farmers.[2]

His financial position was always weak. Shortly after the fall of Peking, Li had control of several provinces—Kansu, Shensi, Shansi, Honan, Shantung, Northern Chih-li, the northern part of Hu-kuang, and the northern part of Southern Chih-li—but the great area south of the Yangtze River, the richer part of the country, was still in the hands of the Ming princes, and Szechuan was under the dominion of Chang Hsien-chung. Not one of the provinces controlled by Li Tzu-ch'eng could be called rich and more than ten years of continual fighting had destroyed many of the cities, towns, and villages. Honan province in particular had suffered irreparable damage. A 1641 report tells us that in the area from the east to the south-west of that province most of the inhabitants had either fled or perished.[3] Over eighty towns in the northwest of the province had been reduced to ruins. Hungry citizens gathered together to rob, and openly defied the government.[4]

After the famines of 1640 and 1641 in Shantung, the province was ravaged by bandits. From Ching-hai 靜海 to Lin-ch'ing in Northern Chih-li, according to an official report, thirty per cent of the inhabitants had died of starvation, thirty per cent had died in a plague, and the remaining forty per cent had become bandits. The price of rice had risen to over twenty-four silver taels a picul and some of the people were reduced to eating corpses.[5] By 1644, the situation in the province had become worse and many of the towns in the west had disappeared.[6] Shensi and Shansi provinces had suffered similar fates, and even the provinces along the Yangtze valley, Hu-kuang and Southern Chih li, normally famous for their abundance of farming products, were now almost depopulated. In 1642, there were hardly any inhabitants left in Yün-yang prefecture and when the government troops passed through it they could find no food.[7] The prefectural city of Ku-ch'eng 穀城 had barely two hundred inhabitants in 1642.[8]

These unfavorable circumstances gravely hindered Li Tzu-ch'eng's activities. He had to supply his forces from whatever he could exact from the provinces he occupied. From east of the capital came the double menace of the Manchus and of Wu San-kuei 吳三桂 (1612–1678), the commander of a strong force in Shan-hai-kuan, who was determined to avenge the death of the Emperor. In the south there was the unpredictable threat of the Ming princes. Faced with these powerful enemies, Li Tzu-ch'eng had to keep his forces strong and feed them well; if he failed in this they would not fight for him. This alone suffices to explain why he could not keep the promises he had made to the people.

Politically, Li Tzu-ch'eng committed a grave error by under-estimating the importance of seeking cooperation from the Ming government officials and the landlord class. Corrupt though they were, they still had great political influence in the capital; but instead of seeking their cooperation, Li humiliated them shamefully, tortur-ing many of them and putting some to death. He did indeed hold government examinations to choose candidates for various offices; but, as an eyewitness tells us, only a few out of a hundred obtained appointments, and the rest were sent away. Ex-officials who still possessed property had to pay in taxes thirty per cent of what they had, and those who had nothing were sent to work as poor laborers. The same eye-witness tells us that in practice, if a family possessed a thousand silver taels, ten thousand were demanded in taxes; if it possessed ten thousand, many more thousands were demanded. Ultimately, many committed suicide because they could not meet these demands.[9] Many of these exorbitant demands were made arbitrarily by the rebel leaders, and Li Tzu-ch'eng disapproved heartily of them. But when he urged his subordinates to be more lenient, they would immediately reply, "We have let you keep the position of emperor; you must leave us free to demand money from the people."[10]

Those who had received posts in the new government, especially officials who had served under the Ming dynasty, had hardly any authority, for the rebels had no respect whatsoever for them. We are told that a newly appointed official of the Board of War happened to meet some of the rebels, when he was coming out from the court. He was asked what appointment he had received and he told them the truth. Upon hearing this, they patted him on the back and said, "That is good. But you must not demand bribes as the officials of the old dynasty did. You must remember that our master is a severe man. He will demand the heads of all corrupt officials!"[11] Even magistrates of districts were unable to avoid the insults of the rebels. It was said that the magistrates of Northern Chih-li often had to supply women to rebels passing through their districts. If the officials displeased the rebels, they suffered physical violence. The soldiers usually took away the better-looking women, leaving the rest for other soldiers who might pass through the same place.[12]

When Li Tzu-ch'eng first entered Peking, many of the government officials of the Ming dynasty were fully willing to cooperate with him. But very soon they detected the attitude of the new government toward them and were greatly disappointed. Many then turned to the example of Wu San-kuei who had sought help from the Manchus to fight the rebels. The Manchus, who had long been waiting for a chance to enter China, saw in this an excellent opportunity and marched in in great force. Their promises to the people were essentially the same as those made earlier by the rebels, exemption from taxes and the restoration of peace and order. But in their political approach there was a highly significant difference. They did not neglect to seek the cooperation of the Ming officials and the landlord class. The proclamation made on the occasion of the accession of the Shun-chih emperor (1644–1661) stated that:

" . . . higher officials of the preceding dynasty (Ming) or their descendants who have taken the initiative in surrendering to us will be employed by us, as soon as they have shown that they are trustworthy, as if they were our own people (the Manchus). If their parents deserve to be raised to the nobility, we will grant them this, according to custom. Officials who approached us when still serving the preceding dynasty are permitted to retain their former ranks."[13]

Some found it difficult to serve a foreign people, so ingenious excuses were invented to dissolve their scruples: "The rebels are our enemies, for they have killed our emperor. Now, the Manchus have helped us to defeat the rebels. Therefore, we have every reason to join them!" The most effective justification offered for the Manchus' intrusion into China was that they had come to avenge the murder of the Chinese emperor by the rebels.[14] The less scrupulous had no difficulty in seeing that the Manchu army was behaving with humanity and justice. They proclaimed that the Manchus had come with the mandate of Heaven to comfort the people and to punish the rebellious.[15] They, therefore, had no hesitation in cooperating with them.

The most potent cause of the rapid dissolution of Li Tzu-ch'eng's government was the collapse of military discipline in his forces. Until the fall of Peking, Li, himself an exemplary soldier, was noted for the strictness of his discipline. He would not countenance the luxurious lives of the nobles and the rich, much less would he tolerate carelessness on this point among his own followers. But once his forces had entered Peking, military discipline so slackened that Li could no longer control his own men. Many of the leaders seized palaces of the nobles and began to live lives of luxury. We are told that Li Tzu-ch'eng used to feast his officials every day in his palace. The scholars, being men of culture, behaved as befitted their dignity. The military men, however, being quite untrained in good manners, cared little for court etiquette, chose their seats without regard for order, poured wine personally into their cups, and ate with their hands, all shocking breaches of the accepted code. One commander of the rebels, Liu Tsung-min 劉宗敏, who had been a blacksmith, kept on addressing Li as "old brother" and nothing that Li could do would stop him. These former leaders of the rebels might be made generals or officials of high rank but their manners betrayed their low birth. One historian has left a vivid description of their manners: "When they sat down they pushed each other, and when they walked they held each other's hands. They cursed and they joked; they pushed and kicked each other. They knew neither how to read nor how to write. . . ." For all this they were greatly despised by the scholars.[16]

The soldiers were no better than their leaders. In the period immediately after the conquest of Peking, Li Tzu-ch'eng tried hard to control them, threatening them with severe punishments. We are told that pillars and other instruments were set up at the Hsi-hua Gate 西華門 for the execution of rebels who had robbed the people, and that many were executed there every day.[17] These measures failed to check the disorders of the rebel soldiers. Frequently they would enter a private house on the pretext of using the kitchen, and then refusing to leave, would rob and rape the women of the household. The scholars, regarding such disorders as intolerable, complained to their leaders, but received from them only the bleak reply that it was better to tolerate the soldiers' misbehavior than to provoke them to revolt. The threat of revolt was no empty one. The soldiers had to eat and their leaders could not support them. They had to be allowed to look for food somewhere.[18]

Remembering that most of the rebels were poor farmers who had been forced to rebel in order to avoid starvation, we can easily understand why after the fall of Peking, they were no longer willing to be subjected to military discipline. For them the aim of the revolt had been achieved. The Ming dynasty had fallen; the corrupt government had been overthrown; the oppressors had disappeared. Their sole desire now was to return to their native places and to start a new life of comfort and peace. Hence, when the news of the advance of Wu San-kuei and the Manchus toward the capital reached Li Tzu-ch'eng, he found great difficulty in inducing his soldiers to take up arms.[19] The *P'ing-k'ou-chih* gives a vivid description of one of the scenes that followed:

"When the rebels learned that the Kuan-tung army was approaching, they all lamented and wanted to return to their homes. None of them had any more will to fight. A certain man when walking in the street one day unintentionally touched the dagger of a rebel. Forthwith he was arrested. The poor man was so frightened that he nearly dropped dead. He and his captors came to a house where several tens of men were at table eating. Some of them had women sitting on their knees and they were joking with one another. When they saw this man come in they all rose and asked if he could write. When they were answered in the affirmative they produced a clay ink pot and an old brush and invited the man to sit on a chair. 'Write for us, because we do not know how to do it,' they said. 'Our parents, wives, and children are in Shensi and we have had no news from them, so we want to send a few lines to comfort them. We became bandits to make money. Now that we have it we do not know how to send it (to our families). Indeed, it is a great hardship to be moving all the time; for this we have lost our homes. We now regret having been seduced by Li Tzu-ch'eng. Tso Liang-yü who is an experienced warrior may appear suddenly with his soldiers from Kiang-nan. Then, we have heard that Wu San-kuei is advancing rapidly. How are we to face them? Li Tzu-ch'eng brought us here and we consider our future very insecure!' Having said this, they all wept.

"Then, one after the other, they produced bracelets and jewels from their pockets and after they had broken them into pieces they put them inside the envelopes, which were despatched, some to Shansi and some to Shensi. These letters were addressed to fathers, sons and wives. (The style of) the Yung-ch'ang 永昌 era (i.e. of Li Tzu-ch'eng) was used in dating the envelopes, though some of the rebels still wished to follow the Ch'ung-chen calendar. When the man had finished writing all the letters, each of the rebels gave him some spare jewels, with which he filled his pockets before leaving the house."[20]

What we have said of Li Tzu-ch'eng can in general be said of Chang Hsien-chung, though it is easy to see that there was less chance of his success. Chang had always been known as a man of ferocious cruelty. His distrust of his own soldiers had caused him to kill a great number of them.[21] He is reported to have said that soldiers who had possessions and kept women were less ready than others to sacrifice themselves for his cause. Hence, when orders were given for mobilization, his soldiers were forced to abandon their belongings and to kill their kept-women. Sometimes, by the end of a long stay in one place the soldiers had raised families, and when orders came to move they were seized with a panic and wept aloud. It is also said that once, in Ch'eng-tu, Chang confined a number of his soldiers in a pagoda and then ordered that cannons be kept firing at the foundation of the building until it had crumbled down and killed all the soldiers. It is also said that once, when a whole rebel group violated his orders, he had them all put into a big junk and brought out to the river to be drowned. In consequence of such cruelty his soldiers both feared and hated him. In the end he was betrayed to the Manchus by one of his own officers.[22]

Cruel to his own, he was still more cruel to the people in general and, cruellest of all to his enemies. We are told that once when passing through Chin-chou 錦州 he saw a beautiful mansion and immediately ordered that the owner be killed.[23] In Ch'eng-tu he pretended to hold a government examination, and when the candidates had assembled, had them all massacred. He is said to have become so habituated to violence that he always kept a weapon by him and even in ordinary conversation would kill anyone who displeased him. He killed government officials, landlords, and scholars, indiscriminately.[24] Toward the end, he was particularly cruel to the people of Szechuan,[25] probably because he resented the strong civilian guard which the people of that province had organized to oppose him. The character of Chang Hsien-chung, especially toward the end of his life, is an enigma to historians. Many think that he must have been insane, since no normal person could have been guilty of such acts of savage folly.

In 1644, when news of the fall of Peking and the death of the emperor reached Nanking, the ministers hastily set about electing a successor to the Ming empire. Under the leadership of Ma Shih-ying 馬士英 and some of the former followers of the eunuch Wei Chung-hsien, they chose Prince Fu who was proclaimed emperor with the reign title of Hung-kuang 弘光 (1645). One historian tells us that Prince Fu was chosen because he was an incompetent ruler and a man of weak character.[26] The real power of the government was thus kept in the hands of Ma Shih-ying and his followers. His election was opposed by many of the more conscientious ministers who favored

Prince Lu 魯王. Under these circumstances, the court divided into two bitterly opposed parties, whose quarrels hastened the fall of the Nanking government. The unhappy reign of Prince Fu lasted for only a few months. Nanking fell into the hands of the Manchus on the 9th of May, 1645, and Prince Fu and his court fled to T'ai-p'ing. Not long after, he was captured by one of his former officers who had surrendered to the Manchus. He was murdered in 1646.

With the fall of Nanking, the center of a resistance to the Manchus moved further south. Three of the Ming princes who had escaped the disaster, established themselves in Chekiang, Fukien, and Canton. Prince Lu 魯王, who had originally come from Shan-tung, fled to T'ai-chou 台州 in Chekiang Province. On the fall of Nanking, he moved to Shao-hsing, in the same province, where he established himself in 1645, with the title of Lu Chien-kuo 魯監國. Prince Lu, we are told, was well liked by the people. Many of the volunteers who put up strong resistance to the Manchus in present Kiangsu were under his leadership. Among these volunteers there were a few great scholars such as Huang Tsung-hsi, his brother Huang Tsung-yen 黃宗炎, and Chu Chih-yü 朱之瑜 (better known as Chu Shun-shui 朱舜水, who later fled to Japan and died there). The Kiangsu resistance did not last long, for the Manchus were advancing rapidly toward the south and in 1646, Prince Lu and his court fled to Fukien where they stayed for two years. In 1648, he returned to Chekiang and continued his resistance to the Manchus from the Chusan Islands, off the Chekiang coast. Meanwhile the Manchus had been concentrating their forces for capturing the province of Fukien, which they took in 1649. In the following year they invaded Chekiang and Prince Lu fled to Amoy. At one time, some of the ministers sought help from Japan to save the empire, but it was already too late and nothing came of this venture. Eventually, Prince Lu resigned his title as Chien-kuo 監國 and the anti-Manchu movement came to an end.

In 1645, while Prince Lu was establishing himself in Chekiang, another scion of the Ming, Prince T'ang 唐王, helped by Cheng Chih-lung 鄭芝龍 (father of Cheng Ch'eng-kung 鄭成功, the famous Koxinga) set up his court in Fu-chow with the reign title of Lung-wu 隆武. Cheng Chih-lung had spent his early days as a pirate but in 1627 he surrendered to the Ming government and in the last years of the dynasty he was in charge of the customs along the southeastern coast. All merchant ships were compelled to carry banners issued by him if they were to be allowed to sail on the southeastern sea. Each merchant ship had to pay a tax of three thousand silver taels yearly. It was said that Cheng's private income amounted to ten million silver taels annually. After the fall of Nanking, Cheng Chih-lung's brother invited Prince T'ang to Fukien, where, with the support of the two Cheng brothers, a new government was organized.²⁷

In all this Cheng Chih-lung had no thought of loyalty to his old masters. His sole thought was to use the influence of Prince T'ang and his court to defend himself and his own interests. In 1646, when a Manchu army led by General Hung Ch'eng-ch'ou attacked Fukien, Cheng Chih-lung had no hesitation in sacrificing the Ming court. He surrendered to the Manchus and Prince T'ang was forced to flee to Chien-ning 建寧, from which he hoped to move to Hunan. On his way he was captured by the Manchu soldiers, who brought him back to Fuchow and he died in their hands.

An examination of the situation in 1646 clearly shows that the Ming empire still had a chance of surviving the Manchu invasion. If, despite all hopes the empire fell, this was because the princes would not cooperate with one another. They divided their forces and manifested no real capacity for government and thus gave the Manchus a chance to succeed in their hazardous project. When Prince Fu ascended the throne in Nanking, the Manchus held only Northern Chih-li. The provinces of Shansi, Shensi, and part of Honan were still occupied by Li Tzu-ch'eng, and Chang Hsien-chung had sole control of Szechuan. The Nanking government had possession of Southern Chih-li, Chekiang, Fukien, Kuangtung, Kuangsi, Yünnan, Kueichou and part of Hu-kuang, Honan and Shantung. The preponderance of manpower and material supplies still lay with the Ming government. Incompetence wasted the supreme opportunity.

The end came very suddenly. Within a short time, the Yellow River valley and more than half of the Yangtze valley were lost to the enemy. By then the Manchus had built up such power that they were able to invade Szechuan from the southwest and they took Southern Chih-li from the southeast. From Chih-li they advanced at their ease to Chekiang and Fukien. Next they turned toward Central China where Wu-ch'ang and Han-yang were occupied. Present Hunan and Kiangsi were soon to become the objects of their invasion.

The armed forces at the disposal of the Hung-kuang (Prince Fu) government were still large. We are told that the troops in present Kiangsu and Anhui numbered no fewer than three hundred thousand men. The thirty-six divisions under General Tso Liang-yü in the area of Wu-ch'ang and Han-yang were estimated at about eight hundred thousand men. If one includes the troops of other provinces under the control of the Ming government, the total must have come to at least something over a million, whereas in those early days the whole Manchu army, including their Chinese and Mongolian soldiers, was only one hundred and eighty-six thousand six hundred strong. But after 1646 the Ming forces repeatedly suffered great defeats. Many of their armies were scattered, others surrendered to the Manchus, and soon the number of soldiers had fallen to less than half of the 1646 number. After every victory, the Manchus recruited into their armies the defeated soldiers, among whom they soon established the Lu-ying-ping system 綠營兵制, using Chinese forces to control Chinese.[28]

In the year 1647, the last of the Ming Princes established himself in Chao-ch'ing 肇慶, north of Canton, with the reign title of Yung-li 永曆. In Canton some of the Ming officials tried to set up Prince T'ang 唐王, in independence of the Yung-li ruler. This attempt, however, did not last long, for the Manchus soon captured Canton. The Yung-li ruler, finding Chao-ch'ing insecure, fled to Wu-chou 梧州, Kuangsi province, and then to Kuei-lin, vigorously pursued by the Manchu army. At this critical moment three hundred Portuguese soldiers under the command of Nicolas Fereira came from Macao to aid the Ming government and for a time the Manchu impetus was checked. The intervention of the Portuguese is said to have been due to the conversion of the imperial family to Catholicism. There was then a Jesuit missionary, Father Andrew Koffler, at the Yung-li court and through him the empress was baptized, taking the name Ann. The prince heir and the dowager also became Christians, the former taking the name Constantine, and the latter Helen. The heroic defender of the Ming dynasty, Ch'ü Shih-ssu 瞿式耜, himself was converted and took the name Thomas. It was he who was responsible for the heroic defence of Kuei-lin and saved it from falling into the hands of the Manchus.[29]

In 1648, for a while, there were great hopes that the Ming government might regain its rule of the empire. Military officers who had surrendered to the Manchus revolted in many provinces. Even the former followers of Li Tzu-ch'eng and Chang Hsien-chung began to join the Ming government in the fight against the Manchus. The Yung-li ruler now had seven provinces under his rule: Yünnan, Kueichou, Kuangtung, Kuangsi, Hunan, Kiangsi and Szechuan. Along the Yellow River valley the Mohammedans were becoming restless, having been influenced by former Ming officials to revolt against the Manchus. Above all, the menace of Cheng Ch'eng-kung 鄭成功, son of Cheng Chih-lung, caused great concern to the Manchus along the coast.[30]

Nevertheless, the Manchus were not deterred from their pursuit of the Ming government. In spite of strong opposition they kept on pouring troops into Yünnan where the Yung-li ruler and his court were then residing. In 1659, the court was forced to retreat to Burma. Two years later (1661), when Wu San-kuei came to seize the emperor, the Burmese were unable to protect him. Under pressure from Wu San-kuei, the Yung-li ruler was delivered to his enemy. He was brought back to Yünnan and was strangled there in the following year.[31]

NOTES

[1] *Wan-Ming min-pien,* 167.

[2] T'ung Shu-yeh 童書業, "Li Tzu-ch'eng szu shih k'ao-i" 李自成死事考異, *Shih-hsüeh chi-k'an* 史學集刊, (April, 1937) 3. 247–266.

[3] *Ming shih,* 275, (ts'e 91) 13ab.

[4] *Ming-shih chi-shih pen-mo,* 78, B. 67.

[5] *Ming shih,* 275, (ts'e 91) 13ab.

[6] *Ming-ch'ing shih-liao,* first series, vol. 1, 74ab.

[7] *Shou-Yün chi-lüeh,* (ts'e 30) 1b–2a.

[8] Ibid., 1–2a.

[9] *Tsai-sheng chi-lüeh,* B. 5. 4a.

[10] *Chia-shen ch'uan-hsin lu,* 4. 56.

[11] *Tsai-sheng chi-lüeh,* B. 5. 45.

[12] Ibid., B. 5. 14b.

[13] *Ming-ch'ing shih-liao,* first series, vol. 1, 97a.

[14] Wen Jui-lin 温睿臨, *Nan-chiang i-shih k'an-pen* 南疆繹史勘本, (Revised by Li Yao 李瑤) (1830), 12, (*ts'e* 7) 12b; cf. "Prince Jui's Letter to Shih K'o-fa" 睿親王與史可法書, *Han-fan-l'ou ku-chin wen-ch'ao chien-pien* 涵芬樓古今文鈔簡編, (*Kuo-hsüeh chi-pen ts'ung-shu* 國學基本叢書, Shanghai, 1933), 19, (*ts'e* 2) 45–46.

[15] *Ming-Ch'ing shih-liao,* first series, vol. 1, 97a; 75a; 84a; 66a; 79a; vol. 2. 126a; 124a.

[16] *K'ou shih pien-nien,* 18, (ts'e 12) 6b.

[17] *Chia-shen ch'uan-hsin lu,* 6, 117.

[18] Ibid., 6, 119; *K'ou-shih pien-nien,* 18, (*ts'e* 12) 7b; *P'ing-k'ou-chih,* 10, (ts'e 3) 8a.

[19] *Tsai-sheng chi-lüeh,* B. 5. 7b.

[20] *P'ing-k'ou-chih,* 10, (ts'e 3) 8a.

[21] *Ao-yang-shih i-shu,* 13ab.

[22] *K'ou-shih pien-nien,* 18, (ts'e 19) 19ab.

[23] Ibid., 18, (ts'e 12) 19b.

[24] *Shu-pi,* 3, 45–49.

[25] Anonymous, *Shu-chi* 蜀記 (T'ung-shih ed.) (*ts'e* 24) 8a. The author of this book gives the number of men killed by Chang Hsien-chung in Szechuan as over six hundred million. The *Ming shih* gives the same number. Cf. *Ming shih,* 309, (*ts'e* 37) 13b. A modern writer (Shao Yüan-chien 蕭遠健,) in an article: "Chang Hsien-chun t'u chuan k'ao-lüeh"

張獻忠屠川考略, published in the *Shih-ta yüeh-k'an* 師大月刊, (30 April, 1935), 18, 227–233, remarks on the impossibility of these numbers. According to the *Ming shih*, he says, the census of Szechuan in 1578 recorded 2,694 (This is either a misquotation or a misprint. The *Ming shih*, 43, (*ts'e* 9) 1a.) gives 262,694 families with a population of 3,102,691 persons). Since rewards were given to the soldiers in proportion to the number of enemies they had killed, they undoubtedly exaggerated these numbers in order to increase their rewards. (Cf. the above mentioned article, p. 233 note 7). However, eyewitnesses and historians testified that the number of people Chang Hsien-chung killed in Szechuan was very great. (Cf. e.g., *Ming-shih chi-shih pen-mo*, 77, (*ts'e* 3,927) 134.

[26] Mei-shih-shih 眉史氏, *Fu-she chi-lüeh* 復社紀略, (CKNLWHLSTS), (ts'e 10).

[27] Inaba Iwakichi 稲葉岩吉, *Ch'ing-ch'ao ch'üan-shih* 清朝全史, tr. by Tan Tao 但燾, (Shanghai, 1924), Chapter 26.

[28] Lo Erh-kang 羅爾綱, *Lu-ying-ping chih* 綠營兵志, Chungking, 1935).

[29] René Grousset, *Histoire de la Chine*, (Paris, (1942), pp. 331–332; J. B. Du Halde, *Description de l'Empire de la Chine*, vol. I, 334 335; Chang Ch'üan-kung 張全恭, "Ch'ü Shih-ssu" 瞿式耜, *Min-tsu tsa-chih* 民族雜誌, 5, (July, 1939) 7.

[30] Wei Yüan 魏源, *Sheng-wu chi* 聖武記, (1846 edition) 1, (ts'e 1) 63a.

[31] So-lu shan-jen 瑣綠山人, *Ming wang shu-lüeh* 明亡述略, (CKNLWHLSTS), (*ts'e* 11) B. 307–308; Huang Tsung-hsi 黃宗羲, *Yung-li chi-nien* 永曆紀年, (CKNLWHLSTS). (*ts'e* 11) 263–267.

CONCLUSION

GREATNESS AND WEAKNESS OF THE MING DYNASTY

Speaking of the emperors of the Ming dynasty, Hsieh Chao-che exclaimed, "In this dynasty of ours T'ai-tsu (the Hung-wu emperor) and Ch'eng-tsu (the Yung-lo emperor) were men of perfection. One being the founder and the other his successor, they matched harmoniously. Their institutions and their activities undoubtedly excelled those of the dynasties that had gone before. Besides, the broadmindedness of Jen-tsung (the Hung-hsi emperor), the conscientiousness and diligence of Hsüan-tsung (the Hsüan-te emperor), the earnestness of Hsiao-tsung (the Hung-chih emperor), the great talent of Shih-tsung (the Chia-ching emperor), and the frugality of Mu-tsung (the Lung-ch'ing emperor) show that they were all gifted monarchs whose qualities were not paralleled by any of the sovereigns who came after the Three Dynasties. Hsüan-tsung and Hsiao-tsung, above all, were famed for their benevolence. Indeed, we are fortunate to have had six or seven good monarchs; no wonder the imperial throne continues indefinitely."[1]

Hsieh omitted such names as Ying-tsung (the Cheng-t'ung or T'ien-shun emperor), Ching-tsung (the Ching-t'ai emperor), Hsien-tsung (the Ch'eng-hua emperor) and Wu-tsung (the Cheng-te emperor), knowing that there was nothing good to be said of these monarchs. If he had mentioned them he would probably have had to detail their faults rather than their virtues. Nor did Hsieh wish to mention the name of the Wan-li emperor, in whose reign he was living, for he had elsewhere shown his poor opinion of what that monarch was doing. From what we have seen of the Ming emperors, it is clear that, even as it stands, Hsieh's remarks are exaggerated. The Hung-wu emperor is probably the only emperor of the Ming dynasty who can fairly be described as a ruler of genius. The Yung-lo emperor was a man of genuine talent. Of the rest, even the best did nothing more than try to maintain the *status quo*.

Yet, despite the weaknesses of the imperial house, it must be admitted that the Ming dynasty takes a great place in the history of China. The very fact that it lasted for nearly three centuries shows that it must have had its good points, otherwise it could not have lasted. Most empires stand firm on the foundation laid by their first rulers. This was certainly true of the Ming dynasty. Years of association with scholars had broadened the founder's outlook on government, and he is said to have had sound knowledge of history. The *Han shu* 漢書 and the *Sung shih* were among his favorite books and he used to read them frequently. "History helps to understand the past and thus to know the present," and the Hung-wu emperor made great use of it.[2] Taught by history, he was able to avoid mistakes and to take precaution against possible abuses. Thus he saw that the military weakness of the imperial dynasties of T'ang and Sung had left them at the mercy of either the military classes or the foreign tribes. For this reason he entrusted to his sons the guarding of the provinces, especially the defence of the borders. In those days the capital was in Nanking, but with his sons settled in important provinces in Central and Northern China, he felt quite safe. On the other hand, he was shrewd enough to restrain the power of his sons lest they should become so strong as to interfere with the policy of the government. Accordingly, civil administration was reserved to government officials and the princes had to be content with living in the provinces as honored guests of the government. This gave the emperor complete rule over the empire without interference from any of his subjects.

Study of T'ang history had warned the Hung-wu emperor against the danger of an overpowerful military class such as had given grievous trouble to that dynasty and had eventually become one of the causes of its downfall. The danger, he thought, arose from entrusting too much power to military leaders. Generals often had a great number of soldiers who obeyed them rather than the government and when this happened the government lost all its authority over the soldiers and was at the mercy of military leaders. To preclude this danger he instituted the Wu-chün tu-tu fu, which secured a two-fold advantage to the government. First, it separated the military leaders from the soldiers, for under it no commander could claim to possess any forces of his own and this diminished the danger of any *coup d'état*. Secondly, the soldiers supported themselves in time of peace. The idea of the army settlement system was, no doubt, derived from the T'ang dynasty's fu-ping system 府兵制, which also had greatly lightened the burden of supporting the army. The Hung-wu emperor was very proud of his ingenious institution: "I keep a million soldiers," he said, "without causing my people to spend one penny!"

Study of history had also revealed that many of the dynasties, especially the Han and T'ang, had been brought to ruin by the empresses and eunuchs. The Hung-wu emperor, therefore, never trusted his eunuchs; in his eyes they were merely servants in the palace. Their duty was to obey orders and they should never be allowed to study lest learning might make them ambitious. "Eunuchs are not to interfere in government affairs. Those who would dare to violate this command will be punished by death!" These words were written on a tablet placed at the entrance of the palace.

Severity was the characteristic note of the Hung-wu emperor's dealings with the empress and the court ladies. Han history illustrated how these women could do irreparable harm to the country. It was a cardinal point of the Hung-wu emperor's policy that empresses and concubines should never be chosen from among the nobles, who might seek excessive influence over the government. He laid down the rule that they should be from among the ordinary people and that their families were to be given honor and riches but never power in the government. The wives of ministers of high rank were allowed to pay homage to the empress twice monthly. Except on these occasions they were not admitted to the palace and the emperor himself never granted them audience. All these precepts were aimed at isolating the inner court from external influences.

The founder of the Ming dynasty knew that the corruption of government officials and sub-officials had been the cause of many revolts against the Yüan dynasty. When he came to the throne he knew how exhausted the poor people were and that to alleviate their sufferings he had first to protect them against greedy officials and sub-officials. Accordingly, he was very strict with these functionaries. In the Ta-kao 大誥 or "Great Precept", written by the monarch himself, permission was granted to the elders of towns and villages to report directly against corrupt officials. "Hereafter, if we wish to free our people from injustice, the best way will be to employ the virtuous elders of villages. They may come to the capital in groups of a hundred or several score or several hundred, nay, even in a group of more than a thousand, at the end of the year and report to us directly the number of good and bad officials. We will investigate thoroughly according as they report to us, rewarding the good, removing the wicked, and if necessary punishing them. . . ."³

Next, the Hung-wu emperor turned his attention to the land-tax, a vital source of income for the country. Since the last days of the Yüan dynasty, landlords had been conspiring with corrupt officials to evade taxes with the result that large farms were often left untaxed and poor farmers were forced to pay for what they did not possess. It was under these circumstances that the "Fish Scale" and the "Yellow Records" systems were instituted to prevent the rich from evading taxes and to protect the poor against injustice.

In order to have good government officials the Hung-wu emperor had students trained after the Confucian pattern. But since Confucian scholars often lacked experience of real life, they were submitted to all sorts of tests in different government offices. Government posts were open to all who passed the examinations, which thus gave equal chances to all. The emperor gave such an impetus to education that schools flourished not only throughout his lifetime but throughout the whole history of his dynasty. Along with the schools there flourished also academies in which eminent scholars lectured on Confucian ideals, forming intellectual groups independent of government influence. Often they held their meetings in temples or monasteries and membership was not confined to any class. They laid stress not only on intellectual life but, still more, on a strict moral life. Throughout the dynasty they exerted great influence on public opinion and not a few of them sacrificed their lives for their principles.

China under Mongol rule had been an amalgam of peoples of the East and peoples of the West. Since the Mongols were the ruling class many of their customs were imposed upon the people. Even when these customs were not imposed, many Chinese either because they admired their conquerors or because they wanted to please them, tried to imitate their manner of living and their language, and even exchanged their Chinese names for Mongol names. When the Hung-wu emperor took up arms his rallying cry was: expel the barbarians from China and restore Chinese rule! "From time immemorial whenever emperors and kings have ruled over the universe, the Middle Kingdom has always been considered the center of government, from which the emperors and kings rule over the barbarians. The barbarians are left outside but they are subject to the Middle Kingdom. It is unheard of that barbarian tribes have ever come to rule the universe."⁴ This proclamation of the Hung-wu emperor's must have made a deep impression on the people. As soon as he came to the throne he tried to delete Mongol customs and to restore the mode of life to a purely Chinese form, based on Confucian ideals. Foreigners were given equal rights on condition that they lived after the manner of the Chinese. The emperor was thus able to weld the people into a single nation and to absorb new blood, which was a source of great vitality to the country.

The second Ming emperor, grandson of the founder and an apparently promising young man, was deposed before he had had time to prove his worth.

The third Ming, the Yung-lo, emperor was a man of high talent, but his usurpation had involved him inextricably in one appalling difficulty: he could not engage the services of loyal, able, and respectable lieutenants. As a usurper, he could not be welcomed by the ministers who followed the Confucian ideals and would rather have died than serve one who was not the legitimate emperor. He could not trust the imperial clansmen, for they might do to him or to his descendants what he had done to his nephew: usurpers cannot claim family loyalty. He therefore determined on the most dangerous step any emperor could take: he turned to the eunuchs for help. The temptation to do so was all the stronger in that the eunuchs seem to have been loyal to him before he came to the throne. For the moment all went well: the eunuchs continued to serve him loyally. Nevertheless, the dynasty, in the long run, was to pay a terrible price for thus abandoning one of the founder's most cherished principles.

During the Yung-lo emperor's reign eunuchs were employed in important embassies, the most important perhaps being that of Cheng Ho, which we have already described. The emperor's greatest mistake was to employ eunuchs as imperial spies. The Tung-ch'ang, instituted by these unscrupulous scoundrels with the approval of the monarch, was the first institution of this kind, and was to do terrible damage to the empire and send many innocent citizens to undeserved death. The step once taken was never retracted. The warnings of the founder of the dynasty against employing eunuchs for high offices were completely forgotten by his descendants.

In spite of this fateful error that his usurpation entailed and of the wound inflicted on dynastic stability, the Yung-lo emperor was considered one of the better emperors of the Ming dynasty. In general he continued the policy of his father and kept his ministers under control. Unfortunately, after the Yung-lo emperor no other really capable rulers appeared. The *Ming shih* remarks disdainfully that in the Ming dynasty besides the founder and the Yung-lo emperor only the Hung-hsi, the Hsüan-te and the Hung-chih emperors were worthy of mention.[5] The historian seems to imply that all the others were too insignificant to be mentioned by name. Yet the Hung-hsi emperor reigned hardly for a year (1424–1425), and his accomplishments are matter for speculation rather than for praise. The Hsüan-te emperor reigned almost immediately after the Hung-wu and Yung-lo emperors and the prosperity of his reign can fairly be attributed to the continuing effects of his predecessors' wisdom. The Hung-chih emperor deserves praise for having reformed the government by sweeping away the abuses of his predecessor and for leading a frugal and virtuous life. His positive achievements, however, were not outstanding.

From the Yung-lo reign onward the eunuchs were ever increasing their power. They owed their ability to do this not only to the encouragement of the Yung-lo emperor, but also to one of the few grave errors made by the founder of the dynasty. By abolishing the office of the prime minister and forbidding his subjects under threat of severe punishment even to mention the restoration of the post, the Hung-wu emperor had made it almost impossible for an emperor of ordinary talent to rule the whole empire satisfactorily or for a pleasure-seeking and negligent emperor to rule it at all. Such emperors, deprived of the help of a prime minister, frequently employed eunuchs to do their work and young eunuchs were trained to become, in some sort, secretaries of the emperors. Chao I tells us that the Ssu-li-chien 司禮監 of the Ming dynasty corresponded to the Shu-mi-yuan 樞密院 of the T'ang dynasty. Both offices pertained to the eunuchs, and both implied acting as secretaries of the emperors.[6] The Chief Eunuch of Ssu-li tai-chien 司禮太監 became so powerful that even the Grand Secretary frequently had to consult him. The notorious Wang Chen 王振, Wang Chih 汪直, Liu Chin 劉瑾, and Wei Chung-hsien 魏忠賢 were all Chief Eunuchs.

In the outer court, ministers who saw the negligence of their master felt that they too could easily evade responsibility in government affairs. Then there was no lack of capable but ambitious ministers, who, taking advantage of the weakness of their imperial masters for their own purposes, tried to please them by pandering to those weaknesses. Once their positions were secure they brought in their own men and eventually their faction would grow so strong as to dominate the whole government. If they met opposition they often fell to enlisting the eunuchs on their side. This happened often after the middle of the sixteenth century, and especially towards the end of the Ming period when several parties were constantly fighting one another.

Such a state of things could not but cause a rapid deterioration of the government. Morality in government was the first casualty. Since all the parties attempted to woo as many as possible to their side, it is clear that they cannot have aimed at enlisting only men of high character. Government examinations became superficial and the demand for scholarship capricious. Sub-officials, having observed that their superiors had no heart for vigilant inspection of their subordinates, began to seize every chance of enriching themselves by extortion from the public. Decline at the highest levels had its inevitable effects: the tax system began to become disorganized and eventually the military organization itself collapsed. It is interesting to compare the quality of the ministers at various periods. Of the one hundred and twenty "Exemplary Officials" (hsün-li 循吏) whose biographies are mentioned in the *Ming shih*, over a hundred belonged to the first sixty years or so of the dynasty. Between the Cheng-t'ung, and the Chia-ching periods about one hundred and thirty-odd years only a few over ten were numbered in the list. Only two of the ministers who held office during the fifty-odd years covered by the Lung-ch'ing and Wan-li reigns were found worthy of this honorable mention. From then on to the fall of the dynasty the list is blank. So greatly had ministerial standards fallen since the great days of the founder.[7]

The abolition of the office of prime minister dealt a terrible blow to the whole system of government. The prime-minister's work was divided among the six Boards, all of which were directly responsible to the emperor. Unhappily the ministers chosen by the emperors were often chosen for their scholarship, without regard to their practical experience in government. Many of them were in fact men of execrable judgment and of no experience at all. Yet these men were sent to far-away provinces, sometimes thousands of miles from their own native places where the dialects and customs were quite foreign to them. Great sums of money were spent on their journeys to the provinces, for they had to travel in state. Then, before they had grown familiar with the duties of their new offices, they would be shifted to some other place. It is, then, not surprising to find that they had to depend almost entirely on their sub-officials, whose already excessive power was thus greatly increased.

The concentration of power in the person of the emperor worked well so long as the emperors were capable men such as the Hung-wu or the Yung-lo emperors. It did not work when the emperor was a weak man devoid of initiative. Hence it must be accounted one of the greatest mistakes, perhaps the greatest, made by the Hung-wu emperor, that he instituted an absolute monarchy in a form that could work only if the emperor was a man of great talent and great energy. He must also be blamed for the rigidity which he sought to impose. He was fully aware that any government institution must be adaptable to the needs of the time; yet he tried to force his descendants to follow exactly the lines that he had laid down. "The government institutions of the Ming dynasty are full of details and are rigid. The power of the government is exclusively dominated by the central government, which makes the emperor a dictator while his ministers are left without authority. All are threatened by the laws, and their power overlaps in a way that does indeed hinder evil-intentioned ministers from doing great harm to the government, but also robs talented officials of all opportunity of distinguishing themselves. Then, many ways are open to them of practising extortion on the people but the attention paid to this is negligible. The late minister Feng Ch'i 馮琦 once remarked that the troubles of the Ming dynasty are not caused by relatives of the empresses, nor by eunuchs, officials, imperial clansmen or enemy countries; what will cause harm to the empire is the lack of contact between the government and the people, and the poverty of the population."[8] Thus the author of the *Ming-chi pai-lüeh*.

All this was especially true of the second half of the dynasty. The Chia-ching emperor spent most of his time in the palace attending Taoistic ceremonies, greatly to the detriment of administrative vigor. Then came the Wan-li emperor whose reign is considered the most disastrous in the Ming dynasty. The fault lay with the emperor, who lived entirely isolated from his ministers and his people at the very time when the country was most in need of his decision and help. From the memorial of Liu Tung-ming 劉東明 one can see clearly how unhappy this period must have been. This memorial, written in the 22nd year of the Wan-li reign (1594), recalls how in recent years wars, floods, famines and calamities of all kinds had occurred one after the other, yet records as still more lamentable the selfishness and jealousy of the court ministers. These men occupied themselves with mutual suspicions and no one cared what was right and what was wrong. Authority fell into the hands of a few ministers and others shunned their responsibilities, so that there was always much talk but never any great achievement. Having described these evils, Liu tried to point out the chief cause of all the evils: "Your Majesty, living in seclusion in the palace, thinks that the empire is as peaceful as before. Alas! Times have changed and the morale of the people is not what it was. This is why I warn Your Majesty to be on the alert. . . . I earnestly implore Your Majesty to realize the change of the times and to start a reform; to give directions for the suppression of the tribes in Szechuan and Kueichou and to instruct the ministers of diverse provinces about the relief works for provinces suffering from flood and famine. If at the same time Your Majesty were to institute inquiries it would help you to understand the conditions of the empire. Furthermore, the presence of Your Majesty would give great encouragement to the people and would thus help to avert disasters of all kinds."[9]

Economic improvements rank among the greatest achievements of the Ming; the Ch'ing dynasty derived its land tax system from that of the Ming. The "Fish Scale Records" and the "Yellow Records" were among the most unmistakably beneficent institutions. The introduction of the i-tiao-pien fa effected a great improvement in the tax system. The fact that from then on the land-tax was levied according to the amount of land owned by farmers and not by the number of males in the household tended to free the farmers from the obligation of *corvée* and thus to give them greater liberty. The "Fish Scale System" lasted to the time of the Republic. The author of the *Ming-tai shih* says that in his native country Wu-chin 武進 the people were still benefiting from tax-exemption on certain fields of mulberry, cotton and jujubes, in accordance with a tradition that had come down from the Hung-wu period.[10]

Industries, whether directly or indirectly under the control of the government, were highly developed, especially the manufacture of porcelain. The porcelain produced in the Yung-lo, Hsüan-te, Ch'eng-hua, Cheng-te, Chia-ching and Wan-li periods is still regarded as of great artistic importance and is valued by connoisseurs. Ching-te-chen remains the unchallenged center of porcelain manufacture even to our day. After the transfer of the capital to Peking, travel became more frequent and the shipbuilding industry developed greatly. Several thousand ships were built by the government for the transportation of grain to the capital and by the T'ien-shun reign the number had increased to over ten thousand. This development of ship-building undoubtedly helped the development of commerce both within and without the empire. The Ming government, it is true, never sought to encourage commerce; on the contrary, there are indications showing that merchants were treated unjustly especially in the early days of the dynasty. Still, because communications were good and commercial taxes low (one thirtieth)—books and farming implements were not taxed—, commerce naturally developed rapidly.

Unfortunately the government of the Ming dynasty never succeeded in stopping the well-to-do from encroaching on the land of poor farmers. In spite of the great effort of the Hung-wu emperor to prevent the encroachments of the landlord class, even the new system of "Fish Scale" and the "Yellow Records" had no permanent effect. Though land reform seems to have made great progress as long as he lived, his descendants were unable to maintain the effort and abuses crept in gradually. By the time of the Hung-chih reign, about a hundred and fifty years after the foundation of the dynasty, the amount of cultivated land was estimated at less than half of what it had been in the Hung-wu period. Much land had fallen into the hands of the nobles, eunuchs and influential landlords.[11]

Land-taxes were constantly being multiplied and the poor farmers, unable to cope with them, had either to abandon their farms or to put themselves under the protection of the well-to-do landlords, which was equivalent to making over their land to them. Great numbers of farmers who had lost everything became vagabonds. They often caused the government much trouble and towards the end of the dynasty they formed part of the rebel forces.

From the Wan-li reign onwards the emperors, not satisfied with their ordinary income, went out of their way to make extraordinary profits at the expense of the people. The financial condition of the empire by this time was extremely precarious and the outbreak of wars with the Japanese, with tribes of Po-chou 播州 in Szechuan, and with the Manchus made things worse. The war in Po-chou, which we have mentioned only *en passant,* started in 1597 and did not end until 1600. Two hundred thousand soldiers took part and it cost the government several million silver taels.[12] The huge sums of money spent on wars came of course from the people in the form of taxes. Often these were extraordinary levies imposed for the upkeep of the soldiers in Liao-tung or for the training of new soldiers. The time came when the people, no longer able to meet the insatiable demands of the government, ran away or revolted. The government was thus placed in a most difficult position, for it still had to find means to support the soldiers. Failing this the soldiers, too, would rebel.

The bad example of the Wan-li emperor served to encourage the evil propensities of highly placed subjects. The eunuchs became more unjust, the officials more corrupt and the imperial families more determined to seize far more than their share. The very fact that the authorities were competing with their subjects for gain was a clear indication of a government decline. The standard of government ethics soon fell very low. At court the ministers were divided into two parties: the righteous who were ready to sacrifice their lives for justice' sake and the wicked who were ready to use any means, however degraded, for obtaining what they desired. Around the emperor there were thousands of eunuchs, who, being greatly favored by the monarch, gradually got control of many activities within the capital and even out in the provinces. Thus they formed a small government independent of the central government. Unscrupulous ministers who wished to secure their own power naturally tried to make allies of the eunuchs. The eunuchs, for their part, gladly accepted the opportunities thus offered of increasing their influence in politics.

Good ministers became ever rarer towards the end of the dynasty, and bad ministers multiplied. Of the five notorious grand secretaries mentioned in the *Ming shih* two belonged to the Ch'ung-chen reign. The ever suspicious emperor had kept on changing his grand secretaries and granted his favors not to outspoken critics but to those who knew how to please him. Under such circumstances there was not much hope of seeing a better government despite the many real excellencies of this last Ming ruler. Ni Yüan-lu 倪元璐 (1593–1644), who witnessed the end of the Ming empire, summed up the situation by saying that the government was in a desperate situation and that all this was due to the strife among the ministers. According to him, between the middle of the Wan-li reign and the very end of the dynasty, a period of thirty-odd years, the government went through three stages.

At first, the emperor shut himself up in his palace and left his ministers to their cat and dog fight. Then came the period when the eunuchs got the upper hand and took over full control of the government. Finally, all authority was once more concentrated in the person of the emperor. Even in this last period the wicked were able to induce the monarch to favor their side and the good thus suffered. What Ni abhorred was the selfishness of the so-called superior men who instead of working for the common good, formed factions and quarrelled among themselves.

The Manchu invasion and the rebel revolts did but hasten a fall that was already, almost certainly, inevitable. Neither could have overthrown the Ming, had the empire been well organized and strong. In the early days of the dynasty there were invasions by Mongols and Japanese pirates, but the government had been able to resist and defeat them. Similarly, early revolts of serious character were firmly suppressed. The empire was then not entirely lacking in capable ministers. The example of Chang Chü-cheng, under whose administration the empire showed every sign of returning to its early glory, shows what a series of capable ministers could have done, even at a late hour. Unfortunately, after Chang's death the hope of a peaceful future vanished gradually. There was still outward glory, but it was like the reflected glory of sunset. The dusk was coming on very rapidly and the dynasty was never again to see the face of the rising sun.

Historians who look back to the Ming dynasty must still admire the splendors of this great empire, and especially the genius of its founder who had laid so solid a foundation that the dynasty was to last for nearly three centuries. Many of its government institutions and its social traditions were to be retained throughout the rule of the Ch'ing dynasty, perhaps even down to our own day. Thus the Grand Secretariat system which originated with the Hung-wu emperor was maintained throughout the Ch'ing period. The office of the censors also retained under the Ch'ing the importance it had received from the Ming. Sun Yat-sen readily praised this office as one that could still render good service to a modern government and in fact the Chien-ch'a yüan 監察院 in the Nationalist government was derived from it. As under the Ming dynasty jurisdiction or criminal cases still belonged in Ch'ing days to the San fa-ssu 三法司, i.e. the Board of Punishments, the Tu-ch'a yüan and the Ta-li ssu. In 1644 when the Manchu government compiled its penal code it based it on the penal code of the Ming dynasty.

Territorially, the Ming empire in its early days came after the Han and T'ang empires at their widest extent.[13] Early in his reign the Hung-wu emperor decided to rid his dominions of the influence of the Mongols, moral as well as physical. Year after year he sent his generals to the desert in order to exterminate the remaining Mongol forces. His attitude towards neighboring countries was on the whole negative. Some of them, such as Korea and the Pescadores, he regarded as subject countries, others as barbarian states. He never encouraged his subjects to trade with foreign countries and on occasion even forbade such trade under severe penalty.

The Yung-lo emperor, being a soldier, continued his father's operations in Mongolia. Under him the empire expanded. Several times he himself led an army to Mongolia and won victories. Annam was conquered by the imperial army in 1407 and was made a province of China. Frequent embassies were sent to Samarkand, Afghanistan, and neighboring countries. Ch'en Ch'eng 陳誠 who led several of these embassies, left us an account of his travels. In his book (*Shih Hsi-yü chi* 使西域記) seventeen countries were mentioned. The greatest achievement of the Yung-lo emperor perhaps was the series of expeditions he sent to the South Seas. There were seven of these, all led by Cheng Ho who brought the Chinese into contact with over fifty countries and small states from the Indian Ocean to the African coast. All these voyages were made from 1405–1433, before the Portuguese reached Cape Verde.

The purpose of these expeditions is not clear, and there are disputes about them among scholars.[14] Probably the Yung-lo emperor, being a usurper, wanted to raise his reputation by sending out expeditions which, by inducing the peoples of foreign lands to pay him homage and by bringing back rare objects, would prove that he was the real son of heaven and therefore the legitimate emperor. The *Huang-Ming t'ung-chi* tells us that on three occasions during the Yung-lo reign foreign countries presented ch'i-lin 麒麟 to the Court: according to ancient Chinese tradition, the ch'i-lin make their appearance only when a sage or sages are ruling. In 1423 embassies consisting of two hundred men from sixteen foreign countries came to pay tribute to the emperor—a magnificent spectacle that led some of the ministers to exclaim "Since the Three Dynasties no one has ever seen such splendor as in our day!"[15] However, it is not unreasonable to suppose that the emperor also had some such secondary purposes as searching for his nephew, the rightful emperor, and establishing trade with foreign countries.

Whatever may have been his purpose, the emperor by sending out these expeditions accomplished something of great moment in the history of China. Politically the Ming dynasty was made known to many neighboring and distant countries. Contemporary documents and writings make it clear that the import of such goods as cloth, metal, medicine and foodstuffs, into China followed the voyage of Cheng Ho, and it is probable that an equal or greater quantity of Chinese goods was exported from China to all the foreign countries then known to the Chinese.[16]

The most momentous consequence of Cheng Ho's expeditions was the impetus it gave to Chinese emigration to the South Seas. The still surviving popularity of legends about Cheng Ho in those regions is a striking indication of the strength of his influence. The *Tung-hsi-yang k'ao* speaks of large numbers of Chinese residents in Java, Sumatra, the Philippines and Malaya. Their arrival must have increased commerce with China and must have opened vast regions to the influence of Chinese civilization.[17] The imperial government paid little heed to this development. Had it taken an active interest in the emigrants the history of China and of all East Asia might have been profoundly modified. Similarly, the neglect of European relations was of great, though negative, importance. Had the Ming government taken more interest in the new European sciences and studied them and put them to use, Chinese society might have developed into something very different from what it became in the succeeding centuries.

After the Yung-lo reign the Ming empire began to lose its military preeminence. Annam revolted and regained its freedom in 1427. In the north, along the Mongol borders, the Yung-lo emperor had committed a serious mistake by handing over part of a region of the utmost strategic importance to some Mongol tribes. We are told that as a safeguard against Mongol invasions the Hung-wu emperor had set up three strategic posts in what is now Jehol and Inner Mongolia, along and outside the Great Wall. Heavy garrisons were placed there in the form of military settlements, and one of the princes was put in charge of them. When the Yung-lo emperor, then known as Prince Yen, was beginning his revolt against his emperor-nephew he took the control of these three places from his brother, Prince Ning 寧王, to guard against a surprise attack from beyond the Great Wall. After his ascent of the throne he removed Prince Ning to Kiangsi and gave these three places as a reward to some Mongol tribes who had taken part in the fighting and were loyal to him. Their chieftains were given government rank and they received a yearly supply of food, cloth and farm equipment. The emperor hoped that these tribes would act as his spies in time of peace, and that they would fight for him in time of war—apparently a model application of the traditional Chinese policy of "letting the barbarian fight against the barbarian" 以夷制夷. But Yung-lo's policy was to prove a failure: one of the three tribes soon joined Aruktai (阿魯台), and gave great trouble to the empire.

The loss of the strategic posts had left K'ai-ping 開平 isolated outside the Great Wall and almost defenceless against the attacks of the nomads. By 1430 the government had decided to give up this region and move inside the Great Wall, abandoning more than three hundred *li* of territory to the Mongols. Hsüan-fu and Ta-t'ung, formerly the second line of defence along the Mongol borders, now became the first, lying thus dangerously exposed to the end of the dynasty; Peking was obviously vulnerable whenever Hsüan-fu and Ta-t'ung were seriously attacked. How great the danger was became apparent in 1449, when, after the destruction of the imperial army at T'u-mu-pu, the Mongol forces marched straight to the outskirts of the capital. In 1550, the peril was greater still when the Mongol troops reached the city wall, and only pure chance saved the capital from falling into the hands of the enemy.

While the Ming government was thus, with whatever mistakes of policy, making a determined effort for the defence of the border lines against the Mongols, they showed a strange neglect of coastal defense. The coast suffered greatly from the Japanese pirates, especially in the 1530's when the destruction was immense. By that time the wei-so army had deteriorated so badly that it was no longer fit to fight. Fortunately, however, some of the generals succeeded in training a new force and the pirates were ultimately suppressed. Next came a war between the Japanese and the Chinese in Korea (1592–1597). It is not easy to see how the Chinese could have extricated themselves from this, had it not been for the sudden death of Hideyoshi (1598), the ruler of Japan. Many Ming soldiers had perished on the battle-field and the war had already cost millions of silver taels.

By the beginning of the seventeenth century there was every sign that the country was exhausted. The author of the *Ming shu* 明書, writing of the Wan-li emperor during that monarch's reign, strove to include every virtue in his praise of the emperor's early days, but when he came to the later years he could only say that by instituting mine taxes he had caused great uneasiness among the people and that his prolonged negligence in government had made him respon-sible for the troubles along the borders and also responsible for the loss of military forces and for the sufferings inflicted on the country. "For this I cannot find excuse for His Majesty," he wrote.[18] It was just at this moment that the Manchus began to invade the empire. The decisive battle at Sarhu 薩爾滸, east of Fu-shun 撫順, was in the long run decisive of the fate of the Ming empire (1619). Within three days the Chinese forces lost an estimated 45,890 dead. In the four great battles fought against the Manchus the Ming forces gained only one victory (1626). Meanwhile the Manchus had conquered Korea and the tribes bordering on Manchuria. Later on they succeeded in dominating Inner Mongolia. They took into their service a large number of the Ming generals and military leaders, thus "using the Chinese to fight against the Chinese."

Society during the Ming period was changing gradually from ancient to modern in China no less than in contemporary Europe. This is especially true of the years, from the middle of the 16th century onward when the people were coming into contact with Europeans. Mutual admiration was aroused when East and West met. Each realized that its own world was not complete and that it had much to learn from the other. The novelty of a new culture greatly attracted the Chinese intelligentsia of the century and the less hidebound scholars welcomed it. The cultural influence affected only the learned class, but the Europeans also affected the daily life of the people by introducing various plants from the New World, in particular sweet potatoes, peanuts, Indian corn and tobacco.[19] The introduction of these plants came too late to produce striking results in the Ming period, but it helped undoubtedly to increase the population in later periods. The monetary system also was affected. By this time silver pesos had been introduced by the Spaniards via Manila and by the Dutch from Japan. The *Wu-tsa-tsu* says that in Fukien and Kuangtung provinces silver became the sole medium of business transaction during the Wan-li period.

The most significant contribution of this period was the introduction of European science and scientific methods into China. There is plentiful evidence that many of the eminent scholars both of the late Ming and of the Ch'ing dynasty were influenced by the scientific method of research of the early Jesuit missionaries.[20] Under these missionaries the foundation of European science was laid, though it did not really flourish till more than a century later.

The science introduced at this period covered a wide range, from the most abstract metaphysics to the most practical matters of daily life. Among the most important of these scientific importations were astronomy and the use of fire-arms, both of which, though they had flourished in earlier times had been neglected and so answered the pressing needs of the time. Both the Chinese and the Mohammedan calendars were known to be inaccurate and a reform was thought necessary. The development of astronomy aroused interest in mathematics which was also studied with great enthusiasm by some scholars. Even geography, recognized as a branch of learning, had flourished from the time of the Ch'in and Han, but later had not been much studied in China before the coming of the missionaries in the 16th century. The map of the world drawn by Ricci fascinated the learned class, and led to the beginnings of cartography in China. Professor Wada Sei 和田清 regards this as the most important event in the history of culture under the Ming dynasty. In due time it was to influence greatly both Japan and Korea.[21]

Eagerness to learn eventually led to the translation of European books into Chinese. It is astonishing to find how many books were translated, especially in the early days when the communication of ideas was by no means easy. In spite of all the difficulties the number of books translated in the later years of the Ming dynasty far exceeded the number of those published in the early days of the Ch'ing dynasty.

Many Chinese scholars applied themselves diligently to the study of science and they left as the fruit of their labors either translation or original works. Some of them studied European languages in order to be able to go directly to the original texts.[22]

While the Far East was becoming daily more deeply interested in Western science, the West was beginning to lay the foundation of Sinology. Intellectual westerners found great attraction in Chinese philosophy and art. Confucius, the "Prince of Chinese Philosophy", was admired and studied. The *Four Books* were for the first time translated into a European language by Ricci, whose Latin version found readers all over Europe. After that, many books were translated from Chinese and written on Chinese culture. It is a matter of history that the ultimate effect of this movement in European thought and arts was profound and prolonged.[23]

The 16th Century was a period of great historic change throughout the world. Europe was in transition from the Middle Ages to the modern era. In Germany and Spain Charles V was still trying to give reality to the tenuous claims of the Holy Roman Empire to supreme power in Europe; England, France and other European countries were manifesting a highly developed sense of nationalism. Feudalism, as a political system, was in its last gasp. Kings were concentrating all political power in their own persons but were finding themselves more and more dependent on the middle class for their revenue. The merchants were increasing their power, wealth and influence and under the protection of their governments were beginning to expand in lands far away. The English East India Company was founded in 1600 for trade with the East. Two years later the Dutch founded a similar organization and in 1604, the French too, set up an East India Company. There was conflict, first between the Portuguese and the Dutch, later between the French and the English, each attempting to secure supremacy at sea and a monopoly of the market in the East.

Had the Ming government grasped the significance of the time and tried to catch up with the foreign countries, the history of China might have taken a very different turn. As we have seen, industry developed rapidly under the Ming dynasty. If to this development there had been added a great expansion of foreign trade, rapid economic progress might have been made, with higher standards of living for the people and greater prosperity for society as a whole. If the government had protected the merchants, trade abroad would probably have flourished, and the modernization of China might have been advanced by a few centuries. However, all this is pure conjecture. The people in general did not want anything new. Yet, independent of their wishes, the hidden force was there; the era of transition had begun.

The Ming line ended in tragedy in 1644, in the third month of the seventeenth year of the Ch'ung-chen reign. Bad news came daily. The rebels were approaching the capital with great speed. An extraordinary meeting of the court was called to see what could be done. One of the ministers proposed that the emperor should transfer the capital to the south and he pointed out a short cut through Shantung which would bring the court to Huai-an 淮安 in present Kiangsu province, in twenty days. He then suggested that money in the imperial treasuries be employed for this journey. On being told that these were empty he proposed that the Board of Revenue might do something to finance the journey. But the emperor who did not trust the Board of Revenue turned to the husband of the imperial princess for advice. Previously this man had himself suggested the idea of transferring the capital to the south and had assured the emperor that he could raise a few hundred thousand soldiers to accompany him on the journey. But now he excused himself by saying that times had changed. The emperor was deeply disappointed. Finally, addressing himself to this imperial relative and to a Marquis, he said, "What if you two accompany me to the south together with your own domestic guards?" Both excused themselves, saying that domestic guards were no equals for the strong force of the rebels. Then, fearing that they might arouse the suspicions of the emperor, they said that they had always been circumspect in their conduct and had never dared to keep domestic guards.[24]

The last day of the dynasty was a day of unrelieved sorrow. In the morning the court met in a silence that was interrupted only by the occasional sobs of the emperor and his ministers. Some of the eunuchs who had been sent as supervisors to different districts had already gone over to the rebels. They now came back only to tell the emperor how powerful the troops of the rebels were: one of them even suggested the abdication of the emperor. Before returning to the rebels, they boasted to colleagues who had remained in the imperial service that they had nothing to worry about, for with the rebels they enjoyed prosperity and honor just as before! A group of the listeners, moved by their ignoble eloquence, decided to surrender to the enemy by opening the gates of the city. It was said that at court that morning the emperor had written with his finger on the table: "I am not an emperor who could cause the ruin of the empire; my ministers are responsible for this." Others said that he had written: "All the court ministers deserve to be killed."[25] It is doubtful that he wrote these last words. He certainly was deserving of pity. Yet, if he had examined his own character for a moment he would have known that he could not so hastily disclaim all responsibility.

Now, the emperor realized that he was alone. In a moment of despair he returned to his palace. Wine was brought in and drinking with solemn restraint he emptied several cups. He ordered that the two princes be sent to the home of their imperial relatives. Then, turning to the empress, he said, "Alas, our reign has come to an end!" Both wept bitterly. Moved by this sad sight the court ladies who were present burst into tears. The emperor, however, waved them away and told them to look to their own safety. The empress turned to her chamber in silence and there she hanged herself. The princess who was then fifteen years of age was summoned by her father. Upon seeing her the emperor sighed and said, "How unhappy you are to have been born into our family!" Then drawing out his sword, he struck her, but his hand faltered and cut off her left arm. Unnerved by this last failure, he lacked the courage to give a second blow. He wrote a last imperial letter begging the enemy to spare his people. Then this heir of such great glory left his palace and climbed a little hill. When he came to the top, he hanged himself. The Ming empire had ended.

NOTES

[1] *Wu-tsa-tsu,* 15, (ts'e 8) 8b, 9a.

[2] *Erh-shih erh-shih cha-chi,* (ts'e 6) 7ab; Wu Han 吳晗, *Chu Yüan-chang chuan* 朱元璋傳, (Kirin, 1949) 266–268.

[3] *Ta-kao* 大誥, paragraph 45. This is quoted from *Chu Yüan-chang chuan,* 243.

[4] *Huang-Ming wen-heng* 皇明文衡, (SPTK newspaper edition), 1, (ts'e 1) 28.

[5] *Ming shih,* 15, (ts'e 4) 12b.

[6] *Kai-yü ts'ung-k'ao,* 398–399.

[7] Meng Shen 孟森, *Ming-tai-shih* 明代史, (Taipei, 1958) 111.

[8] *Ming-ch'i pei-lüeh,* 23, 2. 514.

[9] *Ming-ch'en tsou-i,* 32, (ts'e 2,920) 599.

[10] *Ming-tai shih,* 38.

[11] *Ming hui-yao,* 2, 985.

[12] Li Hua-lung 李化龍 (1554–1611), *P'ing Po ch'üan shu* 平播全書, (TSCCCP), ts'e 3,982–3,988.

[13] T'ung Shih-heng 童世亨, *Li-tai chiang-yü hsing-shih i-lan-t'u* 歷代疆城形勢一覽圖, (Shanghai, 1935) explanatory notes pp. 10, 26, 43.

[14] Wu Han 吳晗, "Shih-liu shih-chi ch'ien chih Chung-kuo yü Nan-yang" 十六世紀前之中國與南洋, *Ch'ing-hua hsüeh-pao* 清華學報, 11, 1; *Yü-kung pan-yüeh-k'an* 禹貢半月刊, 5, 1; 5, 7; 5, 10; 6, 1; 6, 2; 6, 6; 6, 10. See the correspondence section of these numbers. Cf. the same periodical 7,1–2–3 (1937) 239–246, T'ung Yeh-shu 童業書, "Chung lun Cheng Ho hsia Hsi-yang shih-chien chih mao-i hsing chih" 重論鄭和下西洋事件之貿易性質.

[15] *Huang-Ming t'ung-chi*, 5, (ts'e 3) 39a; *Ming-shan-tsang*, 8, (ts'e 4) 25a; *Ch'in hsüan-chi*, 16, (ts'e 5) 16b. From a picture by a contemporary painter it appears that the so-called ch'i lin presented to the court was nothing but an African giraffe. Even contemporary scholars doubted the genuineness of this animal.

[16] *Chung-hsi ch'iao-t'ung-shih*, 3, 201–206.

[17] Concerning these countries cf. Chu Hsieh's book: *Cheng Ho*, 66–67.

[18] *Ming shu*, 16, (ts'e 2) 215.

[19] Ho Ch'iao-yüan 何喬遠 (floruit 1625), *Ching-shan ch'üan-chi* 鏡山全集, (late Ming edition) 7, (ts'e 3) 6b; Wu Chen-fang 吳震芳 (floruit 1680), *Ling-nan tsa-chi* 嶺南雜記, (TSCCCP 3,129), 41. Wu mentioned that in the 38th year of the Kang-hsi reign (1699) in Kuangtung the price of rice went up sky-high; many substituted sweet potatoes; Li Shih-chen 李時珍 (1518–1593), *Pen-ts'ao kang-mu* 本草綱目, (Photographic reprint of the 1889 edition) (Shanghai, 1937) 2.851; Wang Shih-mou 王世懋 (1536–1588), *Hsüeh-p'u tsa-shu* 學圃雜疏, (TSCCCP 1,355), 12; Chao Hsüeh-min 趙學敏 (floruit 1768), *Pen-ts'ao kang-mu shih-i* 本草綱目拾遺, (Shanghai, 1937) 7–11, 43–44; Sung Kung-yü 宋公玉, *Yin-shih shu* 飲食書, (late Ming edition), 5, (ts'e 2) 28ab; *Chi-yüan chi so chi*, B. 39; *Tsao-lin cha-tsu*, B. 150; Yeh Meng-chu 葉夢珠, *Yüeh-shih pien* 閱世編, 7, (this is quoted from *Ming-tai chiang-nan shih-min ching-chi shih-t'an*, 8).

[20] *Ming Ch'ing chien yeh-so-hui-shih i-chu t'i-yao*, 4–5, 7–8; Fang Hao 方豪, *Min-kuo i-lai ti li-shih hsüeh* 民國以來的歷史學, (compiled in the *Chung-hua min-kuo k'o-hsüeh chih* 中華民國科學誌 by Li Hsi-mou 李熙謀, Taipei, 1955) 1.1. On the other hand, there is no doubt that among the scholars quite a number were opposed to things foreign. Because they considered the westerners barbarians they concluded that there was nothing worth learning from them. Cf. Ch'en Teng-yüan 陳登元 "Hsi-hsüeh lai hua shih kuo-jen chih wu-tuan t'ai-tu" 西學來華時國人之武斷態度, *Eastern Miscellany* 東方雜誌, 27, 8, (1930) 61–76.

[21] *Ming Ch'ing chien yeh-so-kui-shih i-chuit'i-yao*; Hsü Tsung-tse 徐宗澤, *Ming-mo Ch'ing-ch'u kuan-shu hsi-hsüeh chih wei-jen* 明末清初灌輸西學之偉人, (Shanghai, 1938); Ayusawa Shintarō 鮎澤信太郎, "Matteo Ricci no sekaizu ni kan suru shi teki kenkyo" マテオ・リウチの世界圖に關する史的研究, *The Journal of Yokohama Municipal University* 橫濱市立大學紀要, August 15th, 1953, Series A–4, No. 18; *Chung-hsi Chiao-t'ung shih*, vols. 4–5.

[22] *Ming Ch'ing chien yeh-so-hui-shih i-chu t'i-yao*, especially cf. 296–299; *Chung-hsi chiao-t'ung-shih*, vol. 4, especially cf. 66–69; Juan Yüan 阮元 (1764–1849), *Ch'ou-jen chuan* 疇人傳, (WYWK, second series); P'an Sheng-chang 潘榿章 (1628–1662), *Chung-ling wen-hsien* 松陵文獻, (Ch'ing edition) 10, (ts'e 2) 16ab; Liu Yi-cheng 柳詒徵, *Chung-kuao wen-hua shih* 中國文化史, (Taipei, 1954) 3.179.

[23] Adolf Reichwein, *China and Europe*, (London, 1925); Lewis A. Mawrick, *China, a model for Europe*, (Texas, 1946); Ralph Ryler Flewelling, "China and European Enlightment", *The Personalist*, (University of Southern California, Winter, 1937) 9–26; Virgile Pinot, *La Chine et la formation de l'esprit philosophique en France (1640–1740)*, (Paris, 1932); Pierre Martino, *L'Orient dans la literature Française au XVIIe et XVIIIe siècle*, (Paris, 1906); M. Jacque Guerin, *La Chinoiserie en Europe au XVIII siècle*, (Paris, 1911); Belevitch-Stankavitch, *Le gout chinois en France au temps de Louis XIV*, (Paris, 1910; Henri Cordier, *La Chine en France au XVIIIe siècle*, (Paris, 1910); Ch'ien Chung-shu 錢鐘書, "China in the English Literature of the 18th Century," *Quarterly Bulletin of Chinese Bibliography*, 2, (June, 1941) 1–2, 7–48; 2 (Sept., 1941) 3–4, 113–152; Phyllis Ackerman, *Wall Paper, its History,*

Design and Use, (New York, 1923); Lady Dilke, *French Furniture and Decoration in the XVIII Century,* (London, 1901); *The China Trade and its Influence,* (Metropolitan Museum of Art, New York, 1941); Edmond Pilon, *Watteau et son Ecole,* (Paris, 1912); Ch'en Shou-yi陳受頤, "Sino-European Cultural contacts since the discovery of the sea route: a bibliographical note," *Nankai Social and Economic Quarterly,* 8, (April, 1935) 1. 44–74; Ch'en Shou-yi, "Daniel Defoe, China's severe critic," *Nankai Social and Economic Quarterly,* 8, (Oct., 1935) 3, 511–550; Ch'en Shou-yi, "Shih-pa-shih-chi ou-chou chih chung-kuo yüan-lin" 十八世紀之歐洲中國園林, *Ling-nan hsüeh-pao* 嶺南學報, 2, 1 (July, 1931) 35–70; Fang Chung 方重, "Shih-pa-shih-chi ti ying-kuo wen-hsüeh yü chung-kuo" 十八世紀之英國文學與中國, *Wen-che kuei-k'an* 文哲季刊, 2, (1941) 2.

[24] *K'ou-shih pien-nien,* 17, (ts'e 11) 7b, 11b.

[25] *Lieh-huang hsiao-chih,* 17, (ts'e 3) 10a; *Ming-chi pei lüeh,* (KHCPTS), 20 b. 340.

APPENDIX

THE INFLUENCE OF THE
SHUI-HU CHUAN ON CONTEMPORARY THOUGHT

During the Ming dynasty literature in the vernacular flourished greatly among the people: books were written not exclusively for the learned, for even the common people could enjoy them. It is to be noted that vernacular literature already existed a few centuries before the Ming dynasty; indeed the discovery of the Tun-huang 敦煌 manuscripts in Kansu province at the beginning of the present century by Sir Aurel Stein and M. Paul Pelliot has revealed that the existence of vernacular literature can be traced back as far as the T'ang dynasty. Up to the time of the new discovery this fact had not been known among scholars. The flourishing of the vernacular at this period can, perhaps, be explained as follows: first, owing to the extensive preaching of Buddhism among the people, it was natural that the language of the people should be used for preaching rather than the classical language which was less familiar to the people. Then, because of the popularization of folklore, scholars often wrote their light poems in simple language within the grasp of the people, and songs composed for musical entertainment were often written in the vernacular. Furthermore, during the T'ang period religious feasts were frequently celebrated with public entertainments near the temples and usually these were performed in the vernacular. Finally, by the end of the T'ang dynasty, printing presses had developed so rapidly that Buddhist scriptures and books of other kinds in the vernacular were common. This tradition continued in the Sung period. Lin-an 臨安 (the modern Hang-chou), capital of the Southern Sung dynasty (1127–1278), seemed especially to have been a place where vernacular literature flourished.[1]

Under Mongol rule, vernacular literature developed very rapidly, represented principally by dramas. The Mongol government never paid serious attention to government examinations with the result that many of the scholars felt that their talent was not appreciated. Accordingly, they took advantage of the situation and devoted their time to the writing of dramas which soon became popular among the people. The fact that over a hundred of these dramas are still extant in our day shows how enthusiastic about them contemporaries must have been.[2]

By the time the Ming took over the government, drama was established as a favorite entertainment of the people and we are told that nobles of the early Ming period greatly encouraged the publication of dramas; this was, perhaps, one reason why vernacular literature became so popular in later days. In the catalogue of the *Yung-lo ta-tien* 永樂大典 one can still see the titles of thirty-three dramas. At the same time novels of all kinds were produced in large quantities; some of these were historical, others social or fairy tales. Since most of these novels depicted the daily life of the people and used their own language they exerted great influence on contemporary thought. Moreover, dramas were composed from these novels and thus even the illiterate were able to enjoy them and we are told that dramas on the stage became a very common form of entertainment for the people from Ch'eng-hua and Hung-chih times.[3]

It is, perhaps, interesting to point out that two novels seem to have greatly influenced contemporary thought and can be said to have indirectly helped to excite the revolts: one is the *Shui-hu chuan* 水滸傳 and the other is the *San-kuo chih yen-i* 三國志演義. The former describes the revolt of the people at the end of the Northern Sung dynasty (circa 1120), and the latter the revolt at the end of the Han dynasty (circa 184 A.D.). Of these two novels the *Shui-hu chuan* had far greater influence on the people for it described the end of the Northern Sung dynasty when the Juchen 女眞 invaded China; these foreigners were the ancestors of the Manchus. The government of the Northern Sung is represented as definitely declining and the officials as corrupt while according to the story, most of the heroes of the novel were good citizens but, because of the oppression by cruel officials, were forced to revolt and their slogan was "To carry out the Way on behalf of Heaven," 替天行道. They were hostile to the government, but kind to the poor. The condition of the Ming dynasty was then very much like that of the Northern Sung so what better inspiration could the people look for than these one hundred and eight heroes?

That these two novels were known to the people of this period can be seen from the writings of contemporary authors. Ch'ien Hsi-yen 錢希言 tells us that the renowned scholar and painter Wen Cheng-ming 文徵明 (1470–1559), and his friends were fond of listening to the telling of the story of Sung Chiang 宋江, the principal character in the novel.[4] Another tells us that the literary critic, Chin Sheng-t'an 金聖歎, who lived in the first half of the 17th century, used to keep only two books on his desk; on the left he had the *Nan-hua-ching* 南華經 of Chuang-tzu 莊子, and on the right, the *Shui-hu chuan*.[5] The same author tells of a learned scholar who, after having listened to the story of the *Shui-hu chuan,* wrote a poem in praise of the novel and considered its author the equal in talent to Tso Ch'iu-ming 左丘明, author of the *Tso Chuan* 左傳, and to Ssu-ma Ch'ien 司馬遷, author of the *Shih chi* 史記.[6] And then we are told that, near the end of the Wan-li reign (circa 1600), there was a very popular card game among the people using cards on which figures of the *Shui-hu chuan* heroes were painted.[7] The famous painter Ch'en Hung-shou 陳洪綬 painted forty of these cards at the request of his friend Chang Tai 張岱 to make a book on behalf of a poor man. In Chang Tai's preface to this little volume in which the paintings were bound, he estimated that these forty pictures would provide an income for his poor friend who had a family of eight.[8] Of course, the painter's name added great value to the pictures but, at the same time, the popularity of the subject painted certainly served as a good advertisement and made the purchasers more enthusiastic. P'eng Sun-i 彭孫貽, who wrote a poem on these pictures of Ch'en Hung-shou, compared the figures to the portraits of the contemporary rebels.[9] A few years ago Chin Ling University 金陵大學 reprinted the *Ying-hsiung-p'u t'u-tsan* 英雄譜圖讚 which was first published during the Ch'ung-chen period. This book contains two parts: illustrations of the *San-kuo-chih yen-i* and illustrations of the *Shui-hu chuan,* each of the illustrations being accompanied by a poem and a few remarks, most of them written by well known contemporary scholars. Some of these remarks actually mirrored the government of the time.[10]

Among the people, there was a more effective way of spreading the stories of these two novels, namely, through story tellers. That story-telling was popular even during the Sung dynasty, we can prove from the writings of scholars of the time.[11] In the late Ming period, we have the testimony of Chang Tai who mentioned some of these story-tellers at the Ch'ing-ming feast 清明 in Yang-chou 揚州[12], particularly Liu Ching-t'ing 柳敬亭, who probably was one of the best story-tellers of this period. Liu was a vagabond in his early days and had developed a talent for story telling, so that he became known at all levels of society and in spite of his high charge—a silver tael for one chapter—he was always kept busy. On a given day he would not go beyond one chapter of any story and those who wished to hear him had to make an appointment ten days ahead, but for a long time he was the guest of the Brigadier General Tso Liang-yü. The *Shui-hu chuan* was one of his favorite stories, although he did not always follow the novel very closely.[13] Story-telling, indeed, communicates a more vivid picture than the written word to the people and it serves as a very effective means of propaganda among the illiterate. We are told that in the later period, when the rebels were ready to besiege a city, they always went into it disguised as scholars, merchants, fortune tellers, coolies, etc. It is very likely that there must also have been a number of story-tellers among them. The same Chang Tai mentioned that on one occasion there was a procession in his village in which thirty-six men and women were dressed up as *Shui-hu chuan* heroes. This novelty attracted many villagers who came from all around to see them. The thirty-six men and women, who were chosen to represent the heroes of the story, were carefully picked from nearby districts and villages and they were highly paid.[14] Even the author of the *Tung-lin tien-chiang lu* 東林 點將錄 was influenced by the *Shui-hu chuan*. In this book, written to ridicule the Tung-lin Party, a nickname is given to each of the prominent leaders of the party after the model of the *Shui-hu chuan*.[15] We see much the same in a later period, when most of the leaders of the rebels had a nickname so that there is some excuse for the author of the *Tsui-wei lu* who felt so indignant with the writer of the *Shui-hu chuan* and blamed him for corrupting innocent people.[16]

Toward the end of the Ch'ung-chen period the government came to the conclusion that the *Shui-hu chuan* had caused serious harm to the people. Accordingly, in 1642, orders came from the emperor to the Board of War and to the Censorate to disperse the vagrants, especially in the Shantung province, which tradition still considered the headquarters of the *Shui-hu chuan* heroes. Again, the emperor demanded that all those who, up to this time, had kept the novel or the blocks for printing this book should burn them without delay. Furthermore, the imperial order was engraved on slabs of stone and placed on the hilltops so that all the public might read it.[17]

Perhaps the *San-kuo chih yen-i* influenced the Manchus more than the rebels. Since this treatise is limited to the rebellions, I refer the reader to the article of Li Kuang-t'ao 李光濤, a modern specialist in the history of the early Ch'ing period: "Ch'ing-t'ai-tsung yü san-kuo yen-i" 清太宗與三國演義 .[18] It is sufficient to recall here that one of the arch-rebels had the nickname of Ts'ao Ts'ao 曹操 an important character of the novel while the notorious Chang Hsien-chung is said to have greatly esteemed both the *San-kuo chih yen-i* and the *Shui-hu chuan*. We are told that he used to have scholars frequently read to him these two novels and that he made great use of the military strategy described in them.[19]

NOTES

[1] Wu Tzu-mu 吳自牧, *Meng-liang lu* 夢粱錄, (PCHSTK), (*ts'e* 243–245); Chou Mi 周密, *Wu-lin chiu-shih* 武林舊事, (PCHSTK), (*ts'e* 250–252); Nai-te-weng 耐德翁, *Tu-ch'eng chi-sheng* 都城紀勝; *Lien-t'ing shih-erh chung* 楝亭十二種, published by Ts'ao Yin 曹寅, reprinted by Ku-shu liu-t'ung ch'u 古書流通處 (Shanghai, 1921) (*ts'e* 1).

[2] Liu Lin-sheng 劉麟生, *Chung-kuo wen-hsüeh-shih* 中國文學史, (Shanghai 1932) 349; Chiang Tsu-i 蔣祖怡, *Chung-kuo jen-min wen-hsüeh-shih* 中國人民文學史, (Shanghai, 1951) 223–224.

[3] Ibid., 228–229.

[4] Ch'ien Hsi-yen 錢希言, *Hsi-hsia* 戲瑕, *Tse-ku chai ch'ung-ch'ao* 澤古齋重鈔, ed. by Ch'en Huang 陳璜 (Shanghai, 1823) 1 (*ts'e* 84).

[5] Hu Ying-lin 胡應麟, *Shao shih-shan fang pi-ts'ung* 少室山房筆叢. This text is quoted from K'ung Ling-ching 孔另境, *Chung-kuo hsiao-shuo shih-liao* 中國小說史料, (Shanghai, 1935) p. 15.

[6] Ibid., 16.

[7] P'ang Tsun-szu 彭遵泗, *Shu-pi* 蜀碧, 4, (CKNLWHLSTS), (*ts'e* 35) 79; *Chi-yüan chi so chi*, 9, (ts'e 14) 48a.

[8] Ch'en Hung-shou 陳洪綬, *Ch'en Lao-lien shui-hu yeh-tzu* 陳老蓮水滸葉子; Chang Tai 張岱, *T'ao-an meng-i* 陶菴夢憶, (Reprinted by the Ch'i-chih shu-chü 啓智書局, Shanghai, 1933) 6.71.

[9] *Ming-jen shih-ch'ao*, First Series, 14, (*ts'e* 4) 18ab.

[10] *Ying-hsiung-p'u t'u-tsan* 英雄譜圖讚, (Originally printed by the Hsiung-fei-ko 雄飛閣 during the Ch'ung-chen reign; reprinted by Chin-ling University 金陵大學) (Nanking, 1949) 4, 79, 80, 100.

[11] Su Shih 蘇軾 (1036–1101), *Tung-p'o chih-lin* 東坡志林, (PCHSTK), 6, (ts'e 323) 4b; Lu Yu 陸游 (1125–1216), *Lu Fang-weng ch'üan chi* 陸放翁全集, (Chi-ku-ko 汲古閣 edition, published by Mao Chin 毛晉 (1598–1659) 33, (*ts'e* 26) 14b.

[12] *T'ao-an meng-i*, 5, 60–61.

[13] Ibid., 5, 56–57.

[14] Ibid., 7. 81.

[15] Wen Ping 文秉 (1609–1669), *Hsien-po chih-shih* 先撥志始, (*Tse-ku-chai Ch'ung-ch'ao ed.*), (*ts'e* 31) A. 68–75.

[16] *Tsui-wei lu*, 31, (ts'e 57) 69b, 70a.

[17] *Ming-mo nung-min ch'i-i shih-liao*, 355–356.

[18] Li Kuang-t'ao 李光濤, "Ch'ing-t'ai-tsung yü San-kuo yen-i", 清太宗與三國演義, *Bulletin of the Institute of History and Philology* 中央研究院歷史語言研究所集刊, 12, 251–272.

[19] Liu Luan 劉鑾, *Wu-shih-hu* 五石瓠. This is quoted from *Chung-kuo hsiao-shuo shih-liao*, 40; cf. *ibid.* where Wang Mo-hsi's 王摩西 *Hsiao-shuo hsiao-hua* 小說小話 is also quoted.

ABBREVIATIONS

1) BIHP   The Bulletin of the Institute of History and Philology 歷史語言研究所集刊.

2) CHHP   *Ch'ing-hua hsueh-pao* 清華學報.

3) CKNLWHLSTS   *Chung-kuo nei-luan wai-hou li shih ts'ung-shu* 中國內亂外禍歷史叢書 ed. by Sheng chou kuo kuang she 神州國光社 (Shanghai, 1936).

4) CKSHCCSCK   *Chung-kuo she-hui ching-chi shih chi-k'an* 中國社會經濟史集刊.

5) CLHP   *Chi-lu hui-pien* 紀錄彙編.

6) CPTCTS   *Chih-pu-ts'u-chai ts'ung-shu* 知不足齋叢書.

7) HFL (ed.)   *Hsien-fen-lou* 涵芬樓.

8) HFLPC   *Hsien-feng-lou pi-chi* 涵芬樓祕笈.

9) HLTTS   *Hsuan-lan-t'ang ts'ung shu* 玄覽堂叢書 ed. by Nanking kuo-li chung-yang t'u-shu-kuan 南京國立中央圖書館 (Nanking, 1947).

10) KHCPTS   *Kuo-hsueh chi-pen tsung-shu* 國學基本叢書.

11) KPL   Kiangsu Provincial Library 蘇江省立圖書館.

12) KSLTSK   Kiangsu sheng-li t'u-shu-kuan 江蘇省立圖書館.

13) MCPS   *Ming-chi pai-shih* 明季稗史 ed. by a certain Liu-yün chü-shih 留雲居士 in the early Ch'ing period. Reprinted edition by the Commercial Press (Shanghai, 1912).

14) PCHSTK   *Pi-chi hsiao-shuo ta-kuan* 筆記小說大觀 ed. by the Chin-pu shu-chü 進步書局 (Shanghai).

15) RK   *Rekishi kenkyu* 歷史研究.

16) SCIS   *Sheng-ch'ao i-shih* 勝朝遺事 ed. by Wu Mi-kuang 吳彌光 (1883).

17) SHPYK   *Shih-hou pan-yüeh k'an* 食貨半月刊.

18) SPTK   *Ssu-pu ts'ung-k'an* 四部叢刊.

19) SZ   *Shigaku zasshi* 史學雜誌.

20) TCFSCTIS   *T'ung-ch'eng Fang-shih ch'i-tai i-shu* 桐城方氏七代遺書 ed. by Fang Ch'ang-han 方昌翰 (Anhui, 1888).

21) TKCCC   *Tse-ku-chai ch'ung-ch'ao* 澤古齋重鈔 ed. by Ch'en Huang 陳璜 (Shanghai, 1823).

22) TSCCCP   *Ts'ung-shu chi-ch'eng ch'u-pien* 叢書集成初編 ed. by the Commercial Press (Shanghai, 1935).

23) WYWK   *Wan-yu wen-k'u* 萬有文庫.

24) YKPYK   *Yü-kung pan-yüeh-k'an* 禹貢半月刊.

BIBLIOGRAPHY

Anonymous, *Ch'ien-pi k'ao* 錢幣考, (TSCCCP), (ts'e 0771).

——, *Ch'ung-chen ch'ang-pien* 崇禎長編, (T'ung-shih 痛史 series, ed. by a certain Lo-t'ien chü-shih 樂天居士), (Shanghai, 1927) (ts'e 13 14).

——, *Huang-ch'ao pen-chi* 皇朝本紀, (CLHP), (ts'e 3).

——, *Liao-hai tan-chung lu* 遼海丹忠錄, (late Ming ed.).

——, *Min-ch'ao tung-huan shih-shih* 民抄董宦事實, (CKNLWHLSTS), (ts'e 35).

——, *P'ing-lo-chuan* 平虜傳, (late Ming ed.).

——, *Shu Chi* 蜀記, (T'ung shih ed.), (ts'e 24).

——, *T'ien-huang yü-tieh* 天潢玉牒, (CLPH), (ts'e 4).

——, *Tu p'ien hsin-shu* 杜騙新書, (Ming edition).

Aoki Masaru 青木正兒, *Chukoku kinsei gikyoku shi* 中國近世戲曲史, (tr. by Wang Ku-lu 王古魯) (Peking, 1958).

Leigh *Ashton* & Basil *Gray, Chinese Art*, (London).

Ayusawa Shintarō 鮎澤信太郎, "Matteo Ricci: no sekaizu ni kan suru shi teki kenkyo" マテオ・リツチの世界圖關する史的研究. *The Journal of Yokohama Municipal University* 橫濱市立大學紀要 (15th Aug., 1953). Series A4, No. 18.

Bernard, Henri, *Matteo Ricci's Scientific Contribution to China,* tr. by Edward C. Werner, (Peiping, 1935).

Boulger, Demetrius Charles, *A Short History of China,* (London, 1900).

Braga, J. M., *China Landfall 1513,* (Macau, 1955).

Ch'a Chi-tso 查繼佐 (1601–1677), *Tsui-wei lu* 罪惟錄, (Photographic reprint by the Commercial Press) (Shanghai, 1928).

Ch'a To 查鐸 (ed. 1570), *I-chai tsou-shu* 毅齋奏疏 (TSCCCP), (ts'e 0,907).

Chang Ho-chung 張和仲, *Ch'ien po nien yen* 千百年眼, (PCHSTK), (ts'e 93–95).

Chang Hsieh 張燮 (ca. 1600), *Tung-hsi-yang k'ao* 東西洋考, (TSCCCP), (ts'e 3,259–3,261).

Chang Hsing-liang 張星烺, *Chung-hsi chiao-t'ung shih-liao hui-pien* 中西交通史料滙編, (Peiping, 1930).

Chang Hsiu-min 張秀民, *Chung-kuo yin-shua-shu ti fa-ming chi ch'i ying-hsiang* 中國印刷術的發明及其影響 (Peking, 1958 and 1978).

Chang Hsüan 張萱, *Hsi-yüan wen-ts'un* 西園文存, (1664 ed.) (ca. 1600), *Hsi-yüan wen-chien-lu* 西園聞見錄, (Reprint of a Ming ms. by the Harvard-Yenching Institute) (Peiping, 1940).

Chang Jui-chao 張瑞朝, *Huang-ming kung-chü k'ao* 皇明貢舉考, (Ming ed.).

Chang Li-hsiang 張履祥 (1611–1674), *Pu nung-shu* 補農書, (*T'ung-hsüeh-chai ts'ung-shu* 通學齋叢書) (ts'e 40).

Chang Tai 張岱 (b. 1597), *T'ao-an meng-i* 陶菴夢憶, (Ch'i-chih shu-chü 啓智書局 ed.) (Shanghai, 1933).

Chang Yang-hao 張養浩 (1269–1329), *Mu-min chung-kao* 牧民忠告, (TSCCCP), (ts'e 0,888).

Chang Ying 張英 (1637–1708), *Heng-ch'an so-yen* 恆產瑣言, *Chin-te ts'ung-shu* 進德叢書 (Shanghai).

Chao Chih-shih 趙吉士 (1628–1706), *Chi-yüan chi so chi* 寄園寄所寄, (Ch'ing ed.).

Chao Hsüeh-min 趙學敏 (circa 1768), *Pen-ts'ao kang-mu shih-i* 本草綱目拾遺, (Shanghai, 1937).

Chao I 趙翼 (1727–1814), *Erh-shih erh-shih cha-chi* 二十二史剳記, (Wen-yüan Shan-fang 文淵山房 ed.) (Shanghai, 1902).

——, *Kai-yü ts'ung-k'ao* 陔餘叢考, (Shanghai, 1957).

Chao Shih-chen 趙士楨, *Shen-ch'i p'u huo-wen* 神器譜或問, (HLTTS), (ts'e 86).

Ch'en Chi-sheng 陳濟生, *Tsai-shang chi-lüeh* 再生紀略, (HLTTS), (ts'e 110).

Ch'en Chien 陳建 (1497–1567), *Huang-ming t'ung-chi* 皇明通紀, (Japanese ed., 19th cent.?).

Ch'en Heng-li 陳恆力, *Pu-nung-shu yen-chiu* 補農書研究 (Shanghai, 1958).

Ch'en Hung-shou 陳洪綬 (1599–1652), *Ch'en Lao-lien shui-hu yeh-tzu* 陳老蓮水滸葉子, (Photographic reprints).

Ch'en Jen-hsi 陳仁錫 (1581–1636), *Huang-ming shih-fa-lu* 皇明世法錄, (Late Ming ed.).

Ch'en Lien 陳璉 (ca. 1410), *Chin-hsüan-chi* 琴軒集, (K'ang-hsi ed.).

Ch'en Lung-cheng 陳龍正 (1585–1645), *Chi-ting wai shu* 幾亭外書, (1631 ed.).

Ch'en Mou-jen 陳懋仁, *Ch'üan-nan tsa-chih* 泉南雜志, (TSCCCP), (ts'e 3).

Ch'en Shih-ch'i 陳詩啓, *Ming-tai kuan-shou-kung-yeh ti yen-chiu* 明代官手工業的研究, (Shanghai, 1956).

Ch'en T'ien 陳田, *Ming-shih chi-shih* 明詩紀事, (KHCPTS).

Ch'en Yi 陳沂 (1469–1538), *Chin-ling shih-chi* 金陵世紀, (Lung-ch'ing 隆慶 ed. 1569).

Ch'en Yi Shan 陳怡山, *Hai-pin wai-shih* 海濱外史, (HFLPC ed., 5th series).

Ch'en Ju-hang 陳汝衡, *Shuo-shu hsiao-shih* 說書小史, (Shanghai, 1936).

——, *Shuo-shu shih-hua* 說書史話, (Peking, 1958).

Ch'en Yüan 陳垣, *Ming-chi T'ien Ch'ien fo-chiao k'ao* 明季滇黔佛教考, (Peking, 1959).

Cheng Chan-to 鄭振鐸, *Ch'a-tu-pen chung-kuo wen-hsüeh-shih* 插圖本中國文學史, (Peking, 1957).

——, *Chung-kuo wen-hsüeh yen-chiu* 中國文學研究, (Peking, 1957).

Cheng Chi-sun 鄭積孫, *Tzu-lin ch'ih-tu* 緇林尺牘, (Shanghai, 1934).

Cheng Ch'in 鄭欽 and *Cheng* Jui 鄭銳, *Po-chung t'ai-shu-ts'ao* 伯仲臺疏草, (TSCCCP), (ts'e 0,912).

Cheng Ho-sheng 鄭鶴聲, *Cheng Ho i-shih hui-pien* 鄭和遺事彙編, (Shanghai, 1948).

Cheng Hsiao 鄭曉 (1499–1566), *Cheng tuan-chien-kung wen-chi* 鄭端簡公文集, (Wan-li ed.).

——, (1499–1566), *Chin-yen lei-pien* 今言類編, (SCIS second series), (ts'e 13–14).

Cheng Lien 鄭廉, *Yü pien chi-lüeh* 豫變紀略, (edited by P'ang Chia-pin 彭家屏) (1743).

Cheng Ta-yü 鄭大郁 (ca. 1640), *Ching-kuo hsiung-liao* 經國雄略, (late Ming ed.).

Cheng T'ien-t'ing 鄭天挺, ed., *Ming-Ch'ing-shih tzu-liao* 明清史資料, vol. I (T'ientsin, 1980).

Ch'eng Pai-erh 程百二, *Fang-yü sheng-lüeh* 方輿勝略, (Wan-li ed.).

Chi Liu-ch'i 計六奇 (ca. 1690), *Ming-chi pei-lüeh* 明季北略, (KHCPTS).

Chi Yün 紀昀 (1724–1805) et. al., *Li-tai chi-kuan-piao* 歷代官職表, (KHCPTS).

Ch'i Po-yü 祁伯裕 (ca. 1595), *Nan-ching tu-ch'a-yüan-chih* 南京都察院志, (T'ien-ch'i 天啓 (1621–1627) ed.).

Chiang Tsu-i 蔣祖怡, *Chung-kuo jen-min wen-hsüeh-shih* 中國人民文學史, (Shanghai, 1951).

Chien-lung Po-shui-hsien chih 乾隆白水縣志.

Ch'ien Ch'ien-i 錢謙益 (1582–1664), *Lieh-ch'ao shih-chi hsiao-chuan* 列朝詩集小傳, (Shanghai, 1957).

Ch'ien Hsi-yen 錢希言, *Hsi-hsia* 戲瑕, (TSCCCP), (ts'e 84–85).

Ch'ien Hsing 錢駴, *Chia-shen ch'uan-hsin lu* 甲申傳信錄, (CKNLWHLSTS), (ts'e 12).

Ch'ien Mu 錢穆, *Chung-kuo li-tai cheng-chih te shih* 中國歷代政治得失, (Hong Kong, 1952).

——, *Kuo-shih ta-kang* 國史大綱, (Chungking, 1944 and Shanghai, 1940).

Chou Hui 周暉, *Chin-ling so-shih* 金陵瑣事, (Wan-li ed.).

Chou I 鄒漪, *Ming-chi i-wen* 明季遺聞, (MCPS second series), (ts'e 1).

Chou I 周怡 (1506–1569), *No-ch'i tsou-i* 訥谿奏議, (TSCCCP), (ts'e 907).

Chou Mi 周密 (1232–1308), *Wu-lin chiu-shih* 武林舊事, (PCHSTK), (ts'e 250–252).

Chou Shun-ch'ang 周順昌 (1584–1626), *Chou Chung-chieh-kung chin-yü-chi* 周忠介公燼餘集, (TSCCCP), (ts'e 2,165).

Chou Te-p'u 鄒德溥, *Sheng-ch'ao t'ai-chiao lu* 聖朝泰交錄, (1634 ed.).

Chu Hsi-tsu 朱希祖 (1879–1944), *Ming-chi shih-liao t'i-pa* 明季史料題跋, (Peking, 1961). *Chu Hsi-tsu hsien-sheng wen-chi* 朱希祖先生文集, 6 vols. (Taipei, 1979).

Chu Hsieh 朱偰, *Cheng Ho* 鄭和, (Peking, 1956). *Ming-Ch'ing liang-tai kung-yüan chien-chih yen-ke t'u-k'ao* 明清兩代宮苑建置沿革圖考, (Shanghai, 1947)

Chu I-tsun 朱彝尊 (1629–1709), *P'u-shu-t'ing chi* 曝書亭集, (KHCPTS).

Chu Kuo-cheng 朱國楨 (1557–1632), *Ta-shih chi* 大事記, (Wan-li ed.).

——, *Yung-chuang hsiao-ptn* 湧幢小品, (PCHSTK), (ts'e 98–100).

Chu Tung-jun 朱東潤, *Chang Chü-cheng ta-chuan* 張居正大傳, (1945). *Chung-kuo wen-hsüeh p'i-p'ing-shih ta-k'ang* 中國文學批評史大綱, (Shanghai, 1947).

Ch'üan-chou-fu chih 泉州府志.

Ch'üan Tzu-wang 全祖望 (1705–1755), *Ch'i-ch'i-t'ing-chi wai-pien* 埼鮚亭集外編, (SPTK), (Shanghai, 1929).

Chuang T'ing-lung 莊廷鑨 (ca. 1650), *Ming-shih ch'ao-lüeh* 明史鈔略, (Photographic reprint by the Commercial Press) (Shanghai, 1935).

Chuang Yün-sheng 莊允升, *T'ang-ming-lü ho-pien* 唐明律合編, (WYWF, second series).

Ch'ung-chen ts'un-shih shu-ch'ao 崇禎存實疏鈔, (Shanghai, 1934).

Chung-hua min-kuo k'o-hsüeh chih 中華民國科學志, compiled by *Li* Hsi-mou 李熙謀, (Taipei, 1955).

Cohn, William, *Chinese Painting*, (London, 1951).

Couling, Samuel, *The Encyclopaedia Sinica*, (London, 1917).

Dehergne, Joseph, *Répertoire des Jésuites de Chine de 1552 à 1800*, (Rome & Paris, 1972).

D'Ohsson, Abraham Constantine Mouradgea (1780–1855), *Histoire des Mongols* 蒙古史, tr. by Feng Ch'eng-chün 馮承鈞, (Shanghai, 1936).

Fan Li-pen 范立本, *Chih-chia chieh-yao* 治家節要, (transcription of the Edo period).

Fang Hao 方豪, *Chung-hsi chiao-t'ung-shih* 中西交通史, (Taipei, 1954). *Li chih-tsao yen-chiu* 李之藻研究, (Taipei, 1066). *Fang Hao liu-shih tzu-ting-kao* 方豪六十自定稿, 2 vols. (Taipei, 1969). *Chung-kuo T'ien-chu-chiao-shih jen-wu chuan* 中國天主教人物傳, 3 vols. (Hongkong & Taipei, 1967–1972).

Fang K'ung-chao 方孔炤 (ca. 1640), *Ch'u-yao hsiao-yen* 芻蕘小言, (TCFSCTIS), (ts'e 5). *Fu-ch'u kung-tu* 撫楚公牘, (TCFSCTIS), (ts'e 5).

Fang Ta-chen 方大鎮 (ca. 1590), *Ning-t'an-chü tsou-i* 甯澹居奏議, (TCFSCTIS), (ts'e 3).

Farmer, Edward L., *Early Ming Government: The Evolution of Duel Capitals*, (Cambridge: Harvard U. Press, 1976).

Fen Wen-lan 范文瀾, *Chung-kuo t'ung shih chien-pien* 中國通史簡編, (Shanghai, 1947).

Feng Kuei-fen 馮桂芬 (1809–1874), *Chiao-pin-lu k'ang-i* 校邠廬抗議, (Kiangsi, 1884).

Feng Ying-ching 馮應京 (ca. 1600), *Ching-shih shih-yung p'ien* 經世實用編, (Ming ed.).

Fletcher, Banister, *A History of Architecture*, (London, 1938).

Four Books The, 四書, (tr. by James Legge) (Shanghai, 1930).

Fu Wei-lin 傅維鱗 (ca. 1670), *Ming Shu* 明書, (TSCCCP).

Fu Yi-ling 傅衣凌, *Ming-ch'ing shih-tai shang-jen chi shang-yeh tzu-pen* 明清時代商人及商業資本, (Peking, 1956).
    Ming-tai Chiang-nan shi-min ching-chi shih-t'an 明代江南市民經濟試探, (Peking, 1961).
    Ming-tai nung-ts'un she-hui ching-chi 明代農村社會經濟, (Peking, 1961).

Giles, Herbert A., *History of Chinese Literature*, (New York and London, 1900).

Goodrich, L. Carrington (ed.), *Dictionary of Ming Biography*, 2 vols. (New York and London, 1976).

Halde, Jean Baptiste du (1674–1743), *Description geographique, historique, chronologique, politique, et physique de l'Empire de la Chine*, (Paris, 1735) 4 vols.

Han-fen-lou ku-chin wen-ch'ao chien-pien 涵芬樓古今文鈔簡編, (compiled by *Wu* Tseng-ch'i 吳曾祺), (KHCPTS), (Shanghai, 1933).

Hevelaque, Emile, *La Chine*, (Paris, 1928).

Ho Ch'iao-yüan 何喬遠 (ca. 1625), *Ching-shan ch'üan-chi* 鏡山全集, (Shen-liu tu-shu-t'ang 深柳讀書堂 ed., printed in the late Ming dynasty).

Ho Liang-ch'en 何良臣, *Chen-chi* 陣紀, (TSCCCP), (ts'e 0,961).

Hsia Hsieh 夏燮, *Ming t'ung-chien* 明通鑑, (Shanghai, 1888).

Hsia Kuang-nan 夏光南, *Yuan-tai Yünnan shih-ti ts'ung-k'ao* 元代雲南史地叢考, (Shanghai, 1935).

Hsia Yün-i 夏允彝 (1596–1645), *Hsing-ts'un lu* 幸存錄, (MCPS first series), (ts'e 4).

Hsiang Meng-yüan 項夢原 (ca. 1600), *Tung-kuan chi-shih* 冬官紀事, (TSCCCP).

Hsiang Ta 向達, *Chung-wai chiao-t'ung hsiao-shih* 中外交通小史, (Shanghai, 1933).

Hsiao Liang-kan 蕭良幹 (?–1602), *Cho-chai shih-i* 拙齋十議, (TSCCCP), (ts'e 0,756).

Hsieh Chao-che 謝肇淛 (ca. 1610), *Hsiao-ts'ao-chai wen-chi* 小草齋文集, (Ming ed.).

——, *Wu-tsa-tsu* 五雜組, (Japanese ed., 1795 and Shanghai ed., 1959).

Hsieh Kuo-chen 謝國楨, *Ming ch'ing chih chi tang-she yün-tung k'ao* 明清之際黨社運動考, (Shanghai, 1934).
    Ming-ch'ing pi-chi t'an-ts'ung 明清筆記談叢, (Shanghai, 1960–1962).
    Ming-tai she-hui ching-chi shih-liao hsüan-pien 明代社會經濟史料選編, (Fukien, 1980).
    Nan-Ming shih-lüeh 南明史略, (Shanghai, 1957).

Hsien-tsung shun-huang-ti shih-lu 憲宗純皇帝實錄, (KSSLTSK photographic reprint).

Hsü Ch'ang-chih 徐昌治 (ca. 1630), *Chao-tai fang-mu* 昭代芳摹, (1636 ed.).

Hsü Chen-ming 徐貞明 (ca. 1585), *Lu shui k'e-tan* 潞水客談, (TSCCCP), (ts'e 3,020).

Hsü Chung-hsi 許重熙 (ca. 1630), Chia-ching i-lai chu-liao 嘉靖以來注略, (late Ming ed.).

Hsü Hsüeh-chü 徐學聚 (ed. 1590), *Kuo-ch'ao tien-hui* 國朝典彙, (1634 ed.).

Hsü Hsüeh-mo 徐學謨 (1522–1593), *Kuei-yu-yüan kao* 歸有園稿, (1612 ed.). *Shih-miao chih-yu-lu* 世廟識餘錄, (1608 ed.).

Hsü Kuang-ch'i 徐光啓 (1562–1633), *Tseng-ting Hsü wen-ting-kung chi* 增訂徐文定公集, (Shanghai, 1909).

Hsü Piao 徐標 (ca. 1640), *Hsiao-chu erh-yen* 小築邇言, (Ch'ung-chen ed.).

Hsü Tsung-tse 徐宗澤, *Ming ch'ing chien yeh-su-hui-shih yi-chu t'i yao* 明清間耶穌會士譯著提要, (Shanghai, 1949).
    Ming-mo Ch'ing-ch'u kuan-shu hsi-hsüeh chih wei-jen 明末清初灌輸西學之偉人, (Shanghai, 1938).

Hsü t'ung-tien 續通典, (WYWK ed.).

Hsü wen-hsien-t'ung-k'ao 續文獻通考, (WYWK ed.).

Hu Wen-huan 胡文煥 (floruit 1596), *Hua-yi feng-t'u chih* 華夷風土志, (Ming ed.).

Huai-tsung ch'ung-chen shih-lu 懷宗崇禎實錄, (KSSLTSK photographic reprint).

Huai-yüan hsien-chih 懷遠縣志, compiled by *Su* Chi-chao 蘇其炤, revised by *Ho* Ping-hsün 何丙勳, (Shensi, 1928).

Huang Chang-chien 黃彰健, *Ming-tai lü-li hui-pien* 明代律例彙編, (Taipei, 1979).
    Ming-Ch'ing-shih yen-chiu ts'ung-kao 明清史研究叢稿, (Taipei, 1977).

Huang Chi-hua 黃緝華, *Ming-tai hai-yün-ho ti yen-chiu* 明代海運及運河的研究, (Taipei, 1961).

Huang Hsi-hsien 黃希賢, *Chu chia pi yung* 居家必用, (Ming ed.).

Huang-ming wen-heng 皇明文衡, (SPTK newspaper ed.).

Huang Ju-liang 黃汝良 (ca. 1590), *Yeh-chi meng sou* 野紀矇搜, (Ming ed.).

Huang Pai-lu 黃伯祿, *Cheng-chiao feng pao* 正教奉褒, (Shanghai, 1904).

Huang Pien 黃汴 (ca. 1560), *I-t'ung lu-ch'eng t'u chih* 一統路程圖志, (1570 ed.).

Huang Tso 黃佐 (1490–1566), *Nan-yung chih* 南雝志, (Ming ed.).

Huang Tsun-so 黃尊素 (1584–1626), *Shuo-lüeh* 說略, (HFLPC, 2nd series), (Shanghai, 1917).

Huang Tsung-hsi 黃宗羲 (1610–1695), *Ming-i tai-fang-lu* 明夷待訪錄, (WYWK ed., 2nd series).
    Ming-ju hsüeh-an 明儒學案, (KHCPTS).
    Nan-lei wen-ting 南雷文定, (TSCCCP), (ts'e 2,463–2,464).
    Yung-li chi-nien 永曆紀年, (CKNLWHLSTS), (ts'e 11).

Huang Yün-mei 黃雲眉, *Ming-shih k'ao cheng* 明史考證, Vol. 1 (Peking, 1979); Vol. 2 (1980).

Huang Yung-ch'üan 黃湧泉, *Ch'en Hung-shou nien-p'u* 陳洪綬年譜, (Peking, 1960).

Hucker, Charles O., (ed.), *Chinese Government in Ming Times: Seven Studies*, (New York, 1969).
    The Ming Dynasty: Its Origins and Evolving Institutions, (Michigan Papers in Chinese Studies No. 34, Ann Arbor, 1978).

Inaba Iwakichi 稻葉岩吉, *Ch'ing-ch'ao ch'üan-shih* 清朝全史, tr. by Tan Tao 但燾, (Shanghai, 1924).

Ishihara Michihiro 石原道博, *Mimmatsu Shinsho Nippon kitsu no kenkyu* 明末清初日本乞師の研究, (Tokyo, 1945).

Jüan Yüan 阮元 (1764–1849), *Ch'ou-jen ch'uan* 疇人傳, (WYWK, 2nd series).

Kao I-han 高一涵, *Chung-kuo nei-ko chih-tu ti yen-ke* 中國內閣制度的沿革, (Shanghai, 1933).
    Chung-kuo yu-shih chih-tu te-yen-ke 中國御史制度的沿革, (Shanghai, 1933).

Kao Tai 高岱 (ca. 1550), *Hung-yu lu* 鴻猷錄, (CLHP ed.).

Kao Tou-shu 高斗樞 (1594–1670), *Shou-yün chi-lüeh* 守鄖紀略, (T'ung-shih ed.) ts'e 30).

K'o Shao-min 柯紹忞 (1850–1933), *Hsin Yüan shi* 新元史, (Shanghai, 1935).

Kato Shige 加藤繁, *Shina Keizaishi kaisetsu* 支那經濟史概說, (Tokyo, 1944).

Ku Ch'i-yüan 顧起元 (1565–1628), *Lai-chen ts'ao-t'ang wen-chi* 嬾眞草堂文集, (1618 ed.).

Ku Chieh-kang 顧頡剛 and *Shih* Nien-tsu 史念祖, *Chung-kuo chiang-yü Yen-ke shih* 中國疆域沿革史, (Shanghai, 1938).

Ku Kung-hsieh 顧公燮, *Hsiao-hsia hsien-chi tse-ch'ao* 消夏閑記摘鈔, (HFLPC), (2nd series) (ts'e 6–8).

Ku Shan-chen 顧山貞, *K'o-tien shu* 客滇述, (T'ung-shih ed.) (ts'e 29).

Ku Yen-wu 顧炎武 (1613–1682), *Jih-chih-lu chi-shih* 日知錄集釋, (WYWK ed.).
    Ming-chi shih-lu 明季實錄, (MCPS, second series) (ts'e 2).

Ku Ying-t'ai 谷應泰 (d. after 1689), *Ming-shih chi-shih pen-mo* 明史紀事本末, (KHCPTS).
    Po-wu yao lan 博物要覽, (Shanghai, 1941).

Kuan-ko shan-jen (*P'eng* Sun-i) 管葛山人 (彭孫貽), (1615–1673).
    P'ing-k'ou-chih 平寇志, (Peiping, 1931).
    Shan-chung wen-chien-lu 山中聞見錄, (Yü-chien-chai ts'ung-shu 玉簡齋叢書 ed., by *Lo*
    Chen-yü 羅振玉) (1st series, 1910).

Kuang ch'ün-fang-p'u 廣羣芳譜, (WYWK, 2nd series).

Kung Ling-ching 孔另境, *Chung-kuo hsiao-shuo shih-liao* 中國小說史料, (Shanghai, 1935).

Kuo Chen-i 郭箴一, *Chung-kuo hsiao-shuo shih* 中國小說史, (Shanghai, 1939).

Kuo Shang-pin 郭尙賓 (ca. 1598), *Kuo chi-chien shu-kao* 郭給諫疏稿, (TSCCCP), (ts'e
    0,908).

Kuo Tzu-chang 郭子章, *Yüeh-ts'ao* 粵草, (Wan-li ed.).

Kuwabara Jitsuzo 桑原隲藏 (1870–1931), *P'u Shou-keng chih shih-chi* 蒲壽庚之事蹟, (tr. by
    Ch'en Yü-ch'ing 陳裕菁) (Shanghai, 1929).

Lan P'u 藍浦, *Ching-te chen t'ao lu* 景德鎭陶錄, (Mi-shu Ts'ung-shu 美術叢書 ed.) (Shang-
    hai, 1947).

Li Chien-nung 李劍農, *Sung Yüan Ming ching-chi-shih k'ao* 宋元明經濟史稿, (Peking, 1957).

Li Ch'ing 李淸, *San-yüan pi-chi* 三垣筆記, (Kiangsu, 1927).

Li Chuo-wu hsien-sheng p'i-p'ing chung-i shui-hu-chuan 李卓吾先生批評忠義水滸傳, (Published
    by Yung-hsing-t'ang, late Ming ed.).

Li Fu-jung 李馥榮, *Yen-yü nang* 灩澦囊, (Tao-kuang ed.).

Li Hsün-chih 李遜之, *Ch'ung-chen ch'ao chi-shih* 崇禎朝記事, (Ch'ang-chou hsien-che i-shu
    常州先哲遺書 ed. by *Sheng* Hsüan-huai 盛宣懷) (Kiangsu, late 19th century ed.).

Li Hua-lung 李化龍 (1554–1611), *P'ing po ch'üan-shu* 平播全書, (TSCCCP), (ts'e 3,982–
    3,988).

Li Kuang-t'ao 李光濤, *Ming-chi liu-k'ou shih-mo* 明季流寇始末, (Taipei, 1965).
    Hsiung T'ing-pi-yü Liao-tung 熊廷弼與遼東, (Taipei, 1976).
    Ming-Ch'ing shih lun-chi 明淸史論集, 2 vols., (Taipei, 1970).

Li Kung 李琳 (1659–1733), *Yüeh-shih ch'i-shih hsü* 閱史郄視續, (TSCCCP), (ts'e 3588).

Li Ma-tou 利瑪竇 (Matteo *Ricci*) (1552–1610), *Ch'i-jen shih-pien* 畸人十篇, (Hong Kong,
    1904).

Li Pang-hua 李邦華 (1574–1644), *Li Chung-wen-kung wen-chi* 李忠文公文集, (1694 ed.).

Li Shao-min 李紹文, *Huang-ming shih-shuo hsin-yü* 皇明世說新語, (Japanese ed., 1754).

Li Shih-chen 李時珍 (1518–1593), *Pen-ts'ao kang-mu* 本草綱目, (Shanghai, 1977).

Li Wen-chih 李文治, *Wan-ming min-pien* 晚明民變, (Shanghai, 1948).

Li Yüeh-kang 李曰剛, *Chung-kuo wen-hsüeh liu-pien shih* 中國文學流變史, Vol. 3, (Taipei,
    1976).

Liang-che hsüeh-cheng 兩浙學政, (1610 ed.).

Liang Chi-ch'ao 梁啓超 (1873–1929), *Yin-ping-shih ch'üan-chi* 飲冰室全集, (Shanghai,
    1916).

Liang Fang-chung 梁方仲, *Ming-tai Liang-chang chih-tu* 明代糧長制度, (Shanghai, 1957).

Liang T'ing-tsang 梁廷燦, *Li-tai ming-jen sheng-tsu nien-piao* 歷代名人生卒年表, (Shanghai,
    1933).

Lin Ch'uan-chia 林傳甲, *Chung-kuo wen-hsüeh-shih* 中國文學史, (Peking circa 1904).

Ling Yang-tsao 凌揚藻, *Li-shao pien* 蠡勺編, (TSCCCP), (ts'e 0,225–0,230).

Liu Hsien-t'ing 劉獻廷 (1648–1695), *Kuang-yang tsa-chi* 廣陽雜記, (Kung-shun-t'ang
    ts'ung-shu 功順堂叢書).

Liu I-cheng 柳詒徵, *Chung-kuo wen-hua shih* 中國文化史, (Taipei, 1954).
    Kuo-shih yao-i 國史要義, (Shanghai, 1948).

Liu Jo-yü 劉若愚 (ca. 1625), *Cho-chung-chih* 酌中志, (TSCCCP), (ts'e 3,966–3,967).

Liu Lin-sheng 劉麟生, *Chung-kuo wen-hsüeh-shih* 中國文學史, (Shanghai, 1932).

Liu Ta-chieh 劉大杰, *Chung-kuo wen-hsüeh fa-chen shih* 中國文學發展史, (Shanghai, 1958).

Lo Erh-kang 羅爾綱, *Lu-ying-ping chih* 綠營兵志, (Chungking, 1935).

Lu Jung 陸容 (1436–1494), *Shu-yüan tsa-chi* 菽園雜記, (TSCCCP), (ts'e 0,329–0,330).

Lu Shih-i 陸世儀 (1611–1672), *Li-ts'ai-i* 理財議, (HLTTS), (ts'e 117).

Lu Yu 陸游 (1125–1210), *Lu Fang-weng ch'üan-chi* 陸放翁全集, (Chi-ku-ko 汲古閣 ed. published by *Mao* Chin 毛晉, 1598–1659).

Lü Chen 呂震 (ca. 1410), *Hsüan te ting-yi p'u chi hsüan-lu po-lun* 宣德鼎彝譜及宣爐博論, (Mei-shu ts'ung-shu ed.), (Shanghai, 1946) Vol. 7.

Lü Pi 呂毖, *Ming-ch'ao hsiao-shih* 明朝小史, (HLTTS), (ts'e 87–92).

Lü Pu-wei 呂不韋, *Lu-shih ch'un-ch'iu* 呂氏春秋, (SPTK).

Lü Tzu-mien 呂思勉, *Chung-kuo t'ung-shih* 中國通史, (Shanghai, 1948).

Lung Wen-pin 龍文彬 (1821–1893), *Ming hui-yao* 明會要, (Shanghai, 1956).

Ma Huan 馬歡, *Ying-yai Sheng-lan* 瀛涯勝覽, (CLHP)

de Magaillans (Magalhães), Gabriel, *Nouvelle relation de la Chine, contenant la description des particularitez les plus considerables de ce grand empire*, (Paris, 1688).

Mao Ch'i-ling 毛奇齡 (1623–1716), *Hou chien lu* 後鑒錄, (SCIS, 2nd series), (ts'e 18). *Sheng-chao t'ung-shih shih-i chi* 勝朝彤史拾遺記, in the *Hsi-ho wen-chi* 西河文集, (WYWK, 2nd series). *Wu-tsung wai-chi* 武宗外紀, (contained in the *Hsi-ho wen-chi* 西河文集, (WYWK ed., 2nd series) (ts'e 8).

Mao Pin 毛霖 (ca. 1726), *P'ing-p'an-chi* 平叛記, (*Yin-li tsai-ssu-t'ang ts'ung-shu* 殷禮在斯堂叢書 published by *Lo* Chen-yü 羅振玉.) (1908) (ts'e 4).

Maspero, Henri, *Melanges Posthumes sur les religions et l'histoire de la Chine, III. Etudes historiques*, (Paris, 1950).

Mei-shih-shih 眉史氏, *Fu-she chi-lüeh* 復社紀略, (CKNLWHLSTS), (ts'e 10).

Meng Shen 孟森, *Ming-tai shih* 明代史, (Taipei, 1958). *Hsin-shih ts'ung-k'an* 心史叢刊, (Hong Kong, 1963). *Ming Ch'ing shih-lun chi-k'an* 明清史論集刊, 2 vols., (Shanghai, 1959).

Mi-chih-hsien-chih 米脂縣志, compiled by *Kao* Chao-hsü 高照煦, (Shensi, 1907).

Ming ch'en tsou-i 明臣奏議, (TSCCCP), (ts'e 913–922).

Ming-Ch'ing shih-liao chia-pien 明清史料甲編, (compiled and edited by the Palace Museum of Peiping), (Peiping, 1931).

Ming Hui-tien 明會典, (Wan-li 萬曆 revision), (WYWK, 2nd series).

Ming-jen shih-ch'ao 明人詩鈔, edited by *Chu* Yen 朱琰, (Ch'ing edition).

Ming-mo nung-min ch'i-i shih-liao 明末農民起義史料, (Peking, 1952).

Ming-shih 明史, (Han-fen-lou 涵分樓 ed.) (Shanghai, 1916).

Ming-shih pen-chi 明史本紀, (Photographic reprint of the 1777 Chien-lung ed.) (Peiping, 1932).

Morant, George Soulie de, *A History of Chinese Art from Ancient Times to the Present Day*, (tr. by G. C. Wheeler) (New York).

Moule, A. C., *The Chinese People*, (London).

Naito Torajirō 内藤虎次郎 (1866–1934), *Shinchoshi tsuron* 清朝史通論, (Tokyo, 1944).

Nai-te-weng 耐得翁, *Tu-ch'eng chi-sheng* 都城紀勝, (Lien-t'ing shih-erh chung 楝亭十二種 ed. by *Ts'ao* Yin 曹寅 (1658–1712).

Omura Seigai 大村西崖, *Chung-kuo mei-shu shih* 中國美術史, (tr. by *Ch'en* Pin-ho 陳彬龢) (Shanghai, 1928).

Ou-yang Chih 歐陽直, *Ou-Yang-shih i-shu* 歐陽氏遺書, (transcription).

Pan Ku 班固 (32 AD-92), *Han-shu* 漢書, (Han-fen-lou ed.) (Shanghai, 1915).

P'an Sheng-chang 潘檉章 (1628–1662), *Chung-ling wen-hsien* 松陵文獻, (Ch'ing ed.).

Pao Ju-chi 包汝楫, *Nan-chung chi-wen* 南中紀聞, (TSCCCP), (ts'e 3,114).

Pao Tsun-p'eng 包遵彭 (compiler), *Ming-shih lun-ts'ung* 明史論叢, 9 vols. (Taipei, 1967).

P'eng Ta-yeh 彭大雅 and *Hsü* Ting 徐霆, *Hei-t'a shih liao* 黑韃事略, (TSCCCP), (ts'e 3,177).

P'eng Tsun-ssu 彭遵泗, *Shu-pi* 蜀碧, (CKNLWHLSTS), (ts'e 22).

P'eng Hsin-wei 彭信威, *Chung-kuo huo-pi shih* 中國貨幣史, (Shanghai, 1958).

Pfister, Louis, *Notices Biographiques et Bibliographiques sur les Jésuites de l'Ancienne Mission de Chine 1552–1773*, (Shanghai, 1932).

Pi Mao-k'ang 畢懋康 (ca. 1630), *Chün-ch'i t'u-shuo* 軍器圖說, (1638 ed.).
  Po-shui-hsien chih 白水縣志, (Chien-lung ed.).

Pi Yüan 畢沅 (1730–1797), Hsü Tzu-chih t'ung-chien 續資治通鑑, (Shanghai).

Po Yü 白愚, *Pien-wei shih-chin lu* 汴圍濕襟錄, (Ching-t'o i-shih 荊駝逸史 series) (Tao-kuang ed.) (ts'e 8).

Pu Shih-ch'ang 卜世昌, *Huang-ming t'ung-chi shu-i* 皇明通紀述遺, (Wan-li ed.).

Shan Shih-yüan 單士元 and *Wang* Pi-wen 王璧文, *Ming-tai chien-chu ta-shih nien-piao* 明代建築大事年表, (Peiping, 1937).

Shang-shu 尙書, (Shanghai, 1887).

Shen Hsün-wei 沈荀蔚, *Shu-nan hsü-lüeh* 蜀難叙略, (MCPS, 2nd series) (ts'e 1).

Shen Kuo-yüan 沈國元, *Liang-ch'ao ts'ung-hsin lu* 兩朝從信錄, (late Ming ed.).

Shen Te-fu 沈德符 (1578–1642), *Yeh-huo pien* 野獲編, (ed. by *Yao* Tsu-en 姚祖恩) (Chekiang, 1827 and Shanghai, 1959).

Shen-shih nung-shu 沈氏農書, written in the late Ming period. (ed. by *Ts'ao* Jung 曹溶 1613–1680, in his Hsüeh-hai lei-pien 學海類編), (Photographic reprint, Shanghai, 1920).

Shih Chi-tsu 史繼祖. *Huang-ming ping-chih k'ao* 皇明兵制考, (Ming ed.).

Shih-i-ch'ao tung-hua-lu 十一朝東華錄, (Ts'un-ku-chai 存古齋 ed) (Shanghai, 1911).

Shih Sheng-han 石聲漢, *Nung-cheng ch'üan-shu chiao-chu* 農政全書校注, 3 vols. (Shanghai, 1979).

Shimizu Taiji 清水泰次, *Chukoku Kinsei shekai keizaishi* 中國近世社會經濟史, (Tokyo, 1950).

Shimizu Taiji and others, *Toyo bunkashi daikei* 東洋文化史大系, Vol. 5, *Min no kobo to siriki no tōzen* 明の興亡と西力の東漸, (Tokyo, 1934).

So-lu shan-jen 瑣綠山人, *Ming wang shu-lüeh* 明亡述略, (CKNLWHLSTS), (ts'e 11).

Ssu-ma Chien 司馬遷 (P.C. 145–86), *Shih-chi* 史記, (HFL ed.).

Su Shih 蘇軾 (1036–1101), *Tung-p'o chih-lin* 東坡志林, (PCHSTK), (ts'e 323).

Sun Ch'eng-tse 孫承澤 (1592–1676), *Ch'un-ming meng-yü-lu* 春明夢餘錄, (Ku-hsiang-chai hsiu-chen shih-chung 古香齋袖珍十種 series) (late 19th century ed.).
  Ssu-ling chin-cheng chi 思陵勤政記, (TSCCCP), (ts'e 3,972).
  Ssu-ling tien-li chi 思陵典禮紀, (TSCCCP), (ts'e 3,972).

Sun Zen E-Tu 孫任以都, *T'ien-kung k'ai-wu, Chinese Technology in the 17th Century*. (Pennsylvania, 1900).

Sung Kung-yü 宋公玉, *Yin-shih-shu* 飲食書, (Late Ming ed.).

Sung P'ei-wei 宋佩韋, *Ming wen-hsüeh-shih* 明文學史, (Shanghai, 1934).

Sung Ying-hsing 宋應星 (ca. 1630), *T'ien-kung-hai-wu* 天工開物, (Shanghai, 1937).

Ta Hsüeh 大學 (The Great Learning). From the *Four Books* translated by James Legge (Shanghai, 1930).

Tai Li 戴笠 (floruit 1680), *Huai-ling liu-k'ou shih-chung-lu* 懷陵流寇始終錄, (other title: *K'ou-shih pien-nien* 寇事編年), (HLTTS, 2nd series).

Tai Ming-shih 戴名世 (1653–1713), *Chieh-i-lu* 孑遺錄, (Kuo ts'ui ts'ung shu 國粹叢書 ed.) (Shanghai, 1905–1909) (ts'e 45).
  Tai-tso kao-huang-ti shih-lu 太祖高皇帝實錄, (KSSLTSK photographic reprint).

T'an Chien 談遷 (1594–1657), *Kuo-ch'üeh* 國榷, (transcription from the copy of Tung-fang wen-hua hui 東方文化會, Peking, now in Toyo Bunko 東洋文庫, Tokyo, Japan.).
Tsao-lin tsa-tsu 棗林雜俎, (PCHSTK), (ts'e 87–92).

Tan Hsi-ssu 譚希思 (ca. 1590), *Huang-ming ta-cheng tsun-yao* 皇明大政纂要, (Wan-li ed.).

T'ang Hsin 唐新, *Chang Chiang-ling hsin-chuan* 張江陵新傳, (Taipei, 1968).

T'ang Shun-chih 唐順之 (1507–1560), *Ching-ch'uan hsien-sheng wai-chi* 荊川先生外集, (SPTK newspaper ed.).

T'ao Hsi-sheng 陶希聖 and *Shen* Jen-yüan 沈任遠, *Ming-Ch'ing cheng-chih chih-tu* 明清政治制度, (Taipei, 1967).

Taylor, Romeyn, *Basic Annals of Ming T'ai-tsu,* (San Francisco, 1975).

Teixeira, Manuel, *Macau e a sua Diocese,* (Macau, 1940).

Ting I 丁易, *Ming-tai t'e-wu cheng-chih* 明代特務政治, (Peking, 1950).

T'o-t'o 脫脫 (1313–1355), *Chin shih* 金史, (Han-fen-lou ed.) (Shanghai, 1915).

Tōyō shiryō shu sei 東洋史料集成, (Tokyo, 1956).

Trigault, Nicolas (1577–1628), *China in the 16th Century: The Journal of Mathew Ricci (1583–1610),* tr. by Louis J. Gallagher, SJ, (New York, 1953).

Ts'ai Chiu-te 采九德, *Wo pien shih-lüeh* 倭變事略, (TSCCCP), (ts'e 3,975).

Tung Chung-shu 董仲舒, *Ch'un-ch'iu fan-lu* 春秋繁露, (SPTK).

T'ung Shih-heng 童世亨, *Li-tai chiang-yü hsing-shih i-lan-t'u* 歷代疆域形勢一覽圖, (Shanghai).

Uchida Sennosuke 內田泉之助 and *Nagasawa* Kikuya 長澤規短也, *Shina bunka shi kōyō* 支那文化史綱要, (Tokyo, 1939).

Wang Ao 王鏊 (1450–1524), *Chen-tse ch'ang-yü* 震澤長語, (Chen-tse hsien-sheng p'ieh-chi 震澤先生別集 ed.) (1901) ts'e 1).

Wang Chia chen 王家楨, *Wang shao-ssu-ma tsou-shu* 王少司馬奏疏, (TSCCCP), (ts'e 911).

Wang Fu-chih 王夫之 (1619–1692), *Ngo-meng* 噩夢, (Peking, 1956).

Wang Hsiao-chuan 王曉傳 (compiler), *Yüan, Ming, Ch'ing san-tai chin-hui hsiao-shuo hsi-chü shih-liao* 元明清三代禁燬小説戲曲史料, (Peking, 1956).

Wang Hui-tsu 汪輝祖 (1730–1807), *Hsüeh-chih i-shuo* 學治臆說, (Kiangsi, early 19th century ed.).

Wang Hung-hsü 王鴻緒 (1645–1723), *Ming-shih k'ao* 明史稿, (Ching-shen-t'ang 敬慎堂 ed.).

Wang Shih-chen 王世貞 (1526–1590), *Chin-i-chih* 錦衣志, (SCIS, second series) (ts'e 15).
Ku pu ku lu 觚不觚錄, (SCIS, second series) (ts'e 15).

Wang Shih-mou 王世懋 (1536–1588), *Erh yu wei t'an chai-lu* 二酉委譚摘錄, (TSCCCP), (ts'e 2,923).
Hsüeh-p'u tsa-shu 學圃雜疏, (TSCCCP), (ts'e 1,353).
Shih-t'u hsüan-ching 仕途懸鏡, (Ch'ing ed.).

Wang Shou-jen 王守仁 (1472–1528), *Wang wen-ch'eng-kung ch'üan-shu* 王文成公全書, (SPTK).

Wang Wen-lu 王文祿 (ca. 1550), *Lung-hsing tz'u-chi* 龍興慈記, (CLHP), (ts'e 4).
Shu-tu 書牘, (TSCCCP), (ts'e 0,755).
Ts'e shu 策樞, (TSCCCP), (ts'e 0,756).

Wang Yü-ch'üan 王毓銓, *Ming-tai ti chün-t'un* 明代的軍屯, (Peking, 1965).

Wei Chieh 衛杰, *Nung-sang ts'ui-pien* 農桑萃編, (Shanghai, 1956).

Wei Ch'ing-yüan 韋慶遠, *Ming-tai huang-ts'e chih-tu* 明代黃冊制度, (Peking, 1961).

Wei Yüan 魏源 (1794–1856), *Sheng-wu chi* 聖武記 (1846 ed.).

Wen Jui-lin 温睿臨 (ca. 1705), *Nan-chiang i-shih k'an-pen* 南疆繹史勘本, (Revised by *Li* Yao 李瑤) (1830 ed.).

Wen Ping 文秉 (1609–1669), *Hsien-po chih-shih* 先撥志始, (TKCCC), (ts'e 31–32).
　　Lieh-huang hsiao-chih 烈皇小識, (MCPS, first series) (ts'e 1–3).

Wu Chen-fang 吳震芳 (floruit 1680), *Ling-nan tsa-chi* 嶺南雜記, (TSCCCP), (ts'e 3,129).

Wu Han 吳晗, *Chu Yüan-chang chuan* 朱元璋傳, (Kirin, 1949).
　　Yu Seng-pu tao huang-ch'uan 由僧鉢到皇權, (Chungking, 1944).
　　Tu shih cha-chi 讀史箚記, (Peking, 1956).

Wu Han 吳晗 and *Fei* Hsiao-t'ung 費孝通, *Huang-ch'üan yü hsin-ch'üan* 皇權與紳權,
　　(Shanghai, 1946).

Wu Tzu-mu 吳自牧, *Meng-liang-lu* 夢梁錄, (PCHSTK), (ts'e 243–245).

Wu Wei-yeh 吳偉業 (1609–1671), *Sui-k'ou chi-lüeh* 綏寇紀略, (TSCCCP), (ts'e 3,990–3,992).

Wu Yen 吳炎 (ca. 1663) and *P'an* Sheng-chang 潘檉章 (1628–1662), *Wu P'an chin-yüeh-fu*
　　吳潘今樂府, (Yin-li tsai-ssu-t'ang ts'ung-shu) (ts'e 2).

Wu Ying-chi 吳應箕 (1594–1645), *Liu-tu chien-wen lu* 留都見聞錄, (*Kuei-ch'ih hsien-che i-shu*
　　貴池先哲遺書 ed. by *Liu* Shih-heng 劉世珩) (Anhui, 1920) (ts'e 13).
　　Lou-shang-t'ang chi 樓山堂集, (TSCCCP), (ts'e 2,167–2,170).

Yabuuchi Kiyoshi 藪內清, *T'ien-kung k'ai-wu yen-chiu lun-wen-chi* 天工開物研究論文集, tr. by
　　Chang Hsiung 章熊 and *Wu* Chieh 吳傑 (Peking, 1959).

Yakisawa Haijime 八木澤元, *Ming-tai chü-tso-chia yen-chiu* 明代劇作家研究 (Chinese
　　translation with no name of the translator.) (Taipei, 1977).

Yamane Yokio 山根幸夫, *Min-tai-shi kenkyū bunken mokuroku* 明代史研究文獻目錄, (Tokyo,
　　1960).
　　Nippon Genson minjin bunsyu mokuroku 日本現存明人文集目錄, (Tokyo, 1966).

Yanai Wataru 箭內亙, *Yüan-tai meng-han se-mu tai-yu k'ao* 元代蒙漢色目待遇考, tr. by
　　Ch'en Chieh 陳捷 and *Ch'en* Ch'ing-ch'üan 陳清泉 (Shanghai, 1933).

Yang Hsüeh-feng 楊雪峰, *Ming-tai ti shen-p'an chih-tu* 明代的審判制度, (Taipei, 1978).

Yeh Ch'ing-ping 葉慶炳 and *Shao* Chiang 邵江 (compilers), *Ming-tai wen-hsüeh p'i-ping
　　tzu-liao hui-pien* 明代文學批評資料滙編, 2 vols. (Taipei, 1979).

Yeh Shao-yüan 葉紹袁 (ca. 1640), *Ch'i-chen chi-wen lu* 啓禎記聞錄, (T'ung-shih ed.)
　　(ts'e 18–20).

Yeh Yung-sheng 葉永盛 (ca. 1590), *Yü-ch'eng tsou-shu* 玉城奏疏, (TSCCCP), (ts'e
　　2,167–2,170).

Yen Chi-heng 顏季亨, *Ching-shih chi-ch'ieh shih-wu* 經世急切時務, (1623 ed.).

Ying-hsiung-p'u t'u-tsan 英雄譜圖讚, (Originally printed by the Hsiung-fei-ko 雄飛閣
　　during the Ch'ung-chen period. Photographic print by the Chin Ling University
　　金陵大學) (Nanking, 1949).

Yule, Henry, *The Book of Ser Marco Polo*, (London, 1926).

Yü Cheng-hsieh 俞正燮 (1775–1840), *Kuei-ssu ts'un-kao* 癸巳存稿, (Shanghai, 1947).

Yü Chi-teng 余繼登 (ca. 1595), *Tien-ku chi-wen* 典故紀聞, (chi-fu ts'ung-shu 畿輔叢書 ed.
　　by *Wang* Hao 王灝) (1878) (ts'e 129–134).

Yü Ping-kuen 余秉權, *Chung-kuo shih-hsüeh lun-wen yin-te* 中國史學論文引得, (Hong Kong,
　　1962); second series. (Cambridge, 1974).

Yü Chien-hua 俞劍華, *Li-tai hua-chia p'ing-chuan* 歷代畫家評傳, (Hong Kong, 1979).

Yü Jen 余寅 (1519–1577), *Huan-li man-chi* 宦歷漫記, (T'ien-chi (1621–1627) ed.).

Yüan Chih 袁袠 (1502–1547), *Shih-wei* 世緯, (CPTCTS).

Yüan Hao 袁顥 (ca. 1415), *Yüan-shih chia-fan ts'ung-shu* 袁氏家範叢書, (Ming ed.).

Yüan Hung-tao 袁宏道 (1568–1610), *Yüan chung-lang ch'üan-chi* 袁中郎全集, (Shanghai,
　　1935).

Chung-kuo k'ao-ku-hsüeh wen-hsien mu lu 中國考古學文獻目錄 1949–1966, (Hong Kong,
　　1979).

Chung-kuo shi-hsüeh lun-wen so-yin 中國史學論文索引, first series 上編 (1900–1937), second series 下編 (1937–1949), (Hong Kong, 1980).

Ming-Ch'ing chin-shih t'i-ming pei-lu so-yin 明清進士題名碑索引, 3 vols. (Shanghai, 1980).

Ming-Ch'ing lieh-k'e chin-shih-t'i-ming pei-lu 明清列科進士題名碑錄, 4 vols. (Taipei, 1969).

Ming-tai she-hui ching-chi-shih lun-chi 明代社會經濟史論集, 3 vols., compiled by Ts'un-ts'ui hsüeh-she 存粹學社, (Hong Kong, 1979).

Wan-Ming pien-ying chu-i hua-chia tso-p'ing chien 晚明變形主義畫家作品展, (Taipei, 1977).

Wen-wu k'ao-ku kung-tso san-shih-nien 文物考古工作三十年, 1949–1979, (Peking, 1979).

PERIODICALS

Acta Asiatica: Bulletin of the Institute of Eastern Culture, 38. (Tokyo, 1980).

Chang Ch'üan-kung 張全恭, "Chu Shih-ssu" 瞿式耜, *Min-tsu tsa-chih* 民族雜誌, 5 (July, 1937) 7.

Chang Hsi-lun 張錫綸, "Ming-tai hu-k'ou t'ao-wang yü t'ien-tu huang-fei chü-li" 明代戶口逃亡與田土荒廢舉例, *(SHPYK,* 3 (1935) 2. 50–53.

Ch'en Teng-yüan 陳登元, "Hsi-hsüeh lai hua shih kuo-jen chih wu-tuan t'ai-tu" 西學來華時國人之武斷態度, *The Eastern Miscellany* 東方雜誌, 27.8.

Chao Tsung-fu 趙宗復, "Li Tzu-ch'eng p'an-luan shih-lüeh" 李自成叛亂史略, *Shih-hsüeh nien-pao* 史學年報, 2 (1937) 4. 127–157.

Fu Ssu-nien 傅斯年, "Ming Cheng-tsu Sheng-mu chi-i" 明成祖生母記疑, *BIHP,* 2 (Peiping, 1932) 4, 406–414.
"Pa ming ch'eng-tsu sheng-mu wen-t'i hui-cheng" 駁明成祖生母問題彙證, *BIHP* (March, 1935) 1.79–81.

Hsiao Yüan-chien 蕭遠健, "Chang Hsien-chung t'u chuan k'ao-lüeh" 張獻忠屠川考略, *Shih-ta yüeh-k'an,* (April, 1935) 18.

Hsieh Yü-ts'ai 解毓才, "Ming-tai wei-so chih-tu hsing-shuai k'ao" 明代衛所制度興衰考, *Shuo-wen yüeh-k'an* 說文月刊, 2 (December, 1942) 9; 10; 11; 12.

Hsü Hung-hsiao 許宏然, "Ming-tai tu-ti cheng-li chih k'ao-ch'a" 明代土地整理之考察, *SHPYK,* 3 (1936) 10. 28–50.

Kitamura Norinao 北村敬直, "Mimmatsu shinsho ni okeru jinushi ni tsuite" 明末清初における地主について *RK* (July, 1949) 140.

Kung Hua-lung 龔化龍, "Ming-tai ts'ai-k'uang shih-yeh ti fa-chan ho liu-tu" 明代採礦事業的發展和流毒, *SHPYK,* 1 (May, 1935) 19. 29–42; 1 (May, 1935) 12, 37–48.

Li Chin-hua 李晉華, "Ming Cheng-tsu sheng-mu wen-t'i hui-chang" 明成祖生母問題彙證, (March, 1935) 1. 55–77.

Li Kuang-t'ao 李光濤, "Ch'ing t'ai-tsung yü san-kuo yen-li" 清太宗與三國演義, *BIHP,* 12, 251–272.
"Chi ming-chi ping-ying chih chi-pi" 記明季兵營之積弊, *Ta-lu tsa-chih* 大陸雜誌, 6 (June, 1953) 12. 15–19.

Li Wen-chih 李文治, "Wan-ming ku-ti fen-p'ei wen-t'i" 晚明土地分配問題, *Hsüeh-yüan* 學原, (1 1947) 6, 48–54.

Liang Fang-chung 梁方仲, "I-t'iao-pien-fa" 一條鞭法, 4 (May, 1936) 1. 1–65.
1. 1–65.
"Ming-tai huang-ts'e k'ao" 明代黃冊考, *Ling-nan hsüeh-pao* 嶺南學報, 10 (June, 1950) 145–172.
"Ming-tai Liang-chang chih-tu" 明代糧長制度, *CKSHCCSCK,* 7 (1946) 2. 107–133.
"Ming-tai yin-k'uang k'ao" 明代銀礦考, *Ching-chi-shih yen-chiu chi-k'an* 經濟史研究集刊, 6 (1939) 1. 65–112.

Liu Ming-shu 劉銘恕, "Cheng Ho hang-hai shih-chi chih ts'ai t'an 鄭和航海事蹟之再探, *Chung-kuo wen-hua yen-chiu hui-k'an* 中國文化研究集刊, (Peiping, 1943)."

Matsumoto Yoshimi 松本善海, "Poverty of the Historical Study of the Ming Dynasty" 明代史研究の貧乏, *RK*, 4 (Sept., 1935) 5.

Pelliot, Paul. "Les grands voyages maritimes chinois au debut de XVᵉ siècle". *T'oung-Pao*, 30 (1930) 237-452.

Shimizu Taiji 清水泰次, "Minchō kōbō no shikan" 明朝興亡の史觀, *SZ*, (November, 1941) 11. 1375-1376 (tr. by *Fang* Chi-sheng 方紀生). "Ming-tai chün-t'un chih peng-k'uei" 明代軍屯之崩潰, *SHPYK*, 4 (1936) 10.
"Min-dai ni okeru bukkyo no torishimari" 明代における佛教の取締, *SZ*, 40 (March, 1929) 3, 263-310.
"Min dai no ryūmin to ryūzaku" 明代の流民と流賊, *SZ*, 46 (March, 1935) 2, 192-230; 3, 348-384.
"Minsho ni okeru gunton no tenkai to sono soshiki" 明初における軍屯の展開とその組織, *SZ*, 44 (May and June 1933) 5, 533-571; 6, 699-742.

Shu Shih-cheng 束世澂, "Ming-chi liu-k'ou chih ch'eng-yen" 明季流寇之成因, *Shih-hsüeh tsa-chih* 史學雜誌, 1 (1929) 3.

Sun Yüan-chen 孫瑗貞, "Ming-tai t'un-t'ien chih yen-chiu" 明代屯田之研究, *SHPYK*, 3 (1935) 2, 26-42.

T'ao Hsi-sheng 陶希聖, "Ming-tai wang-fu chuang-t'ien chih i li" 明代皇府莊田之一例, *SHPYK*, 2 (1935) 7, 34-38

T'ung Shu-yeh 童書業, "Li Tzu-ch'eng ssu-shih k'ao-i" 李自成死事考異, *Shih-hsüeh chi-k'an* 史學集刊, (April, 1937) 3. 247-266.

Ura Ren'ichi 浦廉一, "Kangun (Ujen Cooha) ni tsuite" 漢軍烏眞超哈について. *Kuwabara hakase kanreki kinen tōyōshi rensō* 桑原博士還曆紀念東洋史論叢, (Kyoto, 1931).

Wang Ch'ung-wu 王崇武, "Ming Ch'eng-tsu yü fang-shih" 明成祖與方士, *CKSHCCSCK*, 8 (January, 1949) 1. 12-19.
"Ming Ch'eng-tsu yü fu-chiao" 明成祖與佛教, *CKSHCCSCK*, 8 (January) 1. 1-11.
"Ming-tai min-t'un chih tsu-chih" 明代民屯之組織, *YKPYK*, 7 (1937) 1.2.3. 231-238.
"Ming-tai ti shang-t'un chih-tu" 明代的商屯制度, *YKPYK*, 5 (1936) 12. 1-15.

Wu Han 吳晗, "Ming Cheng-tsu sheng-mu k'ao" 明成祖生母考, *(CHHP)*, 10 (July, 1935) 3. 631-646.
"*T'an ch'ien ho Kuo-ch'üeh*" 談遷和國榷 in *Chung-kuo shih-hsüeh-shih* 中國史學史, 2 vols. compiled by *Wu* Tse 吳澤 and *Yüan* Ying-kuang 袁英光. (Shanghai, 1980), pp. 501-518.

Yang T'ing-hsien 楊廷賢, "Ming-mo nung-min pao-tung chih pei-ching" 明代農民暴動之背景, *SHPYK*, 5 (1937) 8. 18-28.

Yü Teng 于登, "Ming-tai kuo-tzu-chien chih-tu k'ao-lüeh" 明代國子監制度考略, *Chin-ling hsüeh-pao* 金陵學報, 6 (November, 1936) 2. 109-117.
"Ming-tai chien-ch'a chih-tu kai-shu" 明代監察制度概述, *Chin-ling hsüeh-pao* 金陵學報, 6 (November, 1936) 2. 213-229.

Yüan Ying-kuang 袁英光, "*Hsia Hsieh yü Ming-t'ung-chien yen-chiu*" 夏爕與明通鑑研究 *Li-shih yen-chiu* 歷史研究, January 1980, vol. I, 157-172.

Zuzuki Tadashi 鈴木正, "Mintai teishitsu zaisei to bukkyō" 明代帝室財政と佛教, *RK*, 6 (November and December, 1936) 11; 12.

INDEX